The Fountain of Life Opened Up
By John Flavel
This Edition Edited by Anthony Uyl

Woodstock, Ontario, Canada 2018

The Fountain of Life Opened Up
The Fountain of Life Opened Up
By John Flavel (c. 1630-1691)
This Edition Edited by Anthony Uyl

John Flavel, The Fountain of Life
The Fountain of Life opened up: or, A Display of Christ in his essential and mediatorial glory. Containing forty-two sermons on various texts.

Originally Published by:
The Banner of Truth Trust, 3 Murray field Road, Edinburgh EHl2 6EL, PO Box 621, Carlisle, Pennsylvania 17013, U.S.A.
First published by W. Baynes and Son, 1820

The text of The Fountain of Life Opened Up is all in the Public Domain. The layout and Devoted Publishing logo are Copyright ©2018 Devoted Publishing. This edition is published by Devoted Publishing a division of 2165467 Ontario Inc.

What kind of philosophies do you have?
Let us know!

Visit our online store: www.devotedpublishing.com
Contact us at: devotedpub@hotmail.com
Visit us on Facebook: @DevotedPublishing

Published in Woodstock, Ontario, Canada 2018

ISBN: 978-1-77356-219-3

Table of Contents

To his much honoured and beloved Kinsman, Mr. John Flavel, of London, Merchant, and his virtuous Consort, the Author wisheth Grace, Mercy, and Peace. 5

To the Christian Readers, Especially those in the Town and Corporation of Dartmouth, and Parts adjacent, who have either befriended, or attended these Lectures. 7

Sermon 1: Opens the Excellency of the Subject 13

Sermon 2: Sets forth Christ in his essential en primeval Glory 18

Sermon 3: Opens the Covenant of Redemption betwixt the Father and the Redeemer 23

Sermon 4: Opens the admirable love of God in giving his own Son for us 28

Sermon 5: Of Christ's wonderful Person 33

Sermon 6: Of the Authority by which Christ, as Mediator, acted 39

Sermon 7: Of the Solemn Consecration of the Mediator 45

Sermon 8: Of the Nature of Christ's Mediation 50

Sermon 9: The first Branch of Christ's Prophetical Office, consisting in the Revelation of the Will of God 56

Sermon 10: The second Branch of Christ's Prophetical Office, consisting in the Illumination of the Understanding 62

Sermon 11: The Nature and necessity of the Priesthood of Christ 68

Sermon 12: Of the Excellency of our High-Priest's Oblation, being the first Act or Part of His Priestly Office 74

Sermon 13: Of the Intercession of Christ our High-priest, being the second Act or Part of his Priestly Office 80

Sermon 14: A Vindication of the Satisfaction of Christ, as the first Effect or Fruit of his Priesthood 86

Sermon 15: Of the blessed Inheritance purchased by the Oblation of Christ, being the second Effect or Fruit of his Priesthood 92

Sermon 16: Of the Kingly Office of Christ, as it is executed spiritually upon the Souls of the Redeemed 98

Sermon 17: Of the Kingly Office of Christ, as it is providentially executed in the World, for the Redeemed 104

Sermon 18: Of the Necessity of Christ's Humiliation, in order to the Execution of all these his blessed Offices for us; and particularly of his Humiliation by Incarnation 110

Sermon 19: Of Christ's Humiliation in his Life 116

Sermon 20: Of Christ's Humiliation unto Death, in his first preparative Act for it 122

Sermon 21: The second preparative Act of Christ for his own Death 128

Sermon 22: The third preparative Act of Christ for his own Death 134

Sermon 23: The first Preparation for Christ's Death, on his Enemies Part, by the treason at Judas 140

Sermon 24: The second and third Preparatives for the Death of Christ, by his illegal Trial and Condemnation 146

Sermon 25: Christ's memorable Address to the Daughters of Jerusalem, in his Way to the Place of his Execution 152

The Fountain of Life Opened Up

Sermon 26: Of the Nature and Quality of Christ's Death 158

Sermon 27: Of the signal Providence, which directed and ordered the Title affixed to the cross of Christ 164

Sermon 28: Of the manner of Christ's Death, in respect to the Solitariness thereof 169

Sermon 29: Of the manner of Christ's Death, in respect of the Patience thereof 176

Sermon 30: Of the Instructiveness of the Death of Christ, in his seven last Words; the first of which is here illustrated 182

Sermon 31: The second excellent Word of Christ upon the Cross, illustrated 189

Sermon 32: The third of Christ's last Words upon the Cross, illustrated 194

Sermon 33: The fourth excellent Saying of Christ upon the Cross, illustrated 201

Sermon 34: The fifth excellent Saying of Christ upon the Cross, illustrated 208

Sermon 35: The sixth excellent Saying of Christ upon the Cross, illustrated 214

Sermon 36: The seventh and last Word with which Christ breathed out his Soul, illustrated 220

Sermon 37: Christ's Funeral illustrated, in its Manner, Reasons, and excellent Ends 226

Sermon 38: Wherein four weighty Ends of Christ's Humiliation are opened, and particularly applied 233

Sermon 39: Wherein the Resurrection of CHRIST, with its influences upon the Saints Resurrection, is clearly opened, and comfortably applied, being the first Step of his Exaltation 243

Sermon 40: The Ascension of Christ illustrated, and variously improved, being the Second Step of his Exaltation 250

Sermon 41: The Session of Christ at God's right-hand explained and applied, being the third Step of his glorious Exaltation 256

Sermon 42: Christ's Advent to Judgement, being the fourth and last Degree of his Exaltation, illustrated and improved 261

To his much honoured and beloved Kinsman, Mr. John Flavel, of London, Merchant, and his virtuous Consort, the Author wisheth Grace, Mercy, and Peace.

My dear and honoured friends

If my pen were both able, and at leisure, to get glory in paper, it would be but a paper glory when I had gotten it; but if by displaying (which is the design of these papers) the transcendent excellency of Jesus Christ, I may win glory to him from you, to whom I humbly offer them, or from any other into whose hands providence shall cast them, that will be glory indeed, and an occasion of glorifying God to all eternity.

It is not the design of this epistle to compliment, but to benefit you; not to blazen your excellencies, but Christ's; not to acquaint the world how much you have endeared me to yourselves, but to increase and strengthen the endearments betwixt Christ and you, upon your part. I might indeed (this being a proper place for it) pay you my acknowledgements for your great kindnesses to me and mine; of which, I assure you, I have, and ever shall have, the most grateful sense: but you and I are theatre enough to one another, and can satisfy ourselves with the inclosed comforts and delights of our mutual love and friendship. But let me tell you, the whole world is not a theatre large enough to show the glory of Christ upon, or unfold the one half of the unsearchable riches that lie hid in him. These things will be far better understood, and spoken of in heaven, by the noon-day divinity, in which the immediately illuminated assembly do there preach his praises, shall by such a stammering tongue, and scribbling pen as mine, which does but mar them.

Alas! I write his praises but by moon-light; I cannot praise him so much as by halves. Indeed, no tongue but his own (as Nazianzen said of Basil) is sufficient to undertake that task. What shall I say of Christ? The excelling glory of that object dazzles all apprehension, swallows up all expression. When we have borrowed metaphors from every creature that has any excellency or lovely property in it, till we have stript the whole creation bare of all its ornaments, and clothed Christ with all that glory; when we have even worn out our tongues, in ascribing praises to him, alas! we have done nothing, when all is done.

Yes, wo is me! how do I every day behold reasonable souls most unreasonably disaffected to my lovely Lord Jesus! denying love to One, who is able to compel love from the stoniest heart! yea, though they can never make so much of their love (would they set it to sale) as Christ bids for it. It is horrid and amazing to see how the minds of many are captivated and ensnared by every silly trifle; and how others can indifferently turn them with a kind of spontaneity to this object, or to that (as their fancy strikes) among the whole universe of beings, and scarce ever reluctate, recoil, or nauseate, till they be persuaded to Christ. In their unconverted state, it is as easy to melt the obdurate rocks into sweet syrup, as their hearts into divine love.

How do the great men of the world ambitiously court the honours and pleasures of it? The merchants of the earth trade, and strive for the dear-bought treasures of it; whilst the price of Christ (alas! ever too low) falls every day lower and lower upon the exchange of this world! I speak it as a sad truth, if there were no quicker a trade (as dead as they say it is) for the perishing treasures of the earth, than there is for Christ this day in England, the exchange would quickly be shut up, and all the trading companies dissolved.

Dear Sir, Christ is the peerless pearl hid in the field, Mat. 13: 46. Will you be that wise merchant, that resolves to win and compass that treasure, whatever it shall cost you? Ah, Sir, Christ is a commodity that can never be bought too dear.

My dear kinsman, my flesh, and my blood; my soul thirsteth for your salvation, and the salvation of your family. Shall you and I resolve with good Joshua that whatever others do, "we and our families will serve the Lord;" that we will walk as the redeemed by his blood, shewing forth his virtues and praises in the world? that as God has made us one in name, and one in affection, so we may be one in Christ, that it may be said of us, as it was of Austin and Alippous long ago, that they

The Fountain of Life Opened Up

were sanguine Christi conglutinati, glued together by the blood of Christ.

For my own part, I have given in my name to him long since; wo to me, if I have not given in my heart also; for, should I deceive myself in so deep a point as that, how would my profession as a Christian, my calling as a minister, yea, these very sermons now in your hands, rise in judgement to condemn me? which God forbid.

And doubtless, Sir, your eyes have seen both the vanity of all creatures, and the necessity and infinite worth of Christ. You cannot forget what a vanity the world appeared to you, when in the year 1668, you were summoned by the messengers of death (as you and all that were about you then apprehended) to shoot the gulph of vast eternity, when a malignant fever and pleurisy (whereof your physician has given an account to the world) did shake the whole frame of the tabernacle wherein your soul through mercy yet dwells; and long may it dwell there, for the service and praise of your great Deliverer. I hope you have not, nor ever will forget how vain the world appeared to your eye, when you looked back (as it were over your shoulder) and saw how it shrunk away from you; nor will you ever forget the awful apprehensions of eternity that then seized your spirit, or the value you then had for Christ; which things, I hope, still do, and ever will remain with you.

And for you, dear cousin, as it becomes a daughter of Sarah, let your soul be adorned with the excellencies of Christ, and beauties of holiness. A king from heaven makes suit for your love; if he espouse your soul now he will fetch it home to himself at death in his chariot of salvation; and great shall be your joy, when the marriage of the Lamb is come. Look often upon Christ in this glass; he is fairer than the children of men. View him believingly, and you cannot but like and love him. "For (as one well saith) love, when it sees, cannot but cast out its spirit and strength upon amiable objects and things loveworthy. And what fairer things than Christ! O fair sun, and fair moon, and fair stars, and fair flowers, and fair roses, and fair lilies, and fair creatures! but, O ten thousand, thousand times fairer Lord Jesus! Alas, I wronged him in making the comparison this way. O black sun and moon; but O fair Lord Jesus! O black flowers, and black lilies and roses; but O fair fair, ever fair Lord Jesus! O all fair things, black, deformed, and without beauty, when ye are set beside the fairest Lord Jesus! O black heaven, but O fair Christ! O black angels, but O surpassingly fair Lord Jesus."

I hope you both are agreed with Christ, according to the articles of peace propounded to you in the gospel; and that you are every day driving on salvation work, betwixt him and you, in your family, and in your closets.

And now, my dear, friends, if these discoveries of Christ, which I humbly offer to your hands, may be any way useful to your souls, to assist them either in obtaining, or in clearing their in merest in him, my heart shall rejoice, even mine; for none under heaven can be more willing, though many are more able, to help you thither, than is

Your affectionate and obliged,
kinsman and servant
From my Study at Dartmouth, John Flavel.
March 14th, 1671.

John Flavel

To the Christian Readers, Especially those in the Town and Corporation of Dartmouth, and Parts adjacent, who have either befriended, or attended these Lectures.

Honoured and worthy Friends,

Knowledge is man's excellency above the beasts that perish, Psal. 32: 9. the knowledge of Christ is the Christian's excellency above the Heathen, 1 Cor. 1: 23, 24. Practical and saving knowledge of Christ is the sincere Christian's excellency above the self- cozening hypocrite, Heb. 6: 4, 6. but methodical and well digested knowledge of Christ is the strong Christian's excellency above the weak, Heb. 5: 13, 14. A saving, though an immethodical knowledge of Christ, will bring us to heaven, John 17: 2, but a regular and methodical, as well as a saving knowledge of him, will bring heaven into us, Col. 2: 2, 3.

For such is the excellency thereof, even above all other knowledge of Christ, that it renders the understanding judicious, the memory tenacious, and the heart highly and fixedly joyous. How it serves to confirm and perfect the understanding, is excellently discovered by a worthy divine of our own, in these words:

A young ungrounded Christian, when he sees all the fundamental truths, and sees good evidence and reasons of them, perhaps may be yet ignorant of the right order and place of every truth. It is a rare thing to have young professors to understand the necessary truths methodically: and this is a very great defect: for a great part of the usefulness and excellency of particular truths consisteth in the respect they have to one another. This therefore will be a very considerable part of your confirmation, and growth in your understandings, to see the body of the Christian doctrine, as it were, at one view, as the several parts of it are united in one perfect frame; and to know what aspect one point has upon another, and which are their due places. There is a great difference betwixt the sight of the several parts of a clock or watch, as they are disjointed and scattered abroad, and the seeing of them conjointed, and in use and motion. To see here a pin and there a wheel, and not know how to set them all together, nor ever see them in their due places, will give but little satisfaction. It is the frame and design of holy doctrine that must be known, and every part should be discerned as it has its particular use to that design, and as it is connected with the other parts.

By this means only can the true nature of Theology, together with the harmony and perfection of truth, be clearly understood. And every single truth also will be much better perceived by him that sees its place and order, than by any other: for one truth exceedingly illustrates and leads another into the understanding. - Study therefore to grow in the more methodical knowledge of the same truths which you have received; and though you are not yet ripe enough to discern the whole body of theology in due method, yet see so much as you have attained to know, in the right order and placing of every part. As in anatomy, it is hard for the wisest physician to discern the course of every branch of the veins and arteries; but yet they may easily discern the place and order of the principal parts, and greater vessels, (and surely in the body of religion there are no branches of greater or more necessary truth than these) so it is in divinity, where no man has a perfect view of the whole, till he comes to the state of perfection with God; but every true Christian has the knowledge of all the essentials, and may know the orders and places of them all.

And as it serves to render the mind more judicious, so it causes the memory to be more tenacious, and retentive of truths. The chain of truth is easily held in the memory, when one truth links in another; but the loosing of a link endangers the scattering of the whole chain. We use to say, order is the mother of memory; I am sure it is a singular friend to it: hence it is observed, those that write of the art of memory, lay so great a stress upon place and number. The memory would not so soon be overcharged with a multitude of truths, if that multitude were but orderly disposed. It is the incoherence and confusion of truths, rather than their number, that distracts. Let but the understanding receive then regularly, and the memory will retain them with much more facility. A bad memory is a common complaint among Christians: all the benefit that many of you have in hearing, is from the present influence of truths upon your hearts; there is but little that sticks by you, to make a second and third impression upon them. I know it may be said of some of you, that if your affections were not better than your memories, you would need a very large charity to pass for Christians. I confess it is better to have a well ordered heart, than a methodical head; but surely both are better than either. And for you that have constantly attended these exercises, and followed us through the whole series and deduction of these truths, from text to text, and from point to point; who have begun one sabbath where you left another, it will be your inexcusable fault, if these things be not fixed in your understanding and memories, as nails fastened in a sure place: especially as providence has now brought to your eyes, what has been so often sounded in your ears, which is no small help to fix these truths upon you, and prevent that great hazard of them, which commonly attends bare hearing; for now you may have recourse as often as you will to them, view and review them, till they become your own.

But though this be a great and singular advantage, yet is not all you may have by a methodical understanding of the doctrines of Christ: it is more than a judicious understanding them, or faithful remembering them, that you and I must design, even the warm, vital, animating influences of these truths upon our hearts, without which we shall be never the better; yea, much the worse for knowing and remembering them.

Truth is the sanctifying instrument, John 17: 17. the mould into which our souls are cast, Rom. 6: 17. according therefore to the stamps and impressions it makes upon our understandings, and the order in which truths lie there, will be the depth and lastingness of their impressions and influences upon the heart; as, the more weight is laid upon the seal, the more fair and lasting impression is made upon the wax. He that sees the grounds and reasons of his peace and comfort most clearly, is like to maintain it the more constantly.

Great therefore is the advantage Christians have by such methodical systems. Surely they may be set down among the desiderata Christianorum, The most desired things of Christians.

Divers worthy modern pens have indeed undertaken this noble subject before me, Some more succinctly, others more copiously: these have done worthily, and their praises are in the churches of Christ; yet such breadth there is in the knowledge of Christ, that not only those who have written on this subject before me, but a thousand authors more may employ their pens after us, and not interfere with, or straiten another.

And such is the deliciousness of this subject, that, were there ten thousand volumes written upon it, they would never cloy, or become nauseous to a gracious heart. We use to say, one thing tires, and it is true that it does so, except that one thing be virtually and eminently all things, as Christ is; and then one thing can never tire; for such is the variety of sweetness in Christ, who is the deliciae humani generis, the delights of the children of men, that every time he is opened to believers from pulpit or press, it is as if heaven had furnished them with a new Christ; and yet he is the same Christ still.

The treatise itself will satisfy you, that I have not boasted in another man's line, of things made ready to my hand; which I speak not in the least to win any praise to myself from the undertaking, but to remove prejudice from it; for I see more defects in it, than most of my readers will see, and can forethink more faults to be found in it, than I now shall stand to tell thee of, or answer for. It was written in a time of great distractions; and didst thou but know how oft this work has died and revived under my hand, thou wouldst wonder that ever it came to thine.

I am sensible it may fall under some censorious (it may be, envious) eyes, and that far different judgements will pass upon it; for pro captu lectoris habent sua fata libelli: And no wonder if a treatise of Christ be, when Christ himself was to some, "a stone of stumbling, and a rock of offence." I expect not to please every reader, especially the envious; magna debet esse eloquentie, quae invitis placet. It is as hard for some to look upon other men's gifts without envy, as it is to look upon their own without pride; nor will I be any further concerned with such readers, than to pity them; well knowing that every proud, contemptuous and envious censure is a grenado that breaks in the hand of him that casts it.

But to the ingenuous and candid reader, I owe satisfaction for the obscurity of some part of this discourse, occasioned by the conciseness of the stile; to which I have this only to say, that I was willing to crowd as much matter as I could into this number of sheets in thy hand, that I might therein ease thee both in thy pains and thy purse. I confess the sermons were preached in a more relaxed stile, and most of these things were enlarged in the pulpit, which are designedly contracted in the press, that the volume might not swell above the ability of common readers. And it was my purpose at first to have comprised the second part, viz., The application of the redemption that is with Christ unto sinners, in one volume, which occasioned the contraction of this; but that making a just volume itself, must await another season to see the light. If the reader will be but a little the more intent and considerate in reading, this conciseness will turn to his advantage.

This may suffice to show the usefulness of such composure, and prevent offence; but something yet remains with me, to say to the readers in general, to those of this town in special, and to the flock committed by Christ to my charge more especially.

1. To readers in general, according as their different states and conditions may be; there are six things earnestly to be requested of them.

(1.) If you be yet strangers to Christ, let these things begin, and beget your first acquaintance with him. I assure thee, reader, it was a principal part of the design thereof; and here thou wilt find many directions, helps, and sweet encouragements, to assist a poor stranger as thou art, in that great work. Say not, I am an enemy to Christ, and there is no hope of reconciliation; for here thou wilt see, how "God was in Christ reconciling the world to himself." Say not, all this is nothing except God had told thee so, and appointed some to treat with thee about it; "for he has committed unto us the word of this reconciliation." Say not, yea, that may be from your own pity and compassion for us, and not from any commission you have for it; for we "are ambassadors for Christ," 2 Cor. 5: 20.

Say not, O but my sins are greater than can be forgiven: the difficulties of my salvation are too great to be overcome, especially by a poor creature as I am, that am able to do nothing, no, not to raise one penny towards the discharge of that great debt I owe to God. For here thou wilt find, upon thy union with Christ, that there is merit enough in his blood, and mercy enough in his bowels, to justify and save such a one as thou art. Yea, and I will add for thine encouragement, that it is a righteous thing, with God to justify and save thee, that canst not pay him one penny of all the vast sums thou owest him; when, by the same rule of justice, he condemns the most strict, self-righteous Pharisee, that thinks thereby to quit scores with him. It is righteous for a judge to cast him that has paid ninety-nine pounds of the hundred, which he owed, because the payment was not full; and to acquit him, whose surety has paid all, though himself did not, and freely confess that he cannot pay one farthing of the whole debt.

(2.) If thou be a self deceiving soul, that easily takest up thy satisfaction about thine interest in Christ, look to it, as thou valuest thy soul, reader, that a fond and groundless conceit of thine interest in Christ do not effectually and finally obstruct a true and saving, interest in him. This is the common and fatal error in which multitudes of souls are ensnared and ruined: for look as a conceit of great wisdom hinders many from the attaining of it; so a groundless conceit that Christ is already thine, may prove the greatest obstacle between Christ and thee: but here thou will meet with many rules that will not deceive thee, trials that will open thy true condition to thee.

Thou sometimes reflectest upon the state of thy soul, and enquirest, is Christ mine? may I depend upon it, that my condition is safe? Thy heart returns thee an answer of peace, it speaks as thou wouldst have it. But remember, friend, and mark this line, Thy final sentence is not yet come from the mouth of thy Judge; and what if, after all thy self-flattering hopes and groundless confidence, a sentence should come from him quite cross to that of thine own heart? where art thou then? what a confounded person wilt thou be? Christless, speechless, and hopeless, all at once!

O therefore build sure for eternity; take heed lest the loss of thine eternal happiness be at last imputed by thee to the deceitfulness and laziness of thine own heart: lest thy heart say to thee in hell, as the heart of Apollodorus seemed in his sufferings to say to him, I am the cause of all this misery to thee.

(3.) If thou be one whose heart is eagerly set upon this vain world, I beseech thee take heed, lest it interpose itself betwixt Christ and thy soul, and so cut thee off from him for ever. O beware, lest the dust of the earth, getting into thine eyes, so blind thee, that thou never see the beauty or necessity of Christ. The god of this world so blinds the eyes of them that believe not. And what are sparkling pleasures that dazzles the eyes of some, and the distracting cares that wholly divert the minds of others, but as a napkin drawn by Satan over the eyes of them that are to be turned off into hell? 1 Cor. 4: 3, 4.

Some general aims, and faint wishes after Christ you may have; but alas! the world has centered thy heart, intangled thy affections, and will daily find new diversions for them from the great business of life; so that, if the Lord break not this snare, thou wilt never be able to deliver thy soul.

(4.) If thou be a loose and careless professor of Christ, I beseech thee, let the things thou shalt read in this treatise of Christ, convince, shame, reclaim thee from thy vain conversation. Here thou wilt find how contrary thy conversation is to the grand designs of the death and resurrection of Christ. Oh, rethinks as thou art reading the deep humiliation, and unspeakable sorrows Christ underwent for the expiating of sin, thou shouldest thenceforth look upon sin as a tender child would look upon that knife that stabbed his father to the heart! thou shouldst never whet and sharpen it again to wound the Son of God afresh. To such loose and careless professors, I particularly recommend the last general use of this discourse, containing many great motives to reformation and strict godliness in all that call upon the name of the Lord Jesus.

(5.) If thou hast been a profane and vain person, but now art pardoned, and dost experience the superabounding riches of grace, my request to thee is, that thou love Jesus Christ with a more fervent love than ever yet thou hadst for him. Here thou wilt find many great incentives, many mighty arguments to such a love of Christ. Poor soul, consider what thou hast been, what the morning of thy life was, what treasures of guilt thou laidst up in those days; and then think, can such a one as I receive mercy, and that mercy not break my heart? Can I read my pardon, and mine eyes not drop? What! mercy for such a wretch as I! a pardon for such a rebel! O what an ingenuous thaw should this cause upon my heart! if it do not, what a strange heart is thine.

Did the love of Christ break through so many impediments to come to thee? Did it make its way through the law, through the wrath of God, through the grave, through thine own unbelief and great unworthiness, to come to thee? O what a love was the love of Christ to thy soul; And is not thy love strong enough to break through the vanities and trifles of this world, which entangle it, to go to Christ? How poor, how low and weak is thy love to Christ then?

(6.) Lastly, Art thou one that hast through mercy at last attained assurance, or good hope, through grace, of thy interest in Christ? Rejoice then in thy present mercy, and long ardently to be with thine own Christ in his glory. There be many things dispersed through this treatise, of Christ, to animate such joy, and excite such longings. It was truly observed by a worthy author, (whose words I have mentioned more freely than his name in this discourse) That it is in a manner as natural for us to leap when we see the new Jerusalem, as it is to laugh when we are tickled: Joy is not under the soul's command when Christ kisseth it. And for your desires to be with Christ, what consideration can you find in this world strong enough to rein them in? O when you shall consider what he has done, suffered, and purchased for you, where he is now, and how much he longs for your coming, your very hearts should groan out those words, Phil. 1: 23, "I desire to be dissolved, and to be with Christ." The Lord direct your hearts into the love of God, and into the patient waiting for of Christ.

2. Having delivered my message to the reader in general, I have somewhat more particularly to say to you of this place.

You are a people that were born under, and bred up with the gospel. It has been your singular privilege, above many towns and parishes in England, to enjoy more than sixty years together an able and fruitful ministry among you. The dew of heaven lay upon you, as it did upon Gideon's fleece, when the ground was dry in other places about you; you have been richly watered with gospel-showers; you, with Capernaum, have been exalted to heaven in the means of grace. And it must be owned to your praise, that you testified more respect to the gospel than many other places have done, and treated Christ's ambassadors with more civility, whilst they prophesied in sackcloth, than some other places did. These things are praise-worthy in you. But all this, and much more than this, amounts not to that which Jesus Christ expects from you, and which in his name I would now persuade you to. And O that I (the least and unworthiest of all the messengers of Christ to you) might indeed prevail with all that are Christless among you, (1) To answer the long continued calls of God to you, by a thorough and sound conversion, that the long-suffering of God may be your salvation, and you may not receive all this grace of God in vain. O that the damned might never be set a wondering, to see a people of your advantages for heaven, sinking as much below many of themselves in misery, as you now are above them in means and mercy.

Dear friends, my heart's desire and prayer to God for you is that you may be saved. O that I knew how to engage this whole town to Jesus Christ, and make fast the marriage-knot betwixt him and you, albeit after that I should presently go to the place of silence; and see men no more, with the inhabitants of the world. Ah sirs! me thinks I see the Lord Jesus laying the merciful hand of a holy violence upon you: methinks he calls to you, as the angel to Lot saying, "Arise, lest ye be consumed; And "while he lingered, the men laid hold upon his hand, the Lord being merciful unto him. And they brought him without the city, and said, Escape for thy life, stay not in all the plain; escape to the mountain, lest thou be consumed," Gen. 19: 15. How often (to allude to this) has Jesus Christ in like manner laid hold upon you in the preaching of the gospel, and will you not flee for refuge to him? Will you rather be consumed, than to endeavour an escape? A beast will not be driven into the fire, and will you not be kept out? The merciful Lord Jesus, by his admirable patience and bounty, has convinced you how loth he is to leave or lose you. To this day his arms are stretched forth to gather you, and will you not be gathered? Alas for my poor neighbours! Must so many of them perish at last? What shall I do for the daughter of my people?

Lord, by arguments shall they be persuaded to be happy? What will win them effectually to thy Christ? They have many of them escaped the pollutions of the world through the knowledge of the Lord and Saviour. They are a people that love thine ordinances, they take delight in approaching to God; thou hast beautified many of them with lovely and obliging tempers and dispositions. Thus far they are come, there they stick; and beyond this no power but thine can move them. O thou, to whose hand this work is and must be left, put forth thy saving power and reveal thine arm for their salvation; Thou hast glorified thy name in many of them; Lord, glorify it again.

(2.) My next request is, that you will all be persuaded, whether converted or unconverted, to set up all the duties at religion in your families, and govern your children and servants as men that must give an account to God for them in the great day. O that there were not a prayerless family in this town! How little will their tables differ from the manger, where beasts feed together, if God be not owned and acknowledged there, in your eating and drinking? And how can you expect blessings should dwell in your tabernacles, if God be not called on there? Say not, you want time for it, or that your necessities will not allow it; for, had you been more careful of these duties, it is like you had not been exposed to such necessities: besides, you can find time to be idle, you can waste a part of every day vainly; Why could not that time be redeemed for God? Moreover, you will not deny but the success of all your affairs at home and abroad depends upon the blessing of God; and if so, think you it is not the right way, even to temporal prosperity, to engage his presence and blessing with you, in whose hands your all is? Say not, your children and servants are ignorant of God, and therefore you cannot comfortably join with them in those duties, for the neglect of those duties is the cause of their ignorance; and it is not like they will be better, till you use God's means to make them so.

Besides, prayer is a part of natural worship, and the vilest among men are bound to pray, else the neglect of it were none of their sin. O let not a duty, upon which so many and great blessings hang, fall to the ground, upon such silly (not to say wicked) pretences to shift it off. Remember, death will shortly break up all your families, and disband them; and who then think you will have most comfort in beholding their dead? The day of account also hastens, and then who will have the most comfortable appearing before the just and holy God? Set up, I beseech you, the ancient and comfortable duties of reading the scriptures, singing of psalms, and prayer, in all your dwelling-places. And do all these conscientiously, as men that have to do with God; and try the Lord herewith, if he will not return in a way of mercy to you, and restore even your outward prosperity to you again. However, to be sure, far greater encouragements than that lie before you, to oblige you to your duties.

(3.) More especially, I have a few things to say to you that have attended on the ministry, or are under my oversight in a more particular manner, and then I have done. And,

1st, I cannot but observe to you the goodness of our God, yea, the riches of his goodness:

Who freely gave Jesus Christ out of his own bosom for us, and has not withheld his Spirit, ordinances and ministers, to reveal and apply him to us. Here is love that wants an epithet to match it:

Who engaged my heart upon this transcendent subject in the course of my ministry among you: a subject which angels study and admire, as well as we:

Who so signally protected and overshadowed our assemble in those days of trouble, wherein these truths were delivered to you. You then sat down under his shadow with great delight, and his fruit was sweet to your taste: his banner over you was love; your bread was then sure, and your waters failed not: Yea, such was his peculiar indulgence, and special tenderness to you, that he suffered no man to do you harm; and it can hardly be imagined any could attempt it that had but known this, and no worse than this, to be your only design and business:

Who made these meditations of Christ a strong support, and sweet relief to mine, now with Christ, and no less to me, under the greatest exercises and tries that ever befel me in this world; preserving me yet (though a broken vessel) for some farther use and service to your souls:

Who in the years that are past left not himself without witness among us, blessing my labours, to the conversion and edification of many; Some of which yet remain with us, but some are fallen asleep:

Who has made many of you that yet remain, a willing and obedient people, who have in some measure supported the reputation of religion by your stability and integrity in days of abounding iniquity: my joy and my crown; so stand ye fast in the Lord!

Who after all the days of fears and troubles, through which we have past, has at last given us and his churches rest; "that we being delivered out of the hands of our enemies, might serve him without fear in righteousness and holiness (which doing, this mercy may be extended to us) all the days of our life."

In testimony of a thankful heart for these invaluable mercies, I humbly and cheerfully rear up this pillar of remembrance, inscribing it with EBEN-EZER, and JEHOVAH-JIREH!

2dly, As I could not but observe these things to you, so I have a few things to request of you, in neither of which I can bar denial, so deeply Christ's, your own, and my interest lie in them.

(1.) Look to it, my dear friends, that none of you be found Christless at your appearance before him. Those that continue Christless now, will be left speechless then. God forbid that you

The Fountain of Life Opened Up

that have heard so much of Christ, and you that have professed so much of Christ, should at last fall into a worse condition than those that never heard the name of Christ.

(2.) See that you daily grow more Christ-like by conversing with him, as you do, in his precious ordinances. Let it be with your souls, as it is with a piece of cloth, which receives a deeper dye every time it is dipt into a vat. If not, you may not expect the continuance of your mercies much longer to you.

(3.) Get these great truths well digested both in your heads and hearts, and let the power of them be displayed in your lives, else the pen of the scribe, and the tongue of the preacher, are both in vain. These things, that so often warmed your hearts from the pulpit, return now to make a second impression upon them from the press. Hereby you will recover and fix those truths, which, it is like, are in great part already vanished from you.

This is the fruit I promise myself from you: and whatever entertainment it meets with from others in this Christ-despising age, yet two things relieve me; one is, that future times may produce more humble and hungry Christians than this glutted age enjoys, to whom it will be welcome: the other is, that duty is discharged, and endeavours are used to bring men to Christ,, and build them up in him: wherein he does and will rejoice, who is a well-wisher to the souls of men.

John Flavel.

Sermon 1: Opens the Excellency of the Subject

1 COR. 2: 2.
For I determined not to know any thing among you, save Jesus Christ, and him crucified.

The former verse contains an apology for the plain and familiar manner of the apostle's preaching, which was not (as he there tells them) with excellency of speech, or of wisdom; i. e. he studied not to gratify their curiosity with rhetorical strains, or philosophical niceties. In this he gives the reason, "for I determined not to know any thing among you, save Jesus Christ," &c.

"I determined not to know." The meaning is not, that he simply despised, or condemned all other studies and knowledge; but so far only as they stand in competition with, or opposition to the study and knowledge of Jesus Christ. And it is as if he should say, it is my stated, settled judgement; not a hasty, inconsiderate censure, but the product and issue of my most serious and exquisite enquiries. After I have well weighed the case, turned it round, viewed it exactly on every side, balanced all advantages and disadvantages, pondered all things, that are fit to come into consideration about it; this is the result and final determination, that all other knowledge, how profitable, how pleasant soever, is not worthy to be named in the same day with the knowledge of Jesus Christ. This, therefore, I resolve to make the scope and end of my ministry, and the end regulates the mean; such pedantic toys, and airy notions as injudicious ears affect, would rather obstruct than promote my grand design among you; therefore, wholly waving that way, I applied myself to a plain, popular, unaffected dialect, fitted rather to pierce the heart, and convince the conscience, than to tickle the fancy. This is the scope of the words, in which three things fall under consideration;

First, The subject matter of his doctrine, to wit, Jesus Christ. "I determined to know nothing," i. e. to study nothing myself, to teach nothing to you, but "Jesus Christ." Christ shall be the centre to which all the lines of my ministry shall be drawn. I have spoken and written of many other subjects in my sermons and epistles, but it is all reductively the preaching and discovery of Jesus Christ: of all the subjects in the world, this is the sweetest; if there be any thing on this side heaven, worthy our time and studies, this is it. Thus he magnifies his doctrine, from the excellency of its subject-matter, accounting all other doctrines but airy things, compared with this.

Secondly, We have here that special respect or consideration of Christ, which he singled out from all the rest of the excellent truths of Christ, to spend the main strength of his ministry upon; and that is, Christ as crucified: and the rather, because hereby he would obviate the vulgar prejudice raised against him upon the account of his cross; "For Christ crucified was to the Jews a stumbling block, and to the Greeks foolishness," chap. 1: 23. This also best suited his end, to draw them on to Christ; as Christ above all other subjects, so Christ crucified above all things in Christ. There is, therefore, a great emphasis in this word, "and him crucified."

Thirdly, The manner in which he discoursed this transcendent subject to them, is also remarkable; he not only preached Christ crucified, but he preached him assiduously and plainly. He preached Christ frequently; "and whenever he preached of Christ crucified, he preached him in a crucified stile." This is the sum of the words; to let them know that his spirit was intent upon this subject, as if he neither knew, nor cared to speak of any other. All his sermons were so full of Christ, that his hearers might have thought he was acquainted with no other doctrine. Hence observe,

Doct. That there is no doctrine more excellent in itself or more necessary to be preached and, studied, than the doctrine of Jesus Christ, and him crucified.

ALL other knowledge, how much soever it be magnified in the world, is, and ought to be esteemed but dross, in comparison of the excellency of the knowledge of Jesus Christ, Phil. 3: 8. "In him are hid all the treasures of wisdom and knowledge," Col. 2: 3.

Eudoxus was so affected with the glory of the sun, that he thought he was born only to behold it; much more should a Christian judge himself born only to behold and delight in the glory of the Lord Jesus.

The Fountain of Life Opened Up

The truth of this proposition will be made out by a double consideration of the doctrine of Christ.

First, Let it be considered absolutely, and then these lovely properties with which it is naturally clothed, will render it superior to all other sciences and studies.

1st, The knowledge of Jesus Christ is the very marrow and kernel of all the scriptures; the scope and centre of all divine revelations: both Testaments meet in Christ. The ceremonial law is full of Christ, and all the gospel is full of Christ: the blessed lines of both Testaments meet in him; and how they both harmonise, and sweetly concentre in Jesus Christ, is the chief scope of that excellent epistle to the Hebrews, to discover; for we may call that epistle the sweet harmony of both Testaments. This argues the unspeakable excellency of this doctrine, the knowledge whereof must needs therefore be a key to unlock the greatest part of the sacred scriptures. For it is in the understanding of scripture, much as it is in the knowledge men have in logic and philosophy: if a scholar once come to understand the bottom-principle, upon which, as upon its hinge, the controversy turns the true knowledge of that principle shall carry him through the whole controversy, and furnish him with a solution to every argument. Even so the right knowledge of Jesus Christ, like a clue, leads you through the whole labyrinth of the scriptures.

2dly, The knowledge of Jesus Christ is a fundamental knowledge; and foundations are most useful, though least seen. The knowledge of Christ is fundamental to all graces, duties, comforts, and happiness.

(1.) It is fundamental to all graces; they all begin in knowledge; Col. 3: 10. "The new man is renewed in knowledge." As the old, so the new creation begins in light; the opening of the eyes is the first work of the Spirit; and as the beginnings of grace, so all the after-improvements thereof depend upon this increasing knowledge, 2 Pet. 3: 18. "But grow in grace, and in the knowledge of our Lord and Saviour." See how these two, grace and knowledge, keep equal pace in the soul of a Christian in what degree the one increases, the other increases answerable.

(2.) The knowledge of Christ is fundamental to all duties; the duties, as well as the graces of all Christians, are all founded in the knowledge of Christ, Must a Christian believe? That he can never do without the knowledge of Christ: faith is so much dependent on his knowledge, that it is denominated by it, Isa. 53: 11. "By his knowledge shall my righteous servant justify many;" and hence, John 6: 40, seeing and believing are made the same thing. Would a man exercise hope in God? that he can never do without the knowledge of Christ, for he is the author of that hope, 1 Pet. 1: 3, he is also its object, Heb. 6: 19. its ground-work and support, Col. 1: 27. And as you cannot believe or hope, so neither can you pray acceptably without a competent degree of this knowledge. The very Heathen could say, Non loquendum de Deo sine lumine, i. e. Men must not speak of God without light: the true way of conversing with, and enjoying God in prayer, is by acting faith on him through a Mediator: so much comfort and true excellency there is in it, and no more. O then, how indispensable is the knowledge of Christ, to all that do address themselves to God in any duty.

(3.) It is fundamental to all comforts: all the comforts of believers are streams from this fountain. Jesus Christ is the very object matter of a believer's joy, Phil. 3: 3. "Our rejoicing is in "Christ Jesus." Take away the knowledge of Christ, and a Christian is the most sad and melancholy creature in the world: again, let Christ but manifest himself, and dart the beams of his light into their souls, it will make them kiss the stakes, sing in flames, and shout in the pangs of death, as men that divide the spoil.

Lastly, This knowledge is fundamental to the eternal happiness of souls: as we can perform no duty, enjoy no comfort; so neither can we be saved without it, John 17: 3. "This is life eternal, to know thee the only true God, and Jesus Christ whom thou hast sent." And, if it be life eternal to know Christ, then it is eternal damnation to be ignorant of Christ: as Christ is the door that opens heaven, so knowledge is the key that opens Christ. The excellent gifts, and renowned parts of the moral Heathens, though they purchased to them great esteem and honour among men, yet left them in a state of perdition, because of this great defect, they were ignorant of Christ, 1 Cor. 1: 21. Thus you see how fundamental the knowledge of Christ is, essentially necessary to all the graces, duties, comforts and happiness of souls.

3dly, The knowledge of Christ is profound and large; all other sciences are but shadows; this is a boundless, bottomless ocean; no creature has a line long enough to fathom the depth of it; there is height, length, depth and breadth ascribed to it, Eph. 3: 18, yea, it passeth knowledge. There is "a manifold wisdom of God in Christ," Eph. 3: 10. It is of many sorts and forms, of many folds and plates: it is indeed simple, pure and unmixed with any thing but itself, yet it is manifold in degrees, kinds and administrations; though something of Christ be unfolded in one age, and something in another, yet eternity itself cannot fully unfold him. I see something, said Luther, which blessed Austin saw not; and those that come after me, will see that which I see not. It is in the studying of Christ, as in the planting of a new discovered country; at first men sit down by the sea-side, upon the skirts and borders of the land; and there they dwell, but by degrees they search farther and farther into the heart of the country. Ah, the best of us are yet but upon the borders of this vast continent!

4thly, The study of Jesus Christ is the most noble subject that ever a soul spent itself upon; those that rack and torture their brains upon other studies, like children, weary themselves at a low game, the eagle plays at the sun itself. The angels study this doctrine, and stoop down to look into this deep abyss. What are the truths discovered in Christ, but the very secrets that from eternity lay hid in the bosom of God? Eph. 3: 8, 9. God's heart is opened to men in Christ, John 1: 18. This makes the gospel such a glorious dispensation, because Christ is so gloriously revealed therein, 2 Cor. 3: 9. and the studying of Christ in the gospel, stamps such a heavenly glory upon the contemplating soul, ver. 18.

5thly, It is the most sweet and comfortable knowledge; to be studying Jesus Christ, what is it but to be digging among all the veins and springs of comfort? And the deeper you dig, the more do these springs flow upon you. How are hearts ravished with the discoveries of Christ in the gospel? what ecstasies, meltings, transports, do gracious souls meet there? Doubtless, Philip's ecstasy, John 1: 25. "eurekamen Iesoun", "We have found Jesus," was far beyond that of Archimedes. A believer could sit from morning to night, to hear discourses of Christ; "His mouth is most sweet", Cant. 5: 16.

Secondly, Let us compare this knowledge with all other knowledge, and thereby the excellency of it will farther appear.

1. All other knowledge is natural, but this wholly supernatural, Mat. 11: 27. "No man knoweth the Son, but the Father", neither knoweth any the Father, save the Son, and he to whom soever the Son will reveal him." The wisest Heathens could never make a discovery of Christ by their deepest searches into nature; the most eagle-eyed philosophers were but children in knowledge, compared with the most illiterate Christians.

2. Other knowledge is unattainable by many. All the helps and means in the world would never enable some Christians to attain the learned arts and languages; men of the best wits, and most pregnant parts, are most excellent in these; but here is the mystery and excellency of the knowledge of Christ, that men of most blunt, dull and contemptible parts attain, through the teaching of the Spirit, to this knowledge, in which the more acute and ingenious are utterly blind. Mat. 11: 25, "I thank thee, O Father, Lord of heaven and earth, because thou hast hid these things from the wise and prudent, and hast revealed them unto babes." 1 Cor. 1: 26, 27. "You see your calling, brethren, how that not many wise men after the flesh, not many mighty, not many noble are called: but God has chosen the foolish things of the world, to confound the wise," &c.

3. Other knowledge, though you should attain the highest degree of it, would never bring you to heaven, being defective and lame both in the integrity of parts, the principal thing, viz. Christ, being wanting; and in the purity of its nature: for the knowing Heathens grew vain in their imaginations, Rom. 1: 21, and in the efficacy and influence of it on the heart and life, They held the truth in unrighteousness; their lusts were stronger than their light, Rom. 1: 18. But this knowledge has potent influences, changing souls, into its own image, 2 Cor. 3: 18, and so proves a saving knowledge unto men, 1 Tim. 2: 4. And thus I have in a few particulars pointed out the transcendence of the knowledge of Christ.

The use of all this I shall give you in a few inferences, on which I shall not enlarge, the whole being only preliminary to the doctrine of Christ; only for the present I shall hence infer,

Inference 1

The sufficiency of the doctrine of Christ, to make men wise unto salvation. Paul desired to know nothing else; and, indeed, nothing else is of absolute necessity to be known. A little of this knowledge, if saving and effectual upon thy heart, will do thy soul more service, than all the vain speculation and profound parts that others so much glory in. Poor Christian, be not dejected, because thou sees thyself out-stript and excelled by so many in other parts of knowledge; if thou know Jesus Christ, thou knowest enough to comfort and save thy soul. Many learned philosophers are now in hell, and many illiterate Christians in heaven.

Inference 2

If there be such excellency in the knowledge of Christ, let it humble all, both saints and sinners, that we have no more of this clear and effectual knowledge in us, notwithstanding the excellent advantages we have had for it. Sinners, concerning you I may sigh and say with the apostle, 1 Cor. 15: 34. "Some have not the knowledge of Christ, I speak this to your shame". This, O this is the condemnation. And even for you that are enlightened in this knowledge, how little do you know of Jesus Christ, in comparison of what you might have known of him? What a shame is it, that you should need to be taught the very first truths, "when for the time you might have been teachers of others?" Heb. 5: 12, 13, 14. "That your ministers cannot speak unto you as spiritual, but

The Fountain of Life Opened Up

as unto carnal, even as unto babes in Christ," 1 Cor. 3: 1, 2. O how much time is spent in other studies, in vain discourses, frivolous pamphlets, worldly employments? How little is the search and study of Jesus Christ.

Inference 3

How sad is their condition that have a knowledge of Christ, and yet as to themselves it had been better they had never had it! Many there be that content themselves with an unpractical, ineffectual, and merely notional knowledge of him; of whom the apostle saith, "It had been better for them not to have known," 2 Pet. 2: 21. It serves only to aggravate sin and misery; for though it be not enough to save them, yet it puts some weak restraints upon sin, which their impetuous lusts breaking down, exposes them thereby to a greater damnation.

Inference 4

Fourthly, This may inform us by what rule to judge both ministers and doctrine. Certainly that is the highest commendation of a minister, to be an able minister of the New Testament; not of the letter, but of the Spirit, 2 Cor. 3: 6. He is the best artist, that can most lively and powerfully display Jesus Christ before the people, evidently setting him forth as crucified among them; and that is the best sermon, that is most full of Christ, not of art and language. I know that a holy dialect well becometh Christ's ministers, they should not be rude and careless in language or method; but surely the excellency of a sermon lies not in that, but in the plainest discoveries and liveliest applications of Jesus Christ.

Inference 5

Let all that mind the honour of religion, or the peace and comfort of their own souls, wholly sequester and apply themselves to the study of Jesus Christ, and him crucified. Wherefore spend we ourselves upon other studies, when all excellency, sweetness, and desirableness is concentered in this one? Jesus Christ is fairer than the children of men, the chiefest among ten thousands, "as the apple-tree among the trees of the wood;" Quae faciunt divisa beatum, in hoc mixta fluunt. These things which singly ravish and delight the souls of men, are all found conjunctly in Christ. O what a blessed Christ is this! whom to know is eternal life. From the knowledge of Jesus Christ do bud forth all the fruits of comfort, and that for all seasons and conditions. Hence Rev. 22: 2, he is called "the tree of life, which bears twelve manner of fruits, and yields its fruit every month; and the very leaves of this tree are for healing." In Christ souls have, (1.) All necessaries for food and physic. (2.) All varieties of fruits, twelve manner of fruits; a distinct sweetness in this, in that, and in the other attribute, promise, ordinance. (3.) In him are these fruits at all times, he bears fruit every month; there is precious fruit in Jesus Christ, even in the black month; winter fruits as well as summer fruits. O then study Christ, study to know him more extensively. There be many excellent things in Christ, that the most eagle-eyed believer has not yet seen: Ah! tis pity that any thing of Christ should lie hid from his people. Study to know Christ more intensively, to get the experimental taste and lively power of his knowledge upon your hearts and affections: This is the knowledge that carries all the sweetness and comfort in it. Christian, I dare appeal to thy experience, whether the experimental taste of Jesus Christ, in ordinances and duties, has not a higher and sweeter relish than any created enjoyment thou ever tasted in this world? O then separate, devote, and wholly give thyself, thy time, thy strength to this most sweet transcendent study.

Inference 6

Lastly, Let me close the whole with a double caution; one to ourselves, who by our callings and professions are the ministers of Christ; another to those that sit under the doctrine of Christ daily.

First, If this doctrine be the most excellent, necessary, fundamental, profound, noble, and comfortable doctrine, let us then take heed lest, while we study to be exact in other things, we be found ignorant in this. Ye know it is ignominious, by the common suffrage of the civilised world, for any man to be unacquainted with his own calling, or not to attend the proper business of it: it is our calling, as the Bridegroom's friends, to woo and win souls to Christ, to set him forth to the people as crucified among them, Gal. 3: 1, to present him in all his attractive excellencies, that all hearts may be ravished with his beauty, and charmed into his arms by love: we must also be able to defend the truths of Christ against undermining heretics, to instil his knowledge into the ignorant, to answer the cases and scruples of poor doubting Christians. How many intricate knots have we to untie? What pains, what skill is requisite for such as are employed about our work? And shall we spend our precious time in frivolous controversies, philosophical niceties, dry and barren scholastic notions? Shall we study every thing but Christ? Revolve all volumes but the sacred ones? What is observed even of Bellarmine, that he turned with loathing from school divinity, because it wanted the sweet juice of piety, may be convictive to many among us, who are often too much in love with worse employment than what he is said to loathe. O let the knowledge of Christ dwell richly in us.

Secondly, Let us see that our knowledge of Christ be not a powerless, barren, unpractical knowledge: O that, in its passage from our understanding to our lips, it might powerfully melt, sweeten, and ravish our hearts! Remember, brethren, a holy calling never saved any man, without a holy heart; if our tongues only be sanctified, our whole man must be damned. "We and our people must be judged by the same gospel, and stand at the same bar, and be sentenced to the same terms, and dealt with as severely as any other men: We cannot think to be saved by our clergy, or to come off with a Legit ut clericus, when there is wanting the Credit et vixit ut Christianus; as an eminent Divine speaks. O let the keepers of the vineyard look to, and keep their own vineyard: we have a heaven to win or lose, as well as others.

Thirdly, Let us take heed that we withhold not our knowledge of Christ in unrighteousness from the people. O that our lips may disperse knowledge and feed many. Let us take heed of the napkin, remembering the day of account is at hand. Remember, I beseech you, the relations wherein you stand, and the obligations resulting thence: Remember, the great Shepherd gave himself for, and gave you to the flock; your time, your gifts are not yours, but God's; remember the pinching wants of souls, who are perishing for want of Christ; and if their tongues do not, yet their necessities do bespeak us, as they did Joseph, Gen. 47: 15. "Wherefore should we die in thy presence? Give us food, that we may live and not die." Even the sea monsters draw forth their breasts to their young ones, and shall we be cruel! Cruel to souls! Did Christ not think it too much to sweat blood, yea, to die for them? And shall we think it much to watch, study, preach, pray, and do what we can for their salvation? O let the same mind be in you which was also in Christ!

Secondly, To the people that sit under the doctrine of Christ daily, and have the light of his knowledge shining round about them.

First, Take heed ye do not reject and despise this light. This may be done two ways: First, When you despise the means of knowledge by slight and low esteems of it. Surely, if you thus reject knowledge, God will reject you for it, Hos. 4: 6. It is a despising of the richest gift that ever Christ gave to the church; and however it be a contempt and slight that begins low, and seems only to vent itself upon the weak parts, in artificial discourses, and untaking tones and gestures of the speakers; yet, believe it, it is a daring sin that flies higher than you are aware, Luke 10: 16 "He that despiseth you, despiseth me; and he that despiseth me, despiseth him that sent me". Secondly, You despise the knowledge of Christ, When you despise the directions and loving constraints of that knowledge; when you refuse to be guided by your knowledge, your light and your lusts contest and struggle within you. O it is sad when your lusts master your light. You sin not as the heathens sin, who know not God; but when you sin, you must slight and put by the notices of your own consciences, and offer violence to your own convictions. And what sad work will this make in your souls? How soon will it lay your consciences waste?

Secondly, Take heed that you rest not satisfied with that knowledge of Christ you have attained, but grow on towards perfection. It is the pride and ignorance of many professors, when they have got a few raw and undigested notions, to swell with self-conceit of their excellent attainments. And it is the sin, even of the best of saints, when they see (veritas in profundo) how deep the knowledge of Christ lies, and what pains they must take to dig for it, to throw by the shovel of duty, and cry, Dig we cannot. To your work, Christians, to your work; let not your candle go out: sequester yourselves to this study, look what intercourses, and correspondence are betwixt the two world; what communion soever God and souls maintain, it is in this way; count all, therefore, but dross in comparison of that excellency which is in the knowledge of Jesus Christ.

Sermon 2: Sets forth Christ in his essential en primeval Glory

Proverbs 8:30
Then I was by him, [as] one brought up [with him]: and I was daily [his] delight, rejoicing always before him;

These words are a part of that excellent commendation of wisdom, by which in this book Solomon intends two things; first, Grace or holiness, Prov 4: 7. " Wisdom is the principal thing." Secondly, Jesus Christ, the fountain of that grace: and look, as the former is renowned for its excellency, Job 28: 14, 15, so the latter, in this context, wherein the Spirit of God describes the most blessed state of Jesus Christ, the wisdom of the Father, from those eternal delights he had with his Father, before his assumption of our nature: "Then was I by him," &c. that long Evum was wholly swallowed up, and spent in unspeakable delights and pleasures. Which delights were twofold, (1.) The Father and Son delighted one in another (from which delights the Spirit is not here excluded) without communicating that their joy to any other, for no creature did then exist save in the mind of God, verse 30. (2.) They delighted in the salvation of men, in the prospect of that work, though not yet extant, verse 31. My present business lies in the former, viz. the mutual delights of the Father and Son, one with and in another; the account whereof we have in the text; wherein consider,

1. The glorious condition of the non-incarnated Son of God, described by the person with whom his fellowship was, "Then was I by him," or with him; so with him as never was any, in his very bosom, John 1: 18, the only begotten Son was in the bosom of the Father, an expression of the greatest dearness and intimacy in the world; as if he should say, wrapt up in the very soul of his Father, embosomed in God.

2. This fellowship is illustrated by a metaphor, wherein the Lord will stoop to our capacities, (as "One brought up with him"), the Hebrew word "amon" is sometimes rendered a cunning workman, or curious artist, as in Cant. 7: 1, which is the same word. And indeed Christ shewed himself such an artist in the creation of the world; "For all things were made by him, and without him there was nothing made, that was made," John 1: 3. But Montanus, and others, render it nutricius; and so Christ is here compared to a delightful child, spotting before its Father: the Hebrew root "shachak", which our translation renders "rejoicing before him," signifies to laugh, play, or rejoice; so that, look as parents delight to see their children sporting before them, so did the Father delight in beholding this darling of his bosom.

3. This delight is farther amplified by the perpetuity, and uninterruptedness thereof; "I was day by day his delight, rejoicing always before him." These delights of the Father and the Son one in another, knew not a moment's interruption, or diminution: thus did these great and glorious persons mutually let forth their fullest pleasure and delight, each into the heart of the other; they lay as it were embosomed one in another, entertaining themselves with delights and pleasures ineffable, and inconceivable. Hence we observe,

Doct. That the condition and state of Jesus Christ before his incarnation, was a state of the highest and most unspeakable delight and pleasure, in the enjoyment of his Father.

John tells us he was in the bosom of his Father: to lie in the bosom is the posture of dearest love, John 13: 23. "Now there was leaning on Jesus' bosom one of his disciples whom Jesus loved:" but Christ did not lean upon the Father's bosom, as that disciple did in his, but lay in it: and therefore in Isa. 42: 1, the Father calls him, "Mine elect in whom my soul delighteth;" which is variously rendered; the Septuagint, quem suscepit, whom my soul takes, or wraps up: others, complacuit, one that highly pleases and delights my very soul: and 2 Cor. 8: 9, he is said, in this estate, wherein I am now describing him, to be rich: and, Phil. 2: 7. "To be equal with God, and to be in the form of God," (i. e.) to have all the glory and ensigns of the majesty of God; and the riches which he speaks of, was no less than all that God the Father has, John 16: 14. "All that the Father has is mine:" and what he now has in his exalted state, is the same he had before his humiliation, John 17: 5. Now to sketch out (as we are able) the unspeakable felicity of that state of Christ, whilst he lay in that blessed bosom, I shall consider it three ways, negatively, positively, and comparatively.

1. Let us consider that state negatively, by removing from it all those degrees of abasement and sorrow which his incarnation brought him under: as,

First, He was not then abased to the condition of a creature, which was a low step indeed, and that which upon the matter undid him in point of reputation; for by this (saith the apostle) "he made himself of no reputation," Phil. 2: 7, it emptied him of his glory. For God to be made man, is such an abasement as none can express: but then not only to appear in true flesh, but also in the likeness of sinful flesh, as. Rom. 8: 3. O what is this!

Secondly, Christ was not under the law in this estate. I confess it was no disparagement to Adam in the state of innocence, to angels in their state of glory, to be under law to God; but it was an inconceivable abasement to the absolute independent Being to come under law: yea, not only under the obedience, but also under the malediction and curse of the law, Gal. 4: 4. "But when the fulness of time was come, God sent forth his Son, made of a woman, made under the law."

Thirdly, In this state he was not liable to any of those sorrowful consequent and attendants of that frail and feeble state of humanity, which he afterwards assumed, with the nature. As, (1.) He was unacquainted with griefs; there was no sorrowing or sighing in that bosom where he lay, though afterwards he became a man of sorrows, and acquainted with grief," Isa. 53: 3. "A man of sorrows," as if he had been constituted and made up of pure and unmixed sorrows; every day conversing with griefs, as with his intimate companions and acquaintance. (2.) He was never pinched with poverty and wants, while he continued in that bosom, as he was afterwards, when he said, "The foxes have holes, and the birds of the air have nests, but the Son of man has not where to lay his head," Matth. 8: 20. Ah blessed Jesus! thou needest not to have wanted a place to have lain thine head, hadst thou not left that bosom for my sake. (3.) He never underwent reproach and shame in that bosom, there was nothing but glory and honour reflected upon him by his Father, though afterwards he was despised, and rejected of men, Isa 53: 3. His Father never looked upon him without smiles and love, delight and joy, though afterwards he became a reproach of men, and despised of the people, Psalm 22: 6. (4.) His holy heart was never offended with an impure suggestion or temptation of the Devil; all the while he lay in that bosom of peace and love, he never knew what it was to be assaulted with temptations to be besieged and battered upon by unclean spirits, as he did afterwards, Mat. 4: 1, "Then was Jesus led up of the spirit into the wilderness to be tempted of the Devil." It was for our sakes that he submitted to those exercises of spirit, "to be in all points tempted like as we are, that he might be unto us a merciful and faithful high-priest, Heb. 4: 15. (5.) He was never sensible of pains and tortures in soul or body, there were no such things in that blessed bosom where he lay, though afterwards he groaned and sweat under them, Isa. 53: 5. The Lord embraced him from eternity, but never wounded him till he stood in our place and room (6.) There were no hidings or withdrawings of his Father from him; there was not a cloud from eternity upon the face of God, till Jesus Christ had left that bosom. It was a new thing to Christ to see frowns in the face of his Father; a new thing for him to cry, "My God, my God, why hast thou forsaken me?" Mat. 27: 46. (7.) There were never any impressions of his Fathers wrath upon him, as there were afterwards: God never delivered such a bitter cup into his hands before, as that was, Matth. 26: 39. Lastly, There was no death, to which he was subject, in that bosom. All these things were new things to Christ; he was above them all, till for our sakes he voluntarily subjected himself unto them. Thus you see what that state was not.

2. Let us consider it positively, what it was, and guess by some particular considerations (for indeed we can but guess) at the glory of it; as, (1.) We cannot but conceive it to be a state of matchless happiness, if we consider the persons enjoying and delighting in each other: he was with God, John 1: 1. God, you know, is the fountain, ocean and centre of all delights and joys: Psal. 16: 11, "In thy presence is fulness of joy." To be wrapt up in the soul and bosom of all delights, as Christ was, must needs be a state transcending apprehension; to have the fountain of love and delight letting out itself so immediately, and fully, and ever lastingly, upon this only begotten darling of his soul, so as it never did communicate itself to any; judge what a state of transcendent felicity this must be. Great persons have great delights.

(2.) Or if we consider the intimacy, dearness, yea, oneness of those great persons one with another: the nearer the union, the sweeter the communion. Now Jesus Christ was not only near and dear to God, but one with him; I and my Father are one," John 10: 30, one in nature, will, love and delight. There is indeed a moral union of souls among men by love, but this was a natural oneness, no child is so one with his father, no husband so one with the wife of his bosom, no friend so one with his friend, no soul so one with its body, as Jesus Christ and his Father were one. O what matchless delights must necessarily flow from such a blessed union!

(3.) Consider again the purity of that delight with which the blessed Father and Son embraced each other; the best creature delights one in another, are mixed, debased, and allayed; if there be something ravishing and engaging, there is also something cloying and distasting. The purer any delight is, the more excellent. Now, there are no crystal streams flowing so purely from the fountain, no beams of light so unmixed from the sun, as the loves and delights of these holy and glorious persons were: the holy, holy, holy Father embraced the thrice holy Son with a most holy delight and love.

(4.) Consider the constancy of this delight; it was from everlasting, as in verse 23, and from eternity; it never suffered one moment's interruption. The overflowing fountain of God's delight and love never stopped its course, never ebbed; but as he speaks in the text, "I was daily his delight, rejoicing always before him." Once more, consider the fulness at that delight, the perfection of that pleasure; I was delights: so the word is in its original; not only plural, delights, all delights, but also in the abstract, delight itself: as afterwards from the abundance of his sorrows, he was stiled, a man of sorrows, so here, from the fulness of his delights: as though you should say, even constituted and made up of pleasure and delight.

3. Once more, let us consider it comparatively, and this state still yet appear more glorious, comparing it with either the choicest delights that one creature takes in another, or that God takes in the creature, or that the creatures take in God: measure these immense delights, betwixt the Father and his Son, by either of these lines, and you shall find them infinitely short: For, (1.) Though the delights that creatures take in each other, be sometimes a great delight; such was Jacob's delight in Benjamin, whose life is said to be bound up in the lad's life, a dear and high expression, Gen. 44: 30. Such was that of Jonathan in David, whose soul was knit with his soul, "and he loved him as his own soul," 1 Sam. 13: 1, and such is the delight of one friend in another: "there is a friend that is as a man's own soul," Deut. 13: 6, yet all this is but creature-delight, and can in no particular equal the delights betwixt the Father and the Son; for this is but a finite delight, according to the measure and abilities of creatures, but that is infinite, suitable to the infinite perfection of the divine Being; this is always mixed, that perfectly pure. (2.) Or if you compare it with the delight that God takes in the creatures, it is confessed that God takes great delight in some creatures. "The Lord takes pleasure in his saints, he rejoices over them with singing! and resteth in his love," Zeph. 3: 17; Isa. 62: 5. But yet there is a great difference betwixt his delight in creatures, and his delights in Christ; for all his delight in the saints is secondary, and for Christ's sake; but his delights in Christ are primary, and for his own sake: we are accepted in the beloved, Eph. 1: 6, he is beloved, and accepted for himself. (3.) To conclude, compare it once more with the delights that the best of creatures take in God, and Christ, and it must be confessed that is a choice delight, and a transcendent love, with which they love and delight in him; Psal. 73: 25. "Whom have I in heaven but thee? and on earth there is none I desire besides thee." What pangs of love, what raptures of delight did the spouse express to Christ? "O thou whom my soul loveth!" But surely our delight in God is no perfect rule to measure his delight in Christ by: for our love to God (at the best) is still imperfect; that is the burden and constant complaint of saints, but this is perfect; ours is inconstant, up and down, ebbing and flowing, but this is constant. So then, to conclude, the condition and state of Jesus Christ before his incarnation, was a state of the highest and matchless delight, in the enjoyment of his Father. The uses follow.

1. Use of Information

Inference 1

What an astonishing act of love was this then, for the Father to give the delight, the darling, of his soul, out of his very bosom, for poor sinners! all tongues must needs pause and falter, that attempt the expressions of his grace, expressions being here swallowed up: "God so loved the world, that he gave his only begotten Son," John 3: 16. Here is a "sic" without a "sicut"; so loved them: how did he love them? nay, here you must excuse the tongues of angels; which of us would deliver a child, the child of our delights, an only child, to death for the greatest inheritance in the world? what tender parent can endure a parting pull with such a child? when Hagar was taking her last leave (as she thought) of her Ishmael, Gen. 21: 16. the text saith, "she went and sat over against him, a good way off: for she said, Let me not see the death of the child. And she sat over-against him, and lift up her voice, and wept:" though she were none of the best of mothers, nor he the best of children, yet she could not give up the child. O it was hard to part! what an outcry did David make, even for an Absalom! wishing he had died for him. What a hole (as I may say) has the death of some children made in the hearts of some parents, which will never be closed up in this world! yet surely, never did any child lie so close to a parent's heart, as Christ did to his Father's; and yet he willingly parts with him, though his only one, the Son of his delights, and that to death, a cursed death, for sinners, for the worst of sinners. O miranda Dei philanthropic! O the admirable love of God to men! matchless love! a love past finding out! Let all men, therefore, in the business of their redemption, give equal glory to the Father with the Son, John 5: 23. If the Father had not loved thee, he had never parted with such a Son for thee.

Inference 2
From one wonder let our souls turn to another, for they are now in the midst of wonders: adore, and be forever astonished at the love of Jesus Christ to poor sinners; that ever he should consent to leave such a bosom, and the ineffable delights that were there, for such poor worms as we are. O the heights, depths, lengths, and breadths of unmeasurable love! O see, Rom. 5: 6, 7, 8. Read, and wonder; how is the love of Christ commended in ravishing circumstances to poor sinners! You would be loth to leave a creature's bosom, a comfortable dwelling, a fair estate for the best friend in the world; your souls are loth to leave their bodies, though they have no such great content there; but which of you, if ever you found by experience what it is to be in the bosom of God by divine communion, would be persuaded to leave such a bosom for all the good that is in the world? And yet Jesus Christ who was embraced in that bosom after another manner than ever you were acquainted with, freely left it, and laid down the glory and riches he enjoyed there, for your sakes; and as the Father loved him; even so (believers) has he loved you, John 17: 22. What manner of love is this! Who ever loved as Christ loves? Who ever denied himself for Christ, as Christ denied himself for us?

Inference 3
Hence we are informed, That interest in Jesus Christ is the true way to all spiritual preferment in heaven. Do you covet to be in the heart, in the favour and delight of God? Get interest in Jesus Christ, and you shall presently be there. What old Israel said of the children of his beloved Joseph, Thy children are my children; the same God saith of all the dear children of Christ, Gen. 48: 5, 9. You see among men, all things are carried by interest: persons rise in this world as they are befriended; preferment goes by favour: So it is in heaven, persons are preferred according to their interest in the beloved, Eph. 1: 9. Christ is the great favourite in heaven: his image upon your souls and his name in your prayers, makes both accepted with God.

Inference 4
How worthy is Jesus Christ of all our love and delights? You see how infinitely the Father delighteth in him, how he ravishes the heart of God; and shall he not ravish our hearts? I present you a Christ this day, able to ravish any soul that will but view and consider him. O that you did but see this lovely Lord Jesus Christ! Then would you go home sick of love: surely he is a drawing Saviour, John 12: 32. Why do ye lavish away your precious affections upon vanity: None but Christ is worthy of them: when you spend your precious affections upon other objects, what is it but to dig for dross with golden mattocks? The Lord direct our hearts into the love Of Christ. O that our hearts, loves and delights did meet and concentre with the heart of God in this most blessed object! O let him that left God's bosom for you, be embosomed by you, though yours be nothing to God's; he that left God's bosom for you, deserves yours.

Inference 5
If Christ be the beloved darling of the Father's soul, think what a grievous and insufferable thing it is to the heart of God, to see his dear Son despised, slighted, and rejected by sinners: verily, there is no such cut to the heart of God in the whole world. Unbelievers trample upon God's darling, tread under foot him that eternally lay in his bosom, Heb. 10: 29. Smite the Apple of his eye, and how God will bear this, that parable, Mat. 21: 37, to 40, will inform you, surely he will miserably destroy such wretched sinners. If you would study to do God the greatest despight, there is none like this. What a dismal word is that; 1 Cor. 16: 22. "If any man love not our Lord Jesus Christ, let him be Anathema Maranatha," (i. e.) let the great curse of God lie upon that man till the Lord come. O sinners! you shall one day know the price of this sin; you shall feel what it is to despise a Jesus, that is able to compel love from the hardest heart. O that you would slight him no more! O that this day your hearts might fall in love with him! I tell you, if you would set your love to sale, none bids so fair for it as Christ.

2. Use of Exhortation
1. To saints: If Christ lay eternally in this bosom of love, and yet was content to forsake and leave it for your sakes; then, (1.) Be you ready to forsake and leave all the comforts you have on earth for Christ: famous Galleacius left all for this enjoyment. Moses left all the glory of Egypt: Peter, and the other Apostles left all, Luke 18: 28. But what have we to leave for Christ in comparison of what he left for us? Surely Christ is the highest pattern of self-denial in the world. (2.) Let this confirm your faith in prayer: If he, that has such an interest in the heart of God, intercede with the Father for you, then never doubt of audience and acceptance with him; surely

you shall be accepted through the beloved, Eph. 1: 6. Christ was never denied any thing that he asked, John 11: 42. The Father hears him always; though you are not worthy, Christ is, and he ever lives to make intercession for you, Heb. 7: 25.

(3.) Let this encourage thy heart, O saint, in a dying hour, and not only make thee patient in death, but in a holy manner impatient till thou be gone; for whither is thy soul now going, but to that bosom of love whence Christ came? John 17: 24. "Father, I will that they also, whom thou hast given me, be with me where I am:" and where is he but in that bosom of glory and love where he lay before the world was? ver. 5. O then let every believer encourage his soul; comfort ye one another with these words, I am leaving the bosom of a creature, I am going to the bosom of God.

2. To sinners, exhorting them to embrace the bosom-son of God: Poor Wretches! Whatever you are, or have been; whatever guilt or discouragement at present you lie under; embrace Christ, who is freely offered to you, and you shall be as dear to God as the holiest and most eminent believer in the world: but if you still continue to despise and neglect such a Saviour, sorer wrath is treasured up for you than other sinners, even something worse than dying without mercy, Heb. 10: 28. O that these discoveries and overtures of Christ may never come to such a fatal issue with any of your souls, in whose eyes his glory has been this day opened!

Sermon 3: Opens the Covenant of Redemption betwixt the Father and the Redeemer

Isa.53:12.
Therefore will I divide him [a portion] with the great, and he shall divide the spoil with the strong; because he hath poured out his soul unto death: and he was numbered with the transgressors; and he bare the sin of many, and made intercession for the transgressors.

    In this chapter, the gospel seems to be epitomised; the subjectmatter of it is the death of Christ, and the glorious issue thereof: by reading of it, the Eunuch of old, and many Jews since, have been converted to Christ. Christ is here considered absolutely, and relatively; Absolutely, and so his innocence is industriously vindicated, ver. 9. Though he suffered grievous things, yet not for his own sins, "for he had done no violence, neither was any deceit in his mouth;" but relatively considered in the capacity of a surety for us: so the justice of God is so fully vindicated in his sufferings; ver. 6. "The Lord has laid upon him the iniquity of us all." How he came to sustain this capacity and relation of a surety for us, is in these verses plainly asserted to be by his compact and agreement with his Father, before the worlds were made, verse 10, 11,12.
    In this verse we have, 1. His work. 2. His reward. 3. The respect or relation of each to the other. (1.) His work, which was indeed a hard work, to pour out his soul unto death, aggravated by the companions, with whom, being numbered with transgressors; the capacity in which, bearing all the sins of the elect, "he bare the sins of many in and by the manner of his bearing it, viz. meekly, and forgivingly, "he made intercession for the transgressors;" This was his work. (2.) The reward or fruit which is promised him for this work, "therefore will I divide him a portion with the great, and he will divide the spoil with the strong;" wherein is a plain allusion to conquerors in war, for whom are reserved the richest garments, and most honourable captives to follow the conqueror, as an addition to his magnificence and triumph; these were wont to come after them in chains, Isa. 45: 14. see Judges 5: 3 (3.) The respect or relation betwixt that work and this triumph: some will have this work to have no other relation to that glory, than a mere antecedent to a consequent: others give it the respect and relation of a meritorious cause to a reward. It is well observed by Dr. Featly, that the Hebrew particle "lachen", which we render therefore, noting order, is not worth so much contention about it, whether it be the order of casualty, or mere antecedence; neither do I foresee any absurdity in calling Christ's exaltation the reward and fruit of his humiliation: however, it is plain, whether one or other, it is that the Father here agrees and promises to give him, if he will undertake the redemption of the elect, by pouring out his soul unto death; of all which this is the plain result:
    Doct. That the business of man's salvation was transacted upon covenant terms, betwixt the Father and the Son, from all eternity.
    I would not here be mistaken, as though I were now to treat of the covenant of grace, made in Christ betwixt God and us; it is not the covenant of grace, but of redemption, I am now to speak to, which differs from the covenant of grace, in regard of the federates in this, it is God the Father, and Jesus Christ, that mutually covenant; in that, it is God and man: they differ, also in the receptive part, in this it is required of Christ that he should shed his blood, in that it is required of us that we believe. They also differ in their promises; in this, God promises to Christ a name above every name, ample dominion from sea to sea; in that, to us, grace and glory: so that these are two distinct covenants.
    The substance of this covenant of redemption is, dialogue-wise, expressed to us in Isa. 49, where, (as divines have well observed) Christ begins, at the first and second verses, and shows his commission, telling his Father, how he had both called, and prepared him for the work of redemption; "The Lord has called me from the womb - he has made my mouth like a sharp sword, and made me a polished shaft", &c. q. d. by reason of that superabundant measure of the spirit of wisdom and power wherewith I am anointed and filled; my doctrine shall, as a sword, pierce the hearts of sinners; yea, like an arrow, drawn to the head, strike deep into souls standing at a great

distance from God and godliness.

Having told God how ready, and fit he was for his service, he will know of him what reward he shall have for his work, for he resolves his blood shall not be undervalued; hereupon, verse 3, the Father offers him the elect of Israel for his reward, bidding low at first (as they that make bargains use to do) and only offers him that small remnant, still intending to bid higher: But Christ will not be satisfied with these, he values his blood higher than so: therefore, in verse 4 he is brought in complaining, "I have laboured in vain, and spent my strength for nought," q. d. This is but a small reward for so great a suffering, as I must undergo; my blood is much more worth than this comes to, and will be sufficient to redeem all the elect dispersed among the isles of the Gentiles, as well as the lost sheep of the house of Israel. Hereupon the Father comes up higher, and tells him, he intends to reward him better than so; and therefore, verse 6 says, "It is a light thing that thou shouldst be my servant to raise up the tribes of Jacob, and to restore the preserved of Israel; I will also give thee for a light to the Gentiles, that thou mayest be my salvation to the ends of the earth." Thus is the treaty carried on betwixt them, transacting it after the manner of men.

Now, to open this great point, we will here consider, (1.) The persons transacting one with another. (2.) The business transacted. (3.) The quality and manner of the transaction, which is federal. (4.) The articles to which they agree. (5.) How each person performs his engagement to the other. And, Lastly, The antiquity or eternity of this covenant transaction.

(1.) The persons transacting and dealing with each other in this covenant; and indeed they are great persons, God the Father, and God the Son, the former as a Creditor, and the latter as a Surety. The Father stands upon satisfaction, the Son engages to give it. If it be demanded, why the Father and the Spirit might not as well have treated upon our redemption, as the Father and Son! It is answered, Christ is the natural Son of God, and therefore fittest to make us the adopted sons of God. Christ also is the middle person in the Trinity, and therefore fittest to be the mediator and middle person betwixt us and God. The Spirit has another office assigned him, even to apply, as Christ's vicegerent, the redemption designed by the Father, and purchased by the Son for us.

(2.) The business transacted betwixt them; and that was the redemption and recovery of all God's elect: our eternal happiness lay now before them, our dearest and everlasting concerns were now in their hands: the elect (though not yet in being) are here considered as existent, yea, and as fallen, miserable, forlorn creatures: How these may again be restored to happiness (salva justitia Dei) without prejudice to the honour, justice and truth of God; this, this is the business that lay before them.

(3.) For the manner, or quality of the transaction, it was federal, or of the nature of a covenant; it was by mutual engagements and stipulations, each person undertaking to perform his part in order to our recovery.

We find each person undertaking for himself by solemn promise; the Father promiseth that he will "hold his hand, and keep him," Isa. 42: 6. The Son promiseth, he will obey his Father's call to suffering, and not "be rebellious," Isa. 50: 5. And, having promised, each holds the other to his engagement. The father stands upon the satisfaction promised him; and, when the payment was making, he will not abate him one earthing, Rom. 8: 32. "God spared not his own Son," i. e. he abated nothing of the full price he was to have at his hands for us.

And as the Father stood strictly upon the terms of the covenant, so did Christ also; John 17: 45. "I have glorified thee on earth, (saith he to the Father) I have finished the work thou gavest me to do; and now, Father, glorify me with thine own self." As if he had said, Father, the work is done, now where is the wages I was promised? I call for glory as my due, as much my due as the hire of the labourer is his due, when his work is done.

4. More particularly; we will next consider the articles to which they do both agree; or, what it is that each person does for himself promise to the other. And, to let us see how much the Father's heart is engaged in the salvation of poor sinners, there are five things which he promiseth to do for Christ, if he will undertake that work.

First, He promiseth to invest him, and anoint him to a threefold office, answerable to the misery that lay upon the elect as so many bars to all communion with, and enjoyment of God; for, if ever man be restored to that happiness, the blindness of his mind must be cured, the guilt of sin expiated, and his captivity to sin led captive: answerably, Christ must, "of God, be made unto us, wisdom, righteousness, sanctification and redemption," 1 Cor. 1: 30. And he is made so to us as our Prophet, Priest, and King; but he could not put himself into either of these; for if so, he had acted without commissions and consequently all he did had been invalid; Heb. 5: 5. "Christ glorified not himself to be made an High-Priest, but he that said unto him, Thou art my Son". A commission therefore to act authoritatively, in these offices, being necessary to our recovery, the Father engages to him to seal him such a threefold commission.

He promiseth to invest him with an eternal and royal Priesthood, Psal. 110: 4. "The Lord has sworn, and will not repent; Thou art a priest forever, after the order of Melchisedec." This

John Flavel

Melchisedec being King of Righteousness, and king of Salem, that is, Peace, had a royal priesthood; and his descent not being reckoned, it had an adumbration of eternity in it, and so was more apt to type and shadow forth the priesthood of Christ than Aaron's was, Heb. 7: 16, 17, 24, 25, as the apostle accommodates them there.

He promiseth moreover to make him a Prophet, and that an extraordinary one, even the Prince of prophets; the chief Shepherd, as much superior to all others, as the sun is to the lesser stars; so you have it, Isa. 42: 6, 7. "I will give thee for a light to the Gentiles, to open the blind eyes," &c.

And not only so, but to make him king also, and that of the whole empire of the world; so Psal. 2: 6, 7, 8. "Ask of me, and I will give thee the Heathen for thine inheritance, and the utmost ends of the earth for thy possession." Thus he promiseth to qualify and furnish him completely for the work, by his investiture with this threefold office.

Secondly, And forasmuch as he knew it was a hard and difficult work his Son was to undertake, a work that would have broken the backs of all the angels in heaven, and men on earth, had they engaged in it; therefore he promiseth to stand by him, and assist and strengthen him for it: so, Isa. 42: 5, 6, 7. "I will hold thy hand," or take hold of thee with my hands, for so it may be rendered, i. e. I will underprop and support thy humanity, when it is even overweighted with the burden that is to come upon it, and ready to sink down under it; for so you know the case stood with him, Mark 14: 34, and so it was foretold of him, Isa. 53: 7. "He was oppressed," &c. and indeed the humanity needed a prop of no less strength than the infinite power of the Godhead: the same promise you have in the first verse also, "Behold my servant whom I uphold."

Thirdly, He promiseth to crown his work with success, and bring it to an happy issue, Isa. 53: 10. "He shall see his seed, he shall prolong his days, and the pleasure of the Lord shall prosper in his hand." He shall not begin, and not finish; he shall not shed his invaluable blood upon hazardous terms; but shall see and reap the sweet fruits thereof; as the joyful mother forgets her pangs, when she delightfully embraces and kisses her living child.

Fourthly, The Father promiseth to accept him in his work, though millions should certainly perish, Isa. 49: 4. "Surely (saith he) my work is with the Lord." And, verse 5. "I shall be glorious in the eyes of the Lord." His faith has therein respect to this compact and promise. Accordingly the Father manifests the satisfaction he had in him, and in his work, even while he was about it upon the earth, when there came such a "voice from the excellent glory, saying, This is my beloved Son, in whom I am well pleased."

Fifthly, As he engaged to reward him highly for his work, by exalting him to singular and super-eminent glory and honour, when he should have dispatched and finished it. So you read, Psal. 2: 7. "I will declare the decree; the Lord has said unto me, Thou art my Son, this day have I begotten thee." It is spoken of the day of his resurrection, when he had just finished his sufferings. And so the apostle expounds and applies it, Acts 13: 32, 33. For then did the Lord wipe away the reproach of his cross, and invested him with such glory, that he looked like himself again. As if the Father had said, now thou hast again recovered thy glory, and this day is to thee as a new birth-day.

These are the encouragements and rewards proposed and promised to him by the Father. This was the "joy set before him", (as the apostle phraseth it in Heb. 12: 2.) which made him so patiently to "endure the cross, and despise the shame."

And in like manner Jesus Christ restipulates, and gives his engagement to the Father; that, upon these terms, he is content to be made flesh, to divest, as it were, himself of his glory, to come under the obedience and malediction of the law, and not to refuse any, the hardest sufferings it should please his Father to inflict on him. So much is implied in Isa. 50: 5, 6, 7. "The Lord has opened mine ear, and I was not rebellious, neither turned away back; I gave my back to the smilers, and my cheeks to them that pulled off the hair; I hid not my face from shame and spitting: For the Lord God will help me, therefore shall I not be confounded; I have set my face as a flint, and I know that I shall not be ashamed." When he saith, I was not rebellious, "mariti," he meaneth, I was most heartily willing, and content to accept the terms; for there is a Meiosis in the words, and much more is intended than expressed. And the sense of this place is well delivered to us in other terms, Psal. 40: 6, 7, 8, 9, 10. "Then said I, Lo I come, I delight to do thy will, O God, thy law is within my heart." O see with what a full consent the heart of Christ closeth with the Father's offers and proposals; like some echo, that answers your voice twice or thrice over. So does Christ here answer his Father's call, "I come, I delight to do thy will; yea, thy law is in my heart." And thus you see the articles to which they both subscribed, or the terms they agreed on.

(5.) I will briefly show how these articles, and agreements were on both parts, performed, and that precisely and punctually. For, (1.) The Son having thus consented, accordingly he applies himself to the discharge of his work. He took a body, in it fulfilled all righteousness, even to a little, Matth. 3: 15. And at last his out was made an offering for sin, so that he could say as it is, John 17: 4. "Father, I have glorified thee on earth, I have finished the work thou gavest me to do." He went through all the parts of his active, and passive obedience, cheerfully and faithfully. (2.) The Father made good his engagements to Christ, all along, with no less faithfulness than Christ did his. He promised to assist, and hold his hand, and so he did; Luke 22: 43, "And there appeared to him an angel from heaven, strengthening him." That was one of the sorest brunts that ever Christ met with; this was seasonable aid and succour. He promised to accept him in his work, and that he should be glorious in his eyes; so he did: for he not only declared it by a voice from heaven, Luke 3: 22!. "Thou art my beloved Son, in whom I am well pleased:" But it was fully-declared in his resurrection and ascension, which were a full discharge and justification of him. He promised him that "He should see his seed," and so he did; for his very birth-dew was as the dew of the morning; and ever since his blood has been fruitful in the world. He promised gloriously to reward and exalt him; and so he has, Phil. 2: 9, 10, 11, and that highly and super-eminently, "giving him a name above every name in heaven and earth." Thus were the articles performed.

(6.) Lastly, When was this compact made betwixt the Father and the Son? I answer, it bears date from eternity. Before this world was made, then were his delights in us, while as yet we had no existence, but only in the infinite mind and purpose of God, who had decreed this for us in Christ Jesus, as the apostle speaks, 2 Tim. 1: 9. What grace was that which was given us in Christ before the world began, but this grace of redemption, which was from everlasting thus contrived and designed for us, in that way which has been here opened? Then was the council, or consultation of peace betwixt them both, as some take that scripture, Zech. 6: 13.

Next let us apply it to ourselves.

Use 1. The first use that offers itself to us from hence, is the abundant security that God has given the elect for their salvation, and that not only in respect of the covenant of grace made with then, but also of this covenant of redemption made with Christ for them; which indeed is the foundation of the covenant of grace. God's single promise is security enough to our faith, his covenant of grace adds, ex abundanti, farther security; but both these viewed as the effects and fruits of this covenant of redemption, make all fast and sure. In the covenant of grace, we question not the performance on God's part, but we are often stumbled at the grand defects on our parts. But when we look to the covenant of redemption there is nothing to stagger our faith, both the federates being infinitely able and faithful to perform their parts; so that there is no possibility of a failure there. Happy were it, if puzzled and perplexed Christians would turn their eyes from the defects that are in their obedience, to the fulness and completeness of Christ's obedience; and see themselves complete in him, when most lame and defective in themselves.

Use 2. Hence also to be informed, that God the Father, and God the Son, do mutually rely and trust to one another in the business of our redemption. The Father relies upon the Son for the performance of his part; as it is, Isa. 42: 1, " Behold my servant, whom I uphold." Montanus turns it, on whom I lean or depend. As if the Father had said, behold what a faithful servant I have chosen, in whom my soul is at rest: I know he will go through with his work, I can depend upon him. And, to speak plain, the Father so far trusted Christ, that upon the credit of his promise to come into the world, and in the fulness of time to become a sacrifice for the elect, he saved all the Old Testament saints, whose faith also respected a Christ to come; with reference whereto, it is said, Heb. 11: 39, 40. "That they received not the promises, God having provided some better things for us, that they without us should not be made perfect," i. e. without Jesus Christ manifested in the flesh, in our times, though believed on, as to come in the flesh, in their times. And as the Father trusted Christ, so does Christ, in like manner, depend upon, and trust his Father. For, having performed his part, and left the world again, he now trusteth his Father for the accomplishment of that promise made him; Isa. 53: 10. "That he shall see his seed," &c. He depends upon his Father for all the elect that are left behind, yet unregenerated, as well as those already called, that they shall be all preserved unto the heavenly kingdom, according to that, John 17: 11. "And now I am no more in the world, but these are in the world; and I come unto thee: holy Father, keep, through thine own name, those whom thou hast given me." And can it be imagined, that the Father will fail in his trust, who every way acquitted himself so punctually to the Son? It cannot be.

Use 3. Moreover, hence we infer the validity and unquestionable success of Christ's intercession in heaven for believers. You read, Heb. 7: 25. "That he ever lives to make intercession; and, Heb. 12: 24. "That his blood speaks for good things for them." Non, that his blood shall obtain what it pleads in heaven for, is undoubted, and that from the consideration of this covenant of redemption. For here you see that the things he now asks of his Father, are the very same which his Father promised him, and covenanted to give him, before this world was. So that, besides the interest of the person, the very equity of the matter speaks its success, and requires performance. Whatever he asks for us, is as due to him as the wages of the hireling, when the work is ended; if the work be done, and done faithfully, as the Father has acknowledged it is, then the reward is due, and due immediately; and no doubt but he shall receive it from the lands of a righteous God.

Use 4. Hence, in like manner, you may be informed of the consistency of grace with full satisfaction to the justice of God. The apostle, 2 Tim. 1: 9. tells us, "We are saved according to his own purpose and grace, which was given us in Jesus Christ before the world began." i. e. According to the gracious terms of this covenant of redemption; and yet you see notwithstanding, how strictly God stands upon satisfaction from Christ; so then, grace to us, and satisfaction to justice, are not so inconsistent as the Socinian adversaries would make them; what was debt to Christ, is grace to us: when you hear men cry out, Here is grace indeed! pay me all, and I will forgive you; remember, how all mouths are stopped with that one text, Rom. 3: 24. "Being justified freely by his grace;" and yet he adds, "through the redemption that is in Christ."

Use 5. Again, Hence judge of the antiquity of the love of God to believers! what an ancient friend he has been to us; who loved us, provided for us, and contrived all our happiness, before we were, yea, before the world was. We reap the fruits of this covenant now, the seed whereof was sown from eternity; yea, it is not only ancient, but also most free: no excellencies of ours could engage the love of God; for as yet we were not.

Use 6. Hence judge, How reasonable it is that believers should embrace the hardest terms of obedience unto Christ, who complied with such hard terms for their salvation: they were hard and difficult terms indeed, on which Christ received you from the Father's hand: it was, as you have heard, to pour out his soul unto death, or not to enjoy a soul of you. Here you may suppose the Father to say, when driving his bargain with Christ for you:

Father. My son, here is a company of poor miserable souls, that have utterly undone themselves, and now lie open to my justice! Justice demands satisfaction for them, or will satisfy itself in the eternal ruin of them: What shall be done for these souls And thus Christ returns.

Son. O my Father, such is my love to, and pity for them, that rather than they shall perish eternally, I will be responsible for them as their Surety; bring in all thy bills, that I may see what they owe thee; Lord, bring them all in, that there may be no after-reckonings with them; at my hand shalt thou require it. I will rather choose to suffer thy wrath than they should suffer it: upon me, my Father, upon me be all their debt.

Father. But, my Son, if thou undertake for them, thou must reckon to pay the last mite, expect no abatements; if I spare them, I will not spare thee.

Son. Content, Father, let it be so; charge it all upon me, I am able to discharge it: and though it prove a kind of undoing to me, though it impoverish all my riches, empty all my treasures, (for so indeed it did, 2 Cor. 8: 9. "Though he was rich, yet for our sakes he became poor") yet I am content to undertake it. Blush, ungrateful believers, O let shame cover your faces; judge in yourselves now, has Christ deserved that you should stand with him for trifles, that you should shrink at a few petty difficulties, and complain, this is hard, and that is harsh? O if you knew the grace of our Lord Jesus Christ in this his wonderful condescension for you, you could not do it.

Use 7. Lastly, How greatly are we all concerned, to make it sure to ourselves, that we are of this number which the Father and the Son agreed for before the world was; that we were comprehended in Christ's engagement and compact with the Father?

Obj. Yea, but you will say, who can know that, there were no witnesses to that agreement.

Sol. Yes, We may know, without ascending into heaven, or prying into unrevealed secrets, that our names were in that covenant, if, (1.) You are believers indeed; for all such the Father then gave to Christ, John 17: 8. "The men that thou gavest me (for of them he spake immediately before) they have believed that thou didst send me." (2.) If you savingly know God in Jesus Christ, such were given him by the Father, John 17: 6. "I have manifested thy name unto the men thou gavest me." By this they are discriminated from the rest, verse 25. "The world has not known thee, but these have known," &c. (3.) If you are men and women of another world; John 17: 16, "They are not of the world, as I am not of the world." May it be said of you, as of dying men, that you are not men and women for this world, that you are crucified and dead to it, Gal. 6: 14, that you are strangers in it? Heb. 11: 13, 14. (4.) If you keep Christ's word, John 17: 6. "Thine they were, and thou gavest them me; and they have kept thy word." By keeping his word, understand the receiving of the word, in its sanctifying effects and influences into your hearts, and your perseverance in the profession and practice of it to the end, John 17: 17, "Sanctify them through thy truth, thy word is truth". John 15: 7, "If ye abide in me, and my words abide in you, ye shall ask what ye will." Blessed and happy is that soul upon which these blessed characters appear, which our Lord Jesus has laid so close together, within the compass of a few verses, in this 17th chapter of John. These are the persons the Father delivered unto Christ, and he accepted from the Father, in this blessed covenant.

Sermon 4: Opens the admirable love of God in giving his own Son for us

John 3:16.
>   *For God so loved the world, that he gave his only begotten Son, that whosoever believeth in him should not perish, but have everlasting life.*

You have heard of the gracious purpose and design of God, to recover poor sinners to himself by Jesus Christ, and how this design of love was laid and contrived in the covenant of redemption, whereof we last spake.

Now, according to the terms of that covenant, you shall hear from this scripture, how that design was by one degree advanced towards its accomplishment, in God's actual giving or parting with his own Son far us: "God so loved the world, that he gave," &c.

The whole precedent context is spent in discovering the nature and necessity of regeneration, and the necessity thereof is in this text urged and inferred from the peculiar respect and eye God had upon believers, in giving Christ for them; they only reaping all the special and saving benefits and advantages of that gift: "God so loved the world, that he gave his only begotten Son, that whosoever believeth in him should not perish."

In the words are to be considered,

1. The original spring or fountain of our best mercies, the love of God. The love of God is, either benevolent, beneficent, or complacential. His benevolent love, is nothing else but his desire and purpose of saving, and doing us good; so his purpose and grace to Jacob is called love, Rom. 9: 13. "Jacob have I loved;" but this being before Jacob was, could consist in nothing else but the gracious purpose of God towards him. His beneficent love, is his actual doing, good to the persons beloved, or his bestowing the effects of his love upon us, according to that purpose. His complacential love, is nothing else but that delight and satisfaction he finds in beholding the fruits and workings of that grace in us, which he first intended for us, and then actually collated or bestowed on us. This love of benevolence, is that which I have opened to you, under the former head, God's compact with Christ about us, or his design to save us on the articles and terms therein specified.

The love of beneficence, is that which this scripture speaks of; out of this fountain Christ flowed to us, and both ran into that of complacency, for therefore he both purposed and actually bestowed Christ on us, that he might everlastingly delight in beholding the glory and praise of all this reflected on himself, by his redeemed ones. This then is the fountain of our mercies.

2. The mercy flowing out of this fountain, and that is Christ; The mercy, as he is emphatically called, Luke 1: 72. The marrow, kernel, and substance of all other mercies. He gave his only begotten Son: This was the birth of that love, the like whereunto it never brought forth before, therefore it is expressed with a double emphasis in the text, the one is the particle "houtos", so; "he so loved the world;" here is a sic without a sicut: How did he love it? Why, he so loved it; but how much, the tongues of angels cannot declare. And moreover, to enhance the mercy, he is stiled his only begotten Son: to have given a Son had been wonderful; but to give his only begotten Son, that is love inexpressible, unintelligible.

3. The objects of this love, or the persons to whom the eternal Lord delivered Christ, and that is the [world.] This must respect the elect of God in the world, such as do, or shall actually believe, as it is exegetically expressed in the next words, "That whosoever believes in him should not perish:" Those whom he calls the world in that, he stiles believers in this expression; and the word [world] is put to signify the elect, because they are scattered through all parts, and are among all ranks of men in the world; these are the objects of this love; it is not angels, but men, that were so loved; he is called "filantropos", a Lover, a Friend of Men, but never "filangelos" or "filokisos", the Lover or Friend of Angels, or creatures of another species.

4. The manner in which this never-enough celebrated mercy flows to us, from the fountain of divine love, and that is most freely and spontaneously. He gave, not he sold, or barely parted from, but gave. Nor yet does the Father's giving imply Christ to be merely passive; for as the Father is

here said to give him, so the apostle tells us, Gal. 2: 20. That he gave himself; "who loved me, and gave himself for me:" The Father gave him out of good will to men, and he as willingly bestowed himself on that service. Hence the note is,

Doct. That the gift of Christ is the highest and fullest manifestation of the love of God to sinners, that ever was made from eternity to them.

How is this gift of God to sinners signalised in that place of the apostle, 1 Joh. 4: 10, "Herein is love; not that we loved God, but that he loved us, and sent his Son to be the propitiation for our sins?" Why does the apostle so magnify this gift in saying, "Herein is love," as if there were love in nothing else! May we not say, that to have a being, a being among the rational creatures, therein is love? To have our life carried so many years like a taper in the hand of Providence, through so many dangers, and not yet put out in obscurity, therein is love? To have food and raiment, convenient for us, beds to lie on, relations to comfort us, in all these is love? Yea, but if you speak comparatively, in all these there is no love, to the love expressed in sending or giving Christ for us: These are great mercies in themselves, but compared to this mercy, they are all swallowed up, as the light of candles when brought into the sun-shine. No, no, herein is love, that God gave Christ for us. And it is remarkable, that when the apostle would show us, in Rom. 5: 8, what is the noblest fruit that most commends to men the root of divine love that bears it, he shows us this very fruit of it that I am now opening; "But God, saith he, commendeth his love towards us, in that while we were yet sinners, Christ died for us:" this is the very flower of that love.

The method into which I will cast this precious point, shall be this: (1.) To show how Jesus Christ was given by the Father. (2.) How that gift is the fullest and richest manifestation of the love of God that was ever made to the world. (3.) And then draw forth the uses of it.

1. How was Jesus Christ given by the Father, and what is implied therein.

You are not so to understand it, as though God parted with his interest and property in his Son, when he is said to give him; he was as much his own as ever. When men give, they transfer property to another; but when God had given him, he was, I say, still as much his own as ever: but this giving of Christ implies,

(1.) His designation and appointment unto death for us; for so you read, that it was done "according to the determinate counsel of God," Acts 2: 23. Look, as the Lamb under the Law was separated from the flock, and set apart for a sacrifice; though it were still living, yet it was intentionally, and preparatively given, and consecrated to the Lord: so Jesus Christ was, by the counsel and purpose of God, thus chosen, and set apart for his service: and therefore in Isa. 42: 1. God calls him his Elect, or chosen One.

(2.) His giving Christ, implies a parting with him, or setting him (as the French has it) at some distance from himself for a time. There was a kind of parting betwixt the Father and the Son, when he came to tabernacle in our flesh: so he expresseth it, John 16: 28. "I came forth from the Father, and am come into the world; again, I leave the world and go to the Father". This distance that his incarnation and humiliation set him at, was properly as to his humanity, which was really distant from the glory into which it is now taken up, and in respect of manifestation of delight and love, the Lord seemed to carry it as one at a distance from him. Oh! this was it that so deeply pierced, and wounded his soul, as is evident from that complaint, Ps. 32: 1, 2. "My God, my God, why hast thou forsaken me? Why art thou so far from the words of my roaring? O my God, I cry in the day time, but thou hearest not," &c.

(3.) God's giving of Christ, implies his delivering him into the hands of justice to be punished; even as condemned persons are, lay sentence of law, given or delivered into the hands of executioners. So Acts 2: 23. "Him, being delivered by the determinate counsel at God, ye have taken, and by wicked hands have slain:" and so he is said, Rom. 8: 32 "To deliver him up to death for us all." The Lord, when the time was come that Christ must suffer, did, as it were, say, O all ye roaring waves of my incensed justice, now swell as high as heaven, and go over his soul and body; sink him to the bottom; let him go, like Jonah, his type, into the belly of hell, unto the roots of the mountains. Come all ye raging storms, that I have reserved for this day of wrath, beat upon him, beat him down, that he may not be able to look up, Psal. 60: 12. Go justice, put him upon the rack, torment him in every part, till all his "bones be out of joint, arid his heart within him be melted as wax; in the midst of his bowels," Psal. 22: 14. And ye assembly of the wicked Jews and Gentiles, that have so long gaped for his blood, now he is delivered into your hands; you are permitted to execute your malice to the full: I now loose your chain, and into your hand and power is he delivered.

(4.) God's giving of Christ, implies his application of him, with all the purchase of his blood, and settling, all this upon us, as an inheritance and portion, John 6: 32,33, "My Father giveth you the true bread from heaven; for the bread of God is he which cometh down from heaven, and giveth light to the world." God has giveth him as bread to poor starving creatures, that by faith they might eat and live. And so he told the Samaritaness, John 4: 10. "If thou knewest the gift of God, and who it is that saith unto thee, Give me to drink, thou wouldst have asked of him, and he would have given thee living water." Bread and water are the two necessaries for the support of natural life; God has given Christ, you see, to be all that, and more, to the spiritual life.

2. How this gift of Christ was the highest, and fullest manifestation of the love of God, that ever the world saw: and this will be evidenced by the following particulars:

(1.) If you consider how near and dear Jesus Christ was to the Father; he was his Son, "his only Son," saith the text; the Son of his love, the darling of his Soul: His other Self, yea, one with himself; the express image of his person; the brightness of his Father's Glory: In parting with him, he parted with his own heart, with his very bowels, as I may say. "Yet to us a Son is given," Isa. 9: 6, and such a Son as he calls "his dear Son," Col. 1: 13. A late writer tells us, that he has been informed, that in the famine in Germany, a poor family being ready to perish with famine, the husband made a motion to the wife, to sell one of the children for bread, to relieve themselves and the rest: The wife at last consents it should be so; but then they began to think which of the four should be sold; and when the eldest was named, they both refused to part with that, being their first born, and the beginning of their strength. Well, then they came to the second, but could not yield that he should be sold, being the very picture and lively image of his father. The third was named, but that also was a child that best resembled the mother. And when the youngest was thought on, that was the Benjamin, the child of their old age; and so were content rather to perish altogether in the famine, than to part with a child for relief. And you know how tenderly Jacob took it, when his Joseph and Benjamin were rent from him. What is a child, but a piece of the parent wrapt up in another skin? And yet our dearest children are but as strangers to us, in comparison of the unspeakable dearness that was betwixt the Father and Christ. Now, that he should ever be content to part with a Son, and such an only One, is such a manifestation of love, as will be admired to all eternity. And then,

(2.) Let it be considered, To what he gave him, even to death, and that of the cross; to be made a curse for us; to be the scorn and contempt of men; to the most unparalleled sufferings that ever were inflicted or borne by any. It melts our bowels, it breaks our heart, to behold our children striving in the pangs of death: but the Lord beheld his Son struggling under agonies that never any felt before him. He saw him falling to the ground, grovelling in the dust, sweating blood, and amidst those agonies turning himself to his Father, and, with a heart rending cry, beseeching him, "Father, if it be possible, let this cup pass," Luke 22: 42. To wrath, to the wrath, of an infinite God without mixture; to the very torments of hell was Christ delivered, and that by the hand of his own Father. Sure then that love must needs want a name, which made the Father of mercies deliver his only Son to such miseries for us.

(3.) It is a special consideration to enhance the love of God in giving Christ, that in giving him he gave the richest jewel in his cabinet; a mercy of the greatest worth, and most inestimable value, Heaven itself is not so valuable and precious as Christ is: He is the better half of heaven; and so the saints account him, Psal. 73: 25, "Whom have I in heaven but thee?" Ten thousand thousand worlds, saith one, as many worlds as angels can number, and then as a new world of angels can multiply, would not all be the bulk of a balance, to weigh Christ's excellency, love, and sweetness. O what a fair One! what an only One! what an excellent, lovely, ravishing One, is Christ! Put the beauty of ten thousand paradises, like the garden of Eden, into one; put all trees, all flowers, all smells, all colours, all tastes, all joys, all sweetness, all loveliness in one; O what a fair and excellent thing would that be? And yet it should be less to that fair and dearest well-beloved Christ, than one drop of rain to the whole seas, rivers, lakes, and fountains of ten thousand earths. Christ is heaven's wonder, and earth's wonder.

Now, for God to bestow the mercy of mercies, the most precious thing in heaven or earth, upon poor sinners; and, as great, as lovely, as excellent as his Son was, yet not to account him too good to bestow upon us, what manner of love is this!

(4.) Once more, let it be considered on whom the Lord bestowed his Son: upon angels? No, but upon men. Upon man his friend? No, but upon his enemies. This is love; and on this consideration the apostle lays a mighty weight, in Rom. 5: 8, 9, 10. "But God (saith he) commendeth his love towards us, in that while we were yet sinners, Christ died for us, - When we were enemies, we were reconciled to God by the death of his Son." Who would part with a son for the sake of his dearest friends? but God gave him to, and delivered him for enemies: O love unspeakable!

(5.) Lastly, Let us consider how freely this gift came from him: It was not wrested out of his hand by our importunity; for we as little desired as deserved it: It was surprising, preventing, eternal love, that delivered him to us: "Not that we loved him, but he first loved us," 1 John 4: 19. Thus as when you weigh a thing, you cast in weight after weight, till the scales break; so does God, one consideration upon another, to overcome our hearts, and make us admiringly to cry, what manner of love is this! And thus I have shewed you what God's giving of Christ is, and what matchless love is manifested in that incomparable gift.

Next we shall apply this, in some practical corollaries.

Corollary 1. Learn hence, The exceeding preciousness of souls, and at what a high rate God values them that he will give his Son, his only Son out of his bosom, as a ransom for them. Surely this speaks their preciousness: God would not have parted with such a Son for small matters: all the world could not redeem them; gold and silver could not be their ransom; so speaks the apostle, 1 Peter 1: 18. "You were not redeemed with corruptible things, as silver and gold, but with the precious blood of Christ." Such an esteem God had for them, that rather than they should perish, Jesus Christ shall be made a man, yea, a curse for them. Oh then, learn to put a due value upon your own souls: do not sell that cheap, which God has paid so dear for: Remember what a treasure you carry about you; the glory that you see in this world is not equivalent in worth to it. Matth. 16: 26. "What shall a man give in exchange for his soul?"

Corollary 2. If God has given his own Son for the world, then it follows, that those for whom God gave his own Son, may warrantably expect any other temporal mercies from him. This is the apostle's inference, Rom. 8: 32. "He that spared not his own Son, but delivered him up for us all; how shall he not, with him, freely give us all things?" And so 1 Cor. 3: 21, 22. "All is yours, for ye are Christ's" i. e. They hold all other things in Christ, who is the capital, and most comprehensive mercy.

To make out the grounds of this comfortable deduction, let these four things be pondered, and duly weighed in your thoughts. (1.) No other mercy you need or desire, is, or can be so dear to God, as Jesus Christ is: he never laid any other thing in his bosom as he did his Son. As for the world, and the comforts of it, it is the dust of his feet, he values it not; as you see by his providential disposals of it; having given it to the worst of men. "All the Turkish empire," saith Luther, "as great and glorious as it is, is but a crumb which the master of the family throws to the dogs." Think upon any other outward enjoyment that is valuable in your eyes, and there is not so much comparison betwixt it and Christ, in the esteem of God, as is betwixt your dear children and the lumber of your houses, in your esteem. If then God has parted so freely from that which was infinitely dearer to him than these; how shall he deny these, when they may promote his glory, and your good? (2.) As Jesus Christ was nearer the heart of God than all these; so Christ is, in himself, much greater and more excellent than all of them: Ten thousand worlds, and the glory of them all, is but the dust of the balance, if weighed with Christ. These things are but poor creatures, but he is over all, God blessed for ever, Rom. 9: 5. They are common gifts, but he is the Gift of God, John 4: 10. They are ordinary mercies, but he is The mercy, Luke 1: 72. As one pearl, or precious stone is greater in value than ten thousand common pebbles. Now, if God has so freely given the greater, how can you suppose he should deny the lesser, mercies? Will a man give to another a large inheritance, and stand with him for a trifle? how can it be? (3.) There is no other mercy you want, but you are entitled to it by the gift of Christ; it is, as to right, conveyed to you with Christ. So, in the fore cited 1 Cor. 3: 21, 22, 23. "the world is yours, yea, all is yours; for ye are Christ's." So 2 Cor. 1: 20. "For all the promises of God in Christ, in him they are yea, and in him, amen." With him he has given you all things, "eis apolausin", 1 Tim. 6: 17. richly to enjoy: the word signifies rem aliquam cum laetitia percipere, to have the sweet relish and comfort of an enjoyment. So have we in all our mercies, upon the account of our title to them in Christ. (4.) Lastly, If God has given you this nearer, greater, and all comprehending mercy, when you were enemies to him, and alienated from him; it is not imaginable he should deny you any inferior mercy, when you are come into a state of reconciliation and amity with him. So the apostle reasons, Rom. 5: 8, 9, 10. "For if, when we were enemies, we were reconciled to God, by the death of his Son; much more being reconciled, we shall be saved by his life". And thus you have the second inference with its grounds.

Corollary 3. If the greatest love has been manifested in giving Christ to the world, then it follows, that the greatest evil and wickedness is manifested in despising, slighting, and rejecting Christ. It is sad to abuse the love of God manifested in the lowest gift of providence; but, to slight the richest discoveries of it, even in that peerless gift, wherein God commends his love in the most taking and astonishing manner; this is sin with a witness. Blush, O heavens, and be astonished, O earth; yea, be ye horribly afraid! No guilt like this. The most flagitious wretches among the barbarous nations are innocent, in comparison of these. But, are there any such in the world? Dare any slight this gift of God? Indeed, if men's words might be taken, there are few or none that dare do so; but if their lives and practices may be believed, this, this is the sin of the far greater part of the christianised world. Witness the lamentable stupidity and supineness; witness the contempt of the gospel; witness the hatred and persecution of his image, laws and people. What is the language of all this, but a vile esteem of Jesus Christ?

And now, let me a little expostulate with those ungrateful souls, that trample under foot the Son of God, that value not this love that gave him forth. What is that mercy which you so condemn and undervalue? is it so vile and cheap a thing as your entertainment speaks it to be? Is it indeed

The Fountain of Life Opened Up

worth no more than this in your eyes? Surely you will not be long of that opinion! Will you be of that mind, think on, when death and judgement shall have thoroughly awakened you! Oh, no: Then a thousand worlds for a Christ! as it is storied of our crooked-backed Richard, when he lost the field, and was in great danger by his enemies that pressed upon him; Oh now, (said he) a kingdom for a horse! Or think we, that any beside you in the world are of your mind? you are deceived, if you think so, "To them that believe he is precious," through all the world, 1 Pet. 2: 7. and in the other world they are of a quite contrary mind. Could you but hear what is said of him in heaven, in what a dialect the saved of the Lord do extol their Saviour; or could you but imagine the self-revenges, the self torments, which the damned suffer for their folly, and what a value they would set upon one tender of Christ, if it might but again be hoped for; you would see that such as you are the only despisers of Christ. Beside, methinks it is astonishing, that you should despise a mercy in which your own souls are so dearly, so deeply, so everlastingly concerned, as they are in this gift of God. If it were but the soul of another, nay, less, if but the body of another, and yet less than that, if but another's beast, whose life you could preserve, you are obliged to do it; but when it is thyself, yea, the best part of thyself, thine own invaluable soul, that thou ruinest and destroyest thereby, Oh, what a monster art thou, to cast it away thus! What! will you slight your own souls? care you not whether they be saved, or whether they be damned? is it indeed an indifferent thing with you which way they fall at death? have you imagined a tolerable hell? is it easy to perish? are you not only turned God's enemies, but your own too? Oh see what monsters sin can turn men and women into! Oh the stupefying, besetting, intoxicating power of sin! But perhaps you think that all these are but uncertain sounds, with which we alarm you; it may be thine own heart will preach such doctrine as this to thee: Who can assure thee of the reality of these things? why shouldest thou trouble thyself with an invisible world, or be so much concerned for what thine eyes never saw, nor midst ever receive the report from any that have seen them? Well, though we cannot now show you these things, yet shortly they shall be shown you; and your own eyes shall behold them. You are convinced and satisfied that many other things are real which you never saw: but be assured, That "if the word spoken by angels was steadfast, and every transgression and disobedience received a just recompence of reward, how shall we escape, if we neglect so great a salvation, which at first began to be spoken to us by the Lord, and was confirmed to us by them that heard him, God also bearing them witness?" Heb. 2: 2, 3, 4. But if they be certain, yet they are not near; it will be a long time before they come. Poor soul! how dost thou cheat thyself? It maybe not by twenty parts so long a time as thy own fancy draws it forth for thee; thou art not certain of the next moment.

And suppose what thou imagines: What are twenty or forty years when they are past? yea, what are a thousand years to vast eternity? Go trifle away a few days more, sleep out a few nights more, and then lie down in the dust; it will not be long ere the trump of God shall awaken thee, and thine eyes shall behold Jesus coming in the clouds of heaven, and then you will know the price of this sin. Oh, therefore, if there be any sense of eternity upon you, any pity or love for yourselves in you; if you have any concernments more than the beasts that perish, despise not your own offered mercies, slight not the richest gift that ever was yet opened to the world; and a sweeter cannot be opened to all eternity,

Sermon 5: Of Christ's wonderful Person

John 1: 14
And the Word was made flesh, and dwelt among us, &c.

You have heard the covenant of redemption opened. The work therein propounded by the Father, and consented to by the Son, is such as infinitely exceeds the power of any mere creature to perform. He that undertakes to satisfy God, by obedience for man's sin, must himself be God; and he that performs such a perfect obedience, by doing, and suffering all that the law required, in our room, must be man. These two natures must be united in one person, else there could not be a concourse or co-operation of either nature in his mediatory works. How these natures are united, in the wonderful person of our Emmanuel, is the first part of the great mystery of godliness: a subject studied and adored by angels! and the mystery thereof is wrapped up in this text. Wherein we have,

First, The incarnation of the Son of God plainly asserted.

Secondly, That assertion strongly confirmed.

(1.) In the assertion we have three parts.

1. The Person assuming, "ho Logos", the Word, i. e. the second Person or Subsistent in the most glorious Godhead, called the Word, either because he is the scope or principal matter, both of the prophetical and promissory word; or because he expounds and reveals the mind and will of God to men, as verse 18. The only begotten Son which is in the bosom of the Father, he has declared or expounded him.

2. The nature assumed, "sarks", Flesh, i. e. the entire human nature, consisting of a true human soul and body. For so this word "sarks", in Rom. 3: 20, and the Hebrew word "basar" which answers to it, by a usual Metonymy of a part for the whole, is used, Gen. 6: 12. And the word Flesh is rather used here, than Man, on purpose to enhance the admirable condescension and abasement of Christ; there being more of vileness, weakness, and opposition to spirit in this word, than in that, as is pertinently noted by some. Hence the whole nature is denominated by that part, and called flesh.

3. The assumption itself, "egeneto", he was made; not fuit, he was, (as Socinus would render it, designing thereby to overthrow the existence of Christ's glorified body now in heaven) but factus est, it was made, i. e. he took or assumed the true human nature (called flesh, for the reason before rendered) into the unity of his divine person, with all its integral parts and essential properties; and so was made, or became a true and real man, by that assumption. The apostle speaking; of the same act, Heb. 2: 16. uses another word, He took on him, "epilambanetai", fitly rendered he took on him, or he assumed; which assuming, though; inchoative, it was the work of the whole Trinity, God the Father, in the Son, by the Spirit, forming or creating that nature; as if three sisters should make a garment betwixt them, which only one of them wears: yet, terminative, it was the act of the Son only; it was he only that was made flesh. And when it is said, he was made flesh, misconceive not, as if there was a mutation of the Godhead into flesh; for this was performed, "not by changing what he was, but by assuming what he was not," as Augustine well expresseth it. As when the scripture, in a like expression, saith, "He was made sin," 2 Cor. 5: 21, and made a curse, Gal. 3: 13, the nearing is not, that he was turned into sin, or into a curse; no more may we think here the Godhead was turned into flesh, and lost its own being and nature, because it is said he was made flesh. This is the sum of the assertion.

(2.) This assertion ["that the word was made flesh,"] is strongly confirmed. He "dwelt among us," and we saw his glory. This was no phantasm, but a most real and indubitable thing. For, "eskenosen en hemin", pitched his tent, or tabernacled with us. And we are eye-witnesses of it. Parallel to that, 1 John 1: 1, 2, 3. "That which was from the beginning, which we have heard, which we have seen with our eyes, which we have looked upon, and our hands have handled, of the Word of life, &c. declare we unto you." Hence note,

Doct. That Jesus Christ did really assume the true and perfect nature of man, into a personal unions with his divine nature, and still remains true God, and true man, in one person for ever.

The proposition contains one of the deepest mysteries of godliness, 1 Tim. 3: 16. A mystery, by which apprehension is dazzled, invention astonished, and all expression swallowed up. If ever the tongues of angels were desirable to explicate any word of God, they are so here. Great is the interest of words in this doctrine. We walk upon the brink of danger. The least tread awry may engulf us in the bogs of error. Arius would have been content, if the council of Nice would but have gratified him in a letter, "homousios", and "homoiousios". The Nestorians also desired but a letter, "Theodochos", "theotokos". These seemed but small and modest requests, but, if granted, had proved no small prejudice to Jesus Christ, and his truths. I desire therefore the reader would, with greatest attention of mind, apply himself to these truths. It is a doctrine hard to understand, and dangerous to mistake. I am really of his mind that said, It is better not touch the bottom, than not keep within the circle:' Melius est nescire centrum, quam non tenere circulum. He did assume a true human body; that is plainly asserted, Phil. 2: 7, 8, &c. Heb. 2: 14, 16. In one place it is called taking on him the seed of Abraham, and in the text, flesh. He did also assume a true human soul, this is undeniable by its operations, passions, and expiration at last, Matth. 26: 38 and 27: 50. And that both these natures make but one person, is as evident from Rom. 1: 3, 4. "Jesus Christ was made of the seed of David according to the flesh, and declared to be the Son of God with power, according to the Spirit of holiness, by the resurrection from the dead." So Rom. 9: 5, "Of whom, as concerning the flesh, Christ came, who is over all, God blessed for ever. Amen." But that you may have a sound and clear understanding of this mystery, I will (1.) Open the nature; (2.) The effects; and (3.) The reasons or ends of this wonderful union.

First, The nature of this union. There are three illustrious and dazzling unions in scripture: that of three persons in one God, Essentially. That of two distinct natures, and persons; by one spirit Mystically: and this of two distinct natures in one person, Hypostatically. This is my task to open at this time: and, for the more distinct and perspicuous management thereof, I shall speak to it both negatively and positively.

1. Negatively. Think not when Christ assumed our nature, that it was united consubstantially, so as the three persons in the Godhead are united among themselves. They all have but one and the same nature and will; but in Christ are two distinct natures and wills, though but one person.

2. Nor yet that they are limited Physically, as soul and body are united in one person; for death actually dissolves that; but this is indissoluble. So that when his soul expired, and his body was interred, both soul and body were still united to the second person as much as ever.

3. Nor yet is it such a mystical union, as is between Christ and believers. Indeed that is a glorious union; but though believers are said to be in Christ, and Christ in them, yet they are not one person with him. They are not christed into Christ, or godded into God, as blasphemous Familists speak.

Secondly, Positively. But this assumption of which I speak, is that whereby the second Person in the Godhead did take the human nature into a personal union with himself, by virtue whereof the manhood subsists in the second person, yet without confusion, both making but one person, "Theanthropos", or Immanuel, God with us.

So that though we truly ascribe a two-fold nature to Christ, yet not a double person; for the human nature of Christ never subsisted separately and distinctly, by any personal subsistence of its own, as it does in all other men, but from the first moment of conception, subsisted in union with the second person.

To explicate this mystery more particularly, let it be considered;

First, The human nature was united to the second person miraculously and extraordinarily, being supernaturally framed in the womb of the Virgin, by the overshadowing power of the Highest, Luke 1: 34, 35. By reason whereof it may truly and properly be said to be the fruit of the womb, not of the loins of men, nor by man. And this was necessary to exempt the assumed nature from the stain and pollution of Adam's sin, which it wholly escaped; inasmuch as he received it not, as all others do, in the way of ordinary generation, wherein original sin is propagated: but this being extraordinarily produced, was a most pure and holy thing, Luke 1: 35. And indeed this perfect shining holiness, in which it was produced, was absolutely necessary, both in order to its union with the divine Person, and the design of that union; which was both to satisfy for, and to sanctify us. The two natures could not be conjoined in the person of Christ, had there been the least taint of sin upon the human nature. For God can have no fellowship with sin, much less be united to it. Or, supposing such a conjunction with one sinful nature, yet he being a sinner himself, would never satisfy for the sins of others; nor could any unholy thing ever make us holy. "Such an High-priest therefore became us as is holy, harmless, undefiled, separate from sinners, Heb. 7: 26. And such an one he must needs be, whom the Holy Ghost produces in such a peculiar way, "to hagion", that holy thing.

Secondly, As it was produced miraculously, so it was assumed integrally; that is to say, Christ took a complete and perfect human soul and body, with all and every faculty and member pertaining to it. And this was necessary (as both Austin and Fulgentius have well observed) that thereby he might heal the whole nature of that leprosy of sin, which has seized and infected every member and faculty. "Panta anelaben hina panta hagiaze". "He assumed all, to sanctify all;" as Damascen expresseth it. He designed a perfect recovery, by sanctifying us wholly in soul, body, and spirit; and therefore assumed the whole in order to it.

Thirdly, He assumed our nature, as with all its integral parts, so with all its sinless infirmities. And therefore it is said of him, Heb. 2: 17. "That it behaved him," "kata panta homoiotenai", according to all things (that is, all things natural, not formally sinful, as it is limited by the same apostle, Heb. 4: 15.) to be made like into his brethren. But here our divines so carefully distinguish infirmities into personal and natural. Personal infirmities are such as befall particular persons, from particular causes, such as dumbness, blindness, lameness, leprosies, monstrosities, and other deformities. These it was no way necessary that Christ should, nor did he at all assume; but the natural ones, such as hunger, thirst, weariness, sweating, bleeding, mortality, &c., which though they are not in themselves formally and intrinsically sinful; yet are they the effects and consequent of sin. They are so many marks, that sin has left of itself upon our natures. And on that account Christ is said to be sent "in the likeness of sinful flesh", Rom. 8:3. Wherein the gracious condescension of Christ for us is marvellously signalised, that he would not assume our innocent nature, as it was in Adam before the fall, while it stood in all its primitive glory and perfection; But after sin had quite defaced, ruined, and spoiled it.

Fourthly, The human nature is so united with the divine, as that each nature still retains its own essential properties distinct. And this distinction is not, nor can be lost by that union. So that the two understandings, wills, powers &c. viz. The divine and human are not confounded; but a line of distinction runs betwixt them still in this wonderful person. It was the heresy of the Eutychians, condemned by the council of Chalcedon, to affirm, that there was no distinction betwixt the two natures in Christ. Against whom that council determined, that they were united "asunochutos", without any immutation or confusion.

Fifthly, The union of the two natures in Christ, as an inseparable union; so that from the first moment thereof, there never was, nor to eternity shall be, any separation of them.

Doubt. If you ask how the union remained betwixt them, when Christ's human soul and body were separated from each other upon the cross? Is not death the dissolution of the union betwixt soul and body?

Resolution. True, the natural union betwixt his soul and body was dissolved by death for a time, but this hypostatical union remained even then as entire and firm as ever: for, though his soul and body were divided from each other, yet neither of them from the divine nature. Divines assist our conception of this mystery, by an apt illustration. A man that holds in his hand a sword sheathed, when he pleaseth, draws forth the sword; but still holds that in one hand, and the sheath in the other, and then sheaths it again, still holding it in his hand: so when Christ died, his soul and body retained their union with the divine nature, though not (during, that space) one with another.

And thus you are to form and regulate your conceptions of this great mystery. Some adumbrations and imperfect similitudes of it may be found in nature. Among which some commend that union which the soul and body have with each other; they are of different natures, yet both make one individual man. Others find fault with this, because both these united make but one complete human nature; whereas, in Christ's person, there are two natures, and commend to us a more perfect emblem, viz., That of the Cyon and the tree or stock, which have two natures, yet make but one tree. But then we must remember that the Cyon wants a root of its own, which is an integral part, but Christ assumed our nature integrally. This defect is by others supplied in the Misletoe and the Oak, which have different natures; and the Misletoe subsists in union with the Oak, still retaining the difference of nature; and though making but one tree, yet bears different fruits. And so much to the first thing, namely, the nature of this union.

Secondly, For the effects, or immediate results of this marvellous union, let these three be well considered.

1. The two natures being thus united in the person of the Mediator, by virtue whereof the properties of each nature are attributed, and do truly agree in the whole person; so that it is proper to say, the Lord of glory was crucified, 1 Cor. 2: 8, and the blood of God redeemed the Church, Acts 20: 28, that Christ was both in heaven, and in the earth at the same time, John 3: 13.

Yet we do not believe that one nature does transfuse or impart its properties to the other, or that it is proper to say the divine nature suffered, bled, or died; or the human is omniscient, omnipotent, omnipresent; but that the properties of both natures, are so ascribed to the person, that it is proper to affirm any of them of him in the concrete, though not abstractly. The right understanding at this would greatly assist, in teaching the true sense of the forenamed, and many other dark passages in the scriptures.

2. Another fruit of this hypostatical union, is the singular advancement of the human nature in Christ, far beyond and above what it is; capable of in any other person, it being hereby replenished and filled with an unparalleled measure of divine graces and excellencies; in which respect he is

said to be "anointed above, or before his fellows," Gal. 14: 8, and so becomes the object of adoration and divine worship, Acts 7: 59. This the Socinians oppugn with this argument: He that is worshipped with a divine worship, as he is Mediator, is not so worshipped as God; but Christ is worshipped as Mediator. But we say, that to be worshipped as Mediator, and as God, are not opposite, but the one is necessarily included in the other; and therein is further included the ratio formalis sub qua of that divine religious worship.

3. Hence, in the last place, follows, as another excellent fruit of this union, The concourse and co-operation of each nature to his mediatory works; for in them he acts according to both natures: the human nature doing what is human, viz. suffering, sweating, bleeding, dying; and his divine nature stamping all these with infinite value; and so both sweetly concur unto one glorious work and design of mediation. Papists generally deny that he performs any of these mediatory works as God, but only as man; but how boldly do they therein contradict these plain scriptures? See 2 Cor. 5: 10. Heb. 9: 14,15. And so much as to the second thing propounded, viz. the fruits of this union.

Thirdly, The last thing to be opened is the grounds and reasons of this assumption. And we may say, touching that, (1.) That the human nature was not assumed to any intrinsical perfection of the Godhead, not to make that human nature itself perfect. The divine did not assume the human nature necessarily, but voluntarily; not out of indigence, but bounty; not because it was to be perfected by it, but to perfect it, by causing it to lie as a pipe, to the infinite all filling fountain of grace and glory, of which it is the great receptacle. And so, consequently, to qualify and prepare him for a full discharge of his mediatorship, in the offices of our Prophet, Priest, and King. Had he not this double nature in the unity of his person, he could not have been our Prophet: For, as God, he knows the mind and will of God, John 1: 18 and 3: 13, and as man he is fitted to impart it suitably to us, Deut. 18: 15, 16, 17, 18, compared with Acts 3: 22.

As Priest, had he not been man, he could have shed no blood; and if not God, it had been no adequate value for us, Heb. 2: 17. Acts 3: 28.

As King, had he not been man, he had been an heterogeneous, and so no fit head for us. And if not God, he could neither rule nor defend his body the Church.

These then were the designs and ends of that assumption.

Use 1. Let all Christians rightly inform their minds in this truth of so great concernment in religion, and hold it fast against all subtle adversaries, that could wrest it from them. The learned Hooker observes, that the dividing of Christ's person, which is but one, and the confounding of his natures, which are two, has been the occasion of those errors, which have so greatly disturbed the peace of the church. The Arians denied his deity, levelling him with other mere men. The Apollinarians maimed his humanity. The Sabellians affirmed, that the Father and Holy Ghost were incarnated as well as the Son; and were forced, upon that absurdity, by another error, viz. denying the three distinct persons in the Godhead, and affirming they were but three names. The Eutychians confounded both natures in Christ, denying any distinction of them. The Seleusians affirmed, that he unclothed himself of his humanity when he ascended, and has no human body in heaven. The Nestorians so rent the two names of Christ asunder, as to make two distinct persons of them.

But ye (beloved) have not so learned Christ. Ye know he is, (1.) True and very God; (2.) True and very man; that, (3.) these two natures make but one person, being united inseparately; (4.) that they are not confounded or swallowed up one in another, but remain still distinct in the person of Christ. Hold ye the sound words which cannot be condemned. Great things hang upon all these truths. O suffer not a stone to be loosed out of the foundation.

Use 2. Adore the love of the Father, and the Son, who bid so high for your souls, and at this rate were contented you should be recovered.

1. The love of the Father is herein admirably conspicuous, who so vehemently willed our salvation, that he was content to degrade the darling of his soul to so vile and contemptible a state, which was, upon the matter, an undoing to him, in point of reputation; as the apostle intimates, Phil. 2: 7. If two persons be at a variance, and the superior, who also is the wronged person, begin to stoop first, and say, you have deeply wronged me, yea, your blood is not able to repair the wrongs you have done me: however, such is my love to you, and willingness to be at peace with you, that I will part with what is most dear to me in all the world, for peace-sake; yea, though I stoop below myself, and seem, as it were, to forget my own relation and endearments to my own son, I will not suffer such a breach betwixt me and you. John 3: 16. "God so loved the world, that he gave his only begotten Son."

2. And how astonishing is the love of Christ, that would make such a stoop as this to exalt us! Oh, it is ravishing to think, he should pass by a more excellent and noble species of creatures, refusing the angelic nature, Heb. 2: 16, to take flesh; and not to solace and disport himself in it neither, nor experience sensitive pleasures in the body, for, as he needed them not, being at the fountain-head of the highest joys, so it was not at all in his design, but the very contrary, even to make himself a subject capable of sorrows, wounds, and tears. It was, as the apostle elegantly

expresseth it, in Heb. 2: 9, "hopos huper pantos geusetai tanatou"; that he might sensibly taste what relish death has, and what bitterness is in those pangs and agonies. Now, Oh that you would get your hearts suitably impressed and affected with these high impressures of the love both of the Father and the Son! How is the courage of some noble Romans celebrated in history, for the brave adventures they made for the commonwealth; but they could never stoop as Christ did, being so infinitely below him in personal dignity.

Use 3. And here infinite wisdom has also left a famous and everlasting mark of itself; which invites, yea, even chains the eyes of angels and men to itself. Had there been a general council of angels, to advise upon a way of recovering poor sinners, they would all have been in an everlasting demur and loss about it. It could not have entered their thoughts, (though they are intelligencers, and more sagacious creatures) that ever mercy, pardon, and grace, should find such a way as this to issue forth from the heart of God to the hearts of sinners. Oh, how wisely is the method of our recovery laid! So that Christ may be well called, "the power and wisdom of God," 1 Cor. 1: 24; forasmuch as in him the divine wisdom is more glorified than in all the other works of God, upon which he has impressed it. Hence it is, that some of the schoolmen affirm, (though I confess myself unsatisfied with it) that the incarnation of Christ was in itself so glorious a demonstration of God's wisdom and power, and thereupon so desirable in itself, that though man had not sinned, yet Christ would have been made man.

Use 4. Hence also we infer the incomparable sweetness of the Christian religion, that shows poor sinners such a fair foundation to rest their trembling consciences upon. While poor distressed souls look to themselves, they are perpetually puzzled. That is the cry of a distressed natural conscience, Micah 6: 6 "Wherewith shall I come before the Lord?" The Hebrew is "akadem Jehova" how shall I prevent or anticipate the Lord? And so Montanus renders it, in quo praeoccupabo Dominum? Conscience sees God arming himself with wrath, to avenge himself for sin; cries out, Oh, how shall I prevent him; if he would accept the fruit of my body, (those dear pledges of nature,) for the sin of my soul, he should have them. But now we see God coming down in flesh, and so intimately united our flesh to himself, that it has no proper subsistence of its own, but is united with the divine person: hence it is easy to imagine what worth and value must be in that blood; and how eternal love, springing forth triumphantly from it, flourishes into pardon, grace, and peace. Here is a way in which the sinner may see justice and mercy kissing each other, and the latter exercised freely, without prejudice to the former. All other consciences through the world, lie either in a deep sleep in the devil's arms or else are rolling (sea sick) upon the waves of their own fears and dismal presages. Oh, happy are they that have dropped anchor on this ground, and not only know they have peace, but why they have it!

Use 5. Of how great concernment is it, that Christ should have union with our particular persons, as well as with our common nature? For by this union with our nature alone, never any man was, or can be saved. Yea, let me add, that this union with our natures, is utterly in vain to you; and will do you no good, except he have union with your persons by faith also. It is indeed infinite mercy, that God is come so near you, as to dwell in your flesh; and that he has fixed upon such an excellent method to save poor sinners. And has he done all this? is he indeed come home, even to your own doors, to seek peace? does he vail his unsupportable glory under flesh, that he might treat the more familiarly? and yet do you refuse him, and shut your hearts against him? Then hear one word, and let thine ears tingle at the sound of it: Thy sin is hereby aggravated beyond the sin of devils, who never sinned against a mediator in their own nature; who never despised, or refused, because indeed, they were never offered terms of mercy, as you are.

And I doubt not but the devils themselves, who now tempt you to reject, will, to all eternity, upbraid your folly for rejecting this great salvation, which in this excellent way is brought down, even to your own doors.

Use 6. If Jesus Christ has assumed our nature, then he is sensibly touched with the infirmities that attend it, and so has pity and compassion for us, under all our burdens. And indeed this was one end of his assuming it, that he might be able to have compassion on us, as you read, Heb. 2: 17, 18. "Wherefore in all things it behoved him to be made like unto his brethren, that he might be a merciful and faithful High-priest, in things pertaining to God, to make reconciliation for the sins of the people. For in that he himself has suffers, being tempted, he is able to succour them that are tempted." O what a comfort is this to us, that he who is our High-Priest in heaven, has our nature on him, to enable him to take compassion on us!

Use 7. Hence we see, to what a height God intends to build up the happiness of man, in that he has laid the foundation thereof so deep, in the incarnation of his own Son.

They that intend to build high, use to lay the foundation low. The happiness and glory of our bodies, as well as souls, are founded in Christ's taking our flesh upon him: for, therein, as in a model or pattern, God intended to show what in time he resolves to make of our bodies; for he will "metaschematidzein", transform our vile bodies, and make them one day conformable to the glorious body of Jesus Christ, Phil. 3: 21. This flesh was therefore assumed by Christ, that in it might be shown, as in a pattern, how God intends to honour and exalt it. And indeed, a greater honour cannot be done to the nature of man, than what is already done, by this grace of union; nor are our persons capable of higher glory, than what consists in their conformity to this glorious head. Indeed the flesh of Christ will ever have a distinct glory from ours in heaven, by reason of this union; for being the body which the Word assumed, it is two ways advanced singularly above the flesh and blood of all other men, viz. subjectively, and objectively: Subjectively, it is the flesh and blood of God, Acts 20: 28, and so has a distinct and incommunicable glory of its own. And objectively, it is the flesh and blood which all the angels and saints adore. But though in these things it be supereminently exalted, yet it is both the medium and pattern of all that glory which God designs to raise us to.

Use 8. Lastly, How wonderful a comfort is it, that he who dwells in our flesh is God? What joy may not a poor believer make out of this? what comfort one made out of it, I will give you in his own words, "I see it a work of God, (saith he) that experiences are all lost, when summonses of improbation, to prove our charters of Christ to be counterfeit, are raised against poor souls in their heavy trials. But let me be a sinner, and worse than the chief of sinners, yea, a guilty devil, I am sure my well-beloved is God, and my Christ is God. And when I say my Christ is God, I have said all things, I can say no more. I would I could build as much on this, My Christ is God, as it would bear: I might lay all the world upon it."

God and man in one person! Oh! thrice happy conjunction! As man, he is full of experimental sense of our infirmities, wants, and burdens; and, as God, he can support and supply them all. The aspect of faith upon this wonderful Person, how relieving, how reviving, how abundantly satisfying is it? God will never divorce the believing soul, and its comfort, after he has married our nature to his own Son, by the hypostatical, and our persons also, by the blessed mystical union.

Sermon 6: Of the Authority by which Christ, as Mediator, acted

John 6: 27
For him hath God the Father sealed.

    You have heard Christ's compact, or agreement with the Father, in the covenant of redemption; as also what the Father did, in pursuance of the ends thereof, in giving his Son out of his bosom, &c. Also what the Son has done towards it, in assuming flesh. But though the glorious work be thus far advanced, yet all he should act in that assumed body, had been invalid and vain, without a due call, and commission from the Father, so to do: which is the import of the words now before you.

    This scripture is a part of Christ's excellent reply to a self- ended generation, who followed him, not for any spiritual excellencies that they saw in him, or soul-advantages they expected by him, but for bread. Instead of making his service their treat and drink, they only served him, that they might eat and drink. Self is a thing may creep into the best hearts and actions; but it only predominates in the hypocrite. These people had sought Christ from place to place, and having at last found him, they salute him with an impertinent compliment, "Rabbi, whence camest thou hither?" verse 25. Christ's reply is partly dissuasive, and partly directive. He dissuades them from putting the secondary and subordinate, in the place of the principal and ultimate end; not to prefer their bodies to their souls, their fleshly accommodations to the glory of God. "Labour not for the meat that perisheth." Wherein he does not take them off from their lawful labours and callings; but he dissuades them, first, from minding those things too intently: and, secondly, he dissuades them from that odious sin of making religion but a pretence for the belly.

    And it is partly directive, and that in the main end and business of life. "But labour for that meat which endureth to eternal life;" to get bread for your souls to live eternally by. And, that he might engage their diligence in seeking it to purpose, he shows them not only where they may have it, ["which the Son of man shall give you"] but also how they may be fully satisfied, that he has it for them, in the clause I have pitched on; "For him has God the Father sealed."

    In these words are three parts observable.

    1. The Person sealing or investing Christ with authority and power; which is said to be God the Father. Though all the persons in the Godhead are equal in nature, dignity and power, yet in their operation there is an order observed among them; the Father sends the Son, the Son is sent by the Father, the Holy Ghost is sent by both.

    2. The subject in which God the Father lodges this authority, [Him] that is, the Son of man. Jesus Christ, he is the "proton dektikon" the first receptacle of it, and he must here be understood exclusively. God the Father has so sealed him, as he never sealed any other before him, or that shall arise after him. No name is given in heaven, or earth, but this name by which we are saved, Acts 4: 12. "The government is upon his shoulders," Isa. 9.

    3. Here is farther observable, the way and manner of the Father's delegating and committing this authority to Christ; and that is, by sealing him. Where we have both a metonymy, the symbol of authority being put for the authority itself, and a metaphor, sealing, which is a human act, for the ratifying and confirming an instrument, or grant, being here applied to God. Like as princes, by sealed credentials, confirm the authority of those that are sent by them; as the Dutch Annotators well express the meaning of it. Hence we note,

    Doct. That Jesus Christ did not of himself undertake the work of our redemption, but was solemnly sealed unto that work by God the Father.

    When I say, he did not of himself undertake this work, I mean not that he was unwilling to go about it, for his heart was as fully and ardently engaged in it, as the Father's was: so he tells us, Psal. 40: 7. "Lo, I come to do thy will, O God; thy law is in my heart." But the meaning is, he came not without a due call, and full commission from his Father. And so it is to be understood in opposition to intrusion, not voluntary susception; and this is the meaning of that scripture, John 8: 24. "I proceeded and came from God; neither came I of myself, but he sent me." And this the apostle plainly expresseth, and fully clear; Heb. 5: 4, 5 "And no man taketh this honour to himself, but he that is called of God, as was Aaron: so also, Christ glorified not himself to be made an Highpriest; but he that said unto him, Thou art my Son." And on the account of these sealed credentials, he received from the Father, he is called the Apostle and High-priest of our profession, Heb. 3: 1: i. e. one called and sent forth by the Father's authority. Our present business, then, is to open Christ's commission, and to view the great seal of heaven by which it was ratified.

And, to preserve a clear method in the explication of this great truth, into which your faith and comfort is resolved, I shall,

First, Show what was the work and office to which the Father sealed him.

Secondly, What his sealing to this work does imply.

Thirdly, How, and by what acts, the Father sealed him to it.

Fourthly, Why it was necessary that he should be thus sealed and authorised by his Father; and then improve it in its proper uses.

First, What was that office, or work, to which his Father sealed him? I answer, more generally, he was sealed to the whole work of mediation for us, thereby to recover and save all the elect, whom the Father had given him; so John 17: 2 "It was to give eternal life to as many as were given him": it was to "bring Jacob again to him," Isa. 49: 5, or as the apostle expresses it, 1 Pet. 3: 18 "That he might bring us to God." More particularly, in order to the sure, and full effecting of this most glorious design, he was sealed to the offices of a Prophet, Priest, and King, that so he might bring about and compass this work.

1. God sealed him a commission to preach the glad tidings of salvation to sinners. This commission Christ opened and read in the audience of the people, Luke 4: 17, 18, 19, 20, 21. "And when he had opened the book, he found the place where it was written, The Spirit of the Lord is upon me, because he has anointed me to preach the gospel to the poor, he has sent me to heal the broken-hearted, to preach deliverance to the captives, and the recovering of sight to the blind, to set at liberty them that are bruised; to preach the acceptable year of the Lord. And he closed the book, &c. And he began to say unto them, this day is this scripture fulfilled in your ears."

2. He also sealed him to the priesthood, and that the most excellent; authorising him to execute both the parts of it, viz. oblatory and intercessory. He called him to offer up himself a sacrifice for us. "I have power (saith he) to lay down my life, this commandment have I received of my Father," John 10: 18. And upon that account, his offering up of his blood is, by the apostle, stiled an act of obedience, as it is, Phil. 2: 8. "He became obedient unto death." He also called him to intercede for us; Heb. 7: 21, 24, 25. "These priests were made without an oath; but this with an oath; by him that said unto him, The Lord sware, and will not repent, thou art a priest for ever:" because his sacrifice is virtually continued, in his living for ever to make intercession, as it is, verse 24. Yea,

3. He called him to his regal office; he was set upon the highest throne of authority by his Father's commission, as it is, Matth. 28: 18. "All power in heaven and earth is given to me." To all this was Christ sealed and authorised by his Father.

Secondly, What does the Father's sealing of Christ to this work and office imply? There are divers things implied in it: As,

1. The validity and efficacy of all his mediatory acts. For, by virtue of this his sealing whatever he did was fully ratified. And in this very thing lies much of a believer's comfort and security, forasmuch as all acts done without commission and authority (how great, or able soever the person that does them is, yet) are in themselves null and void. But what is done by commission and authority, is authentic, and most allowable among men. Had Christ come from heaven, and entered upon his mediatory work without a due call, our faith had been stumbled at the very threshold; but this greatly satisfies.

2. It imports the great obligation lying upon Jesus Christ to be faithful in the work he was sealed to: for, the Father, in this commission, devolves a great trust upon him, and relies upon him for his most faithful discharge thereof. And, indeed, upon this very account Christ reckons himself specially obliged to pursue the Father's design and end, John 9: 4. "I must work the works of him that sent me". And John 5: 30. "I seek not mine own will, but the will of the Father which has sent me." Still his eye is upon that work and will of his Father. And he reckons himself under a necessity of punctual and precise obedience to it; and, as a faithful servant, will have his own will swallowed up in his Father's will.

3. It imports Christ's complete qualification, or instrumental fitness to serve the Father's design and end of our recovery. Had not God known him to be every way fit, and qualified for the work, he would never have sealed him a commission for it. Men may, but God will not seal an unfit, or incapable person, for his work. And, indeed, whatever is desirable in a servant, was eminently found in Christ: for faithfulness, none like him. Moses indeed was faithful to a pin, but still as a servant: but Christ as a Son, Heb. 3: 2. He is the faithful and true witness, Rev. 1: 5. For

zeal, none like him. The zeal of God's house did eat him up, John 2: 16, 17. He was so intent upon his Fathers works that he forgot to eat bread, counting his work his meat and drink, John 4: 32. Yea, and love to his Father carried him on through all his work, and made him delight in the hardest piece of his service; for he served him as a Son, Heb. 3: 5, 6. All that ever he did was done in love. For wisdom, none like him. The Father knew him to be most wise, and said of him before he was employed, "Behold my servant shall deal prudently," Isa. 52: 13. To conclude, for self-denial, never any like him; he sought not his own glory, but the glory of him that sent him, John 8: 50. Had he not been thus faithful, zealous, full of love, prudent, and self-denying, he had never been employed in this great affair.

4. It implies Christ's sole authority in the church, to appoint and enjoin what he pleaseth; and this is his peculiar prerogative. For, the commission God sealed him in the text, is a single, not a joint commission; he has sealed him, and none beside him. Indeed there were some that pretended a call and commission from God; but all that were before him were thieves and robbers, that came not in at the door, as he did, John 10: 8. And he himself foretells, that after him some should arise, and labour to deceive the world with a feigned commission, and a counterfeit seal, Matth. 24: 24. "There shall arise false Christs, and false prophets, and shall show great signs and wonders: insomuch, that if it were possible, they should deceive the very elect." But God never commissioned any besides him, neither is there any other name under heaven, Acts 4: 12. Thus you see how the validity of his acts, his obligation to be faithful, his complete qualifications, and sole authority in the church, are imported in his sealing.

Thirdly, Let us enquire how God the Father sealed Jesus Christ to this work, and we shall find that he was sealed by four acts of the Father.

1. By solemn designation to this work. He singled him out and set him apart for it: and therefore the prophet Isaiah, chap. 42: 1. calls him God's elect. And the apostle Peter, 1 Pet. 2: 4. Chosen of God. This word which we render Elect, does not only signify one that in himself is eximious, worthy, and excellent, but also one that is set apart and designed, as Christ was, for the work of mediation. And so much is included in Johns 10: 36. where the Father is said to sanctify him, i. e. to separate, and devote him to this service.

2. He was sealed, not only by solemn designation, but also supereminent and unparalleled sanctification. He was anointed, as well as appointed to it. The Lord filled him with the Spirit, and that without measure, to qualify him for this service. So Isa. 61: 1, 2, 3 "The Spirit of the Lord is upon me, because he has anointed me to preach," &c. Yea, the Spirit of the Lord was not only upon him, but he was full of the Spirit, Luke 4: 1. and so full as was never any beside him, for God "anointed him with the oil of gladness, above his fellows," Psalm 45: 7. Believers are his fellows, or co-partners of this Spirit; they have an anointing also, but not as Christ had; in him it dwelt in its fulness, in them according to measure. It was poured out on Christ, our Head, abundantly, and ran down to the hem of his garment. "God gave not the Spirit to him by measure," John 3: 34. God filled Christ's human nature, to the utmost capacity, with all fulness of the Spirit of knowledge, wisdom, love, &c. beyond all creatures for the plenary and more effectual administration of his mediator chip: he was full extensively, with all kinds of grace; and full intensively, with all degrees of grace. "It pleased the Father that in him should all fulness dwell, Col. 1: 19. as light in the sun, or water in a fountain, that he might not only fill all things, as the apostle speaks, Eph 1: 22. but that he might be prompt, expedite, and every way fit to discharge his own work, which was the next and immediate end of it: so that the holy oil that was poured out upon the head of kings and priests, whereby they were consecrated to their offices, was but typical of the Spirit, by which Christ was consecrated, or sealed, to his offices.

3. Christ was sealed by the Father's immediate testimony from heaven, whereby he was declared to be the person whom the Father had solemnly designed and appointed to his work. And God gave this extraordinary testimony of him at two remarkable seasons, the one was just at his entrance on his public ministry, Mat. 3, and the other but a little before his sufferings, Matth. 17: 5. This voice was not formed by such organs and instruments of speech, as ours are, but by creating a voice in the air which the people heard sounding therein: by this God owned, approved, and as by a seal ratified his work.

4. Christ was sealed by the Father, in all those extraordinary miraculous works wrought by him, in which the Father gave yet more full and convincing testimonies to the world, that this was he whom he had appointed to be our Mediator. These were convictive to the world, that God had sent him, and that his doctrine was of God. "God anointed Jesus of Nazareth with the Holy Ghost and power, who went about doing good, and healing all that were oppressed of the devil; for God was with him," Acts 10: 38. And so, John 5: 36. "I have a greater witness than that of John; for the works which the Father has given me to finish, the same works that I do, bear witness of me, that the Father has sent me." Therefore he still referred those that doubted of him, or of his doctrine, to the seal of his Father, even the miraculous works he wrought in the power of God, Matth. 11: 3, 4,

5. And thus the Father sealed him.

Fourthly and lastly, We will enquire why it was necessary Christ should be sealed by his Father to this work: and there are these three weighty reasons for it.

1. Else he had not corresponded with the types which prefigured him, and in him it was necessary that they should be all accomplished. You know, under the Law, the kings and high priests had their inaugurations by solemn unctions; in all which this consecration, or sealing of Christ to his work, was shadowed out: and therefore you shall find, Heb. 5: 4, 5. "No man taketh this honour to himself, but he that is called of God, as was Aaron:" so also (mark the necessary correspondence betwixt Christ and them) "Christ glorified not himself to be made an High Priest; but he that said unto him, Thou art my Son."

2. Moreover, here the hearts of believers are the more engaged to love the Father, inasmuch as it appears hereby that the Father's love, and good will to them, was the original and spring of their redemption. For had not the Father sealed him such a commission, he had not come; but now he comes in the Father's name, and in the Father's love, as well as his name; and so all men are bound to ascribe equal glory and honour to them both, as it is, John 5: 23.

3. And especially Christ would not come without a commission, because, else you had no ground for your faith in him. How should we have been satisfied that this is indeed the true Messiah, except he had opened his commission to the world, and shewed his Father's seal annexed to it? If he had come without his credentials from heaven, and only told the world that God had sent him, and that they must take his bare word for it, who could have rested his faith on that testimony? And that is the true meaning of that place, John 5: 31. "If I bear witness of myself, my witness is not true." How so? You will say, does not that contradict what he said, John 8: 14. "Though I bear record of myself, yet my record is true." Therefore you must understand truth, not as it is opposed to reality; but the meaning is, if I had only given you my bare word for it, and not brought other evidence from my Father, my testimony had not been authentic and valid, according to human laws; but now all doubtings are precluded. Let us next improve this.

Inf. 1. Hence we infer the unreasonableness of infidelity, and how little rejecters of Christ can have to pretend for their so doing. You see he has opened his commission in the gospel, shown the world his Father's hand and seal to it, given as ample satisfaction as reason itself could desire, or expect; yet even his own received him not; John 1: 11. And he knew it before hand, and therefore complained by the prophet, Isa. 53: 1. "Who has believed our report?" &c. Yea, and that he is believed on in the world, is by the apostle put among the great mysteries of godliness, 1 Tim. 3: 16. A man that well considers with what convincing evidence Christ comes, would rather think it a mystery, that any should not believe. But, Oh the brutish obstinacy, and devilish enmity, that is in nature to Jesus Christ! Devilish did I say? You must give me that word again, for he compelled the devil's assent; "We know thee, whom thou art." And it is equally as wonderful to see the facility that is in nature to comply (meanwhile) with any, even the most foolish imposture. Let a false Christ arise, and he shall deceive many, as it is, Matth. 24: 24. Of this Christ complains, and not without great reason, John 5:43, "I am come in my Father's name, and ye receive me not: If another come in his own name, him will ye receive," q. d. You are incredulous to none but me: every deceiver, every pitiful cheat, that has but wit, or rather wickedness, enough to tell you the Lord has sent him, though you must take his own single word for it, he shall obtain and get disciples; but though I come in my Father's name, i. e. shewing you a commission signed and sealed by him, doing those works which none but a God can do, yet ye receive me not. But in all this, we must adore the justice of God, permitting it to be so, giving men up to such unreasonable obstinacy and hardness. It is a sore plague that lies upon the world, and a wonder that we all are not engulfed in the same infidelity.

Inf 2. If Christ was sealed to his work by his Father, then how great is the sin of those that reject and despise such as are sent and sealed by Jesus Christ? For look, as he came to us in his Father's name, so he has sent forth, by the same authority, ministers in his name; and as he acts in his Father's, so they in his, authority. "As thou hast sent me into the world, even so have I also sent them into the world," John 17: 18. And so, John 20: 21. "As my Father has sent me, so have I sent you." You may think it a small matter to despise or reject a minister of Christ, (a sin, in the guilt whereof, I think no age has been plunged deeper than this;) but hear, and let it be a warning to you for ever: in so doing you despise, and put the slight both upon the Father that sent Jesus, and upon Christ that sent them: so that it is a rebellion, that however it seems to begin low in some small piques against their persons, or some little quarrels at their parts and utterance, tones, methods or gestures; yet it runs high, even to the fountain-head of the most supreme authority. You that set yourselves against a minister of Christ, set yourselves against God the Father, and God the Son; Luke 10: 16. "He that heareth you, heareth me; and he that despiseth you, despiseth me; and he that despiseth me, despiseth him that sent me." God expects that you behave yourselves, under the word spoken by us, as if he himself spake it; yea, he expects submission to his word in the mouths of his ministers from the greatest on earth. And therefore it was that God so severely punished Zedekiah, "because he humbled not himself before Jeremiah the prophet, speaking from the mouth of the Lord," 2 Chron. 36: 12. God was angry with a great king for not humbling himself before a poor prophet. Yet here you must distinguish both of Persons, and of Acts. This reverence and submission is not due to them as men, but as men in office, as Christ's ambassadors; and must involve that respect still in it. Again, we owe it not to them, commanding or forbidding in their own names, but in Christ's, not inventing their own spleen, but the terrors of the Lord; and then to resist is a high rebellion and affront to the sovereign authority of heaven. And, by the way, this may instruct ministers, that the way to maintain that veneration and respect that is due to them, in the consciences of their hearers, is by keeping close to their commission.

Inf. 3. Hence also we infer, how great an evil it is to intrude into the office of the ministry without a due call. It is more than Christ himself would do; he glorified not himself: the honours and advantages attending that office, have invited many, to run before they were sent. But surely this is an insufferable violation of Christ's order. Our age has abounded with as many church-levellers as state-levellers. I wish the ministers of Christ might at last see and consider, what they were once warned of by a faithful watchman: I believe (saith he) God has permitted so many to intrude into the ministers' calling, because ministers have too much meddled with, and intruded into other men's callings.'

Inf. 4. Hence be convinced of the great efficacy that is in all gospel ordinances duly administered: For Christ having received full commission from his Father, and by virtue thereof having instituted and appointed these ordinances in the church, all the power in heaven is engaged to make them good, to back and second them, to confirm and ratify them. Hence, in the censures of the church, you have that great expression, Matth. 18: 18. "Whatsoever ye bind or loose on earth, shall be bound or loosed in heaven." And so, for the word and sacraments, Matth. 18: 18, 19, 20. "All power in heaven and earth is given unto me: Go therefore, &c. They are not the appointments of men; your faith stands not in the wisdom of men, but in the power of God. That very power, God the Father committed to Christ, is the fountain whence all gospel institutions flow. And he has promised to be with his officers, not only the extraordinary officers of that age, but with his ministers, in succeeding ages, to the end of the world. O therefore, when we come to an ordinance, come not with slight thoughts, but with great reverence, and great expectations, remembering Christ is there to make all good.

Inf. 5. Again, here you have another call to admire the grace and love, both of the Father and Son to your souls: It is not lawful to compare them, but it is duty to admire them. Was it not wonderful grace in the Father to seal a commission for the death of his Son, for the humbling him as low as hell, and in that method to save you, when you might have expected he should have sealed your Mittimus for hell, rather than a commission for your salvation? He might rather have set his irresistible seal to the sentence of your damnation, than to a commission for his Son's humiliation for you. And no less is the love of Christ to be wondered at, that would accept such a commission, as this for us, and receive this seal, understanding fully (as he did) what were the contents of that commission, that the Father delivered him thus sealed, and knowing that there could be no reversing of it afterwards.

O then, love the Lord Jesus, all ye his saints, for still you see more and more of his love breaking out upon you. I commend to you a sealed Saviour this day; O that every one that reads these lines might, in a pang of love, cry out with the enamoured spouse, Cant. 8: 6. "Set me as a seal upon thy heart, as a seal upon thy arm; for love is strong as death, jealousy is cruel as the grave; the coals thereof are coals of fire, which have a most vehement flame."

Inf. 6. Once more; Has God sealed Christ for you? Then draw forth the comfort of his sealing for you, and be restless till ye also be sealed by him.

1. Draw out the comfort of Christ's sealing for you. Remember that hereby God stands engaged, even by his own seal, to allow and confirm whatever Christ has done in the business of our salvation. And on this ground you may thus plead with God: Lord, thou hast sealed Christ to this office, and therefore I depend upon it, that thou allowest all that he has done, and all that he has suffered for me, and wilt make good all that he has promised me. If men will not deny their own seals, much less wilt thou.

2. Get your interest in Christ sealed to you by the Spirit, else you cannot have the comfort of Christ's being sealed for you. Now the Spirit seals two ways, Objectively and Effectually; the first is by working those graces in us, which are the conditions of the promises: the latter is by shining upon his own work, and helping the soul to discern it, which follows the other, both in order of nature, and of time. And these sealings of the Spirit are to be distinguished, both ex parte subjecti, or the quality of the person sealed, which always is a believer, Eph. 1: 13. for there can be no reflex, till there have been a direct Act of faith; and ex parte materiae, by the matter of which that comfort is made: which if it be of the Spirit, is ever consonant to the written word, Isa. 8: 20. And

partly ab effectis, by its effects: for it commonly produces in the sealed soul, great care and caution to avoid sin, Eph. 4: 30. Great love to God, John 14: 22. Readiness to suffer any thing, for Christ, Rom. 5: 3, 4, 5. Confidence in addresses to God, 1 John 5: 13, 14, and great humility and self-abasement; as in Abraham, who lay on his face when God sealed the covenant to him, Gen. 17: 1, 2, 3. This, O this brings home the sweet and good of all, when this seal is super-added to that.

Sermon 7: Of the Solemn Consecration of the Mediator

John 17: 19.
And for their sakes I sanctify myself.

Jesus Christ being fitted with a body, and authorised by a commission, now actually devotes, and sets himself apart to his work. In the former sermon you heard what the Father did; in this you shall hear what the Son has done towards the farther advancement of that glorious design of our salvation: He sanctified himself for our sakes. Wherein observe, (1.) Christ's sanctifying of himself. (2.) The end or design of his so doing.

1. You have Christ's sanctifying of himself. The word "hagiadzo" is not here to be understood for the cleansing, purifying, or making holy that which was before unclean and unholy, either in a moral sense, as we are cleansed from sin by sanctification; or in a ceremonial sense, as persons and things were sanctified under the law; though here is a plain allusion to those legal rites; But Christ's sanctifying himself, imports, (1.) His separation, or setting apart to be an oblation or sacrifice. So Beza, nempe ut sacerdos et victima, as the priest and sacrifice. I sanctify myself, imports, (2.) His consecration, or dedication of himself to this holy use and service. So the Dutch Annotations, I sanctify myself, (i. e.) I give up myself for a holy sacrifice. And so our English Annotations, I sanctify, (i. e.) I consecrate and voluntarily offer myself a holy and unblemished sacrifice to thee for their redemption. And thus under the Law, when any day, person, or vessel, was consecrated and dedicated to the Lord, it was so entirely for his use and service, that to use it afterward in any common service, was to profane and pollute it, as you see Dan. 5: 3.

2. The end of his so sanctifying himself [for their sakes, and that they might be sanctified, where you have the Finis cujus, the end for whom, for their (i. e.) for the elect's sake, for them whom thou gavest me; and the Finis cui, the end for which, that they might be sanctified. Where you also see that the death of Christ wholly respects us; he offered not for himself as other priests did, but for us, that we may be sanctified. Christ is so in love with holiness, that at the price of his blood he will buy it for us. Hence the observation is;

Doct. That Jesus Christ did dedicate, and wholly set himself apart to the work of a Mediator, for the elect's sake.

This point is a glass, wherein the eye of your faith may see Jesus Christ preparing himself to be offered up to God for us, fitting himself to die. And to keep a clear method, I shall open these two things, in the doctrinal part; First, what his sanctifying himself implies: Secondly, How it respects us.

First, What is implied in this phrase, "I sanctify myself". And there are seven things carried in it.

1. This phrase "I sanctify myself" implies the personal union of the two natures in Christ; for what is that which he here calls himself, but the same that was consecrated to be a sacrifice, even his human nature? This was the sacrifice. And this also was himself: So the apostle speaks, Heb. 9: 14. "He through the eternal Spirit, offered up himself to God, without spot." So that our nature, by that assumption, is become himself. Greater honour cannot be done it, or greater ground of comfort proposed to us. But having spoken of that union in the former sermon, shall remit the reader thither.

2. This sanctifying, or consecrating himself to be a sacrifice for us, implies, the greatness and dreadfulness of that breach which sin made between God and us. You see no less a sacrifice than Christ himself must be sanctified to make atonement. Judge of the greatness of the wound by the breadth of the plaister. "Sacrifice and offering, and burnt-offering for sin, thou wouldest not; but a body hast thou prepared me," Heb. 10: 5. All our repentance, could we shed as many tears for sin, as there have fallen drops of rain since the creation, could not have been our atonement: "But God was in Christ, reconciling the world to himself." And had he not sanctified Christ to this end, he would have sanctified himself upon us, in judgement and fury for ever.

3. This his sanctifying Himself, implies his free and voluntary undertaking of the work. It is not, I am sanctified, as if he had been merely passive in it, as the lambs that typed him out were, when pluckt from the fold, but it is an active verb he useth here, I sanctify myself; he would have none think that he died out of a necessity of compulsion, but out of choice: therefore he is solid to "offer up himself to God", Heb. 10:14. And John 9:18, "I lay down my life of myself; no man taketh it from me." And although it is often said "his Father sent him, and gave him"; yet his heart was as much set on that work, as if there had been nothing but story, ease, and comfort in it; he was under no constraint, but that of his own love. Therefore, as when the scripture would set forth the willingness of the Father to this work, it saith, God sent his Son, and God gave his Son; so when it would set forth Christ's willingness to it, it saith, he offered himself, gave himself; and, here in the text, sanctified himself: The sacrifice that struggled, and came not without force to the altar, was reckoned ominous and unlucky by the Heathen: our Sacrifice dedicated himself; he died out of choice, and was a free-will offering

4. His sanctifying himself implies his pure and perfect holiness, that he had no spot or blemish in him. Those beasts that prefigured him, were to be without blemish, and none else were consecrated to that service. So, and more than so, it behaved Christ to be, Heb. 7: 26. "Such an High-Priest became us, who is holy, harmless, undefiled, separate from sinners:" And what it became him to be, he was. Therefore in allusion to the lambs offered under the law, the apostle calls him a Lamb without blemish, or spot, 1 Pet. 1: 19. Every other man has a double spot on him, the heart spot, and the life-spot; the spot of original, and the spots of actual sin. But Christ was without either, he had net the spot of original sin, for he was not by man; he came in a peculiar way into the world, and so escaped that: nor yet of actual sins; for, as his nature, so his life was spotless and pure, Isa. 53: 9. "He did no iniquity." And though tempted to sin externally, yet he was never defiled in heart or practice; he came as near as he could for our sakes, yet still without sin, Heb. 4: 15. If he sanctifies himself for a sacrifice, he must be as the law required, pure and spotless.

5. His sanctifying himself for our sakes, speaks the strength of his love, and largeness of his heart to poor sinners, thus to set himself wholly and entirely apart for us: so that what he did and suffered, must all of it have a respect and relation to us. He did not (when consecrated for us) live a moment, do an act, or speak a word, but it had some tendency to promote the great design of our salvation. He was only and wholly, and always doing your work, when consecrated for your sakes. His incarnation respects you; Isa. 9: 6. "For to us a child is born, to us a son is given." And he would never have been the son of man, but to make you the sons and daughters of God. God would not have come down in the likeness of sinful flesh, in the habit of a man, but to raise up sinful man unto the likeness of God. All the miracles he wrought Were for you, to confirm your faith. When he raised up Lazarus, John 11: 42. "Because of the people which stand by, I said it, that they might believe that thou hadst sent me." While he lived on earth, he lived as one wholly set apart for us: and when he died, he died for us, Gal. 3: 13. "he was made a curse for us." When he hanged on that cursed tree, he hanged there in our room, and did but fill our place. When he was buried, he was buried for us: for the end of it was, to perfume our graves, against we come to lie down in them. And when he rose again, it was, as the apostle saith, "for our justification," Rom. 4: 25. When he ascended into glory, he protested it was about our business, that he went to prepare places for us: and if it had not been so, he would have told us, John 14: 2. And now he is there, it is for us that he there lives; for he "ever lives to make intercession for us," Heb. 7: 25. And when he shall return again to judge the world, he will come for us too. "He comes (whenever it be) to be glorified in his saints, and admired in them that believe," 2 Thess. 1: 10. He comes to gather his saints home to himself, that where he is, there they all may be in soul and body with him for ever. Thus you see how, as his consecration for us does speak him set apart for our use; so he did wholly bestow himself, time, life, death, and all upon us; living and dying for no other end, but to accomplish this great work of salvation for us.

6. His sanctifying himself for us plainly speaks the vicegerency of his death, that it was in our room or stead. When the priest consecrated the sacrifice, it was set apart for the people. So it is said of the scapegoat; "And Aaron shall lay both his hands upon the head of the live goat, and confess over him all the iniquities of the children of Israel, and all their transgressions in all their sins, putting them upon the head of the goat, and shall send him away by the hand of a fit man into the wilderness," Levit. 16: 21. Thus Isa. 53: 6, 7. He stood in our room, to bear our burden. And as Aaron laid the iniquities of the people upon the goat, so were ours laid on Christ; it was said to him in that day, On thee be their pride, their unbelief, their hardness of heart, their vain thoughts, their earthly-mindedness, &c. Thou art consecrated for them, to be the sacrifice in their room. His death was in our stead, as well as for our good. And so much his sanctifying himself [for us] imports.

7. His sanctifying himself, imparts the extraordinariness of his person: for it speaks him to be both Priest, Sacrifice, and altar, all in one: a thing unheard of in the world before. So that this name might well be called Wonderful. I sanctify myself: I sanctify, according to both natures; myself, i.

e. my human nature, which was the sacrifice upon the altar of my divine nature; for it is the altar that sanctifies the gift. As the three offices never met in one person before, so these three things never met in one priest before. The priests indeed consecrated the bodies of beasts for sacrifices, but never offered up their own souls and bodies as a whole burnt offering, as Christ did. And thus you have the import of this phrase, I sanctify myself for their sakes.

Secondly, I shall show you briefly the habitude and respect that all this has to us; for unto us the scriptures every where refer it. So in 1 Cor. 5: 7. "Christ our passover is sacrificed for us." Eph. 5: 2. "He loved the church, and gave himself for it." See Tit. 2: 14. This will be made out, by a threefold consideration of Christ's death. And,

1. Let it be considered, that he was not offered up to God for his own sins for he was most holy. Isa. 53: 9. No iniquity was found in him. Indeed, the priests under the law offered for themselves, as well as the people; but Christ did not so, Heb. 7: 27. "He needed not daily, as those High-priests, to offer up sacrifice, first for his own sins, and then for the people's." And indeed had he been a sinner, what value or efficacy could have been in his sacrifice? He could not have been the sacrifice, but would have needed one. Now, if Christ were most holy, and yet put to death, and cruel sufferings, either his death or sufferings must be an act of injustice and cruelty, or it must respect others, whose persons and cause he sustained in that suffering capacity. He could never have suffered or died by the Father's hand, had he not been a sinner by imputation. And in that respect, as Luther speaks, he was the greatest of sinners; or, as the prophet Isaiah speaks, all our sins were made to meet upon Him; not that he was intrinsically, but was made so, so, by imputation, as is clear from 2 Cor. 5: 21. "He was made sin for us, who knew no sin." So that hence it is evident, that Christ's death, or sacrifice, is wholly a respective or relative thing.

2. It is not to be forgotten here, that the scriptures frequently call the death of Christ a price, 1 Cor. 6: 20, and a ransom, Matt. 20: 28, or counterprice. To whom then does it relate, but to them that were, and are in bondage and captivity? If it was to redeem any, it must be captives: but Christ himself was never in captivity; he was always in his Father's bosom, as you have heard; but we were in cruel bondage and thraldom, under the tyranny of sin and Satan: and it is we only that have the benefit of this ransom.

3. Either the death of Christ must relate to believers, or else he must die in vain. As for the angels, those that stood in their integrity needed no sacrifice, and those that fell, are totally excluded from any benefit by it: he is not a Mediator for them. And among men that have need of it, unbelievers have no share in it, they reject it; such have no part in it. If then he neither died for himself, as I proved before, nor for angels, nor unbelievers; either his blood must be shed with respect to believers, or, which is most absurd, and never to be imagined, shed as water upon the ground, and totally cast away, so that you see by all this, it was for our sakes, as the text speaks, that he sanctified himself. And now we may say, Lord, the condemnation was thine, that the justification might be mine; the agony thine, that the victory might be mine; the pain was thine, and the ease mine; the stripes thine, and the healing balm issuing from them mine; the vinegar and gall were thine, that the honey and sweet might be mine; the curse was thine, that the blessing might be mine; the crown of thorns was thine, that the crown of glory might be mine; the death was thine, the life purchased by it mine; thou paidst the price that I might enjoy the inheritance.

We come next to the inferences of truth deducible from this point, which follow.

Inference 1. If Jesus Christ did wholly set himself apart for believers, how reasonable is it that believers should consecrate and set themselves apart wholly for Christ? Is he all for us, and shall we be nothing for him? What he was, he was for you? Whatever he did, was done for you; and all that he suffered, was suffered for you. O then, "I beseech you, brethren, by the mercies of God, present your bodies,", i. e. your whole selves, (for so body is there synecdochically put to signify the whole person) I say, "present your bodies a living sacrifice, holy, acceptable to God, which is your reasonable service," Rom. 12: 1. As your good was Christ's end, so let his glory be your end. Let Christ be the "end of your conversation," Heb. 13: 7. As Christ could say, To me to live is you; so do you say, "For us to live is Christ," Phil. 1: 21. O that all who profess faith in Christ, could subscribe cordially to that profession, Rom. 14: 8. "None of us liveth to himself, and no man dies to himself; but whether we live, we live to the Lord; and whether we die, we die to the Lord; so then whether we live or die, we are the Lord's." This is to be a Christian indeed. What is a Christian, but an holy dedicated thing to the Lord? And what greater evidence can there be, that Christ set himself apart for you, than your setting yourselves apart for him?

This is the marriage covenant, Hos. 3: 3 "Thou shall be for me, and not for another; so will I be for thee." Ah, what a life is the life of a Christian; Christ all for you, and you all for him. Blessed exchange! Soul, (saith Christ) all I have is thine, Lord, (saith the soul) and all I have is thine. Soul, (saith Christ) my person is wonderful, but what I am, I am for thee: my life was spent in labour and travail, but lived for thee. And Lord, (saith the believers, my person is vile, and not worth thy accepting; but such as it is, it is thine; my soul, with all and every faculty; my body, and every member of it, my gifts, time, and all my talents are thine.

And see that as Christ bequeathed and made over himself to you, so ye, in like manner, bestow and make over yourselves to him. He lived not, neither died (as you hear) for himself, but you. O that you, in like manner, would down with self, and exalt Christ in the room of it. Wo, wo is me, (saith one) that the holy profession of Christ is made a shewy garment by many to bring home a vain fame; and Christ is made to serve men's ends. This is to stop an oven with a king's robes. Except men martyr and slay the body of sin, in sanctified self-denial, they shall never be Christ's martyrs and faithful witnesses. O if I could be master of that house-idol, myself, mine own, mine own wit, will, credit, and ease, how blessed were I! O but we have need to be redeemed from ourselves, rather than from the devil and the world. Learn to put out yourselves, and to put in Christ for yourselves. I should make a sweet bargain, and give old for new, if I could shuffle out self, and substitute Christ my Lord in place of myself; to say, not I, but Christ; not my will, but Christ's; not my ease, not my lusts, not my credit, but Christ, Christ. - O wretched idol, myself, when shall I see thee wholly decourted, and Christ wholly put in thy room? O if Christ had the full place and room of myself, that all aims, purposes, thoughts and desires would coast and land upon Christ, and not upon myself.'

He set himself apart for you believers, and no others: no, not for angels but for you: Will ye also set yourselves apart peculiarly for Christ? be his, and no others? Let not Christ and the world share anal divide your hearts in two halves betwixt them; let not the world step in and say, half mine. You will never do Christ right, nor answer this grace, till you can say, as it is, Psal. 73: 25, "Whom have I in heaven but thee? and on earth there is none that I desire in comparison of thee." None but Christ, none but Christ, is a proper motto for a Christian.

He left the highest and best enjoyments, even those in his Father's bosom, to set himself apart for death and suffering for you: Are you ready to leave the bosom of the best and sweetest enjoyments, you have in this world, to serve him? If you stand not habitually ready to leave father, mother, wife, children, lands, yea, and life too, to serve him, you are not worthy of him, Matt. 10: 37.

He was so wholly given up to your service, that he refused not the worst and hardest part of it, even bleeding, groaning, dyingwork; his love to you sweetened all this to him; Can you say so too; do you "account the reproaches of Christ greater riches than the treasures of Egypt, as Moses did?" Heb. 11: 26.

He had so entirely devoted himself to your work, that He could not be at rest till it was finished: he was so intent upon it, that he "forgot to eat bread," John 4: 31 ,32. So it should be with you; his service should be meat and drink to you. To conclude:

He was so wholly given up to your work and service, that he would not suffer himself to be in the least diverted, or taken off from it: and if Peter himself counsel him to favour himself, he shall hear, "Get thee behind me, Satan." O happy were it if our hearts were but so engaged for Christ! In Galen's time it was proverbial, when they would express the impossibility of a thing, You may as soon take off a Christian from Christ. Thus you see what use you should make of Christ's sanctifying himself for you.

Inf. 2. If Christ has sanctified or consecrated himself for us; learn hence, what a horrid evil it is, to use Christ or his blood, as a common and unsanctified thing. Yet so some do, as the apostle speaks, Heb. 10: 29. The apostate is said to tread upon the Son of God, as if he were no better than the dirt under his feet, and to count his blood an unholy (or common) thing. But wo to them that do so, they shall be counted worthy of something worse than dying without mercy, as the apostle there speaks.

And as this is the sin of the apostate, so it is also the sin of all those that without faith approach, and so profane the table of the Lord, unbelievingly and unworthily handling those awful things. Such "eat and drink judgement to themselves, not discerning the Lord's body," 1 Cor. 11:29. Whereas the body of Christ was a thing of the deepest sanctification that ever God created; sanctified (as the text tells us) to a far more excellent and glorious purpose than ever any creature in heaven or earth was sanctified. It was therefore the great sin of those Corinthians, not to discern it, and not to behave themselves towards it, when they saw and handled the signs of it, as became so holy a thing.

And as it was their great sin, so God declared his just indignation against it, in those sore strokes inflicted for it. As they discerned not the Lord's body, so neither did the Lord discern their bodies from others in the judgements that were inflicted. And, as one well observes, God drew the model and platform of their punishment, from the structure and proportion of their sin. And truly, if the moral and spiritual seeds and originals of many of our outward afflictions and sicknesses were but duly sifted out, possibly we might find a great part of them in the bowels of this sin.

The just and righteous God will build up the breaches we make upon the honour of his Son, with the ruins of that beauty, strength and honour which he has given our bodies. O then, when you draw nigh to God in that ordinance, take heed to sanctify his name, by a spiritual discerning of this most holy, and most deeply sanctified body of the Lord; sanctified beyond all creatures, angels or men, not only in respect of the Spirit which filled him, without measure with inherent holiness, but also in respect of its dedication to such a service as this, it being set apart by him to such holy, solemn ends and uses, as you have heard.

And let it, for ever, be a warning to such as have lifted up their hands to Christ in a holy profession, that they never lift up their heel against him afterwards by apostasy. The apostate treads on God's dear Son, and God will tread upon him for it. "Thou hast trodden down all that err from thy statutes," Psal. 119: 118.

Inf. 3. What a choice pattern of love to saints have we here before us! Calling all that are in Christ to an imitation of him, even to give up ourselves to their service, as Christ did; not in the same kind, so none can give himself for them, but as we are capable. You see here how his heart was affected to them, that he would sanctify himself as a sacrifice for them. See to what a height of duty the apostle improves this example of Christ, 1 John 3: 16. "hereby perceive we the love of God, because he laid down his life for us, and we ought also to lay down our lives for the brethren." Some Christians came up fairly to this pattern in primitive times; Priscilla and Aquila laid down their necks for Paul, Rom. 16: 4. i. e. eminently hazarded their lives for him; and he himself could "rejoice, if he were offered up upon the sacrifice and service of their faith," Phil. 2: 17. And in the next times, what more known, even to the enemies of Christianity, than their fervent love one to another? Ecce quam mutuo se diligunt, et mori volunt pro alterutris! See how they love one another, and are willing to die one for another!

But alas! the primitive spirit is almost lost in this degenerate age: instead of laying down life, how few will lay down twelve pence for them? I remember, it is the observation of a late Worthy, upon Mat. 5: 44. That he is persuaded there is hardly that man to be found this day alive, that fully understands and fully believes that scripture. O, did men think what they do for them, is done for Christ himself, it would produce other effects than are yet visible.

Infer. 4. Lastly, If Christ sanctified himself, that we might be sanctified by [or in] the truth; then it will follow, by sound consequence, That true sanctification is a good evidence that Christ set apart himself to die for us. In vain did he sanctify himself (as to you) unless you be sanctified. Holy souls only can claim the benefit of the great Sacrifice. O try then, whether true holiness (and that is only to be judged by its conformity to its pattern, 1 Pet. 1: 15. "As he that called you is holy, so be ye holy"); whether such a holiness as is, and acts (according to its measure) like God's holiness, in the following particulars, be found in you.

1. God is universally holy in all his ways; so Psal. 145: 17. "His works are all holy:" whatever he does, it is still done as becomes a holy God: he is not only holy in all things, but at all times unchangeably holy. Be ye therefore holy in all things and at all times too, if ever you expect the benefit of Christ's sanctifying himself to die for you.

O brethren, let not the feet of your conversation be as the feet of a lame man, which are unequal, Prov. 20: 7. Be not sometimes hot, and sometimes cold; at one time careful, at another time careless; one day in a spiritual rapture, and the next in a fleshly frolic: but be ye holy "en pase anastrofe", 1 Pet. 1: 15. "in all manner of conversation," in every creek and turning of your lives: and let your holiness hold out to the end. "Let him that is holy, be holy still," Rev. 21: 11. Not like the hypocrite's paint, but as a true natural completion.

2. God is exemplarily holy, Jesus Christ is the great pattern of holiness. Be ye examples of holiness too, unto all that are about you. "Let your light so shine before men, that they may see your good works," Matth. 5: 16. As wicked men infect one another by their examples, and diffuse their poison and malignity, wherever they come; so do ye disseminate godliness in all places and companies; and let those that frequently converse with you, especially those of your own families, receive a deeper dye and tincture of heavenliness every time they come nigh you, as the cloth does by every new dipping into the vat.

3. God delights in nothing but holiness, and holy ones; he has set all his pleasure in the saints. Be ye holy herein, as God is holy. Indeed, there is this difference betwixt God's choice and yours; he chooses not men, because they are holy, but that they may be so; so you are to chose them for your delightful companions, that God has chosen and made holy. "Let all your delights be in the saints, even them that excel in virtue," Psal. 16: 3.

4. God abhors and hates all unholiness; do ye so likewise that ye may be like your Father which is in heaven. And when the Spirit of holiness runs down this upon you, a sweeter evidence the world cannot give, that Christ was sanctified for you. Holy ones may confidently lay the hand of their faith on the head of this great sacrifice, and say, "Christ our passover is sacrificed for us."

Sermon 8: Of the Nature of Christ's Mediation

1 Tim. 2: 5.
And one Mediator betwixt God and Man, the man Christ Jesus.

Great and long preparations bespeak the solemnity and greatness of the work for which they are designed; A man that had but seen the heaps of gold, silver and brass, which David amassed in his time, for the building of the temple, might easily conclude before one stone of it was laid, that it would be a magnificent structure. But lo, here is a design of God as far transcending that, as the substance does the shadow. For, in deed, that glorious temple was but the type and figure of Jesus Christ, John 2: 19, 21, and a weak adumbration of that living, spiritual temple which he was to build, cementing the lively stones thereof together with his own blood, 1 Pet. 2: 5, 6. that the great God might dwell and walk in it, 2 Cor. 6: 16. The preparations for that temple were but of few years, but the consultations and preparations for this were from eternity, Prov. 8: 31. And as there were preparations for this work (which Christ dispatched in a few years) before the world began; so it will be matter of eternal admiration and praise, when this world shall be dissolved. What this astonishing glorious work is, this text will inform your as to the general nature of it: it is the work of mediation betwixt God and man, managed by the sole hand of the man Christ Jesus.

In this scripture (for I shall not spend time to examine the words in their contexture) you have a description of Jesus the Mediator: and he is here described four ways, viz. by his work or office, a Mediator; by the singularity of his mediation, one Mediator; and by the nature and quality of his person, employed in this singular way of mediation, the man; and lastly, his name Jesus Christ.

1. He is described by the work, or office he is employed about "Mesites", a Mediator, a middle person. So the word imports a fit, indifferent, and equal person, that comes between two persons that are at variance, to compose the difference and make peace. Such a middle, equal, indifferent person is Christ; a day's man, to lay his hand upon both; to arbitrate and award justly and give God his due, and that without ruin to poor man.

2. He is described by the singularity of his mediation, one Mediator, and but one. Though there be many mediators of reconciliation among men, and many intercessors in a petitionary way, betwixt God and man; yet but "heis Mesites", one only mediator of reconciliation betwixt God and man: and it is as needless and impious to make more mediators than one, as to make more Gods than one. There is one God, and one Mediator betwixt God and men.

He is described by the nature and quality of his person, "anthropos Christos" &c. the man Christ Jesus. This description of him by one nature, and that the human nature also (wherein, as you shall see anon, the Lord especially consulted our encouragement and comfort); I say, his being so described to us, hath, through the corruption of men, been improved to the great dishonour of Jesus Christ, both by the Arians and Papists. The former took occasion from hence to affirm, that he was but "psilos anthropos", a mere man.

The latter allow him to be the true God, but on this weak ground affirm, that he performed not the work of mediation as God, but only as man. Thus what the Spirit ordered for our comfort, is wickedly retorted to Christ's dishonour; for I doubt not but he is described by his human nature in this place; not only because in this nature he paid that ransom (which he speaks of in the words immediately following) but especially for the drawing of sinners to him; seeing he is the man Christ Jesus, one that clothed himself in their own flesh; and to encourage the faith of believers, that he tenderly rewards all their wants and miseries, and that they may safely trust him with all their concerns, as one that will carefully mind them as his own, and will be for them a merciful and faithful High Priest, in things pertaining to God.

4. He is described by his names; by his appellative name Christ, and his proper name Jesus. The name Jesus, notes his work about which he came; and Christ, the offices to which he was anointed; and in the execution of which he is our Jesus. "In the name Jesus, the whole gospel is contained, it is the light, the food, the medicine of the soul," as one speaks. The note from hence is,

John Flavel

Doct. That Jesus Christ is the true and only Mediator betwixt God and men.

"Ye are come to Jesus the Mediator of the new covenant," Heb. 12: 24. "And for this cause he is the Mediator of the New Testament," &c. Heb. 9: 14. I might show you a whole vein of scriptures running this way; but to keep a profitable and clear method, I shall show,

First, What is the sense of this word "Mesites", a Mediator.

Secondly, What it implies, as it is applied to Christ.

Thirdly, How it appears that he is the true and only Mediator betwixt God and men.

Fourthly, In what capacity he performed his mediatory work.

First, What is the sense and import of this word "Mesites", a Mediator? The true sense and importance of it, is a middle Person, or one that interposes betwixt two parties at variance, to make peace betwixt them. So that as Satan is medium disjungens, a medium of discord; so Christ is medium conjungens, a medium of concord and peace. And he is such a Mediator, both in respect of his person and office; in respect of his person, he is a Mediator, i. e. one that has the same nature both with God and us, true God, and true man; and in respect of his Office or work, which is to interpose, to transact the business of reconciliation between us and God. The former some call his substantial, the latter his energetical, or operative mediation: Though I rather conceive that which is called his substantial mediation, is but the aptitude of his person to execute the mediatorial function; and that it does not constitute two kinds of mediation. His being a middle person, fits and capacitates him to stand in the midst betwixt God and us. This, I say, is the proper sense of the word; though "Mesites", a Mediator, is rendered variously; sometimes an umpire or arbitrator; sometimes a messenger that goes betwixt two persons; sometimes an interpreter, imparting the mind of one to another; sometimes a reconciler or peace-maker. And in all these senses Christ is the "Mesites", the middle person in his mediation of reconciliation or intercession; i. e. either in his mediating, by suffering to make peace, as he did on earth; or to continue, and maintain peace, as he does in heaven, by meritorious intercession. Both these ways he is the only Mediator. And he manageth this his mediation,

1. As an umpire or arbitrator; one that layeth his hands upon both parties, as Job speaks, chap. 9: 33. so does Christ, he layeth his hands (speaking after the manner of men) upon God, and saith, Father, wilt thou be at peace with them, and re admit them into thy favour? If thou wilt, thou shalt be fully satisfied for all that they have done against thee. And then he layeth his hand upon man, and saith, poor sinner, be not discouraged, thou shalt be justified and saved.

2. As a messenger or ambassador, so he came to impart the mind of God to us, and so he presents our desires to God; and in this sense only Socinus would allow Christ to be Mediator. But therein he endeavours to undermine the foundation, and to exclude him from being, Mediator by a suretiship; which is,

3. The third way of his mediation. So the apostle speaks, Heb. 7: he is "enguos", the surety, or pledge. Which, as the learned David Pareus well expresseth it, is one that engageth to satisfy another, or gives caution or security by a pledge in the hand for it. And indeed, both these ways, Christ is our mediator by suretiship, viz. in a way of satisfaction, coming under our obligation to answer the law; this he did on the cross and in a way of caution, a surety for the peace, or good behaviour. But to be more explicit and clear, I shall,

Secondly, In the next place enquire, what it implies and carries in it, for Christ to be a Mediator betwixt God and us. And there are, mainly, these five things in it.

1. At the first sight, it carries in it a most dreadful breach and jar betwixt God and men; else no need of a Mediator of reconciliation. There was indeed a sweet league of amity once between them, but it was quickly dissolved by sin; the wrath of the Lord was kindled against man, pursuing him to destruction, Psal. 5: 5. " Thou hatest all the workers of iniquity." And man was filled with unnatural enmity against his God, Rom. 1: 30. "theostugeis", haters of God; this put an end to all friendly commerce and intercourse between him and God. Reader, say not in thy heart, that it is much, that one sin, and that seemingly so small, should make such a breach as this, and cause the God of mercy and goodness so to abhor the works of his hands, and that as soon as he had made man: for it was a heinous and aggravated evil. It was upright, perfect man, created in the image of God, that thus sinned: he sinned when his mind was most bright, clear and apprehensive; his conscience pure and active; his will free, and able to withstand any temptation: his conscience pure and undefiled; he was a public as well as a perfect man, and well knew that the happiness or misery of his numberless offspring was involved in him.

The condition he was placed in, was exceeding happy: no necessity or want could arm and edge temptation: he lived amidst all natural and spiritual pleasures and delights, the Lord most delightfully conversing with him; yea, he sinned while as yet his creation-mercy was fresh upon him; and in this sin was most horrible ingratitude: yea, a casting off the yoke of obedience almost as soon as God had put it on. God now saw the work of his hands spoiled, a race of rebels now to be propagated, who, in their successive generations would be fighting against God: he saw it, and his just indignation sparkled against man, and resolves to pursue him to the bottom of hell.

2. It implies, a necessity of satisfaction and reparation to the justice of God. For the very design and end of this mediation was to make peace, by giving full satisfaction to the party that was wronged. The Photinians, and some others, have dreamed of a reconciliation with God, founded not upon satisfaction, but upon the absolute mercy, goodness, and free-will of God. "But concerning that absolute goodness and mercy of God, reconciling sinners to himself, there is a deep silence throughout the scriptures:" and whatever is spoken of it, upon that account, is as it works to us through Christ, Eph. 1: 3, 4, 5. Acts 4: 12. John 6: 40. And we cannot imagine, either how God could exercise mercy to the prejudice of his justice, which must be, if we must be reconciled without full satisfaction; or how such a full satisfaction should be made by any other than Christ. Mercy, indeed moved in the heart of God to poor man; but from his heart it found no way to vent itself for us, but through the heart blood of Jesus Christ: and in him the justice of God was fully satisfied, and the misery of the creature fully cured. And so, as Augustine speaks, "God neither lost the severity of his justice in the goodness of mercy, nor the goodness of his mercy in the exactness of his severity." But if it had been possible God could have found out a way to reconcile us without satisfaction, yet it is past doubt now, that he has pitched and fixed on this way. And for any now to imagine to reconcile themselves to God by any thing but faith in the blood of this mediator, is not only most vain in itself, and destructive to the soul, but most insolently derogatory to the wisdom and grace of God.

And to such I would say, as Tertullian to Marcion, whom he calls the murderer of truth, "spare the only hope of the whole world, O thou who destroyest the most necessary glory of our faith!" All that we hope for is but a fantasy without this. Peace of conscience can be rationally settled on no other foundation but this; for God having made a law to govern man, and this law violated by man; either the penalty must be levied on the delinquent, or satisfaction made by his surety. As good no law, as no penalty for disobedience; and as good no penalty, as no execution. He therefore that will be made a mediator of reconciliation betwixt God and man, must bring God a price in His hand, and that adequate to the offence and wrongs done him, else he will not treat about peace; and so did our Mediator.

3. Christ being a Mediator of reconciliation and intercession, implies the infinite value of his blood and sufferings, as that which in itself was sufficient to stop the course of God's justice, and render him not only placable, but abundantly satisfied and well pleased, even with those that before were enemies. And so much is said of it. Col. 1: 21, 22. "And ye that were sometimes alienated, and enemies in your minds by wicked works, yet now has he reconciled, in the body of his flesh through death, to present you holy, and unblamable, and unreproveable in his sight." Surely, that which can cause the holy God, justly incensed against sinners, to lay aside all his wrath, and take an enemy into his bosom, and establish such an amity as can never more be broken, but to rest in his love, and to joy over him with singing, as it is, Zeph. 3: 17, this must be a most excellent and efficacious thing.

4. Christ's being a Mediator of reconciliation, implies the ardent love and large pity that filled his heart towards poor sinners. For he does not only mediate by way of entreaty, going betwixt both, and persuading and begging peace; but he mediates, (as you have heard) in the capacity of a surety, by putting himself under an obligation to satisfy our debts. O how compassionately did his heart work towards us, that when he saw the arm of justice lifted up to destroy us, would interpose himself, and receive the stroke, though he knew it would smite him dead! Our Mediator, like Jonah his type, seeing the stormy sea of God's wrath working tempestuously, and ready to swallow us up, cast in himself to appease the storm. I remember how much that noble act of Marcus Curtius is celebrated in the Roman history, who being informed by the oracle, that the great breach made by the earthquake could not be closed, except something of worth were cast into it, heated with love to the commonwealth, he went and cast in himself. This was looked upon as a bold and brave adventure. But what was this to Christ?

5. Christ being a mediator betwixt God and man, implies as the witness of his person, so his authoritative call to undertake it. And indeed the Father, who was the wronged person, called him to be the umpire and arbitrator, trusting his honour in his hands. Now Christ was invested with this office and power virtually, soon after the breach was made by Adam's fall; for we have the early promise of it, Gen. 3: 15. Ever since, till his incarnation, he was a virtual and effectual Mediator; and, on that account, he is called, "the Lamb slain from the beginning of the world," Rev. 13: 8. And actually, from the time of his incarnation. But having discussed this more largely in a former discourse, I shall dismiss it here, and apply myself to the third thing proposed, which is,

Thirdly, How it appears that Jesus Christ is the true and only Mediator betwixt God and men. I reply, it is manifest he is so,

1. Because he, and no other, is revealed to us by God. And if God reveal him, and no other, we must receive him, and no other as such. Take but two scriptures at present, that in 1 Cor. 8: 5. "The heathen have many gods, and many lords," i. e. many great gods, supreme powers and ultimate objects of their worship; and lest these great gods should be defiled by their immediate and unhallowed approaches to them, they therefore invented heroes, demigods, intermediate powers, that they were as agents, or lord mediators betwixt the gods and them, to convey their prayers to the gods, and the blessings of the gods back again to them. "But unto us (saith he) there is but one God, the Father, of whom are all things, and we by him," i. e. one supreme essence, the first spring and fountain of blessings, and one Lord, i. e. one Mediator, "by whom are all things, and we by him." By whom are all things which come from the Father to us, and by whom are all our addresses to the Father: So Acts 4: 12. "Neither is there salvation in any other; for there is none other name under heaven given among men whereby we must be saved." No other name, i. e. no other authority, or rather, no other person authorised under heaven, i. e. the whole world: for heaven is not here opposed to earth, as though there were other intercessors in heaven besides Christ: no, no, in heaven and earth God has given him, and none but him, to be our Mediator. One sun is sufficient for the whole world; and one Mediator for all men in the world. So that the scriptures affirm this is he, and exclude all others.

2. Because he, and no other, is fit for, and capable of this office. Who but he that has the divine and human nature united in his single person, can be a fit day's-man to lay his hand upon both? Who but he that was God, could support under such sufferings, as were, by divine justice, exacted for satisfaction! Take person of the greatest spirit, and put him an hour in the case Christ was in, when he sweat blood in the garden, or uttered that heart-rending cry upon the cross, and he had melted under it as a moth.

3. Because he is alone sufficient to reconcile the world to God by his blood, without accessions from any other. The virtue of his blood reached back as far as Adam, and reaches forward to the end of the world; and will be as fresh, vigorous, and efficacious then, as the first moment it was shed. The sun makes day before it actually rises, and continues day sometimes after it is set: so do does Christ, who is the same yesterday, to-day, and forever; so that he is the true and only Mediator betwixt God and men: no other is revealed in scripture; no other is sufficient for it; no other needed beside him.

Fourthly, The last thing to be explained is, in what capacity he executed his mediatory work. About which we affirm, according to scripture, that he performs that work as God-man, in both natures. Papists, in denying Christ to act as mediator, according to his divine nature, do at once spoil the whole mediation of Christ of all its efficacy, dignity and value, which arise from that nature, which they deny to co-operate, and exert its virtue in his active and passive obedience. They say, the apostle, in my text, distinguishes the Mediator from God, in saying, "there is one God and one Mediator." We aptly reply, that the same Apostle distinguishes Christ from man, Gal. 1: 1. "Not by man, but by Jesus Christ." Does it thence follow that Christ is not true man? Or that according to his divine nature only, he called Paul? But what need I stay my reader here; Had not Christ, as Mediator, power to lay down his life, and power to take it up again? John 10: 17,18. Had he not, as Mediator, all power in heaven and earth to institute ordinances, and appoint officers? Matt. 28: 18. To baptise men with the Holy Ghost and fire? Matt. 3: 11. To keep those his Father gave him in this world? John 17: 12. To raise up the saints again in the last day? John 6: 54. Are these, with many more I might name, the effects of the mere human nature? Or, were they not performed by him as God-man? And besides, how could he, as Mediator, be the object of our faith, and religious adoration, if we are not to respect him as God-man? But I long now to be at the application of this: and the first inference from it, is this,

Inference 1. That it is a dangerous thing to reject Jesus Christ the only Mediator betwixt God and man. Alas! there is no other to interpose and screen thee from the devouring fire, the everlasting burnings! O it is a fearful thing to fall into the hands of the living God! And into his hands you must needs fall, without an interest in the only Mediator. Which of us can dwell with devouring fire? Who can endure the everlasting burnings? Isa. 33: 14. You know how they singed and scorched the green tree, but what would they do to the dry tree? Luke 23: 31. Indeed, if there were another plank to save after the shipwreck; any other way to be reconciled to God, besides Jesus the Mediator, somewhat might be said to excuse this folly; but you are shut up to the faith of Christ, as to your last remedy, Gal. 3: 23. You are like starving beggars, that are come to the last door. O take heed of despising, or neglecting Christ! If so, there's none to intercede with God for you; the breach betwixt him and you can never be composed. I remember, here, the words of Eli, to his profane sons, who caused men to abhor the offerings of the Lord, 1 Sam. 2: 25. "If one man sin against another, the judge shall judge him; but if a man sin against the Lord, who shall entreat for him?" The meaning is, common trespasses betwixt men, the civil magistrate takes cognisance of it, and decides the controversy by his authority, so that there is an end of that strife; but if man sin against the Lord, who shall entreat or arbitrate in that case? Eli's sons had despised the Lord's sacrifices, which were sacred types of Christ, and the stated way that men had then to act faith on the Mediator in. Now, (saith he) if a man thus sin against the Lord, by despising Christ shadowed out in that way, who shall entreat for him? What hope, what remedy remains?

I remember, it was the saying of Luther, and he spake it with deep resentment, Nolo Deum absolutum, "I will have nothing to do with an absolute God," i.e. with God without a Mediator. thus the devils have to do with God: but will ye, in whose nature Christ is come, put yourselves into their state and case? God forbid!

Inf. 2. Hence also be informed, how great an evil it is to join any other Mediators, either of reconciliation, or meritorious intercession with Jesus Christ. O this is a horrid sin, and that which both pours the greatest contempt upon Christ, and brings the surest and sorest destruction upon the sinner! I am ashamed my pen should English what mine eyes have seen in the writings of Papists, ascribing as much, yea, more to the mediation of Mary than to Christ, with no less than blasphemous impudence, thus commenting upon scripture: "What is that which the Lord saith, I have trod the wine-press alone, and of the people there was no man with me? true Lord, there was no man with thee, but there was a woman with thee, who received all these wounds in her heart which thou receivedst in thy body." I will not blot my paper with more of this, but refer the learned reader as under, where he may (if he have a mind to see more) be informed not only what blasphemy hath dropped from single pens, but even from councils, to the reproach of Jesus Christ, and his blood.

How do they stamp their own sordid works with the peculiar dignity and value of Christ's blood; and therein seek to enter at the gate which God has shut to all the worlds because Jesus Christ the prince entered in thereby, Ezek. 44: 2, 3. He entered into heaven in a direct immediate way, even in his own name, and for his own sake; this gate, saith the Lord, shall be shut to all others; and I wish men would consider it, and fear, lest while they seek entrance into heaven at the wrong door, they do not for ever shut against themselves, the true and only door of happiness.

Inf. 3. If Jesus Christ be the only Mediator of reconciliation betwixt God and men; then reconciled souls should thankfully ascribe all the peace, favours, and comforts they have from God, to their Lord Jesus Christ. Whenever you have had free admission, and sweet entertainment with God in the more public ordinances, or private duties of his worship; when you have had his smiles, his seals, and with hearts warmed with comfort, are returning from those duties, say, O my soul, thou mayest thank thy good Lord Jesus Christ for all this! had not he interposed as a Mediator of reconciliation, I could never have had access to, or friendly communion with God to all eternity.

Immediately upon Adam's sin, the door of communion with God was locked, yea, chained up, and no more coming nigh the Lord: not a soul could have any access to him, either in a way of communion in this world, or of enjoyment in that to come. It was Jesus the Mediator that opened that door again, and in him it is that we have boldness, and access with confidence, Eph. 3: 12. "We can now come to God by a new and living way, consecrated for us through the vail, that is to say, his flesh," Heb. 10: 20. The vail had a double use, as Christ's flesh answerable has: it hid the glory of the Sanctum Sanctorum, and also gave entrance into it. Christ's incarnation rebates the edge of the divine glory and brightness, that we may be able to bear it and converse with it; and it gives admission into it also. O thank your dear Lord Jesus for your present and future heaven! these are mercies which daily emerge out of the ocean of Christ's blood, and come swimming in it to our doors. Blessed be God for Jesus Christ!

Inf. 4. If Jesus Christ is the true and only Mediator, both of reconciliation and meritorious intercession betwixt God and men, how safe and secure then is the condition and state of believers? Surely, as his mediation, by sufferings, has fully reconciled, so his mediation, by intercession, will everlastingly maintain that state of peace betwixt them and God, and prevent all future breaches. "Being justified by faith, we have peace with God, through our Lord Jesus Christ," Rom. 5: 1. It is a firm and lasting peace, and the Mediator that made it, is now in heaven to maintain it for ever, and prevent new jars, Heb. 9: 24. "There to appear in the presence of God for us;" according to the custom of princes and states, who, being confederated, have their agents residing in each others courts, who upon all occasions appear in the presence of the prince, in the name and behalf of those whom they represent, and negotiate for.

And here it is proper to reflect upon the profound and incomprehensible wisdom of God, who has made an advantage to us, even out of our sin and misery. Come, see and adore the wisdom of our God, that has so improved, reduced, and disposed the fall of Adam, as to make a singular advantage thereby to advance his offspring to a better state! It was truly said by one of the ancients upon this account, "That Job was a happier man on the dunghill, than Adam was in paradise". His holiness indeed was perfect, his happiness was great: but neither of them permanent and indefeasible, as our happiness by the Mediator is. So that, in the same sense some divines call Judas's treasons foelix scelus, a happy wickedness: we may call Adam's fall, foelix lapsus, a happy fall, because ordered and over-ruled by the wisdom of God, to such an advantage for us. And to that purpose Austin somewhere sweetly speaks, "O how happily did I fall in Adam, who rose again more happy in Christ!" Thus did the Lord turn a poison into an antidote, thus did that dreadful fall make way for a more blessed and fixed state. Now are we so confirmed, fixed, and established in Christ, by the favour of God, that there can be no more such fatal breaches, and dreadful jars betwixt God and his reconciled ones for ever. The bone that is well set, is stronger where it is knit, than it was before. blessed be God for Jesus Christ!

Inf. 5. Did Jesus Christ interpose betwixt us and the wrath of God, as a Mediator of reconciliation? did he rather chose to receive the stroke upon himself, than to see us ruined by it? How well then does it become the people of God, in a thankful sense of this grace, to interpose themselves betwixt Jesus Christ and the evils they see like to fall upon his name and interest in the world? O that there were but SUCH a heart in the people of God! I remember it is a saving of Jerome, when he heard the revilings and blaspheming of many against Christ, and his precious truths, "O (said he) that they would turn their weapons from Christ to me, and be satisfied with my blood!" And much to the same sense is that sweet one of Bernard, "Happy were I, if God would vouchsafe to use me as a shield." And David could say, "The reproaches of them that reproached thee, fell on me, Psal. 69: 9. Ten thousand of our names are nothing to Christ's name: his name is "kalon onoma", a worthy name; and no man that gives up his name as a shield to Christ, but shall thereby secure and increase the true honour of it. And though wicked men, for the present may bespatter them, yet Jesus Christ will take it out of the dirt, (as one speaks), wipe it clean, and give it us again. Oh, it is the least one can do, to interpose ourselves and all that is dear to us, betwixt Christ and the wrath of men, when he (as you hear) interposed himself betwixt you and the eternal wrath of God!

Sermon 9: The first Branch of Christ's Prophetical Office, consisting in the Revelation of the Will of God

Acts 3: 22.
A prophet shall the Lord your God raise up unto you of your brethren, like unto me; him shall ye hear in all things whatsoever he shall say unto you.

Having, in the former discourses, shown you the solemn preparations, both on the Father's part, and on the Son's, for the blessed design of reconciling us by the meritorious mediation of Christ: and given you a general prospect of that his mediation, in the firmer sermon; method now requires, that I proceed to show how he executes this his mediation, in the discharge of his blessed offices of Prophet, Priest and King.

His prophetical office consists of two parts; one external, consisting in a true and full revelation of the will of God to men, according to John 17: 6. "I have manifested thy name to the men thou gavest me." The other in illuminating the mind, and opening the heart to receive and embrace that doctrine. The first part is contained in the words before us; "A prophet shall the Lord your God raise up," &c.

Which words are those of Moses, recorded in Deut. 18: 15. And here, by Peter, pertinently applied to Christ, to convince the incredulous Jews, that he is the true and only Messiah, and the great Prophet of the church; whose doctrine it was highly dangerous to condemn, though out of the mouths of such (otherwise contemptible) persons as he and John were. And it is well observed by Calvin, he singles out this testimony of Moses, rather than any other, because of the great esteem they had for Moses, and his writings, beyond any others. Now in the words themselves are two general parts.

First, Christ, according to the prophetical office, described.
Secondly, Obedience to him, as such a prophet, strictly enjoined.

First, You have here a description of Christ in his prophetical office; "A prophet shall the Lord your God raise up unto you of your brethren, like unto me." Where Christ is described,

1. By his title, Prophet, and that, princeps prophetarum, the prince of the prophets, or the great and chief shepherd, as he is stiled, Heb. 13: 10. 1 Pet. 5: 4. It belongs to a prophet to expound the law, declare the will of God, and foretell things to come: all these meet, and that, in a singular and eminent manner, in Christ our prophet, Matth. 5: 21, &c. John 1: 18. 1 Pet. 1: 11.

2. He is described by his type; a prophet like unto Moses, who therein typified and prefigured him. But is it not said of Moses, in Deut. 34: 10. "that there arose not a prophet since in Israel, like unto Moses, whom the Lord knew face to face?" True, of mere men there never arose so great a prophet in Israel, as Moses was, either in respect of his familiarity with God, or of his miracles which he wrought in the power of God: but Moses himself was but a star to this sun. However, in these following particulars, Christ was like him. He was a prophet that went between God and the people, carried God's mind to them, and returned theirs to God, they not being able to hear the voice of God immediately, Deut. 18: 16, 17. "According to all that thou desires of the Lord thy God in Horeb, in the day of the assembly, sayings Let me not again hear the voice of the Lord my God, neither let me see this great fire any more, that I die not." And upon this their request, God makes the promise which is cited in the text; verse 17, 18. "They have well spoken that which they have spoken. I will raise them up a prophet like unto thee," &c. Moses was a very faithful prophet, precisely faithful, and exact in all things that God gave him in charge, even to a pin of the tabernacle. "Moses verily was faithful in all his house, as a servant, for a testimony of those things which were to be spoken after: but Christ as a Son over his own house," Heb. 3: 5, 6. Again, Moses confirmed his doctrine by miracles, which he wrought in the presence, and to the conviction of gainsayers. Herein, Christ our Prophet is also like unto Moses, who wrought many, mighty, and uncontrolled miracles, which could not be denied, and by them confirmed the gospel which he preached. Lastly, Moses was that prophet which brought God's Israel out of literal Egypt, and

Christ his out of spiritual Egypt, whereof that bondage was a figure. Thus he is described by his likeness to Moses, his type.

3. He is described by his stock and original, from which, according to his flesh, he sprang; "I will raise him up from among thy brethren. Of Israel, as concerning the flesh, Christ came," Rom. 9: 5. And "it is evident that our Lord sprang out of Judah," Heb. 7: 14. He honoured that nation by his nativity. Thus the prophet is described.

Secondly, Here is a strict injunction of obedience to this Prophet, Him shall ye hear in all things, &c. By hearing, understand obedience. So words of sense are frequently put in scripture, to signify those affections that are moved by, and use to follow those senses. And this obedience is required to be yielded to this prophet only, and universally, and under great penalties. It is required to be given to him only, for so [him] in the text must be understood, as exclusive of all others. It is true, we are commanded to obey the voice of his ministers, Heb. 13: 17. But still it is Christ speaking them, by whom we pay our obedience: He that heareth you, heareth me: We obey them in the Lord, i.e. commanding or forbidding in Christ's name and authority. So when God said, Deut. 6: 13, ["Thou shalt serve him,"] Christ expounds it exclusively, Matth. 4: 10. "Him only shalt thou serve." He is the only Lord, Jude 4. and therefore to him only our obedience is required. And as it is due to him only, so to him universally; "Him shall ye hear in all things:" his commands are to be obeyed, not disputed. A judgement of discretion indeed is allowed to Christians, to judge whether it be the will of Christ or no. We must "prove what is that holy, good, and acceptable will," Rom. 12: 2. "His sheep hear his voice, and a stranger they will not follow: they know his voice, but know not the voice of strangers," John 10: 4, 5. But when his will is understood and known, we have no liberty of choice, but are concluded by it, be the duty commanded never so difficult, or the sin forbidden never so tempting: and this is also required severely, under penalty of being destroyed from among the people, and of God's requiring it at our hands, as it is in Deut. 18, i.e. of revenging himself in the destruction of the disobedient. Hence the observation.

Doct. That Jesus Christ is called and appointed by God to be the great Prophet and teacher of the Church.

He is anointed to preach good tidings to the meek, and sent to bind up the broken hearted, Isa. 61: 1. When he came to preach the gospel among the people, then was this scripture fulfilled, Matt. 11: 27. "Yea, all things are delivered him of his Father; so as no man knoweth whom the Father is, but the Son, and he to whom the Son will reveal him." All light is now collected into one body of light, the Sun of righteousness; and he "enlighteneth every man that comets into the world," John 1: 9. And though he dispensed knowledge variously, in times past, speaking in many ways and divers manners, to the fathers; yet now the method and way of revealing the will of God to us is fixed and settled in Christ: In these last times he has spoken to us by his Son

Twice has the Lord solemnly sealed him to this office, or approved and owned him in it, by a miraculous voice from the most excellent glory, Matth. 3: 17 and Matth. 17: 5.

In this point there are two things doctrinally to be discussed and opened, viz. What Christ's being a Prophet to the church implies: and how he executes and discharges this his office.

First, What is implied in Christ's being a Prophet to the church: And it necessarily imports these three things.

1. The natural ignorance and blindness of men in the things of God. This shows us that "vain man is born as the wild ass's colt." the world is involved in darkness: The people sit as in the region and shadow of death till Christ arise upon their souls, Matt. 4: 15, 16,17. It is true, in the state of innocence man had a clear apprehension of the will of God, without a Mediator: but now that light is quenched in the corruption of nature, "and the natural man receiveth not the things of God," 1 Cor. 2: 14. These things of God are not only contrary to corrupt and carnal reason, but they are also above right reason. Grace indeed uses nature, but nature can do nothing without grace. The mind of a natural man has not only a native blindness, by reason whereof it cannot discern the things of the Spirit, but also a natural enmity, Rom. 8: 7, and hates the light, John 3: 19, 20. So that until the mind be healed, and enlightened by Jesus Christ, the natural faculty can no more discern the things of the Spirit, than the sensitive faculty can discern the things of reason. The mysteries of nature may be discovered by the light of nature; but when it comes to supernatural mysteries, there, omnis Platonicorum caligavit subtilitus, as Cyprian somewhere speaks, the most subtle, searching, penetrating wit and reason, is at a loss.

2. It implies the divinity of Christ, and proves him to be true God, forasmuch as no other can reveal to the world, in all ages, the secrets that lay hid in the heart of God, and that with such convincing evidence and authority. He brought his doctrine from the bosom of His Father; John 1: 18. "The only begotten Son, Who is in the bosom of the Father, he has revealed him." The same words which his Father gave him he has given us, John 17: 8. He spake to us that which he had seen with his Father, John 8: 38. What man can tell the bosom-counsels and secrets of God? Who but he that eternally lay in that bosom can expound them?

Besides, other prophets had their times assigned them to rise, shine, and set again by death, Zech. 1: 5. "Your fathers, where are they? And do the prophets live for ever?" But Christ is fixed and perpetual sun, that gives light in all ages of the world: for he is "the same yesterday, today, and for ever," Heb. 13: 8. Yea, and the very beams of his divinity shone with awfulness upon the hearts of them that heard him; so that his very enemies were forced to acknowledge, that, "never any man spake like him," John 7: 46.

3. It implies Christ to be the original and fountain of all that light which is ministerially diffused up and down the world by men. Ministers are but stars, which shine with a borrowed light from the sun: so speaks the apostle, 2 Cor. 3: 6, 7. "For God, who commanded the light to shine out of darkness, has shined into our hearts, to give the light of the knowledge of the glory of God, in the face of Jesus Christ." Those that teach men, must be first taught by Christ. All the prophets of the Old, and all the prophets, pastors, and teachers of the New-Testament, have lighted their candles at his torch: it was Christ that "gave them a mouth and wisdom," Luke 21: 15. What Paul received from the Lord, he delivered to the church, 1 Cor. 11: 23 Jesus Christ is the chief Shepherd, 1 Pet. 5: 4. and all the under-shepherds receive their gifts and commissions from him. These things are manifestly implied in Christ's prophetical office.

Secondly, We shall next enquire how he executes and discharges this his office, or how he enlightens and teacheth men the will of God. And this he has done variously, gradually, plainly, powerfully, sweetly, purely, and fully.

1. Our great Prophet has revealed unto men the will of God variously; not holding one even and constant tenor in the manifestations of the Father's will, but as the apostle speaks, "polumeros kai polutropos", at sundry times, and in divers manners, Heb. 1: 1. Sometimes he taught the church immediately, and in his own person, John 18: 20. He declared God's righteousness in the great congregation, Psal. 22: 22. And sometimes mediately, by his ministers and officers, deputed to that service by him. So he dispensed the knowledge of God to the church before his incarnation; it was Christ that in the time, and by the ministry of Noah, went and preached to the spirits in prison, as it is 1 Pet. 3: 19, that is, to men and women then alive, but now separated from the body, and imprisoned in hell for their disobedience. And it was Christ that was with the church in the wilderness, instructing and guiding them by the ministry of Moses and Aaron, Acts 7: 37, 38; and so he has taught the church since his ascension. He cannot now be personally with us, having other business to do for us in heaven; but, however, he will not be wanting to teach us by his officers, whom, for that end, he has set and appointed in the church, Eph. 4: 11, 12.

2. He has dispensed his blessed light to the church gradually. The discoveries of light have been "polumeros", that is, in many parts or parcels; sometimes more obscure and cloudy; as to the Old-Testament believers, by visions dreams, Urim, Thummim, vocal oracles, types, sacrifices, &c. which, though comparatively, were but a weak glimmering light, and had no glory compared to that which now shines, 2 Cor. 3: 7, 8, 9, 10, 11. yet it was sufficient for the instruction and salvation of the elect in those times, but now is light sprung up gloriously in the gospel-dispensation: "And we all with open face, behold as in a glass, the glory of the Lord." It is to us not a twilight, but the light of a perfect day; and still is advancing in the several ages of the world. I know more (saith Luther) than blessed Austin knew; and they that come after me, will know more than I know.

3. Jesus Christ, our great Prophet, has manifested to us the will of God plainly and perspicuously. When he was on earth himself, he taught the people by parables, and "without a parable he spake nothing," Matt. 13: 3, 4. He clothed sublime and spiritual mysteries in earthly metaphors, bringing them thereby to the low and dull capacities of men, speaking so familiarly to the people about them, as if he had been speaking earthly things to them, John 3: 12. And so (according to his own example) would he have his ministers preach, "using great plainness of speech," 2 Cor. 3: 12. and by manifestation of the truth, "commending themselves to every man's conscience," 1 Cor. 4: 2. Yet not allowing them to be rude and careless in expression, pouring out undigested, crude, immethodical words; no, a holy serious, strict, and grave expression befits the lips of his ambassadors: and who ever spake more weightily, more logically, persuasively than that apostle, by whose pen Christ has admonished us to beware of vain affections and swelling words of vanity? But he would have us stoop to the understandings of the meanest, and not give the people a comment darker than the text; he would have us rather pierce their ears, than tickle their fancies; and break their hearts than please their ears. Christ was a very plain preacher.

4. Jesus Christ discovered truth powerfully, speaking "as one having authority, and not as the Pharisees," Matt. 7: 29. They were cold and dull preachers, their words did even freeze betwixt their lips; but Christ spake with power; there was heat as well as light in his doctrine: and so there is still, though it be in the mouth of poor contemptible men, 2 Cor. 10: 4. "The weapons of our warfare are not carnal, but mighty through God, to the casting down of strongholds: it is still quick and powerful, sharper than a two edged sword; and piercing, to the dividing asunder of soul and spirit, and of joints and marrow," Heb. 4: 12. The blessed apostle imitated Christ; and being filled

with his spirit, spake home and freely to the hearts of men. So many words, so many claps of thunder, (as ones said of him) which made the hearts of sinners shake and tremble in their breasts. All faithful and able ministers are not alike gifted in this particular; but, surely, there is a holy seriousness and spiritual grace and majesty in their doctrine, commanding reverence from their hearers.

5. This Prophet, Jesus Christ, taught the people the mind of God in a sweet, affectionate, and taking manner; his words made their hearts burn within them, Luke 24: 32. It was prophesied of him, Isa. 42: 2. "He shall not cry, nor lift up, nor cause his voice to be heard on high. A bruised reed he shall not break, and smoking flax he shall not quench. He knew how to speak word in season to the weary soul," Isa. 61: 1. "He gathered the Lambs with his arms, and gently led those that were with young," Isa. 4: 11. How sweetly did his words slide to the melting hearts about him! he drew with cords of love, with the bands of a man: he discouraged none, upbraided none that were willing to come to him: his familiarity and free condescensionds to the most vile and despicable sinners, were often made the matter of his reproach. Such is his gentle and sweet carriage to his people, that the church is called the Lamb's wife, Rev. 19: 7.

6. He revealed the mind of God purely to men; his doctrine had not the least dash of error to debase it; his most enviously observant hearers could find nothing to charge him with: he is "the faithful and true witness," Rev. 1: 5, and he has commanded his ministers to preserve the simplicity and purity of the gospel, and not to blend and sophisticate it, 2 Cor. 4: 2.

7. And lastly, He revealed the will of God perfectly and fully, keeping back nothing needful to salvation. So he tells his disciples, John 15: 15. "All things that I have heard of my Father, I have made known unto you." He was "faithful as a Son over his own house," Heb. 3: 6. Thus you have a brief account of what is implied in this part of Christ's prophetical office, and how he performed it.

Inference 1. If Jesus Christ, who is now passed into the heavens, be the great Prophet and Teacher of the church; hence we may justly infer the continual necessity of a standing ministry of the church: for by his ministers he now teacheth us, and to that intent has fixed them in the church, by a firm constitution, there to remain to the end of the world, Matt. 28: 20. He teacheth men more personally, but ministerially. His ministers supply the want of his personal presence, 2 Cor. 5: 10. "We pray you in Christ stead." These officers he gave the church at his ascension, i.e. when he ceased to teach them any longer with his own lips; and so set them in the church that their succession shall never totally fail: for so the word "etheto", he has set, 1 Cor. 12: 28. plainly implies. They are set by a sure establishment, a firm and unalterable constitution, even as the times and seasons, which the Father hath put ["etheto"] in his own power: it is the same word, and it is well they are so firmly set and fixed there; for how many adversaries in a}l ages have endeavoured to shake the very office itself? pretending that it is needless to be taught by men, and wresting such scriptures as these to countenance their error, Joel 2: 28, 29, "I will pour out my Spirit upon all flesh: and your sons and daughters shall prophesy," &c. And Jer. 31: 34. "These shall teach no more every man his neighbour, and every man his brother, saying, Know the Lord; for they shall all know me from the least of them to the greatest of them." As to that of Joel, it is answered, That if an Old-Testament prophecy may be understood according to a New-Testament interpretation, then that prophecy does no way oppose, but confirm the gospel ministry. How the apostle understood the prophet in that his prophecy, may be seen in Acts 2: 17, when the Spirit was poured out on the day of Pentecost upon the apostles. And surely he must be a confident person indeed, that thinks not an apostle to be as good an expositor of the prophet, as himself. And for that in Jer. 31 we say,

1. That if it conclude against ministerial teachings, it must equally conclude against Christian conferences.

2. We say that cannot be the sense of one scripture which contradicts the plain sense of other scriptures: but so this would, Eph. 4: 11,12. 1 Cor. 12: 28.

3. And we say, the sense of that text is not negative, but comparative. Not that they shall have no need to be taught any truth, but no such need to he taught the first truths: That there is a God, and who is this true God: They shall no more teach every "man his brother, saying, allow the Lord! for they shall all "know me." To conclude, God has given ministers to the church for the work of conversion and edification, "till we all come into the unity of the faith, to a perfect man," Eph. 4: 11, 12. So that when all the elect are converted, and all those converts become perfect men; when there is no error in judgement or practice, and no seducer to cause it, then, and not till then, will a gospel ministry be useless. But (as it is well observed) there is not a man that opposes a gospel ministry, but the very being of that man is a sufficient argument for the continuance of it.

Inf. 2. If Christ be the great Prophet of the church, and such a Prophet; then it follows, that the weakest Christians need not be discouraged at the dullness and incapacity they find in themselves: for Christ is not only a patient and condescending teacher, but he can also, as he has often done, reveal that to babes, which is hid from the wise and learned, Matth. 11: 25. "The testimonies of the Lord are sure, making wise the simple," Psal. 19: 7. Yea, and such as you are, the Lord delights to

The Fountain of Life Opened Up

choose, that his grace may be the more conspicuous in your weakness, 1 Cor. 1: 26, 27. You will have nothing of your own to glory in; you will not say, as a proud wretch once said, Ego et Deus meus; "I and my God did this." Jesus Christ affects not social glory, he will not divide the praise with any. Well then, be not discouraged; others may know more, in other things than you, but you are not incapable of knowing so much as shall save your souls, if Christ will be your teacher, in other knowledge they excel you: but if ye know Jesus Christ, and the truth as it is in him, one drop of your knowledge is worth a whole sea of their gifts: one truth sucked in faith and prayer from the breast of Christ is better than ten thousand dry notions beaten out by racking the understanding. It is better in kind, the one being but natural, the other super natural, from the saving illuminations and inward teachings of the Spirit: and so is one of those better things that accompany salvation. It is better in respect of effects; other knowledge leaves the heart as dry, barren, and unaffected, as if it had its seat in another man's head; but that little you have been taught of Christ, sheds down its gracious influence upon your affections, and slides sweetly to your melting hearts. So that as one "preferred the most despicable work of a plain rustic Christian, before all the triumphs of Alexander and Caesar;" much more ought you so prefer one saving manifestation of the Spirit, to all the powerless illuminations of natural men.

Inf. 3. If Christ be the great Prophet and teacher of the church; it follows, That prayer is a proper mean for the increase of knowledge: Prayer is the golden key that unlocks that treasure. When Daniel was to expound that secret which was contained in the king's dream, about which the Chaldean magicians had racked their brains to no purpose; what course does Daniel take? Why, "he went to his house, (saith the text, Dan. 2: 17, 18) and made the thing known to Hananiah, Michael, and Azariah his companions; that they would desire mercies of the God of heaven concerning his secret." And then was the secret revealed to Daniel. Luther was wont to say, "Three things made a divine; meditation, temptation, and prayer." Holy Mr. Bradford was wont to study upon his knees. Those truths that are got by prayer, leave an unusual sweetness upon the heart. If Christ be our teacher, it becomes all his saints to be at his feet.

Inf. 4. If Christ be the great Prophet and teacher of the church, We may thence discern and judge of doctrines, and it may serve us as a test to try then by. For such as Christ is, such are the doctrines that flow from him; every error pretends to derive itself from him; but as Christ was holy, humble, heavenly, meek, peaceful, plain and simple, and in all things alien, yea, contrary to the wisdom of the world, the gratifications of the flesh, such are the truths which he teacheth. They have his character and image engraven on them. Would you know then whether this or that doctrine be from the Spirit of Christ or no? Examine the doctrine itself by this rule. And whatsoever doctrine you find to encourage and countenance sin, to exalt self, to be accommodated to earthly designs and interests, to wrap and bend to the humours and lusts of men; in a word, what doctrine soever directly, and as a proper cause makes them that profess it carnal, turbulent, proud, sensual, &c. you may safely reject it, and conclude this never came from Jesus Christ. The doctrine of Christ is after godliness; his truth sanctifies. There is a Gustus spirituals judicii, a spiritual taste, by which those that have their senses exercised, can distinguish things that differ. "The spiritual man judgeth all things," 1 Cor. 2: 15. "His ear tries words, as his mouth tasteth meats," Job 34: 3. Swallow nothing (let it come never so speciously) that has not some relish of Christ and holiness in it. Be sure, Christ never revealed any thing to men, that derogates from his own glory, or prejudices and obstructs the ends of his own death.

Inf. 5. And as it will reeve us for a test of doctrines, so it serves for a test of ministers; and hence you may judge who are authorised and sent by Christ the great Prophet, to declare his will to men. Surely those whom he sends have his Spirit in their hearts, as well as his words in their mouths. And according to the measures of grace received, they faithfully endeavour to fulfil their ministry for Christ, as Christ did for his Father: "As my Father has sent me (saith Christ) so send I you," John 20: 21. They take Christ for their pattern in the whole course of their ministration, and are such as sincerely endeavour to imitate the great Shepherd, in these six particulars following:

1. Jesus Christ was a faithful Minister, the "faithful and true witness," Rev. 1: 5. He declared the whole mind of God to men. Of him it was prophetically said, Psal. 40: 10. "I have not hid thy righteousness within my heart; I have declared thy faithfulness, and thy salvation; I leave not concealed thy lovingkindness and thy truth from the great congregation." To the same sense, and almost in the same words, the apostle Paul professed, in Acts 20: 20. "I have kept back nothing that was profitable unto you; and ver. 35. "I have shewed you all things." Not that every faithful minister does in course of his ministry, anatomise the whole body of truth, and fully expound and apply each particular to the people: No, that is not the meaning, but of those doctrines which they have opportunity of opening, they do not out of fear, or to accommodate and secure base low ends, with hold the mind of God, or so corrupt and abuse his words, as to subject truth to their own, or other men's lusts: "They preach not as pleasing men, but God," 1 Thess. 2: 4. "For if we yet please men, we cannot be the servants of Christ," Gal. 1: 10. Truth must be spoken, though the greatest on

earth be offended.

    2. Jesus Christ was a tender-hearted Minister, full of compassion to souls. He was sent to bind up the broken in heart, Isa. 61: 1. He was full of bowels to poor sinners. "He grieved at the hardness of men's hearts, Mark 3: 5. He mourned over Jerusalem, "and said, O Jerusalem, Jerusalem! how oft would I have gathered thy children, as a hen gathers her brood under her wings!" Matth. 23: 27. His bowels yearned when he saw the multitude, as sheep having no shepherd, Matth. 9: 37. These bowels of Christ must be in all the under shepherds. "God is my witness, (saith one of them) how greatly I long after you all, in [or after the pattern of] the bowels of Christ Jesus," Phil. 1: 8. He that shows a hard heart, unaffected with the dangers and miseries of souls, can never show a commission from Christ to authorise him for ministerial work.

    3. Jesus Christ zeal a laborious painful Minister, he put a necessity on himself to finish his work in his day; a work infinitely great, in a very little time; John 9: 4. "I must work the works of him that sent me, while it is day: the night cometh, when no man can work." O how much work did Christ do in a little time on earth! "He went about doing good," Acts 10: 38. He was never idle. When he sits down at Jacob's well, to rest himself, being weary, presently he falls into his work, preaching the gospel to the Samaritaness. In this must his ministers resemble him; "striving according to his working, that worketh in them mightily" Col. 1: 28, 29. An idle minister seems to be a contradictions in adjecto; as who should say, a dark light.

    4. Jesus Christ delighted in nothing more than the success of his ministry; to see the work of the Lord prosper in his hand, this was meat and drink to him. When the seventy returned, and reported the success of their first embassy, "Lord, even the devils are subject to us through thy name!" "Why, (saith Christ) I beheld Satan fall as lightning from heaven." As if he had said, You tell me no news, I saw it when I sent you out at first: I knew the gospel would make work where it came. "And in that hour Jesus rejoiced in spirit," Luke 10: 17, 18, 21. And is it not so with those sent by him? do not they value the success of their ministry at a high rate? It is not (saith one) the expense, but the recoiling of our labours back again upon us, that kills us. Ministers would not die so fast, nor be grey-headed so soon, could they but see the travail of their souls. "My little children, (saith Paul) of whom I travail again in birth, "palin odino", till Christ be formed in you", Gal. 4: 19. As for those that have the name of shepherds only, who visit the flock only once a year, about shearing time; who have "the instruments of a foolish shepherd," (forcipes et mulctra) the shears and pail, Zech. 11: 15, woeful will be their condition at appearing of this great Shepherd.

    5. Jesus Christ was a minister that lived up to his doctrine: his life and doctrine harmonised in all things. He pressed to holiness in his doctrine, and was the great pattern of holiness in his life, Matt. 11: 28 "Learn of me, I am meek and lowly." And such his ministers desire to approve themselves, Phil. 4: 9. "What ye have heard, and seen in me, that do." He preached to their eyes, as well as ears, His life was a comment on his doctrine. They might see holiness acted in his life, as well as sounded by his lips. He preached the doctrine, and lived the application.

    6. And lastly, Jesus Christ was a minister that minded and maintained sweet, secret communion with God, for all his constant public labours. If he had been preaching and healing all the day, yet he would redeem time from his very sleep to spend in secret prayer; Matt. 14: 23. "When he had sent the multitude away, he went up into a mountain apart to pray, and was there alone." O blessed pattern! Let the keepers of the vineyards remember they have a vineyard of their own to keep, a soul of their own that must be looked after as well as other men's. Those that, in these things, imitate Christ, are surely sent to us from him, and are worthy of double honour: They are a choice blessing to the people.

Sermon 10: The second Branch of Christ's Prophetical Office, consisting in the Illumination of the Understanding

Luke 24: 45.
Then opened he their understandings, &c.

Knowledge of spiritual things is well distinguished into intellectual and practical: the first has its seat in the mind, the latter in the heart. This latter, divines call a knowledge peculiar to saints; and, in the apostle's dialect, it is "huperechon tes gnoseos Christou Iesou", Phil. 3: 8. "The eminency, or excellency of the knowledge of Christ."

And indeed, there is but little excellency in all those petty notions which furnish the lips with discourse, unless by a sweet and powerful influence they draw the conscience and will to the obedience of Christ. Light in the mind is necessarily antecedent to the sweet and heavenly motions and elevations of the affections: For the farther any man stands from the light of truth, the farther he must needs be from the heat of comfort. Heavenly quickening are begotten in the heart, while the sun of righteousness spreads the beams of truth into the understanding, and the soul sits under those its wings; yet all the light of the gospel spreading and diffusing itself into the mind, can never savingly open and change the heart, without another act of Christ upon it; and what that is, the text informs you; "Then opened he their understandings, that they might understand the scriptures".

In which words we have both an act of Christ upon the disciples' understandings, and the immediate end and scope of that act.

1. Christ's act upon their understandings: He opened their understandings. By understanding is not here meant the mind only, in opposition to the heart, will, and affections, but these were opened by and with the mind. The mind is to the heart, as the door to the house: what comes in to the heart, comes in at the understanding, which is introductive to it; and although truths sometimes go no farther than the entry, never penetrate the hearts, yet, here, this effect is undoubtedly included.

Expositors make this expression parallel to that in Acts 16: 14. "The Lord opened the heart of Lydia." And it is well observed, that it is one thing to open the scriptures, that is, to expound them, and give the meaning of them, as Paul is said to do in Acts 18: 3, and another thing to open the mind or heart, as it is here. There are, as a learned man truly observes, two doors of the soul barred against Christ; the understanding by ignorance; and the heart by hardness: both these are opened by Christ. The former is opened by the preaching of the gospel, the other by the internal operation of the Spirit. The former belongs to the first part of Christ's prophetical office, opened in the foregoing sermon: the latter, to that special internal part of his prophetical office, to be opened in this.

And that it was not a naked act upon their minds only, but that their hearts and minds did work in fellowship, being both touched by this act of Christ, is evident enough by the effects mentioned, ver. 52, 53. "They returned to Jerusalem with great joy, and were continually in the temple, praising and blessing God." It is confessed, that before this time Christ had opened their hearts by conversion; and this opening is not to be understood simply, but secundum quid, in reference to those particular truths, in which, till now, they were not sufficiently informed, and so their hearts could not be duly affected with them. They were very dark in their apprehensions of the death and resurrection of Christ; and consequently their hearts were sad and dejected about that which had befallen him, ver. 17. But when he opened the scriptures and their understandings and hearts together, then things appeared with another face, and they returned, blessing and praising God.

2. Here is farther to be considered, the design and end of this act upon their understandings: That they might understand the scriptures: Where let it be marked, reader, that the teachings of Christ, and his Spirit, were never designed to take men off from reading, and studying, and searching the scriptures, as some vain notionists, have pretended, opposing those things which are

subordinated, but to make their studies and duties the more fruitful, beneficial, and effectual to their souls: or that they might this way receive the end or blessing of all their duties. God never intended to abolish his Word, by giving his Spirit; and they are true fanatics (as Calvin upon thus place calls them) that think, or pretend so. By this means he would at once impart more light, and make that they had before more operative and useful to them, especially in such a time of need as this was. Hence we observe,

Doct. That the opening of the mind and heart, effectually to receive the truths of God, is the peculiar prerogative and office of Jesus Christ.

One of the great miseries under which lapsed nature labours, is spiritual blindness. Jesus Christ brings that eye-salve which only can cure it. Rev. 3: 18. "I counsel thee to buy of me eye-salve, that thou mayest see." Those to whom the Spirit has applied it, can say, as it is 1 John 5: 20. "We know that the Son of God is come, and has given us an understanding, that we may know him that is true; and we are in him that is true, even in his Son Jesus Christ: this is the true God, and eternal life.

"To the spiritual illumination of a soul, it suffices not that the object be revealed, nor yet that man, the subject of that knowledge have a due use of his own reason; but it is further necessary that the grace and special assistance of the holy Spirit be superadded, to open and mollify the heart, and so give it a due taste and relish of the sweetness of spiritual truth." By opening the gospel, he reveals truth to us, and, by opening the heart, in us. Now, though this cannot be without that, yet it is much more excellent to have truth revealed in us, than to us. This divines call praecipuum illud "apogelesma" muneris prophetici; "the principal perfective effect of the prophetical office," the special blessing promised in the new covenant, Heb. 8: 10. "I will put my laws in their mind, and write them in their hearts."

For explication of this part of Christ's prophetical office, I shall as in the former, show what is included in the opening of their understanding, and by what acts Christ performs it. And,

First, Give you a brief account of what is included in this act of Christ; take it in the following particulars.

1. It implies the transcendent nature of spiritual things, far exceeding the highest flight and reach of natural reason. Jesus Christ must by his Spirit open the understandings of men, or they can never comprehend such mysteries. Some men have strong natural parts, and by improvement of them are become eagle-eyed in the mysteries of nature. Who more acute than the heathen sages? Yet, to them the gospel seemed foolishness, 1 Cor. 1: 20. Austin confesses, that before his conversion, he often felt his spirit swell with offence and contempt of the gospel; and he despising it, said dedignabar esse parvulus; "he scorned to become a child again." Bradwardine, that profound doctor, learned usque ad stuporem, even to a wonder, professes that when he read Paul's epistles, he condemned them, because in them he found not a metaphysical wit. Surely, it is possible a man may, with Berengarius, be able to dispute de omni scibili, of every point of knowledge; to unravel nature from the cedar in Lebanon, to the hyssop on the wall; and yet be as blind as a bat in the knowledge of Christ. Yes, it is possible a man's understanding may be improved by the gospel, to a great ability in the literal knowledge of it, so as to be able to expound the scriptures orthodoxly, and enlighten others by them, as it is Mat. 7: 22. The Scribes and Pharisees were well acquainted with the scriptures of the Old Testament; yea, such were their abilities, and esteem among the people for them, that the apostle stiles them the princes of this world, 1 Cor. 2: 8. And yet notwithstanding Christ truly calls them blind guides, Mat. 23. Till Christ open the heart, we can know nothing of him, or of his will, as we ought to know it. So experimentally true is that of the apostle, 1 Cor. 2: 14, 15. "The natural man receiveth not the things of the Spirit of God, for they are foolishness to him; neither can he know them, because they are spiritually discerned. But he that is spiritual, judgeth all things; yet he himself is judged of no man." The spiritual man can judge and discern the carnal man, but the carnal man wants a faculty to judge of the spiritual man: as a man that carries a dark lantern, can see another by its light, but the other cannot discern him. Such is the difference betwixt persons whose hearts Christ has, or has not opened.

2. Christ's opening the understanding, implies the insufficiency of all external means, how excellent soever they are in themselves, to operate savingly upon men, till Christ by his power opens the soul, and so makes them effectual. What excellent preachers were Isaiah and Jeremiah to the Jews? The former spake of Christ more like an Evangelist at the New than a Prophet of the Old Testament; the latter was a most convictive and pathetical preacher: yet the one complains, Isa. 53: 1, "Who has believed our report? and to whom is the arm of the Lord revealed?" The other laments the successlessness of his ministry, Jer. 6: 18. "The bellows are burnt, the lead is consumed of the fire, the founder melteth in vain." Under the New Testament, what people ever enjoyed such choice helps and means, as those that lived under the ministry of Christ and the apostles? Yet how many remained still in darkness? Matt. 11: 27. "We have piped to you, but ye have not danced; we have mourned unto you, but ye have not lamented". Neither the delightful airs of mercy, nor the doleful

ditties of judgement, could effect or move their hearts.

And indeed if you search into the reason of it, you will be satisfied, that the choicest of means can do nothing upon the heart, until Christ by his Spirit open it, because ordinances work not as natural causes do: for then the effect would always follow unless miraculously hindered; and it would be equally wonderful, that all that hear should not be converted, as that the three children should be in the fiery furnace so long, and yet not be burned: no, it works not as a natural, but as a moral cause, whose efficacy depends on the gracious and arbitrary concurrence of the Spirit. "The wind bloweth where it listeth," John 3: 8. The ordinances are like the pool of Bethesda, John 5: 4. At a certain time an angel came down and troubled the waters, and then they had a healing virtue in them. So the Spirit comes down at certain times in the word, and opens the heart; and then it becomes the power of God to salvation. So that when you see souls daily sitting under excellent and choice means, and remain dead still, you may say as Martha did to Christ of her brother Lazarus, Lord, if thou hadst been here they had not remained dead. If thou hadst been in this sermon, it had not been so ineffectual to them.

3. It implies the utter impotency of man to open his own heart, and thereby make the word effectual to his own conversion and salvation. He that at first said, "let there be light," and it was so, must shine into our hearts, or they will never be savingly enlightened, 2 Cor. 4: 4, 6. A double misery lies upon a great part of mankind, viz. Impotency and Pride. They have not only lost the liberty and freedom of their wills, but with it have so far lost their understanding and humility as not to own it. But, alas! Man is become a most impotent creature by the fall; so far from being able to open his own heart, that he cannot know the things of the Spirit, 1 Cor. 2: 14. cannot believe, John 6: 44. cannot obey, Rom. 8: 7. cannot speak one good word, Matt. 12: 34, cannot think one good thought, 2 Cor. 3: 5, cannot do one good act, John 15: 5. O what a helpless, shiftless thing is a poor sinner! Suitably to this state of impotence, conversion is in scripture called regeneration, John 3: 3, a resurrection from the dead, Eph. 2: 5. a creation, Eph. 2: 10. a victory, 2 Cor. 10: 5. Which does not only imply man to be purely passive in his conversion to God, but a renitency, and opposition made to that power which goes forth from God to recover him.

Lastly, Christ's opening the understanding imports his divine power, whereby he is able to subdue all things to himself. Who but God knows the heart? Who but God can unlock and open it at pleasure? No mere creature, no not the angels themselves, who for their large understandings are called intelligences, can command or open the heart. We may stand and knock at men's hearts, till our own ake; but no opening till Christ come. He can fit a key to all the cross wards of the will, and with sweet efficacy open it, and that without any force or violence to it. These things are carried in this part of his office, consisting in opening the heart: which was the first thing propounded for explication.

Secondly, In the next place, let us see by what acts Jesus Christ performs this work of his, and what way and method he takes to open the hearts of sinners.

And there are two principal ways, by which Christ opens the understandings and hearts of men, viz. by his Word and Spirit.

1. By his word; to this end was Paul commissioned and sent to preach the gospel, Acts 26: 18. "To open their eyes, and turn them from darkness to light, and from the power of Satan to God." The Lord can, if he pleases, accomplish this immediately; but though he can do it, he will not do it ordinarily without means, because he will honour his own institutions. Therefore you may observe, that when Lydia's heart was to be opened, "there appeared unto Paul a man of Macedonia, who prayed him, saying, come over into Macedonia, and help us," Acts 19: 9. God will keep up his ordinances among men: and though he has not tied himself, yet he has tied us, to them. Cornelius must send for Peter: God can make the earth produce corn, as it did at first, without cultivation and labour; but he that shall now expect it in the neglect of means, may perish for want of bread.

2. But the ordinances in themselves cannot do it, as I noted before; and therefore Jesus Christ has sent forth the Spirit, who is his Prorex, his vicegerent, to carry on this work upon the hearts of his elect. And when the Spirit comes down upon the souls in the administration of the ordinances, he effectually opens the heart to receive the Lord Jesus, by the healing of faith. He breaks in upon the understanding and conscience by powerful convictions and compunctions? so much that word, John 16: 8. imports, "He shall convince the world of sin;" convince by clear demonstration, such as enforces assent, so that the soul cannot but yield it to be so; and yet the door of the heart is not opened, till he has also put forth his power upon the will, and, by a sweet and secret efficacy, overcome all its reductions, and the soul be made willing in the day of his power. When this is done, the heart is opened: saving light now shines in it; and this light set up, the Spirit in the soul is,

1. A new light in which all things appear far otherwise than they did before. The names Christ and sin, the words heaven and hell have another sound in that man's ears, than formerly they had. When he comes to read the same scriptures, which possibly he had read a hundred times before, he wonders he should be so blind as he was, to overlook such great, weighty, and concerning things as

he now beholds in them; and saith, Where were mine eyes, that I could never see these things before?

2. It is a very affecting light; a light that has heat and powerful influences with it, which makes deep impressions on the heart. Hence they whose eyes the great Prophet opens, are said to be "brought out of darkness into his marvellous light," 1 Pet. 2: 9. The soul is greatly affected with what it sees. The beams of light are contracted and twisted together in the mind; and being reflected on the heart and affections, soon cause them to smoke and burn. "Did not our hearts burn within us, whilst he talked with us, and opened to us the scriptures?"

3. And it is a growing light, like the light of the morning which "shines more and more unto the perfect day," Prov. 4: 18. When the Spirit first opens the understanding, he does not give it at once a full sight of all truths, or a full sense of the power, sweetness and goodness of any truth; but the soul in the use of means grows up to a greater clearness day by day: its knowledge grows extensively in measure, and intensively in power and efficacy. And thus the Lord Jesus by his Spirit opens the understanding. Now the use of this follows in five practical deductions.

Inference 1. If this be the work and office of Jesus Christ, to open the understandings of men; hence we infer the miseries that lie upon those men, whose understandings, to this day, Jesus Christ has not opened; of whom we may say, as it is, Deut. 24: 4. "To this day Christ has not given them eyes to see." Natural blindness, whereby we are deprived of the light of this world, is sad; but spiritual blindness is much more so. See how dolefully their case is represented, 2 Cor. 4: 3, 4. "But if our gospel be hid, it is hid to them that are lost: whose eyes the God of this world has blinded, lest the light of the glorious gospel of Christ, who is the image of God, should shine unto them:" he means a total and final concealment of the saving power of the word from them. Why, what if Jesus Christ withhold it, and will not be a prophet to them, what is their condition? Truly no better than lost men. It is hid "tois apollumenois", to them that are to perish, or be destroyed. This blindness, like the covering of the face, or tying the handkerchief over the eyes, is in order to their turning off into hell. More particularly, because the point is of deep concernment, let us consider,

1. The judgement inflicted, and that is spiritual blindness. A sore misery indeed! Not an universal ignorance of all truths, O no! in natural and moral truths they are oftentimes acute, and sharp sighted men; but in that part of knowledge which wraps up eternal life, John 17:2, there they are utterly blinded: as it is said of the Jews, upon whom this misery lies, that blindness in part is happened to Israel. They are learned and knowing persons in other matters, but they know not Jesus Christ; there is the grand and sad defect.

2. The subject of this judgement, the mind, which is the eye of the soul. If it were put upon the body, it would not be so considerable; this falls immediately upon the soul, the noblest part of man, and upon the mind, the highest and noblest faculty of the soul, whereby we understand, think, and reason. This in scripture is called "pneuma", the spirit, the intellectual, rational faculty, which the philosophers call "to hegemonikon", the leading directive faculty; which is to the soul what the natural eye is to the body. Now the soul being the most active and restless thing in the world, always working, and its leading, directive power blind, judge what a sad and dangerous state such a soul is in; just like a fiery, highmettled horse, whose eyes are out, furiously carrying his rider up on rocks, pits and dangerous precipices. I remember Chrysostom, speaking of the loss of a soul, saith that the loss of a member of the body is nothing to it; for, saith he, If a man lose an eye, ear, hand or foot, there is another to supply its want: Omnia Deus dedit duplicia, "God has given us those members double;" animam vero unam, "but he has not given us two souls," that if one be lost, yet the other may be saved: Surely it were better for thee, reader, to have every member of thy body made the seat and subject of the most exquisite racking torments, than for spiritual blindness to befal thy soul. Moreover,

3. Consider the indiscernableness of this judgement to the soul on whom it lies: they know it not, no more than a man knows that he is asleep. Indeed it is "the spirit of a deep sleep poured out upon them from the Lord," Isa. 29: 10. like that which befal Adam when God opened his side, and took out a rib. This renders their misery the more remediless: "Because ye say you see, therefore your sin remaineth," John 9: 41. Once more,

4. Consider the tendency and effects of it. What does this tend to but eternal ruin? for hereby we are cut off from the only remedy. The soul that is so blinded, can never see sin, nor a Saviour; but, like the Egyptians, during the palpable darkness, sits still, and moves not after its own recovery. And as ruin is that to which it tends, so in order thereto, it renders all the ordinances and duties under which that soul comes, altogether useless and ineffectual to its salvation. He comes to the word, and sees others melted by it, but to him it signifies nothing. O what a heavy stroke of God is this! Most wretched is their case, to whom Jesus Christ will not apply this eye-salve, that they may see. Did you but understand the misery of such a state, if Christ should say to you, as he did to the blind man, Mat. 20: 33. That wilt thou that I should do for thee?" You would return as he did, "Lord, that my eyes may be opened."

The Fountain of Life Opened Up

Infer. 2. If Jesus Christ be the great Prophet of the church, then surely he will take special care both of the church and the under shepherds appointed by him to feed them: else both the objects and instruments upon and by which he executes his office, must fail and consequently this glorious office be in vain. Hence he is said "to walk among the golden candlesticks," Rev. 1: 13: and Rev. 2: 1. "to hold the stars in his right hand." Jesus Christ instrumentally opens the understandings of men by preaching of the gospel; and whilst there is an elect soul to be converted, or a convert to be farther illuminated, means shall not fail to accomplish it by.

Infer. 3. Hence you that are yet in darkness, may be directed to whom to apply yourselves for saving knowledge. It is Christ that has the sovereign eye-salve, that can cure your blindness; he only has the key of the house of David; he opens, and no man shutteth. O that I might persuade you to set yourselves in his way, under the ordinances, and cry to him, "Lord, that my eyes may be opened." Three things are marvellously encouraging to you so to do

1. God the Father has put him into this office, for the cure of such as you be, Isa. 49: 6. "I will give thee for a light to the Gentiles, that thou mayest be my salvation to the end of the earth". This may furnish you with an argument to plead for a cure. Why do you not go to God, and say, Lord, didst thou give Jesus Christ a commission to open the blind eyes? Behold me, Lord, such a one am I, a poor, dark, ignorant soul. Didst thou give him to be thy salvation to the ends of the earth? No place nor people excluded from the benefit of that right; and shall I still remain in the shadow of death? O that unto me he might be a saving light also? The best and most excellent work that ever thou wroughtest, brings thee no glory till it comes into the light! O let me see and admire it!

2. It is encouraging to think, that Jesus Christ has actually opened the eyes of them that are as dark and ignorant as you are. He has revealed those things to babes, that have been hid from the wise and prudent, Mat. 11: 25. "The law of the Lord is perfect, making wise the simple," Psal. 19: 7. And if you look among those whom Christ has enlightened, you will not find "many wise after the flesh, many mighty or noble; but the foolish, weak, base, and despised; these are they op whom he has glorified the riches of his grace," 1 Cor. 1: 26, 27.

3. And is it not yet farther encouraging to you that hitherto he has mercifully continued you under the means of light? Why is not the light of the gospel put out? Why are times and seasons of grace continued to you, if God have no farther design of good to your souls? Be not therefore discouraged, but wait on the Lord in the use of means, that you may yet be healed.

Quest. If you ask, What can we do to put ourselves into the way of the Spirit, in order to such a cure?

Sol. I say, though you cannot do any thing, that can make the gospel effectual, yet the Spirit of God can make those means you are capable of using effectual, if he please to concur with them. And it is a certain truth, that your inability to do what is above your power, does no ways excuse you from doing what is within the compass of your power to do. I know no act that is saving, can be done without the concurrence of spiritual grace; yea, and no act that has a remote order and tendency thereto, without a more general concourse of God's assistance: but herein he is not behind hand with you. Let me therefore advise,

1. That you diligently attend upon an able, faithful, and searching ministry. Neglect no opportunity God affords you; for how know you but that may be the time of mercy to your soul? If he that lay so many years at the pool of Bethesda, had been wanting but that hour when the angel came down and troubled the waters, he had not been healed.

2. Satisfy not yourselves with hearing, but consider what ye hear. Avow time to reflect upon what God has spoken to you. What power is there in man more excellent, or more appropriate to the reasonable nature, than its reflective and self-considering power? There is little hope of any good to be done upon your souls, till you begin to go alone, and become thinking men and women: Here all conversion begins. I know, a severer task can hardly be imposed upon a carnal heart. It is a hard thing to bring a man and himself together upon this account: but this must be, if ever the Lord do your souls good. Psal. 4: 4. "Commune with your own hearts."

3. Labour to see, and ingenuously confess the insufficiency of all your other knowledge to do you good. What if you had never so much skill and knowledge in other mysteries? What if you be never so well acquainted with the letter of the scripture? What if you had an angelical illumination? This can never save thy soul. No, all thy knowledge signifies nothing till the Lord show thee by special light the deplorable sight of thy own heart, and a saving sight of Jesus Christ, thy only remedy.

Inf. 4. Since then there is a common light, and special saving light, which none but Christ can give, it is therefore the concernment, of every one of you to try what your light is. "We know, (saith the apostle, 1 Cor. 8: 1.) that we all have knowledge." O but what, and whence is it? Is it the light of life springing from Jesus Christ, that bright and morning star, or only such as the devils and damned have? These lights differ,

1. In their very kind and natures. The one is heavenly, supernatural, and spiritual, the other earthly, and natural, the effect of a better constitution or education, James 3: 15, 17.

2. They differ most apparently in their effects and operations. The light that comes in a special way from Christ, is humbling, abasing, and soul-emptying light: by it a man sees the vileness of his own nature and practice, which begets self-loathing in him; but natural light, on the contrary, puffs up, exalts, and makes the heart swell with self-conceitedness, 1 Cor. 8: 1.

The light of Christ is practical and operative, still urging the soul, yet lovingly constraining it to obedience. No sooner did it shine into Paul's heart, but presently he asks, "Lord, what wilt thou have me to do?" Acts 9: 13. It brought forth fruit on the Colossians, from the first day it came to them, Col. 1: 6; but the other spends itself in impractical notions, and is detained in unrighteousness, Rom. 1: 18. The light of Christ is powerfully transformative of its subjects, changing the man, in whom it is, into the same image, from glory to glory, 2 Cor. 3: 18. But common light leaves the heart as dead, as carnal and sensual, as if no light at all were in it.

In a word, All saving light endears Jesus Christ to the soul; and as it could not value him before it saw him, so when once he appears to the soul in his own light, he is appreciated and endeared unspeakably: then none but Christ; all is but dung, that he may win Christ: none in heaven but him, nor in earth desirable in comparison of him. But no such effect flows from natural common knowledge.

3. They differ in their issues. Natural common knowledge vanisheth, as the apostle speaks, 1 Cor. 13: 8. It is but a Mayflower, and dies in its month. "Does not their excellency that is in them go away?" Job 4: 21. But this that springs from Christ is perfected, not destroyed by death: it springs up into everlasting life. The soul in which it is subjected, carries it away with it into glory. John 17: 2. this light is life eternal. Now turn in, and compare yourselves with these rules: let not false light deceive you.

Inf. 5. Lastly, How are they obliged to love, serve, and honour Jesus Christ, whom he has enlightened with the saving knowledge of himself? O that with hands and hearts lifted up to heaven, ye would adore the free grace of Jesus Christ to your souls? How many round about you have their eyes closed, and their hearts shut up! How many are in darkness, and there are like to remain, till they come to the blackness of darkness, which is reserved for them? O what a pleasant thing is it for your eyes to see the light of this world! But what is it for the eye of your mind to see God in Christ? To see such ravishing sights as the objects of faith are? and to have such a pledge as this given you of the blessed visions of glory? for in this light you shall see light. Bless God, and boast not: rejoice in your light, but be proud of it; and beware ye sin not against the best and highest light in this world. If God were so incensed against the Heathens for disobeying the light of nature, what is it in you to sin with eyes clearly illuminated with the purest light that shines in this world? You know, God charges it upon Solomon, 1 Kings 11: 9. that he turned from the way of obedience after the Lord, had appeared, to him twice. Jesus Christ intended when he opened your eyes, that your eyes should direct your feet. Light is a special help to obedience, and obedience is a singular help to increase your light.

Sermon 11: The Nature and necessity of the Priesthood of Christ

Heb. 9: 23.
It was therefore necessary that the patterns of things in the heavens should be purified with these; but the heavenly things themselves with better sacrifices than these.

Salvation (as to the actual dispensation of it) is revealed by Christ as a Prophet, procured by him as a Priest, applied by him as a King. In vain it is revealed, if not purchased; in vain revealed and purchased, if not applied. How is it revealed, both to us, and in us, by our great Prophet, has been declared. And now, from the prophetical office, we pass on to the priestly office of Jesus Christ, who as our Priest, purchased our salvation. In this office is contained the grand relief for a soul distressed by the guilt of sin. When all other reliefs have been essayed, it is the blood of this great sacrifice, sprinkled by faith upon the trembling conscience, that must cool, refresh, and sweetly compose and settle it. Now, seeing so great a weight hangs upon this office, the apostle industriously confirms and commends it in this epistle, and more especially in this ninth chapter; showing how it was figured to the world by the typical blood of the sacrifices, but infinitely excels them all: and as in many other most weighty respects, so principally in this, that the blood of these sacrifices did but purify the types or patterns of the heavenly things; but the blood of this sacrifice purified or consecrated the heavenly things themselves, signified by those types.

The words read, contains an argument to prove the necessity of the offering up of Christ, the great sacrifice, drawn from the proportion betwixt the types, and the things typified. If the sanctuary, mercy-seat, and all things pertaining to the service of the tabernacle, were to be consecrated by blood; those earthly, but sacred types, by the blood of bulls and lambs, &c. Much more the heavenly things shadowed by them, ought to be purified or consecrated by better blood than the blood of beasts. The blood consecrating these, should as much excel the blood that consecrated those, as the heavenly things themselves do, in their own nature, excel those earthly shadows of them. Look, what proportion there is between the type and anti-type, the like proportion also is betwixt the blood that consecrates them; earthly things with common, heavenly things with the most excellent blood.

So then, there are two things to be especially observed here: First, The nature of Christ's death and sufferings: It had the nature, use and end of a sacrifice, and of all the sacrifices the most excellent. Secondly, The necessity of his offering it up: it was necessary to correspond with all the types and prefiguration of it under the law: but especially it was necessary for the expiating of sin, the propitiating of a justly incensed God, and the opening, a way for reconciled ones to come to God in. The point I shall give you from it is,

Doct. That the sacrifice of Christ, our High Priest, is most excellent in itself; and most necessary for us.

Sacrifices are of two sorts, eucharistical, or thank-offerings, in testification of homage, duty and service; and in token of gratitude for mercies freely received; and ilastical, or expiatory, for satisfaction to justice, and thereby the atoning and reconciling of God. Of this last kind was the sacrifice offered by Jesus Christ for us: to this office he was called by God, Heb. 5: 5. In it he was confirmed by the unchangeable oath of God, Psal. 110: 4. for it, he was singularly qualified by his incarnation, Heb. 10: 6, 7. and all the ends of it he has fully answered, Heb. 9: 11, 12.

My present design is, from this scripture, to open the general nature and absolute necessity of the priesthood of Christ; shewing what his priesthood implies in it, and how all this was indispensably necessary in order to our recovery from the deplorable state of sin and misery.

First then, we will consider what it supposes and implies; and then, wherein it consists. And there are six things which it either pre-supposeth, or necessarily includeth in it.

1. At first sights it supposes man's revolt and fall from God; and a dreadful breach made thereby betwixt God and him, else no need of an atoning sacrifice. "If one died for all, then were all dead", 2 Cor. 5: 14. dead in law, under sentence to die, and that eternally. In all the sacrifices, from Adam to Christ, this was still preached to the world, that there was a fearful breach betwixt God

and man; and even so, that justice required our blood should be shed. And the fire flaming on the altar, which wholly burnt up the sacrifice, was a lively emblem of that fiery indignation that should devour the adversaries. But above all, when Christ, that true and great Sacrifice, was offered up to God, then was the fairest glass that ever was in the world, set before us, therein to see our sin and misery by the fall.

2. His priesthood, supposes the unalterable purpose of God to take vengeance for sin; he will not let it pass. I will not determine what God could do in this case, by his absolute power; but I think it is generally yielded, that, by his ordinate power, he could do no less than punish it in the person of the sinner, or of his surety.

Those that contend for such a forgiveness, as is an act of charity, like that whereby private persons forgive one another, must at once suppose God to part with his right, cedendo de jure suo, and also render the satisfaction of Christ altogether useless, as to the procurement of forgiveness; yea, rather an obstacle, than a means to it. Surely, the nature and truth of God oblige him to punish sin. "He is of purer eyes than to look upon iniquity," Heb. 1: 13. And beside, the word is gone out of his mouths that the sinner shall die.

3. The priesthood of Christ pre-supposeth the utter impotency of men to appease God, and, recover his favour by any thing he could do or suffer. Surely God would not come down to assume a body to die, and be offered up for us, if at any cheaper rate it could have been accomplished; there was no other way to recover man and satisfy God. Those that deny the satisfaction of Christ, and talk of his dying to confirm the truth, and give us an example of meekness, patience, and self-denial, affirming these to be the sole ends of his death, do not only therein root up the foundations of their own comfort, peace and pardon, but most boldly impeach and tax the infinite wisdom. God could have done all this at a cheaper rate: the sufferings of a mere creature are able to attain these ends: the deaths of the martyrs did it. But who by dying can satisfy and reconcile God? what creature can bring him an adequate and proportionable value for sin? yea, for all the sin that ever was, or shall be transmitted to the natures, or committed by the persons, of all God's elect, from Adam, to the last that shall be found alive at the Lord's coming? surely, none but Christ can do this.

4. Christ's priesthood implies the necessity of his being God- man. It was necessary he should be a man, in order to his passion, compassion, and derivation of his righteousness and holiness to men. Had he not been a man, he had had no sacrifice to offer, no soul or body to suffer in. The Godhead is impatible, immortal, and above all those sufferings and miseries Christ felt for us. Besides, his being man, fills him with bowels of compassion, and tender sense of our miseries: this makes him a merciful and faithful High priest, Heb. 4: 15. and not only fits him to pity, but to sanctify us also; for "he that sanctifieth, and they that are sanctified, are both of one," Heb. 2: 11,14, 17. And as necessary it was our High-priest should be God, since the value and efficacy of our sacrifice results from thence.

5. The priesthood of Christ implies the extremity of his sufferings. In sacrifices, you know, there was a destruction, a kind of annihilation of the creature to the glory of God. The shedding of the creature's blood, and burning its flesh with fire, was but an umbrage, or faint resemblance of what Christ endured, when he made his soul an offering for sin.

And lastly, It implies the gracious design of God to reconcile us at a dear rate to himself in that he called and confirmed Christ in his priesthood by an oath, and thereby laid out a sacrifice, of infinite value, for the world. Sins, for which no sacrifice is allowed, are desperate sins, and the case of such sinners is helpless: But if God allow, yea, and provide a sacrifice himself, how plainly does it speak his intentions of peace and mercy? These things are manifestly presupposed, or implied in Christ's priesthood.

"This priesthood of Christ is that function, wherein he comes before God, in our name and place, to fulfil the law, and offer up himself to him a sacrifice of reconciliation for our sins; and by his intercession to continue and apply the purchase of his blood to them for whom he shed it:" All this is contained in that famous scripture, Heb. 10: 7, 8, 9, 10,11, 12, 13. Or, more briefly, the priesthood of Christ is that whereby he expiated the sins of men, and obtained the favour of God for them, Col. 1: 20, 22. Rom. 5: 10. But because I shall insist more largely upon the several parts and fruits of this office, it shall here suffice to speak this much as to its general nature; which was the first thing proposed for explication.

Secondly, The necessity of Christ's priesthood comes next to be opened. Touching which, I affirm, according to the scriptures, it was necessary, in order to our salvation, that such a Priest should, by such a sacrifice, appear before God for us.

The truth of this assertion will be cleared by these two principles, which are evident in the scripture, viz. That God stood upon full satisfaction, and would not remit one sin without it: and that fallen man is totally incapable of tendering him any such satisfaction; therefore Christ, who only can, must do it, or we perish.

The Fountain of Life Opened Up

1. God stood upon full satisfaction, and could not remit one sin without it. This will be cleared from the nature of sin; and from the veracity and wisdom of God.

(1.) From the nature of sin, which deserves that the sinner should suffer for it. Penal evil; in a course of justice, follows moral evil. Sin and sorrow ought to go together; betwixt these is a necessary connection, Rom. 6: 13. "The wages of sin is death."

(2.) The veracity of God requires it. The word is gone out of his mouth; Gen. 2: 17. "in the day that thou eatest thereof, thou shalt surely die:" certo ac statim morieris. From that time he was instantly and certainly obnoxious and liable to the death of soul and body. The law pronounces him cursed, "that continues not in all things that are written therein to do them," Gal. 3: 9. Now, though man's threatening are often vain and insignificant things, yet God's shall surely take place; "not one little of the law shall fail, till all be fulfilled," Matt. 5: 18. God will be true in his threatening, though thousands and millions perish.

(3.) The wisdom of God, by which he governs the rational world, admits not of a dispensation or relaxation of the threatenings without satisfaction: for, as good no king, as no laws for government; as good no law, as no penalty; and as good no penalty, as no execution. To this purpose one well observes; "It is altogether indecent, especially to the wisdom and righteousness of God, that that which provoketh the execution, should procure the abrogation of his law; that that should supplant and undermine the law, for the alone preventing whereof the law was before established." How could it be expected, that men should fear and tremble before God, when they should find themselves more scared than hurt by his threats against sin! So then God stood upon satisfaction, and would admit no treaty of peace, on any other ground.

Object. Let none here object, that reconciliation upon this only score of satisfaction, is derogatory to the riches of grace; or that we allow not God what we do men, viz. to forgive an injury freely, without satisfaction.

Sol. Free forgiveness to us, and full satisfaction made to God by Jesus Christ for us, are not "asurata", things inconsistent with each other, as in its proper place shall be more fully cleared to you. And for denying that to God which we allow to men, you must know, that man and man stand on even ground: man is not capable of being wronged and injured by man, as God is by man, there is no comparison between the nature of the offences.

To conclude, man only can freely forgive man; in a private capacity, so far as wrong concerns himself; but ought not to do so in a public capacity, as he is judge, and bound to execute justice impartially. God is our Law-giver and Judge: he will not dispense with violations of the law, but strictly stands upon complete satisfaction.

2. Man can render to God no satisfaction of his own, for the wrong done by his sin. He finds no way to compensate and make God amends, either by doing, or by suffering his will.

(1.) Not by doing: this way is shut up to all the world; none can satisfy God, or reconcile himself to him this way; for it is evident our best works are sinful; "All our righteousness is as filthy rags," Isa. 64: 6. And it is strange any should imagine, that one sin should make satisfaction for another. If it be said, not what is sinful in our duties, but what is spiritual, pure and good, may ingratiate us with God? it is at hand to reply, that what is good in any of our duties, is a debt we owe to God, yea, we owe him perfect obedience; and it is not imaginable how we should pay one debt by another; quit a former by contracting a new engagement. If we do any thing that is good, we are be holden to grace for it, John 15: 5. 2 Cor. 3: 5. 1 Cor. 15: 10. In a word, those that have had as much to plead on that score as any now living, have quitted, and utterly given up all hopes of appeasing and satisfying the justice of God, that way. It is like, holy Job feared God, and eschewed evil as much as any of you; yet he saith, Job 9: 20, 21. "If I justify myself, mine own mouth shall condemn me; if I say I am perfect, it shall also prove me perverse. Though I were perfect, yet would I not know my soul; I would despise my life." It may be David was a man as much after the heart of God as you; yet he said, Psal. 143: 2. "Enter not into judgement with thy servant; for in thy sight shall no man be justified." It is like Paul lived as holy, heavenly, and fruitful a life as the best of you, and far, far beyond you; yet he saith, 1 Cor. 4: 4. "I know (or am conscious to myself) of nothing, yet am I not hereby justified." His sincerity might comfort him, but could not justly him. And what need I say more? The Lord has shut up this way to all the world; and the scriptures speak it roundly and plainly: Rom. 3: 20. " Therefore, by the deeds of the law, there shall no flesh be justified in his sight." Compare Gal. 3: 21. Rom. 8: 3.

(2.) And as man can never reconcile himself to God by doing, so neither by suffering: that is equally impossible; for no sufferings can satisfy God, but such as are proportionable to the offence we suffer for. And if so, an infinite suffering must be borne: I say infinite, for sin is an infinite evil, objectively considered, as it wrongs an infinite God. Now sufferings may be said to be infinite, either in respect of their height, exceeding all bounds and limits; the letting out of the wrath and fury of an infinite God: or in respect of duration, being endless and everlasting. In the first sense, no creature can bear an infinite wrath, it would swallow us up. In the second, it may be borne as the damned do; but then, ever to be suffering, is never to have satisfied.

So that no man can be his own priest, to reconcile himself to God by what he can do or suffer. And therefore, one that is able by doing and suffering, to reconcile him, must undertake it, or we perish. Thus you see plainly and briefly the general nature and necessity of Christ's priesthood.

From both these, several useful corollaries, or practical deductions, offer themselves.

Corollary 1. This shows, in the first place, the incomparable excellency of the reformed Christian religion above all other religions, known to, or professed in the world. What other religions seek, the Christian religion only finds, even a solid foundation for true peace and settlement of conscience. While the Jews seek it in vain in the law, the Mahometan in his external and ridiculous observances; the Papist in his own merits; the believer only finds it in the blood of this great Sacrifice; this, and nothing less than this, can pacify a distressed conscience, labouring under the weight of its own guilt. Conscience demands no less to satisfy it, than God demands to satisfy him. The grand inquest of conscience is, is God satisfied? If he be satisfied, I am satisfied. Woeful is the state of that man, that feels the worm of conscience nibbling on the most tender part of the soul, and has no relief against it; that feels the intolerable scalding wrath of God burning within, and has nothing to cool it. Hear me, you that slight the troubles of conscience, that call them fancies and melancholy whimsies; if you ever had had but one sick night for sin, if you had ever felt that shame, fears horror, and despair, which are the dismal effects of an accusing and condemning conscience, you would account it an unspeakable mercy to hear of a way for the discharge of a poor sinner from that guilt: you would kiss the feet of that messenger that could bring you tidings of peace; you would call him blessed, that should direct you to an effectual remedy. Now, whoever thou art, that finest away in thine iniquities, that droopest from day to day under the present wounds, the dismal presages of conscience, know that thy soul and peace can never meet, till thou art persuaded to come to this blood of sprinkling.

The blood of this sacrifice speaks better things than the blood of Abel. The blood of this sacrifice is the blood of God, Acts xx. 2-7. Invaluably precious blood, 1 Pet. 1: 18. One drop of it infinitely excels the blood of all mere creatures, Heb. 10: 4, 5, 6. Such is the blood that must do thee good. Lord, I must have such blood (saith conscience) as is capable of giving thee full satisfaction, or it can give me no peace. The blood of all the cattle upon a thousand hills cannot do this. What is the blood of beasts to God? the blood of all the men in the world can do nothing in this case. What is our polluted blood worth? No, no, it is the blood of God, that must satisfy both thee and me.

Yea, Christ's blood is not only the blood of God, but it is blood shed in thy stead, and in thy place and room, Gal. 3: 13. "He was made a curse for us." And so it becomes sin-pardoning blood, Heb. 9: 22. Eph. 1: 7. Col. 1: 14. Rom. 3: 26. And consequently, conscience-pacifying, and soul quieting blood, Col. 1: 20. Eph. 2: 13, 14. Rom. 3: 26. O bless God, that ever the news of this blood came to thine ears. With hands and eyes lifted up to heaven, admire that grace that cast thy lot in a place where this joyful sound rings in the ears of poor sinners. What had thy case been, if thy mother had brought thee forth in the deserts of Arabia, or in the wastes of America! Or that if thou hadst been nursed up by a popish father, who could have told thee of no other remedy when in distress for sin, but to go such a pilgrimage, to whip and lash thyself, to satisfy an angry God! Surely the pure light of the gospel shining upon this generation, is a mercy never to be duly valued, never to be enough prized.

Corollary 2. Hence also be inferred of the necessity of faith, in order to a state and sense of peace with God: for to what purpose is the blood of Christ our sacrifice shed, unless it be actually and personally applied, and appropriated by faith? You know when the sacrifices under the law were brought to be slain, he that brought it was to put his hand upon the head of the sacrifice, and so it was accepted for him, to make an atonement, Lev. 1: 4. not only to signify, that how it was no more his, but God's, the property being transferred by a kind of manumission; nor yet that he voluntarily gave it to the Lord as his own free act; but principally it noted the putting off his sins, and the penalty due to him for them, upon the head of the sacrifice: and so it implied in it an execration, as if he had said, upon thy head be the evil. So the learned observe; the ancient Egyptians were wont expressly to imprecate, when they sacrificed; if any evil be coming upon us or upon Egypt, let it turn and rest upon this head, laying their hand, at these words, on the sacrifice's head. And upon that ground, saith the Historian, none of them would eat of the head of any living creature. You must also lay the hand of faith upon Christ your sacrifice, not to imprecate, but apply and appropriate his to your own souls, he having been made a curse for you.

To this the whole gospel tends, even to persuade sinners to apply Christ, and his blood to their own souls. To this he invited us, Matth. 11: 28. "Come unto me all ye that labour, and are heavy laden, and I will give you rest." For this end our sacrifice was lifted up upon the altar; John 3: 14, 15. "As Moses lifted up the serpent in the wilderness, so must the Son of man be lifted up: that whosoever believeth in him should not perish, but have everlasting life." The effects of the law, not only upon the conscience, filling it with torments, but upon the whole person, bringing death upon it, are here shadowed out by the stingings of fiery serpents; and Christ by the brazen serpent which Moses exalted for the Israelites, that were stung, to look unto. And as by looking to it they were healed; so by believing, or looking to Christ in faith, our souls are healed. Those that looked not to the brazen serpent, died infallibly; so must all that look not to Jesus, our sacrifice, by faith. It is true, the death of Christ is the meritorious cause of remission, but faith is the instrumental applying cause; and as Christ's blood is necessary in its place, so is our faith in its place also. For to the actual remission of sin, and peace of conscience, there must be a co-operation of all the causes of remission and peace. As there is the grace and love of God for an efficient and impulsive cause, and the death of Christ our sacrifice, the meritorious cause; so of necessity there must be faith, the instrumental cause. And these con-causes do all sweetly meet in their influences, and activities, in our remission, and tranquillity of conscience; and they are all (suo genare) in their kind and place absolutely necessary to the procuring and applying of it.

What is the need that the blood of Christ is shed, if I have no interest in it, no saving influences from it? O be convinced, this is the end, the business of life. Faith is the Phoenix-grace, as Christ is the Phoenix-mercy. He is the gift, John 4: 10. And this is "the work of God," John 6: 29. The death of Christ, the offers and tenders of Christ, never saved one soul in themselves, without believing application. But, wo is me! how do I see sinners, either not at all touched with the sense of sin, and so being whole, need not the physician; or if any be stung and wounded with guilt, how do they lick themselves whole with their own duties and reformations! As physicians say of wounds, let them be kept clean, and nature will find balsam of its own to heal them: If it be so in spiritual wounds, what need Christ to have left the Father's bosom, and come down to die in the quality and nature of a sacrifice for us? O if men can but have health, pleasure, riches, honours, and any way make a shift to still a brawling conscience, that it may not check or interrupt them in these enjoyments, Christ may go where he will for them.

And I am assured, till God show you the face of sin, in the glass of the law, make the scorpions and fiery serpents, that lurk in the law, and in your own consciences, to come hissing about you, and smiting you with their deadly stings, till you have had some sick nights, and sorrowful days for sin, you will never go up and down seeking an interest in the blood of his sacrifice with tears.

But, reader, if ever this be thy condition, then wilt thou know the worth of a Christ; then wilt thou have a value for the blood of sprinkling. As I remember it is storied of our crook-backed Richard, when he was put to a rout in a field-battle, and flying on foot from his pursuing enemies; he cried out, O now saith he, a kingdom for a horse. So wilt thou cry, A kingdom for a Christ; ten thousand worlds now, if I had them, for the blood of sprinkling.

Corollary 3. Is Christ your High-priest, and is his priesthood so indispensably necessary to our salvation? Then, freely acknowledge your utter impotency to reconcile yourselves to God by any thing you can do, or suffer; and let Christ have the whole glory of your recovery ascribed to him. It is highly reasonable that he that laid down the whole price, should have the whole praise. If any man think, or say, he could have made an atonement for himself, he does therein cast no light reproach upon that profound wisdom which laid the design of our redemption in the death of Christ. But of this I have spoken elsewhere. And therefore,

Corollary 4. In the last place, I rather choose to persuade you to see your necessity of this priest, and his most excellent sacrifice; and accordingly to make use of it. The best of you have polluted natures, poisoned in the womb with sin; those natures have need of this sacrifice, they must have the benefit of this blood to pardon and cleanse them, or be eternally damned. Hear me, ye that never spent a tear for the sin of nature, if the blood of Christ be not sprinkled upon your natures, it had been better for you, that you had been the generation of beasts, the offspring of dragons or toads. They have a contemptible, but not a vitiated sinful nature, as you have.

Your actual sins have need of the priest, and his sacrifice, to procure remission for them. If he take them not away by the blood of his cross, they can never be taken away, they will lie down with you in the dust; they will rise with you and follow you to the judgement seat, crying, We are thy works, and we will follow thee. All thy repentance and tears, couldst thou weep as many as there be drops in the ocean, can never take away sin. Thy duties, even the best of them, need this sacrifice. It is in the virtue thereof that they are accepted of God. And were it not that God had respect to Christ's offering, he would not regard, or look towards thee, or any of thy duties. Thou couldst no more come near to God, than thou couldst approach a devouring fire, or dwell with everlasting burnings.

Well then, say, I need such a price every way. Love him in all his offices. See the goodness of God in providing such a sacrifice for thee. Meat, drink, and air, are not more necessary to maintain thy natural life, than the death of Christ is to give and maintain thy spiritual life.

John Flavel

O then, let thy soul grow big whilst meditating of the usefulness and excellency of Christ, which is thus displayed and unfolded in every branch of the gospel. And, with a deep sense upon thy heart, let thy lips say, Blessed be God, for Jesus Christ.

Sermon 12: Of the Excellency of our High-Priest's Oblation, being the first Act or Part of His Priestly Office

Heb.10:14
For by one offering he hath perfected for ever them that are sanctified.

After this more general view and consideration of the priesthood of Christ, method requires that we come to a nearer and more particular consideration of the parts thereof, which are his oblation and intercession, answerable to the double office of the High-priest, offering the blood of the sacrifices without the holy place, which typed out Christ's oblation, and then once a year bringing the blood before the Lord into the most holy place, presenting it before God, and with it sprinkling the mercy-seat, wherein the intercession of Christ (the other part or act of his priesthood) was in a lively manner typified to us.

My present business is to open and apply the oblation of Christ; the efficacy and excellency whereof is excellently illustrated, by a comparison with all other oblations, in the precedent context, and with a singular encomium commended to us in these words, from the singularity of it. It is but one offering; one not only specifically, but one numerically considered; but once offered, and never more to be repeated: for Christ dies no more, Rom. 6: 9. He also commends it from the efficacy of it; by it he has perfected it, i.e. not only purchased a possibility of salvation, but all that we need to our full perfection. It brings in a most entire, complete and perfect righteousness: all that remains to make us perfectly happy, is but the full application of the benefits procured by this oblation for us. Moreover, it is here commended from the extensiveness of it; not being restrained to a few, but applicable to all the saints, in all the ages and places of the world: for this indefinite, them that that sanctified, is equivalent to a universal, and is as much as if he had said, To all and every saint, from the beginning to the end of the world. Lastly, He commends it from its perpetuity; it perfects for ever, that is, it is of everlasting efficacy: it shall abide as fresh, vigorous and powerful to the end of the world, as it was the first moment it was offered up. All runs into this sweet truth:

Doct. That the oblation made unto God by Jesus Christ, is of unspeakable value, and everlasting efficacy, to perfect all them that are, or shall be sanctified, to the end of the world.

Out of this fountain flow all the excellent blessings that believers either have, or hope for. Had it not been for this, there had been no such things in rerum natura, as justification, adoption, salvation, &c. peace with God and hopes of glory, pardon of sin, and divine acceptation: these and all other our best mercies, had been but so many entia, rationis, mere conceits. A man, as one saith, might have happily imagined such things as these, as he may golden mountains, and rivers of liquid gold, and rocks of diamonds: but these things could never have had any real existence extra mentem, had not Christ offered up himself a sacrifice to God for us. It is "the blood of Christ, who through the eternal Spirit offered up himself without spot to God, that purges the conscience from dead works," Heb. 9: 14. that is, from the sentence of condemnation and death, as it is reflected by conscience, for our works sake.

His appearing before God as our priest, with such an offering for us, is that which removes our guilt and fear together: "He appeared to put away sin by the sacrifice of himself," Heb. 9: 29. Now, forasmuch as the point before us is of so great weight in itself, and so fundamental to our safety and comfort, I shall endeavour to give you as distinct and clear an account of it, as can consist with that brevity which I must necessarily use. And therefore, reader, apply thy mind attentively to the consideration of this excellent Priest that appears before God, and the sacrifices he offers, with the properties and adjuncts thereof; the person before whom he brings, and to whom he offers it; the persons for whom he offers; and the end for which this oblation is made.

First, The Priest that appears before God with an oblation for us, is Jesus Christ, God-man: the dignity of whose person dignified, and derived an inestimable worth to the offering he made. There were many priests before him, but none like unto him, either for the purity of his person, or the perpetuity of his priesthood: they were sinful men, and offered for their own sins, as well as the sins of the people, Heb. 5: 3. "but he was holy, harmless, undefiled, separate from sinners," Heb. 7: 2. He could stand before God, even in the eye of his justice, as a lamb without spot. Though he made his soul an offering for sin, "yet he had done no iniquity, nor was any guile found in his mouth," Isa. 53: 9. and indeed his offering had done us no good, if the least taint of sin had been found on him. They were mortal men, that "continued not by reason of death," Heb. 7: 25, but Christ is "a Priest for ever," Psal. 110: 4.

Secondly, The oblation or offering he made, was not the blood of beasts, but his own blood, Heb. 9: 12. And herein he transcended all other priests, that he had something of his own to offer; he had a body given him to be at his own dispose, to this use and purpose, Heb. 10: 10. he offered his body: "yea, not only his body, but his soul was made an offering for sin," Isa. 53: 10. We had made a forfeiture of our souls and bodies by sin, and it was necessary the sacrifice of Christ should be answerable to the debt we owed. And when Christ came to offer his sacrifice, he stood not only in the capacity of a priest, but also in that of a surety: and so his soul stood in the stead of ours, and his body in the stead of our bodies. Now the excellency of this oblation will appear in the following adjuncts and properties of it. This oblation being for the matter of it, the soul and body of Jesus Christ, is therefore,

1. Invaluably precious. So the apostle styles it, 1 Pet. 1: 19. "Ye were redeemed "timioi aimati", with the precious blood of the Son of God:" and such it behoved him to offer. For it being offered as an expiatory sacrifice, it ought to be equivalent, in its own intrinsic value to all the souls and bodies that were to be redeemed by it. And so it was, and more also for there was a redundancy of value, an over plus of merit, which went to make a purchase for the redeemed, as will be opened in its place. So that, as one rich diamond is more worth than a thousand pebbles: one piece of gold, than many counters; so the soul and body of one Christ, are much more excellent than all the souls and bodies in the world.

And yet I dare not affirm, as some do, that by reason of the infinite preciousness of Christ's blood, one drop thereof had been sufficient to have redeemed the whole world: for if one drop had been enough, why was all the rest, even to the last drop, shed? Was God cruel, to exact more from him than was needful and sufficient: Besides, we must remember, that the passions of Christ, which were inflicted on him as the curse of the law, these only are the passions which are sufficient for our redemption from the curse of the law; now it was not a drop of blood, but death which was contained in the curse: this therefore was necessary to be inflicted. But surely as none but God can estimate the weight and evil of sin, so none but he can comprehend the worth and preciousness of the blood of Christ, shed to expiate it. And being so infinitely precious a thing which was offered up to God, it must,

2. Needs be a most complete and all-sufficient oblation, fully to expiate the sins of all for whom it was offered, in all ages of the world. The virtue of this sacrifice reacheth backward as far as Adam, and reacheth forward to the last person of the elect springing from him. That the efficacy of it thus reacheth back to Adam, is plain: for, on the account thereof, he is stiled "The Lamb slain from the foundation of the world," Rev. 13: 8.

And to the same sense a judicious expositor understands those words of Christ, John 8: 58. "Before Abraham was, I am." And, look, as the sun at midday extends his light and influence, not only forward towards the West, but also backward towards the East, where he arose; so did this most efficacious sacrifice reach all the elect in the virtue of it, who died before Christ came in the flesh. It is therefore but a vain cavil, that some make against the satisfaction of Christ, to render it needless, when they say, many were saved without it, even as many as were saved before the death of Christ. For they say, the effect cannot be before the cause, which is true of physical, but not of moral causes; and such was Christ's satisfaction. As for example, a captive is freed out of prison from the time that his surety undertakes for him, and promises his ransom; here the captive is actually delivered, though he ransom that delivered him be not yet actually paid. So it was in this case; Christ had engaged to the Father to satisfy for them, and upon that security they were delivered.

And the virtue of this oblation not only reaches those believers, that lived and died before Christ's day, but it extends itself forward to the end of the world. Hence Heb. 13: 8. Christ is said to be "the same yesterday, to-day, and for ever;" i.e. "He is not so a Saviour to us that now live, as that he was not their Saviour also, that believed in him, before us, from the beginning: yet not so a Saviour both to them and us, as that he shall not be the same to all that shall believe on him to the world's end."

To the same sense are those words, Heb. 11: 40. rightly paraphrased, "God having provided some better thing for us, that they without us should not be made perfect:" q. d. God has appointed the accomplishment of the promise of sending the Messiah, to be in the last times, that they (viz. that lived before Christ, should not be perfected, that is, justified and saved by any thing done in their time, but by looking to our time, and Christ's satisfaction made therein; whereby they and we are perfected together. No tract of time can wear out the virtue of this eternal sacrifice. It is as fresh, vigorous, and potent now, as the first hour it was offered. And though he actually offer it no more, yet he virtually continues it by his intercession now in heaven; for there he is still a Priest. And therefore, about sixty years after his ascension, when he gave the Revelation to John, he appears to him in his priestly garment, Rev. 1: 13. "Clothed in a garment down to the feet, and girt about the paps with a golden girdle:" in allusion to the priestly ephod, and curious girdle.

And as the virtue of this oblation reaches backward and forward, to all ages, and to all believers, so to all the sins of all believers, which are fully purged and expiated by it: this no other oblation could do. The legal sacrifices were no real expiations, but rather remembrances of sins, Heb. 9: 9, 12. Heb. 10: 3. And all the virtue they had, consisted in their typical relation to this sacrifice, Gal. 3: 23. Heb. 9: 13. And, separate from it, were altogether weak, unprofitable, and insignificant things, Heb. 7: 18. But this blood cleanseth from all sins, 1 John 1: 7. and sin, originating, or originated, or actual, flowing from them both. It expiates all fully, without exception, and finally, without revocation. So that by his being made sin for us, we are made not only righteous, but "the righteousness of God in him," 2 Cor. 5: 21.

3. And lastly, to name no more; being so precious in itself, and so efficacious to expiate sin, it must needs be a most grateful oblation to the Lord, highly pleasing and delightful in his eyes. And so indeed it is said, Eph. 5: 2. "He gave himself for us, an offering, and a sacrifice to God, for a sweet smelling savour." Not that God took any delight or content in the bitter sufferings of Christ, simply and in themselves considered; but with relation to the end for which he was offered, even our redemption and salvation.

Hence arose the delight and pleasure God had in it; this made him take pleasure in bruising, him, Isa. 53: 10. God smelled a savour of rest in this sacrifice. The meaning is, that as men are offended with a stench, and their stomachs rise at it, and on the contrary delighted with sweet doors and fragrances; so the blessed God speaking after the manner of man, is offended, and filled with loathing, and abhorrence by our sins; but infinitely pleased and delighted in the offering of Christ for them, which came up as an odour of sweet smelling savour to him, Whereof the costly perfumes under the law were types and shadows. This was the oblation.

Thirdly, This oblation he brings before God, and to him he offers it up: So speaks the apostle, Heb. 9: 14. "Through the eternal Spirit he offered himself without spot to God." As Christ sustained the capacity of a surety, so God of a creditor, who exacted satisfaction from him; that is, he required from him, as our surety, the penalty due to us for our sin. And so Christ had to do immediately with God, yea, with a God infinitely wronged, and incensed by sin against us. To this incensed Majesty, Christ our High priest approached, as to a devouring fire, with the sacrifice.

Fourthly, The persons for whom, and in whose stead he offered himself to God, was the whole number of God's elect, which were given him of the Father, neither more nor less: So speak the scriptures. He laid down his life for the sheep, John 10: 15. for the church, Acts 20: 28. for the children of God, John 11: 50, 51, 52!. It is confessed, there is sufficiency of virtue in this Sacrifice to redeem the whole world, and on that account some divines affirm he is called the "Saviour of the world," John 4: 42 et alibi. We acknowledge also, that he purchased the services of others, besides the elect, to be useful to them, as they many ways are. In which sense others take those scriptures that speak so universally of the extent of his death. We also acknowledge that the elect being scattered in all parts, and among all ranks of men in the world, and unknown to those that are to tender Jesus Christ to men by the preaching of the gospel; the stile of the gospel (as it was necessary) is by such indefinite expressions suited to the general tenders they are to make of him: but that the efficacy and saving virtues of this all-sufficient sacrifice, is co-extended with God's election, so that they all, and no others can, or shall reap the special benefits of it, is too clear in the scriptures to be denied, Eph. 5: 23. John 17: 2, 9, 19, 20. John 10: 26, 27, 28. 1 Tim. 4: 10.

Fifthly, The design and end of this oblation was to atone, pacify, and reconcile God, by giving him a full and adequate compensation or satisfaction for the sins of these his elect: so speaks the apostle, Col. 1: 20. "And having made peace, through the blood of his cross, by him to reconcile all things unto himself; by him, I say, whether they be things in earth, or things in heaven." So 2 Cor. 5: 19. "God was in Christ, reconciling the world to himself." Reconciliation is the making up of that breach caused by sin, between us and God, and restoring us again to his favour and friendship. For this end Christ offered up himself to God; I say, not for this end only, but more especially; hence it is called "hilasmos", a propitiation; and so the Seventy render that place, Numb. 15: "hilasmos krios", the propitiating ram. But here I would not be mistaken, as though the reconciliation were made only between us and God the Father, by the blood of the cross; for we were reconciled by it to the whole Trinity. Every sin being made against the divine Majesty, it must needs follow, that the three Persons, having the same divine essence, must be all offended by the commission, and so all reconciled by the expiation and remission of the same. But reconciliation is said to be with the Father, because, though the works of the Trinity, ad extra, be undivided, and what one does, all do;

and what is done to one, is done to all; yet by this form and manner of expression (as a learned man well observes), the scriptures point out the proper office of each Person. The Father receives us into favour; the Son mediates, and gives the ransom which procures it; the Spirit applies and seals this to the persons and hearts of believers. However, being reconciled to the Father, we are also reconciled to the Son, and Spirit, as they are one God in three Persons. And if it be objected, that then Christ offered up a sacrifice, or laid down a price to reconcile us to himself; I shall more fairly and directly meet with, and satisfy that objection, when I come to speak of Christ's satisfaction, which is one of the principal fruits of this excellent oblation. For the present, this may inform you about the nature and precious worth of Christ's oblation. The uses whereof follow in these five practical inferences.

Inference 1. Hence it follows, That actual believers are fully freed from the guilt of their sins, and shall never more come under condemnation.

The obligation of sin is perfectly abolished by the virtue of this sacrifice. When Christ became our sacrifice, he both bare, and bare away our sins. First, They were laid upon him, then expiated by him; so much is imported in that word, Heb. 9: 28. "Christ was once offered to bear the sins of many". To bear, the word is a full and emphatical word, signifying not only to bear, but to bear away. So John 1: 29. "Behold the Lamb of God, "ho arion", that taketh away the sins of the world;" not only declaratively, or by way of manifestation to the conscience; but really, making a purgation of sin, as it is in Hebrews 1: 3, "katarismon poiesamenos", word for word, a purgation being made, and not declared only. Now, how great a mercy is this, "that by him, all that believe should be justified from all things from which they could not be justified by the law of Moses," Acts 13: 39. What shall we call this grace? surely, we should do somewhat more than admire it, and faint under the sense of such a mercy. "Blessed is he whose transgression is forgiven, whose sin is covered," Psal. 32: or, O the blessedness or felicities of him that is pardoned! who can express the mercies, comforts, happiness of such a state as this? Reader, let me beg thee, if thou be one of this pardoned number, to look over the cancelled bonds, and see what vast sums are remitted to thee. Remember what thou wast in thy natural estate: possibly thou wast in that black bill, 1 Cor. 6: 3. What, and yet pardoned! full and finally pardoned, and that freely, as to any hand that thou hadst in the procurement of it! what can't thou do less, than fall down at the feet of free grace, and kiss those feet that moved so freely towards so vile a sinner? It is not long since thy iniquities were upon thee, and thou pinedst away in them. Their guilt could by no creature power be separated from thy soul. Now they are removed from thee, as far as the East from the West, Psal. 103: 11. So that, when the East and West, which are the two opposite points of heaven, meet, then thy soul and its guilt may meet again together.

O the unspeakable efficacy of Christ's sacrifice, which extends to all sins! 1 John 1: 7. "The blood of Christ cleanseth from all sins, sins past and present, without exception. And some divines of good note affirm, all sins to come also; for, (saith Mr. Paul Blains), original sin, in which all future sins are, as fruits in the root, is pardoned; and if these were not pardoned, they would void and invalidate former pardons. And lastly, it would derogate from the most plenary satisfaction of Christ. But the most say, and I think, truly, that all the past sins of believers are pardoned, without revocation, all their present sins without exception; but not their sins to come by way of anticipation: and yet for them there is a pardon of course, which is applied on their repentance, and application, of Christ's blood; so that none of them shall make void former pardons. O let these things slide sweetly to thy melting heart.

Inf. 2. From this oblation Christ made of himself to God for our sins, we infer the inflexible severity of divine Justice, which could be no other way diverted from us, and appeased, but by the blood of Christ. If Christ had not presented himself to God for us, Justice would not have spared us: And if he do appear before God as our surety, it will not spare him; Rom. 8: 32. "He spared not his own Son, but delivered him up to death for us all." If forbearance might have been expected from any, surely it might from God, "who is very pitiful, and full of tender mercy," James 5: 11. yet God in this case spared not. If one might have expected sparing mercy and abatement from any, surely Christ might most of all expect it from his own Father; yet you hear, God spared not his own Son. Sparing mercy is the lowest degree of mercy, yet it was denied to Christ: he abated him not a minute of the time appointed for his suffering, nor one degree of wrath he was to bear; nay, though in the garden Christ fell upon the ground, and sweat clodders of blood, and in that unparalleled agony scrued up his spirit to the highest intention, in that pitiful cry, "Father, if it be possible, let this cup pass;" and though he brake out upon the cross, in that heart-rending complaint, "My God, my God, why hast thou forsaken me?" yet no abatement; Justice will not bend in the least; but having to do with him on this account, resolves upon satisfaction from his blood. If this be so, what is the case of thy soul, reader, if thou be a man or woman that has no interest in this sacrifice? For if these things be done in (Christ) the green tree, what will be done to (thee) the dry tree? Luke 23: 31 "That is, if God so deal with me, that I am not only innocent, but like a green and fruitful tree, full of all delectable fruits of holiness, yet if the fire of his indignation thus seize upon me, what will be your condition, that are both barren and guilty, void of all good fruit, and full of all unrighteousness," and so like dry scary wood, are fitted as fuel to the fire? Consider with thyself, man, how canst thou imagine thou canst support that infinite wrath that Christ grappled with in the room of God's elect! He had the strength of a Deity to support him, Isa. 42: 1. "Behold my servant whom I uphold." He had the fulness of his Spirit to prepare him, Isa. 61: 11. He had the ministry of an angel, who came post from heaven to relieve him in his agony, Luke 22: 43. He had the ear of his Father to hear him, for he cried, "and was heard in that he feared," Heb. 5: 7. He was assured of the victory, before the combat; he knew he should be justified, Isa. 50: 8. and yet for all this he was sore amazed, and sorrowful even to death, and his heart was melted like wax in the midst of his bowels. If the case stood thus with Christ, notwithstanding all these advantages he had to bear the wrath of God for a little time; how dost thou think, a poor worm as thou art, to dwell with everlasting burnings, or contend with devouring fire? Luther saw ground enough for what he said, when he cried, out, "I will have nothing to do with an absolute God," i. e. with a God out of Christ: for, "it is a fearful thing to fall into the hands of the living God." Wo and alas for evermore to that man who meets a just and righteous God without a Mediator! Whoever thou art that readest these lines, I beseech thee, by the mercies of God, by all the regard and love thou hast to thy own soul, neglect not time, but make quick and sure work of it. Get an interest in this sacrifice quickly, what else will be thy state when vast eternity opens to swallow thee up? what wilt thou do, man, when thine eye-strings and heart strings are breaking? O what a fearful shriek will thy conscience give, when thou art presented before the dreadful God, and no Christ to screen thee from his indignation! Happy is that man who can say in a dying hour, as one did, who being desired, a little before his dissolution, to give his friends a little taste of his present hopes, and the grounds of them, cheerfully answered, I will let you know how it is with me: then stretching forth his hand, said,

"Here is the grave, the wrath of God, and devouring flame, the just punishment of sin, on the one side: and here am I, a poor sinful soul, on the other side: but this is my comfort, the covenant of grace, which is established upon so many sure promises, has saved all. There is an act of oblivion passed in heaven: I will forgive their iniquities, and their sins will I remember no more. This is the blessed privilege of all within the covenant, among whom I am one." O it is sweet at all times, especially at such a time, to see the reconciled face of God, through Jesus Christ, and hear the voice of peace through the blood of the cross.

Inf. 3. Has Christ offered up himself a sacrifice to God for us? Then let us improve, in every condition, this sacrifice, and labour to get hearts duly affected with such a sight as faith can give us of it. Whatever the condition or complaint of any Christian is, the beholding the Lamb of God, that taketh away the sin of the world, may give him strong support, and sweet relief. Do you complain of the hardness of your hearts, and want of love to Christ? Behold him as offered up to God for you; and such a sight, (if any in the world will do it) will melt your hard hearts. Zech. 12: 10. "They shall look upon me whom they have pierced, and shall mourn." It is reported of Johannes Milieus, that he was never observed to speak of Christ and his sufferings, but his eyes would drop. Art thou too little touched and unaffected with the evil of sin? Is it thy complaint, Christian, that thou canst not make sin bear so hard upon thy heart as thou wouldst? Consider but what thou hast now read; realise this sacrifice by faith, and try what efficacy there is in it to make sin for ever bitter as death to thy soul. Suppose thine own Father had been stabbed to the heart with such a knife, and his blood were upon it, wouldst thou delight to see, or endure to use that knife any more? sin is the knife that stabbed Christ to the heart; this shed his blood. Surely, you can never make light of that which lay so heavy upon the soul and body of Jesus Christ.

Or is your heart pressed down even to despondency, under the guilt of sin, so that you cry, how can such a sinner as I be pardoned? my sin is greater than can be forgiven? "Behold the Lamb of God, that taketh away the sin of the world." Remember that no sin can stand before the efficacy of his blood. 1 John 1: 7. "The blood of Jesus Christ cleanseth from all sin." This sacrifice makes unto God full satisfaction.

Are you at any time staggering through unbelief filled with unbelieving suspicions of the promises? Look hither, and you shall see them all ratified and established in the blood of the cross, so that hills and mountains shall sooner start from their own basis and centres, than one little of the promise fail. Heb. 9: 17, 18, 19.

Do you at any time find year hearts fretting, disquieted, and impatient under every petty cross and trial? See how quietly Christ your sacrifice came to the altar, how meekly and patiently he stood under all the wrath of God and men together This will silence, convince, and shame you.

In a word, here you will see so much of the grace of God, and love of Christ, in providing and becoming a sacrifice for you: you will see God taking vengeance against sin, but sparing the sinner:

you will see Christ standing as the body of sin alone; for, "he was made sin for us, that we might be made the righteousness of God in him:" that whatever corruption burdens, this, in the believing application, will support; whatever grace is defective, this will revive it.

Blessed be God for Jesus Christ.

Sermon 13: Of the Intercession of Christ our High-priest, being the second Act or Part of his Priestly Office

Heb. 7: 25.
Wherefore he is able also to save them to the uttermost that come unto God by him, seeing he ever liveth to make intercession for them.

Having dispatched the first part, or act of Christ's priesthood, consisting in his Oblation; we come to the other branch of it, consisting in his Intercession, which is nothing else but the virtual continuation of his offering once made on earth; that being medium reconciliationis, the means of reconciling; this, medium applicationis, the way and means of his applying to us the benefits purchased by it.

This second part, or branch of his priesthood, was typified by the High-priest's entering with the blood of the sacrifice and sweet incense into the holy place: Lev. 16: 12, 13, 14. "And he shall take the censer full of burning coals of fire, from off the altar before the Lord, and his hands full of sweet incense beaten small, and bring it within the vail. And he shall put the incense upon the fire before the Lord, that the cloud of the incense may cover the mercy-seat that is upon the testimony, that he die not. And he shall take the blood of the bullock, and sprinkle it with his finger upon the mercy-seat, eastward," &c

Christ's offering himself on earth, answered to the killing of the sacrifice without; and his entering into heaven, there to intercede, was that which answered to the priest's going with blood, and his hands full of incense, within the vail. So that this is a part, yea, a special part of Christ's priesthood; and so necessary to it, that if he had not done this, all his work on earth had signified nothing; nor had he been a priest, i. e. a complete and perfect priest, if he had remained on earth, Heb. 8: 4. because the very design and end of shedding his blood on earth had been frustrated, which was to carry it before the Lord into heaven. So that this is the principal perfective part of the priesthood: he acted the first part on earth, in a state of deep abasement in the form of a servant; but he acts this in glory, whereto he is taken up, that he may fulfil his design in dying, and give the work of our salvation its last completing act. So much is imported in this scripture, which tells us, by reason hereof, he "is able to save to the uttermost," &c.

The words contain an encouragement to believers, to come to God in the way of faith, drawn from the intercession of Christ in heaven for them. In which you may take notice of these principal parts.

1. The quality of the persons here encouraged, who are described by a direct act of faith, as poor recumbents that are going out of themselves to God by faith; but conscious of great unworthiness in themselves, and thence apt to be discouraged.

2. The encouragement propounded to such believers, drawn from the ability of Jesus Christ, in whose name they go to the Father, to save them to the uttermost, i.e. fully, perfectly, completely; for so this emphatical word, "eis to panteles", signifies, the saving us wholly, thoroughly, completely, and altogether; giving our salvation its last act and completion.

The ground or reason of this his saving ability: "Seeing he ever liveth to make intercession;" i.e. he has not only offered up his blood to God upon the tree, as a full price to purchase pardon and grace for believers; but lives in heaven, and that for every to apply unto us, in the way of intercession, all the fruits, blessings, and benefits, that that precious blood of his deserves, and has procured us a price for them. The words thus opened, the point I shall single out, from among many that lie in them, as most suitable to my design and purpose, is this;

John Flavel

Doct. That Jesus our High-priest lives for ever, in the capacity of a potent Intercessor, in heaven for believers.

Here we will enquire, First, What it is for Christ to be an intercessor. Secondly, By what acts he performs that work in heaven. Thirdly, Whence the potency and prevalence of his intercession is. Fourthly, and lastly, How he lives for ever to make intercession for us.

First, What it is for Christ to be an intercessor for us. To intercede in general, is to go betwixt two parties, to intreat, argue, and plead with one for the other. And of this there are two sorts; 1. Ex charitate, ut fratres, that whereby one Christian prays and pleads with God for another, 1 Tim. 2: 1. 2. Ex officio mediatorio, that whereby Christ, as an act of office, presents himself before God to request for us. Betwixt these two is this difference, that the former is performed not in our own, but in another's name; we can tender no request to God immediately, or for our own sake, either for ourselves, or for others: John 16: 23 "Whatsoever ye shall ask the Father in my name, he will give it you." But the latter, which is proper to Christ, is an intercession with God for us, in his own name, and upon the account of his own proper merit; the one is a private act of charity, the other a public act of office; and so he is our advocate or court friend, as Satan is or accuser or court-adversary. Satan is "ho antidikos", one that charges us before God, 1 Pet. 5: 8. and continually endeavours to make breaches between us and God. Christ is "ho parakletos", our attorney, or advocate, that pleads for us, and continues peace and friendship between us and God, 1 John 2: 2. "If any man sin, we have an advocate with the Father, Jesus Christ the righteous."

And thus to make intercession, is the peculiar and incommunicable prerogative of Jesus Christ, none but he can go in his own name to God. And in that sense we are to understand that place, Ezek. 44: 2, 3. "Then said the Lord unto me, This gate shall be shut, it shall not be opened, and no man shall enter in by it, because the Lord the God of Israel has entered in by it, therefore it shall be shut. It is for the prince, the prince he shall sit in it, to eat bread before the Lord," &c. The great broad gate, called here the prince's gate, signifies that abundant and direct entrance that Christ had into heaven by his own merits, and in his own name; this, saith the Lord, shall be shut, no man shall enter in by it; all other men must come thither, as it were, by collateral or side doors, which looked all towards the altar, viz. by virtue of the Mediator, and through the benefit of his death imputed to them.

And yet, though God has for ever shut up and barred this way to all the children of men, telling us that no man shall ever have access to him in his own name, as Christ the Prince had; how do some, notwithstanding, strive to force open the Prince's gate? So do they, that found the intercession of saints upon their own works and merits, thereby robbing Christ of his peculiar glory; but all that so approach God, approach a devouring fire; Christ only, in the virtue of his blood, thus comes before him, to make intercession for us.

Secondly, We will enquire wherein the intercession of Christ in heaven consists, or by what acts he performs his glorious office there. And the scriptures place it in three things:

1. In his presenting himself before the Lord in our names, and upon our accounts. So we read in Heb. 9: 28. "Christ is entered into heaven itself, now to appear in the presence of God for us." The apostle manifestly alludes to the High-priest's appearing in the holy of holies, which was the figure of heaven, presenting to the Lord the names of the twelve tribes of Israel, which were on his breast and shoulders, Exod. 28: 9,12, 28, 29. To which the church is supposed to allude in that request, Cant. 8: 6. "Set me as a seal upon thine heart, as a seal upon thine arm." Now the very sight of Christ, our High priest in heaven, prevails exceedingly with God, and turns away his displeasure from us. As when God looks upon the rainbow, which is the sign of the covenant, he remembers the earth in mercy: so when he looks on Christ, his heart must needs be towards us, upon his account; and therefore in Rev. 4: 3, Christ is compared to a rainbow encompassing the throne.

Christ performs his intercession-work in heaven, not by a naked appearing in the presence of God only, but also by presenting his blood, and all his sufferings to God, as a moving plea on our account. Whether he makes any proper oral intercession there, as he did on earth, is not so clear; some incline to it, and think it is countenanced by Zechariah, chap. 1: 12,13. Where Christ our Intercessor presents a proper vocal request to the Father, in the behalf of his people; saying "O Lord of hosts, how long wilt thou not have mercy on Jerusalem, and on the cities of Judah, against which thou hast had indignation these threescore and ten years? And the Lord answered him with good and comfortable words." And so Acts 2: 23. as soon as he came to heaven, he is said (and that is the first fruits of his intercession) to obtain the promise of the Holy Ghost. But sure I am, an interceding voice is by an usual prosopopeia attributed to his blood; which in Heb. 12: 24. is said "to speak better things than that of Abel." Now Abel's blood and so Christ's, do cry unto God, as the hire of the labourers unjustly detained, or the whole creation, which is in bondage, through our sins, is said to cry and groan in the ears of the Lord, Jam. 5: 4. Rom. 8: 22. not vocally, but efficaciously. A rare illustration of this efficacious intercession of Christ in heaven, we have in that famous story of Amintas, who appeared as an advocate for his brother AEchylus, who was strongly accused, and very likely to be condemned to die. Now Amintas having performed great services, and merited highly of the common-wealth, in whose service one of his hands was cut off in the field; he comes into the court in his brother's behalf, and said nothing, but only lifted up his arm, and shewed them cubitum sine manu, an arm without a hand, which so moved them, that, without a word speaking, they freed his brother immediately.

And thus if you look into Rev. 5: 6. you shall see in what posture Christ is represented, visionally there, as standing between God and us; "And I beheld, and lo, in the midst of the throne, and the four beasts, and in the midst of the elders stood a Lamb as it had been slain;" i.e. bearing in his glorified body the marks of death and sacrifice. Those wounds he received for our sins on earth, are, as it were, still fresh bleeding in heaven: a moving and prevailing argument it is with the Father, to give out the mercies he pleads for.

3. And lastly, He presents the prayers of his saints to God, with his merits; and desires that they may for his sake be granted. He causes a cloud of incense to ascend before God with them, Rev. 8: 3. All these were excellently typified out by the going in of the High-priest before the Lord, with the names of the children of Israel on his breast, with the blood of the sacrifice, and his hands full of incense, as the apostle explains them in Heb. 7 and Heb. 9.

Thirdly, And that this intercession of Christ is most potent, successful, and prevalent with God, will be evinced, both from the qualification of this our Advocate, from his great interest in the Father, from the nature of the place he useth with God, and from the relation and interest believers have, both in the Father to whom, and the Son by whom this intercession is made.

1. Our intercessor in the heavens is every way able and fit for the work he is engaged in there. Whatever is desirable in an advocate, is in him eminently. It is necessary that he who undertakes to plead the cause of another, especially if it be weighty and intricate, should be wise, faithful, tender-hearted, and one that concerns himself in the success of his business. Our Advocate Christ, wants no wisdom to manage his work; he is the wisdom of God, yea, only wise, Jude 25. There is much folly in the best of our duties, we know not how to press an argument home with God; but Christ has the art of it. Our business is in a wise hand: he is no less faithful than wise, therefore he is called "a faithful High-priest, in things pertaining to God," Heb. 2: 17. He assures us we may safely trust our concerns with him, John 14: 2. "In my Father's house are many mansions; if it were not so, I would have told you;" q. d. Do you think I could deceive you? men may cheat you, but I will not; your own hearts may and daily do deceive you, but so will not I. And for tender heartedness, and sensible feelings for your conditions, there is none like him: Heb. 4: 15. "For we have not an High-priest who cannot be touched with the feeling of our infirmities, but was in all points tempted like as we are, yet without sin." We have not one that cannot sympathise, so it is in the Greek: and on purpose that he might the better sympathise with us, he came as near to our conditions, as the holiness of his nature could permit. He suffered himself to be in all points tempted like as we are, sin only excepted.

And then for his concernment and interest in the success of his suit; he not only reckons, but has really made it his own interest, yea, more his own than it is ours: For now by reason of the mystical union, all our wants and troubles are his, Eph. 1: 23, yea, his own glory and completeness, as Mediator, is deeply interested in it; and therefore we need not doubt but he will use all care and diligence in that work. If you say, so he may, and yet not speed for all that, for it depends upon the Father's grant: True, but then,

2. Consider the great interest he has in the Father, with whom he intercedes. Christ is his dear Son, Col. 1: 13. the beloved of his soul, Eph. 1: 6. Betwixt him and the Father, with whom, when he intercedes, there is an unity, not only of nature, but will; and so he always hears him, John 11: 42. Yea, and he said to his dear Son, when he came first to heaven, "Ask of me, and I will give thee," Psal. 2: 8. Moreover,

He must needs speed in his suit, if you consider the nature of his intercession, which is just and reasonable for the matter, urgent and continual, for the manner of it. The matter of his requesting most equal: what he desires is not desired gratis, or upon terms unbecoming the holiness and righteousness of God to grant; he desires no more but what he has deserved, and given a valuable consideration to the Father for. And so the justice of God does, not only not oppose, but furthers and pleads for the granting, and fulfilling his requests.

Here you must remember, that the Father is under a covenant tie and bond to do what he asks; for Christ having fully performed the work on his part, the mercies he intercedes for, are as due as the hire of the labourer is, when the work is faithfully done. And as the matter is just, so the manner of his intercession is urgent and continual. How importunate a suitor he is, may be gathered from that specimen, given of it in John 17, and for the constancy, of it, my text tells us, "he ever lives to make intercession:" It is his great business in heaven, and he follows it close. And to close all,

4. Consider who they are for whom he makes intercession: The friends of God, the children of God; those that the Father himself loves, and his heart is propense and ready enough to grant the best and greatest of mercies to: which is the meaning of John 15: 26, 27. "The Father himself loveth you." And it must needs be so, for the first corner stone of all these mercies was laid by the Father himself in his most free election. He also delivered his Son for us; and "how shall he not with him freely give us all things?" Rom. 8: 32. So then there can remain no doubt upon a considering heart, but that Christ is a prevalent and successful intercessor in heaven. There only remains one thing more to be satisfied, and that is,

Fourthly, In what sense he is to live for ever to make intercession. Shall he then be always at his work? employed in begging new favours for us to eternity? How then shall the people of God be perfect in heaven, if there be need of Christ's intercession to eternity for them?

I answer, by distinguishing the essence and substance of Christ's offices, from the way and manner of administration. In the first sense it is eternal: for his mediatory kingdom, as to the essence of it, is to abide for ever; Christ shall never cease to be a Mediator; the church shall never want a head; for "of his kingdom, there shall be no end," Luke 1: 33. However, Christ, as a Mediator, being employed in a kind of subordinate way, 1 Cor. 3: 23, when he shall have accomplished that design for which he became a Mediator, "Then shall he deliver up the kingdom (in the sense we spake before) to the Father, and so God shall be all in all," 1 Cor. 15: 24. Then shall the divinity of Christ, which was so emptied and obscured in his undertaking this temporary dispensatory kingdom, be more gloriously manifested, by the full possession, use, and enjoyment of that natural, divine, eternal kingdom, which belongs to all the three co-essential and co-equal persons, reigning with the same power, majesty, and glory, in the unity of the Divine Essence, and common acts, in all, and over all, infix nicely and immutably for ever.

And so Christ continues to be our Mediator; and yet that affords no argument that our happiness shall be incomplete, but rather argues the perfection of the church, which thenceforth shall be governed no more as it now is, nor have any farther use of ordinances, but shall be ruled more immediately, gloriously, triumphantly, and ineffably in the world to come. The substance of his Mediatorship is not changed, but the manner of the administration only.

Use 1. Does Christ live for ever in heaven to present his blood to God in the way of intercession for believers? How sad then is their case, that have no interest in Christ's blood; bit instead of pleading for them, it cries to God against then, as the despisers and abusers of it! Every unbeliever despises it: The apostate treads it under foot. He that is an intercessor for some, will be an accuser of others. To be guilty of a man's blood is sad; but to have the blood of Jesus accusing and crying to God against a soul, is unspeakable terrible. Surely when he shall make inquisition for blood, when the day of his vengeance is come, he will make it appear by the judgements he will execute, that this is a sin never to be expiated, but vengeance shall pursue the sinner to the bottom of hell. Oh! what do men and women do, in rejecting the gracious offer of Christ! what, tread upon a Saviour! and cast contempt, by unbelief and hardness of heart, upon their only remedy! I remember I have read of a harlot that killed her child, and said that it smiled upon her when she went to stab it. Sinner, does not Christ smile upon thee in the gospel? And wilt thou, as it were, stab him to the heart by thine infidelity? Wo, and alas for that man, against whom this blood cries in heaven!

Use 2. Doth Christ live for ever to make intercession? Hence let believers fetch relief, and draw encouragement against all the causes and grounds of their fears and troubles; for surely this answers them all.

1. Hence let them be encouraged against all their sinful infirmities, and lamented weaknesses. It is confessed these are sad things; they grieve the Spirit of God, sadden your own hearts, cloud your evidences; but having such a High-priest in heaven, can never be your ruin. 1 John 2: 1, 2. "My little children, these things write I unto you, that you sin not: and if any man sin, we have an Advocate with the Father, Jesus Christ the righteous." [My little children.] Children, especially little children, when first beginning to take the foot, are apt to stumble at every straw; so are raw, young and unexperienced Christians: but what if they do? Why though it must be far from them to take encouragement so to do from Christ and his intercession, yet if by surprizal they do sin, let them not be utterly discouraged: for we have an Advocate, he stops whatever plea may be brought in against us by the Devil, or the law, and answers all by his satisfaction: he gets out fresh pardons for new sins. And this Advocate is with [the Father:] he does not say with his Father, though that had been a singular support in itself, nor yet with our Father, which is a sweet encouragement singly considered, but with [the Father] which takes in both, to make the encouragement full. Remember, you that are cast down, under the sense of sin, that Jesus, your friend, in the court above, "is able to save to the uttermost." Which is, as one calls it, a reaching word, and extends itself so far, that thou canst not look beyond it. "Let thy soul be set on the highest mount that any creature was ever set on, and enlarged to take in view the most spacious prospect both of sin and misery, and difficulties

of being saved, that ever yet any poor humble soul did cast within itself; yea, join to these all the hindrances and objections that the heart of man can invent against itself and salvation: lift up thine eyes, and look to the utmost thou canst see; and Christ, by his intercession, is able to save thee beyond the horizon and utmost compass of thy thoughts, even to the utmost."

2. Hence draw abundant encouragement against all heart- straitenings, and deadness of Spirit in prayer. Thou complainest thy heart is dead, wandering, and contracted in duty: O, but remember Christ's blood speaks, when thou canst not; it can plead for thee, and that powerfully, when thou art not able to speak a word for thyself: to this sense that scripture speaks, Cant. 3: 6. "Who is this that cometh out of the wilderness like pillars of smoke, perfumed with myrrh, and frankincense, with all powders of the merchant?" The duties of Christians go up many times, as pillars or clouds of smoke from them, more smoke than fire, prayers smoked and sullied with their offensive corruptions; but, remember, Christ perfumes them with myrrh, &c. He, by his intercession, gives them a sweet perfume.

3. Christ's intercession is a singular relief to all that come unto God by him, against all sinful damps and slavish fears from the justice of God. Nothing more promotes the fear of reverence; nothing more suppresseth unbelieving despondencies, and destroys the spirit of bondage. So you find it, Heb. 10: 19, 20, 21. "Having therefore, brethren, boldness to enter into the holiest, by the blood of Jesus, by a new and living way, which he has consecrated for us through the vail, that is to say, his flesh; and having a High priest over the house of God, let us draw near with a true heart, en pleroforia pisteos', in full assurance of faith": or let us come unto God, as a ship comes with full sail into the harbour. O what a direct and full gale of encouragement does this intercession of Christ give to the poor soul that lay a-ground, or was wind-bound before?

4. The intercession of Christ gives admirable satisfaction and encouragement to all that corns to God, against the fears of de setting him again by apostasy. This, my friends, this is your principal security against these matters of fear. With this he relieved Peter, Luke 22: 31, 32. "Simon, (saith Christ) Satan has desired to have you, that he may sift you as wheat; but I have prayed for thee, that thy faith fail not," q. d. Satan will fan thee, not to get out thy chaff, but bolt out thy flour: his temptations are levelled against thy faith; but fear not, my prayer shall break his designs, and secure thy faith against all his attempts upon it. Upon this powerful intercession of Christ, the apostle builds his triumph against all that threatens to bring him, or any of the saints, again into a state of condemnation. And see how he drives on that triumph, from the resurrection, and session of Christ at the Father's right hand; and especially from the work of intercession, which he lives there to perform: Rom. 8: 34, 35. "Who is he that condemneth. It is Christ that died; yea, rather that is risen again, who is even at the right hand of God, who also maketh intercession for us. Who shall separate us from the love of Christ?"

5. It gives sweet relief against the defects and wants that yet are in our sanctification. We want a great deal of faith, love, heavenly-mindedness, mortification, knowledge. We are short and wanting in all. There are "husteremata", the remains, or things wanting, as the apostle calls them, 1 Thess. 3: 10. Well, if grace be but yet in its weak beginnings, and infancy in thy soul, this may encourage, that by reason of Christ's intercession, it shall live, grow, and expatiate itself in thy heart. He is not only the author, but the finisher of it, Heb. 12: 2. He is ever begging new and fresh mercies for you in heaven; and will never cease till all your wants be supplied. He saves "eis to panteles", to the uttermost, i.e. as I told you before, to the last, perfective, completing act of salvation. So that this is a fountain of relief against all your fears.

Use 3. Does Christ live for ever to make intercession? Then let those who reap on earth the fruits of that his work in heaven, draw instruction thence about the following duties, to which it leads them as by the hand.

1. Do not forget Christ in an exalted state. You see though he be in all the glory above, at God's right hand, and enthroned king, he does not forget you: he, like Joseph, remembers his brethren in all his glory. But, alas, how oft does advancement make us forget him? As the Lord complains in Hosea 13: 5, 6 "I did know thee in the wilderness, in the land of great drought: but when they came into Canaan, according to their pastures, so were they filled: they were filled, and their heart was exalted; therefore have they forgotten me." As if he had said, O my people, you and I were better acquainted in the wilderness, when you were in a low condition, left to my immediate care, living by daily faith. O then you gave me many a sweet visit; but now you are filled, I hear no more of you. Good had it been for same saints, if they had never known prosperity.

2. Let the intercession of Christ in heaven for you, encourage you to constancy in the good ways of God. To this duty it sweetly encourages also, Heb. 4: 14. "seeing then that we have a great High-priest that is passed into the heavens, Jesus the son of God, let us hold fast our profession." Here is encouragement to perseverance on a double account. One is, that Jesus, our head, is already in heaven; and if the head be above water, the body cannot drown. The other is from the business he is there employed about, which is his priesthood; he is passed into the heavens, as our great

High-priest, to intercede, and therefore we cannot miscarry.

3. Let it encourage you to constancy in prayer: O do not neglect that excellent duty, seeing Christ is there to present all your petitions to God; yea, to perfume as well as present them. So the apostle, Heb. 4: 16. infers from Christ's intercession; "Let us therefore come boldly unto the throne of grace, that we may obtain mercy, and find grace to help in time of need."

4. Hence be encouraged to plead for Christ on earth, who continually pleads for you in heaven. If any accuse you, he is there to plead for you: and if any dishonour him on earth, see that you plead his interest, and defend his honour. Thus you have heard what his intercession is, and what benefits we receive by it.

Blessed be God for Jesus Christ.

Sermon 14: A Vindication of the Satisfaction of Christ, as the first Effect or Fruit of his Priesthood

Gal. 3: 13.
Christ has redeemed us from the curse of the law, being made a curse for us.

You have seen the general nature, necessity and parts of Christ's priesthood, viz. oblation and intercession. Before you part from this office, it is necessary you should farther take into consideration the principal fruits and effects of his priesthood; which are, complete satisfaction and the acquisition or purchase of an eternal inheritance. The former viz. The satisfaction, made by his blood, is manifestly contained in this excellent scripture before us, wherein the apostle (having shown before, at ver. 10. that whosoever "continues not in all things written in the law, to do them, are cursed)" declares how, notwithstanding the threats of the law, a believer comes to be freed from the curse of it, namely, by Christ's bearing that curse for him, and so satisfying God's justice, and discharging the believer from all obligations to punishment.

More particularly, in these words you have the believer's discharge from the curse of the law, and the way and manner thereof opened.

1. The believers discharge; Christ has redeemed us from the curse of the law. The law of God has three parts, commands promises, and threatening or curses. The curse of the law is its condemning sentence, whereby a sinner is bound over to death, even the death of soul and body. The chain, by which it binds him, is the guilt of sin; and from which none can loose the soul but Christ. This curse of the law is the most dreadful thing imaginable; it strikes at the life of a sinner, yea, his best life, the eternal life of the soul: and when it has condemned, it is inexorable, no cries nor tears, no reformation nor repentance can loose the guilty sinner; for it requires for its reparation that which no mere creature can give, even an infinite satisfaction. Now from this curse Christ frees the believer; that is, he dissolves the obligation to punishment, cancels the hand-writing, looses all the bonds and chains of guilt, so that the curse of the law has nothing to do with him for ever.

2. We have here the way and manner in and by which this is done; and that is by a full price paid down, and that price paid in the room of the sinner, both making up a complete and full satisfaction. He pays a full price, every way adequate and proportionable to the wrong. So much this word, "hemas exegorasen", which we translate redeemed, imports; he has bought us out, or fully bought us, that is, by a full price. This price with which he so fully bought or purchased our freedom from the curse, is not only called "lutron", Mat. 20: 28. or ransom, but more emphatically "antilutron", in 1 Tim. 2: 5, 6 which might be translated an adequate or fully answerable ransom. And so his freeing us by this price, is not only expressed by "egorasas toi Theoi hemas", "Thou hast bought us to God by thy blood," Rev. 5: 9. but "exegorasen hemas", he has fully, perfectly, bought us out.

And as the price or ransom paid was full, perfect, and sufficient in itself; so it was paid in our room, and upon our account: so saith the text, "By his being made a curse for us," the meaning is not, that Christ was made the very curse itself, changed into a curse; no more than when the word is said to be made flesh, the divine nature was converted into flesh, but it assumed or took flesh; and so Christ took the curse upon himself; therefore it is said, 2 Cor. 5: 21. "He was made sin for us who knew no sin;" that is, our sin was imputed to our surety, and laid upon him for satisfaction. And so this word "huper" [for] implies a substitution of one, in the place and stead of another. Now the price being full, and paid in lieu of our sins, and thereupon we fully redeemed or delivered from the curse, it follows, as a fair and just deduction, that,

Doct. The death of Christ; has made a full satisfaction to God for all the sins of his elect.

"He (to wit our surety, Christ) was oppressed, and he was afflicted," saith the prophet, Isa. 52: 7. it may be fitly rendered, (and the words will bear it without the least force) it was exacted, and answered. But how, being either way translated, it establisheth the satisfaction of Christ, may be seen in our learned Annotations on that place. So Col. 1: 14. "In whom we have apolutrosin dia tou haimatos', redemption through his blood, even the forgiveness of sin." Here we have the benefit, viz. redemption interpreted by way of opposition, "even the remission of sins;" and the matchless price that was laid down to purchase it, the blood of Christ. So again, Heb. 9: 12. "By his own blood he entered once into the holy place, having obtained aionian lutrosin', eternal redemption for us." Here is eternal redemption, the mercy purchased: his own blood, the price that procured it.

Now forasmuch as this doctrine of Christ's satisfaction is so necessary, weighty and comfortable in itself, and yet so much opposed and intricated by several enemies to it; the method I shall take for the clearing, establishing, and preparing it for use, shall be,

First, To open the nature of Christ's satisfaction, and shew what it is.

Secondly, To establish the truth of it, and prove that he made full satisfaction to God for all the sins of the elect.

Thirdly, To answer the most considerable objections made against it.

And lastly, To apply it.

First, What is the satisfaction of Christ, and what does it imply? I answer, satisfaction is the act of Christ, God-man, presenting himself as our surety in obedience to God and love to us; to do and to suffer all that the law required of us: thereby freeing us from the wrath and curse due to us for sins.

1. It is the act of God-man; no other was capable of giving satisfaction for an infinite wrong done to God. But by reason of the union of the two natures in his wonderful person, he could do it, and has done it for us. The human nature did what was necessary in its kind; it gave the matter of the sacrifice: the divine nature stamps the dignity and value upon it, which made it an adequate compensation: so that it was opus "Theandrikon", the act of God-man; yet so, that each nature retained its own properties, notwithstanding their joint influence into the effect. If the angels in heaven had laid down their lives, or if the blood of all the men in the world had been poured out by justice, this could never have satisfied, because that "axiosis", worth and value which this sacrifice has, would have still been wanting. "It was God that redeemed the church with his own blood," Acts 20: 18. If God redeem with his own blood, he redeems as God-man, without any dispute.

2. If he satisfy God for us, he must present himself before God, as our surety, in our stead, as well as for our good; else his obedience had signified nothing to us; to this end he was "made under the law," Gal. 4: 4. comes under the same obligation with us, and that as a surety, for so he is called, Heb. 7: 22. Indeed his obedience and sufferings could be exacted from him upon no other account. It was not for any thing he had done that he became a curse. It was prophesied of him, Dan. 9: 26. "The Messiah shall be cut off, but not for himself;" and being dead, the scriptures plainly assert it was for our sins, and upon our account: so 1 Cor. 15: 3. "Christ died for our sins, according to the scriptures."

And it is well observed by our divines, who assert the vicegerency and substitution of Christ in his sufferings, that all those Greek particles which we translate [for] when applied to the sufferings of Christ do note the meritorious, deserving, procuring cause of those sufferings. So you find, Heb. 10: 12. "He offered one sacrifice huper hamartion', for sins." 1 Pet. 3: 18. "Christ once suffered, peri' for sins." Rom. 4: 25. "He was delivered, dia', for our offences." Mat. 20: 28. "He gave his life a ransom, anti', for many." And there are that confidently affirm this last particle is never used in any other sense in the whole book of God; as "an eye for an eye, a tooth for a tooth," i.e. one in lieu of another. Just as those whom the Greeks called "antipsuchoi", men that exchanged their lives, or gave life for life, staking down their own to deliver another's, as Philumene did for Aristides. And so the poet Virgil speaks: Si fratrem Pollux alterna morte redemit.

And indeed, this very consideration is that which supports the doctrine of imputation, the imputation of our sins to Christ, and the imputation of Christ's righteousness unto us, Rom. 5: 19. For how could our sins be laid on him, but as he stood in our stead? or his righteousness be imputed to us, but as he was our surety, performing it in our place; so that to deny Christ's sufferings in our stead, is to lose the corner-stone of our justification, and overthrow the very pillar which supports our faith, comfort and salvation. Indeed if this had not been, he would have been the righteous Lord, but not the Lord our righteousness, as he is stiled, Jer. 33: 16. So that it was but a vain distinction, to say it was for our good, but not in our stead: for had he not been in our stead, we could not have had the good of it.

3. The internal moving cause of Christ's satisfaction for us, was his obedience to God, and love to us. That it was an act of obedience, is plain from Phil. 2: 8. "He became obedient unto death, even the death of the cross." Now obedience respects a command, and each a command Christ received to die for us, as himself tells us, John 10: 18. "I lay down my life of myself; I have power to lay it down, and power to take it again: this commandment have I received of my Father." So that it was an act of obedience with respect to God, and yet a most free and spontaneous act with respect to himself. And that he was moved to it out of pity and love to us, himself assures us: Gal. 5: 2. "Christ loved us, and gave himself for us an offering and a sacrifice to God." Upon this Paul

The Fountain of Life Opened Up

sweetly reflected, Gal. 2: 20. "Who loved me and gave himself for me." As the external moving cause was our misery, so the internal was his own love and pity for us.

    4. The matter of Christ's satisfaction, was his active and passive obedience to all the law of God required. I know there are some that doubt whether Christ's active obedience have any place here, and so whether it be imputed as any part of our righteousness. It is confessed, that scripture most frequently mentions his passive obedience, as that which made the atonement, and procures our redemption, Matth. 20: 28. and 26: 28. Rom. 3: 24, 25 and elsewhere: but his passive obedience is never mentioned exclusively, as the sole cause, or matter of satisfaction. But in those places where it is mentioned by itself, it is put for his whole obedience, both active and passive, by an usual trope; and in other scriptures it is ascribed to both, as Gal. 4: 4. he is said, "to be under the law, to redeem them that were under the law." Now his being "made under the law" to this end, cannot be restrained to his subjection to the curse of the law only, but to the commands of it also. So Rom. 5: 19. "As by one man's disobedience, many were made sinners; so by the obedience of one, shall many be made righteous." It were a manifest injury to this text also, to restrain it to the passive obedience of Christ only. To be short, this twofold obedience of Christ, stands opposed to a twofold obligation that fallen man is under; the one to do what God requires, the other to suffer what he has threatened for disobedience. We owe him active obedience as his creatures, and passive obedience as his prisoners. Suitably to his double obligation, Christ comes under the commandment of the law, to fulfil it actively, Matth. 3: 15. and under the malediction of the law, to satisfy it passively. And whereas it is objected by some, if he fulfilled the whole law for us by his active, what need then of his passive obedience? We reply, great need; because both these make up that one, entire, and complete obedience, by which God is satisfied, and we justified. It is a good rule of Alsted, *obedientia Christi est una copulativa*; the whole obedience of Christ, both active and passive, make up one entire perfect obedience; and therefore there is no reason why one particle, either of the one, or of the other, should be excluded.

    5. The effect and fruit of this his satisfaction, is our freedom, ransom, or deliverance from the wrath and curse due to us for our sins. Such was the dignity, value, and completeness of Christ's satisfactions, that in strict justice it merited our redemption and full deliverance; not only a possibility that we might be redeemed and pardoned, but a right whereby to be so, as the learned Dr. Twiss judiciously argues. If he be made a curse for us, we must then be redeemed from the curse, according to justice; so the apostle argues, Rom. 3: 25, 56. "Whom God has set forth to be a propitiation, through faith in his blood, to declare his righteousness for the remission of sins that are past, through the forbearance of God; to declare, I say, at this time, his righteousness, that God might be just, and the justifier of him that believeth in Jesus." Mark the design and end of God in exacting satisfaction from Christ, it was to declare his righteousness in the remission of sin to believers; and lest we should lose the emphatical word, he doubles it, to declare, I say, his righteousness. Every one can see how his mercy is declared in remission: but he would have us take notice, that his justification of believers is an act of justice; and that God, as he is a just God, cannot condemn the believer, since Christ has satisfied his debts. This attribute seems to be the main bar against remission; but now it is become the very ground and reason why God remits. O how comfortable a text is this! Doth Satan or conscience set forth thy sin in all its discouraging circumstances and aggravations? God has set forth Christ to be a propitiation. Must justice be manifested, satisfied and glorified? So it is in the death of Christ, ten thousand times more than ever it could in thy damnation. Thus you have a brief account of the satisfaction made by Jesus Christ.

    Secondly, We shall gather up all that has been said to establish the truth of Christ's satisfaction; proving the reality of it, that it is not an improper, catachrestical, fictitious satisfaction, by divine acceptiltation, as some have very diminutively called it; but real, proper, and full, and as such accepted by God. For his blood is the stood of a Surety, Heb. 7: 22. who came under the same obligations of the law with us, Gal. 4: 4. and though he had no sin of his own, yet standing before God as our Surety, the iniquities of us all were laid upon him, Isa. 53: 6. and from him did the Lord, with great severity, exact satisfaction for our sins, Rom. 8: 32. punish them upon his soul, Matth. 27: 46. and upon his body, Acts 2: 23. and with this obedience of his Son, is fully pleased and satisfied, Eph. 5: 2. and has in token thereof raised him from the dead, and set him at his own right hand, 1 Tim. 3: 16. and for his righteousness-sake acquitted and discharged believers, who shall never more come into condemnation, Rom. 8: 1, 34. All this is plain in scripture; and our faith in the satisfaction of Christ, is not built on the wisdom of man, but the everlasting sealed truth of God: yet such is the perverse nature of man, and the pride of his heart, that whilst he should be humbly adoring the grace of God, in providing such a Surety for us, he is found accusing the justice, and diminishing the mercy of God, and raising all the objections which Satan and his own heart can invent, to overturn that blessed foundation upon which God has built up his own honour, and his people's salvation.

Thirdly, In the next place, therefore, we shall reject those doctrines, and remove the principal of those objections that are found militating against the satisfaction of Christ.

And, in the first place, we reject with deep abhorrence that doctrine, which ascribes to man any power, in whole, or in part, to satisfy God for his own, or other men's sins. This, no mere creature can do by active obedience, were it so complete that he could never sin in thought, word, or deed, any more, but live the most holy life that ever any lived: for all this would be no more than his duty as a creature, Luke 17: 10. and so can be no satisfaction for what he is by nature, or has done against God as a sinner. Nor yet by suffering; for we have offended an infinite God, and can never satisfy him by our finite sufferings.

We also, with like detestation, reject that doctrine which makes the satisfaction of Christ either impossible, or fictitious, and inconsistent with grace, in the free pardon of sin. Many are the cavils raised against Christ's satisfaction; the principal are such as these that follow:

Object. The doctrine of Christ's satisfaction is absurd, for Christ (say we) is God; if so then, God satisfied himself, than which what can be more absurd to imagine?

Sol. I answer, God cannot properly be said to satisfy himself for that would be the same thing as to pardon, simply, without any satisfaction. But there is a twofold consideration of Christ; one in respect of his Essence and Divine Nature, in which sense he is the object both of the offence, and of the satisfaction made for it. Another in respect of his person and economy, or office; in which sense he properly satisfies God, being in respect of his manhood another, and inferior to God, John 14: 28. The blood of the man Christ Jesus is the matter of the satisfaction, the Divine Nature dignifies it, and makes it of infinite value. A certain family had committed treason against the king, and are all under the condemnation of the law for it' the king's son moved with pity and love, resolves to satisfy the law, and yet save the family; in order whereunto he marries a daughter of the family, whereby her blood becomes royal blood, and worth the blood of the whole family whence she sprang; this princess is by her husband executed in the room of the rest. In this case the king satisfies not himself for the wrong, but is satisfied by the death of another, equivalent in worth to the blood of them all. This similitude answers not to all the particulars, as indeed nothing in nature does, or can; but it only shows what it was that satisfied God, and how it became so satisfactory.

Object. If Christ satisfied by paying our debt, then he should have endured eternal torments; for so we should, and the damned shall.

Sol. We must distinguish betwixt what is essential, and what is accidental in punishment. The primary intent of the law is reparation and satisfaction; he that can make it at one entire payment (as Christ could and did) ought to be discharged. He that cannot (as no mere creature can) ought to lie for ever, as the damned do, under sufferings.

Object. If God will be satisfied for our sins before he pardon them, how then is pardon an act of grace.

Sol. Pardon could not be an act of pure grace, if God received satisfaction from us; but if he pardon us upon the satisfaction received from Christ, though it be of debt to him, it is of grace to us: for it was grace to admit a Surety to satisfy, more grace to provide him, and most of all to apply his satisfaction to us, by uniting us to Christ, as he has done.

Object. But God loved us before Christ died for us; for it was the love of God to the world that moved him to give his only-begotten Son. Could God love us, and yet not be reconciled and satisfied?

Sol. God's complacent love is indeed inconsistent with an unreconciled state: He is reconciled to every one he so loves. But his benevolent love, consisting in his purpose of good, may be before actual reconciliation and satisfaction.

Object. Temporal death, as well as eternal, is a part of the curse, if Christ have fully satisfied by bearing the curse for us, how is it, that those for whom he bare it, die as well as others?

Sol. As temporal death is a penal evil, and part of the curse, so God inflicts it not upon believers; but they must die for other ends, viz. to be made perfectly happy in a more full and immediate enjoyment of God, than they can have in the body: and so, death is theirs by way of privilege, 1 Cor. 3: 22. They are not death's by way of punishment. The same may be said of all the afflictions with which God, for gracious ends, now exercises his reconciled ones. Thus much may suffice to establish this great truth.

Inference 1. If the death of Christ was that which satisfied God for all the sins of the elect, then certainly there is an infinite evil in sin, since it cannot be expiated but by an infinite satisfaction. Fools make a mock at sin, and there are but few souls in the world that are duly sensible of, and affected with its evil; but certainly, if God should damn thee to all eternity, thy eternal sufferings could not satisfy for the evil that is in one vain thought. It may be you may think this is harsh and severe, that God should hold his creatures under everlasting sufferings for sin, and never be satisfied with them any more. But when you have well considered, that the object against whom you sin, is the infinite blessed God, which derives an infinite evil to the sin committed against him; and when you consider how God dealt with the angels that fell, for one sin, and that but of the mind; (for having no bodily organs, they could commit nothing externally against God:) you will alter your minds about it. O the depth of the evil of sin! If ever you will see how great and horrid an evil sin is, measure it in your thoughts, either by the infinite holiness and excellency of God, who is wronged by it; or by the infinite sufferings of Christ, who died to satisfy for it; and then you will have deeper apprehensions of the evil of sin.

Inf. 2. If the death of Christ satisfied God, and thereby redeemed the elect from the curse: then the redemption of souls is costly; souls are dear things, and of great value with God. "Ye know, (says the apostle,) that ye were not redeemed with corruptible things, as silver and gold, from your vain conversation, received by tradition; but with the precious blood of the Son of God, as of a lamb without spot," 1 Pet. 1: 18, 19. Only the blood of God is found an equivalent price for the redemption of souls. Gold and silver may redeem from Turkish, but not from hellish bondage. The whole creation sold to the utmost worth of it, is not a value for the redemption of one soul. Souls are very dear; he that paid for them found them so: yet how cheaply do sinners sell their souls, as if they were but low priced commodities! but you that sell your souls cheap, will buy repentance dear.

Inf. 3. If Christ's death satisfied God for our sins, how unparalleled is the love of Christ to poor sinners! It is much to pay a pecuniary debt to free another, but who will pay his own blood for another? We have a noted instance of Zaleucus, that famous Locrensian lawgiver, who decreed, that whoever was convicted of adultery, should have both his eyes put out. It so fell out that his own son was brought before him for that crime: hereupon the people interposing, made suit for his pardon. At length the father, partly overcome by their importunities, and not unwilling to show what lawful favour he might to his son, he first put out one of his own eyes, and then one of his son's; and so shewed himself both a merciful father, and a just lawgiver; so tempering mercy with justice, that both the law was satisfied, and his son spared. This is written by the historian as an instance of singular love in his father, to pay one half of the penalty for his son. But Christ did not divide, and share in the penalty with us, but bare it all. Zaleucus did it for his son, who was dear to him; Christ did it for enemies, that were fighting and rebelling against him: Rom. 5: 8. "While we were yet sinners, Christ died for us." "O would to God (said a holy one) I could cause paper and ink to speak the worth and excellency, the high and loud praises of our brother ransomer! O the ransomer needs not my report; but O if he would take it, and make use of it! I should be happy if I had an errand to this world but for some few years, to spread proclamations, and out-cries, and love-letters of the highness [the highness evermore] of the ransomer, whose clothes were wet, and dyed in blood; howbeit, that after that, my soul and body should go back to their mother nothing."

Inf. 4. If Christ by dying, has made full satisfaction, then God is no loser in pardoning the greatest of sinners that believe in Jesus; and consequently his justice can be no bar to their justification and salvation. He is just to forgive us our sins, 1 John 1: 9. What an argument is here for a poor believer to plead with God! Lord, if thou save me by Jesus Christ, thy justice will be fully satisfied at one full payment; but if thou damn me, and require satisfaction at my hands, thou canst never receive it: I shall make but a dribbling payment, though I lie in hell to eternity, and shall still be infinitely behind with thee. Is it not more for thy glory to receive it from Christ's hand, than to require it at mine? One drop of his blood is more worth than all my polluted blood. O how satisfying a thing is this to the conscience of a poor sinner that is objecting the multitude, aggravations, and amazing circumstances, of his sins, against the possibility of their being pardoned! Can such a sinner as I be forgiven? Yes, if thou believest in Jesus, thou mayest; for so God will lose nothing in pardoning the greatest transgressors: "Let Israel hope in the Lord; for with the Lord there is mercy, and with him is plenteous redemption," Psal. 130: 7. i.e. a large stock of merit lying by him in the blood of Christ, to pay him for all that you have done against him.

Inf 5. Lastly, If Christ has made such a full satisfaction as you have heard, How much is it the concernment of every soul to abandon all thoughts of satisfying God for his own sins and retake himself to the blood of Christ, the ransomer, by faith, that in that blood they may be pardoned? It would grieve one's heart to see how many poor creatures are drudging and tugging at a task of repentance, and revenge upon themselves, and reformation, and obedience, to satisfy God for what they have done against him: And alas! it cannot be, they do but lose their labour, could they swelter their very hearts out, weep till they can weep no more, cry till their throats be parched, alas, they can never recompence God for one vain thought; for such is the severity of the law, that when it is once offended, it will never be made amends again by all that we can do: it will not discharge the sinner, for all the sorrow in the world. Indeed, if a man be in Christ, sorrow for sin is something, and renewed obedience is something; God looks upon them favourably, and accepts them graciously in Christ: but out of him they signify no more than the intreaties and cries of a condemned malefactor, to reverse the legal sentence of the judge. You may toil all the days of your life, and at night go to bed without a candle. To that sense that scripture sounds, Isa. 1. 11. "Behold, all ye that kindle a fire, that compass yourselves about with sparks; walk in the light of your fire, and in the sparks that you have kindled: This shall ye have of mine hand, ye shall lie down in sorrow." By fire, and the light of it, some understand the sparkling pleasures of this life, and the sensitive joys of the creatures: but generally it is taken for our own natural righteousness, and all acts of duties, in order to our justification by them before God. And so it stands opposed to that faith of recumbence spoken of in the verse before. By their compassing themselves about with these sparks, understand their dependence on these their duties, and glorying in them. But see the fatal issue, Ye shall lie down in sorrow, that shall be your recompence from the hand of the Lord that is all the thanks and reward you must expect from him, for slighting Christ's, and preferring your own righteousness before his. Reader, be convinced, that one act of faith in the Lord Jesus pleases God more than all the obedience, repentance, and strivings to obey the law, through thy whole life, can do. And thus you have the first special fruits of Christ's priesthood, in the full satisfaction of God, for all the sins of believers.

Sermon 15: Of the blessed Inheritance purchased by the Oblation of Christ, being the second Effect or Fruit of his Priesthood

Gal. 4: 4, 5.

But when the fulness of the time was come, God sent forth his Son, made of a woman, made under the law, To redeem them that were under the law, that we might receive the adoption of sons.

This scripture gives us an account of a double fruit of Christ's death, viz. the payment of our debt, and the purchase of our inheritance.

1. The payment of our debt, expressed by our redemption, or buying us out from the obligation and curse of the law, which has been discoursed in the last exercise.

2. The purchase of an inheritance for those redeemed ones, expressed here by their receiving the adoption of sons, which is to be our present subject. Adoption is either civil, or divine. Of the first, the civil law gives this definition: that it is,

"A lawful act, an imitation of nature, invented for the comfort of them that have no children of their own. Divine adoption is that special benefit whereby God, for Christ's sake, accepteth us as sons, and makes us heirs of eternal life with him."

Betwixt this civil and sacred adoption, there is a twofold agreement, and disagreement. They agree in this, that both flow from the pleasure and good-will of the adoptant; and in this, that both confer a right to privileges, which we have not by nature: but in this they differ, one is an act imitating nature, the other transcends nature; the one was found out for the comfort of them that had no children; the other for the comfort of them that had no father. This divine adoption is, in scripture, either taken properly for that act or sentence of God, by which we are made sons, or for the privileges with which the adopted are invested: and so it is taken Rom. 8: 23, and in this scripture now before us. We lost our inheritance by the fall of Adam; we receive it, as the text speaks, by the death of Christ, which restores it again to us by a new and better title. The doctrine hence, is this,

Doct. That the death of Jesus Christ has not only satisfied for our debts, but over and above purchased a rich inheritance for the children of God.

"For this end, or cause, he is the Mediator of the New Testament; that, by means of death, for the redemption of the transgressions that were under the first Testament, they which are called, might receive the promise of the eternal inheritance," Heb. 9: 15.

We will here, First, See what Christ paid. Secondly, What he purchased. Thirdly, For whom.

First, that Christ paid. Our divines comprise the virtue and fruits of the priesthood of Christ in these two things, viz. Solutio debiti, et acquisitio haereditatis, payment and purchase. Answerable, the obedience of Christ has a double relation, relatio legalis justitiae, the relation of a legal righteousness; and adequate and exactly proportioned price. And it has also in it ratio superlegalis meriti, the relation of a merit over and beyond the law.

To object (as some do) "the satisfaction of Christ was more than sufficient", according to our doctrine, "and therefore could not be intended, for the payment of our debt," is a senseless cavil. For surely, if Christ paid more than was owing, he must needs pay all that was owing to Divine Justice. And truly it is but a bad requital of the love of Jesus Christ, who, beside the payment of what he owed, would manifest his bounty by the redundancy of his merit, which he paid to God to purchase a blessed inheritance for us. This over plus of satisfaction (which was the price of that inheritance I am now to open) is not obscurely hinted, but plainly expressed twice in Rom. 5: 15. "But not as the offence, so also is the free gift: for if through the offence of one many be dead, pollo mallon', much more the grace of God, and the gift of grace, which is by one man, Jesus Christ, eperisseuse'" has abounded or flowed abundantly unto many." So ver. 17. "For if by one man's offence, death reigned by one, pollo mallon', much more they which receive ten perissean', the overflowing, or abundance of grace, and of the gift of righteousness, shall reign in life by one, Jesus Christ." In both which places Christ and Adam are compared as the two roots or common heads of mankind, both agreeing in this property of communicating their conditions to those that are theirs; yet there is a great deal of difference betwixt them! for in Christ the power is all divine, and therefore infinitely more active and effectual: He communicates abundantly more to his, than they lost in Adam; so that his blood is not only sufficient to redeem all those that are actually redeemed by it, but even the whole world also. And were there so many worlds of men as there are men in the world, it would be sufficient for them also; and yet still there would be an over plus of value: for all those worlds of men would rise but to a finite bulk; but this blood is infinite in its worth and dignity. Since then there is not a whole world, no not half, but the far less part redeemed by the blood of Christ, which was sufficient for so many; great must be the surplusage and redundancy of merit? Here our divines rightly distinguish betwixt the substance and accidents of Christ's death and obedience. Consider Christ's suffering, as to the substance of it, it was no more than what the law required; for, neither the justice, nor love of the Father would permit that Christ should suffer more than what was necessary for him to bear, as our Surety; but, as to the circumstances, the person of the sufferer, the cause and efficacy of his sufferings, &c. it was much more than sufficient: a superlegale meritum, a merit above and beyond what the law required; for, though the law required the death of the sinner, who is but a poor contemptible creature, it did not require that one, perfectly innocent, should die, it did not require that God should shed his blood: it did not require blood of such value and worth as this was. I say, none of this the law required, though God was pleased, for the advancement and manifestation of his justice and mercy in the highest, to admit, and order this, by way of commutation, admitting him to be our antipsuchos', or ransomer, by dying for us. And, in(teed, it was a most gracious relaxation of the law, that admitted of such a commutation as this; for hereby it comes to pass, that justice is fully satisfied, and yet we live and are saved; which, before, was a thing that could not be imagined. Yea, now we are not only redeemed from wrath, by the adequate compensation made for our sins by Christ's blood and sufferings, substantially considered; but entitled to a most glorious inheritance, purchased by his blood, considered as the blood or an innocent, as the blood of God, and therefore as most excellent and efficacious blood, above what the law demanded. And this is the meaning of Athanasius, when he saith, "That Christ recompensed, or made amends for small things with great:" he means not, that sin, considered absolutely, and in itself, is small, O no, but compared with Christ's blood, and the infinite excellency and worth of it, it is so. And Chrysostom, to the same purpose, "Christ paid much more (saith he) than he owed and so much more, as the immense ocean is more than a small drop." So that it was rightly determined by holy Anselm: "No man (saith he) can pay to God what he owes him; Christ only paid more than he owed him." By this you see, how rich a treasure lies in Christ, to bestow in a purchase for us, above what he paid to redeem us; even as much as his soul and body were more worth than ours, for whom it was sacrificed; which is so great a sum, that all the angels in heaven, and men on earth, can never compute and sum up, so as to show us the total of it. And this was that inexhaustible treasure that Christ expended, to procure and purchase the fairest inheritance for believers. Having seen the treasure that purchased, let us next enquire into the inheritance purchased by it.

    Secondly, This inheritance is so large, that it cannot be surveyed by creatures: nor can the boundaries and limits thereof be described, for it comprehends all things; 1 Cor. 3: 22. "All is yours, ye are Christ's, and Christ is God's." Rev. 21: 7. "He that overcomes shall inherit all things". And yet I do not think, or say, that Dominium fundatur in gratia, that temporal dominion is founded in grace: no, that is at the cast and disposal of Providence. But Christ, by his death, has restored a right to all things to his people.

    But, to be more particular, I shall distribute the saints inheritance, purchased by Christ, into three heads; all temporal good things, all spiritual good things, and all eternal good things are theirs.

    1. All temporal good things. 1 Tim. 6: 7. "He hath given us all things richly to enjoy". Not that they have the possession, but the comfort and benefit of all things: others have the sting, gall, wormwood, baits and snares of the creature; saints only have the blessing and comfort of it. So that this little that a righteous man has, is (in this among other respects) better than the treasures of many wicked: which is the true key to open that dark saying of the apostle, 2 Cor. 6: 10. "As having nothing, and yet possessing all things." They only possess, others are possessed by the world. The saints utuntur mundi, et fruuntur Deo, "use the world, and enjoy God" in the use of it. Others are deceived, defiled, and destroyed by the world; but these are refreshed and furthered by it.

    2. All spiritual good things are purchased by the blood of Christ for them; as Justification, which comprises remission of sins and acceptance of our persons by God: Rom. 3: 24. "Being justified freely by his grace, through the redemption that is in Christ." Sanctification is also purchased for them; yea, both initial and progressive sanctification: for of "God, he is made unto us,

not only wisdom and righteousness, but sanctification also," 1 Cor. 1: 30. These two, viz. our justification and sanctification, are two of the most rich and shining robes in the wardrobe of free grace. How glorious and lovely do they render the soul that wears them! These are like the bracelets, and jewels Isaac sent to Rebecca. Adoption into the family of God is purchased for us by his blood; "For ye are all the children of God by faith in Jesus Christ," Gal. 3: 26. Christ, as he is the Son, is haeres natus,, "the heir by nature;" as he is Mediator, he is haeres constitutus, "the heir by appointment," appointed heir of all things, as it is, Heb. 1: 2. By the Sonship of Christ, we being united to him by faith, become sons; and if sons, then heirs. "O what manner of love is this, that we should be called the sons of God", 1 John 3: 1. That a poor beggar should be made an heir, yea, an heir of God, and joint heir with Christ! Yea, that very faith, which is the bond of union, and consequently, the ground of all our communion with Christ, is the purchase of his blood also: 2 Pet. 1: 1. "To them that have "obtained like precious faith with us, through the righteousness of God and our Saviour Jesus Christ." This most precious grace is the dear purchase of our Lord Jesus Christ; yea, all that peace, joy, and spiritual comfort, which are sweet fruits of faith, are with it purchased for us by this blood.

So speaks the apostle in Rom. 5: 1, 2, 3. "Being justified by faith, we have peace with God, through our Lord Jesus Christ," &c. Moreover the Spirit himself, who is the author, fountain, and spring of all graces and comforts, is procured for us by his death and resurrection: Gal. 3: 13, 14. "Christ has redeemed us from the curse of the law, being made a curse for us; for it is written, cursed is every one that hangeth on a tree: that the blessing of Abraham might come upon the Gentiles through Jesus Christ, that we might receive the promise of the Spirit through faith." That Spirit that first sanctified, and since has so often sealed, comforted, directed, resolved, guided, and quickened your souls, had not come to perform any of these blessed offices upon your hearts, if Christ had not died.

3. All eternal good things are the purchase of his blood. Heaven, and all the glory thereof is purchased for you that are believers, with this price. Hence that glory, whatever it be, is called "an inheritance incorruptible, undefiled, and that fadeth not away, reserved in heaven for you": To the lively hope whereof you are begotten again, "by the resurrection of Christ from the dead," 1 Pet. 1: 3, 4. Not only present mercies are purchased for us, but things to come also, as it is, 1 Cor. 3: 22. Man is a prudent and prospecting creature, and is not satisfied that it is well with him for the present, unless he have some assurance it shall be well with him for time to come. His mind is taken up about what shall be hereafter; and from the good or evil things to come, he raiseth up to himself vast hopes or fears.

Therefore to complete our happiness, and fill up the uttermost capacity of our souls, all the good of eternity is put into the account and inventory of the saints estate and inheritance. This happiness is ineffably; it is usually distinguished into what is essential, and what is accessory to it. The essentials of it, as far as we in our embodied state can conceive, is either the objective, subjective, or formal happiness to be enjoyed in heaven.

The objective happiness is God himself, Psal. 73: 25. "Whom have I in heaven but thee?" If it could be supposed (saith one) that God should withdraw from the saints in heaven, and say, Take heaven, and divide it among you; but as for me, I will withdraw from you; the saints would fall a weeping in heaven, and say, Lord, take heaven, and give it to whom thou wilt; it is no heaven to us, except thou be there: Heaven would be very Bochim to the saints without God. In this, our glory in heaven consists, to be ever with the Lord, 1 Thess. 4: 17. God himself is the chief part of a saint's inheritance, in which sense, as some will understand, Rom. 8: 1. they are called heirs of God.

The subjective glory and happiness is the attemperation and suiting of the soul and body to God. This is begun in sanctification, and perfected in glorification. It consists in removing from both all that is indecent, and inconsistent with a state of such complete glory and happiness, and in superinducting and clothing it with all heavenly qualities.

The immunities of the body are its freedom from all nature infirmities; which as they come in, so they go out with sin. Thenceforth there shall be no diseases, deformities, pains, flaws, monstrosities; their good physician death has cured all this, and their vile bodies shall be made like unto Christ's glorious body, Phil. 3: 21. and be made a spiritual body, 1 Cor. 15: 44. For agility, like the chariots of Aminadab; for beauty, as the top of Lebanon; for incorruptibility, as if they were pure spirits.

The soul also is discharged and freed from all darkness and ignorance of mind, being now able to discern all truths in God, that crystal ocean of truth. The leaks of the memory stopt for ever; the roving of the fancy perfectly cured; the stubbornness and reluctance of the will for ever subdued, and retained in due and full subjection to God. So that the saints in glory shall be free from all that now troubles them; they shall never sin more nor be once tempted so to do, for no serpent hisses in that paradise; they shall never grieve nor groan more, for God shall wipe away all tears from their eyes. They shall never be troubled more, for God will then recompense tribulation to their troublers, and to them that are troubled, rest; they shall never doubt more, for fruition excludes doubting.

The formal happiness is the fulness of satisfaction resulting from the blessed sight and enjoyment of God, by a soul so attempered to him, Psal. 17: 15. "When I awake I shall be satisfied with thy likeness." This sight of God, in glory, called the beatifical vision, must needs yield ineffable satisfaction to the beholding soul, inasmuch as it will be an intuitive vision. The intellectual or mental eye shall see God, 1 John 3: 2. The corporeal glorified eye shall see Christ, Job 19: 26, 27. What a ravishing vision will this be! and how much will it exceed all reports and apprehensions we had here of it! Surely one half was not told us. It will be a transformative vision, it will change the beholder into its own image and likeness. "We shall be like him, for we shall see him as he is," 1 John 3: 2. As iron put into the fire, becomes all fiery; so the soul, by conversing with God, is changed into his very similitude. It will be an appropriative vision; "Whom I shall see for myself," Job 19: 26, 27. In heaven interest is clear and undoubted, fear is cast out: no need of marks and signs there; for what a man sees and enjoys, how can he doubt of? It will be a ravishing vision; these we have by faith are so, how much more those in glory? How was Paul transported, when he was in a visional way wrapt up into the third heaven, and heard the unutterable things, though he was not admitted into the blessed society, but was with them, as the angels are in our assemblies, a stander by, a looker-on. If a spark do so inflame, what is it to lie down like a Phoenix in her bed of spices! Like a Salamander to live and move in the fire of love! It will also be an eternal vision; vacabimus et videbimus, (as Augustinus said) we shall then be at leisure for this employment, and have no diversions from it for ever. No evening is mentioned to the seventh day's sabbath; no night in the new Jerusalem. And therefore,

Lastly, It will be a fully satisfying vision: God will then be all in all, Etiam ipsa curiositas satietur, "Curiosity itself will be satisfied." The blessed soul will feel itself blessed, filled, satisfied in every part. Ah, what a happiness is here! to look and love, is drink and sing, and drink again at the fountain head of the highest glory! And if at any time its eye be turned from a direct to a reflex sight upon what it once was, how it was wrought on, how fitted for his glory, how wonderfully distinguished by special grace from them that are howling in flames, whilst himself is shouting aloud upon his bed of everlasting rest; and this will enhance the glory.

And so also will the accessories of this blessedness be; The place where God is enjoyed, the empyrean heaven, the city of God, whither Christ ascended, where the great assembly are met. Paradise and Canaan were but the types of it; more excelling and transcending the royal palaces or earthly princes, than they do a pigeon-hole. The company also with whom he is enjoyed, adds to the glory. A blissful society indeed! store of good neighbours in that city. There we shall have familiar converse with angels, whose appearances now are insupportable by poor mortals. There will be sweet and full closings also betwixt the saints; Luther and Zwinglius are there agreed. Here they could not fully close with one another, and no wonder, for they could not fully close with themselves. But there is perfect harmony and unity; all meeting and closing in God, as lines in the centre. This is a blessed glimpse of your inheritance.

Thirdly, All this is purchased for believers: hence it is called, "the inheritance of the saints in light," Col. 1: 12. "All is yours, for ye are Christ's," that is the tenure, 1 Cor. 3: 23. So Rom. 8: 30. "Whom he did predestinate, them he also called; and whom he called, them he also justified; and whom he justified, them he also glorified." Only those that are sons, are heirs, Rom. 8: 17. The unrighteous shall not inherit, 1 Cor. 6: 9. "It is the Father's good pleasure, to give the kingdom to the little flock," Luke 12: 32.

Inf. 1. Has Christ not only redeemed you from wrath, but purchased such an eternal inheritance also by the overplus of his merit for you? O how well content should believers then be with their lot of providence in this life, be it what it will! Content did I say? I speak too low; overcome, ravished, filled with praises and thanksgivings; how low, how poor, how afflicted soever for the present they are. O let not such things as grumbling, repining, fretting at providence, be found, or once named among the expectants of this inheritance! Suppose you had taken a beggar from your door, and adopted him to be your son, and made him heir of a large inheritance, and after this he should contest and quarrel with you for a trifle; could you bear it? How to work the spirit of a saint into contentment with a low condition here, I have laid down several rules in another discourse, to which, for the present I refer the reader.

Infer. 2. With what weaned affections should the people of God walk up and down this world, content to live, and willing to die? For things present are theirs if they live, and things to come are theirs if they die. Paul expresses himself in a frame of holy indifference, Phil. 1: 23 "Which to chose I know not." Many of them that are now in fruition of their inheritance above, had vitam in patientia, mortem in desiderio, "Life in patience, and death in desire," while they tabernacled with us. "O (cried one) what would I give to have a bed made to my wearied soul in Christ's bosom? " - I cannot tell you what sweet pain and delightful torments are in his love; I often challenge time for holding us asunder; I profess to you, I have no rest till I be over head and ears in love's ocean. If Christ's love (that fountain of delights) were laid open to me as I would wish, O how overcome would this my soul be! I half call his absence cruel; and the mask and vail on his face a cruel covering, that hideth such a fair, fair face from a sick soul. I dare not challenge himself, but his absence is a mountain of iron upon my heavy heart. O when shall we meet! How long is the dawning of the marriage-day! O sweet Lord Jesus, take wide steps! O my Lord, come over mountains at one stride! O my beloved, flee like a roe, or young hart upon the mountains of separation! O if he would fold the heavens together like an old cloak, and shovel time and days out of the way, and make really in haste the Lamb's wife for her husband! Since he looked upon me, my heart is not mine own."

Who can be blamed for desiring to see that fair inheritance which is purchased for him! But, truly, should God hold up the soul by the power of faith, from day to day, to such sights as these, who would be content to live a day more on earth! How should we be ready to pull down the prison walls, and not have patience to wait till God open the door! As the Heathen said, "Victurosque dii celant, ut vivere durent." And truly the wisdom of God is in this specially remarkable, in giving the new creature such an admirable crisis, and even temper, as that scripture, 2 Thess. 3: 5. expresses, "The Lord direct your hearts into the love of God and patient waiting for Christ." Love inflames with desire, patience allays that fervour. So that fervent desires (as one happily expresses it) are allayed with meek submission; mighty love with strong patience. And had not God twisted together these two principles in the Christian's constitution, he had framed a creature to be a torment to itself, to live upon a very rack.

Inf. 3. Hence we infer the impossibility of their salvation that know not Christ, nor have interest in his blood. Neither Athens, nor merely nominal Christians, can inherit heaven. I know some are very indulgent to the Heathen, and many formal Christians are too much so to themselves: but union by faith with Jesus Christ, is the only way revealed in scripture, by which we hope to come to the heavenly inheritance. I know it seems hard, that such brave men, as some of the Heathens were, should be damned: but the scripture knows no other way to glory, but Christ put on, and applied by faith. And it is the common suffrage of modern sound divines, that no man, by the sole conduct of nature, without the knowledge of Christ, can be saved. There is but one way to glory for all the world, John 14: 6. "No man cometh to the Father but by me." Gal. 3: 14. "The blessing of Abraham comes upon the Gentiles through faith." Scripture asserts the impossibility of being or doing, any thing that is truly evangelically good, out of Christ, John 15: 5. "Without me ye can do nothing." And Heb. 11: 6. "Without faith it is impossible to please God."

Scripture every where connects and chains salvation with vocation, Rom. 8: 30. and vocation with the gospel, Rom. 10: 14. To those that plead for the salvation of Heathens, and profane Christians. we may apply that tart rebuke of Bernard, that while some labour to make Plato a Christian, he feared they therein did prove themselves to be Heathens.

Inf. 4. How greatly are we all concerned to clear up our title to the heavenly inheritance! It is horrible to see how industrious many are for an inheritance on earth, and how careless for heaven. By which we may plainly see how vilely the noble soul is depressed by sin, and sunk down into flesh, minding only the concernments of the flesh. Hear me, ye that labour for the world, as if heaven were in it; what will ye do when at death you shall look back over your shoulder, and see what you have spent your time and strength for, shrinking and vanishing away from you? When you shall look forward, and see vast eternity opening its mouth to swallow you up; O then what would you give for a well-grounded assurance of an eternal inheritance!

O, therefore if you have any concernment for your poor souls; if it be not indifferent to you what becomes of them, whether they be saved, or whether they be damned, "give all diligence to make your calling and election sure," 2 Pet. 1: 10. "Work out your own salvation with fear and trembling; for it is God that worketh in you both to will and to do of his own good pleasure," Phil. 2: 12. Remember it is salvation you work for, and that is no trifle. Remember, it is your own salvation, and not another's. It is for thy poor soul that thou art striving; and what hast thou more?

Remember, now God offers you his helping hand; now the Spirit waits upon you in the means, but of the continuance thereof you have no assurance; for it is of his own good pleasure, and not at yours. To your work, souls, to your work. Ah, strive as men that know what an inheritance in heaven is worth.

And, as for you that have solid evidence that it is yours; O, that with hands and eyes lifted up to heaven, you would adore that free grace, that has entitled a child of wrath to a heavenly inheritance! Walk as becomes heirs of God, and joint heirs with Christ. Be often looking heavenward when wants pinch here. O look to that fair estate you have reserved in heaven for you, and say, I am hastening home; and when I come thither, all my grants shall be supplied. Consider what it cost Christ to purchase it for thee; and with a deep sense of what he has laid out for thee, let thy soul say,

Blessed be God for Jesus Christ.

Sermon 16: Of the Kingly Office of Christ, as it is executed spiritually upon the Souls of the Redeemed

2 Cor. 10: 5.
Casting down imaginations, and every high thing that exalteth itself against the knowledge of God, and bringing into captivity every thought to the obedience of Christ.

We now come to the Regal office, by which our glorious Mediator executes and dischargeth the undertaken design of our redemption. Had he not, as our Prophet, opened the way of life and salvation to the children of men, they could never have known it; and if they had clearly known it, except, as their Priest, he had offered up himself, to impetrate and obtain redemption for them, they could not have been redeemed virtually by his blood; and if they had been so redeemed, yet had he not lived in the capacity of a King, to apply this purchase of his blood to them, they would have had no actual, personal benefit by his death; for what he revealed as a Prophet, he purchased as a Priest; and what he so revealed and purchased as a Prophet and Priest, he applies as a King: first subduing the souls of his elect to his spiritual government; then ruling them as his subjects, and ordering all things in the kingdom of Providence for their good. So that Christ has a twofold kingdom, the one spiritual and internal, by which he subdues and rules the hearts of his people; the other providential and external, whereby he guides, rules, and orders all things in the world, in a blessed subordination to their eternal salvation. I am to speak from this text of his spiritual and internal kingdom.

These words are considered two ways, either relatively or absolutely. Considered relatively, they are a vindication of the apostle from the unjust censures of the Corinthians, who very unworthily, interpreted his gentleness, condescension, and winning affability, to be no better than a fawning upon them for self-ends; and the authority he exercised, no better than pride and imperiousness. But hereby he lets them know, that as Christ needs not, so he never used such carnal artifices: The weapons of our warfare (saith he) are not carnal, but mighty, through God, &c.

Absolutely considered, they hold forth the efficacy of the gospel, in the plainness and simplicity of it, for the subduing of rebellious sinners to Christ: and in them we have these three things to consider,

1. The oppositions made by sinners against the assaults of the gospel, viz. imaginations, or reasonings, as the word "logismous" may be fitly rendered. He means the subtleties, slights, excuses, subterfuges, and arguing of fleshly-minded men; in which they fortify and entrench themselves against the convictions of the word: yea, and there are not only such carnal seasonings, but many proud, high conceits with which poor creatures swell, and scorn to submit to the abasing, humble, self denying way of the gospel. These are the fortifications erected against Christ by the carnal mind.

2. We have here the conquest which the gospel obtains over sinners, thus fortified against it; it casts down and overthrows, and takes in these strong holds. Thus Christ spoils Satan of his armour in which he trusted, by shewing the sinner that all this can be no defence to his soul against the wrath of God. But that is not all: in the next place,

3. You have here the improvement of the victory. Christ does not only lead away these enemies spoiled, but brings them into obedience to himself, i.e. makes them, after conversion, subjects of his own kingdom, obedient, useful, and serviceable to himself; and so is more than a conqueror. They do not only lay down their arms, and fight no more against Christ with them; but repair to his camp, and fight for Christ, with those reasons of theirs that were before employed against him: as it is said of Jerome, Origin, and Tertullian, that they came into Canaan, laden with Egyptian gold; i.e. they came into the church full of excellent learning and abilities, with which they eminently served Jesus Christ. "O blessed victory, where the conqueror, and conquered, both triumph together!" And thus enemies and rebels are subdued, and made subjects of the spiritual kingdom of Christ. Hence the doctrinal note is,

Doct. That Jesus Christ exercises a Kingly power over the souls of all whom the gospel subdues to his obedience.

No sooner were the Colossians delivered out of the power of darkness, but they were immediately translated into the kingdom of Christ, the dear Son, Col. 1: 13.

This kingdom of Christ, which is our present subject, is the internal spiritual kingdom, which is said to be within the saints, Luke 17: 20, 21. "The kingdom of God is within you." Christ sits as an enthroned king in the hearts, consciences, and affections of his willing people, Psal. 110: 3. And his kingdom consists in "righteousness, peace, and joy in the Holy Ghost," Rom. 14: 17. and it is properly monarchical, as appears in the margin.

In the prosecution of this point, I will speak doctrinally to these three heads.

First, How Christ obtains the throne in the hearts of men.

Secondly, How he rules in it, and by what acts he exercises his kingly authority.

Thirdly, What are the privileges of those souls over whom Christ reigns. And then apply it.

First, We will open the war and manner in which Christ obtains a throne in the hearts of men, and that is by conquest: for though the souls of the elect are his by donation, and right of redemption; the Father gave them to him, and he died for them; yet Satan has the first possession: and so it fares with Christ, as it did with Abraham, to whom God gave the land of Canaan by promise and covenant, but the Canaanites, Perizites, and sons of Anak, had the actual possession of it, and Abraham's posterity must fight for it, and win it by inches, before they enjoy it. The house is conveyed to Christ by him that built it, but the strong man armed keeps the possession of it, till a stronger than he comes and ejects him, Luke 11: 20, 21, 22. Christ must fight his way into the soul, though he have a right to enter, as into his dearly purchased possession. And so he does; for when the time of recovering them is come, he sends forth his armies to subdue them; as it is Psal. 110: 3. "Thy people shall be willing in the day of thy power." The Hebrew may as fitly be rendered, and so is by some, "in the day of thine armies;" when the Lord Jesus sent forth his armies of prophets, apostles, evangelists, pastors, teachers, under the conduct of his Spirit, armed with that two edged sword, the word of God, which is sharp and powerful, Heb. 4: 12. But that is not all: he causes armies of convictions, and spiritual troubles, to begird and straiten them on every side, so that they know not what to do. These convictions, like a shower of arrows, strike, point blank, into their consciences; Acts 2: 37. "When they heard this, they were pricked to the heart, and said, Men and brethren, what shall we do?" Christ's arrows are sharp in the hearts of his enemies, whereby the people fall under him, Psal. 45: 5, 6. By these convictions he batters down all their loose vain hopes, and levels them with the earth.

Now all their weak pleas and defences, from the general mercy of God, the example of others, &c. prove but as paper walls to them. These shake their hearts, even to the very foundation, and overturn every high thought there, that exalts itself against the Lord. This day, in which Christ sits down before the soul, and summons it by such messengers as these, is a day of distress within: yea, such a day of trouble, that none is like it. But though it be so, yet Satan has so deeply entrenched himself in the mind and will, that the soul yields not at the first summons, till its provisions within are spent, and all its towers of pride, and walls of vain confidence, be undermined by the gospel, and shaken down about its ears: and then the soul desires a parley with Christ. O now it would be glad of terms, any terms, if it may but save its life: let all go as a prey to the conqueror. Now it sends many such messengers as these to Christ, who is come now to the very gates of the soul; mercy, Lord, mercy, O were I but assured thou wouldest receive, spare, and pardon me, I would open to thee the next moment! Thus the soul is shut up to the faith of a Christ, as it is, Gal. 3: 23. and reduced now to the greatest strait and loss imaginable; and now the merciful King, whose only design is to conquer the heart, hangs forth the white flag of mercy before the soul, giving it hopes it shall be spared, pitied, and pardoned, though so long in rebellion against him, if yet it will yield itself to Christ. Many staggering, hesitations, irresolutions, doubts, fears, scruples, half-resolves, reasonings for and against, there are at the council table of man's own heart, at this time. Sometimes there is no hope; Christ will slay me, if I go forth to him, and then it trembles. But then, who ever found him so that tried him? Other souls have yielded, and found mercy beyond all their expectations. O but I have been a desperate enemy against him. Admit it, yet thou hast the word of a King for it; "Let the wicked forsake his way, and the unrighteous man his thoughts; and let him turn to the Lord, and he will have mercy on him; and to our God, for he will abundantly pardon him", Isa. 55: 7.

But the time of mercy is past, I have stood out too long: yet if it were so, how is it that Christ has not made short sock, and cut me off? set fire, hell fire to my soul, and withdrawn the siege? Still he waiteth that he may be gracious, and is exalted that he may have compassion. A thousand such debates there are, till, at last, the soul considering, if it abide in rebellion, it must needs perish; if it go forth to Christ, it can but perish: and being somewhat encouraged by the messages of grace sent into the soul, at this time, such as in Heb. 8: 25. "Wherefore he is able to save to the uttermost, all that come unto God by him;" and, John 6: 37. "He that cometh to me, I will in nowise cast out;" and in Matt. 11: 28. "Come unto me all ye that labour, and are heavy laden and I will give you rest." It is, at last, resolved to open to Christ; and saith, "Stand open ye everlasting gates, and be ye opened ye everlasting doors, and the King of glory shall come in." Now, the will spontaneously opens to Christ: that royal fort submits and yields; all the affections open to him. The will brings Christ the keys of all the rooms in the soul. Concerning the triumphant entrance of Christ into the soul, we may say, as the Psalmist rhetorically speaks concerning the triumphant entrance of Israel into Canaan, Psal. 114: 5, 6. "The mountains skipped like rams, and the little hills like lambs; what aileth thee, O thou sea, that thou fleddest? Thou Jordan, that thou wast driven back?" So here, in a like rhetorical triumph, we may say, the mountains and hills skipped like rams, and the fixed and obstinate will, starts from its own basis and centre; the rocky heart rends in twain. A poor soul comes into the word, full of ignorance, pride, self-love, desperate hardness, and fixed resolutions to go on in its way: and, by an hour's discourse, the tide turns, Jordan is driven back. What aileth thee, thou stout will, that thou surrenderest to Christ! thou hard heart, that thou relents, and the waters gush out? And thus the soul is won to Christ; he writes down his terms, and the soul willingly subscribes them. Thus it comes in to Christ by free and hearty submission, desiring nothing more than to come under the government of Christ, for the time to come.

Secondly, Let us see how Christ rules in the souls of such as submit to him. And there are six things in which he exerts his kingly authority over them.

1. He imposes a new law upon them, and enjoins them to be severe and punctual in their obedience to it. The soul was a Belialite before, and could endure no restraint; its lusts gave it laws. "We ourselves were sometimes foolish, disobedient, serving diverse lusts and pleasures," Tit. 3: 3. Whatever the flesh craved, and the sensual appetite whined after, it must have, cost what it would; if damnation were the price of it, it would have it, provided it should not be present pay. Now, it must not be any longer "anomos Theoi, all' ennomos toi Christoi", without law to God; but under law to Christ. Those are the articles of peace which the seal willingly subscribes in the day of its admission to mercy, Mat. 11: 29. "Take my yoke upon you, and learn of me." This "Law of the spirit of life which is in Christ Jesus makes them free from the law of sin and death," Rom. 8: 2. Here is much strictness, but no bondage; for the law is not only written in Christ's statute-book, the bible, but copied out by his spirit upon the hearts of his subjects, in correspondent principles; which makes obedience a pleasure, and self-denial easy. Christ's yoke is lined with love, so that it never galls the necks of his people: 1 John 5: 3. "His commandments are not grievous." The soul that comes under Christ's government, must receive law from Christ; and under law every thought of the heart must come.

2. He rebukes and chastises souls for the violations and transgressions of his law. That is another act of Christ's regal authority: "whom he loves he rebukes and chastens," Heb. 12: 6, 7. These chastisements of Christ are either by the rod of providence upon their bodies, and outward comforts, or upon their spirits and inward comforts. Sometimes his rebukes are smart upon the outward man, 1 Cor. 11: 30. "for this cause, many among you are weakly and sick, and many sleep." They had not that due regard to his body that became them, and he will make their bodies to smart for it. And he had rather their flesh should smart, than their souls should perish. Sometimes he spares their outward, and afflicts their inner man, which is a much smarter rod. He withdraws peace, and takes away joy from the spirits of his people. The hidings of his face are sore rebukes. however, all is for emendation, not for destruction. And it is not the least privilege of Christ's subjects to have a seasonable and sanctified rod to reduce them from the ways of sin: Psal. 23: 3. "Thy rod and thy staff, they comfort me." Others are suffered to go on stubbornly in the way of their own hearts; Christ will not spend a rod upon them for their good, will not call them to account for any of their transgressions, but will reckon with them for all together in hell.

3. Another regal act of Christ, is the restraining and keeping back his servants from iniquity, and withholding them from those courses which their own hearts would incline, and lead them to; for, even in them, there is a spirit bent to backsliding, but the Lord in tenderness over them, keeps back their souls from iniquity, and that when they are upon the very brink of sin: "My feet were almost gone, my steps were well nigh slipt," Psal. 73: 2. Then does the Lord prevent sin, by removing the occasion providentially, or by helping them to resist the temptation, graciously assisting their spirits in the trial, so that no temptation shall befall them, but a way of escape shall be opened, that they may be able to bear it, 1 Cor. 10: 13. And thus his people have frequent occasions to bless his name for his preventing goodness, when they are almost in the midst of all evil. And this I take to be the meaning of Gal. 5: 16. "This, I say then, walk in the Spirit, and ye shall not fulfil the lusts of the flesh;" tempted by them, you may be, but fulfil them ye shall not; my spirit shall cause the temptation to die, and wither away in the womb, in the embryo of it, so that it shall not come to a full birth.

4. He protects them in his ways, and suffers them not to relapse from him into a state of sin, and bondage to Satan and more. Indeed, Satan is restless in his endeavours to reduce them again to his obedience; he never leaves tempting and soliciting for their return; and where he finds a false professor he prevails; but Christ keeps his, that they depart not again. John 17: 12. "All that thou hast given me I have kept, and none of them is lost, but the son of perdition." They are "kept by the mighty power of God, through faith unto salvation," 1 Pet. 1: 5. Kept, as in a garrison, according to the importance of that word. None more solicited, none more safe than the people of God. They are "preserved in Christ Jesus," Jude 1. It is not their own grace that secures them, but Christ's care, and continual watchfulness. "Our own graces left to themselves would quickly prove but weights, sinking us to our own ruin," as one speaks. This is his covenant with them, Jer. 32: 4. "I will put my fear in their hearts, that they shall not depart from me." Thus, as a king he preserves them.

5. As a king he Regards their obedience, and encourages their sincere service. Though all they do for Christ be duty, yet he has united their comfort with their duty; "this I had, because I kept thy precepts," Psal. 119: 56. They are engaged to take this encouragement with them to every duty, that he whom they seek "is a bountiful rewarder of inch as diligently seek him", Heb. 11: 6. O what a good master do the saints serve! Hear how a king expostulates with his subjects, Jer. 2: 31. "Have I been a barren wilderness, or a land of darkness to you?" q. d. Have I been such a hard master to you? Have you any reason to complain of my service? To whomsoever I have been strait-handed, surely I have not been so to you. You have not found the ways or wages of sin like mine.

6. He pacifies all inward troubles, and commands peace when their spirits are tumultuous. This "peace of God rules in their hearts" Col. 3: 15. it does "brabeuein" act the part of an umpire, in appeasing strife within. When the tumultuous affections are up, and in a hurry; when anger, hatred, and revenge begin to rise in the soul, this hushes and stills all. "I will hearken (saith the church) what God the Lord will speak, for he will speak peace to his people, and to his saints," Psal. 75: 8. He that saith to the raging sea, be still, and it obeys him; he can only pacify the disquieted spirit. They say of frogs, that if they be croaking never so much in the night, bring but a light among them, and they are all quiet: such a light is the peace of God among our disordered affections. These are Christ's regal acts. And he puts them forth upon the souls of his people, powerfully, sweetly, suitably.

(1.) Powerfully: whether he restrains from sin, or impels to duty, he does it with a soul determining efficacy: for "his kingdom is not in word, but in power," 1 Cor. 4: 20. And those whom his Spirit leads, go bound in the spirit, to the fulfilling and discharge of their duties, Acts 20:22. And yet,

(2.) He rules not by compulsion, but most sweetly. His law is a law of love, written upon their hearts. The church is the Lamb's wife, Rev. 19: 7. "a bruised reed he shall not break, and smoking flax he shall not quench," Isa. 42: 2, 3. "I beseech you by the meekness and gentleness of Christ," saith the apostle, 2 Cor. 10: 1. For he delighteth in free, not in forced obedience. He rules Children, not slaves; and so his kingly power is mixed with fatherly love. His yoke is not made of iron, but gold.

(3.) He rules them suitably to their natures in a rational way; Hos. 11: 4. "I drew them with the cords of man, with bands of love;" i.e. in a way proper to convince their reason, and work upon their ingenuity. And thus his eternal kingdom is administered by his Spirit, who is his prorex, or vicegerent in our hearts.

Thirdly, and lastly, we will open the privileges pertaining to all the subjects of this spiritual kingdom. And they are such as follow.

1. These souls, over whom Christ reigns, are certainly and fully set free from the curse of the law. "If the Son makes you free, then are you free indeed," John 8: 36. I say not, they are free from the law as a rule of life; such a freedom were no privilege to them at all: but free from the rigorous exactions, and terrible maledictions of it; to hear our liberty proclaimed from this bondage, is the joyful sound indeed, the most blessed voice that ever our ears heard. And this all that are in Christ shall hear, "If we be led by the Spirit, we are not under the law," Gal. 5: 18. "Blessed are the people that hear this joyful sound," Psal. 89: 15.

2. Another privilege of Christ's subjects, is, freedom from the dominion of sin. Rom. 6: 14. "Sin shall not reign over them; for they are not under the law, but under grace." One heaven cannot bear two suns; nor one soul two kings: when Christ takes the throne, sin quits it. It is true, the being of sin is there still; its defiling and troubling power remains still; but its dominion is abolished. O joyful tidings! O welcome day!

3. Another privilege of Christ's subjects, is, protection in all troubles and dangers to which their souls or bodies are exposed. "This man shall be the peace, when the Assyrian shall come into our land, and when he shall tread in our palaces," Mic. 5: 5. Kings owe protection to their subjects: none so able, so faithful in that work as Christ; all "thou gavest me, I have kept, and none is lost," John 17: 12.

4. Another privilege of Christ's subjects, is, a merciful and tender bearing of their burdens and infirmities. They have a meek and patient king; "Tell the daughters of Sion, thy king cometh meek and lowly;" Mat. 21: 5. Mat. 11: 29. "Take my yoke, and learn of me, for I am meek and lowly." The meek Moses could not bear the provocations of the people, Numb. 11: 12. but Christ bears them all: "He carries the lambs in his arms, and gently leads them that be with young," Isa. 42: 11. He is one that can have compassion upon the ignorant, and them that are out of the way.

5. Again, Sweet peace, and tranquillity of soul, is the privilege of the subjects of this kingdom: for this kingdom "consisteth in peace, and joy in the Holy Ghost," Rom. 14: 17. And till souls come under his sceptre, they shall never find peace: "Come unto me, ye that are weary, I will give you rest." Yet do not mistake, I say not, they have all actual peace, at all times: no, they often break that peace by sin; but they have the root of peace, the ground work and cause of peace. If they have not peace, yet they have that which is convertible into peace at any time. They also are in a state of peace, Rom. 5: 11. "Being justified by faith, we have peace with God." This is a feast every day, a mercy which they only can duly value, that are in the depths of trouble for sin.

6. And lastly, everlasting salvation is the privilege of all over whom Christ reigns. Prince and Saviour are joined together, Acts 5: 31. He that can say, "thou shalt guide me with thy counsels," may add what follows, "and afterwards bring me to glory," Psal. 73: 24. Indeed, the kingdom of grace does but breed up children for the kingdom of glory. And to speak as the thing is, it is the kingdom of heaven here begun. The difference betwixt them is not specifical, but only gradual: and therefore this, as well as that, bears the name of the kingdom of heaven. The king is the same, and the subjects the same. The subjects of this are shortly to be translated to that kingdom. Thus I have named, and indeed but named, some few of those inestimable privileges of Christ's subjects. We next apply it.

Inference 1. How great is their sin and misery who continue in bondage to sin and Satan and refuse the government of Christ! Who had rather sit under the shadow of that bramble, than under the sweet and powerful government of Christ. Satan writes his laws in the blood of his subjects, grinds them with cruel oppression, wears them out with bondage to divers lusts, and rewards their service with everlasting misery. And yet how few are weary of it, and willing to come over to Christ! "Behold (saith one of Christ's heralds) Christ is in the fields sent of God to recover his right and your liberty. His royal standard is pitched in the gospel, and proclamation made, that if any poor sinners, weary of the Devil's government, and laden with the miserable chains of his spiritual bondage, (so as these irons of his sins enter into his very soul, to afflict it with the sense of them) shall thus come and repair to Christ, he shall have protection from God's justice, the Devil's wrath, and sin's dominion; in a word, he shall have rest, and that glorious," Isa. 11: 10.

And yet how few stir a foot towards Christ, but are willing to have their ears bored, and be perpetual slaves to that cruel tyrant? O when will sinners be weary of their bondage, and sigh after deliverance! If any such poor soul shall read these lines, let them know, and I do proclaim it in the name of my royal Master, and give him the word of a King for it, he shall not be rejected by Christ, John 6: 37. Come, poor sinner, come, the Lord Jesus is a merciful King, and never did, nor will hang up that poor penitent, that puts the rope about his own neck, and submits to mercy.

Inf. 2. How much does it concern us to enquire and know whose government we are under, and who is king over our souls; Whether Christ or Satan be in the throne, and sways the sceptre over our souls?

Reader, the work I would now engage thy soul in, is the same that Jesus Christ will thoroughly and effectually do in the great day. Then will he gather out of his kingdom every thing that offends, separate the tares and wheat, divide the whale world into two ranks or grand divisions, how many divisions and subdivisions soever there be in it now. It nearly concerns thee therefore to know who is Lord and King in thy soul. To help thee in this great work, make use of the following hints; for I cannot fully prosecute these things as I would.

1. "To whom do you yield your obedience? His subjects and servants ye are to whom ye obey," Rom. 6: 16. It is but a mockery to give Christ the empty titles of Lord and King, whilst ye give your real service to sin and Satan. What is this but like the Jews, to bow the knee to him, and say, Hail master, and crucify him? "Then are ye his disciples, if ye do whatsoever he commands you," John 15: 14. He that is Christ's servant in jest, shall be damned in earnest. Christ does not compliment with you; his pardons, promises, and salvation are real; O let your obedience be so too! Let it be sincere and universal obedience; this will evidence your unfeigned subjection to Christ. Do not dare to enterprise any thing, till you know Christ's pleasure and will, Rom. 12: 2. Enquire of Christ, as David did of the Lord, 1 Sam. 23: 9, 10. 11. Lord, may I do this or that? or shall I forbear? I beseech thee tell thy servant.

2. Have you the power of godliness, or a form of it only? There be many that do but trifle in religion, and play about the skirts and borders of it; spending their time about jejune and barren controversies: but as to the power of religion, and the life of godliness, which consist in communion

with God in duties and ordinances, which promote holiness, and mortify their lusts, they concern not themselves about these things. But surely "the kingdom of God is not in words, but in power," 1 Cor. 4: 20. It is not meat and drink, (i. e. dry disputes about meats and drinks) "but righteousness and peace, and joy in the Holy Ghost; for he that in these things serves Christ, is acceptable to God, and approved of men," Rom. 14: 17, 18. O I am afraid when the great host of professors shall be tried by these rules, they will shrink up into a little handful, as Gideon's host did.

3. Have ye the special saving knowledge of Christ? All his subjects are translated out of the kingdom of darkness, Col 1: 13. The devil, that ruleth over you in the days of your ignorance, is called the ruler of the darkness of this world; his subjects are all blind, else he could never rule them. As soon as their eyes are opened, they run out of his kingdom, and there is no retaining them in subjection to him any longer. O enquire then whether you are brought out of darkness into this marvellous light! do you see your condition, how sad, miserable, wretched it is by nature? do you see your remedy, as it lies only in Christ, and his precious blood? Do you see the true way of obtaining interest in that blood by faith? does this knowledge run into practice, and put you upon lamenting heartily your misery by sin? thirsting vehemently after Christ and his righteousness? striving continually for a heart to believe and close with Christ? This will evidence you indeed to be translated out of the kingdom of darkness into the kingdom of Christ.

4. With whom do you delightfully associate yourselves? Who are your chosen companions? You may see to whom you belong by the company you join yourselves to. What do the subjects of Christ among the slaves of Satan? If the subjects of one kingdom be in another king's dominion, they love to be together with their own countrymen rather than the natives of the place; so do the servants of Christ, They are a company of themselves, as it is said, Acts 4: 23. "They went to their own company." I know the subjects of both kingdoms are here mingled, and we cannot avoid the company of sinners except we go out of the world, 1 Cor. 5: 10. but yet all your delights should be in the saints and in the excellent of the earth, Psal. 16: 3.

5. Do you live holy and righteous lives? If not, you may claim interest in Christ as your King, but he will never allow your claim. "The sceptre of his kingdom is a sceptre of righteousness," Psal. 45: 6. If ye oppress, go beyond, and cheat your brethren, and yet call yourselves Christ's subjects, what greater reproach can you study to cast upon him? What is Christ the King of cheats? Does he patronise such things as these? No, no, pull off your vizards, and fall into your own places; you belong to another prince, and not to Christ.

Inf. 3. Does Christ exercise such a kingly power over the souls of all them that are subdued by the gospel to him? O then let all that are under Christ's government walk as the subjects of such a King. Imitate your King; the examples of kings are very influential upon their subjects. Your King has commanded you not only to take his yoke upon you, but also to learn of him, Matth. 11: 29. Yea, and "if any man say that he is Christ's, let him walk even as Christ walked," 1 John 2: 6. Your King is meek and patient, Isa. 53: 7. as a lamb for meekness: shall his subjects be lions for fierceness? Your King was humble and lowly; Matth. 21: 5. "Behold thy King cometh meek and lowly." Will you be proud and lofty? Does this become the kingdom of Christ? Your King was a self-denying King; he could deny his outward comforts, ease, honour, life, to serve his Father's design, and accomplish your salvation, 2 Cor. 8: 9. Phil. 2: 1, 2, 3, 4, 5, 6, 7, 8. shall his servants be self-ended, and self-seeking persons, that will expose his honour, and hazard their own souls for the trifles of time? God forbid. Your king was painful, laborious, and diligent in fulfilling his work, John 9: 3. Let not his servants be lazy and slothful. O imitate your King, follow the pattern of your King: this will give you comfort now, and boldness in the day of judgement, if as he was, so ye are in this world, 1 John 4: 17.

Sermon 17: Of the Kingly Office of Christ, as it is providentially executed in the World, for the Redeemed

Eph. 1: 22.
And has put all things under his feet, and gave him to be the head, over all things to the church.

The foregoing verses are spent in a thankful and humble adoration of the grace of God, in bringing the Ephesians to believe in Christ. This effect of that power that raised their hearts to believe in Christ, is here compared with that other glorious effect of it, even the raising of Christ himself from the dead: both these owe themselves to the same efficient cause. It raised Christ from a low estate, even from the dead, to a high, a very high and glorious state; to be the head both of the world, and of the church; the head of the world by way of dominion, the head of the church by way of union, and special influence, ruling the world for the good of his people in it. "He gave him is be the head over all things to the church."

In this scripture let these four things be seriously regarded.

1. The dignity and authority committed to Christ; "He has put all things under his feet;" which implies, full, ample and absolute dominion in him, and subjection in them over whom he reigns. This power is delegated to him by the Father: for besides the essential, native, ingenite power and dominion over all, which he has as God, and is common to every person in the Godhead, Psal. 22: 28. there is a mediatory dispensed authority, which is proper to him as Mediator, which he receives as the reward or fruit of his suffering, Phil. 2: 8.

2. The subject recipient of this authority, which is Christ, and Christ primarily, and only: he is the "proton dektikon", first receptacle of all authority and power. Whatever authority any creature is clothed with, is but ministerial and derivative, whether it be political, or ecclesiastical. Christ is the only Lord, Jude, ver. 4. The fountain of all power.

3. The object of this authority, the whole creation; all things are put under his feet: he rules from sea to sea, even to the utmost bounds of God's creation, "Thou hast given him power over all flesh," John 17: 2. all creatures, rational, and irrational animate, and inanimate, angels, devils, men, winds, seas, all obey him.

4. And especially, take notice of the finis cui, the end for which he governs and rules the universal empire; it is for the church, i. e. for the advantage, comfort, and salvation of that chosen remnant he died for. He purchased the church; and that he might have the highest security that his blood should not be lost, God the Father has put all things into his hand, to order and dispose all as he pleaseth. For the furtherance of that his design and end, as he bought the persons of some, so the services of all the rest; and that they might effectually serve the end they are designed to, Christ will order them all in a blessed subordination and subserviency thereunto. Hence the point is,

Doct. That all the affairs of the kingdom of providence are ordered and determined by Jesus Christ, for the special advantage, and everlasting good of his redeemed people.

John 17: 2. "As thou hast given him power over all flesh, that he should give eternal life to as many as thou hast given him." Hence it comes to pass, that "all things work together for good to them that love God, to them that are called according to his purpose," Rom. 8: 28.

That Jesus Christ has a providential influence upon all the affairs of this world is evident, both from scripture assertions, and rational observations, made upon the acting of things here below

The first chapter of Ezekiel contains an admirable scheme or draught of providence. There you see how all the wheels, i. e. the motions and revolutions here on earth, are guided by the spirit that is in them. And, ver. 26. it is all run up into the supreme cause; there you find one like the Son of man, which is Jesus Christ, sitting upon the throne, and giving forth orders from thence for the government of all: and if it were not so, how is it that there are such strong combinations, and predispositions of persons and things to such ends and issues, without any communications of councils, or holding of intelligence with one another? As in Israel's deliverance out of Egypt, and innumerable more instances have appeared. Certainly, if ten men, from several places, should all meet at one place, and about one business, without any fore-appointment among themselves, it would argue their motions were secretly over-ruled by some invisible agent. How is it that such marvellous effects are produced in the world by causes that carry no proportion to them? Amos 5: 9 and 1 Cor. 1: 27 and as often, the most apt and likely means are rendered wholly ineffectual? Psal. 33: 16. In a word, if Christ has no such providential influx, how are his people in all ages preserved in the midst of so many millions of potent and malicious enemies, amongst whom they live as sheep in the midst of wolves? Luke 10: 3. How is it that the bush burns, and yet is not consumed Exod. 3: 2.

But my business, in this discourse, is not to prove that there is a Providence, which none but Atheists deny. I shall chose rather to show by what acts Jesus Christ administers this kingdom, and in what manner; and what use may be made thereof.

First, He rules and orders the kingdom of Providence, by supporting, permitting, restraining, limiting, protecting, punishing, and rewarding those over whom he reigns providentially.

1. He supports the world, and all creatures in it, by his power. "My Father works hitherto, and I work," John 5: 17. "And in him (that is, in Christ) all things consist," Col. 1: 17. It is a considerable part of Christ's glory to have a whole world of creatures owing their being and hourly conservation to him. The parts of the world are not coupled and fastened together as the parts of the house, whose beams are pinned and nailed to each other; but rather as several rings of iron, which hang together by the virtue of a loadstone. This goodly fabric was razed to the foundation when sin entered, and had tumbled into everlasting confusion, had not Christ stept in to shore up the reeling world. For the sake of his redeemed that inhabits it, he does and will prop it by his omnipotent power. And when he has gathered all his elect out of it into the kingdom above, then will he set fire to the four quarters of it, and it shall lie in ashes. Meanwhile, he is "given for a covenant to the people, to establish the earth," Isa. 49: 8.

2. He permits and suffers the worst of creatures in his dominion, to be and act as they do. "The deceived, and the deceiver, are his," Job 12: 16. Even those that fight against Christ and his people, receive both power and permission from him. Say not, that it is unbecoming the most Holy to permit such evils, which he could prevent if he pleased. For as he permits no more than he will overrule to his praise, so that very permission of his, is holy and just. Christ's working is not confounded with the creature's. Pure sun beams are not tainted by the noisome vapours of the dung hill on which they shine. His holiness has no fellowship with their iniquities; nor are their transgressions at all excused by his permissions of them. "He is a rock, his work is perfect, but they have corrupted themselves," Deut. 32: 4, 5. This holy permission is but the withholding of those restraints from their lusts, and denying those common assistances which he is no way bound to give them. Acts 14: 16. "He suffered all nations to walk in their own ways." And yet should he permit sinful creatures to act out all the wickedness that is in their hearts, there would neither remain peace nor order in the world. And therefore,

3. He powerfully restrains creatures by the bridle of providence, from the commission of those things, to which their hearts are propense enough, Psal. 76: 10. "The remainder of wrath thou wilt restrain," or gird up; letting forth just so much as shall serve his holy ends, and no more. And truly this is one of the glorious mysteries of Providence, which amazes the serious and considerate soul; to see the spirit of a creature fully set to do mischief; power enough, as one would think, in his hand to do it, and a door of opportunity standing open for it; and yet the effect strangely hindered. The strong propensions of the will are inwardly checked, as in the case of Laban, Gen. 31: 24. or a diversion, and rub is strangely cast in their way; as in the case of Sennacherib, 2 Kings 19: 7, 8. so that their hands cannot perform their enterprises. Julia had two great designs before him, one was to conquer the Persian, the other to root out the Galileans, as he, by way of contempt, called the Christians: but he will begin with the Persian first, and then make a sacrifice of all the Christians to his idols. He does so, and perishes in the first attempt. O the wisdom of Providence!

4. Jesus Christ limits the creatures in their acting, assigning them their boundaries and lines of liberty; to which they may, but beyond it cannot, go. Rev. 2: 10. "Fear none at these things that ye shall suffer; behold, the devil shall cast some of you into prison, and ye shall have tribulation ten days." They would have cast them into their graves, but it shall only be into prisons: They would have stretched out their hands, upon them all; no, but only some of them shall be exposed: They would have kept them there perpetually; no, it must be but for ten days, Ezek. 22: 6. "Behold, the princes of Israel were in thee, every one to their power to shed blood." They went as far as they had power to go, not as far as they had will to go. Four hundred and thirty years were determined upon the people of God in Egypt; and then, even in that very night, God brought them forth; for then "the time of the promise was come," Acts 7: 17.

The Fountain of Life Opened Up

5. The Lord Jesus providentially protects his people amidst a world of enemies and dangers. It was Christ that appeared unto Moses in the flaming bush, and preserved it from being consumed. The bush signified the people of God in Egypt; the fire flaming on it, the exquisite sufferings they there endured: the safety of the bush, amidst the flames, the Lord's admirable care and protection of his poor suffering ones. None so tenderly careful as Christ. "as birds flying, so he defends Jerusalem," Isa. 31: 5; i. e. as they fly swiftly towards their nests, crying when their young are in danger, so will the Lord preserve his. They are "preserved in Christ Jesus", Jude 1, as Noah and his family were in the ark. Hear how a Worthy of our own expresses himself on this point.

"That we are at peace in our houses, at rest in our beds; that we have any quiet in our enjoyments, is from hence alone. Whose person would not be defiled, or destroyed? whose habitation would not be ruined? whose blood almost would not be shed, if wicked men had power to perpetrate all their conceived sin? It may be, the ruin of some of us has been conceived a thousand times. We are beholden to this Providence, of obstructing sin, for our lives, our families, our estates, our liberties, and whatsoever is or may be dear to us. For may we not say sometimes with the Psalmist, Psal. 57: 4. My soul is among lions, and I lie even among them that are set on fire, even the sons of men, whose teeth are spears, and their tongue a sharp sword? And how is the deliverance of men contrived from such persons? Psal. 8: 6. God breaks their teeth in their mouths, even the great teeth at the young lions. He keeps this fire from burning, - some he cuts off and destroys: some he cuts short in their power: some he deprives of the instruments whereby alone they can work: some he prevents in their desired opportunities, or diverts by other objects for their lust; and oftentimes causeth them to spend them among themselves, one upon another. We may say, therefore, with the Psalmist, Psal. 104: 24. O Lord, how manifold are thy works! in wisdom hast thou made then all; the earth is full of thy riches."

6. He punishes the evil doers, and repays, by providence into their own lap, the mischief they do, or but intend to do, unto them that fear him. Pharaoh, Sennacherib, both the Julians, and innumerable more, are the lasting monuments of his righteous retribution. It is true, a sinner may do evil a hundred times, and his days be prolonged; but oft-times God hangs up some eminent sinners in chains, as spectacles and warnings to others. Many a heavy blow has Providence given to the enemies of God, which they were never able to recover. Christ rules, and that with a rod of iron, in the midst of his enemies, Psal. 110: 2.

7. And lastly, He rewards by Providence the services done to him and his people. Out of this treasure of Providence God repays oftentimes those that serve him, and that with a hundredfold reward now in this life, Matth. 19: 29. This active, vigilant Providence has its eye upon all the wants, straits, and troubles of the creatures: but especially upon such as religion brings us unto. What huge volumes of experiences might the people of God write upon this subject? and what a pleasant history would it be, to read the strange, constant, wonderful, and unexpected acting of Providence, for them that have left themselves to its care?

Secondly, We shall next enquire how Jesus Christ administers this providential kingdom.

And here I must take notice of the means by which, and the manner in which he does it. The means, or instruments, he uses in the governing the providential kingdom, (for he is not personally present with its himself), are either angels or men, "the angels are ministering creatures, sent forth by him for the good of them that shall be heirs of salvation," Heb. 1: 14. Luther tells us, they have two offices, superius canere, et inferius vigilare, "to sing above and watch beneath." These do us many invisible offices of love. They have dear and tender respects and love for the saints. To them, God, as it were, puts forth his children to nurse, and they are tenderly careful of them whilst they live, and bring them home in their arms to their Father when they die. And as angels, so men are the servants of Providence; yea, bad men as well as good. Cyrus, on that account, is called God's servant: they fulfil his will, whilst they are prosecuting their own lusts. "The earth shall help the woman," Rev. 12: 16. But good men delight to serve Providence; they and the angels are fellow servants in one house, and to one master, Rev. 19: 10. Yea, there is not a creature in heaven, earth, or hell, but Jesus Christ can providentially use it and serve his ends, and promote his designs by it. But whatever the instrument be Christ uses, of this we may be certain, that his providential working is holy, judicious, sovereign, profound, irresistible, harmonious, and to the saints peculiar.

1. It is holy. Though he permits, limits, orders and overrules many unholy persons and actions, yet he still works like himself, most holily and purely throughout. "The Lord is righteous in all his ways, and holy in all his works, Psal. 145: 17. it is easier to separate light from a sunbeam, than holiness from the works of God. The best of men cannot escape sin in their most holy actions; they cannot touch, but are defiled. But no sin cleaves to God, whatever he has to do about it.

2. Christ's providential working is not only most pure and holy, but also most wise and judicious. Ezek. 1: 20. "The wheels are full of eyes:" They are not moved by a blind impetus, but in deep counsel and wisdom. And, indeed, the wisdom of Providence manifests itself principally in the choice of such states for the people of God, as shall most effectually promote their eternal

happiness. And herein it goes quite beyond our understandings and comprehensions. It makes that medicinal and salutiferous, which we judge as destructive to our comfort and good, as poison. I remember, it is a note of Suarez, speaking of the felicity of the other world: "Then (saith he) the blessed shall see in God all things and circumstances pertaining to them, excellently accommodated and attempered;" then shall they see that the crossing of their desires was the saving of their souls; and that otherwise they had perished. The most wise Providence looks beyond us. It eyes the end, and suits all things thereto, and not to our fond desires.

3. The providence of Christ is most supreme and sovereign. "Whatsoever he pleaseth, that he does in heaven and in earth, and in all places," Psal. 135: 6. "He is Lord of lords, and King of kings," Rev. 19: 16. The greatest monarchs on earth are but as little bits of clay, as the worms of the earth to him: they all depend on him, Prov. 8: 15, 16. "By me kings reign, and princes decree justice; by me princes rule, nobles, even all the judges of the earth."

4. Providence is profound and inscrutable. The judgements of Christ are "a great deep, and his footsteps are not known," Psal. 36: 6. There are hard texts in the works as well as in the words of Christ. The wisest heads have been at a loss in interpreting some Providence, Jer. 12: 1, 2. Job 21: 7. The angels had the hands of a man under their wings, Ezek. 1: 8. i. e. they wrought secretly and mysteriously.

5. Providence is irresistible in its designs and motions; for all providences are but fulfilling and accomplishments of Gods immutable decrees. Eph. 1: 11. "He works all things according to the counsel of his own will." Hence Zech. 6: 1. the instruments by which God executed his wrath, are called "chariots coming from betwixt two mountains of brass," i.e. "the firm and immutable decrees of God." When the Jews put Christ to death, they did but do what "the hand and counsel of God had before determined to be done," Acts 4: 28. so that none can oppose or resist providence. "I will work, and who shall let it?" Isa 43: 13.

6. The providence of Christ are harmonious. There are secret chains, and invisible connections betwixt the works of Christ. We know not how to reconcile promises and providence together, nor yet providence one with another; but certainly they all work together, Rom. 8: 28. as adjutant causes, or con-causes standing under, and working by the influence of the first cause. He does not do, and undo; destroy by one providence, what he built by another. But, look, as also seasons of the year, the nipping frosts, as well as the halcyon days of summer, do all conspire and conduce to the harvest; so it is in providence.

7. And lastly, The providence of Christ work in a special and peculiar way for the good of the saints. His providential is subordinated to his spiritual kingdom. "He is the Saviour of all men, especially of them that believe," 1 Tim. 4: 1. These only have the blessings of providence. Things are so laid and ordered, as that their eternal good shall be promoted and secured by all that Christ does.

Inference 1. If so, See then, in the first place, to whom you are beholden for your lives, liberties, comforts, and all that you enjoy in this world. Is it not Christ that orders all for you? He is, indeed in heaven, out of your sight; but though you see him not, he sees you, and takes care of all your concerns. When one told Silentiarius of a plot laid to take away his life, he answered, Si Deus mei curam non habet, quid vivo? "If God take no care of me, how do I live?" how have I escaped hitherto? "In all thy ways acknowledge him," Prov. 3: 6. It is he that has espied out that state thou art in, as most proper for thee. It is Christ that does all for you that is done. He looks down from heaven upon all that fear him; he sees when you are in danger by temptation, and casts in a providence, you know not how, to hinder it. He sees when you are sad, and orders reviving providence, to refresh you. He sees when corruptions prevail, and orders humbling providence to purge them. Whatever mercies you have received, all along the way you have gone hitherto, are the orderings of Christ for you. And you should carefully observe how the promises and providence have kept equal pace with one another, and both gone by step with you until now.

Inf. 2. Has God left the government of the whole world in the hands of Christ, and trusted him over all? Then do you also leave your particular concerns in the hands of Christ too, and know that the infinite wisdom and love, which rules the world, manages every thing that relates to you. It is in a good hand, and infinitely better than if it were in your own. I remember when Melanchton was under some despondencies of spirit about the estate of God's people in Germany, Luther chides him thus for it, "Let Philip cease to rule the world." It is none of our work to steer the course of providence, or direct its motions, but to submit quietly to him that does. There is an itch in men, yea, in the best of men, to be disputing with God: "Let me talk with thee of thy judgement," saith Jeremiah, chap. 12: 1, 2. Yea, how apt are we to regret at providence, as if they had no conducency at all to the glory of God, or to our good, Exod. 5: 22. yea, to limit providence to our way and time? Thus, the "Israelites tempted God, and limited the holy One," Psal. 78: 18, 41. How often also do we, unbelievingly, distrust providence as though it could never accomplish what we profess to expect and believe? Ezek. 37: 11. "Our bones are dry, our hope is lost; we are cut off for our part."

The Fountain of Life Opened Up

So Gen. 18: 13, 14. Isa. 40: 17. There are but few Abrahams, among believers, who "against hope, believed in hope, giving glory to God," Rom. 4: 20. And it is but too common for good men to repine and fret at providence, when their wills, lusts, or humours are crossed by it: this was the great sin of Jonah. Brethren, these things ought not to be so; did you but seriously consider, either the design of providence, which is to bring about the gracious designs and purposes of God upon you, which were laid before this world was, Eph. 1: 11. or that it is a lifting up of thy wisdom against his, as if thou couldst better order thine affairs, if thou hadst but the conduct and management of them; or that you have to do herein faith a great and dreadful God, in whose hands you are as the clay in the potter's hands, that he may do what he will with you, and all that is yours, without giving you an account of any of his matters, Job 33: 13. or whether providence has cast others, as good, by nature, as yourselves, tumbled them down from the top of health, wealthy honours and pleasures, to the bottom of hell; or, lastly, did you but consider how often it has formerly baffled and befouled yourselves; you would retract, with shame, your rash, headlong censures of it, and enforce you, by the sight of its births and issues, to confess your folly and ignorance, as Asaph did, Psal. 73: 22. I say, if such considerations as these could but have place with you in your troubles and temptations, they would quickly mould your hearts into a better and more quiet frame.

O that I could but persuade you to resign all to Christ. He is a cunning workman, as he is called, Prov. 8: 30. and can effect what he pleaseth. It is a good rule, De operibus Dei non est judicandum, ante quintum actum. "Let God work out all that he intends, but have patience till he has put the last hand to his works and then find fault with it, if you can." You have heard of the patience of Job, "and have seen the end of the Lord," James 5: 11.

Inf. 3. If Christ be Lord and king over the providential kingdom, and that, for the good of his people, let none that are Christ's henceforth stand in a slavish fear of creatures. It is a good note that Grotius has upon my text; "It is a marvellous consolation (saith he) that Christ has so great an empire, and that he governs it for the good of his people, as a head consulting the good of the body." Our head and husband, is Lord-general of all the hosts of heaven and earth; no creature can move hand or tongue without his leave or order: the power they have is given them from above, John 19: 11, 12. The serious consideration of this truth will make the feeblest spirit cease trembling, and set it a singing; Psal. 47: 7. "The Lord is king of all the earth, sing ye praises with understanding,:" that is, (as some well paraphrase it) every one that has understanding of this comfortable truth. Has he not given you abundant security in many express promises, that all shall issue well for you that fear him? Rom. 8: 28. "All things shall work together for good, to them that love God," And Eccl. 8: 12. verily "it shall be well with them that fear God,: even with them that fear before him. And suppose he had not, yet the very understanding of our relation to such a king, should, in itself, be sufficient security: for, he is the universal, supreme, absolute, meek, merciful, victorious, and immortal king.

He sits in glory, at the Father's right hand; and, to make his seat the easier, his enemies are a footstool for him. His love to his people is unspeakably tender and fervent, he that touches them, "touches the apple of his eye," Zech. 2. And, it is hardly imaginable, that Jesus Christ will sit still, and suffer his enemies to thrust out his eyes. Till this be forgotten, the wrath of man is not feared; Isa. 2: 12, 13. "He that fears a man that shall die, forgets the Lord his Maker." He loves you too well to sign any order to your prejudice, and without his order, none can touch you.

Inf. 4. If the government of the world be in the hands of Christ, Then our engaging and entitling of Christ to all our affairs and business, is the true and ready way to their success and prosperity. If all depend upon his pleasure, then sure it is your wisdom to take him along with you to every action and business; it is no lost time that is spent in prayer, wherein we ask his leave, and beg his presence with us: and, take it for a clear truth, that which is not prefaced with prayer, will be followed with trouble. How easily can Jesus Christ dash all your designs, when they are at the very birth and article of execution, and break off, in a moment, all the purposes of your hearts? It is a proverb among the Papists, that Mass and meat hinder no man. The Turks will pray five times a day, how urgent soever their business be. Blush you that enterprise your affairs without God: I reckon that business as good as done, to which we have got Christ's leave, and engaged his presence to accompany us.

Inf. 5. Lastly, Eye Christ in all the events of providence; see his hand in all that befall you, whether it be evil or good. "The works of the Lord are great, sought out of all them that have pleasure therein," Psal. 111: 2.

How much good might we get, by observation of the good or evil that befall us throughout our course!

John Flavel

1. In all the evils of trouble and afflictions that befall you, eye Jesus Christ: and set your hearts to the study of these four things in affliction.

(1.) Study his sovereignty and dominion; for he creates and forms them: they rise not out of the dust, nor do they befall you casually; but he raises them up, and gives them their commission, Jer. 18: 11. "Behold, I create evil, and devise a device against you." He elects the instrument of your trouble; he makes the rod as afflictive as he pleaseth; he orders the continuance and end of your troubles; and they will not cease to be afflictive to you, till Christ say, Leave off, it is enough. The Centurion wisely considered this, when he told him, Luke 7: 8. "I have soldiers under me, and I say to one, Go, and he goes; to another, Come, and he comes:" meaning, that as his soldiers were at his beck and command, so diseases were at Christ's beck, to come and go as he ordered them.

(2.) Study the wisdom of Christ in the contrivance of your troubles. And his wisdom shines out many ways in them, it is evident in chasing such kinds of trouble for you: this, and not that, because this is more apt to work upon, and purge out the corruption that most predominates in you: In the degrees of your troubles, suffering them to work to such a height, else not reach their end; but no higher, lest they overwhelm you.

(3.) Study the tenderness and compassions of Christ over his afflicted. O think if the devil had but the mixing of my cup, how much more bitter would he make it! There would not be one drop of mercy, no, not of sparing mercy in it, which is the lowest of all sorts of mercy: but here is much mercy mixed with my troubles; there is mercy in this, that it is no worse. Am I afflicted? "It is of the Lord's mercy I am not consumed," Lam. 3: 2. It might have been hell as well as this; there is mercy in his supports under it. Others have, and I might have been left to sink and perish under my burdens. Mercy, in deliverance out of it; this might have been everlasting darkness, that should never have had a morning. O the tenderness of Christ over his afflicted!

(4.) Study the love of Christ to thy soul, in affection. Did he not love thee, he would not sanctify a rod to humble or reduce thee, but let thee alone to perish in thy sin. Rev. 3: 19. "Whom I love, I rebuke and chasten." This is the device of love, to recover thee to thy God, and prevent thy ruin. O what an advantage would it be thus to study Christ, in all your evils that befall you!

2. Eye and study Christ in all the good you receive from the hand of providence. Turn both sides of your mercies, and view them in all their lovely circumstances.

Eye them in their suitableness: how conveniently providence has ordered all things for thee. Thou hast a narrow heart, and a small estate suitable to it: Hadst thou more of the world, it would be like a large sail to a little boat, which would quickly pull thee under water: thou hast that which is most suitable to thee of all conditions.

(2.) Eye the seasonableness of thy mercies, how they are timed to an hour. Providence brings forth all its fruits in due season.

(3.) Eye the peculiar nature of thy mercies. Others have common, thou special ones; others have but a single, thou a double sweetness in thy enjoyments, one natural from the matter at it, another spiritual from the way in which, and end for which it comes.

(4.) Observe the order in which providence sends your mercies. See how one is linked strangely to another, and is a door to let in many. Sometimes one mercy is introductive to a thousand.

(5.) And lastly, Observe the constancy of them, "they are new every morning," Lam. 3: 23. How assiduously does God visit thy soul and body! Think with thyself, if there be but a suspension of the care of Christ for one hour, that hour would be thy ruin. Thousands of evils stand round about thee, watching when Christ will but remove his eye from thee, that they may rush in and devour thee.

Could we thus study the providence of Christ in all the good and evil that befall us in the world, then in every state we should be content, Phil 4: 11. Then we should never be stopt, but furthered in our way by all that falls out; then would our experience swell to great volumes, which we might carry to heaven with us; and then should we answer all Christ's ends in every state he brings us into. Do this, and say,

Thanks be to God for Jesus Christ.

Sermon 18: Of the Necessity of Christ's Humiliation, in order to the Execution of all these his blessed Offices for us; and particularly of his Humiliation by Incarnation

Phil. 2:8
And being found in fashion as a man, he humbled himself, and became obedient to death, even the death of the cross.

You have heard how Christ was invested with the offices of prophet, priest, and king, for the carrying on the blesses design of our redemption; the execution of these offices necessarily required that he should be both deeply abased, and highly exalted. He cannot as our Priest, offer up himself a sacrifice to God for us, except he be humbled, and humbled to death. He cannot, as a King, powerfully apply the virtue of that his sacrifice, except he be exalted, yea, highly exalted. Had he not stooped to the low estate of a man, he had not, as a Priest, had a sacrifice of his own to offer; as a Prophet, he had not been fit to teach us the will of God, so as that we should be able to bear it; as a King, he had not been a suitable head to the church: and, had he not been highly exalted, that sacrifice had not been carried within the vail before the Lord. Those discoveries of God could not have been universal, effectual and abiding. The government of Christ could not have secured, protected, and defended the subjects of his kingdom.

The infinite wisdom prospecting all this, ordered that Christ should first be deeply humbled, then highly exalted: both which states of Christ are presented to us by the apostle in this context.

He that intends to build high, lays the foundation deep and low. Christ must have a distinct glory in heaven, transcending that of angels and men, (for the saints will know him from all others by his glory, as the sun is known from the lesser stars.) And, as he must be exalted infinitely above them, so he must first, in order thereunto, be humbled and abased as much below them: "His form was marred more than any man's; and his visage more than the sons of men." The ground colours are a deep sable, which afterwards are laid on with all the splendour and glory of heaven.

Method requires that we first speak to this state of Humiliation.

And, to that purpose, I have read this scripture to you, which presents you the Son under an (almost) total eclipse. He that was beautiful and glorious, Isa. 4: 2. yea, glorious as the only begotten of the Father, John 1: 14. yea, the glory, James 2: 1. yea, the splendour and "brightness of the Fathers glory," Heb. 1: 3. was so veiled, clouded, and debased, that he looked not like himself; a God, no, nor scarce as a man; for, with reference to this humbled state, it is said, Psal. 22: 6. "I am a worm, and no man:" q. d. rather write me worm, than man: I am become an abject among men, as that word, Isa 53: 8. signifies. This humiliation of Christ we have here expressed in the nature, degrees, and duration or continuance of it.

1. The nature of it, "etapeinosen heauton", he humbled himself. The word imports both a real and voluntary abasement. Real; he did not personate a humbled man, nor act the part of one, in a debased state, but was really, and indeed humbled; and that not only before men, but God. As man, he was humbled really, as God in respect of his manifestative glory: and, as it was real, so also voluntary: It is not said he was humbled, but he humbled himself: he was willing to stoop to this low and abject state for us. And, indeed, the voluntariness of his humiliation made it most acceptable to God, and singularly commends the love of Christ to us, that he would chose to stoop to all this ignominy, suffering, and abasement for us.

2. The degrees of his humiliation; it was not only so low as to become a man, a man under law; but he humbled himself to become "obedient to death, even the death of the cross." Here you see the depth of Christ's humiliations both specified, it was unto death, and aggravated, even the

death of the cross: not only to become a man but a dead corpse, and that too hanging on a tree, dying the death of a malefactor.

3. The duration, or continuance of this his humiliation: it continued from the first moment of his incarnation, to the very moment of his vivification and quickening in the grave. So the terms of it are fixed here by the apostle; from the time he was found in fashion as a man, that is, from his incarnation, unto his death on the cross, which also comprehends the time of his abode in the grave; so long his humiliation lasted. Hence the observation is,

Doct. That the estate of Christ, from his conception to his resurrection, was a state of deep abasement and humiliation.

We are now entering upon Christ's humbled state, which I shall cast under three general heads, viz. his humiliation, in his incarnation, in his life, and in his death. My present work is to open Christ's humiliation, in his incarnation, imported in these words, He was found in fashion as a man. By which you are not to conceive that he only assumed a body, as an assisting form, to appear transiently to us in it, and so lay it down again. It is not such an apparition of Christ in the shape of a man, that is here intended; but his true and real assumption of our nature, which vas a special part of his humiliation; as will appear by the following particulars.

1. The incarnation of Christ was a most wonderful humiliation of him, inasmuch as thereby he is brought into the rank and order of creatures, who is over all, "God blessed for ever," Rom. 9: 5. This is the astonishing mystery, 1 Tim. 3: 16. that God should be manifest in the flesh; that the eternal God should truly and properly be called the Man Christ Jesus, 1 Tim. 2: 5. It was a wonder to Solomon, that God would dwell in that stately and magnificent temple at Jerusalem, 2 Chron. 6: 18. "But will God in very deed dwell with men on earth! Behold the heaven, and heaven of heavens cannot contain thee; how much less this house which I have built?" But it is a far greater wonder that God should dwell in a body of flesh, and pitch his tabernacle with us, John 1: 14. It would have seemed a rude blasphemy, had not the scriptures plainly revealed it, to have thought, or spoken of the eternal God, as born in time; the world's Creator a creature; the Ancient of Days, as an infant of days.

The Heathen Chaldeans told the king of Babel, that the "dwelling of the gods is not with flesh," Dan. 2: 11. But now God not only dwells with fleshy but dwells in flesh; yea, was made flesh, and dwelt among us.

For the sun to fall from its sphere, and be degraded into a wandering atom; for an angel to be turned out of heaven, and be converted into a silly fly or worm, had been no such great abasement; for they were but creatures before, and so they would abide still, though in an inferior order or species of creatures. The distance betwixt the highest and lowest species of creatures, is but a finite distance. The angel and the worm dwell not so far asunder. But for the infinite glorious Creator of all things, to become a creature, is a mystery exceeding all human understanding. The distance betwixt God and the highest order at creatures, is an infinite distance. He is said to humble himself; to behold the things that are done in heaven. What a humiliation then is it, to behold the things in the lower world! but to be born into it, and become a man! Great indeed is the mystery of godliness. "Behold, (saith the prophet, Isa. 40: 15, 18) the nations are as the drop of a bucket, and are counted as the small dust of the balance; he taketh up she isles as a very little thing. All nations before him are as nothing, and they are accounted to him less than nothing, and vanity." If, indeed, this great and incomprehensible Majesty will himself stoop to the state and condition of a creature, we may easily believe, that being once a creature, he would expose him to hunger, thirst, shame, spitting, death, or any thing but sin. For that once being a man, he should endure any of these things, is not so wonderful, as that he should become a man. This was the low step, a deep abasement indeed!

2. It was a marvellous humiliation to the Son of God, not only to become a creature, but an inferior creature, a man, and not an angel. Had he taken the angelical nature, though it had been a wonderful abasement to him, yet he had staid (if I may so speak) nearer his own home, and been somewhat liker to a God, than now he appeared, when he dwelt with us: for angels are the highest and most excellent of all created beings: For their nature, they are pure spirits; for their wisdom, intelligences; for their dignity, they are called principalities and powers; for their habitation, they are stiled the heavenly host, and for their employment, it is to behold the face of God in heaven. The highest pitch, both of our holiness and happiness in the coming world, is expressed by this, we shall be "isangeloi", "equal to the angels," Luke 20: 36. As man is nothing to God, so he is much inferior to the angels; so much below them, that he is not able to bear the sight of an angel, though in a human shape, rendering himself as familiarly as may be to him, Judges 42: 22. When the Psalmist had contemplated the heavens, and viewed the celestial bodies, the glorious luminaries, the moon and stars which God had made, he cries out, Psal. 8: 5. "What is man, that thou art mindful of him, or the son of man that thou visitest him!" Take man at his best when he came a perfect and pure piece out of his Maker's hand, in the state of innocence: yet he was inferior to angels. They always bare the image of God, in a more eminent degree than man, as being wholly spiritual

substances and so more lively representing God, than man could do, whose noble soul is immersed in matter, and closed up in flesh and blood: yet Christ chooses this inferior order and species of creatures, and passeth by the angelical nature; Heb. 2: 16. "He took not on him the nature of angels but the seed of Abraham."

3. Moreover, Jesus Christ did not only neglect the angelical, and assume the human nature; but he also assumed the human nature, after sin had blotted the original glory of it, and withered up the beauty and excellency thereof. For he came not in our nature before the fall, whilst as yet its glory was fresh in it; but he came, as the apostle speaks, Rom. 8: 3 "In the likeness of sinful flesh," i.e. in flesh that had the marks, and miserable effects, and consequent of sin upon it. I say not that Christ assumed sinful flesh, or flesh really defiled by sin, That which was born of the Virgin was a holy thing. For by the power of the Highest (whether by the energetical command and ordination of the Holy Ghosts as some; or by his benediction and blessing, I here dispute not) that whereof the body of Christ was to be formed, was so sanctified, that no taint or spot of original pollution remained in it. But yet though it had not intrinsical native uncleanness in it, it had the effects of sin upon it; yea, it was attended with the whole troop of human infirmities, that sin at first let into our common nature, such as hunger, thirst, weariness, pain, mortality, and all these natural weaknesses and evils that clog our miserable natures, and make them groan from day to day under them.

By reason whereof, though he was not a sinner, yet he looked like one: and they that saw and conversed with him, took him for a sinner; seeing all these effects of sin upon him. In these things he came as near to sin as his holiness could admit. O what a stoop was this! to be made in the likeness of flesh, though the innocent flesh of Adam, had been much; but to be made in the likeness of sinful flesh, the flesh of sinners, rebels; flesh, though not defiled, yet miserably defaced by sin! O what is this! and who can declare it! And indeed, if he will be a Mediator of reconciliation, it was necessary it should be so. It behaved him to assume the same nature that sinned, to make satisfaction in it. Yea, these sinless infirmities were necessary to be assumed with the nature, forasmuch as his bearing them was a part of his humiliation, and went to make up satisfaction for us. Moreover, by them our High Priest was qualified from his own experience, and filled with tender compassion to us.

But O the admirable condescensions of a Saviour, to take such a nature! to put on such a garment when so very mean and ragged! Did this become the Son of God to wear? O grace unsearchable!

4. And yet more, by this his incarnation he was greatly humbled, inasmuch as this so veiled, clouded, and disguised him, that during the time he lived here, he looked not like himself, as God; but as a poor, sorry, contemptible sinner, in the eyes of the world; they scorned him. This fellow said, Matth. 26: 61. Hereby "he made himself of no reputation," Phil. 2: 6. It blotted his honour and reputation. By reason hereof he lost all esteem and honour from those that saw him, Matth. 13: 55. "Is not this the carpenter's son?" To see a poor man travelling up and down the country, in hunger, thirst, weariness, attended with a company of poor men; one of his company bearing the bag, and that which was put therein, John 13: 29. Who that had seen him, would ever have thought this had been the Creator of the world, the Prince of the kings of the earth? "He was despised, and we esteemed him not." Now which of you is there that would not rather chose to endure much misery as a man, than to be degraded into a contemptible worm, that every body treads upon, and no man regards it? Christ looked so unlike a God in this habit, that he was scarce allowed the name of a man; a worm rather than a man.

And think with yourselves now, was not this astonishing self-denial? That he, who from eternity had his Father's smiles and honours, he that from the creation was adored, and worshipped by angels, as their God, must now become a footstool for every miscreant to tread on; and not to have the respects due to a man; sure this was a deep abasement. It was a black cloud that for so many years darkened, and shut up his manifestative glory, that it could not shine out to the world; only some weak rays of the Godhead shone to some few eyes, through the chinks of his humanity, as the clouded sun sometimes opens a little, and casts some faint beams, and is muffled up again. "We saw his glory, as of the only begotten Son:" but the world knew him not, John 1: 14. If a prince walk up and down in a disguise, he must expect no more honour than a mean subject. This was the case of our Lord Jesus Christ, this disguise made him contemptible, and an object of scorn.

5. Again, Christ was greatly humbled by his incarnation, inasmuch as thereby he was put at a distance from his Father, and that ineffable joy and pleasure he eternally had with him. Think not, reader, but the Lord Jesus lived at a high and inimitable rate of communion with God while he walked here in the flesh: but yet to live by faith, as Christ here did, is one thing; and to be in the bosom of God, as he was before, is another. To have the ineffable delights of God perpetuated and continued to him, without one moment's interruption from eternity, is one thing; and to have his soul sometimes filled with the joy of the Lord, and then all overcast with clouds of wrath again; to cry, and God not hear, as he complains, Psal. 32: 2. nay, to be reduced to such a low ebb of spiritual

comforts, as to be forced to cry out so bitterly, as he did, Psal. 22: 1. "My God, my God, why hast thou forsaken me?" This was a thing Christ was very unacquainted with, till he was found in habit as a man.

6. And lastly, It was a great stoop and condescension of Christ if he would become a man, to take his nature from such obscure parents, and chose such a low and contemptible state in this world as he did. He will be born, but not of the blood of nobles, but of a poor woman in Israel, espoused to a carpenter: yea, and that too, under all the disadvantages imaginable; not in his mother's house, but an inn; yea, in the stable too. He suited all to that abased state he was designed for; and came among us under all the humbling circumstances imaginable: "You know the grace of our Lord Jesus Christ (saith the apostle) how that though he was rich, yet for our sakes he became poor," 2 Cor. 8: 9. And thus I have shown you some few particulars of Christ's humiliation in his incarnation. Next we shall infer some things from it that are practical.

Inference 1. Hence we gather the fullness and completeness of Christ's satisfaction, as the sweet first-fruits of his incarnation. Did man offend and violate the law of God? Behold, God himself is become man to repair that breach, and satisfy for the wrong done. The highest honour that ever the law of God received, was to have such a person as the man Christ Jesus is, to stand before its bar, and make reparation to it. This is more than if it had poured out all our blood, and built up its honour upon the ruins of the whole creation.

It is not so much to see all the stars in heaven overcast, as to see one sun eclipsed. The greater Christ was, the greater was his humiliation; and the greater his humiliation was, the more full and complete was his satisfaction; and the mote completeness there is in Christ's satisfaction, the more perfect and steady is the believers consolation. If he had not stooped so low, our joy and comfort could not be exalted so high. The depth of the foundation is the strength of the superstructure.

Inf. 2. Did Christ for our sakes stoop from the majesty, glory and dignity he was possessed of in heaven, to the mean and contemptible state of a man? What a pattern of self-denial is here presented to Christians? What objection against, or excuses to shift off this duty, can remain, after such an example as is here propounded? Brethren, let me tell you, the pagan world was never acquainted with such an argument as this, to press them to self-denial. Did Christ stoop, and cannot you stoop? did Christ stoop so much, and cannot you stoop at the least? Was he content to become any thing, a worm, a reproach, a curse; and cannot you digest any abasement? Do the least slights and neglects rankle your hearts, and poison them with discontent, malice and revenge; O how unlike Christ are you! Hear; and blush in hearing, what your Lord saith in John 13: 14. "If I then your Lord and Master, wash your feet; ye ought also to wash one another's feet." "The example obliges not, (as a learned man well observes) to the same individual act, but it obliges us to follow the reason of the example;" i.e. after Christ's example, we must be ready to perform the lowest and meanest offices of love and service to one another. And indeed to this it obliges most forcibly; for it is as if a master, seeing a proud, sturdy servant, that grudges at the work he is employed about, as if it were too mean and base, should come and take it out of his hand; and when he has done it, should say, does your Lord and Master think it not beneath him to do it; and is it beneath you? I remember it is an excellent saying that Bernard has upon the nativity of Christ: saith he, "What more detestable, what more unworthy, or what deserves severer punishment, than for a poor man to magnify himself, after he has seen the great and high God, so humbled, as to become a little child? It is intolerable impudence for a worm to swell with pride, after it has seen majesty emptying itself; to see one so infinitely above us, to stoop so far beneath us." O how convincing and shaming should it be! Ah how opposite should pride and stoutness be to the Spirit of a Christian! I am sure nothing is more so to the spirit of Christ. Your Saviour was lowly, meek, self-denying, and of a most condescending spirit; he looked not at his own things, but yours, Phil. 2: 4. And does it become you to be proud, selfish, and stout? I remember Jerome, in his epistle to Pamachius, a godly young nobleman, advised him to be eyes to the blind, feet to the lame; yea, saith he, if need be, I would not have you refuse to cut wood, and draw water for the saints: And what, saith he, is this to buffeting and spitting upon, to crowning with thorns, scourging and dying! Christ did undergo all this, and that for the ungodly.

Inf. 3. Did Christ stoop so low as to become a man to save us? Then those that perish under the gospel must needs perish without apology. What would you have Christ do more to save you? Lo, he has laid aside the robes of majesty and glory, put on your own garments of flesh, come down from his throne, and brought salvation home to your own doors. Surely, the lower Christ stooped to save us, the lower we shall sink under wrath that neglect so great salvation. The Lord Jesus is brought low, but the unbeliever will lay him yet lower, even under his feet: he will tread the Son of God under foot, Heb. 10: 28. For such (as the apostle there speaks) is reserved something worse than dying without mercy. What pleas and excuses others will make at the judgement seat, I know not; but once, it is evident, you will be speechless. And, as one well observes, the vilest sinners among the Gentiles, nay, the devils themselves, will have more to say for themselves than you.

The Fountain of Life Opened Up

I must be plain with you; I beseech you consider, how Jews, Pagans, and Devils will rise up in judgement against you. The Jew may say, I had a legal yoke upon me, which neither I nor my fathers were able to bear; Christ invited me only into the garden of nuts, where I might sooner break my teeth with the hard shells of ceremonies, than get the kernel of gospel promises. - In the best of our sacrifices, the smoke filled our temple; smoke only to provoke us to weep for a clearer manifestation. We had but the old edition of the covenant of grace, in a character very darkly intelligible: You have the last edition, with a commentary of our rejection, and the world's reception, and the Spirit's effusion. You had all that heart could wish. - I perish eternally, may the poor Pagan say, without all possibility of reconciliation, and have only sinned against the covenant of works; having never heard of a gospel covenant, nor of reconciliation by a Mediator. O had I but heard one sermon! had Christ but once broke in upon my soul, to convince me of my undone condition, and to have shown a righteousness to me! But woe is me! I never had so much as one offer of Christ. - But so have I, must you say that refuse the gospel: I have, or might have beard thousands of sermons; I could scarce escape hearing one or other shewing me the danger of my sin, and my necessity of Christ. But notwithstanding all I heard, I wilfully resolved I would have nothing to do with him. I could not endure to hear strictness pressed upon me: It was all the hell I had upon earth, that I could not sin in quiet. - Nay, may the devil himself say, it is true, I was ever since my fall maliciously set against God. But alas! as soon as I had sinned, God threw me out of heaven, and told me he would never have mercy upon me: and though I lived in the time of all manner of gracious dispensations, I saw sacrifices offered, and Christ in the flesh, and the gospel preached; yet how could all this chose but enrage me the more, to have God, as it were, say, Look here, Satan, I have provided a remedy for sin, but none for thine! This set me upon revenge against God, as far as I could reach him. But alas! alas! had God entered into any covenant with me at all; had God put me on any terms, though never so hard for the obtaining of mercy; had Christ been but once offered to me, What do you think would I not have done? &c.

O poor sinners! Your damnation is just, if you refuse grace brought home by Jesus Christ himself to your very doors. The Lord grant this may not be thy case who readest these lines.

Inf. 4. Moreover; hence it follows, that none does, or can love like Christ: His love to man is matchless. The freeness, strength, antiquity, and immutability of it, puts a lustre on it beyond all examples. Surely it was a strong love indeed, that made him lay aside hit glory, to be found in fashion as a man, to become any thing, though never so much below himself, for our salvation. We read of Jonathan's love to David, which passed the love of women; of Jacob's love to Rachel, who for her sake endured the heat of summer, and cold of winter; of David's love to Absalom; of the primitive Christians love to one another, who could die one for another but neither had they that to deny which Christ had, nor had he those inducements from the object of his love that they had. His love, like himself, is wonderful.

Inf. 5. Did the Lord Jesus so deeply abase and humble himself for us? What an engagement has he thereby put on us, to exalt and honour him, who for our sakes was so abused? It was a good saying of Bernard, "By how much the viler he was made for me, by so much the dearer he shall be to me." And O that all, to whom Christ is dear, would study to exalt and honour him, these four ways.

1. By frequent and delightful speaking of Him, and for Him. When Paul had once mentions(I his name, he knows not how to part with it, but repeats it no less than ten times in the compass of ten verses, in 1 Cor. 1. It was Lambert's motto, "None but Christ, none but Christ." It is said of Johannes Milius, that after his conversion, he was seldom or never observed to mention the name of Jesus, but his eyes would drop; so dear was Christ to him. or. Fox never denied any beggar that asked an alms in Christ's name, or for Jesus' sake. Julius Palmer, when all concluded he was dead, being turned as black as a coal on the fire, at last moved his scorched lips, and was heard to say, Sweet Jesus, and fell asleep. Plutarch tells us, that when Titus Flaminius had freed the poor Grecians from the bondage with which they had been long ground by their oppressors, and the herald was to proclaim in their audience the articles of peace he had concluded for then, they so pressed upon him, (not being half of them able to hear), that he was in great danger to have lost his life in the press; at last, reading them a second time, when they came to understand distinctly how their case stood, they shouted for joy, "Soter, Soter," "a Saviour, a Saviour," that they made the cry heavens ring gain with their acclamations, and the very birds fell down astonished. And all that night the poor Grecians, with instruments of music, and songs of praise, danced and sung about his tent, extolling him as a god that had delivered them. But surely you have more reason to be exalting the Author of your salvation, who, at a dearer rate, has freed you from a more dreadful bondage. O ye that have escaped the eternal wrath of God, by the humiliation of the Son of God, extol your great Redeemer, and for ever celebrate his praises!

2. By acting your faith on him, for whatsoever lies in the promises yet unaccomplished. In this you see the great and most difficult promise fulfilled, Gen. 3: 15. "The seed of the woman shall break the serpent's head;" which contained this mercy of Christ's incarnation for us in it: I say, you see this fulfilled; and seeing that which was most improbable and difficult is come to pass, even Christ come in the flesh, methinks our unbelief should be removed for ever, and all other promises the more easily believed. It seemed much more improbable and impossible to reason, that God should become a man, and stoop to the condition of a creature, than being a man, to perform all that good which his incarnation and death procured. Unbelief usually argues from one of these two grounds, Can God do this? or, Will God do that? It is questioning either his power or his will; but after this, let it cease for ever to cavil against either. His power to save should never be questioned by any that know what sufferings and infinite burdens he supported in our nature: and surely his willingness to save should never be put to a question, by any that consider how low he was content to stoop for our sakes.

3. By drawing nigh to God with delight, "through the veil of Christ's flesh," Heb. 10: 19. God has made this flesh of Christ a veil betwixt the brightness of his glory and us: it serves to rebate the unsupportable glory, and also to give admission to it, as the veil did in the temple. Through this body of flesh, which Christ assumed, are all decursus et recurs us gratiarum, "outlets of grace from God to us; and through it, also, must be all our returns to God again." It is made the great medium of our communion with God.

4. By applying yourselves to him, under all temptations and troubles, of what kind soever, as to one that is tenderly sensible of your case, and most willing and ready to relieve you. O remember, this was one of the inducements that persuaded and invited him to take your nature, that he might be furnished abundantly with tender compassion for you, from the sense he should have of your infirmities in his own body. Heb. 2: 17. "Wherefore in all things it behaved him to be made like unto his brethren, that he might be a merciful and faithful High-priest, in things pertaining to God, to make reconciliation for the sins of the people." You know by this argument the Lord pressed the Israelites to be kind to strangers; for, (saith he) "you know the heart of a stranger," Exod. 22: 9. Christ, by being in our nature, knows experimentally what our wants, fears, temptations, and distresses are, and so is able to have compassion. O let your hearts work upon this admirable condescension of Christ, till they be filled with it, and your lips say,

Thanks be to God for Jesus Christ.

Sermon 19: Of Christ's Humiliation in his Life

Phil. 2: 8.
And being found in fashion as a man, he humbled himself; and became obedient to death, even the death of the cross.

This scripture has been once already under consideration, and, indeed, can never be enough considered: It holds forth the humbled state of the Lord Jesus, during the time of his abode on earth. The sum of it was delivered you before in this point:

Doct. That the state of Christ, from his conception to his resurrection, was a state of deep debasement and humiliation.

The humiliation of Christ was proposed to you under these three general heads or branches; of his humiliation in his incarnation; his humiliation in his life; and his humiliation in his death. How he was humbled by incarnation, has been opened above in the 18th sermon. How he was humbled in his life, is the design of this sermon: yet expect not that I should give you here an exact history of the life of Christ. The scriptures speak but little of the private part of his life, and it is not my design to dilate upon all the memorable passages that the evangelists (those faithful narrators of the life of Christ) have preserved for us; but only to observe and improve those more observable particulars in his life, wherein especially he was humbled: and such are these that follow.

First, The Lord Jesus was humbled in his very infancy, by his circumcision according to the law. For being of the stock of Israel, he was to undergo the ceremonies, and submit to the ordinances belonging to that people, and thereby to put an end to them; for so it became him to fulfil all righteousness. Luke 2: 21. "And when eight days were accomplished for the circumcising of the child, his name was called Jesus." Hereby the Son of God was greatly humbled, especially in these two respects.

1. In that hereby he obliged himself to keep the whole law, though he was the Law-maker; Gal. 5: 3. "For I testify again to every man that is circumcised, that he is a debtor to do the whole law." The apostle's meaning is, he is a debtor in regard of duty, because he that thinks himself bound to keep one part of the ceremonial law, does thereby bind himself to keep it all; for where all the parts are inseparably united, (as they are in the law of God) we pull all upon us, by engaging or meddling with any one. And he that is a debtor in duty to keep the whole law, quickly becomes a debtor in regard of penalty, not being able to keep any part of it. Christ therefore coming as our surety, to pay both those debts, the debt of duty, and the debt of penalty to the law; He, by his circumcision, obliges himself to pay the whole debt of duty by fulfilling all righteousness: and though his obedience to it was so exact and perfect, that he contracted no debt of penalty for any transgression of his own, yet he obliges himself to pay the debt of penalty which he had contracted, by suffering all the pains due to transgressors. This was that intolerable yoke that none were able to bear but Christ, Acts 15: 10. And it was no small measure of Christ to bind himself to the law, as a subject made under it: For he was the Law-giver, above all law: and herein that sovereignty of a God (one of the choice flowers in the crown of heaven) was obscured and veiled by his subjection.

2. Hereby he was represented to the world not only as a subject, but also as a sinner: for though he was pure and holy, yet this ordinance passing upon him, seemed to imply as if corruption had indeed been in him, which must be cut off by mortification. For this was the mystery principally intended by circumcisions: it served to mind and admonish Abraham, and his seed, of the natural guiltiness, uncleanness, and corruption of their hearts and nature. So Jer. 4: 4, "Circumcise yourselves unto the Lord, and take away the foreskins of your hearts, ye men of Judah;" i.e. the sinfulness and corruption of them. Hence the rebellious and immortified are called "stiff-necked and uncircumcised in heart," as it is Acts 7: 51. And as it served in convince of natural uncleanness, so it signified and sealed "the putting off the body of the sins of the flesh," as the apostle phraseth it, Col. 2: 11. Now, this being the end of God in the institution of this ordinance for Abraham and his ordinary seed, Christ, in his infancy, by submitting to it, did not only veil his sovereignty by subjection, but was also represented as a sinner to the world, though most holy and

pure in himself.

Secondly, Christ was humbled by persecution, and that in the very morning of his life: he was banished almost as soon as born. Matth. 2: 13. "Flee into Egypt (saith the angel to Joseph) and be thou there until I bring thee word, for Herod will seek the young child to destroy him." Ungrateful Herod! was this entertainment for a Saviour? what, raise a country against him, as if a destroyer, rather than a Saviour, had landed upon the coast? what, deny him the protection of those laws, under which he was born, and that before he had broken the least punctilio of them? The child of a beggar may claim the benefit and protection of law, as his birth-right; and must the Son of God be denied it! But herein Herod fulfilled the scriptures, whilst venting his own lusts; for so it was foretold, Jer. 31: 15. And this early persecution was not obscurely hinted in the title of the 22d Psalm, that psalm which looks rather like a history of the New, than a prophecy of the Old Testament; for as it contains a most exact description of Christ's sufferings, so it is fitted with a most suitable title, To the chief musician upon Aijeleth Shahar, which signifies the Hind of the morning, or that deer which the Hunter rouses betides in the morning, and singles out to hunt down that day; and so they did by him, as the 16th verse will tell you; for, (saith he), "Dogs have compassed me, the assembly of the wicked have enclosed me." Upon which Musculus sweetly and ingeniously descants: "O what sweet venison, (saith he) is the flesh of Christ! abundantly sweeter to the believing soul, than that which the nobles of this world esteem most delicate: and lest it should want the highest and richest savour to a delicate palate, Christ, our hart, was not only killed, but hunted to the purpose before he was killed; even as great men use, by hunting and chasing, before they cut the throat of the deer, to render its flesh more sweet, tender, and delicate:" Thus was Christ hunted betides out of the country he was born in. And, no doubt but where such dogs scent and wind the Spirit of Christ in any, they would pursue them also to destruction, did not a gracious Providence rate them off. But to returns, how great a humiliation is this to the Son of God, not only to become an infant, but in his infancy, to be hurried up and down, and driven out of his own land as a vagabond!

Thirdly, Our Lord Jesus Christ was yet more humbled in his life, by that poverty and outward meanness which all along attended his condition: he lived poor and low all his days, so speaks the apostle, 2 Cor. 8: 9. "Though he was rich, yet for our sakes he became poor;" so poor, that he was never owner of a house to dwell in, but lived all his days in other men's houses, or lay in the open air. His outward condition was more neglected and destitute than that of the birds of the air, or beasts of the earth; so he told that scribe, who professed such readiness and resolution to follow him, but was soon cooled, when Christ told him, Matth. 8: 20. "The foxes have holes, and the birds of the air have nests; but the Son of man has not where to lay his head.

It was a common saying, among the Jews, when the Messiah comes, he will not find a place to sit down in. Sometimes he feeds upon barley bread and broiled fish, and sometimes he was hungry, and had nothing to eat, Mark 11: 12. As for money, he was much a stranger to it; when the tribute-money was demanded of him, he and Peter were not so well furnished to make half-a-crown betwixt them to pay it, but must work a miracle for it, Matt. 17 ult.

He came hot to be ministered unto, but to minister, Mat. 20: 28. not to amass earthly treasures, but to bestow heavenly ones. His great and heavenly soul neglected and despised those things, that too many of his own too much admire and prosecute. He spent not a careful thought about those things that eat up thousands and ten thousands of our thoughts. Indeed he came to be humbled, and to teach men by his example the vanity of this world, and pour contempt upon the ensnaring glory of it; and therefore went before us in a chosen and voluntary poverty: yet he lived not a mendicant life neither; but was sometimes fed by ordinary, and sometimes by miraculous and extraordinary ways. He had wherewith to support that precious body of his, till the time was come to offer it up to God; but would not indulge and pamper that flesh, which he purposely assumed to be humbled in.

Fourthly, Our dear Jesus was yet further humbled in his life, by the horrid temptations wherewith Satan assaulted him, than which nothings could be more grievous to his holy heart. The Evangelist gives us an account of this in Luke 4 from the first to the fourteenth verse: in which context you find how the bold and envious spirit meets the Captain of our salvation in the field, comes up with him in the wilderness, when he was solitary, and had not a second with him, verse 1. There he keeps him fasting forty days and forty nights, to prepare him to close with his temptation: all this while Satan was pointing and edging that temptation, with which at last he resolves to try the breast of Christ by a home thrust. verse 2. By this time he supposes Christ was hungry, (as indeed he was) and now he thought it was time to make his assault, which he does in a very suitable temptation at first, and with variety of temptations, trying several weapons upon him afterwards But whom he had made a thrust at him with that first weapon, in which he especially trusted, "command that these stones may be made bread," verse 3, and saw how Christ had put it by, verse 4, then he changes postures and assaults him with temptations to blasphemy, even "to fall down and worship

The Fountain of Life Opened Up

the Devil." But when he saw he could fasten nothing on him, that he was as pure fountain water in a crystal phial, how much soever agitated and shaken, no dregs, or filthy sediment would rise, but he remained pure still: I say, seeing this, he makes a politic retreat, quits the field for a season, verse 13. yet leaves it cum animo revertendi, with a resolution to return to him again. And thus was our blessed Lord Jesus humbled by the temptations of Satan: and what can you imagine more burdensome to him that was brought up from eternity with God, delighting in the holy Father, to be now shut into a wilderness with the Devil, there to be baited so many days, and have his ears filled, though not defiled, with horrid blasphemy, quantum mutatus AB illo? O how was the case altered with Christ! From what, to what was he now come? A chaste woman would account it no common misery to be dogged up and down, and solicited by some vile ruffian, though there were no danger of defilement.

A man would account it no small unhappiness to be shut up five or six weeks together with the Devil, though appearing in a human shape, and to hear no language but that of hell spoken all that time; and the more holy the man is, the more would he be afflicted to hear such blasphemies malignantly spat upon the holy and reverend name of God; much more to be solicited by the devil to join with him in it. This, I say, would be accounted no small misery for a man to undergo. How great a humiliation then must it be to the great God, to be humbled to this! to see a slave of his house, setting upon himself the Lord! His jailer coming is take him prisoner, if he can! A base apostate spirit, daring to attempt such things as these upon him! Surely this was a deep abasement to the Son of God,

Fifthly, Our blessed Lord Jesus was yet more humbled in his life than all this, and that by his own sympathy with others, under all the burdens that made him groan. For he, much more than Paul, could say, who is afflicted, and I burn not? He lived all his time as it were in an hospital among the sick and wounded. And so tender was his heart, that every groan for sin, or under the effects of sin, pierced him so, that it was truly said, "himself bare our sicknesses, and took our infirmities," Matth. 8: 16, 17. It was spoken upon the occasion of some poor creatures that were possessed by the devil, and brought to him to be dispossessed. It is said of him, John 11: 33 "That when he saw Mary weeping, and the Jews also weeping which came with her, he groaned in the Spirit, and was troubled." And verse 35. Jesus wept: yea, his heart flowed with pity for them that had not one drop of pity for themselves. Witness his tears spent upon Jerusalem, Luke 19: 41, 42. He foresaw the misery that was coming, though they never foresaw, nor feared it. O how it pierced him to think of the calamities hanging over that great city! Yea, he mourned for them that could not mourn for their own sins. Therefore it is said, Mark 3: 5. "He was grieved for the hardness of the people's hearts." So that the commendation of a good physician, that he does as it were die with every patient, was most applicable to our tender-hearted Physician. This was one of those things that made him "a man of sorrows, and acquainted with grief." For the more holy any is, the more he is grieved and afflicted for the sin of others; and the more tender any man is, the more he is pierced with beholding the miseries that lie upon others. And it is sure, never any heart more holy, or more sensible, tender and compassionate than Christ's.

Sixthly, Lastly, That which yet helped to humble him lower, was the ungrateful, and most base and unworthy entertainment the world gave him. He was not received or treated like a Saviour, but as the vilest of men. One would think that he who came from heaven, "to give his life a ransom for many," Matt. 20: 28. He that was, "not sent to condemn the world, but that the world through him might be saved", John 3: 17. He that came "to dissolve the works of the devil," 1 John 3: 8. knock off the chains, "open the prison-doors, proclaim liberty to the captives," Isa. 61: 1. I say, when such a Saviour arrived, O with what acclamations of joy, and demonstration of thankfulness, should he have been received? One would have thought they should even kiss the ground he trod upon: but instead of this, he was hated, John 15: 13. He was despised by them, Matt. 13: 55. So reproached that he became "the reproach of men," as who should say, a corner for every one to spit in; a butt for every base tongue to shoot at, Psal. 22: 6. Accused of working his miracles by the power of the devil, Mat. 12: 24. He was trod upon as a worm, Psal. 22: 6;. They buffeted him, Matt. 26: 67. smote him on the head, Matt. 27: 30. arrayed him as a fool, ver. 20. spat in his face, ver. 30. despised him as the basest of men, "this fellow said," Matt. 26: 61. One of his own followers sold him, another forswore him, and all forsook him in his greatest troubles, All this was a great abasement to the Son of God, who was not thus treated for a day, or in one place, but all his days, and in all places. "He endured the contradiction of sinners against himself." In these particulars I have pointed out to you something of the humble life Christ lived in the world. From all these particulars some useful inferences will be noted.

Inference 1. From the first degree of Christ's humiliation, in submitting to be circumcised, and thereby obliging himself to fulfil the whole law, it followeth, that justice itself may set both hand and seal to the acquittances and discharges of believers. Christ hereby obliged himself to be the law's pay-master, to pay its utmost demand; to bear that yoke of obedience that never any before him could bear. And as his circumcision obliged him to keep the whole law; so he was most precise and punctual in the observation of it: so exact, that the sharp eye of Divine Justice cannot espy the least flaw in it; but acknowledges full payment, and stands ready to sign the believer a full acquittance. Rom. 3: 15. "That God may be just, and the justifier of him that believes in Jesus." Had not Christ been thus obliged, we had never been discharged. Had not his obedience been an entire, complete, and perfect thing, our justification could not have been so. He that has a precious treasure, will be loth to adventure it in a leaky vessel: wo to the holiest man on earth, if the safety of his precious soul were to be adventured on the bottom of the best duty that ever he performed. But Christ's obedience and righteousness is firm and sound; a bottom that we may safely adventure all in.

Inf. 2. From the early flight of Christ into Egypt we infer, That the greatest innocence and piety cannot exempt from persecution and injury. Who more innocent than Christ? And who more persecuted? The world is the world still. "I have given them thy word, and the world has hated them," John 17: 14. The world lies in wait as a thief for them that carry this treasure; they who are empty of it may sing before him, he never stops them: but persecution follows piety as the shadow does the body, 2 Tim. 3: 12. "All that will live godly in Christ Jesus, must suffer persecution." Whosoever resolves to live holy, must never expect to live quietly. It is godliness, and godliness in Christ Jesus, i.e. such as is derived from Christ, tulle godliness; and it is true godliness as it is manifested in practice. All that will live godly, that will exert holiness in their lives, which convinces and galls the consciences of the ungodly. It is this enrages, for there is an enmity and antipathy betwixt them: and this enmity runs in the blood; and it is transmitted with it from generation to generation, Gal. 4: 29. "As then he that was born after the flesh, persecuted him that was born after the Spirit; even so it is now." Mark, so it was, and so still it is. "Cain's club is still carried up and down crimsoned with the blood of Abel," said Bucholtzer: but thus it must be, to conform us unto Christ: and O that your spirits, as well as your conditions, may better harmonise with Christ. He suffered meekly, quietly, and self-denyingly; be ye like him. Let it not be said of you, as it is of the hypocrite, whose lusts are only hid, but not mortified by his duties, that he is like flint, which seems cold; but if you strike him, he is all fiery. To do well, and suffer ill, is Christ-like.

Inf. 3. From the third particular of Christ's humiliation, I infer, that such as are full of grace and holiness, may be destitute and empty of creature-comforts. What an overflowing fulness of grace was there in Christ? and yet to what a low ebb did his outward comforts sometimes fall? and as it fared with him, so with many others now in glory with him, whilst they were in the way to that glory; 1 Cor. 4: 11. "Even to this present hour, we both hunger and thirst, and are naked, and buffeted and have no certain dwelling-place." Their souls were richly clothed with robes of righteousness, their bodies naked or meanly clad. Their souls fed high, even on hidden manna, their bodies hungry. Let us be content (saith Luther) with our hard fare; for do we not feast with angels upon that bread of life? Remember, when wants pinch hard, that these fix no marks of Gods hatred upon you. He has dealt no worse with you than he did with his own Son. Nay, which of you is not better accommodated than Christ was? If you be hungry or thirsty, you have some refreshments; you have beds to lie on; the Son of man had not where to lay his head; the Heir of all things had sometimes nothing to eat. And remember you are going to a plentiful country, where all your wants will be supplied; "poor in the world, rich in faith, and heirs of the kingdom which God has promised," James 2: 5. The meanness of your present, will add to the lustre of your future condition.

Inf. 4. From the fourth particular of Christ's humiliation in his life, by Satan's temptations, we infer, That those in whom Satan has no interest, may have most trouble from him in this world, John 14: 30. "The Prince of this world comes, and has nothing in me." Where he knows he cannot be a conqueror he will not cease to be a troubler. This bold and daring spirit adventures upon Christ himself; for doubtless he was filled with envy at the sight of him, and would do what he could though to no purpose, to obstruct the blessed design in his hand. And it was the wisdom and love of Christ to admit him to come as near him as might be, and try all his darts upon him; that by this experience he might be filled with pity to succour them that are tempted. And as he set on Christ, so much more will he adventure upon us; and but too oft comes off a conqueror. Sometimes he shoots the fiery darts of blasphemous injections. These fall as flashes of lightning on the dry thatch, which instantly sets all in a combustion, And just so it is attended with an after thunderclap of inward horror, that shivers the very heart, and strikes all into confusion within.

Divers rules are prescribed in this case to relieve poor distressed ones. One adviseth to think seriously on that which is darted suddenly, and to do by your hearts as men used to do with young horses, that are apt to start and boggle at every thing in the way; we bring them close to the things they fright at, make them look on them, and smell to them, that time and better acquaintance with such things, may teach them not to start. Others advise to diversions of the thoughts, as much as

The Fountain of Life Opened Up

may be, to think quite another way. These rules are contrary to one another, and I think signify but little to the relief of a poor soul so distressed.

The best rule, doubtless, is that of the apostle, Eph. 6: 16. "Above all, taking the shield of faith, wherewith ye shall be able to quench all the fiery darts of the wicked." Act your faith, my friends, upon your tempted Saviour, who passed through temptations before you: and particularly exercise faith on three things in Christ's temptations.

1. Believingly consider, how great variety of temptations were tried upon Christ; and of what a horrid blasphemous nature that was, fall down and worship me.

2. Believingly consider, that Christ came off a perfect conqueror in the day of his trial, beat Satan out of the field. For he saw what he attempted on Christ was as impossible as to batter the body of the sun with snow-balls.

3. Lastly, Believe that the benefits of those his victories and conquests are for you; and that for your sakes he permitted the tempter to come so near him: as you find, Heb. 2: 18.

Object. Heb. 4: 15. If you say, true, Christ was tempted as well as I; but there is a vast differences betwixt his temptations and mine: fir the prince of this world came, and found nothing in him, John 14:13. He was not internally defiled, though externally assaulted; but I am defiled by them as well as troubled.

Sol. This is a different case. True, it is so, and must be so, or else it had signified nothing to your relief: For had Christ been internally defiled, he had not been a fit Mediator for you; nor could you have had any benefit, either by his temptations, or sufferings for you. But he being tempted, and yet still escaping the defilement of sin, has not only satisfied for the sins you commit when tempted, but also got an experimental sense of the misery of your condition, which is in him, (though now in glory) as a spring of pity and tender compassion to you. Remember, poor tempted Christian, "the God of peace shall shortly tread Satan under thy feet," Rom. 16: 20. Thou shalt set thy foot on the neck of that enemy: and as soon as both thy feet are over the threshold of glory, thou shalt cast back a smiling look, and say, now, Satan, do thy worst; now I am there where thou canst not come. Mean while, till thou be out of his reach, let me advise thee to go to Jesus Christ, and open the matter to him; tell him how that base spirit falls upon thee, yea, sets upon thee, even in his presence: entreat him to rebuke and command him off: beg him to consider thy case, and say, Lord, dost thou remember how thy own heart was once grieved, though not defiled, by his assaults? I have grief and guilt together upon me. Ah Lord, I expect pity and help from thee; thou knowest the heart of a stranger, the heart of a poor and tempted one. This is singular relief in this case. O try it!

Inf. 5. Was Christ yet more humbled, by his own sympathy with others in their distresses? Hence we learn, that a compassionate spirit, towards such as labour under burdens of sin, or affliction, is Christ like, and truly excellent: this was the Spirit of Christ: O be like him! Put on as the elect of God, bowels of mercy, Col. 3: 12. "Weep with them that weep, and rejoice with them that rejoice," Rom. 12: 15. It was Cain that said "Am I my brother's keeper?" Blessed Paul was of a contrary temper, 2 Cor. 11: 29. "Who is weak, and I am not weak? Who is offended, and I burn not?" Three things promote sympathy in Christians, one is the Lords pity for them; he does as it were suffer with them; "in all their afflictions he was afflicted;" Isa. 63: 9. Another is, the relation we sustain to God's afflicted people: they are members with us in one body, and the members should have the same care of one another, 1 Cor. 12: 25. The last is, we know not how soon ourselves may need from others, what others now need from us. "Restore him with the spirit of meekness, considering thyself, lest thou also be tempted," Gal. 6: 1.

Inf. 6. Did the world help on the humiliation of Christ by their base and vile usage of him? Learn hence that the judgement the world gives of persons, and their worth, is little to be regarded. Surely it dispenses its smiles and honours very preposterously and unduly, in this respect, among others, the saints are styled persons, "of whom the world is not worthy" Heb. 11: 38. i.e. it does not deserve to have such choice spirits as these are, left in it, since it knows not how to use or treat them. It was the complaint of Salvian, above eleven hundred years ago? "if any of the nobility (saith he) do but begin to turn to God, presently he loses the honour of nobility! O in how little honour is Christ among Christian people, when religion shall make a man ignoble! So that (as he adds) many are compelled to be evil, lest they should be esteemed vile." And indeed, if the world gives us any help to discover the true worth and excellency of men by, it is by the rule of contraries, for the most part. Where it fixes its marks of hatred, we may usually find that which invites our respect and love. It should trouble us the less to be under the slights and disrespects of a blind world. "I could be even proud upon it, (saith Luther) that I see I have an ill name from the world." And Jerome "blessed God that counted him worthy to be hated of the world." Labour to stand right in the judgement of God, and trouble not thyself for the rash and headlong censures of men. Let wicked men, saith one, cut the throat of my credit, and do as they like best with it; when the wind of their calumnies has blown away my good name from me in the way to heaven, I know Christ will take my name out of the mire, and wash it, and restore it to me again.

Inf. 7. From the whole of Christ's humiliation in his life, learn you to pass through all the troubles of your life with a contended, composed spirit, as Christ your fore-runner did. He was persecuted, and bare it meekly: poor, and never murmured; tempted, and never yielded to the temptation; reviled, and reviled not again. When ye therefore pass through any of these trials, look to Jesus, and consider him. See how he that passed through those things before you, managed himself in like circumstances; yea, not only beat the way by his pattern, and example for you, but has in every one of those conditions left a blessing behind him, for them that follow his steps.

Thanks be to God for Jesus Christ.

Sermon 20: Of Christ's Humiliation unto Death, in his first preparative Act for it

John 17: 11.
And now I am no more in the world, but these are in the world, and I come to thee. Holy Father, keep through thine own name those whom thou hast given me, that they may be one, as we [are].

We now come to the last and lowest step of Christ's humiliation, which was in his submitting to death, even the death of the cross. Out of this death of Christ the life of our soul springs up; and in this blood of the cross, all our mercies swim to us. The blood of Christ runs deep to some eyes; the judicious believer sees multitudes, multitudes of inestimable blessings in it. By this crimson fountain I resolve to sit down; and concerning the death of Christ, I shall take distinctly into consideration the preparations made for it; the nature and quality of it; the deportment and carriage of dying Jesus; the funeral solemnities with which he was buried; and lastly, the blessed designs and glorious ends of his death.

The preparatives for his death were six;. Three on his own part, and three more by his enemies. The preparations made by himself for it, were the solemn recommendation of his friends to his Father; the institution of a commemorative sign, to perpetuate and refresh the memory of his death in the hearts of his people, till he come again. And his pouring out his soul to God, by prayer in the garden; which was the posture he chose to be found in, when they should apprehend him.

This scripture contains the first preparative of Christ for death, whereby he sets his house in order, prays for his people, and blesses them before he dies. The love of Christ was ever tender and strong to his people; but the greatest manifestation of it was at parting. And this he manifested two ways especially; viz. in leaving singular supports, and grounds of comfort with them in his last heavenly sermon, in chap. 14, 15, 16, and in pouring out his soul most affectionately to the Father for them in this heavenly prayer, chap. 17. In this prayer he gives them a specimen, or sample, of that his glorious intercession-work, which he was just then going to perform in heaven for them. Here his heart overflowed, for he was now leaving them, and going to the Father. The last words of a dying man are remarkable, how much more a dying Saviour? I shall not launch out into that blessed ocean of precious matter contained in this chapter, but take immediately into consideration the words that I read, wherein I find a weighty petition, strongly followed and set home with many mighty arguments.

1. We have here Christ's petition, or request in behalf of his people, not only those on the place, but all others that then did, or afterwards should believe on him. And the sum of what he here requests for them is, that his Father would keep them through his name. Where you have both the mercy, and the means of attaining it. The mercy is to be kept. Keeping implies danger, And there is a double danger obviated in this request; danger in respect of sin, and danger in respect of ruin and destruction. To both these the people of God lie open in this world.

The means of their preservation from both is the name, i.e. the power of God. This name of the Lord is that "strong tower to which the righteous fly, and are safe," Prov. 18: 10. Alas! It is not your own strength or wisdom that keeps you; but ye are kept by the mighty power of God. This protecting power of God, does not, however, exclude our care and diligence, but implies it; therefore it is added, "Ye are kept by the mighty power of God, through faith, unto salvation," 1 Pet. 1: 5. God keeps his people, and yet they are to keep themselves in the love of God, Jude, ver. 21. to keep their hearts with all diligence, Prov. 4: 23. This is the sum of the petition

2. The arguments with which he urgeth and presses on this request, are drawn partly from his own condition, "I am no more in the world;" i.e. I am going to die; within a very few hours I shall be separated from them, in regard of my corporeal presence. Partly from their condition: "but these are in the world;" i.e. I must leave them in the midst of danger; and partly from the joint interest his Father and himself had in them; "Keep those that thou hast given me:" with several other most

prevalent pleas, which, in their proper places, shall be anon produced, and displayed, to illustrate and confirm this precious truth which this scripture affords us,

Doct. That the fatherly care, and tender love of our Lord Jesus Christ, was eminently discovered in that pleading prayer he poured out for his people at his parting with them.

It pertained to the priest and father of the family to bless the rest, especially when he was to be separated from them by death. This was a rite in Israel. When good Jacob was grown old, and the time was come that he should be gathered to his fathers, then "he blessed Joseph, Ephraim and Manasseh, saying, God, before whom my fathers Abraham and Isaac did walk, the God which fed me all my life long unto this day, the angel which redeemed me from all evil, bless the lads", Gen. 48: 15, 16. This was a prophetical and patriarchal blessing: not that Jacob could bless as God blesses; he could speak the words of blessing, but he knew the effect, the real blessing itself depended upon God. And though he blessed authoritatively, yet not potestatively; i. e. he could as the mouth of God, pronounce blessings, but could not confer them. Thus he blessed his children, as his father Isaac had also blessed him before he died, Gen. 28: 3. and all these blessings were delivered prayer-wise,

Now when Jesus Christ comes to die, he will bless his children also, and therein will discover how much dear and tender love he had for them: "Having loved his own, which were in the world, he loved them to the end," John 13: 1. The last act of Christ in this world, was an act of blessing, Luke 24: 50, 51.

To prepare this point for use, I will here open, First, The mercies which Christ requested of the Father for them. Secondly, The arguments used by him to obtain these mercies. Thirdly, Why he thus pleaded for them when he was to die. Fourthly, and lastly, How all this gives full evidence of Christ's tender care and love to his people.

First, We will enquire what those mercies and special favours were, which Christ begged for his people, when he was to die. And, we find, among others, these five special mercies desired for them, in this context.

1. The mercy of preservation, both from sin and danger: so in the text; "Keep, through thine own name, those whom thou hast given me", which is explained, ver. 15. "I pray not that thou shouldst take them out of the world, but that thou shouldst keep them from the evil." We, in ours, and the saints that are gone, in their respective generations, have reaped the fruit of this prayer. How else comes it to pass, that our souls are preserved amidst such a world of temptations, and these assisted and advantaged by our own corruptions? How is it else, that our persons are not ruined and destroyed amidst such multitudes of potent and malicious enemies, that are set on fire of hell? Surely, the preservation of the burning bush, of the three children amidst the flames; of Daniel in the den of lions; are not greater wonders, than these our eyes do daily behold. As the fire would have certainly consumed, and the lions, without doubt, have rent and devoured, had not God, by the interposition of his own hand, stopped and hindered the effect; so would the sin that is in us, and the malice that is in others, quickly ruin our souls and bodies, were it not that the same hand guards and keeps us every moment. To that hand, into which this prayer of Christ delivered your souls and bodies, do you owe all your mercies and salvations, both temporal and spiritual.

2. Another mercy he prays for, is the blessing of union among themselves. This he joins immediately with the first mercy of preservation, and prays for it in the same breath, verse 11. "That they may be one, as we are." And well might he join them together in one breath; for this union is not only a choice mercy in itself, but a special means of that preservation he had prayed for before: their union with one another, is a special means to preserve them all.

3. A third desirable mercy that Christ earnestly prayed for, was, that his "joy might be fulfilled in them," verse 13. He would provide for their joy, even when the hour of his greatest sorrow was at hand; yea, he would not only obtain joy for them, but full joy: "that my joy might be fulfilled in them." It is as if he had said, O my Father, I am to leave these dear ones in a world of troubles and perplexities; I know their hearts will be subject to frequent despondencies; O let me obtain the cordials of divine joy for them before I go: I would not only have them live, but live joyfully; provide for fainting hours reviving cordials.

4. And as a continued spring to maintain all the aforementioned mercies, he prays "they all may be sanctified through the word of truth, verse 17. i. e. more abundantly sanctified than yet they were, by a deeper radication of gracious habits and principles in their heart. This is a singular mercy in itself, to have holiness spreading itself over and through their souls, as the light of the morning. Nothing is in itself more desirable. And it is also a singular help to their perseverance, union and spiritual joy, which he had prayed for before, and are all advanced by their increasing sanctification.

5. And lastly, as the complement and perfection of all desirable mercies, he prays, "that they may be with him, where he is, to behold his glory," verse 24. This is the best and ultimate privilege they are capable of. The end of his coming down from heaven, and returning thither again, all runs

The Fountain of Life Opened Up

into this, to bring many sons and daughters unto glory. You see Christ asks no trifles, no small things for his people; no mercies, but the best that both worlds afford, will suffice him on their behalf.

Secondly, Let us see how he follows his requests, and with what arguments he pleads with the Father for these things: and, among others, I shall single out six choice ones, which are urged in this text, or the immediate context.

The first argument is drawn from the joint interest, that both himself, and his Father, have in their persons, for whom he prays, "All mine are thine, and thine are mine," verse 10. As if he should say, Father, behold, and consider the persons I pray for, they are not aliens, but Christians: yea, they are thy children as well as mine: the very same on whom thou hast set thy eternal love, and in that love hast given them to me; so that they are both thine and mine: great is our interest in them, and interest draws care and tenderness. Every one cares for his own, provides for, and secures his own. Property, (even amongst creatures) is fundamental to our labour, care, and watchfulness; they would not so much prize life, health, estates, or children, if they were not their own. Lord these are thine own by many ties or titles: O therefore keep, comfort, sanctify, and save them, for they are thine. What a mighty plea is this? Surely, Christians, your intercessor is skilful in his work, your advocate wants no eloquence or ability to plead for you.

The second argument, and that a powerful one, treads as I may say, upon the very heel of the former, in the next words, "And I am glorified in them;" q. d. my glory and honour are infinitely dear to thee; I know thy heart is entirely upon the exalting and glorifying of thy Son. Now, what glory have I in the world, but what comes from my people? Others neither can, nor will glorify one; nay, I am daily blasphemed and dishonored by them: these are they from whom my active glory and praise in the world must rise. It is true, both thou and I have glory from other creatures objectively; the works that we have made, and impress our power, wisdom and goodness upon, do so glorify us: and honour we have from our very enemies accidentally; their very wrath shall praise us: but for active and voluntary praise, whence comes this but from the people that were formed for that very purpose? Should these then miscarry and perish, where shall my manifestative and active glory be? and from whom shall I expect it? So that here his property and glory are pleaded with the Father, to prevail for those mercies; and they are both great, and valuable things with God. What dearer, what nearer to the heart of God?

Arg. 3. And yet, to make all fast and sure, he adds, in the beginning of this verse 11 a third argument, in these words, "And now I am no more in the world." Where we must consider the sense of it, as a proposition, and the force of it, as an argument. This proposition, "I am no more in the world," is not to be taken simply and universally, as if, in no sense, Christ should be any more in this world: but only respectively, as to his corporeal presence; this was, in a little time, to be removed from his people, which had been a sweet spring of comfort to them,, in all their troubles. But now it might have been said to the pensive disciples, as the sons of the prophets said to Elisha, a little before Elijah's translation, "Know ye not that your master shall be taken from your heads today?" This comfortable enjoyment must be taken from them; this is the sense. And here lies the argument; Father, consider the sadness and trouble I shall leave my poor children under. Whilst I was with them, I was a sweet relief to their souls, whatever troubles they met with; in all doubts, fears, and dangers, they could repair to me, and in their straits and wants I still supplied them; they had my counsels to direct them, my reproofs to reduce them, and my comforts to support them; yea, the very sight of me was an unspeakable joy and refreshment to their souls: but now the hour is come, and I must be gone. All the comfort and benefit they had from my presence among them, is cut off. and, except thou do make up all this to them another way, what will become of these children, when their Father is gone? What will be the case of the poor sheep, and tender lambs, when the shepherd is smitten? Therefore, O my Father, look thou after them, see to them, for they are thine as well as mine; I am glorified in them, and now leaving them, and removing out of this world from them.

Arg. 4. And yet, to move and engage the Father's care and love for them, he subjoins another great consideration, in the very next words drawn from the danger he leaves them in; "But these are in the world." The world is a sinful, infecting, and unquiet place; it lies in wickedness: And a hard thing it will be for such poor, weak, imperfect creatures to escape the pollutions of it; or, if they do, yet the troubles, persecutions, and strong oppositions of it they cannot escape. Seeing therefore I must leave thine own dear children, as well as mine, and those from whom the glory is to rise, in the midst of a sinful, troublesome, dangerous world, where they can neither move backward nor forward, without danger of sin or ruin: O, since the case stands so, look after them, provide for them, and take special care for them all. Consider who they are, and where I leave them. They are thy children, to be left in a strange country; thy soldiers, in the enemies quarters; thy sheep, in the midst of wolves; thy precious treasure, among thieves.

Arg. 5. And yet he has not done, for he resolves to strive hard for the mercies he had asked, and will not come off with a denial; and therefore adds another argument in the next words, And I come to thee. As his leaving them was an argument, so his coming to the Father is a mighty argument also. There is much in these words, I come to thee. [I,] thy beloved Son, in which thy soul delighteth; I, to whom thou never deniedst any thing. It is not a stranger, but a son; not an adopted, but thine only begotten Son. It is I that [come.] I am now coming to thee apace, my Father. I come to thee swimming through a bloody ocean. I come, treading every step of my way to thee in blood, and unspeakable sufferings; and all this for the sake of those dear ones I now pray for; yea, the design and end of my coming to thee, is for them. I am coming to heaven in the capacity of an advocate, to plead with thee for them. And I come to [Thee] my Father, and their Father; my God, and their God. Now then, since I, that am so dear, come through such bitter pangs, to thee, so dear, so tender-hearted a Father; and all this on their score and account: Since I do but now, as it were, begin, or give them a little taste of that intercession work, which I shall live for ever to perform for them in heaven; Father, hear, Father, grant what I request. O give a comfortable earnest of those good things which I am coming to thee for, and which I know thou wilt not deny me.

Arg. 6. And, to close up all, he tells the Father how careful he had been to observe, and perform that trust which was committed to him; "While I was with them in the world, I kept them in thy name; those that thou gavest me, I have kept, and none of them is lost, but the son of perdition ver. 12.

And thus lies the argument: Thou committedst to me a certain number of elect souls, to be redeemed by me; I undertook the trust, and said, if any of these be lost, at my hand let them be required, I will answer for them every one to thee. In pursuance of which trust, I am now here on the earth, in a body of flesh. I have been faithful to a point. I have redeemed them (for he speaks of that as finished and done, which was now ready to be done) I have kept them also, and confirmed them hitherto; and now, Father, I commit them to thy care. Lo, here they are, not one is lost, but the son of perdition, who was never given. With how great care have I been careful for them! O let them not fail now; Let not one of them perish.

Thus you see what a nervous, argumentative, pleading prayer Christ poured out to the Father for them at parting.

Thirdly, The next enquiry is, why he thus prayed and pleaded with God for them, when he was to die?

And certainly it was not because the Father was unwilling to grant the mercies he desired for them: No, they came not with difficulty, nor were they wrestled by mere importunity, out of the hand of an unwilling and backward person. For, he tells us, John 16: 27. "The Father himself loveth you," i. e. he is propense enough of his own accord to do you good. But the reasons of this exceeding importunity, are,

1. He foresaw a great trial then at hand, yea, and all the aftertrials of his people as well as that. He knew how much they would be sifted, and put to, in that hour, and power of darkness, that was coming. He knew their faith would be shaken, and greatly staggered by the approaching difficulties, when they should see their Shepherd smitten, and themselves scattered, the Son of man delivered into the hands of sinners, and the Lord of life hang dead upon the tree, yea, sealed up in the grave. He foresaw what straits his poor people would fall into, betwixt a busy devil, and a bad heart; therefore he prays and pleads with such importunity and ardency for them, that they might not miscarry.

2. He was now entering upon his intercession-work in heaven, and he was desirous in this prayer to give us a specimen, or sample, of that part of his world, before he left us; that by this we might understand what he would do for us, when he should be out of sight. For this being his last prayer on earth, it shows us what affections and dispositions he carried hence with him, and satisfies us, that he who was so earnest with God on our behalf, such a mighty pleader here, will not forget us, or neglect our concerns in the other world. Yet, reader, I would have thee always remember, that the intercession of Christ in heaven is carried much higher than this; it is performed in a way more suitable to that state of honour to which he is now exalted. Here he used prostrations of body, cries and tears in his prayers: there, his intercession is carried in a more majestic way, and with more state, becoming an exalted Jesus. But yet in this he has left us a special assistance, to discover much of the frame, temper, and working of his heart, now in heaven towards us.

3. And lastly, he would leave this as a standing monument of his father-like care, and love to his people, to the end of the world. And for this it is conceived Christ delivered this prayer so publicly, not withdrawing from the disciples to be private with God, as he did in the garden; but he delivers it in their presence, "These things which I speak in the world," ver. 13. This, with the circumstances of place, [in the world], does plainly speak it to be a public prayer. And not only was it publicly delivered, but it was also, by a singular providence, recorded at large by John, though omitted by the other evangelists; that so it might stand to all generations, for a testimony of Christ's

The Fountain of Life Opened Up
tender care and love to his people.

Fourthly, If you ask how this gives evidence of Christ's tender care and love to his people? which is the last enquiry; I answer, in few words, for the thing is plain and obvious; it appears in these two particulars.

1. His love and care was manifested in the choice of mercies for them. He does not pray for health, honour, long life, riches, &c. but for their preservation from sin, spiritual joy in God sanctification and eternal glory. No mercies but the very best in God's treasure will content him. He was resolved to get all the best mercies for his people; the rest he is content should be dispenses promiscuously by Providence: but these he will settle as an heritage upon his children. O see the love of Christ! look over all your spiritual inheritance in Christ, compare it with the richest, fairest, sweetest inheritance on earth; and see what poor things these are to yours. O the care of a dear father! O the love of a tender Saviour!

2. Besides, what an evidence of his tenderness to you, and great care for you, was this, that he should so intently, and so affectionately mind, and plead your concerns with God, at such a time as this was, even when a world of sorrow encompassed him on every side; a cup of wrath mixed, and ready to be delivered into his hand: at that very time when the clouds of wrath grew black, a storm coming, and such as he never felt before; when one would have thought, all his care, thoughts, and diligence, should have been employed on his own account, to mind his own sufferings? No, he does as it were forget his own sorrows, to mind our peace and comfort. O love unspeakable!

Corollary 1. If this be so, that Christ so eminently discovered his care and love for his people, in this his parting hour; then hence we conclude, The perseverance of the saints is unquestionable. Do you hear how he pleads! how he begs! how he fills his mouth with arguments! how he chooses his words, and sets them in order, how he winds up his spirit to the very highest pitch of zeal and fervency? and can you doubt of success? Can such a Father deny the importunity, and strong seasonings and pleading of such a Son; O, it can never be! he cannot deny him: Christ has the art and skill of prevailing with God: He has (as in this appears) the tongue of the learned. If the heart or hand of God were hard to be opened, yet this would open them; but when the Father himself loves us, and is inclined to do us good, who can doubt of Christ's success? "That which is in motion, is the more easily moved" The cause Christ manageth in heaven for us is just and righteous. The manner in which he pleads is powerful and therefore the success of his suit is unquestionable.

The apostle professeth, 2 Cor. 1: 3. "We can do nothing against the truth." He means it in regard of the bent of his heart; he could not move against truth and righteousness. And if a holy man cannot, much less will a holy God. If Christ undertake to plead the cause of his people with the Father, and use his oratory with him, there is no doubt of his prevailing. Every word in this prayer is a chosen shaft, drawn to the head by a strong and skilful hand; you need not question but it goes home to the white, and hits the mark aimed at. Does he pray, "Father, keep, through thine own name, those thou hast given me?" Sure they shall be kept, if all the power in heaven can keep them. Think on this, when dangers surround your souls or bodies, when fears and doubts are multiplied within: when thou art ready to say in thy haste, All men are liars, I shall one day perish by the hand of sin or Satan; think on that encouragement Christ gave to Peter, Luke 22: 31. "I have prayed for thee."

Corollary 2. Again, hence we learn, that argumentative prayers are excellent prayers. The strength of every thing is in its joints; there lies much of the strength of prayer also: how strongly jointed, how nervous and argumentative was this prayer of Christ. Some there are indeed, that think we need not argue and plead in prayer with God, but only present the matter of our prayers to him, and let Christ alone (whose office it is) to plead with the Father; as if Christ did not present our pleas and arguments, as well as simple desires to God; as if the choicest part of our prayers must be kept back, because Christ presents our prayers to God. No, no, Christ's pleading is one thing, ours another: "His and ours are not opposed, but subordinate;" his pleading does not destroy, but makes ours successful. God calls us to plead with him, Isa. 1: 18. "Come now let us reason together." "God (as one observes) reasoneth with us by his word and providences outwardly, and by the motions of his Spirit inwardly: let we reason with him by framing (through the help of his Spirit) certain holy arguments, grounded upon allowed principles, drawn from his nature, name, word, or works." And it is condemned as a very sinful defect in professors, that they did not plead the church's cause with God; Jer. 30: 13. "There is none to plead thy cause that thou mayest be bound up." What was Jacob's wrestling with the angels but his holy pleading and importunity with God? and how well it pleased God, let the event speak, Gen. 32: 24. Hos. 12: 4. "As a prince he prevailed, and had power with God." On which instance, a Worthy thus glosseth: "Let God frown, smite or wound, Jacob is at a point, a blessing he came for, and a blessing he will have; I will not let thee go, (saith he) unless thou bless me. His limbs, his life might go, but there is no going from Christ without a pawn, without a blessing." This is the man, now what is his speed? The Lord admires him, and honours him to all generations. "What is thy name?" saith he; q. d. I never met with such a man, titles of honour are not worthy of thee: thou shalt be called, not Jacob a shepherd with men, but Jacob a prince with God. Nazianzen said of his sister Gorgonia, That she was modestly impudent with God; there was no putting her off with a denial. The Lord, on this account, has honoured his saints with the title of, His recorders, men fit to plead with him as that word [maskir] signifies: Isa. 62: 6. "Ye that make mention of the Lord, keep not silence, give him no rest." It notes the office of him that recorded all the memorable matters of the king, and used to suggest seasonable items and memorandums of things to be done.

By these holy pleadings, "the King is held in his galleries," as it is Cant. 7: 5. I know we are not heard, either for our much speaking, or our excellent speaking; it is Christ's pleading in heaven that makes our pleading on earth available: but yet surely, when the Spirit of the Lord shall suggest proper arguments in prayer, and help the humble suppliant to press them home believingly and affectionately, when he helps us to weep and plead, to groan and plead, God is greatly delighted in such prayers. "Thou hast said, I will surely do thee good," said Jacob, Gen. 32: 12. It is thine own free promise; I did not go on mine own head, but thou badest me go, and encouragedst me with this promise. O this is pleasing to God, when by his spirit of adoption we can come to God, crying, Abba Father; Father, hear, forgive, pity, and help me. Am I not thy child, thy son, or daughter? To whom may a child be bold to go, with whom may a child have hope to speed, if not with his father? Father, hear me. The fathers of our flesh are full of bowels, and pity their children, and know how to give good things to them, when they ask them. When they ask bread or clothes, will they deny them? And is not the Father of spirits more full of bowels, more full of pity? Father, hear me. This is that kind of prayer, which is melody in the ears of God.

Corollary 3. What an excellent pattern is here, for all that have the charge and government of others committed to them, whether magistrates, ministers, or parents, to teach them how to acquit themselves towards their relations, when they come to die?

Look upon dying Jesus, see how his care and love to his people flamed out, when the time of his departure was at hand. Surely, as we are bound to remember our relations every day, and to lay up a stock of prayers for them in the time of our health, so it becomes us to imitate Christ in our earnestness with God for them, when we die. Though we die, our prayers die not with us: they out-live us, and those we leave behind us in the world, may reap the benefit of them, when we are turned to dust.

For my own part, I must profess before the world, that I have a high value for this mercy, and do, from the bottom of my heart, bless the Lord, who gave me a religious and tender father, who often poured out his soul to God for me: he was one that was inwardly acquainted with God; and being full of bowels to his children, often carried them before the Lord, prayed and pleaded with God for them, wept and made supplications for them. This stock of prayers and blessings left by him before the Lord, I cannot but esteem above the fairest inheritance on earth. O it is no small mercy to have thousands of fervent prayers lying before the Lord, filed up in heaven for us. And O that we would all be faithful to this duty! Surely our love, especially to the souls of our relations, should not grow cold when our breath does. O that we would remember this duty in our lives, and, if God give opportunity and ability, fully discharge it when we die; considering, as Christ did, we shall be no more, but they are in this world, in the midst of a defiled, tempting, troublesome world; it is the last office of love that ever we shall do for them. After a little while we shall be no longer sensible how it is with them; for, (as the church speaks Isa 63: 16. "Abraham is ignorant of us, and Israel acknowledgeth us not") what temptations and troubles may befall them, we do not know. O imitate Christ your pattern.

Corollary 4. To conclude; Hence we may see, what a high esteem and precious value Christ has of believers; this was the treasure which he could not quit, he could not die till he had secured it in a safe hand; "I come unto thee, holy Father, keep through thine own name those whom thou hast given me".

Surely believers are dear to Jesus Christ; and good reason, for he has paid dear for them: let his dying language, this last farewell, speak for him, how he prized them. The Lord's portion "is his people, Jacob is the lot of his inheritance," Deut. 32: 9. "They are a peculiar treasure to him, above all the people of the earth," Exod. 19: 5. What is much upon our hearts when we die, is dear to us indeed. O how precious, how dear should Jesus Christ be to us! Were we first and last upon his heart; did he mind us, did he pray for us, did he so wrestle with God about as, when the sorrows of death compassed him about? How much are we engaged, not only to love him, and esteem him, whilst we live, but to be in pangs of love for him, when we feel the pangs of death upon us! to be dying him, when our eye-strings break! To have hot affections for Christ, when our hands and feet grow cold! The very last whisper of our departing souls should be this,

Blessed be God for Jesus Christ.

Sermon 21: The second preparative Act of Christ for his own Death

1 Corinthians xi. 23-25
> *The Lord Jesus the [same] night in which he was betrayed took bread: And when he had given thanks, he brake [it], and said, Take, eat: this is my body, which is broken for you: this do in remembrance of me. After the same manner also [he took] the cup, when he had supped, saying, This cup is the new testament in my blood: this do ye, as oft as ye drink [it], in remembrance of me.*

Christ had no sooner recommended his dear charge to the Father, but (the time of his death hastening on) he institutes his last supper, to be the lasting memorial of his death, in all the churches, until his second coming; therein graciously providing for the comfort of his people, when he should be removed out of their sight. And this was the second preparative act of Christ, in order to his death: he will set his house in order, and then die.

- This his second act manifests no less love than the former. It is like the plucking off the ring from his finger, when ready to lay his neck upon the block, and delivering it to his dearest friends, to keep that as a memorial of him: "Take this, &c. in remembrance of me."

In the words read, are four things noted by the apostle, about this last and lovely act of Christ, viz. the Author, Time, Institution, and End of this holy, solemn ordinance.

1. The author of it, The Lord Jesus: It is an effect of his lordly power, and royal authority; Matth. 28: 18. "And Jesus came, and spake unto them, saying, All power is given unto me in heaven and earth: Go ye therefore." The government is upon his shoulders, Isa. 9: 6. He shall bear the glory, Zech. 6: 13. Who but he that came out of the bosom of the Father, and is acquainted with all the counsels that are there, knows what will be acceptable to God? And who but he can give creatures, by his blessing, their sacramental efficacy and virtue? Bread and wine are naturally fit to refresh and nourish our bodies; but what fitness have they to nourish souls? Surely none, but what they receive from the blessing of Christ that institutes them.

2. The Time when the Lord Jesus appointed this ordinance. "In the same night in which he was betrayed:" it could not be sooner, because the passover must first be celebrated; nor later, for that night he was apprehended. It is therefore emphatically expressed "en tei nukti", in that same night, that night for ever to be remembered. He gives, that night, a cordial draught to his disciples before the conflict: he settles, that night, an ordinance in the church, for the confirmation and consolation of his people, in all generations, to the end of the world. By instituting it that night, he gives abundant evidence of his care for his people, in spending so much of that little, very little, time he had left, on their account.

3. The Institution itself; in which we have the memorative, significative, instructive signs, and they are bread and wine; and the glorious mysteries represented and shadowed forth by them, viz. Jesus Christ crucified; the proper New-Testament nourishment of believers. Bread and wine are choice creatures, and do excellently shadow forth the flesh and blood of crucified Jesus; and that both, in their natural usefulness, and manner of preparation. Their usefulness is very great; bread is a creature necessary to uphold and maintain our natural life; therefore it is called the staff of bread, Isa. 3: 1. Because as a feeble man depends and leans upon his staff, so do our feeble spirits upon bread. Wine was made to cheer the heart of man, Judg. 11: 13. They are both useful and excellent creatures; their preparations, to become so useful to us, are also remarkable. The corn must be ground in the mill, the grapes torn and squeezed to pieces in the winepress, before we can either have bread or wine. And when all this is done, they must be received into the body, or they nourish not. So that these were very fit creatures to be set apart for this use and end.

If any object, It is true, they are good creatures, but not precious enough to be the signs of such profound and glorious mysteries: it was worth creating a new creature, to be the sign of the new covenant.

Let him that thus objects, ask himself, whether nothing be precious without pomp? The preciousness of these elements is not so much from their own natures, as their use and end; and that makes them precious indeed. A loadstone at sea is much more excellent than a diamond, because more useful. A penny-worth of wax applied to the label of a deed, and sealed, may in a minute have its value raised to thousands of pounds. These creatures receive their value and estimation on a like account. Nor should it at all remain a wonder to thee, why Christ should represent himself by such mean and common things, when thou hast well considered that the excellency of the picture, is its similitude and conformity to the original; and that Christ was in a low, sad, and very abased state, when this picture of him was drawn; he was then a man of sorrows. These then, as lively sighs, shadow forth a crucified Jesus, represent him to us in his red garments. This precious ordinance may much more than Paul, say to us, "I always bear about in my body the dying of the Lord Jesus:" That is the thing it signifies.

4. Lastly take notice of the use, design, and end of this institution. "Eis ten emen anamnesin", in remembrance, or for a memorial of me. O there is much in this: Christ knew how apt our base hearts would be to lose him, amidst such a throng of sensible objects as we here converse with; and how much that forgetfulness of him and of his sufferings, would turn to our prejudice and loss; therefore does he appoint a sign to be remembered by: "As oft as you do this, ye show forth the Lord's death till he come." Hence we observe, suitable to the design of this discourse,

Doct. That the sacramental memorial Christ left with his people, is a special mark of his care and love for them.

What! To order his picture (as it were) to be drawn when he was dying, to be left with his spouse! To rend his own flesh, and set abroach his own blood to be meat and drink for our souls! O what manner of love was this! It is true, his picture in the sacrament is full of scars and wounds: but these are honourable scars, and highly grace and commend it to his spouse, for whose dear sake he here received them.

"They are marks of love and honour." And he would be so drawn, or rather he so drew himself, that as oft as his people looked upon the portraiture of him, they might remember, and be deeply affected with those things he here endured for their sakes. These are the wounds my dear husband Jesus received for me. These are the marks of that love which passes the love of creatures. O see the love of a Saviour! This is that heavenly Pelican that feeds his young with his own blood. We have read of pitiful and tender women that have eaten the flesh of their own children, Lam. 4: 10. But where is that woman recorded that gave her own flesh and blood to be meat and drink to her children? Surely the spouse may say of the love of Christ, what David in his lamentations, said of the love of Jonathan, "Thy love to me was wonderful, passing the love of women." But to prepare the point to be meat indeed, and drink indeed to thy soul, I shall discuss briefly these three things, and hasten to the application.

First, What it is to remember the Lord Jesus in the sacrament.

Secondly, What aptitude there is in that ordinance, so to bring him to our remembrance.

Thirdly, How the care and love of Christ is discovered, by leaving such a memorial of himself with us.

Remembrance, properly, is the return of the mind to an object, about which it has been formerly conversant; and it may so return to a thing, it has conversed with before, two ways; speculatively and transiently; or affectingly, and permanently. A speculative remembrance is only to call to mind the history of such a person and his sufferings: that Christ was once put to death in the flesh. An affectionate remembrance, is when we so call Christ and his death to our minds, as to feel the powerful impressions thereof upon our hearts. Thus, Mat. 26: 75. "Peter remembered the word of the Lord, and went out, and wept bitterly." His very heart was melted with that remembrance; his bowels were pained, he could not hold, but went out and wept abundantly. Thus Joseph, when he saw his brother Benjamin, whose sight refreshed the memory of former days and endearments, was greatly affected, Gen. 43: 29, 30. "And he lift up his eyes, and saw his brother Benjamin, his mother's son: and said, Is this your younger brother, of whom ye spake to me? and he said, God be gracious to thee my son. And Joseph made haste, for his bowels did yearn upon his brother, and he sought where to weep; and he entered into his chamber, and wept there." Such a remembrance of Christ is that which is here intended. This is indeed a gracious remembrance of Christ: the former has nothing of grace in it. The time shall come when Judas that betrayed him, and the Jews that pierced him, shall historically remember what was done; Rev. 1: 7. "Behold he comets with clouds, and every eye shall see him; and they also which pierced him, and all kindreds of the earth shall wail because of him." Then I say, Judas shall remember; This is he whom I perfidiously betrayed. Pilate shall remember; This is he whom I sentenced to be hanged on the tree though I was convinced of his innocence. Then the soldiers shall remember; This is that face we spit upon, that head we crowned with thorns; Lo, this is he whose side we pierced, whose hands and feet we once nailed to the cross. But this remembrance will be their torment, not their benefit. It is not therefore a bare historical, speculative, but a gracious, affectionate, impressive remembrance of Christ, that is here intended: and such a remembrance of Christ supposes and includes,

The Fountain of Life Opened Up

    1. The saving knowledge of him. We cannot be said to remember what we never knew; nor to remember, savingly, what we never knew savingly. There have been many previous, sweet end gracious transactions, dealings, and intimacies betwixt Christ and his people, from the time of their first happy acquaintance with him: much of that sweetness they have had in former considerations of him, and hours of communion with him, is lost and gone; for nothing is more volatile, hazardous, and inconstant, than our spiritual comforts: but now at the Lord's table, there our old acquaintance is renewed, and the remembrance of his goodness and love refreshed and revived: "We will remember thy love more than wine; the upright love thee," Cant. 1: 4.

    2. Such a remembrance of Christ includes faith in it. Without discerning Christ at a sacrament, there is no remembrance of him; and, without faith, no discerning Christ there. But when the precious eye of faith has spied Christ, under that vail, it presently calls up the affections, saying "Come see the Lord." These are the wounds he received from me. This is he that loved me, and gave himself for me. This is his flesh, and that his blood; sic oculus, sic ille manus, &c. so his arms were stretched out upon the cross to embrace me; so his blessed head hung down to kiss me. Awake my love, rouse up my hope, flame out my desires; Come forth, all ye powers and affections of my soul; come, see the Lord. No sooner does Christ by his Spirit call to the believer but faith hears; and discerning the voice, turns about, like Mary, saying, Rabboni, my Lord, my Master.

    3. This remembrance of Christ includes suitable impressions made upon the affections, by such a sight and remembrance of him: and therein lies the nature of that precious thing which we call communion with God. Various representations of Christ are made at his table. Sometimes the soul there calls to mind the infinite wisdom, that so contrived and laid the glorious and mysterious design and project of redemption: the effect of this is wonder and admiration. O the manifold wisdom of God! Eph. 3: 10. O the depths, the heights, the length, the breadth of this wisdom! I can as easily span the heavens as take the just dimensions of it. Sometimes a representation of the severity of God is made to the soul at that ordinance. O how inflexible and severe is the justice of God! What, no abatement! no sparing mercy; no, not to his own Son? This begets a double impression on the heart.

    (1.) Just and deep indignation against sin; Oh cursed sin! It was thou used my dear Lord so; for thy sake he underwent all this. If thy vileness had not been so great, his sufferings had not been so many. Cursed sin! thou wast the knife that stabbed him: thou the sword that pierced him. Ah what revenge it works! I remembered that it is storied of one of the kings of France, that hearing the bishop (as I remember it was Remegius) read the history of Christ's trial and execution, and hearing how barbarously they had used him, he was moved, with so tragical and pathetical a history, to great indignation against Pilate, the Jews, and the rude and bloody soldiers, and could not contain himself, but cried out, as the bishop was reading, "O that I had been there with my Frenchmen, I would have cut all their throats who so barbarously used my Saviour."

    To allude to this: when the believer considers and remembers, that sin put Christ to all that shame and ignominy, and that he was wounded for our transgressions, he is filled with hatred of sin, and cries out, O sin, I will revenge the blood of Christ upon thee! thou shalt never live a quiet hour in my heart. And,

    (2.) It produces an humble adoration of the goodness and mercy of God, to exact satisfaction for our sins, by such bloody stripes, from our surety. Lord, if this wrath had seized on me, as it did on Christ, what had been my condition then! If these things were done to the green tree, what had been the case of the dry tree?

    Sometimes representations, (and not common ones), are made of the love of Christ, who assumed a body and soul, on purpose to bear the wrath of God for our sins. And when that surpassing love breaks out in its glory upon the souls, how is the soul transported and ravished with it! crying out, what manner of love is this! here is a love large enough to go round the heavens, and the heaven of heavens! Who ever loved after this rate, to lay down his life for enemies! O love unutterable and inconceivable! How glorious is my love in his red garments! Sometimes the fruits of his death are there gloriously displayed; even his satisfaction for sin, and the purchase his blood made of the eternal inheritance: And this begets thankfulness and confidence in the soul, Christ is dead, and his death has satisfied for my sin. Christ is dead, therefore my soul shall never die. Who shall separate me from the love of God? These are the fruits, and this is the nature of that remembrance of Christ here spoken of.

    Secondly, What aptitude or condecency is there in this ordinance, to bring Christ so to remembrance?

    Much every way; for it is a sign, by him appointed to that end, and has (as divines well observe) a threefold use and consideration, viz. as it is memorative, significative, and instructive.

    1. As it is memorative, and so it has the nature and use of a pledge or token of love, left by a dying to a dear surviving friend. And so the sacrament, as was said before, is like a ring pluckt off from Christ's finger, or a bracelet from his arm; or rather his picture from his breast, delivered to us

with such words as these; "As oft as you look on this, remember me; let this help to keep me alive in your remembrance when I am gone, and out of your sight." It induces to it also,

2. As it is a significative sign, most aptly signifying both his bitter sufferings for us, and our strict and intimate union with him; both which have an excellent usefulness to move the heart, and its deepest affections, at the remembrance of it. The breaking of the bread, and shedding forth the wine, signify the former; our eating, drinking, and incorporating them, is a lively signification of the other.

3. Moreover, this ordinance has an excellent use and advantage for this affectionate remembrance of Christ, as it is an instructive sign. And it many ways instructs us, and enlightens our mind, particularly in these truths, which are very affecting things.

1. That Christ is the bread on which our souls live, proper meat and drink for believers, the most excellent New-Testament food. It is said, Psal. 78: 25. "Man did eat angels food:" he means the manna that fell from heaven, which was so excellent, that if angels, who are the noblest creatures, did live upon material food, they would choose this above all to feed on. And yet this was but a type and weak shadow of Christ, on whom believers feed. Christ makes a royal feast of his own flesh and blood, Isa. 25: 6. All our delicates are in him.

2. It instructs us that the New Testament is now in its full force, and no substantial alteration can be made in it, since the testator is dead, and by his death has ratified it. So that all the excellent promises and blessings of it are now fully confirmed to the believing soul, Heb. 9: 16, 17. All these, and many more choice truths, are we instructed in by this sign: And all these ways it remembers us of Christ, and helps powerfully to raise, warm, and affect our hearts with that remembrance of him.

Thirdly, The last enquiry is, How Christ has, hereby, left such a special mark of his care for, and love to his people. And that will evidently appear, if you consider these five particulars.

1. This is a special mark of the care and love of Christ, inasmuch as hereby he has made abundant provision for the confirmation and establishment of the faith of his people to the end of the world. For this being an evident proof that the New Testament is in its full force, (Matth. 26: 28. "This is the cup of the New testament in my blood,") it tends as much to our satisfaction, as the legal execution of a deed, by which we hold and enjoy our estate. So that when he saith, Take, eat, it is as much as if God should stand before you at the table with Christ, and all the promises in his hand; and say, I deliver this to thee as my deed. What think you, does this promote and confirm the faith of a believer? if it does not, what does?

2. This is a special mark of Christ's care and love, inasmuch as by this he has made like abundant provision for the enlargement of the joy and comfort of his people. Believers are at this ordinance, as Mary was at the sepulchre, with fear and great joy, Matth. 28: 8. Come, reader, speak thy heart, if thou be one that heartily lowest Jesus Christ, and hast gone many days, possibly years, mourning and lamenting because of the inevidence and cloudiness of thine interest in him; who hast sought him sorrowing, in this ordinance, and in that, in one duty, and another: if at last Christ should take off that mask, that cruel covering (as one calls it) from his face, and be known of thee in breaking of bread: suppose he should, by his Spirit, whisper thus in thine ear as thou sittest at his table, Dost thou indeed so prize, esteem, and value me? Will nothing but Christ and his love content and satisfy thee? Then, as sweet, lovely, and desirable as I am, know that I am thine: take thine own Christ into the arms of thy faith this day: Would not this create in thy soul, a joy transcendent to all the joys and pleasures in this world? What thinkest thou of it?

3. Here is a signal mark of Christ's care and love, inasmuch as this is one of the highest, and best helps for the mortification of the corruption of his people. Nothing tends more to the killing of sin, than this does. Christ's blood, as it is food to faith, so it is poison to our lusts. O what a pill is wrapt up in that bread! what an excellent potion is in that cup to purge the soul? One calls that table, an altar, on which our corruptions are sacrificed and slain before the Lord. For how can they that there see what Christ suffered for sin, live any longer therein?

4. Moreover his care and love appear in providing an ordinance so excellently adapted, to excite and blow up his people's love into lively flame. When Joseph made himself known to his brethren, "I am Joseph your brother, whom ye sold, be not grieved:" O! what showers of tears and dear affections were there? How did they fall upon each others necks! so that the Egyptians wondered at the matter. How does the soul (if I may so speak) passionately love Jesus Christ at such a time? O what a Christ is my Christ! "The fairest among ten thousand." What has he done, what has he suffered for me! what great things has my Jesus given, and what great things has he forgiven me: A world, a thousand worlds cannot show such another. Here the soul is melted down by love at his feet; it is pained with love.

5. To conclude; Christ's care and love are further manifested to his people, in this ordinance, as it is one of the strongest bonds of union betwixt them that can be: 1 Cor. 10: 17. "We being many, are one bread, and one body; for we are all partakers of that one bread." And though, through our corruptions, it falls out, that what was intended for a bond of union proves a bone of contention,

yet, inasmuch as by this it appears how dearly Christ loved them; for as much also as here they are sealed up to the same inheritance, their dividing corruptions here slain, their love to Christ, and consequently to each other, here improved; it is certainly one of the strongest ties in the world, to wrap up gracious hearts in a bundle of love.

And thus I have dispatched the doctrinal part of this point. The improvement of it is in the following inferences.

Inference 1. Did Christ leave this ordinance with his church to preserve his remembrance among his people: Then surely Christ foresaw, that, notwithstanding what he is, has done, suffered, and promised yet to do for his people, they will for all this be still apt to forget him.

A man would think that such a Christ should never be one whole hour together out of his people's thoughts and affections: that wherever they go, they should carry him up and down with them, in their thoughts, desires, and delights: that they should let their thoughts work towards Christ as the longing thoughts of her that is with child do work after that she longs for: that they should lie down with Christ in their thoughts at night, and when they awake be still with him that their very dreams in the night should be sweet visions of Christ, and all their words savour of Christ.

But O the baseness of these hearts! Here we live and converse in a world of sensible objects, which, like a company of thieves, rob us of our Christ, and lay the dead child in his room. Wo is me, that it should be so with me, who am so obliged to love him! Though he be in the highest glory in heaven, he does not forget us; he has graven us upon the palms of his heads; we are continually before him. He thinks on us, when we forget him. The whole honour and glory paid him in heaven by the angels, cannot divert his thoughts one moment from us; but every trifle that meets us in the way, is enough to divert our thoughts from him. Why do we not abhor and loathe ourselves for this? What! Is it a pain, a burden, to carry Christ in our thoughts about the world? As much a burden, if thy heart be spiritual, as a bird is burdened by carrying his own wings.

Will such thoughts intrude unseasonably, and thrust greater things than Christ out of our minds? For shame, Christian, for shame, let not thy heart play the wanton, and gad from Christ after every vanity. In heaven nothing else takes up the thoughts of saints to eternity; and yet there is no tiring, no satiety. O learn to live nearer that heavenly life. Never leave praying and striving, till thou canst say as it is, Psal. 63: 5. "My soul shall be satisfied as with marrow and fatness, and my mouth shall praise thee with joyful lips; whilst I remember thee on my bed, and meditate on thee in the night watches."

Inf. 2. Hence also we infer, that sacrament-seasons are heart melting seasons; because therein the most affecting and heart-melting recognitions and representations of Christ are made. As the gospel offers him to the ear, in the most sweet, affecting sounds of grace; so the sacrament to the eye, in the most pleasing visions that are on this side heaven.

There, hearts that will not yield a tear under other ordinances, can pour out floods: Zech. 12: 10. "They shall look upon me whom they have pierced, and mourn." Yet I dare not affirm, that every one whose heart is broken by the believing sight of Christ there, can evidence that it is so by a dropping eye. No, we may say of tears, as it is said of love, Cant. 8: 7. If some Christians would give all the treasures of their houses for them, they cannot be purchased: yet they are truly humbled for sin, and seriously affected with the grace of Christ. For the support of such, I would distinguish, and have them to do so also, betwixt what is essential to spiritual sorrow, and what is contingent. Deep displeasure with thyself for sin, hearty resolutions and desires of the complete mortification of it, this is essential to all spiritual sorrow; but tears are accidental, and in some constitutions rarely found. If thou hast the former, trouble not thyself for want of the latter, though it is a mercy when they kindly and undissembledly flow from a heart truly broken.

And surely, to see who it is that thy sins have pierced, how great, how glorious, how wonderful a Person that was, that was so humbled, abased, and brought to the dust, for such a wretched thing as thou art, cannot but tenderly affect the considering soul. If it was for a lamentation in the captivity, "that princes were hanged up by the hands, and the faces of the elders not reverenced," Lam. 5: 12. And if at the death of Abner, David could lament, and say, "A prince, and a great man is fallen in Israel this day," 2 Sam. 3: 38. If he could pathetically lament the death of Saul and Jonathan, saying, "Daughters of Israel, weep over Saul, who clothed you in scarlet; the beauty of Israel is slain upon the high places!" Ah! how much more should it affect us, to see the beauty of heaven fallen, the Prince of life hang dead upon a tree! O let the place where you assemble to see this sight of your crucified Jesus, be a Bochim, a place of lamentation.

Inf. 3. Moreover hence it is evident, that the believing and affectionate remembrance of Christ, is of singular advantage at all times to the people of God. For it is the immediate end of one of the greatest ordinances that ever Christ appointed to the church.

To have frequent recognitions of Christ, will appear to be singularly efficacious and useful to believers, if you consider,

1. If at any time the heart be dead and hard, this is the likeliest means in the world to dissolve, melt, and quicken it. Look hither hard heart; hard indeed if this hammer will not break it. Behold the blood of Jesus.

2. Art thou easily overcome by temptations to sin? This is the most powerful restraint in the world from sin: Rom. 6: 2 "How shall we that are dead to sin, live any longer therein?" We are crucified with Christ, what have we to do with sin? Have such a thought as this, when thy heart is yielding to temptation. How can I do this, and crucify the Son of God afresh! Has he not suffered enough already on earth; shall I yet make him groan as it were for me in heaven! Look, as David poured the water brought from the well of Bethlehem, on the ground, though he was athirst, for he said, it is the blood of the men? i.e. they eminently hazarded their lives to fetch it; much more should a Christian pour out upon the ground, yea, despise and trample under foot, the greatest profit or pleasure of sin; saying, Nay, I will have nothing to do with it, I will on no terms touch it, for it is the blood of Christ: it cost blood, infinite, precious blood to expiate it. If there were a knife in your house that had been thrust to the heart of your father, you would not take pleasure to see that knife, much less to use it.

3. Are you afraid your sins are not pardoned, but still stand upon account before the Lord? What more relieving, what more satisfying, than to see the cup of the New Testament in the blood of Christ, which is "shed for many for the remission of sins?" Who shall lay any thing to the charge of God's elect? It is Christ that died."

4. Are you staggered at your sufferings, and hard things you must endure for Christ in this world? Does the flesh shrink back from these things, and cry, spare thyself? What is there in the world more likely to steel and fortify thy spirit with resolution and courage, than such a sight as this? Did Christ face the wrath of men, and the wrath of God too? Did he stand as a pillar of brass, with unbroken patience, and steadfast resolution, under such troubles as never met in the like height upon any mere creature, till death beat the last breath out of his nostrils? And shall I shrink for a trifle? Ah, he did not serve me so! I will arm myself with the like mind, 1 Pet. 2: 2.

5. Is thy faith staggered at the promises? Can't thou not rest upon a promise? Here is what will help thee against hope to believe in hope, giving glory to God. For this is God's seal added to his covenant, which ratifies and binds fast all that God has spoken.

6. Dost thou idle away precious time vainly, and live unusefully to Christ in thy generation? What more apt both to convince and cure thee, than such remembrance of Christ as this? O when thou considerest thou art not thine own, thy time, thy talents are not thine own, but Christ's; when thou shalt see thou art bought with a price (a great price indeed) and so art strictly obliged to glorify God, with thy soul and body, which are his, 2 Cor. 5: 14. This will powerfully awaken a dull, sluggish, and lazy spirit. In a word, what grace is there that this remembrance of Christ cannot quicken? What sin cannot it mortify? What duty cannot it animate? O it is of singular use in all cases to the people of God.

Inf. 4. Lastly we infer; Though all other things do, yet Christ neither does, nor can grow stale. Here is an ordinance to preserve his remembrance fresh to the end of the world. The blood of Christ does never dry up. The beauty of this rose of Sharon is never lost or withered. He is the same yesterday, to-day, and for ever. As his body in the grave saw no corruption, so neither can his love, or any of his excellencies. When the saints shall have fed their eyes upon him in heaven, thousands and millions of years, he shall be as fresh, beautiful, and orient as at the beginning. Others beauties have their prime, and their fading time; but Christ abides eternally. Our delight in creatures is often most at first acquaintance; when we come nearer to them, and see more of them, the edge of our delight is abated: but the longer you know Christ, and the nearer you come to him, still the more do you see of his glory. Every farther prospect of Christ entertains the mind with a fresh delight. He is as it were a new Christ every day, and yet the same Christ still.

Blessed be God for Jesus Christ.

Sermon 22: The third preparative Act of Christ for his own Death

Luke 22:41-44

And he was withdrawn from them about a stone's cast, and kneeled down, and prayed, Saying, Father, if thou be willing, remove this cup from me: nevertheless not my will, but thine, be done. And there appeared an angel unto him from heaven, strengthening him. And being in an agony he prayed more earnestly: and his sweat was as it were great drops of blood falling down to the ground.

The hour is now almost come, even that hour of sorrow, which Christ had so often spoken of. Yet a little, a very little while, and the Son of man is betrayed into the hands of sinners. He has affectionately recommended his children to his Father. He has set his house in order, and ordained a memorial of his death to be left with his people, as you have heard. There is but one thing more to do, and then the tragedy begins. He recommended us, he must also recommend himself by prayer to the Father; and when that is done, he is ready, let Judas with the black guard come when they will.

This last act of Christ's preparation for his own death, is contained in this scripture; wherein we have an account, 1. Of his prayer. 2. Of the agony attending it. 3. His relief in that agony, by an angel that came and comforted him.

1. The prayer of Christ; in a praying posture he will be found when the enemy comes; he will be taken upon his knees: he was pleading hard with God in prayer, for strength to carry him through this heavy trial, when they came to take him. And this prayer was a very remarkable prayer, both for the solitariness of it, he withdrew about a stone's cast, verse 41. from his dearest intimates, no ear but his Father's shall hear what he had now to say; and for the vehemency and importunity of it; these were those "iketerias", Heb. 5: 7. strong cries that he poured out to God in the days of his flesh. And for the humility expressed in it; he fell upon the ground, he rolled himself as it were in the dust, at his Father's feet. And in divers other respects it was a very remarkable prayer, as you will hear anon.

2. This scripture gives you also an account of the agony of Christ, as well as of big prayer, and that a most strange one: such as in all respects never was known before in nature. It was a sweat as it had been blood, which, [as] is neither an hyperbole, as some would make it: nor yet a similitude of blood; as others fancy, but a real bloody sweat. For so [as] is sometimes taken for the very thing itself, as John 1: 14. And as a worthy divine of our own well notes, that if the Holy Ghost had only intended it for a similitude or resemblance, he would rather have expressed it, as it were drops of water, than as it were drops of blood, for sweat more resembles water than blood.

3. You have here his relief in this his agony and that by an angel dispatched post from heaven to comfort him. The Lord of angels now needed the comfort of an angel. It was time to have a little refreshment when his face and body too stood as full of drops of blood, as the drops of dew are upon the grass. Hence we note,

Doct. That our Lord Jesus Christ was praying to his Father in an extraordinary agony, when they came to apprehend him in the garden.

To open and explain this last act of preparation on Christ's part for our use, I shall at this time speak of these particulars. First, The place where he prayed. Secondly, The time when he prayed. Thirdly, The matter of his prayer. And lastly, The manner how he prayed.

First, For the circumstance of place, where was this last and remarkable prayer poured out to God? It was in the garden: St. Matthew tells us it was called Gethsemane, which signifies, (as Pareus on the place observes) "the valley of fatness, viz. of olives, which grew in that valley or garden most plentifully". This garden lay very near to the city of Jerusalem. The city had twelve gates, five of which were on the east side of it, among which the most remarkable were the fountain gate, so called of the fountain Siloe. Through this gate Christ rode into the city in triumph, when he came from Bethany, the other was the sheep-gate, so called from the multitude of sheep driven in at it for the sacrifice, for it stood close by the temple; and close by this gate was the garden called Gethsemane, where they apprehended Christ, and led him through this gate, as a sheep to the slaughter. Betwixt this garden and the city, ran the brook Cedron, which rose from a hill upon the south, and ran upon the east part of the city, between Jerusalem and the mount of olives: and over this brook Christ passed into the garden, John 18: 1. To which the Psalmist alludes in Psal. 110: 7. "He shall drink of the brook in the way; therefore he shall lift up the head." For this brook running through the valley of Jehosaphat, that fertile soil, together with the filth of the city which it washed away, gave the waters a black tincture, and so fitly resembled those grievous sufferings of Christ, in which he tasted both the wrath of God and men.

Now, Christ went not into this garden to hide, or shelter himself from his enemies. No, that was not his end; for if so, it had been the most improper place he could have chosen, it being the accustomed place where he was wont to pray, and a place well known to Judas, who was now coming to seek him, as you may see, John 18: 2. "And Judas, which betrayed him, knew the place, for Jesus ofttimes resorted thither with his disciples." So that he repairs thither, not to shun, but to meet the enemy; to offer himself as a prey to the wolves, which there found him, and laid hold upon him. He also resorted thither for an hour or two of privacy before they came, that he might there freely pour out his soul to God. So much for the circumstances of place where he prayed.

Secondly, We shall consider the time when he entered into this garden to pray: and it was in the shutting in of the evening: for it was after the passover and the supper were ended. Then (as Matthew has it, chap. 26: 36.) Jesus went over the brook into the garden, betwixt the hours of nine and ten in the evening, as it is conjectured; and so he had betwixt two and three hours time to pour out his soul to God. For it was about midnight that Judas and the soldiers came and apprehended him there. So that it being immediately before his apprehension, it shows us in what frame and posture Christ desired to be found: and by it he left us an excellent pattern, what we ought to do, when imminent dangers are near us, even at the door. It becomes a soldier to die fighting, "and a minister to die preaching," and a Christian to die praying. If they come, they will find Christ upon his knees, wrestling mightily with God by prayer. He never spent one moment of the time of his life idly; but these were the last moments he had to live in the world, and here you may see how they were filled up and employed.

Thirdly, Next let us consider the matter of his prayers or the things about which he poured out his soul to God in the garden, that evening. And verse 42 informs us what that was: he prayed, saying, "Father, if thou be willing, remove this cup from me; nevertheless, not my will, but thine be done." These words are involved in many difficulties, as Christ himself was when he uttered them. By the cup, understand that portion of sorrows then to be distributed to him by his Father. Great afflictions and bitter trials are frequently expressed, in scripture, under the metaphor of a cup. So, that dreadful storm of wrath upon the wicked, in Psal. 11: 6. "Upon the wicked he shall rain snares, fire, and brimstone and a horrible tempest; this shall be the portion of their cup," i.e. the punishment allotted to them by God for their wickedness. And an exceeding great misery, by a large or deep cup. So Ezek. 23: 32, 33, "Thou shalt drink of thy sister's cup deep and large; thou shalt be laughed to scorn, and had in derision; it containeth much. Thou shalt be filled with drunkenness and sorrow, with the cup of astonishment and desolation, with the cup of thy sister Samaria." And when an affliction is compounded of many bitter ingredients, stinging and aggravating considerations and circumstances, then it is said to be mixed. "In the hand of the Lord there is a cup, and the wine is red, (noting a bloody trial) it is full of mixture, and he poureth out the same but the dregs thereof all the wicked of the earth shall wring them out and drink them:" i.e. their shall have the worst part of the judgement for their share. Thus afflictions and calamities are expressed by the metaphor of a cup; great calamities by a deep and large cup; afflictions compounded of many aggravating circumstances, by a mixed cup. And from the effect it has on those that must drink it, is called a cup of trembling, Isa. 57: 17. "Thou hast drunken at the hand of the Lord, the cup of his fury, the dregs of the cup of trembling." Such a cup now was Christ's cup; a cup of wrath; a large and deep cup, that contained more wrath than ever was drunk by any creature, seen the wrath of an infinite God. A mixed cup, mixed with God's wrath and man's in the extremity. And all the bitter aggravating circumstances that ever could be imagined; great consternation and amazement; this was the portion of his cup.

By the passing of the cup from him, understand his exemption from suffering that dreadful and horrid wrath of God, which he foresaw to be now at hand. For as the coming of the cup to a man, does, in scripture-phrase, note his bearing and suffering of evil, as you find it, Lam. 4: 21. "Rejoice and be g}ad, O daughter of Edom, that dwellest in the land of Uz; the cup also shall pass through unto thee; thou shalt be drunken, and make thyself naked;" which is an ironical reproof at the Idumeans, the deadly enemies of the Jews, who wickedly insulted over them, when the cup was at their mouths: as if the Lord had said, you have laughed and jeered at my people, when my hand was on them; you rejoiced to see their calamities: well, make yourselves merry still if you can, the cup shall pass through unto thee; thy turn is coming, then laugh if thou canst. So, on the contrary, the passing away of the cup, notes freedom from, or our escaping of those miseries. And so Christ's meaning, in this conditional request, is, Father, if it be thy will, excuse me from this dreadful wrath; my soul is amazed at it. Is there no way to shun it? Cannot I be excused? Or if it be possible, spare me. This is the meaning of it. But then here is the difficulty, how Christ, who knew God had from everlasting determined he should drink it, who had compacted and agreed with him in the covenant of redemption so to do, who came (as himself acknowledges) for that end into the world, John 18: 37, who foresaw this hour all along, and professed when he spake of this bloody baptism with which he was to be baptised, that he was "straitened till it was accomplished," Luke 12: 50. How (I say) to reconcile all this with such a petition, that now when the cup was delivered to him, it might pass, or he excused from suffering; this is the knot, this is the difficulty.

What! did he now repent of his engagement? Was all he said before but a nourish, before he saw the enemy? Does he nor begin to wish to be disengaged, and that he had never undertaken such a work? Is that the meaning of it? No, no, Christ never repented of his engagement to the Father, never was willing to let the burden lie on us, rather than on himself; there was not such a thought in his holy and faithful heart; but the resolution of this doubt depends upon another distinction, which will clear his meaning in it.

1st, You must distinguish of prayers. Some are absolute and peremptory; and so to have prayed that the cup might pass, would have been chargeable with such absurdities, as were but now mentioned: others are conditional and submissive prayers, "If it may be, if the Lord please." And such was this, If you be willing; if not, I will drink it. But you will say, Christ knew what was the mind of God in that case; he knew what transactions had of old been betwixt his Father and him; and therefore though he did not pray absolutely, yet it is strange he would pray conditionally it might pass. Therefore in the

2d Place, you must distinguish of the natures according to which Christ acted. He acted sometimes as God, and sometimes as man. Here he acted according to his human nature; simply expressing and manifesting in this request the reluctance it had at such sufferings, wherein he shewed himself a true man, in shunning that which is destructive to his nature.

As Christ had two distinct natures so two distinct wills. And (as one well observes) in the life of Christ, there was an intermixture of power and weakness, of the divine glory, and human frailty. At his birth a star shone, but he was laid in a manger. The devil tempted him in the wilderness, but there angels ministered to him. As man he was deceived in the fig-tree, but as God he blasted it. He was caught by the soldiers in the garden, but first made them fall back. So here, as man he feared and shunned death; but as God-man he willingly submitted to it.

"It was (as Deodatus well expresses it) a purely natural desire, mere man, by which for a short moment he apprehended and shunned death and torments; but quickly recalled himself to obedience, by a deliberate will, to submit himself to God. And besides that, this desire was but conditional, under the will of God, accepted by Christ; but from the contemplation of which he was a while diverted by the extremity of horrors; therefore there was no sin in it, but only a short conflict of nature, presently overcome by reason, and a firm will: or a small suspension, quickly overcome by a most strong resolution. Finally, this sacred deliberation in Jesus was not made simply, or in an instant, but with a short time, and with a counterpoise, which is the natural property of the soul in its motions, and voluntary actions."

In a word, as there was nothing of sin in it, it being a pure and sinless affection of nature; so there was much good in it, and that both as it was a part of his satisfaction for our sin, to suffer inwardly such fears, tremblings, and consternation: and as it was a clear evidence, that he was in all things made like unto his brethren, except sin. And lastly, as it serves notably to express the grievousness and extremity of Christ's sufferings, whose very prospect and appearance, at some distance, was so dreadful to him.

If the learned reader desire to see what is further said on this point, let him read what the judicious and learned Parker, in his excellent book "de descensu", has collected upon that case.

Fourthly, Let us consider the manner how he prayed, and that was,

1. Solitarily, He does not here pray in the audience of his disciples, as he had done before, but went at a distance from them. He had now private business to transact with God. He left some of them at the entering into the garden; and for Peter, James, and John, that went farther with him than the rest, he bids them remain there, while he went and prayed. He did not desire them to pray with him, or for him; no, he must tread the winepress alone. Nor will he have them with him, possibly lest it should discourage them to see and hear how he groaned, sweat, trembled, and cried, as one in an agony, to his Father.

Reader, there are times and cases, when a Christian would not be willing, that the dearest and most intimate friend he has in the world, should be privy to what passes betwixt him and his God.

2. It was an humble prayer; that is evident by the postures into which he cast himself; sometimes kneeling, and sometimes prostrate upon his face. He creeps in the very dust, lower he cannot fall; and his heart was as low as his body. He is meek and lowly indeed.

3. It was a reiterated prayer; he prays, and then returns to the disciples, as a man in extremity turns every way for comfort: so Christ prays, "Father, let this cup pass," but in that the Father hears him not; though as to support he was heard. Being denied deliverance by his Father, he goes and bemoans himself to his pensive friends, and complains bitterly to them, "my soul is exceeding sorrowful even unto death." He would ease himself a little, by opening his condition to them; but alas, they rather in crease than ease his burden. For he finds them asleep, which occasioned that gentle reprehension from him, Mat. 26: 40. "What, could you not watch with me one hour?" What, not watch with me? Who may expect it from you more than I? Could you not watch? I am going to die for you, and cannot you watch with me? What! cannot you watch with me one hour? Alas! what if I had required great matters from you? What: not an hour, and that the parting hour too! Christ finds no ease from them, and back again he goes to that sad place, which he had stained and purpled with a bloody sweat, and prays to the same purpose again. O how he returns upon God over and over, as if he resolved to take no denial! But, however, considering it must be so, he sweetly falls in with his Father's will, Thy will be done.

4. And lastly, It was a prayer accompanied with a strange and wonderful agony: so saith verse 44. "and being in an agony, he prayed more earnestly; and his sweat was it were great drops of blood falling down to the ground." Now he was red indeed in his apparel, as one that trod the wine-press. "It was not a faint thin dew, but a clotted sweat, "trumboi haimator", clodders of blood falling upon the ground. It is disputed whether this sweat was natural or preternatural. That some in extremity have sweat kind of bloody thin dew, is affirmed. I remember Thuanus gives us two instances that come nearest to this, of any thing I ever observed or heard of. "The one was a captain, who by a cowardly and unworthy fear of death was so overwhelmed with anguish, that a kind of bloody dew or sweat stood on all his body. The other is of a young man condemned for a small matter to die by Sixtus 5 who poured out tears of blood from his eyes, and sweat blood from his whole body."

These are rare and strange instances, and the truth of them depends upon the credit of the relator; but certainly for Christ whose body had the most excellent crests and temperament, to sweat clotted blood, or globules of blood, as some render it; and that in a cold night, when others needed a fire within doors to keep them warm, John 18: 18. I say, for him to sweat such streams through his garments, falling to the ground on which he lay, must be concluded a preternatural thing. And indeed it was not wonderful that such a preternatural sweat should stream from all parts of his body, if you do but consider what an extraordinary load pressed his soul at that time, even such as no mere man felt, or was able to stand under, even the wrath of a great and terrible God, in the extremity of it. "Who (saith the prophet Nahum, chap. 1: 6.) can stand before his indignation? And who can abide in the fierceness of his anger? His fury is poured out like fire, and the rocks are thrown down by him."

The effects of this wrath, as it fell at this time upon the soul of Christ in the garden, are largely and very emphatically expressed by the several Evangelists who wrote this tragedy. Matthew tells us, his soul was "exceeding sorrowful, even unto death," Matth. 26: 38. "The word signifies beset with grief round about." And it is well expressed by that phrase of the psalmist, "The sorrows of death compassed me about, the pains of hell got hold upon me." Mark varies the expression, and gives it us in another word no less significant and full, Mark 14: 33. "He began to be sore amazed and very heavy," "Sore amazed, it imports so high a degree of consternation and amazement, as when the hair of the head stands up through fear." Luke has another expression, for it in the text; he was "en agonia", in an agony. An agony is the labouring and striving of nature in extremity. And John gives it us in another expression, John 12: 27. "Now is my soul troubled." The original word is a very full word. And it is conceived the Latins derive that word which signifies hell, from this, by which Christ's troubles are here expressed. This was the load which oppressed his soul, and so straitened it with fear and grief, that his eyes could not vent or ease sufficiently by tears; but the innumerable pores of his body are set open, to give vent by letting out streams of blood. And yet all this while, no hand of man was upon him. This was but a prelude, as it were, to the conflict that was at hand. This bloody sweat in which he prayed, was but as the giving or sweating of the stones before a great rain. Now he stood as it were, arraigned at God's bar, and had to do immediately with him. And you know "it is a fearful thing to fall into the hands of the living God." The uses of this follow in this order.

Inference 1. Did Christ pour out his soul to God so ardently in the garden, when the hour of his trouble was at hand? Hence we infer, That prayer is a singular preparative for, and relief under, the greatest troubles.

It is sweet, when troubles find us in the way of our duty. The best posture we can wrestle with afflictions in, is to engage them upon our knees. The naturalist tells us, if a lion find a man prostrate, he will do him no harm. Christ hastened to the garden to pray, when Judas and the soldiers were hastening thither to apprehend him. O! when we are nigh to danger it is good for us to draw nigh to our God. Then should we be urging that seasonable request to God, Psal. 22: 11. "Be not far from me, for trouble is near; for there is none to help." We be to him, whom death or trouble finds afar off from God. And as prayer is the best preparative for troubles, so the choicest relief under them. Griefs are eased by groans. The heart is cooled and disburdened by spiritual evaporations. You know it is some relief if a man can pour out his complaint into the bosom of a faithful friend, though he can but pity him; how much more to pour out our complaints into the bosom of a faithful God, who can both pity and help us; Luther was wont to call prayers the leeches of his cares and sorrows; they suck out the bad blood. It is the title of Psal. 102, A prayer for the afflicted, when he is overwhelmed, and poureth out his complaint before the Lord. It is no small ease to open our hearts to God. When we are as full of grief, as Elihu was of matter, let us say as he did, Job 32: 19. "Behold, Lord, my heart is as wine which has no vent, it is ready to burst as new bottles. I will speak that I may be refreshed."

To go to God when thou art full of sorrow, when thy heart is ready to burst within thee, as it was with Christ in this day of his trouble; and say, Father, thus and thus the case stands with thy poor child; and so and so it is with me; I will not go up and down complaining from one creature to another, it is to no purpose to do so; nor yet will I leave my complaint upon myself: but I will tell thee, Father, how the case stands with me; for to whom should children make their moan, but to their Father? Lord, I am oppressed, undertake for me. What thinkest thou, reader, of this? Is it relieving to a sad soul? Yes, yes; if thou be a Christian that hast had any experience this way, thou wilt say there is nothing like it; thou wilt bless God for appointing such an ordinance as prayer, and say, Blessed be God for prayer: I know not what I should have done, nor how in all the world I should have waded through the troubles I have passed, if it had not been for the help of prayer.

Inf. 2. Did Christ withdraw from the disciples to seek God by prayer? Thence it follows, That the company of the best men is not always seasonable. Peter, James, and John, were three excellent men, and yet Christ saith to them, Tarry ye here, while I go and pray yonder. The society of men is beautiful in its season, and no better than a burden out of season. I have read of a good man, that when his stated time for closet-prayer was come, he would say to the company that were with him, whatever they were, Friends, I must beg your excuse for a while, there is a friend waits to speak with me. The company of a good man is good, but it ceases to be so, when it hinders the enjoyment of better company. One hour with God is to be preferred to a thousand days enjoyment of the best men on earth. If thy dearest friends in the world intrude unseasonably betwixt thee and thy God, it is neither rude nor unmannerly to bid them give place to better company; I mean, to withdraw from them, as Christ did from the disciples, to enjoy an hour with God alone. In public and private duties we may admit of the company of others to join with us; and if they be such as fear God, the more the better: but in secret duties, Christ and thou must whisper it over betwixt yourselves; and then the company of the wife of thy bosom, or thy friend, that is as thine own soul, would not be welcome. "When thou prayest, enter into thy closet, and when thou hast shut thy door, pray to thy Father which is in secret," Mat. 6: 6. It is as much as if Christ had said, See all clear; be sure to retire in as great privacy as may be; let no ear but God's hear what thou hast to say to him. This is at once a good note of sincerity, and a great help to spiritual liberty and freedom with God.

Inf. 3. Did Christ go to God thrice upon the same account? Thence learn, that Christians should not be discouraged, though they have sought God once and again, and no answer of peace comes. Christ was not heard the first time, and he goes a second: he was not answered the second, he goes the third and last time, yet was not answered in the thing he desired, viz. that the cup might pass from him; and yet he has no hard thoughts of God, but resolves his will into his Father's. If God deny you in the things you ask, he deals no otherwise with you than he did with Christ. "O my God (saith he) I cry in the day-time, but thou hearest not; and in the night, and am not silent." Yet he justifies God, "but thou art holy," Psal. 22: 2. Christ was not heard in the thing he desired, and yet heard in that he feared, Heb. 5: 7.

The cup did not pass as he desired, but God upheld him, and enabled him to drink it. He was heard as to support, he was not heard as to exemption from suffering: his will was expressed conditionally; and therefore though he had not the thing he so desired, yet his will was not crossed by the denial. But now, when we have a suit depending before the throne of grace, and cry to God once and again, and no answer comes; how do your hands hang down, and your spirits wax feeble!

Then we complain with the church, Lam. 3: 8. "When I cry and shout, he shutteth out my prayers; thou coverest thyself with a cloud, that our prayers cannot pass through." Then, with Jonah we conclude "we are cast out of his sight." Alas! we judge by sense according to what we see and feel; and cannot live by faith on God, when he seems to hide himself, put us off, and refuse our requests. It calls for an Abraham's faith, to "believe against hope, giving glory to God." If we cry, and no answer comes presently, our carnal reason draws a headlong hasty conclusion. Sure I must expect no answer: God is angry with my prayers: The seed of prayer has lain so long under the clods, and it appears not; surely it is lost, I shall hear no more of it.

Our prayers may be heard, though their answer be for the present suspended. As David acknowledged, when he coolly considered the matter, Psal. 31: 22. "I said in my haste, I am cut off from before thine eyes; nevertheless thou heardest the voice of my supplication, when I cried unto thee." No, no, Christian; a prayer sent up in faith, according to the will of God, cannot be lost, though it be delayed. We may say of it as David said of Saul's sword, and Jonathan's bow, that they never returned empty.

Inf. 4. Was Christ so earnest in prayer, that he prayed himself into every agony? Let the people of God blush to think how unlike their spirits are to Christ, as to their prayers-frames!

O what lively, sensible, quick, deep, and tender apprehensions and sense of those things about which he prayed, had Christ? Though he saw his very blood starting out from his hands, and his clothes died in it: yet being in an agony, he prayed the more earnestly. I do not say Christ is imitable in this; no, but his fervour in prayer is a pattern for us, and serves severely to rebuke the laziness, dullness, torpor, formality, and stupidity, that are in our prayers. How often do we bring the sacrifice of the dead before the Lord! how often do our lips move, and our hearts stand still! O how unlike Christ are we! his prayers were pleading prayers! full of mighty arguments and fervent affections. O that his people were in this more like him!

Inf. 5. Was Christ in such an agony before any hand of man was upon him, merely from the apprehensions of the wrath of God, with which he now contested? "Then surely it is a dreadful thing to fall into the hands of the living God; for our God is a consuming fire."

Ah, what is divine wrath, that Christ staggered when the cup came to him! Could not he bear, and dost thou think to bear it? Did Christ sweat clots of blood at it, and dost thou make light of it? Poor wretch, if it staggered him, it will confound thee. If it made him groan, it will make thee howl, and that eternally. Come, sinner, come; dost thou make light of the threatening of the wrath of God against sin? Dost thou think there is no such matter in it, as these zealous preachers make of it? Come look here upon my text, which shows thee the face of the Son of God standing as full of purple drops under the sense and apprehension of it, as the drops of dew that hang upon the grass. Mark how he cries, "Father if it be possible, let this cup pass." O any thing of punishment rather than this. Hear what he tells the disciples; "My soul, (saith he,) is sorrowful even to death: amazed, and very heavy." Fools make a mock at sin, and the threatening that lie against it.

Inf. 6. Did Christ meet death with such a heavy heart? Let the hearts of Christians be the lighter for this, when they come to die. The bitterness of death was all squeezed into Christ's cup. He was made to drink up the very dregs of it, that so our death might be the sweeter to us. Alas! there is nothing now left in death that is frightful or troublesome, beside the pain of dissolution, that natural evil of it. I remember it is storied of one of the martyrs, that being observed to be exceeding jocund and merry when he came to the stake, one asked him, What was the reason his heart was so light, when death, (and that in such a terrible form too) was before him? O said he, my heart is so light at my death, because Christ's was so heavy at his death.

Inf. 7. To conclude, what cause have all the saints to love their dear Lord Jesus with an abounding love? Christian, open the eyes of thy faith, and fix them upon Christ, in the posture he lay in the garden, drenched in his own blood; and see whether he be not lovely in these his dyed garments. He that suffered for us more than any creature could or did, may well challenge more love than all the creatures in the world. O what has he suffered, and suffered upon thy account! it was thy pride, earthliness, sensuality, unbelief; hardness of heart, that laid on more weight in that day that he sweat blood.

Sermon 23: The first Preparation for Christ's Death, on his Enemies Part, by the treason at Judas

Matth. 26:47,48,49.

And while he yet spake, lo, Judas, one of the twelve, came, and with him a great multitude with swords and staves, from the chief priests and elders of the people. Now he that betrayed him gave them a sign, saying, Whomsoever I shall kiss, that same is he: hold him fast. And forthwith he came to Jesus, and said, Hail, master; and kissed him.

The former sermons give you an account how Christ improved every moment of his time, with busy diligence, to make himself ready for his death. He has commended his charge to the Father, instituted the blessed memorial of his death, poured out his soul to God in the garden, with respect to the grievous sufferings he should undergo; and now he is ready, and waits for the coming of the enemies, being first in the field.

And think you that they were idle on their parts? No, no, their malice made them restless. They had agreed with Judas to betray him. Under his conduct, a band of soldiers was sent to apprehend him. The hour, so long expected, is come. For "while he yet spake," saith the text, "lo, Judas, one of the twelve, came, and with him a great multitude, with swords and staves."

These words contain the first preparative act, on their part, for the death of Christ, even to betray him, and that by one of his own disciples. Now they execute what they had plotted, ver. 14, 15. And in this paragraph you have an account, 1. Of the traitor, who he was. 2. Of the treason, what he did. 3. Of the manner of its execution, how it was contrived and effected. Lastly, Of the time, when they put this hellish plot in execution.

1. We have here a description of the traitor: and it is remarkable how carefully the several Evangelists have described him, both by his name, surname, and office, "Judas, Judas Iscariot, Judas Iscariot, one of the twelve;" that he might not be mistaken for Jude or Judas the apostle. God is tender of the names and reputations of his upright-hearted servants. His office, "one of the twelve," is added to aggravate the fact, and to show how that prophecy was accomplished in him, Psal. 41: 9. "Yea, mine own familiar friend, in whom I trusted, which did eat of my bread, has lift up his heel against me." Lo, this was the traitor, and this was his name and office.

2. You have a description of the treason, or an account what this man did. He led an armed multitude to the place where Christ was, gave them a signal to discover him, and encouraged them to lay hands on him, and hold him fast. This was that hellish design which the devil put into his heart, working upon that principle, or lust of covetousness, which was predominant there. What will not a carnal heart attempt, if the devil suit a temptation to the predominant lust, and God withhold restraining grace!

3. You have here the way and manner in which the hellish plot was executed. It was managed both with force and with fraud. He comes with a multitude, armed with swords and staves, in case they should meet with any resistance. And he comes to him with a kiss, which was their signal, lest they should mistake the man. For they aimed neither at small nor great, save only at the King of Israel, the King of glory. Here was much ado, you see, to take a harmless Lamb, that did not once start from them, but freely offered himself to them.

4. And lastly, When this treasonable design was executed upon Christ. And it was executed upon him while he stood among his disciples, exhorting them to prayer and watchfulness, dropping heavenly and most seasonable counsels upon them. "While he yet spake, lo, Judas, and with him a multitude, came with swords and staves." Surely, it is no better than a Judas's trick, to disturb and afflict the servants of God in the discharge of their duties. This was the traitor and his treason; thus it was executed and at this time. Hence we observe,

John Flavel

Doct. That is was the lot of our Lord Jesus Christ, to be betrayed into the hands of his mortal enemies, by the assistance of a false and dissembling friend.

Look, as Joseph was betrayed and sold by his brethren; David by Achitophel, his old friend; Samson by Delilah, that lay in his bosom; so Christ by Judas, one of the twelve; a man, his friend, his familiar, that had been so long conversant with him: he that by profession had lifted up his hand to Christ, now by treason lifts up his heel against him; he bids the soldiers bind those blessed hands, that not long before had washed the traitor's feet.

In the point before us, we will,

First, Consider Judas, according to that eminent station and place he had under Christ.

Secondly, We will consider his treason, according to the several aggravations of it.

Thirdly, We will enquire into the cause or motives that put him upon such a dreadful, hellish design as this was.

Fourthly, and lastly, we will view the issue, and see the event of this treason, both as to Christ and as to himself. And then apply it.

First, As for the person that did this, he was very eminent by reason of that dignity Christ had raised him to. For,

1. He was one of the twelve; one retained not in a more general, and common, but in the nearest, and most intimate and honourable relation and service to Jesus Christ. There were in Christ's time several sorts and ranks of persons that had relation to him. There were secret disciples; men that believed, but kept their stations, and abode with their relations in their callings. There were seventy also whom Christ sent forth; but none of these were so much with Christ or so eminent in respect of their place, as the twelve, they were Christ's family, day and night conversant with him: it was the highest dignity that was conferred upon any: and of this number was Judas. The ancients have much extolled the apostolical dignity. Some stiled these twelve, pedes Christi, the feet of Christ: because they, as it were, carried Christ up and down the world. Others, oculi Dei, the very eyes of God; they were his watchmen, that took care for the concernments of his name and gospel in the world. Others, mammae ecclesiae, the breasts of the church; they fed and nourished the children of God by their doctrine. Now, to be one of this number, one of the twelve, what a dignity was this.

2. Yea, he being one of the twelve, was daily conversant with Christ: often joined with him in prayer, often sat at his feet, bearing the gracious words that came out of his mouth. It was one of Austin's three wishes, that he had seen Christ in the flesh: Judas not only saw him but dwelt with him, travelled with him, and eat and drank with him. And during the whole time of his abode with him, all Christ's carriage towards him was very obliging and winning; yea, such was the condescension of Christ to this wretched man, that he washed his feet, and that but a little before betrayed him.

3. He was a man of unsuspected integrity among the apostles. When Christ told them, One of you shall betray me; none thought on him, but every one rather suspected himself; Lord, is it I? saith one, and so said they all; but none pointed at Judas, saying, Thou art he.

4. To conclude, in some respect, he was preferred to the rest. For he had not only a joint commission with them to preach the gospel to others, (though, poor unhappy wretch, himself became a cast-away) but he had a peculiar office, he bare the bag, i.e. he was Almoner, or the steward of the family, to take care to provide for the necessary accommodations of Christ and them. Now who could ever have suspected, that such a man as this should have sold the blood of Christ for a little money? that ever he should have proved a perfidious traitor to his Lord, who had called him, honoured him, and carried himself so tenderly towards him? And yet so it was; "Lo, Judas, one of the twelve, came, and with him a multitude:" O whither will not a busy devil and a bad heart carry a man!

Secondly, But what did this man do? and what are the just aggravations of his fact? Why, he most basely and unworthily sold and delivered Christ into his enemies hands, to be butchered and destroyed; and all this for thirty pieces of silver.

Blush, O heavens, and be astonished, O earth, at this! In this fact, most black and horrid aggravations appear.

1. Judas had seen the majesty of a God on him whom he betrayed. He had seen the miracles that Christ wrought, which none but Christ could do. He knew that by the finger of God he had raised the dead, cast out devils, healed the sick. He could not choose but observe and see the rays and awful beams of divine majesty shining in his very face, in his doctrine, and in his life; to betray a man, to sell the blood of the poorest innocent in the world, is horrid; but to sell the blood of God, O what is this! Here is a wickedness that no epithet can match! Yea,

2. This wickedness he committed after personal warnings and premonitions given him by Christ, he had often told them in general, that one of them should betray him, Mark 14: 20. He also denounced a dreadful woe upon him that should do it, ver. 21. "the Son of man goes indeed, as it is

written of him; but wo to that man by whom the Son of man is betrayed; good had it been for that man if he had never been born." This was spoken in Judas's presence. And one would have thought so dreadful a doom as Christ passed upon the man! that should attempt this, should have affrighted him far enough from the thoughts of such a wickedness. Nay, Christ comes nearer to him than this, and told him he was the man: for when Judas (who was the last that put the question to Christ) asked him, "Master, is it I?" Christ's answer imports as much as a plain affirmation, "Thou hast said," Matt. 26: 25. Moreover,

3. He does it not out of a blind zeal against Christ, as many of his other enemies did; of whom it is said, 1 Cor. 2: 8. "That had they known him, they would not have crucified the Lord of glory:" but he did it for money to make his market of Christ. He sold Christ as a man would sell an ox, or a sheep to the butcher for profit. He was fully of the mind of the Pope, whose motto was "The smell or savour of gain is sweet? let it arise out of what it will." If he can get any thing by Christ's blood, it shall be a vendible commodity with him. "what will ye give me, (saith he) and I will betray him?" Matth. 26: 15.

4. He sells him, and he sells him at a low rate too, which showed how vile an esteem he had of Christ. He is content to part with him for thirty pieces of silver. If these pieces, or shekels, were the shekels of the sanctuary, they amounted but to three pounds fifteen shillings. But it is supposed they were the common shekels, which were mostly used in buying and selling; and then his price, that he put upon the Saviour of the world, was but one pound seventeen shillings and six pence. A goodly price (as the prophet calls it) that he was valued at! Zech. 11: 12,13. I confess, it is a wonder, he asked no more, knowing how much they longed for his blood; and that they offered no more for him: how then should the scriptures have been fulfilled? O what a sale was this! to sell that blood, which all the gold and silver in the world is not worth one drop of, for a trifle! still the wickedness of the fact rises higher and higher.

5. He left Christ in a most heavenly and excellent employment, when he went to make this soul-undoing bargain. For if he went away from the table, as some think, then he left Christ instituting and administering those heavenly signs of his body and blood: there he saw, or might have seen, the bloody work he was going about, acted as in a figure before him. If he sat out that ordinance, as others suppose he did, then he left Christ singing an heavenly hymn, and preparing to go where Judas was preparing to meet him. When the Lord Jesus was in the most serious and heavenly exercise, the wretch slinked away from him into the city, or else went under pretence to buy some necessaries. But his design was not to buy, but to sell, whatever his pretences were. Nay,

What he did, was not done by the persuasions of any. The high-priest sent not for him, and without doubt, was surprised when he came to him on such on errand. For it could never enter into any of their hearts, that any of his own disciples could ever be drawn into a confederacy against Him. No, he went as a volunteer, offering himself to this work: which still heightens the sin, and makes it out of measure sinful.

7. The manner in which he executes his treasonable design adds further malignity to the fact, He comes to Christ with fawning words and carriage, "Hail, Master, and kissed him." Here is honey in the tongue, and poison in the heart. Here is hatred hid under lying lips. This was the man; and this was his fact. Let us enquire,

Thirdly, The cause and motives of this wickedness, how he came to attempt and perpetrate such a villany. Maldonate the Jesuit criminates the Protestant divines, for affirming that God had a hand in ordering and over-ruling this fact.

But we say, that Satan and his own lust was the impulsive cause of it: that God, as it was a wicked treason, permitted it; and as it was a delivering Christ to death, was not only the permitter, but the wise and holy director and orderer of it, and in the wisdom of his providence over-ruled it, to the great good and advantage of the church; in respect of which happy issue, Judas's treason is called foelix scelus, "a happy wickedness." Satan inspired the motion, Luke 23: 3, 4. "Then entered Satan into Judas, surnamed Iscariot, and he went his way", &c. his own lusts, like dry tinder, kindled presently: his heart was covetous; there was predisposed matter enough for the devil to work on, so that it was but touch and take. Ver. 25. They covenanted to give him money, and he promised, &c.

The holy God disposed and ordered all this to the singular benefit and good of his people: Acts 4: 28. they did whatsoever "his hand and counsel had before determined to be done." And by this determinate counsel of God, he was taken and slain, Acts 2: 23. Yet this no ways excuses the wickedness of the instruments: for what they did, was done from the power of their own lusts, most wickedly; what he did was done in the unsearchable depth of his own wisdom, most holy. God knows how to serve his own ends by the very sins of men, and yet have no communion at all in the sin he so over-rules. If a man let a dog out of his hand in pursuit of a hare, the dog hunts merely for a prey; but he that lets him go, uses the sagacity and nimbleness of the dog to serve his own ends by it. Judas minded nothing but his own advantage to get money: God permitted that lust to work, but over ruled the issue to his own eternal glory, and the salvation of our souls.

Fourthly and lastly, But what was the end and issue of this fact? As to Christ, it was his death; for the hour being come, he does not meditate an escape, nor put forth the power of his Godhead to deliver himself out of their hands. Indeed he shewed what he could do, when he made them go back and stagger with a word. He could have obtained more than twelve legions of angels to have been his life-guard; one of whom had been sufficient to have coped with all the Roman legions: but how then should the scriptures have been fulfilled, or our salvation accomplished? No, he resists not, but Judas, delivering him into their hands at that time, was his death.

And what got he as a reward of his wickedness? It ended in the ruin both of his soul and body. For immediately a death-pang of despair seized his conscience; which was so intolerable, that he ran to the halter for a remedy; and so falling headlong, he burst asunder, and all his bowels gushed out, Acts 1: 18. And now he that had no bowels for Christ, has none for himself. As for his soul, it went to its own place, ver. 25. even the place appointed for the son of perdition, as Christ calls him, John 17: 12. His name retains an odious stench to this day, and shall to all generations: it is a bye-word, a proverb of reproach. This was his end; we will next improve it.

Corollary 1. Hence in the first place we learn, That the greatest professors had need to be jealous of their own hearts, and look well to the grounds and principles of their professions. One of the ancients would have had this epitaph engraven upon Judas's tomb-stone, "eis eme tis horaon eusebes ekso", "Let every one that beholds me, learn to be godly indeed, to be sincere in his profession, and to love Christ more unfeignedly than I did." O professors, look to your foundation, and build not upon the sand, as this poor creature did. That is sound advice, indeed, which the apostle gives, 1 Cor. 10: 12. "Let him that thinks he standeth, take heed lest he fall." O beware of a loose foundation. If you begin your profession as Judas did, no wonder if it shall end as his did.

1. Beware therefore that you hold not the truth in unrighteousness: Judas did so: he knew much, but lived not up to what he knew, for he was still of a worldly spirit in the height of his profession. His knowledge never had any saving influence upon his heart, he preached to others, but he himself was a cast-away. He had much light, but still walked in darkness. He had no knowledge to do himself good.

2. Beware you live not in a course of secret sin. Judas did so, and that was his ruin. He made a profession indeed, and carried it smoothly but he was a thief, John 12: 6. He made no conscience of committing the sin, so he could but cover and hide it from men. This helped on his ruin, and so it will thine, reader, if thou be guilty herein. A secret way of sinning, under the covert of profession, will either break out at last to the observation of men, or else slide thee down insensibly to hell, and leave thee there only this comfort, that no body shall know thou art there.

3. Beware of hypocritical pretences of religion to accommodate self-ends. Judas was a man that had notable skill this way. He had a mind to fill his own purse, by the sale of that costly ointment which Mary bestowed upon our Saviour's feet. And what a neat cover had he fitted for it, to do his business clearly; Why, saith he, "This might have been sold for three hundred pence, and given to the poor." Here was charity to the poor, or rather poor charity; for this was only a blind to his base self ends. O Christian, be plain hearted, take heed of craft and cunning in matters of religion: This spoiled Judas.

4. Beware of self-confidence. Judas was a very confident man of himself. "Last of all, Judas said, Master, is it I?" Matth. 26: 25. But he that was last in the suspicion was first in the transgression. "He that trusteth in his own heart, is a fool," saith Solomon, Prov. 28: 26. Such a fool was this great professor. It will be your wisdom to keep a jealous eye upon your own hearts; and still suspect their fairest pretences.

5. If you will not do as Judas did, nor come to such an end as he did, take heed you live not unprofitably under the means of grace. Judas had the best means of grace that ever man enjoyed. He heard Christ himself preach, he joined often with him in prayer, but he was never the better for it all; it was but as the watering of a dead stick, which will never make it grow, but rot it the sooner. Never was there a rotten branch so richly watered as he was. O it is a sad sign and a sad sin too, when men and women live under the gospel from year to year, and are never the better. I warn you to beware of these evils, all ye that profess religion. Let these footsteps by which Judas went down to his own place, terrify you from following him in them.

Corollary 2. Learn hence also, That eminent knowledge and profession put a special and eminent aggravation upon sin. Judas Iscariot, one of the twelve. Poor wretch! better had it been for him, if he had never been numbered with them, nor enlightened with so much knowledge as he was endowed with: for this rent his conscience to pieces, when he reflected on what he had done, and presently run into the gulph of despair. To sin against clear light, is to sin with an high hand. It is that which makes a sad waste of the conscience. That, without doubt, which now torments this poor soul in hell, is that he should go against his light, against his profession, to gratify a base lust to his eternal ruin. Had he known no better, it had been more excusable. Those that had a hand in the death of Christ, through mistake and ignorance, were capable to receive the pardon of their sin by that blood they so shed, Acts 3: 17,19 compared. Take heed therefore of abusing knowledge, and putting a force upon conscience.

Corollary 3. Learn hence in the third place, That unprincipled professors will sooner or later become shameful apostates. Judas was an unprincipled professor, and see what he came to; ambition invited Simon Magus to the profession of Christ, he would be "eis megas", "some great one," and how quickly did the rottenness of his principles discover itself in the ruin of his profession? That which wants a root, must needs wither, as Christ speaks, Matth. 13: 20, 21. That which is the predominant interest, will prevail, and sway with us in the day of our trial. Hear me, all you that profess religion, and have given your names to Christ; if that profession be not built upon a solid and real work of grace upon your hearts, you shall never honour religion, nor save your souls by it. O it is your union with Christ, that, like a spring, maintains your profession. "So much as you are united to Christ, so much constancy, steadiness, and evenness, you will manifest in the duties of religion, and no more."

O brethren, when he that professes Christ for company, shall be left alone as Paul was; when he that makes religion a stirrup to help himself into the saddle of preferment and honour, shall see that he is so advanced to be drawn forth into Christ's camp and endure the heat of the day, and not to take his pleasure; in a word, when he shall see all things about him discouraging and threatening, his dearest interest on earth exposed for religion's sake, and he has no faith to balance his present losses with his future hopes; I say, when it comes to this, you shall then see the rottenness of many hearts discovered; and Judas may have many fellows, who will part with Christ for the world, as he did. O therefore look well to your foundation.

Corollary 4. Moreover, in this example of Judas you may read this truth; That men and women are never in more imminent danger, than when they meet with temptations exactly suited to their master-lusts, to their own iniquity. O pray, pray, that ye may be kept from a violent suitable temptation. Satan knows that when a man is tried here, he falls by the root. The love of this world was all along Judas' master sin, and some conjecture he was a married man, and had a great charge; but that is conjectural: this was his predominant lust. The devil found out this, and suited it with a temptation which fully hit his humour, and it carries him immediately. This is the dangerous crisis of the soul. Now you shall see what it is, and what it will do. Put money before Judas, and presently you shall see what the man is.

Corollary 5. Hence, in like manner, we are instructed, That no man knows where he shall stop, when he first engages himself in a way of sin.

Wickedness, as well as holiness, is not born in its full strength, but grows up to it by insensible degrees. So did the wickedness of Judas. I believe, he himself never thought he should have done what he did; and if any should have told him, in the first beginning of his profession, Thou shalt sell the blood of Christ for money, thou shalt deliver him most perfidiously into their hands that seek his life; he would have answered as Hazael did to Elisha, "But what, is thy servant a dog, that he should do this great thing?" 2 Kings 8: 13. His wickedness first discovered itself in murmuring and discontent, taking a pique at some small matters against Christ, as we may find, by comparing John 6 from verse 60 to 70, with John 12 from verse 3 to 9. but see to what it grows at last. That lust or temptation that at first is but a little cloud as big as a man's hand, may quickly overspread the whole heaven. It is our engaging in sin, as in the motion of a stone down the hill, vires acquirit eundo, "it strengthens itself by going;" and the longer it runs, the more violent. Beware of the smallest beginnings of temptations. No wise man will neglect or slight the smallest spark of fire, especially if he see it among many barrels of gun-powder. You carry gun-powder about you, O take heed of sparks.

Corollary 6. Did Judas sell Christ for money? What a potent conqueror is this love of this world! How many has it cast down wounded! What great professors have been dragged at its chariot wheels as its captives? Hymenaeus and Philetus, Ananias and Sapphire, Demas and Judas, with thousands and ten thousands, since their days, led away in triumph. It "drowns men in perdition," 1 Tim. 6: 9. In that pit of perdition, this son of perdition fell, and never rose more. O you that so court and prosecute it; that so love and admire it; make a stand here; pause a little upon this example; consider to what it brought this poor wretch, whom I have presented to you dead, eternally dead, by the mortal wound that the love of this world gave him: it destroyed both soul and body. Pliny tells us, that the Mermaids delight to be in green meadows, into which they draw men by their enchanting voices; but, saith he, there always lie heaps of dead men's bones by them. A lively emblem of a bewitching world! Good had it been for many professors of religion, if they had never known what the riches, and honours, and pleasures of this world meant.

Corollary 7. Did Judas fancy so much happiness in a little money, that he would sell Christ to get it? Learn then, That which men promise themselves much pleasure and contentment in the day of sin, may prove the greatest curse and misery to them that ever befell them in the world. Judas thought it was a brave thing to get money! he fancied much happiness in it: but how sick was his conscience as soon as he had swallowed it! O take it again, saith he! It griped him to the heart. He knows not what to do, to rid himself of that money. Give me children, saith Rachel, or I die: she has children, and they prove her death. O mortify your fancies to the world; put no necessity upon riches. "They that will be rich, fall into temptations, and many hurtful lusts, which drown men in perdition," 1 Tim. 6: 9. You may have your desires with a curse. He that brings home a pack of fine clothes infected with the plague, has no such great bargain of it, how cheap soever he bought them.

Corollary 8. Was there one, and but one of the twelve, that proved a Judas, a traitor to Christ? Learn thence, that it is a most unreasonable thing to be prejudiced at religion, and the sincere professors of it, because some that profess it prove naught and vile.

Should the eleven suffer for one Judas? Alas, they abhorred both the traitor and his treason. As well might the High-priest and his servants have condemned Peter, John, and all the rest, whose souls abhorred the wickedness. If Judas proved a vile wretch, yet there were eleven to one that remained upright: if Judas proved naught, it was not his profession made him so, but his hypocrisy; he never learned it from Christ. If religion must be charged with all the miscarriages of its professors, then there is no pure religion in the world. Name that religion among the professors whereof there is not one Judas. Take heed, reader, of prejudices against godliness on this account. The design of the devil, without doubt, is to undo thee eternally by them. "Wo to the world because of offences," Matth. 18: 7. And what if God do permit these things to fall out, that thou mayest be hardened in iniquity, confirmed in sin by such occasions, and so the destruction brought about this way: Blessed is he that is not offended at Christ.

Corollary 9. Did Judas, one of the twelve, do so? Learn thence, That a drop of grace, is better than a sea of gifts. Gifts have some excellency in them, but the way of grace is the more excellent way, 1 Cor. 12: 31. Gifts as one saith, are dead graces, but graces are living gifts. There is many a learned head in hell. These are not the things that accompany salvation. Gifts are the gold that beautifies the temple; but grace is as the temple which sanctifies the gold. One tear, one groan, one breathing at an upright heart, is more than the tongues of angels.

Poor Christian, thou art troubled that thou canst not speak and pray so neatly, so handsomely, as some others can? but canst thou go into a corner, and there pour out thy soul affectionately, though not rhetorically, to thy Father? trouble not thyself. It is better for thee to feel one divine impression from God upon the heart, than to have ten thousand fine notions floating in thy head; Judas was a man of parts; but what good did they do him?

Corollary 10. Did the devil win the consent of Judas to such a design as this? Could he get no other but the hand of an apostle to assist him? Learn hence, That the policy of Satan lies much in the choice of his instruments he works by. No bird, (saith one) like a living bird to tempt others into the net. Pelagius Socinus, &c. were fit for that work the devil put them upon. Austin told an ingenious young scholar, "The devil coveted him for an ornament." He knows he has a foul cause to manage, and therefore will get the fairest hand he can to manage it with the less suspicion.

Corollary 11. Did Judas one of the twelve, do this? Then certainly, Christians may approve and join with such men on earth, whose faces they shall never see in heaven. The apostles held communion a long time with this man, and did not suspect him. O please not yourselves therefore, that you have communion with the saints here, and that they think and speak charitably of you. "All the churches shall know, (saith the Lord) that I am he that searcheth the heart and reins, and will give to every man as his work shall be," Rev. 2: 23. In heaven we shall meet many that we never thought to meet there, and miss many we were confident we should see there.

Corollary 12. Lastly, Did Judas, one of the twelve, a man so obliged, raised and honoured by Christ, do this? Cease then from man, be not too confident, but beware of men. "Trust ye not in a friend, put no confidence in a guide, keep the door of thy lips from her that lieth in thy bosom," Micah 7: 5. Not that there is no sincerity in any man, but because there is so much hypocrisy in many men, and so much corruption in the best of men, that we may not be too confident, nor lay too great a stress upon any man. Peter's modest expression of Sylvanus is a pattern for us; "Sylvanus, a faithful brother unto you (as I suppose") 1 Pet. 5: 12. The time shall come, saith Christ, that "brother shall betray brother to death," Mat. 10: 11. Your charity for others may be your duty, but your too great confidence may be your snare. Fear what others may do, but fear thyself more.

Sermon 24: The second and third Preparatives for the Death of Christ, by his illegal Trial and Condemnation

Luke 23:23,24

And they were instant with loud voices, requiring that he might be crucified. And the voices of them and of the chief priests prevailed. And Pilate gave sentence that it should be as they required.

Judas has made good his promise to the high-priest, and delivered Jesus a prisoner into their hands. These wolves of the evening, no sooner seize the Lamb of God, but they thirst and long to be sucking his precious innocent blood; their revenge and malice admit no delay, as fearing a rescue by the people.

When Herod had taken Peter, he committed him to prison, "intending after Easter to bring him forth to the people," Acts 12:4. But these men cannot sleep till they have his blood, and therefore the preparation of the passover being come, they resolve in all haste to destroy him; yet lest it should look like a downright murder, it shall be formalised with a trial. This his trial and condemnation are the two last acts by which they prepared for his death, and are both contained in this context; in which we may observe, 1. The indictment. 2. The sentence to which the judge proceeded.

1. The indictment drawn up against Christ, wherein they accuse him of many things, but can prove nothing. They charge him with sedition and blasphemy, but falter shamefully in the proof. However, what is wanting in evidence, shall be supplied with glamour and importunity. For saith the text, "They were instant with loud voices, requiring that he might be crucified; and their voices prevailed". When they can neither prove the sedition and blasphemy they charged him with, then, Crucify him, Crucify him, must serve the turn, instead of all witnesses and proofs.

The sentence pronounced upon him; Pilate gave sentence, that it should be as they required: i. e. he sentenced Christ to be nailed to the cross, and there to hang till he was dead. From both these we may observe these two doctrinal conclusions.

Doct. 1. That the trial of Christ for his life, was managed most maliciously, and illegally against him, by his unrighteous judges.

Doct. 2. Though nothing could be proved against our Lord Jesus Christ worthy of death, or of bonds; yet he was condemned to be nailed to the cross, and there to hang till he died.

I shall handle these two points distinctly in their order, beginning with the first, namely,

Doct. 1. That the trial of Christ for his life, was managed most maliciously and illegally against him, by his unrighteous judges.

Reader, here thou mayest see the Judge of all the world standing himself to be judged; he that shall judge the world in righteousness, judged most unrighteously; he that shall one day come to the throne of judgement, attended with thousands, and ten thousands of angels and saints, standing as a prisoner at man's bar, and there denied the common right which a thief or murderer might claim, and is commonly given them.

To manifest the illegality of Christ's trial, let the following particulars be heedfully weighed.

1. That he was inhumanely abused, both in words and actions, before the court met, or any examination was taken of the fact: for as soon as they had taken him, they forthwith bound him, and led him away to the High-priest's house, Luke 22: 54. And there they that held him, mocked him, smote him, blind-folded him, struck him on the face, and bid him prophesy who smote him; and many other things blasphemously spake they against him, ver. 63, 64, 65. How illegal and barbarous a thing was this? When they were but binding Paul with thongs, he thought himself abused contrary to law, and asked the centurion that stood by, "Is it lawful fat for you to scourge a man that is a Roman, and uncondemned?" q. d. Is this legal! What, punish a man first, and judge him afterwards! But Christ was not only bound, but horribly abused by them all that night, dealing with him as the lords of the Philistine did with Samson, to whom it was sport to abuse him. No rest had Jesus that night; no more sleep for him now in this world: O it was a sad night to him: and this

under Caiaphas's own roof.

2. As he was inhumanely abused before he was tried, so he was examined and judged by a court that had no authority to try him. Luke 22: 66. "As soon as it was day, the elders of the people, and the chief priests, and the scribes came together and led him into their council." This was the ecclesiastical court, the great Sanhedrin, which, according to its first constitution, should consist of seventy grave, honourable, and learned men; to whom were to be referred all doubtful matters, too hard for inferior courts to decide. And these were to judge impartially and uprightly for God, as men in whom was the Spirit of God, according to God's counsel to Moses, Numbers 11: 16, &c. In this court the righteous and innocent might expect relief and protection. And that is conceived to be the meaning of Christ's words, Luke 13: 33 "It cannot be that a prophet perish out of Jerusalem;" that is, there righteousness and innocence may expect protection. But now, contrary to the first constitution, it consisted at a pack of malicious Scribes and Pharisees, men full of revenge, malice, and all unrighteousness: and over these Caiaphas (a head fit for such a body) at this time presided. And though there was still some face of a court among them, yet their power was so abridged by the Romans, that they could not hear and determine, judge and condemn in capital matters, as formerly. For as Josephus their own historian informs us, Herod in the beginning of his reign took away this power from them; and that scripture seems to confirm it, John 18: 31. "It is not lawful for us to put any man to death;" and therefore they bring him to Pilate's bar. He also understood him to be a Galilean, and Herod being Tetrarch of Galilee, and at that time in Jerusalem, he is sent to him, and by him remitted to Pilate.

3. As he was at first heard and judged by a court that had no authority to judge him; so when he stood at Pilate's bar, he was accused of perverting the nation, and denying tribute to Caesar, than which nothing was more notoriously false. For as all his doctrine was pure and heavenly, and malice itself could not find a flaw is it; so he was always observant of the laws under which he lived, and scrupulous of giving the least just offence to the civil powers. Yea, he not only paid the tribute himself though he might have pleaded exemption, but charged it upon others as their duty so to do, Mat. 22: 24. "Give unto Caesar the things that are Caesar's." And yet with such palpable untruths is Christ charged.

4. Yea, and what is more abominable and unparalleled; to compass their malicious designs, they industriously labour to suborn else witnesses to take away his life, not sticking at the grossest perjury, and manifest injustice, so they might destroy him. So you read, Mat. 26: 59. "Now the chief priests and elders, and all the council, sought false witnesses against Jesus to put him to death." Abominable wickedness! for such men, and so many, to complot to shed the blood of the innocent, by known and studied perjury! What will not malice against Christ transport men to?

5. Moreover, the carriage of the court was most insolent and base towards him during the trial: for whilst he stood before them as a prisoner, yet uncondemned, sometimes they are angry at him for his silence! and when he speaks, and that pertinently to the point, they smite him on the mouth for speaking, and scoff at what he speaks. "To some of their light, frivolous and ensnaring questions, he is silent, not for want of an answer, but because he heard nothing worthy of one." And to fulfil what the prophet Isaiah had long before predicted of him; "He was oppressed, and he was afflicted, yet he opened not his mouth: he is brought as a lamb to the slaughter, and as a sheep before her shearers is dumb, so he opened not his mouth," Isa. 53: 7. As also to leave us a precedent when to speak, and when to be silent, when we for his name sake shall be brought before governors: for such reasons as these he sometimes answers not a word, and then they are ready to condemn him for a mute. "Answerest thou nothing? (saith the high-priest) what is it that these witness against thee?" Mat. 26: 62. "Hearest thou not how many things they witness against thee?" saith Pilate, Mat. 27: 13.

And when he makes his defence in words of truth and soberness, they smite him for speaking, John 18: 22. "And when he had thus spoken, one of the officers which stood by, struck Jesus with the palm of his hand, saying, answerest thou the high priest so?" And what had he spoken to exasperate them? Had he spoken impertinently? Not at all; what he said was but this, when they would have had him ensnare himself with his own lips: "Jesus answered, I spake openly in the world, I ever taught in the synagogue, and in the temple, whither the Jews always resort, and in secret have I said nothing. Why askest thou me? Ask them that heard me, behold they know what I said;" q. d. I am not obliged to accuse and ensnare myself, but you ought to proceed secundum allegata et probata, according to what is alleged and proved. Did he deserve a blow on his mouth for this? O who but himself could have so patiently digested such abuses! Under all this he stands in perfect innocence and patience, making no other return to that wretch that smote him, but this, "If I have spoken evil, bear witness of the evil but if well, why smites thou me?"

6. Lastly, To instance in no more: he is condemned to die by that very mouth which had once and again professed he found no fault in him. He had heard all that could be alleged against him, and saw it was a perfect piece of malice and envy. When they urge Pilate to proceed to sentence

The Fountain of Life Opened Up

him; "Why, saith he, what evil has he done?" Mat. 27: 23. Nay, in the preface to the very sentence itself, he acknowledges him to be a just person, Mat. 27: 24. "When Pilate saw he could prevail nothing, but that rather a tumult was made, he took water, and washed his hands before the multitude, and said, I am innocent of the blood of this just person, see ye to it." Here the innocence of Christ brake out like the sun wading out of a cloud; convincing the conscience of his judge that he was just; and yet he must give sentence on him, for all that, to please the people.

Inference 1. Was Christ thus used when he stood before the great council, the scribes and elders of Israel? Then surely "great men are not always wise, neither do the aged understand judgement," Job 32: 9. Here were many great men, many aged men, many politic men in council; but not one wise or good man among them. In this council were men of parts and learning, men of great abilities, and by so much the more pernicious, and able to do mischief. Wickedness in a great or learned man, is like poison given in wine, the more operative and deadly. Christ's greatest enemies were such as these. Heathen Pilate had more pity for him than superstitious Caiaphas. Luther tells us, that his greatest adversaries did not rise out of the ale-houses or brothel-houses, but out of monasteries, convents, and religious houses.

Inf. 2. Hence also we learn, That though we are not obliged to answer every captious, idle, or ensnaring question, yet we are bound faithfully to own and confess the truth, when we are solemnly called thereto.

It is true, Christ was sometimes silent, and as a deaf man that heard not; but when the question was solemnly put, "Art thou the Christ, the Son of the blessed? Jesus said, I am," Mat. 14: 61, 62. He knew that answer would cost his life, and yet he durst not deny it. On this account the apostle saith, "he witnessed a good confession before Pontius Pilate," 1 Tim. 6: 13. Herein Christ has ruled out the way of our duty, and by his own example, as well as precept, obliged us to a sincere confession of him, and his truth, when we are required lawfully so to do, i.e. when we are before a lawful magistrate, and the questions are not curious or captious; when we cannot hold our peace, but our silence will be interpretatively a denying of the truth; finally, when the glory of God, honour of his truth, and edification of others, are more attainable by our open confession, than they can be by our silence; then must we with Christ, give direct, plain, sincere answers.

It was the old Priscillian error, to allow men to deny or dissemble their profession, when an open confession would infer danger. But you know what Christ has said, Mat. 10: 33. "Whosoever shall deny me before men, him will I deny before my Father which is in heaven." Christ will repay him in his own coin. It was a noble saying of courageous Zwinglius, "What deaths would I not choose? What punishment would I not undergo? Yea, into what vault of hell would I not rather choose to be thrown, than to witness against my conscience? Truth can never be bought too dear, nor sold cheap. The Lord Jesus, you see, owns truth with the imminent and instant hazard of his life. The whole Cloud of witnesses have followed him therein, Rev. 14: 1. We ourselves once openly owned the ways of sin; and shall we not do as much for Christ, as we then did for the devil? Did we then glory in our shame, and shall we now be ashamed of our glory? Do not we hope Christ will own us at the great day? Why, if we confess him, he also will confess us. O think on the reasonableness of this duty.

Inf. 3. Once more, hence it follows, That to bear the reviling contradictions, and abuses of men, with a meek, composed, and even spirit, is excellent and Christ-like. He stood before them as a lamb; he rendered not railing for railing? he endured the contradictions of sinners against himself. Imitate Christ in his meekness. He calls you so to do, Mat. 11: 28. This will be convincing to your enemies, comfortable to yourselves, and honourable to religion: and as for your innocence, God will clear it up as Christ's was.

You have heard the illegal trial of Christ, how insolently it was managed against him; well, right or wrong, innocent or guilty, his blood is resolved upon; it is bought and sold before-hand; and if nothing else will do it, menaces and clamours shall constrain Pilate to condemn him. Whence our second note was,

Doct. 2. That though nothing could be proved against our Lord Jesus Christ worthy of death or of bonds, yet was he condemned to be nailed to the cross, and there to hang till he died.

For the explication of this, I shall open the following particulars. First, Who gave the sentence. Secondly, Upon whom it was given. Thirdly, What sentence it was that was given. Fourthly, In what manner Christ received it.

First, Who, and what was he, that durst attempt such a thing as this? Why, this was Pilate, who succeeded Valerius Gratus in the presidentship of Judea, (as Josephus tells us) in which trust he continued about ten years. This cruel, cursed act of his against Christ was in the eighth year of his government. Two years after, he was removed from his place and office by Vitellius, president of Syria, for his inhuman murdering of the innocent Samaritans. This necessitated him to go to Rome to clear himself before Caesar; but before he came to Rome, Tiberius was dead, and Caius in his room. Under him, saith Eusebius, Pilate killed himself. "He was a man not very friendly or benevolent to the Jewish nation, but still suspicious of their rebellions and insurrections; this jealous humour the priests and scribes observed, and wrought upon it to compass their design against Christ." Wherefore they tell him so often of Christ's sedition, and stirring up the people; and that if he let him go, he is none of Caesar's friends, which very consideration prevailed with him to do what he did. But how durst he attempt such a wickedness as this, though he had stood ill in the opinion of Caesar? What! give judgement against the Son of God? for it is evident, by many circumstances in this trial, that he had many inward fears and convictions upon him, that he was the Son of God: By these he was scared, and sought to release him, John 19: 8, 12. the fear of a Deity fell upon him; his mind was greatly perplexed, and dubious about this prisoner whether he was a God or a man. And yet the fear of Caesar prevailed more than the fear of a Deity; he proceeds to give sentence.

O Pilate! thou was not afraid to judge and sentence an innocent, a known innocent, and one whom thou thyself suspectest at least to be more than man! But see in this predominance of self-interest, what man will attempt, and perpetrate, to secure and accommodate self.

Secondly, Against whom does Pilate give sentence? Against a malefactor? No, his own mouth once and again acknowledged him innocent. Against a common prisoner? No, but one whose fame no doubt had often reached Pilate's ears, even the wonderful things wrought by him, which none but God could do: one that stood before him as the picture, or rather as the body, of innocency and meekness. Ye have condemned and killed the just, and he resisteth you not, Jam. 5: 6. Now was that word made good, Psal. 94: 21. "They gather themselves together against the soul of the righteous, and condemn the innocent blood."

Thirdly, But what was the sentence that Pilate gave? We have it not in the form in which it was delivered: but the sum of it was, that it should be as they required. Now what did they require? why, crucify him, crucify him. So that in what formalities soever it was delivered, this was the substance and effect of it, I adjudge Jesus of Nazareth to be nailed to the cross, and there to hang till he be dead. Which sentence against Christ was,

1. A most unjust and unrighteous sentence: the greatest perversion of judgement and equity that was ever known to the civilised world, since seats of judicature were first set up. What! to condemn him before one accusation was proved against him. And if what they accused him of (that he said he was the Son of God) had been proved, it had been no crime, for he really was so; and therefore no blasphemy in him to say he was. Pilate should rather have come down from his seat of judgement, and adored him, than sat there to judge him. O it was the highest piece of injustice that ever our ears heard of!

As it was an unrighteous, so it was a cruel sentence, delivering up Christ to their wills. This was that misery which David so earnestly deprecated, Psal. 27: 12. "O deliver me not over to the will of mine enemies." But Pilate delivers Christ over to the will of his enemies, men full of enmity, rage, and malice, whose greatest pleasure it was to glut themselves with his blood, and to satiate their revengeful hearts with such a spectacle of misery. For lo, as soon as these wolves had gripped their prey, they were not satisfied with that cursed, cruel, and ignominious death of the cross, to which Pilate had adjudged him, but they are resolved he shall die over and over; they will contrive many deaths in one; now they saw as a tyrant did once, moriatur, at sentiat se mori; "let him die, so as he may feel himself to die." To this end they presently strip him naked; scourge him cruelly; array him in scarlet, and mock him; crown him with a bush of plaited thorns; fasten that crown upon his head by a blow with a cane, which set them deep into his sacred temples; sceptered him with a reed, spat in his face, stript off his mock-robes again; put the cross upon his back, and compelled him to bear it. All this, and much more, they express their cruelty by, as soon as they had him delivered over to their will. So that this was a cruel sentence.

3. As it was a cruel, so it was a rash and hasty sentence. The Jews are all in haste; consulting all night, and early up by the break of day in the morning, to get him to his trial. They spur on Pilate, with all arguments they can to give sentence. His trial took up but one morning, and a great part of that was spent in sending him from Caiaphas to Pilate, and from Pilate to Herod, and then back; again to Pilate; so that it was a hasty and headlong sentence that Pilate gave. He did not sift and examine the matter, but handles it very slightly. The trial of many a mean man has taken up ten times more debates and time than was spent about Christ. "They that look but slightly into the cause, easily pronounce and give sentence." But that which was then done in haste, they have had time enough to repent for since.

4. As it was a rash and hasty, so it was an extorted, forced sentence. They squeeze it out of Pilate by mere glamour, importunity, and suggestions of danger. In courts of judicature, such arguments should signify but little; not importunity, but proof, should carry it: but timorous Pilate bends like a willow at this breath of the people: he had neither such a sense of justice, nor spirit of courage, as to withstand it.

5. As it was an extorted, so it was a hypocritical sentence, masking horrid murder under the pretence and formality of law. It must look like a legal procedure to palliate the business. Loth he was to condemn him lest innocent blood should glamour in his conscience; but since he must do it, he will transfer the guilt upon them, and they take it; "his blood be on us, and on our children for ever," say they. Pilate calls for water, washes his hands before them, and tells them, "I am free from the blood of this just person." But stay; free from his blood, and yet condemn a known innocent person? Free from his blood, because he washed his hands in water? No, no, he could never be free, except his soul had been washed in that blood he shed. O the hypocrisy of Pilate! Such juggling as this will not serve his turn, when he shall stand as a prisoner before him who now stood arraigned at his bar.

6. And lastly, As it was hypocritical, so it was an unrevoked sentence: it admitted not of a reprieve, no, not for a day; nor does Christ appeal to any other judicature, or once desire the least delay; but away he is hurried in haste to the execution. Blush, O ye heavens! and tremble, O earth! at such a sentence as this! Now is Christ dead in law, now he knows whether he must he carried, and that presently. His soul and body must feel that, the very sight of which put him into an agony but the night before.

Fourthly, and lastly, In what manner did Christ receive this cruel and unrighteous sentence? He received it like himself, with admirable meekness and patience. He does as it were wrap himself up in his own innocence, and obedience to his Father's will, and stands at the bar with invincible patience, and meek submission. He does not at once desire the judge to defer the sentence, much less fall down and beg for his life, as other prisoners use to do at such times. No, but as a sheep he goes to the slaughter, not opening his mouth. Some apply that expression to Christ, Jam. vs. 6. "Ye have condemned and killed the Just, and he resisteth you not." From the time that Pilate gave sentence, till he was nailed to the cross, we do not read that ever he said any thing, save only to the women that followed him out of the city to Golgotha: and what he said there, rather manifesting his pity to them, than any discontent at what was now come upon him; "Daughters of Jerusalem, (saith he) weep not for me, but weep for yourselves and for your children," Luke 23: 28, &c. O the perfect patience and meekness of Christ. The inferences from hence are.

Inference 1. Do you see what was here done against Christ, under pretence of law? What cause have we to pray for good laws, and righteous executioners of them?

O! It is a singular mercy to live under good laws, which protect the innocent from injury. Laws are hedges about our lives, liberties, estates, and all the comforts we enjoy in this world. Times will be evil enough, when iniquity is not discountenanced and punished by law; but how evil are those times like to prove when iniquity is established by law! As the Psalmist complains, Psal. 94: 20. "It was the complaint of Pliny to Trojan, that whereas crimes were wont to be the burden of the age, now laws were so; and that he feared the commonwealth which was established would be subverted by laws." It is not likely that virtue will much flourish, when "judgement springs up as hemlock in the furrows of the field," Hos. 10: 4. How much therefore is it our concernment to pray, that "judgement may run down as a mighty stream?" Amos 5: 24. "That our officers may be peace, and our exactors righteousness?" Isa. 60: 17. It was not therefore without great reason, that the apostle exhorted, that "supplications, prayers, intercessions, and giving of thanks be made for all men; for kings, and all that are in authority, that we may lead a quiet and peaceful life in all godliness and honesty;" 1 Tim. 2: 1, 2. Great is the interest of the church of God in them; they are instruments of much good or much evil.

Inf. 2. Was Christ condemned in a court of judicature? How evident then is it, that there is a judgement to come after this life? Surely things will not be always carried as they are in this world. When you see Jesus condemned, and Barabbas released, conclude, that a time will come when innocence shall be vindicated, and wickedness shamed. On this very ground, Solomon concludes, and very rationally, that God will call over things hereafter at a more righteous tribunal: "And moreover, I saw under the sun the place of judgement, that wickedness was there; and the place of righteousness, that iniquity was there. I said in my heart, God shall judge the righteous, and the wicked: for there is a time there for every purpose and for every work," Eccles. 3: 16, 17. Some indeed, on this ground, have denied the divine providence; but Solomon draws a quite contrary conclusion, God shall judge: Surely, he will take the matter into his own hand, he will bring forth the righteousness of his people as the light, and their just dealing as the noon-day. It is a mercy, if we be wronged in one court, that we can appeal to another where we shall be sure to be relieved by a just impartial Judge. "Be patient therefore, my brethren (saith the apostle) until the coming of the Lord," James 5: 6, 7, 8.

Inf. 3. Again here you see how conscience may be over-borne and run down by a fleshly interest. Pilate's conscience bid him beware, and forbear: His interest bid him act; his fear of Caesar was more than the fear of God. But O! what a dreadful thing is it for conscience to be ensnared by the fear of man? Prov. 29: 25. To guard thy soul, reader, against this mischief, let such considerations as those be ever with thee.

    1. Consider how dear those profits, or pleasures cost, which are purchased with the loss of inward peace! There is nothing in this world good enough to recompense such a loss, or balance the misery of a tormenting conscience. If you violate it, and prostitute it for a fleshly lust, it will remember the injury you did it many years after; Gen. 42: 21. Job 13: 26. It will not only retain the memory of what you did, but it will accuse you for it: Mat. 27: 4. It will not fear to tell you that plainly, which others dare not whisper. It will not only accuse, but it will also condemn you for what you have done. This condemning voice of conscience is a very terrible voice.

    You may see the horror of it in Cain, the vigour of it in Judas, the doleful effects of it in Spira. It will, from all these its offices, produce shame, fear, and despair, if God give not repentance to life. The shame it works will so confound you, that you will not be able to look up; Job 31: 14. Psal. 1: 5. The fear it works will make you wish for a hole in the rock to hide you; Isa. 2: 9, 10, 15, 19. And its despair is a death pang. The cutting off of hope, is the greatest cut in the world. O! who can stand under such a load as this? Prov. 17: 14.

    2. Consider the nature of your present actions; they are seed sown for eternity, and will spring up again in suitable effects, rewards, and punishments, when you that did them are turned to dust. Gal. 6: 7. "What a man sows, that shall he reap:" And as sure as the harvest follows the seed time, so sure shall shame, fear, and horror, follow sin, Dan. 12: 2. What Zeuxis, the famous limner, said of his work, may much more truly be said of ours, aeternitati pingo, I paint for eternity, said he, when one asked him why he was so curious in his work. Ah! how bitter will those things be in the account and reckoning, which were pleasant in the acting, and committing? It is true, our actions, physically considered, are transient; how soon is a word or action spoken or done, and there is an end of it? But morally considered, they are permanent, being put upon God's book of account. O! therefore take heed what you do; so speaks speak, so act, as they that must give an account.

    3. Consider, how by these things men do but prepare for their own torment in a dying hour. There is bitterness enough in death, you need not add more gall and wormwood to increase the bitterness of it. What is the violencing and wounding of conscience now, but the sticking so many pins or needles in your death bed, against you come to lie down on it? This makes death bitter indeed. How many have wished in a dying hour, they had rather lived poor and low all their days, than to have strained their consciences for the world? Ah! how is the face and aspect of things altered in such an hour.

    No such considerations as these had any place in Pilate's heart; for if so, he would never have been courted, or scared in such an act as this.

    Inf. 4. Did Christ stand arraigned and condemned at Pilate's bar? Then the believer shall never be arraigned and condemned at God's bar. This sentence that Pilate pronounced on Christ gives evidence that God will never pronounce sentence against such: for had he intended to have arraigned them, he would never have suffered Christ, their surety, to be arraigned and condemned for them. Christ stood at this time before a higher judge than Pilate; he stood at God's bar as well as his. Pilate did but that which God's own hand and counsel had before determined to be done, and what God himself, at the same time, did; though God did it justly and holier, dealing with Christ as a creditor with a surety; Pilate most wickedly and basely, dealing with Christ as a corrupt judge, that shed the blood of a known innocent to pacify the people. But certain it is, that out of his condemnation flows our justification: and had not sentence been given against him, it must have been given against us.

    O what a melting consideration is this! that out of his agony comes our victory; out of his condemnation, our justification; out of his pain, our ease; out of his stripes, our healing: out of his gall and vinegar, our honey; out of his curse, our blessing; out of his crown of thorns, our crown of glory; out of his death, our life: if he could not be released, it was that you might. If Pilate gave sentence against him, it was that the great God might never give sentence against you. If he yielded that it should be with Christ as they required, it was that it might be with our souls as well as we can desire. And therefore,

    Thanks be to God for his unspeakable gift

Sermon 25: Christ's memorable Address to the Daughters of Jerusalem, in his Way to the Place of his Execution

Luke 23:27,28,&c.

And there followed him a great company of people, and of women, which also bewailed and lamented him. But Jesus turning unto them said, Daughters of Jerusalem, weep not for me, but weep for yourselves, and for your children.

The sentence of death once given against Christ, the execution quickly follows. Away they lead him from Gabbatha to Golgotha, longing as much to be nailing him to the cross, and feeding their eyes with his torments, as the eagle does to be tearing the flesh, and drinking the blood of that lamb she has seized in her talons, and is carrying away to the top of some rock to devour.

The Evangelist here observes a memorable passage that fell out in their way to the place of execution; and that is, the laments lions and wailing of some that followed him out of the city, who expressed their pity and sorrow for him most tenderly and compassionately: all hearts were not hard, all eyes were not dry. "There followed him a great company of people, and of women, which also bewailed and lamented him," &c.

In this paragraph we have two parts, viz. the lamentation of the daughters of Jerusalem for Christ, and Christ's reply to them.

1. The lamentation of the daughters of Jerusalem for Christ. Concerning them, we briefly enquire who they were, and why they mourned.

(1.) Who they were? The text calls them "daughters", i.e. inhabitants of Jerusalem"; for it is a Hebraism; as "daughters of Zion, daughters of Israel". And it is like the greatest part of them were women; and there were many of them, a troop of mourners, that followed Christ out of the city towards the place of his execution, with lamentations and wailings.

(2.) What the principle, or ground of these their lamentations was, is not agreed by those that have pondered the story. Some are of opinion their tears and lamentations were but the effects and fruits of their more tender and ingenuous natures, which were moved and melted with so tragical and sad a spectacle as was now before them. It is well observed by a judicious author, "That the tragical story of some great and noble personage, full of he royal virtue and ingenuity (yet inhumanely and ungratefully used) will thus work upon ingenuous spirits who read or hear of it, - which when it reaches no higher, is so far from being faith, that it is but a carnal and fleshly devotion, springing from fancy, which is pleased with such a story and the principles of ingenuity stirred towards one, who is of a noble spirit, and yet abused. Such stories use to stir up a principle of humanity in men unto a compassionate love; which Christ himself at his suffering found fault with, as being not spiritual, nor raised enough in those women that went weeping to see the Messiah so handled. Weep not for me, (saith he) i.e. weep not so much for this, to see me so unworthily handled by those for whom I die." This is the principle from which some conceive those tears to flow.

But Calvin attributes it to their faith, "looking upon these mourners as a remnant reserved by the Lord in that miserable dispersion; and though their faith was but weak, yet he judges it credible that there was a secret seed of godliness in them, which afterwards grew to a maturity, and brought forth fruit". And to the same sense others give their opinion also.

2. Let us consider Christ's reply to them; "weep not for me, ye daughters of Jerusalem," &c. Strange, that Christ should forbid them to weep for him, yea for him under such unparalleled sufferings and miseries. If ever there was a heart melting object in the world, it was here. O who could hold, whose heart was not petrified, and more obdurate than the senseless rocks? This reply of Christ undergoes a double sense and interpretation, suitable to the different construction of their sorrows. Those that look upon their sorrows as merely natural, take Christ's reply in a negative sense, prohibiting such tears as those. They that expound their sorrows as the fruit of faith, tell us, though the form of Christ's expression be negative, yet the sense is comparative, as Mat. 9: 13. "I

will have mercy, and not sacrifice," i.e. mercy rather than sacrifice. So here, weep rather upon your own account, than mine; reserve your sorrows for the calamities coming upon yourselves and your children. You are greatly affected, I see, with the misery that is upon me; but mine will be quickly over, yours will be long. In which he shows his merciful and compassionate disposition, who was still more mindful of the troubles and burdens of others than of his own.

And indeed, the days of calamity coming upon them and their children were doleful days. What direful and unprecedented miseries befell them at the breaking up and devastation of the city, who has not read or heard? And who can refrain from tears that hears or reads it?

Now if we take the words in the first sense, as a prohibition of their merely natural and carnal affections, expressed in tears and lamentations for him, no otherwise than they would have been upon any other like tragical story; then the observation from it will be this,

Doct. 1. That melting affections and sorrows, even from the sense and consideration of the sufferings of Christ, are no infallible signs of grace.

If you take it in the latter sense, as the fruit of their faith, as tears flowing from a gracious principle; then the observation will be this,

Doct. 2. That the believing meditation of what Christ suffered for us, is of great force and efficacy to melt and break the heart.

I shall rather choose to prosecute both these branches, than to decide the controversy; especially since the notes gathered from either may be useful to us. And therefore I shall begin with the first, viz.

Doct. 1. That melting affections and sorrows, even from the sense of Christ's sufferings, are no infallible marks of grace.

In this point I have two things to do, to prepare it for use.

First, To show, what the melting of the affections by way of grief and sorrow is.

Secondly, That they may be so melted, even upon the account of Christ, and yet the heart remain unrenewed.

First, What the melting of the affections, by way of grief and sorrow, is.

Tears are nothing else but the juice of a mind oppressed, and squeezed with grief. Grief compresses the heart; the heart so compressed and squeezed, vents itself sometimes into tears, sighs, groans, &c. and this is two-fold: gracious, and wholly supernatural; or common, and altogether natural. The gracious melting or sorrow of the soul, is likewise two-fold; habitual or actual. Habitual bodily sorrow is that gracious disposition, inclination, or tendency of the renewed heart to mourn and melt, when any just occasion is presented to the soul that calls for such sorrow. It is expressed, Ezek. 36: 26. "By taking away the heart of stone, and giving a heart of flesh;" i.e. a heart impressive, and yielding to such arguments and considerations as move it to mourning.

Actual sorrow is the expression and manifestation of that its inclination upon just occasions; and it is expressed two ways, either by the internal effects of it, which are the heaviness, shame, loathing, resolution, and holy revenge begotten in the soul upon the account of sin: or also by more external and visible effects, as sighs, groans, tears, &c. The former is essential to godly sorrow, the latter contingent and accidental, much depending upon the natural temperature and constitution of the body.

Natural and common meltings are nothing else but the effects of a better temper, and the fruit of a more ingenuous spirit, and easier constitution, which shows itself on any other, as well as upon spiritual occasions: as Austin said, he could weep plentifully when he read the story of Dido. The history of Christ is a very tragical and pathetical history, and may melt an ingenuous nature, where are is no renewed principles at all. So that,

Secondly, Our affections may be melted, even upon the score and account of Christ; and yet that is no infallible evidence of a gracious heart. And the reasons for it are,

1. Because we find all sorts of affections discovered by such as have been no better than temporary believers. The stony ground hearers in Mat. 13: 20. "received the word with joy," and so did Johns hearers also, who for "a season rejoiced in his light," John 3: 35. Now, if the affections of joy under the word may be exercised, why not of sorrow also? If the comfortable things revealed in the gospel may stir up the one, by a parity of reason, the sad things it reveals may answerably work upon the other. Even those Israelites whom Moses told they should fall by the sword, and not prosper, for the Lord would not be with them, because they were turned away from him; yet when Moses rehearsed the message of the Lord in their ears, they mourned greatly, Numb. 14: 39. I know the Lord pardoned many of them their iniquities, though he took vengeance on their inventions; and yet it is as true, that with many of them God was not well pleased, 1 Cor. 10: 5. Many instances of their weeping and mourning before the Lord we find in this sacred history; and yet their hearts were not steadfast with God.

The Fountain of Life Opened Up

2. Because though the object about which our affections and passions are moved, may be spiritual; yet the motives and principles that set them on work, may be but carnal and natural ones. When I see a person affected in the hearing of the word, or prayer, even unto tears, I cannot presently conclude, surely this is the effect of grace; for it is possible, the pathetical quality of subject matter, the rhetoric of the speaker, the very affecting tone, and modulation of the voice, may draw tears as well as faith working upon the spirituality, and deep concernment the soul hath in those things.

Whilst Austin was a Manichee, he sometimes heard Ambrose; and, saith he, "I was greatly affected in hearing him, even, unto tears many times:" howbeit, it was not the heavenly nature of the subject, but the abilities and rare parts of the speaker that so affected him. And this was the case of Ezekiel's hearers, chap. 33: 32.

Again, 3. These motions of the affections may rather be a fit and mood, than the very frame and temper of the soul. Now there is a vast difference betwixt these; there are times and seasons, when the roughest and most obdurate hearts may be pensive and tender: but that is not its temper and frame, but only a fit, a pang, a transient passion. So the Lord complains of them, Hos. 6: 4. "O Ephraim, what shall I do unto thee? O Judah, what shall I do unto thee? for your goodness is as a morning cloud and as the early dew, it goeth away. And so he complains, Psal. 78: 34, 35, 36. When he slew them, then they sought him: and they returned and enquired early after God. And the remembered that God was their rock, and the most high God their redeemer; nevertheless they did flatter him with their lips, and lied unto him with their tongues." For had this remembrance of God been the gracious temper of their souls, it would have continued with them; they would not have been thus wavering thus hot and cold with God, as they were. Therefore we conclude, that we cannot infer a work of grace upon the heart, simply and mere from the meltings and thaws that are sometimes upon it. And hence, for your use, I shall infer, that,

Inference 1. If such as sometimes feel their hearts thawed and melted with the consideration of the sufferings of Christ, may yet be deceived; What cause have they to fear and tremble, whose hearts are as unrelenting as rocks, yielding to nothing that is proposed, or urged upon them? How many such are there, of whom we may say, as Christ speaks of the inflexible Jews, "We have piped unto you, but ye have not danced; we have mourned unto you, but you have not lamented" Mat. 11: 17. They must inevitably come short of heaven, who come so short of those that do come short of heaven. If those perish that have rejoiced under the promises, and mourned under the threats of the word; what shall become of them that are as unconcerned, and unteached by what they hear, as the seats they sit on, or the dead that lie under their feet? Who are given up to such hardness of heart, that nothing can touch or affect them? One would think, the consideration of the sixth chapter to the Hebrew should startle such men and women, and make them cry out, Lord, what will become of such a senseless, stupid, dead creature as I am? If they that shave been enlightened, and have tasted of the heavenly gift, and were made partakers of the Holy Ghost, and have tasted the good word of God, and the powers of the world to come, may, notwithstanding such high raised affections as these, so fall away, that it shall be impossible to renew them again by repentance, what shall we then say, or think of his estate, to whom the most penetrating and awakening truths are no more than a tale that is told? The fire and hammer of the gospel can neither melt nor break them; they are iron and brass, Jer. 6: 28, 29.

Inference 2. If such as these may eternally miscarry; then let us look carefully to their foundation, and see that they do not bless themselves in a thing of nought. It is manifest from 1 Cor. 10: 12. that many souls stand exceeding dangerously, who are yet strongly conceited of their own safety. And if you please to consult those scriptures in the margin, you shall find vain confidence to be ruling folly over the greatest part of men; and that which is the utter overthrow, and undoing of multitudes of professors.

Now there is nothing more apt to beget and breed this vain soul-undoing confidence, than the stirrings and meltings of our affections about spiritual things, whilst the heart remains unrenewed all the while. For (as a grave divine has well observed) such a man seems to have all that is required of a Christian, and herein to have attained the very end of all knowledge; which is operation and influence upon the heart and affections.

Indeed (thinks such a poor deluded soul) if I did hear, read, or pray, without any inward affections, with a dead, cold, and unconcerned heart, or if I did make a show of zeal and affection in duties, and had it not, well might I suspect myself to be a self-cozening hypocrite; but it is not so with me, I feel my heart really melted many times, when I read the sufferings of Christ; I feel my heart raised and ravished with strange joys and comforts, when I hear the glory of heaven opened in the gospel: Indeed if it were not so with me, I might doubt the root of the matter is wanting; but if to my knowledge, affections be added; a melting heart joined with a knowing head, then I may be confident all is well. I have often heard ministers cautioning and warning their people not to rest satisfied with idle and unpractical notions in their understandings, but to labour for impressions upon their hearts; this I have attained, and therefore what danger of me? I have often heard it given as a mark of a hypocrite, that he has light in his head, but it sheds not down its influence upon the heart: whereas in those that are sincere, it works on their heart and affections: So I find it with me, therefore I am in a most safe estate. O soul! of all the false signs of grace, none more dangerous than those that most resemble true ones; and never does the devil more surely and incurably destroy, than when transformed into an angel of light. What if these meltings of thy heart be but a flower of nature? What if thou art more beholden to a good temper of body, than a gracious change of spirit for these things? Well, so it may be. Therefore be not secure, but fear, and watch. Possibly, if thou wouldest but search thine own heart in this matter, thou mayest find, that any other pathetical, moving story, will have the like effects upon thee. Possibly too, thou mayest find, that, notwithstanding all thy raptures and joys at the hearing of heaven, and its glory, yet after that pang is over, thy heart is habitually earthly, and thy conversation is not there. For all thou canst mourn at the relations of Christ's sufferings, thou art not so affected with sin, that was the meritorious cause of the sufferings of Christ, as to crucify one corruption, or deny the next temptation, or part with any way of sin that is gainful, or pleasurable to thee for his sake.

Why now, reader, if it be so with thee, what art thou the better for the influence of thy affections? Dost thou think in earnest, that Christ has the better thoughts of thee, because thou canst shed tears for him, when notwithstanding thou every day fiercest and woundest him? O! be not deceived. Nay, for ought know, thou mayest find, upon a narrow search, that thou puttest thy tears in the room of Christ's blood, and divest the confidence and dependence of thy soul to them; and if so, they shall never do thee any good.

O therefore search thy heart, reader be not too confident: take not up too easily upon such poor weak grounds as these, a soul-undoing confidence. Always remember the wheat and tares resemble each other in their first springing up; that an egg is not liker to an egg, than hypocrisy, in some shapes and forms into which it can cast itself, is like a genuine work of grace. O remember that among the ten virgins, that is, the reformed professors of religion that have cast off and separated themselves from the worship and defilements of Antichrist, five of them were foolish.

There be first, that shall be last; and last, that shall be first, Mat. 19: 30. Great is the deceitfulness of our hearts, Jer. 17: 9. And many are the subtleties and devices of Satan, 2 Cor. 11: 3. Many also are the astonishing examples of self-deceiving souls recorded in the word. Remember what you lately read of Judas. Great also will be the exactness of the last judgement. And how confident soever you be, that you shall speed well in that day, yet still remember that trial is not yet past. Your final sentence is not yet come from the mouth of your Judge. This I speak not to affright and trouble, but excite and warn you. The loss of a soul is no small loss, and, upon such grounds as these, they are every day cast away.

This may suffice to be spoken to the first observation, built on this supposition, that it was but a pang of mere natural affection in them. But if it were the effect of a better principle, the fruit of their faith, as some judge; then I told your the observation from it would be this,

Doct. 2. That the believing meditation of what Christ suffered for us, is of great force and efficacy to melt and break the heart.

It is promised, Zech. 12: 10. that "they shall look upon him whom they have pierced, and mourn for him, as one mourneth for his only son, and shall be in bitterness for him, as one that is in bitterness for his first-born." Ponder seriously here, the spring and motive, They shall look upon me; it is the eye of faith that melts and breaks the heart. The effect of such a sight of Christ; they shall look and mourn; be in bitterness and sorrow. True repentance is a drop out of the eye of faith; and the measure or degree of that sorrow caused by a believing view of Christ. To express which, two of the fullest instances of grief we read of, are borrowed; that of a tender father, mourning over a dear and only son; that of the people of Israel, mourning over Josiah, that peerless prince, in the valley of Megiddo.

Now to show you how the believing meditation of Christ, and his sufferings, come kindly and savingly to break and melt down the gracious heart, I shall propound these four considerations of the heart-breaking efficacy of faith, eyeing a crucified Jesus.

First, The very realising of Christ and his sufferings by faith, is a most affecting and melting thing. Faith is a true glass that represents all those his sufferings and agonies to the life. It presents them not as a fiction, or idle tale, but as a true and faithful narrative. This (saith faith) is a true and faithful saying, that Christ was not only clothed in our flesh; even he that is over all, God blessed for ever, the only Lord, the Prince of the kings of the earth, became a man; but it is also most certain, that in this body of his flesh, he grappled with the infinite wrath of God, which filled his soul with horror and amazement; that the Lord of life did hang dead upon the tree; that he went as a lamb to the slaughter, and was as a sheep dumb before the shearer; that he endured all this, and more than any finite understanding can comprehend, in my room and stead; for my sake he there groaned and bled; for my pride, earthliness, lust, unbelief, hardness of heart, he endured all this. I say, to realise the sufferings of Christ thus, is of great power to affect the coldest, dullest heart. You cannot imagine the difference there is in presenting things as realities, with convincing and satisfying evidences, and our looking on them as a fiction or uncertainty.

Secondly, But faith can apply as well as realise; and if it do so, it must needs overcome the heart.

Ah! Christian, canst thou look upon Jesus as standing in thy room, to bear the wrath of a Deity for thee? Canst thou think on it, and not melt? That when thou, like Isaac, wast bound to the altar, to be offered up to justice, Christ, like the ram, was caught in the thicket, and offered in thy room. When thy sins had raised a fearful tempest, that threatened every moment to entomb thee in a sea of wrath, Jesus Christ was thrown over to appease that storm! Say, reader, can thy heart dwell one hour upon such a subject as this? Canst thou with faith, present Christ to thyself, as he was taken down from the cross, drenched in his own blood, and say, These were the wounds that he received for me; this is he that loved me, and gave himself for me: out of these wounds comes that balm that heals my soul; out of these stripes my peace: When he hanged upon the cross, he bore my name upon his breast, like the high priest. It was love, pure love, strong love to my poor soul; to the soul of an enemy that drew him down from heaven, and all the glory he had there, to endure these sorrows in soul and body for me.

O you cannot hold up your hearts long to the piercing thoughts of this, but your bowels will be pained, and, like Joseph, you will seek a place to vent your hearts in.

Thirdly, Faith cannot only realise and apply Christ, and his death, but it can reason and conclude such things from his death, as will fill the soul with affection to him, and break the heart in pieces, in his presence. When it views Christ as dead, it infers, Is Christ dead for me? then was I dead in law, sentenced and condemned to die eternally; 2 Cor. 5: 14. "If one died for all, then were all dead." How woeful was my case when the law had passed sentence on me! I could not be sure when I lay down, but that it might be executed before I rose; nothing but a puff of breath betwixt my soul and hell.

Again, Is Christ dead for me? then I shall never die. If he be condemned, I am acquitted. "Who shall lay any thing to the charge of God's elect? It is God that justifieth, it is Christ that died," Rom. 8: 34. My soul is escaped as a bird out of the snare of the fowler; I was condemned, but am now cleared; I was dead, but am now alive; O the unsearchable riches of Christ! O love past finding out!

Again, Did God give up Christ to such miseries and sufferings for me? How shall he withhold any thing from me? He that "spared not his own Son, will doubtless with him freely give me all things", Rom. 8: 32. Now I may rest upon him for pardon, peace, acceptance, and glory for my soul. Now I may rely upon him safely for provision, protection, and all supplies for my body. Christ is the root of these mercies; he is more than all these, he is nearer and dearer to God than any other gift. O what a blessed, happy, comfortable state has he now brought my soul into!

To conclude, Did Christ endure all these things for me? then it is past doubt, he will never leave nor forsake me: It cannot be that after he has endured all this, he will cast off the souls for whom he endured it. Here the soul is evangelically broken, considering the mercies that emerge and flow to it out of the sea of Christ's blood.

Fourthly, and lastly, Faith can not only realise, apply, and infer, but it can also compare the love of Christ in all this, both with his dealings with others, and with the soul's dealing with Christ, who loved it. To compare Christ's dealings with others, is most affecting: he has not dealt with every one, as with me; nay, few there are that can speak of such mercies as I have from him. How many are there that have no part nor portion in his blood? Who must bear that wrath in their own persons, that he bare himself for me! He espied me out, and singled me forth to be the object of his love, leaving thousands and millions still unreconciled; not that I was better than they, for I was the greatest of sinners, far from righteousness, as unlikely as any to be the object of such grace and love: my companions in sin are left, and I am taken. Now the soul is full, the heart grows big, too big to contain itself.

Yea, faith helps the soul to compare the love of Christ to it, with the returns it has made to him for that love. And what, my soul! has thy carriage to Christ been, since this grace that wants a name, appeared to thee? Hast thou returned love for love? Love suitable to such love? Hast thou prized, valued, and esteemed this Christ, according to his own worth in himself, or his kindness to thee? Ah no, I have grieved, pierced, wounded his heart a thousand times since that, by my ingratitude; I have suffered every trifle to jostle him out of my heart? I have neglected him a thousand times, and made him say, Is this thy kindness to thy friend? Is this the reward I shall have for all that I have done, and suffered for thee? Wretch that I am, how have I requited the Lord! This shames, humbles and breaks the heart.

And when from such sights of faith, and considerations as these, the heart is thus affected, it affords a good argument, indeed, that thou art gone beyond all the attainments of temporary believers? flesh and blood has not revealed this.

Inference 1. Have the believing meditations of Christ, and his sufferings, such heart melting influences? Then sure there is but little faith among men. Our dry eyes and hard hearts are evidences against us, that we are strangers to the sights of faith.

God be merciful to the hardness of your hearts. How is Christ and his love slighted among men! How shallow does his blood run to some eyes? O that my head were waters, and mine eyes fountains of tears for this! What monsters are carnal hearts? We are as if God had made us without affections, as if all ingenuity and tenderness were dried up. Our ears are so accustomed to the sounds of Christ, and his blood, that now they are become as common things. If a child die, we can mourn over our dead: but who mourns for Christ as for an only son? We may say of faith, when men and women sit so unaffected under the gospel, as Martha said of Christ concerning her brother Lazarus, If thou (precious faith) hadst been here, so many hearts had not been dead this day, and in this duty. Faith is that burning-glass which contracts the beams of the grace, and love, and wisdom, and power of Jesus Christ together, reflects these on the heart, and makes it burn; but without it, we feel nothing savingly.

Inf. 2. Have the believing meditations of Christ, and his sufferings, such heart melting influences? Then surely the proper order of raising the affections, is to begin at the exercise of faith. It grieves me to see how many poor Christians strive with their own dead hearts, endeavouring to raise and affect them, but cannot: they complain and strive, strive and complain, but can discover no love to the Lord, no brokenness of heart; they go to this ordinance and that, to one duty and another, hoping that now the Lord will affect it, and fill the sails; but come back disappointed and ashamed, like the troops of Tema. Poor Christian, hear me one word; possibly it may do thy business, and stand thee in more stead, than all the methods thou hast yet used. If thou wouldst indeed get a heart evangelically melted for sin, and broken with the kindly sense of the grace and love of Christ, thy way is not to force thy affections, nor to vex thyself, and go about complaining of a hard heart, but set thyself to believe, realise, apply, infer, and compare by faith as you have been directed; and see what this will do: "They shall look on me whom they have pierced, and mourn." This is the way and proper method to raise the heart, and break it.

Inf. 3. Is this the way to get a truly broken heart? Then let those that have attained brokenness of heart this way, bless the Lord whilst they live, for so choice a mercy; and that upon a double account.

1. For as much as a heart so affected and melted, is not attainable by any natural or unrenewed person; if they would give all they have in the world, it cannot purchase one such tear, or groan over Christ; mark, what characters of special grace it bears, in the description that is made of it, in that aforementioned place, Zech. 12: 10. Such a frame as this is not born with us, or to be acquired by us; for it is there said to be poured out by the Lord upon us, "I will pour upon them," &c. There is no hypocrisy or dissimulation in these mournings, they being compared to the mourning of a man for his only son: an sure parents hearts are not untouched when they behold such sights.

Nature is not the principle of it, but faith; for it is there said, they shall look on me; i.e. believe and mourn. Self is not the end and centre of these sorrows; it is not so much for damning ourselves, as for piercing Christ: "They shall look on me whom they have pierced, and shall mourn;" so that this is sorrow after God, and not a flesh of nature, as discoursed in the former point. Therefore you have cause to bless the Lord, whilst you live for such a special mercy as this is. And

2. As it is the right, so it is the choicest, and most precious gift that can be given you; for it is ranked among the prime mercies of the new covenant, Ezek. 36: 26. This shall be the covenant; "A new heart also will I give you, and a new spirit will I put within you; and I will take away the stony heart out of your flesh, and I will give you an heart of flesh." What wouldest thou have given sometimes for such a heart as now thou hast, though it be not yet as thou wouldest have it? And however you value and esteem it, God himself sets no common value on it: for mark what he saith of it, Psal. 51: 17. "The sacrifices of God are a broken heart: a broken and a contrite spirit, O God, thou wilt not despise;" i. e. God is more delighted with such a heart, than with all the sacrifices in the world; one groan, one tear, flowing from faith, and the spirit of adoption, are more to him, than the cattle upon a thousand hills. And to the same sense he speaks again, Isa. 66: 1, 2. "Thus saith the Lord, The heaven is my throne, and the earth is my footstool, Where is the house that ye build to me? And where is the place of my rest? - But to this man will I look, even to him that is poor, and of a contrite spirit, and trembleth at my word;" q. d. All the magnificent temples and glorious structures in the world, give me no pleasure in comparison of such a broken heart as this.

O then, for ever bless the Lord, that has done that for you, which none else could do, and which he has done but for few besides you.

Sermon 26: Of the Nature and Quality of Christ's Death

Acts 2:23
Him, being delivered by the determinate counsel and foreknowledge of God, ye have taken, and by wicked hands have crucified and slain.

Having considered, in order, the preparative acts for the death of Christ, both on his own part, and on his enemies part, we now come to consider the death of Christ itself, which was the principal part of his humiliation, and is the chief pillar of our consolation. Here we shall in order consider,

First, The kind and nature of the death he died.

Secondly, The manner in which he bare it, viz. patiently, solitarily, and instructively; dropping divers holy and instructive lessons upon all that were about him, in his seven last words upon the cross.

Thirdly, The funeral solemnities at his burials

Fourthly, and lastly, The weighty ends and great designs of his death. In all which particulars, as we proceed to discuss and open them, you will have an account of the deep debasement and humiliation of the Son of God.

In this text, we have an account of the kind and nature of that death which Christ died: as also of the causes of it, both principal and instrumental.

First, The kind and nature of the death Christ died, which is here described more generally, as a violent death, Ye have slain him: and more particularly, as a most ignominious, cursed, dishonourable death; ye have crucified him.

Secondly, The causes of it are here likewise expressed: and that both principal and instrumental. The principal cause, permitting, ordering, and disposing all things about it, was the determinate counsel and fore-knowledge of God. There was not an action or circumstance but came under this most wise and holy counsel and determination of God.

The instruments effecting it were their wicked hands. This fore-knowledge and counsel of God, as it did no way necessitate or enforce them to it; so neither does it excuse their fact from the least aggravation of its sinfulness. It did no more compel or force their wicked hands to do what they did, than the mariner's hoisting up his sails, to take the wind to serve his design, compels the wind. And it cannot excuse their action from one circumstance of sin; because God's end and manner of acting was one thing, their end and manner of acting another. His, most pure and holy; theirs, most malicious and daringly wicked. Idem quod duo faciunt, non est idem. To this purpose a grave divine well expresses it.

In respect of God, Christ's death was justice and mercy. In respect of man, it was murder and cruelty. In respect of himself, it was obedience and humility. Hence our note is,

Doct. That our Lord Jesus Christ was not only put to death, but to the worst of deaths, even the death of the cross.

To this the apostle gives a plain testimony, Phil. 2: 8. "He became obedient to death, even the death of the cross;" where his humiliation is both specified; he was humbled to death; and aggravated by a most emphatical reduplication, even the death of the cross. So Acts 5: 30. "Jesus whom ye slew and hanged on a tree;" q.d. it did not suffice you to put him to a violent death, but you also put him to the most base, vile and ignominious death; "you hanged him on a tree."

On this point we will discuss these three particulars, viz. The nature or kind, the manner and reasons of Christ's death upon the tree.

1. I shall open the kind or nature of his death, by shewing you that it was a violent, painful, shameful, cursed, slow, and succourless death.

First, It was a violent death that Christ died. Violent in itself, though voluntary on his part. "He was cut off out of the land of the living," Is 53: 8. And yet "he laid down his life of himself; no man took it from him," John 10: 17. I call his death violent, because he died not a natural death, i.e. he lived not till nature was consumed with age, as it is in many who live till their, balsamum radicale, "radical moisture," like the oil in the lamp, be quite consumed, and then go out like an expiring lamp. It was not so with Christ: for he was but in the flower and prime of his time when he died. And indeed, he must either die a violent death, or not die at all; partly, because there was no sin in him, to open a door to natural death; as it does in all others. Partly, because else his death had not been a sacrifice acceptable and satisfactory to God for us. That which died of itself was never offered up to God; but that which was slain, when it was in its full strength and health. The temple was a type of the body of Christ, John 2: 19. Now, when the temple was destroyed, it did not drop down as an ancient structure decayed by time, but was pulled down by violence, when it was standing in its full strength. Therefore he is said to suffer death, and to be put to death for us in the flesh, 1 Pet. 3: 18. That is the first thing. It was a violent, though a voluntary death. For violent is not opposed to voluntary, but to natural.

Secondly, The death of the cross was a most painful death. In deed in this death were many deaths, contrived in one. The cross was a rack as well as a gibbet. The pains which Christ suffered upon the cross, are by the apostle emphatically stiled "tas odinas tou tanatou", Acts 2: 24. "The pains of death:" but properly they signify the pangs of travail: yea, the birth-pangs, the most acute sorrows of a travailing woman. His soul was in travail, Isa. 53, his body in bitter pangs; and being as Aquinas speaks, optime complectionatus, of the most excellent crests, exact and just temperament; his senses were more acute and delicate than ordinate; and all the time of his suffering, so they continued; not in the least blunted, dulled, or rebated, by the pains he suffered.

"The death of Christ, doubtless, contained the greatest and acutest pains imaginable: because these pains of Christ alone, were intended to equalise all that misery which the sin of men deserved," all that pain which the damned shall, and the elect deserve to feel. Now, to have pains meeting at once upon one person, equivalent to all the pains of the damned; judge you what a plight Christ was in.

Thirdly, The death of the cross was a shameful death: not only because the crucified were stripped quite naked, and so exposed as spectacles of shame, but mainly, because it was a kind of death which was appointed for the basest, and vilest of men.

The free-men when they committed capital crimes, were not condemned to the cross. No, that was looked upon as the death appointed for slaves. Tacitus calls it servile supplicium, the punishment of a slave: and to the same sense Juvenal speaks, pone crucem servo, put the cross upon the back of a slave. As they had a great esteem of a free man, so they manifested it, even when they had forfeited their lives, in cutting them off by more honourable kinds of death. This, by hanging on the tree, was always accounted most ignominious. To this day we say of him that is hanged, He dies the death of a dog: and yet it is said of our Lord Jesus, Heb. 12: 2. He not only endured the cross, but also despised the shame. Obedience to his Father's will, and zeal for our salvation, made him digest the shame of it, and despise the baseness that was in it.

Fourthly, The death of the cross was a cursed death. Upon that account he is said to be "made katara', a curse for us; For it is written, Cursed is every one that hangeth on a tree," Gal. 3: 13. "His body shall not remain all night upon the tree, but thou shalt in any wise bury him that day; for he that is hanged is accursed of God." The very symbol of lifting them up betwixt heaven and earth carried much shame in it. For it implies this in it, that the person so used, was so execrable, base, and vile, that he deserved not to tread upon the earth or touch the surface of the ground any more. And the command for burying them that day, does not at all mitigate, but rather aggravates this curse: speaking the person to be so abominable, that as he is lifted up into the air, and hanging between heaven and earth, as unworthy ever to set foot more upon the earth; so when dead, they were to hasten to bury him, that such an abominable sight might be removed as soon as might be, from before the eyes of men; and that the earth might not be defiled, by his lying on the surface of it, when taken down.

However, as the learned Junius has judiciously observed, this curse is only a ceremonial curse; for otherwise it is neither in it self, nor by the law of nature, or by civil law, more execrable than any other death. And the main reason why the ceremonial law attached the curse to this, rather than to any other death, was principally with respect to the death Christ was to die. And therefore, reader, see and admire the providence of God, that Christ should die by a Roman, and not by a Judaic law. For crucifying, or hanging on a tree, was a Roman punishment, and not in use among the Jews. But the scriptures cannot be broken.

Fifthly, The death of the cross was a very slow and lingering death. They died leisurely. Which still increaseth and aggravateth the misery of it. If a man must die a violent death, it is a favour to be dispatched: as they that are pressed to death, beg for more weight. And it is a favour to those that are hanged, to be smitten on the breast, or plucked by the heels by their friends. On the contrary, to hang long in the midst of tortures, to have death coming upon us with a slow pace, that we may feel every tread of it, as it comes on, is a misery.

The Fountain of Life Opened Up

The tyrant that heard the poor martyr was dead under his first torments, said, as one disappointed, Evasit, "He has escaped me." For he intended to have kept him much longer under torments. And it was the cruel counsel of another to his executioner; "Let him die so as he may feel himself how he dies." And surely in this respect it was worse for Christ, than any other that ever was nailed to the tree. For all the while he hanged there, he remained full of life and acute sense. His life departed not gradually, but was whole in him to the last. Other men die gradually, and, towards their end, their sense of pain is much blunted. They falter, and expire by degrees, but Christ stood under the pains of death in his full strength. His life was whole in him. This was evident by the mighty out-cry he made when he gave up the ghost, which argued him to be full of strength, contrary to the experience of all other men. Which made the centurion when he heard it, to conclude, "Surely this was the Son of God," Mark 15: 37, 39.

Sixthly, It was a succourless and helpless death to Christ. Sometimes they gave to malefactors amidst their torments, vinegar and myrrh, to blunt, dull, and stupefy their senses. And if they hanged long, would break their bones to dispatch them out of their pains. Christ had none of this favour. Instead of vinegar and myrrh, they gave him vinegar and gall to drink, to aggravate his torments. And for the breaking of his bones he prevented it, by dying before they came to break his legs. For the scriptures must be fulfilled, which say, Not a bone of him shall be broken.

This now was the kind and nature of that death he died. Even the violent, painful, shameful, cursed, slow, and succourless death of the cross. An ancient punishment both among the Romans and Carthaginians. But in honour of Christ, who died this death, Constantine the Great abrogated it by law, ordaining that none should ever be crucified any more, because Christ died that death.

Secondly, As to the manner of the execution. They that were condemned to the death of the cross, (saith a learned Antiquary of our own) bare their cross upon their own shoulders, to the place of execution. They were stripped of all their clothes, for they suffered naked. And then were fastened to the cross with nails.

The manner how that was done, one gives us in these swords, They stretched him out (meaning Christ) like another Isaac upon his own burden, the cross; that so they might take measure of the holes. And though the print of his blood upon it, gave them the true length of his body; yet how strictly do they take it longer than the truth. Thereby at once to crucify and rack him. Then being nailed, like as Moses lifted up the serpent, so was the Son of man lifted up. And when the cross, with the Lord fastened on it, fell into its socket, or basis, it jerked the whole, and every part of his sacred body. And the whole weight hanging upon his nailed hands, the wounds by degrees grew wider and wider: till at last he expired in the midst of those tortures.

And that the equity of their proceedings might the better appear to the people, the cause of the punishment was written in capital letters, and fixed to the tree over the head of the malefactor. Of this appendant to this kind of death, I shall speak distinctly in the next sermon, before I come to handle the manner of his death: there being so much of providence in that circumstance, as invites us to spend more than a few transient thoughts upon it. Meanwhile, in the next place,

Thirdly, We will enquire briefly into the reasons why Christ died this, rather than any other kind of death. And amongst others, these three are obvious.

First, Because Christ must bear the curse in his death, and a curse by law was affixed to no other kind of death, as it was to this.

The learned Masius upon Joshua 8:29. commenting upon the death of king Ai, who was hanged upon the tree, until the evening, tells us, "That the principal reason of the malediction and execrableness of his death was, because the death of Christ was prefigured in that mystery." Christ came to take away the curse from us by this death; and so must be made a curse. On him must all the curses of the moral law lie, which were due to us. And that nothing might be wanting to make it a full curse, the very death he died, must also have a ceremonial curse upon it.

Secondly, Christ died this, rather than any other kind of death; to fulfil the types, and prefiguration that of old were made with respect to it. All the sacrifices were lifted up from the earth, upon the altar. But especially the brazen serpent prefigured this death, Numb. 19: 9. Moses made a serpent of brass, and put it upon a pole. And, saith Christ, John 3: 14. "As Moses lifted up the serpent in the wilderness, so must the Son of man be lifted up," that so he might correspond with that lively type, made of him in the wilderness.

Thirdly, Christ died this, rather than any other death, because it was predicted of him, and in him must all the predictions, as well as types, be fully accomplished. The psalmist spake in the person of Christ, of this death, as plainly as if he had rather been writing the history of what was done, than a prophecy of what was to be done, so many years afterwards, Psal. 22: 16, 17. "For dogs have compassed me about, the assembly of the wicked have inclosed me: they pierced my hands and feet; I may tell all my bones; they look and stare upon me." Which has a manifest reference to the distension of all his members upon the tree, which was a rack to him. So Zech. 12: 10. "They shall look upon me, whom they have pierced." Yea, Christ himself had foretold the death he should die, in the forecited, John 3: 14. saying, "He must be lifted up," i.e. hanged between heaven and earth. And the scriptures must be fulfilled.

Thus you have a brief account both of the kind, manner, and reasons of this death of Christ. The improvement of it, you have in the following inferences of truth, deducible from it.

Inference 1. Is Christ dead? and did he die the violent, painful, shameful, cursed, slow, and succourless death of the cross? Then surely there is forgiveness with God, an plenteous redemption for the greatest of sinners, that by faith apply the blood of the cross to their poor guilty souls. So speaks the apostle, Col. 1: 14. "In whom we have redemption through his blood, even the forgiveness of sins." And 1 John 1: 7. "The blood of Christ cleanseth us from all sin." Two things will make this demonstrable.

First, That there is a sufficient efficacy in this blood of the cross, to expiate the greatest sins.

Secondly, That the efficacy of it is designed and intended by God for believing sinners. How clearly do both these propositions lie in the word?

First, That there is sufficient efficacy in the blood of the cross, to expiate and wash away the greatest sins. This is manifest, for it is precious blood, as it is called, 1 Pet. 1: 18. "Ye were not redeemed with corruptible things, as silver and gold; but with the precious blood of the Son of God." This preciousness of the blood of Christ riseth from the union it has with that person, who is over all, God blessed for ever. And on that account is stiled the blood of God, Acts 20: 28: and so it becomes royal, princely blood: Yea, such for the dignity, and efficacy of it, as never was created, or shall ever run in any other veins but his. The blood of all the creatures in the world, even a sea of human blood bears no more proportion to the precious. and excellent blood of Christ, than a dish of common water, to a river of liquid gold. On the account of its invaluable preciousness, it becomes satisfying and reconciling blood to God. So the apostle speaks, Col. 1: 20. "And (having made peace through the blood of his cross) by him to reconcile all things to himself; by him, I say, whether they be things in earth, or things in heaven." The same blood which is redemption to them that dwell on earth, is confirmation to them that dwell in heaven. Before the efficacy of this blood, guilt vanishes, and shrinks away as the shadow before the glorious sun. Every drop of it has a voice, and speaks to the soul that sits trembling under its guilt better things than the blood of Abel, Heb. 10: 24. It sprinkles us from all evil, i.e. an unquiet and accusing conscience, Heb. 10: 22. For having enough in it to satisfy God, it must needs have enough in it to satisfy conscience.

Conscience can demand no more for its satisfaction, nor will it take less than God demands for his satisfaction. And in this blood is enough to give both satisfaction.

Secondly, As there is sufficient efficacy in this blood to expiate the greatest guilt; so it is as manifest, that the virtue and efficacy of it, is intended and designed by God for the use of believing sinners. Such blood as this washed, without doubt, for some weighty end, that some might be the better for it. Who they are for whom it is intended, is plain enough from Acts 13: 39. "And by him all that believe, are justified from all things, from which they could not be justified by the law of Moses."

That the remission of the sins of believers was the great thing designed in the pouring out of this precious blood of Christ, appears from all the sacrifices that figured it to the ancient church. The shedding of that typical blood, spake a design of pardon. And the putting of their hands upon the head of the sacrifice, spake the way and method of believing, by which that blood was then applied to them in that way; and is still applied to us in a more excellent way. Had no pardon been intended, no sacrifices had been appointed.

Moreover, let it be considered, this blood of the cross is the blood of a surety; that came under the same obligations with us, and in our name or stead shed it: and so of course frees and discharges the principal offender, or debtor, Heb. 7: 22. Can God exact satisfaction from the blood and death of his own Son, the surety of believers, and yet still demand it from believers? It cannot be. "Who (saith the apostle) shall lay any thing to the charge of God's elect? It is God that justifieth. Who shall condemn? It is Christ that died," Rom. 8: 33, 34. And why are faith and repentance prescribed as the means of pardon? Why does God every where in his word, call upon sinners to repent, and believe in this blood? encouraging them so to do, by so many precious promises of remission; and declaring the inevitable and eternal ruin, of all impenitent, and unbelieving ones, who despise and reject this blood? What, I say, does all this speak, but the possibility of a pardon for the greatest of sinners; and the certainty of a free, full, and final pardon for all believing sinners? O what a joyful sound is this! What ravishing voices of peace, pardon, grace, and acceptance, come to our ears from the blood of the cross?

The greatest guilt that ever was contracted upon a trembling, shaking conscience, can stand before the efficacy of the blood of Christ no more, than the sinner himself can stand before the justice of the Lord, with all that guilt upon him.

Reader, the word assures thee, whatever thou hast been, or art, that sins of as deep a dye as thine, have been washed away in this blood. "I was a blasphemer, a persecutor, injurious; but I obtained mercy," saith Paul, 1 Tim. 1: 13. But it may be thou wilt object; this was a rare and singular instance, as it is a great question whether any other sinner shall find the like grace that he did. No question of it at all, if you believe in Christ as he did; for he tells us, ver. 16. "For this cause I obtained mercy that in me first, Jesus Christ might show forth all long suffering, for a pattern to them which should hereafter believe on him to life everlasting." So that upon the same grounds he obtained mercy, you may obtain it also.

Those very men who had a hand in the shedding of Christ's blood, had the benefit of that blood afterwards pardoning them, Acts 2: 36. There is nothing but unbelief and impenitence of heart can bar thy soul from the blessings of this blood.

Inf. 2. Did Christ die the cursed death of the cross for believers, then though there be much of pain, there is nothing of curse in the death of the saints. It still wears its dart, by which it strikes; but has lost its sting, by which it hurts and destroys. A serpent that has no sting, may hiss and affright, but we may take him in our hand, without danger. Death poured out all its poison, and lost its sting in Christ's side, when he became a curse for us.

But what speak I of the innocence and harmlessness of death to believers? It is certainly their friend and great benefactor. As there is no curse, so there are many blessings in it. "Death is yours," 1 Cor. 3: 22. Yours as a special privilege and favour. Christ has not only conquered it, but is more than a conqueror; for he has made it beneficial, and very serviceable to the saints. When Christ was nailed to the tree, then he said as it were to death, which came to grapple with him there, "Death, I will be thy plague; O grave, I will be thy destruction:" and so he was; for he swallowed up death in victory, spoiled it of its power. So that, though it may now affright some weak believers, yet cannot hurt them at all.

Inf. 3. If Christ died the cursed death of the cross for us, how cheerfully should we submit to, and bear any cross for Jesus Christ? He had his cross, and we have ours; but what feathers are ours compared with his? His cross was a heavy cross indeed, yet how patiently and meekly did he support it! "he endured his cross," we cannot endure or bear ours, though they be not to be named with his. Three things would marvellously strengthen us to bear the cross of Christ, and bring up a good report upon it in the world.

First, That we shall carry it but a little way. Secondly, Christ bears the heaviest end of it. Thirdly, Innumerable blessings and mercies grow upon the cross of Christ.

First, We shall bear it but a little way. It should be enough to me (saith a holy one) that Christ will have joy and sorrow halfers of the life of the saints. And that each of them should have a share of our days, as the night and day are kindly partners of time, and take it up betwixt them. But if sorrow be the greediest halfer of our days here, I know joy's day shall dawn, and do more than recompense all our sad hours.

Let my Lord Jesus, (since he will do so) weave my bit-and-span length of time with white and black; well and woe. - Let the rose be neighbour with the thorn. - "When we are over the water, Christ shall cry, down crosses, and up heaven for evermore; down hell, and down death, and down sin, and down sorrow; and up glory, up life, up joy for evermore. It is true, Christ and his cross are not separable in this life; howbeit Christ and his cross part at heaven's door: for there is no house room for crosses in heaven. One tear, one sigh, one sad heart, one fear, one loss, one thought of trouble cannot find lodging there." - Sorrow and the saints are not married together! or suppose it was so, heaven shall make a divorce. Life is but short, and therefore crosses cannot be long. Our sufferings are but for a while, 1 Pet. 5: 10. They are but the sufferings of the present time, Rom. 8: 18.

Secondly, As we shall carry the cross of Christ but a little way, so Christ himself bears the heaviest end of it. And as one happily expresses, he saith of their crosses, half mine. He divideth sufferings with them, and takes the largest share to himself. "O how sweet a sight (saith one sweetly) is it to see a cross betwixt Christ and us. To hear our Redeemer say, at every sigh, at every blow, and eatery loss of a believer, half mine. For they are called the sufferings of Christ, and the reproach of Christ, Col. 2: 24. Heb. 11: 26. As when two are partners or owners of a ship, half of the gain, and half of the loss, belongeth to either of the two. So Christ in our sufferings, is half gainer, and half loser, with us: yea, the heaviest end of the black tree lieth on your Lord. It falleth first upon him, and but rebounds from him upon you:" "The reproaches of them that reproached thee, are fallen upon me," Psal. 69: 9. Nay, so speak as the thing is, Christ does not only bear half, or the better part, but the whole of our cross and burden. Yea, he bears all, and more than all; for he bears us and our burden too, or else we would quickly sink, and faint under it.

Thirdly, As we have not far to carry it, and Christ carries the heaviest part; yea, all the burden for us; yea, us and our burden too; so, in the last place, it is reviving to think what an innumerable multitude of blessings and mercies are the fruit and offspring of a sanctified cross. Since that tree was so richly watered with the blood of Christ; what store of choice, and rich fruits does it bear to believers?

Our sufferings (saith one) are washed in the blood of Christ, as well as our souls. "For Christ's merits bought a blessing to the crosses of the sons of God. Our troubles owe us a free passage through him. Devils, and men, and crosses, are our debtors; and death, and all storms are our debtors, to blow our poor tossed bark over the water freight free: and to set the travellers in their own known ground. Therefore we shall die, and yet live. - I know no man has a velvet cross, but the cross is made of what God will have it; but verily, howbeit, it be no warrentable market to buy a cross, yet I dare not say, O that I had liberty to sell Christ's cross, lest therewith also I should sell joy, comfort, sense of love, patience, and the kind visits of a bridegroom. I have but small experience of sufferings for Christ, but let my Judge and witness in heaven, lay my soul in the balance of justice; if I find not a young heaven, and a little paradise of glorious comforts, and soul-delighting love-kisses of Christ in suffering for him and his truth. - My prison is my palace, my sorrow is with child of joy; my losses are rich losses, my pain easy pain, my heavy days are holy days and happy days. I may tell a new tale of Christ to my friends. O what owe I to the file, and to the hammer, and to the furnace of my Lord Jesus! who has now let me see how good the wheat of Christ is, that goes through his mill, and his oven, to be made bread for his own table. Grace tried is better than grace, and more than grace. It is glory in its infancy."

"Who knows the truth of grace without a trial. - O how little getteth Christ of us, but what he winneth (to speak so) with much toil and pains? And how soon would faith freeze without a cross? Bear your cross therefore with joy."

Inf. 4. Did Christ die the death, yea, the worst of deaths for us? Then it follows, that our mercies are brought forth with great difficulty; and that which is sweet to us in the fruition, was costly, and hard to Christ in the acquisition. Surely, upon every mercy we have this motto written, The price of Blood, Col. 1: 14. "In whom we have redemption through his blood:" Upon which a late neat writer delivers himself thus. "The way of grace is here considerable; life comes through death; God comes in Christ; and Christ comes in blood: the choicest mercies come through the greatest miseries; prime favours come swimming in blood to us. Through a red sea Israel came to Canaan. Many a man lost his life, and much blood shed; the very land flowing with milk and honey was first made to flow with blood, ere Israel could inherit the promise. Seven nations were destroyed, ere the land of Canaan was divided to the Israelites, Acts 13: 19. - "Sin makes mercy so deadly hard to bring forth. To christen every precious child, every Benjamin Benoni, every son of God's right-hand, a son of sorrow and death to her that brings him forth. Adam's sweets had no bitter till he transgressed God's will: one mercy did not die to bring forth another, till he died. But oh! how should this raise the value of our mercies? What, the price of blood, the price of precious blood, the blood of the cross! O what an esteem should this raise!"

"Things (as the same ingenious author adds) are prized rather as they come, than as they are. Far fetched and dear bought makes all the price, and gives all the worth with us weak creatures. Upon this ground the scripture, when it speaks of our great fortune, tells the great price it cost, as eyeing our weakness, who look more at what things cost, than at what they are. And as knowing if any thing will take with us, this will, To him that loved us and washed us from sins in his own blood," Rev. 1: 5.

"Man is a legal creature, and looks much at what is given for a thing. What did this cost? Why, it cost Christ's own blood. Colour is more than the cloth with us, and scarlet colour is a general taking colour with us: and therefore is Christ's garment dipped in blood, and he admired in this habit. Who is this that comes from Edom, with garments dyed red from Bozra?"

Beware then you abuse not any of the mercies that Christ brought forth with so many bitter pangs and throes. And let all this endear Christ more than ever to you, and make you in a deep sense of his grace and love, to say,

Thanks be to God for Jesus Christ.

Sermon 27: Of the signal Providence, which directed and ordered the Title affixed to the cross of Christ

Luke 23:38

And a superscription also was written over him in letters of Greek, and Latin, and Hebrew, THIS IS THE KING OF THE JEWS.

Before I pass on to the Manner of Christ's death, I shall consider the title affixed to the cross; in which very much of the wisdom of Providence was discovered. It was the manner of the Romans, that the equity of their proceedings might the more clearly appear to the people, when they crucified any man, to publish the cause of his death, in a table written in capital letters, and placed over the head of the crucified. And that there might be at least, a show and face of justice in Christ's death, he also shall have his title or superscription.

The worst and most unrighteous actions labour to cover and shroud themselves under pretension of equity. Sin is so shameful a thing, that it cares not to own its name. Christ shall have a table written for him also. This writing one evangelist calls the Accusation, "aitia", Matth. 27: 37. Another calls it the Title, "titlos", John 19: 19. Another the Inscription or Superscription, "epigrafe", so the text. And another the Superscription of his Accusations, "epigrafe tes aitias", Mark 15: 26. In short, it was a fair legible writing, intended to express the fact or crime, for which the person died.

This was their usual manner, though sometimes we find it was published by the voice of the common crier. As in the case of Attalus the martyr, who was led about the amphitheatre, one proclaiming before him, this is Attalus the Christian. But it was customary and usual to express the crime in a written table, as the text expresses it. Wherein these three things offer themselves to your consideration.

First, The character or description of Christ, contained in that writing. And he is described by his kingly dignity: This is the king of the Jews. The very office, which but a little before, they had reproached and derided, bowing the knee to him in mockery, saying, Hail King of the Jews: the Providence of God so orders it, that therein he shall be vindicated and honoured. This is the King of the Jews: Or, as the other evangelists complete it, This is Jesus of Nareth the King of the Jews.

Secondly, The person that drew his character or title. It was Pilate; he that but now condemned him: he that was his judge, shall be his herald, to proclaim his glory. For the title is honourable. Surely, this was not from himself, for he was Christ's enemy; but rather than Christ should want a tongue to clear him, the tongue of an enemy shall do it.

Thirdly, The time when this honour was done him: It was when he was at the lowest ebb of his glory; when shame and reproach were heaped on him by all hands. When all the disciples had forsaken him, and were fled. Not one left to proclaim his innocence, or speak a word in his vindication. Then does the providence of God as strangely, as powerfully, over-rule the heart and pen of Pilate, to draw this title for him, and affix it to his cross. Surely we must look higher than Pilate in this thing, and see how Providence serves itself by the hands of Christ's adversities. Pilate writes in honour of Christ, and stiffly defends it too. Hence our observation is,

Doct. 1. That the dignity of Christ was openly proclaimed, and defended by an enemy; and that, in the time of his greatest reproaches and sufferings.

To open this mystery of providence to you, that you may not stand idly gazing upon Christ's title, as many then did; we must, First, Consider the nature and quality of this title. Secondly, What hand the Providence of God had in this matter. Thirdly, and then draw forth the proper uses and improvements of it.

First, To open the nature and quality of Christ's title or inscription; let it be thoroughly considered, and we shall find,

First, That it was an extraordinary title, varying from all examples of that kind; and directly crossing the main design and end of their own custom. For, as I hinted before, the end of it was to clear the equity of their proceedings, and show the people how justly they suffered those punishments inflicted on them for such crimes. But lo, here is a title expressing no crime at all, and so vindicating Christ's innocence t. This some of them perceived, and moved Pilate to change It, not, This is, but, This is he that said, I am the King of the Jews. In that, as they conceived, lay his crime. O how strange and wonderful a thing was this! But what shall we say! it was a day of wonders and extraordinary things. As there was never such a person crucified before, so there was never such a title affixed to the cross before.

Secondly, As it was an extraordinary, so it was a public title, both written and published with the greatest advantage of spreading itself far and near, among all people, that could be, "for it was written in three languages, and to those most known in the world at that time." The Greek tongue was then known in most parts of the world. The Hebrew was the Jews native language. And the Latin the language of the Romans. So that it being written both in Hebrew, Greek, and Latin, it was easy to be understood both by Jews and Gentiles.

And indeed, unto this the providence of God had a special eye, to make it notorious and evident to all the world; for even so all things designed for public view, and knowledge were written. Joseph us tells us of certain pillars, on which was engraven in letters of Greek, and Latin, "It is a wickedness for strangers to enter into the holy place". So the soldiers of Gordian, the third emperor, when he was slain upon the borders of Persia, raised a monument for him, and engraved his memorial upon it, in Greek, Latin, Persia, Judaic, and Egyptian letters, that all people might read the same. And as it was written in three learned languages, so it was exposed to view in a public place; and at that time, when multitudes of strangers, as well as Jews, were at Jerusalem; it was at the time of the passover; so that all things concurred to spread and divulge the innocence of Christ, vindicated in this title.

Thirdly, As it was a public, so it was an honourable title. Such was the nature of it, saith Bucer; that in the midst of death, Christ began to triumph by it. And by reason thereof, the cross began to change its own nature, and instead of a rack, or engine of torture, it became a throne of majesty. Yea, it might be called now, as the church itself is, The pillar and ground of truth; for it held out much of the gospel, much of the glory of Christ; as that pillar does, to which a royal proclamation is affixed.

Fourthly, It was a vindicating title: it cleared up the honour, dignity, and innocence of Christ, against all the false imputations, calumnies, and blasphemies, which acre cast upon him before, by the wicked tongues, both of Jews and Gentiles.

They had called him a deceiver, an usurper, a blasphemer; they rent their clothes, in token of their detestation of his blasphemy; because he made himself the Son of God, and King of Israel. But now in this, they acknowledged him to be both Lord and Saviour. Not a mock king, as they had made him before. So that herein the honour of Christ was fully vindicated.

Fifthly, Moreover it was a predicting and presaging title. Evidently foreshowing the propagation of Christ's kingdom, and the spreading of his name and glory among all kindreds, nations, tongues, and languages. As Christ has right to enter into all the kingdoms of the earth, by his gospel, and set up his throne in every nation: so it was presaged by this title that he should do so. And that both Hebrews, Greeks, and Latins should be called to the knowledge of him. Nor is it a wonder, that this should be predicted by wicked Pilate, when Caiaphas himself, a man every way as wicked as he, had prophesied to the same purpose, John 11: 51, 52. For being High-Priest that year, he prophesied, That Jesus should die for that nation, and not for that nation only, but that also he should gather together in one, the children of God that were scattered abroad. Yea, many have prophesied in Christ's name, who, for all that, shall never be owned by him, Matth. 7: 22.

Sixthly, And lastly, It was an immutable title. The Jews endeavoured, but could not persuade Pilate to alter it. To all their importunities he returns this resolute answer, "What I have written, I have written;" as if he should say, Urge me no more, I have written his title, I cannot, I will not, alter a letter, a point thereof. "Surely the constancy of Pi]ate at this time can be attributed to nothing but divine special Providence." Most wonderful! that he, who before was as inconstant as a reed shaken by the wind, is now as fixed as a pillar of brass.

And yet more wonderful], that he should write down that very particular in the title of Christ, This is the King of the Jews, which was the very thing that so scared him but a little before, and was the very consideration that moved him to give sentence. What was now become of the fear of Caesar? that Pilate dares to be Christ's herald, and publicly to proclaim him, a King of the Jews. This was the title.

Secondly, We shall next enquire what hand the Divine Providence had in this business.

And indeed, the providence of God in this hour, acted gloriously, and wonderfully, these five ways.

First, In over-ruling the heart and hand of Pilate in the draught and stile of it, and that contrary to his own inclination. I doubt not but Pilate himself was ignorant of, and far enough from designing that which the wisdom of providence aimed at in this matter. He was a wicked man, and had no love to Christ. He had given sentence of death against him; yet this is he that proclaimed him to be Jesus, King of the Jews. It so over-ruled his pen, that he could not write what was in his own heart and intention, but the quite contrary; even a fair and public testimony of the kingly office of the Son of God, This is the King of the Jews.

Secondly, Herein the wisdom of Providence was gloriously displayed, in applying a present, proper, public remedy to the reproaches and blasphemies which Christ had then newly received in his name and honour. The superstitious Jews wound him, and Heathen Pilate prepares a plaister to heal him: they reproach, he vindicates; they throw the dirt, he washes it off. Oh the profound and inscrutable wisdom of Providence!

Thirdly, Moreover, Providence eminently appeared at this time in keeping so timorous a person, a man of so base a spirit, that would not stick at any thing to please the people, from receding, or giving ground in the least to their importunities. Is Pilate become a man of such resolution and constancy? whence is this? but from the God of the spirits of all flesh, who now flowed in so powerfully upon his spirit, that he could not choose but write; and when he had written, had no more power to alter what he had written, than he had to refuse to write it.

Fourthly, Herein also much of the wisdom of Providence appeared, in casting the ignominy of the death of Christ upon those very men who ought to bear it. Pilate was moved by divine instinct, at once to clear Christ, and accuse them. For it is as if he had said, you have moved me to crucify your king, I have crucified him, and now let the ignominy of his death rest upon your heads, who have extorted this from me. He is righteous, the crime is not his but yours.

Fifthly, And lastly, The providence of God wonderfully discovered itself (as before was noted) in fixing this title to the cross of Christ, when there was so great a confluence of all sorts of people to take notice of it. So that it could never have been more advantageously published, than it was at this time. So that we may say, How wonderful are the works of God! "His ways are in the sea, his paths in the great deeps; his footsteps are not known:" His providence has a prospect beyond the understandings of all creatures.

Inference 1. Hence it follows, That the providence of our God can, and often does over-rule the counsels and actions of the worst of men to his own glory.

It can serve itself by them that oppose it, and bring about the glory and honour of Christ, by those very men, and means, which are designed to lay it in the dust. "Surely the wrath of man shall praise thee", Psal. 76: 10. The Jews thought when they crowned Christ with thorns, bowed the knee, and mocked him, led him to Golgotha and crucified him; that now they had utterly despoiled him of all his kingly dignities; and yet even there he is proclaimed a king. Thus the dispersion of the Jews, upon the death of Stephen, spread the gospel far and near, "For they went everywhere preaching the word," Acts 8: 4. Thus Paul's bonds for the gospel fell out to the furtherance of the gospel, Phil. 1: 12. O the depth of Divine Wisdom! to propagate and establish the interest of Jesus Christ, by those very means that seem to import its destruction: that extracts a medicine out of poison! How great a support should this be to the faith of God's people! When all things seem to run cross to their hopes and happiness! "Let Israel therefore hope in the Lord, for with the Lord there is mercy, and with him is plenteous redemption," Psal. 130: 7. i.e. He is never at a loss for means to promote and serve his own ends.

Inf. 2. Hence likewise it follows, That the greatest services performed to Christ accidentally and undesignedly, shall never be accepted nor rewarded of God. Pilate did Christ an eminent piece of service. He did that for Christ that not one of his own disciples at that time durst do; and yet this service was not accepted of God, because he did it not designedly for his glory, but from the mere overrulings of providence.

If there be first a willing mind, it is accepted, according to what a man has, saith the apostle, 1 Cor. 8: 12. The eye of God is first and mainly upon the will; if that be sincere and right for God, small things will be accepted; and if not, the greatest shall be abhorred. So 1 Cor. 9: 17. If I do this thing (i.e. preach the gospel) willingly, I have a reward; but if against my will, a dispensation is committed to me, q.d. If I upon pure principles of faith and love, from my heart, designing the glory of God, and delighting to promote it by my ministry, do cheerfully and willingly apply myself to the preaching of the gospel, I shall have acceptance and reward with God; but if my work be a burden to me, and the service of God esteemed as a bondage, why then providence may use me for the dispensing of the gospel to others, but I myself shall lose both reward and comfort. As it does not excuse my sin, that God can bring glory to himself out of it; so neither does it justify an action that God has praise and honour accidentally by it. Paul knew that even the strife and envy in which some preached Christ, should turn to his salvation; and yet he was not at all beholden to them for promoting his salvation that way. So Pilate here promotes the honour of Jesus Christ to whom he had no love, and whose glory he did not at all design in this thing; and therefore has neither acceptance nor reward with God.

John Flavel

O therefore, whatever you do for Christ, do it heartily, designedly, for his glory: of a ready and willing mind; with pure and sincere aims at his glory; for this is that the Lord more respects, than the greatest services by accident.

Inf. 3. Would not Pilate recede from what he had written on Christ's behalf? How shameful a thing is it for Christians to retract what they have said or done on Christ's behalf? When Pilate had asserted him to be king of the Jews, he maintained his assertion, and all the importunity of Christ's enemies shall not move him an hairs breadth from it. "that I have written, I have written," q. d. I have said it, and I will not revoke it. Did Pilate say, "What I have written, I have written:" and shall not we say, What we have believed, we have believed: and what we have professed, we have professed? that we have engaged to Christ, we have engaged. We will stand to what we have done for him: we will never recant our former ownings of and appearances for Christ.

As God's election, so your profession must be irrevocable. O let him that is holy be holy still. That counsel given by a reverend divine in this case, is both safe and good. "Be sure, (saith he) you stand on good ground, and then resolve to stand your ground against all the world. Follow God, and fear not men. Art thou godly! repent not whatsoever thy religion cost thee. Let sinners repent, but let not saints repent. Let saints repent of their faults, but not of their faith: of their iniquities, but not of their righteousness. Repent not of your righteousness, lest you afterward repent of your repentance. - Repent not of your seal, or your forwardness, or activity in the holy ways of the Lord. - Wish not yourselves a step farther back, or a cubit lower in your stature, in the grace of God. wish not any thing undone, concerning which God will say, Well done."

In Galen's time it was a proverbial expression, when any one would show the impossibility of a thing; you may as soon turn a Christian from Christ as do it.

A true heart choice of Christ is without reserves, and what is without reserves, will be without repentance. There is a stiffness and stoutness of spirit which is our sin. But this is our glory, in the matters of God, saith Luther, I assume this title, Cedo nulli, "I yield to none:" If ye be hot and cold, off and on; profess, and retract your profession. He that condemned Christ with his lips, will condemn you by his example. Resolute Pilate shall be your judge.

Inf. 4. Did Pilate affix such an honourable, vindicating title to the cross? Then the cross of Christ is a dignified cross. Then the cross and sufferings of Christ are attended with glory and honour. Remember when your hearts begin to startle at the sufferings and reproaches of Christ, there is an honourable title upon the cross of Christ. And as it was upon his, so it will be upon your cross also, if ye suffer for Christ. Moses saw it, which made him esteem the very reproaches of Christ, above all the treasures of Egypt, Heb. 11: 26. How did the martyrs glory in their sufferings for Christ! calling their chains of iron, chains of gold; and their manacles, bracelets.

I remember it is storied of Ludovicus Marsacus, a knight of France, that when he, with divers other Christians of an inferior rank and degree in the world, were condemned to die for religion. and the gaoler had bound them with chains, but did not bind him being a more honourable person than the rest: he was offended greatly by that omission, and said, "Why do not you honour me with a chain for Christ also, and create me a knight of that it lustrous order?"

"To you (saith the apostle) it is given in the behalf of Christ not only to believe, but also to suffer for his sake," Phil. 1: 29. There is a two-fold honour attending the cross of Christ; one in the very sufferings themselves; another, as the reward and fruit of them. To be called out to suffer for Christ, is a great honour. Yea, an honour peculiar to the saints. The damned suffer from Christ, the wicked suffer for their sins. The angels glorify Christ by their active but not their passive obedience. This is reserved as a special honour for saints.

And as there is a great deal of honour in being called forth to suffer on Christ's account; so Christ will confer special honour upon his suffering saints, in the day of their reward, Mat. 10: 32. "He that confesses me before men, him will I confess also before my Father which is in heaven." O Sirs, one of these days the Lord will break out of heaven, with a shout, accompanied with myriads of angels, and ten thousands of his saints, those glittering courtiers of heaven. The heavens and earth shall flame and melt before him; and it shall be very tempestuous round about him; the graves shall open, the sea and earth shall yield up their dead. You shall see him ascending the awful throne of Judgement, and all flesh gathered before his face; even multitudes, multitudes that no man can number. And then to be brought forth by Christ before that great assembly of angels and saints: and there to have an honourable mention and remembrance made of your labours, and sufferings, your pains, patience and self-denial, of all your sufferings, and losses for Christ; and to hear from his mouth, Well done, good and faithful servant: O what honour is this! Yet this shall be done to the man that now chooses sufferings for Christ, rather than sin; That esteems his reproaches greater riches than the treasures of Egypt.

I tell you, It is an honour the angels have not. I make no doubt, but they would be glad, (had they bodies of flesh as we have), to lay their necks on the block for Christ. But this is the saints peculiar privilege. The apostles went away from the council rejoicing, that they were honoured to be dishonoured for Christ: Or, as we translate it, "counted worthy to suffer shame for him," Acts 5: 41. Surely, if there be any stigmata laudis, "marks of honour," they are such as we receive for Christ's sake. If there be any shame that has glory in it, it is the reproach of Christ, and the shame you suffer for his name.

Inf. 5. Did Pilate so stiffly assert and defend the honour of Christ? What doubt can then be made of the success of Christ's interest, and the prosperity of his cause: when the very enemies thereof are made to serve it?

Rather than Christ shall want honour, Pilate, the man that condemned him, shall do him honour. And as it fared with his person, just so with his interest also. How often have the people of God received mercies from the hands of their enemies? Rev. 12: 16. "The earth helped the woman," i.e. wicked men did the church service. So that this may singularly relieve us against all our despondencies and fears of the miscarriage of the interest of Christ.

That people can never be ruined, who thrive by their losses; conquer by being conquered; multiply by being diminished: Whose worst enemies are made to do that for them, which friends cannot or dare not do. See you a Heathen Pilate proclaiming the honour and innocence of Christ; God will not want instruments to honour Christ by. If others cannot, his very enemies shall.

Inf. 6. Did Pilate vindicate Christ in drawing up such a title to be affixed to his cross? then hence it follows, That God will, sooner or later, clear up the innocency and integrity of his people, who commit their cause to him. Christ's name was clouded with many reproaches; wounded through and through, by the blasphemous tongues of his malicious enemies. He committed himself to him that judgeth righteously, 1 Pet. 2: 23. and see how soon God vindicates him. That is sweet and seasonable counsel for us, when our names are clouded with unjust censures, Psal. 37: 5, 6. "Commit thy way unto the Lord; trust also in Him, and he shall bring it to pass. He shall brings forth thy righteousness as the light, and thy judgement as the noon day." Joseph was accused of incontinence; David of treason; Daniel of disobedience; Elijah of troubling Israel; Jeremiah of revolting; Amos of preaching against the king; the Apostles of sedition, rebellion, and alteration of laws; Christ himself of gluttony, sorcery, blasphemy, sedition, but how did all these honourable names wade out of their reproaches, as the sun out of a cloud! God cleared all their honour for them even in this world. "Slanders (saith one) are but as soap, which though it soils and daubs for the present, yet it helps to make the garment more clean and shining." "When hair is shaven, it comes the thicker, and with a new increase: so when the razor of censure has (saith one) made your heads bare, and brought on the baldness of reproach, be not discouraged, God has a time to bring forth your righteousness as the light, by an apparent conviction, to dazzle and discourage your adversaries."

The world was well changed, when Constantine kissed the hollow of Paphnutius' eye, which was ere while put out for Christ. Scorn and reproach is but a little cloud, that is soon blown over. But suppose ye should not be vindicated in this world, but die under a cloud upon your names; be sure God will clear it up, and that to purpose in that great day. Then shall the righteous, (even in this respect) shine forth as the sun, in the Kingdom of their Father. Then every detracting mouth shall be stopped, and no more cruel arrows of reproach shot at the white of your reputation.

Be patient therefore, my brethren, unto the coming of the Lord. "The Lord comes with ten thousands of his saints, to execute judgement upon all; and to convince all that are ungodly, of all their ungodly deeds, which they have ungodly committed. And of all their hard speeches which ungodly sinners have spoken against him," Jude 14, 15. Then shall they retract their censures, and alter their opinions of the saints. If Christ will be our compurgator, we need not fear who are our accusers. If your names, for his sake, be cast out as evil, and spurned in the dirt; Christ will deliver it you again in that day whiter than the snow in Salmon.

Inf. 7. Did Pilate give this title to cast the reproach of his death upon the Jews, and clear himself of it? How natural is it to men to transfer the fault of their own actions from themselves to others? For when he writes, This is the king of the Jews, he wholly charges them with the crime of crucifying their king: and it is as if he had said, Hereafter let the blame and fault of this action lie wholly upon your heads, who have brought the guilt of his blood upon yourselves and children.

I am clear, you have extorted it from me. O where shall we find a spirit so ingenuous, to take home to itself the shame of its own actions, and charge itself freely with its own guilt? Indeed it is the property of renewed, gracious hearts to remember, confess, and freely bewail their own evils, to the glory of God: and that is a gracious heart indeed, which in this case judgeth, that the glory, which by confession, goes to the name of his God, is not so much glory lost to his own name, but it is the power of grace moulding our proud natures into another thing, that must bring them to his.

Sermon 28: Of the manner of Christ's Death, in respect to the Solitariness thereof

Zechariah 13:7
Awake, O sword, against my shepherd, and against the man [that is] my fellow, saith the LORD of hosts: smite the shepherd, and the sheep shall be scattered: and I will turn mine hand upon the little ones.

In the former sermons, we have opened the nature and kind of death Christ died; even the cursed death of the cross. Wherein, nevertheless his innocence was vindicated, by that honourable title providentially affixed to his cross. Method now requires that we take into consideration the manner in which he endured the cross, and that was solitarily, meekly, and instructively.

His solitude in suffering is plainly expressed in this scripture now before us, it cannot be doubted, but the prophet in this place speaks of Christ, if you consider Matth. 26: 31. where you shall find these words applied to Christ by his own accommodation of them, "Then said Jesus unto them, all ye shall be offended because of me this night, for it is written, I will smite the shepherd, and the sheep shall be scattered." Besides, the title here given [God's fellow] is too big for any creature in heaven or earth besides Christ.

In these words we have four things particularly to consider. First, The commission given to the sword by the Lord of hosts. Secondly, The person against whom it is commissioned. Thirdly, The dismal effect of that stroke. Fourthly and lastly, The gracious mitigation of it.

First, The commission given to the sword by the Lord of hosts. "Awake, O sword, and smite, saith the Lord of hosts." The Lord of hosts, at whose beck and command all the creatures are. Who, with a word of his mouth, can open all the armouries in the world, and command what weapons and instruments of death he pleaseth, calls here for the sword; not the rod, gently to chasten; but the sword to destroy. The rod breaks no bones, but the sword opens the door to death and destruction. The strokes and thrusts of the sword are mortal; and he bids it awake. It signifies both "to rouse up," as one that awakes out of sleep, and "to rouse or awake with triumph and rejoicing." So the same word is rendered, Job 31: 29. Yea, he commands it, "to awake and smite." And it is as if the Lord had said, Come forth of thy scabbard, O sword of justice, thou hast been hid there a long time, and hast, as it were, been asleep in thy scabbard, now awake and glitter, thou shalt drink royal blood, such as thou never sheddest before.

Secondly, The person against whom it is commissioned, "my shepherd, and the man that is my fellows." This shepherd can be no other than Christ, who is often in scripture stiled "a Shepherd, yea, the chief Shepherd, the Prince of pastors." Who redeemed, feeds, guides, and preserves the flock of God's elect, 1 Pet. 5: 4. John 10: 11. This is he whom he also stiles the man his fellow. Or his neighbour, as some render it. And so Christ is, with respect to his equality and unity with the Father, both in essence and will. His next neighbour. His other self. You have the sense of it in Phil. 2: 6. He was in the form of God, and thought it no robbery to be equal with God.

Against Christ his fellow, his next neighbour, the delight of his soul, the sword here receives its commission.

Thirdly, you have here the dismal consequent of this deadly stroke upon the shepherd. And that is the scattering of the sheep. By the sheep understand here, that little flock, the disciples, which followed this shepherd till he was smitten i.e. apprehended by his enemies, and they were scattered, i.e. dispersed; they all forsook him and fled. And so Christ was left alone, amidst his enemies. Not one durst make a stand for him, or own him in that hour of his danger.

Fourthly, And lastly, Here is a gracious mitigation of this sad dispersion, "I will turn my hand upon the little ones." By little ones he means the same that before he called sheep; but the expression is designedly varied, to show their feebleness and weakness, which appeared in their relapse from Christ. And by turning his hand upon them, understand God's gracious reduction, and gathering of them again after their sad dispersion, so that they shall not be lost, though scattered for the present. For after the Lord was risen, he went before them into Galilee, as he promised, Matth. 26: 31. And gathered them again by a gracious hand, so that not one of them was lost but the son of perdition.

The words thus opened, I shall observe suitably to the method I have proposed.

Doct. That Christ's dearest friends forsook and left him alone, in the time of his greatest distress and danger.

This doctrine containing only matter of fact, and that also so plainly delivered by the pens of the several faithful Evangelists, I need spend no longer time in the proof of it, than to refer you to the several testimonies they have given to it. But I shall rather choose to fit and prepare it for use, by explaining these four questions.

First, Who were the sheep that were scattered from their shepherd, and left him alone?
Secondly, What evil was there in this their scattering?
Thirdly, What were the grounds and causes of it?
Fourthly, and lastly, What was the issue and event of it?

First, Who were these sheep that were dispersed and scattered from their shepherd when he was smitten. It is evident they were those precious elect souls that he had gathered to himself, who had long followed him, and dearly loved him, and were dearly beloved of him. They were persons that had left all and followed him, and, till that time, faithfully continued with him in his temptations, Luke 22: 28. And were all resolved so to do, though they should die with him, Matth. 26: 35. These were the persons.

Secondly, But were they as good as their word? Did they indeed stick faithfully to him? No, they all forsook him and fled. These sheep were scattered. This was not indeed a total and final apostasy, that is the fall proper to the hypocrite, the temporary believer, who, like a comet, expires when that earthly matter is spent that maintained the blaze for a time.

These were stars fixed in their orb, though clouded and overcast for a time. This was but a mist or fog, which overspreads the earth in the morning till the sun be risen, and then it clears up and proves a fair day. But though it was not a total and final apostasy; yet it was a very sinful and sad relapse from Jesus Christ, as will appear by considering the following aggravations and circumstances of it. For,

First, This relapse of theirs was against the very articles of agreement, which they had sealed to Christ at their first admission into his service; he had told them, in the beginning, what they must resolve upon, Luke 14: 26, 27. "If any man come to me, and hate not his father and mother, and wife, and children, and brethren, and sisters, yea, and his own life also, he cannot be my disciple. And whosoever does not bear his cross, and come after me, cannot be my disciple." Accordingly they submitted to these terms, and told him they had left all and followed him, Mark 10: 28. Against this engagement made to Christ, they now sin. Here was unfaithfulness.

Secondly, As it was against the very terms of their admission, so it was against the very principles of grace implanted by Christ in their hearts. They were holy sanctified persons, in whom dwelt the love and fear of God. By these they were strongly inclined to adhere to Christ, in the time of his sufferings, as appears by those honest resolves they had made in the case. Their grace strongly inclined them to their duty, their corruptions swayed them the contrary way. Grace bid them stand, corruption bid them fly. Grace told them it was their duty to share in the sufferings as well as in the glory of Christ. Corruption represented these sufferings as intolerable, and bid them shift for themselves whilst they might. So that here must needs be a force and violence offered to their light, and the loving constraints thereof; which is no small evil.

For though I grant it was a sudden, surprising temptation, yet it cannot be imagined that this fact was wholly deliberate; nor that, for so long time, they were without any debate or seasonings about their duty.

Thirdly, As it was against their own principles, so it was much against the honour of their Lord and Master. By this their sinful flight they exposed the Lord Jesus to the contempt and scorn of his enemies. This some conceive is imported in that question which the High-priest asked him, John 18: 19. "The High priest then asked Jesus of his disciples, and of his doctrine." He asked him of his disciples, how many he had, and what was become of them now? And what was the reason they forsook their master, and left him to shift for himself when danger appeared? But to those questions Christ made no reply. He would not accuse them to their enemies, though they had deserted him. But, doubtless, it did not a little reflect upon Christ, that there was not one of all his friends that durst own their relation to him, in a time of danger.

Fourthly, As it was against Christ's honour, so it was against their own solemn promise made to him before his apprehension, to live and die with him. They had passed their word, and given their promise that they would not flinch from him, Matth. 26: 35. "Peter said to him, though I should die with thee, yet will I not deny thee. Likewise also said all the disciples." This made it a perfidious relapse. Here they break promise with Christ who never did so with them. He might have told then when he met them afterwards in Galilee, as the Roman soldier told his general, when he refused his petition after the war was ended, I did not serve ye so at the battle of Actium.

Fifthly, As it was against their solemn promise to Christ, so it was against Christ's heart-melting expostulations with them, which should have abode in their hearts while they lived. For when others that followed him went back, and walked no more with him, Jesus said to these very men, that now forsook him at last, Will ye also go away? There is an emphasis in [ye] q.d. What, ye that from eternity were given to me! Ye whom I have called, loved, and honoured above others, for whose sakes I am ready and resolved to die. "Will ye also forsake me?" John 6: 67. What ever others do, I expect other things from you.

Sixthly, As it was against Christ's heart-melting expostulations with them, so it was against a late direful example presented to them in the fall of Judas. In him, as in a glass, they might see how fearful a thing it is to apostatise from Christ. They had heard Christ's dreadful threats against him. They were present when he called him the son of perdition, John 18: 11. They had heard Christ say of him, "Good had it been if he had never been born." An expression able to scare the deadest heart. They saw he had left Christ the evening before. And that very day, in which they fled, he hanged himself. And yet they fly. For all this they forsake Christ.

Seventhly, As it was against the dreadful warning given them in the fall of Judas, so it was against the law of love, which should have knit them closer to Christ, and to one another.

If to avoid the present shock of persecution, they had fled, yet surely they should have kept together, praying, watching, encouraging, and strengthening one another. This had made it a lesser evil: but as they all forsook Christ, so they forsook one another also; for it is said, John 16: 32 "They shall go every man to his own, and leave Christ alone," (i.e. saith Beza) every man to his own house, and to his own business. They forsook each other, as well as Christ. O what an hour of temptation was this!

Eighthly, and lastly, This their departure from Christ, was accompanied with some offence at Christ. For so he tells them, Matth. 26: 31. "All ye shall be offended because of me this night." The word is, "skandalisthesesthe", you shall be scandalised at me, or in me. Some think the scandal they took at Christ was this, that when they saw he was fallen into his enemies' hands, and could no longer defend himself; they then began to question whether he were the Christ or no, since he could not defend himself from his enemies. Others, more rightly, understand it of their shameful flight from Christ, seeing it was not now safe to abide longer with him. That seeing he gave himself into their hands, they thought it advisable to provide as well as they could for themselves, and somewhere or other, to take refuge from the present storm, which had overtaken him. This was the nature and quality of the fact. We enquire,

Thirdly, Into the grounds and reasons of it. Which were three.

First, God's suspending wonted influences and aids of grace from them. They were not wont to do so. They never did so afterwards. They would not have done so now, had there been influences of power, zeal, and love from heaven upon them. But how then should Christ have borne the heat and burden of the day? How should he tread the wine-press alone? How should his sorrows have been extreme, unmixed, succourless (as it behaved them to be) if they had stuck faithfully to him in his troubles? No, no, it must not be; Christ must not have the least relief or comfort from any creature; and therefore, that he might be left alone, to grapple hand to hand with the wrath of God, and of men; the Lord for a time withholds his encouraging, strengthening influences from them; and then, like Samson when he had lost his locks, they were weak as other men.

"Be strong in the Lord, and in the power of his might," saith the apostle, Eph. 6: 10. If that be with-held, our resolutions and purposes melt away before a temptation, as snow before the sun.

Secondly, As God permitted it, and with-held usual aid from them; so the efficacy of that temptation was great, yea, much greater than ordinary. As they were weaker than they were used to be, so the temptation was stronger than any they had yet met withal. It is called, Luke 22: 53. "Their hour and the power of darkness." A sifting, winnowing hour, ver. 46. O it was a black and cloudy day. Never had the disciples met with such a whirlwind, such a furious storm before. The devil desired but to have the winnowing of them in that day, and so would have sifted and winnowed them, that their faith had utterly failed, had not Christ secured it by his prayer for them. So that it was an extraordinary trial that was upon them.

Thirdly and lastly, That which concurred to their shameful relapse, as a special cause of it, was the remaining corruptions that were in their hearts yet unfortified. Their knowledge was but little, and their faith not much. Upon the account of their weakness in grace, they were called little ones in the text. And as their graces were weak, so their corruptions were strong. Their unbelief, and carnal fears grew powerfully upon them.

Do not censure them, reader, in thy thoughts, nor despise them for this their weakness. Neither say in thy heart, Had I been there as they were, I would never have done as they did. They thought as little of doing what they did, as you, or any of the saints do; and as much did their souls detest and abhor it: but here thou mayest see, whither a soul that fears God may be carried, if his corruptions be irritated by strong temptation, and God withholds usual influences.

Fourthly and lastly, Let us view the issue of this sad apostasy of theirs. And you shall find it ended far better than it began. Though these sheep were scattered for a time, yet the Lord made good his promise, in turning his hand upon these little ones, to gather them. The morning was over cast, but the evening was clear.

Peter repents of his perfidious denial of Christ, and never denied him more. All the rest likewise returned to Christ, and never forsook him any more. He that was afraid at the voice of a damsel, afterwards feared not the frowns of the mighty. And they that durst not own Christ now, afterwards confessed him openly before councils, and rejoiced that they were counted worthy to suffer for his sake, Acts 5: 41. They that were now as timorous as hares, and started at every sound, afterward became as bold as lions, and feared not any danger, but sealed their confession of Christ with their blood. For though, at this time, they forsook him, it was not voluntarily, but by surprisal. Though they forsook him, they still loved him; though they fled from him, there still remained a gracious principle in them; the root of the matter was still in them, which recovered them again.

To conclude: Though they forsook Christ, yet Christ never forsook them: he loved them still; "Go tell the disciples, and tell Peter, that he goes before you into Galilee," Mark 16: 7. q.d. Let them not think that I so remember their unkindness, as to own them no more: No, I love them still.

The use of this is contained in the following inferences.

Inf. 1. Did the disciples forsake Christ, though they had such strong persuasions and resolutions never to do it? Then we see, That self-confidence is a sin too incident to the best of men. They little thought their hearts would have proved so base and deceitful, as they found them to be when they were tried. "Though all men forsake thee (saith Peter) yet will not!" Good man, he resolved honestly, but he knew not what a feather he should be in the wind of temptation, if God once left him to his own fears.

Little reason have the best of saints to depend upon their inherent grace, let their stock be as large as it will. The angels left to themselves, quickly left their own habitations, Jude 6. Upon which, one well observes, That the best of created perfections, are of themselves defectible. Every excellency without the prop of divine preservation, is but a weight which tends to a fall. The angels in their innocence, were but frail, without God's sustentation; even grace itself is but a creature, and therefore purely dependant. It is not from its being and nature, but from the assistance of something without it, that it is kept from annihilation. What becomes of the stream, if the fountain supply it not? What continuance has the reflection in the glass, if the man that looks into it, turn away his face? The constant supplies of the Spirit of Jesus Christ, are the food and fuel of all our graces. The best men will show themselves but men if God leave them. He who has set them up, must also keep them. It is safer to be humble with one talent, than proud with ten; yea, better to be an humble worm, than a proud angel. Adam had more advantage to maintain his station than any of you. For though he were left to the liberty of his own mutable and self-determining will; and though he was created upright, and had no inherent corruption to endanger him, yet he fell.

And shall we be self confident, after such instances of human frailty! Alas, Christian! What match art thou for principalities and powers, and spiritual wickedness! "Be not high-minded, but fear." When you have considered well the example of Noah, Lot, David, and Hezekiah, men famous and renowned in their generations, who all fell by temptations; yea, and that when one would think they had never been better provided to cope with them. Lot fell after, yea, presently after the Lord had thrust him out of Sodom, and his eyes had seen the direful punishment of sin. Hell, as it were, rained upon them out of heaven. Noah, in like manner, immediately after God's wonderful, and astonishing preservation of him in the ark; when he saw a world of men and women, perishing in the floods for their sins. David, after the Lord had settled the kingdom on him, which for sin he rent from Saul, and given him rest in his house. Hezekiah was but just up from a great sickness, wherein the Lord wrought a wonderful salvation for him. Did such men, and at such times, when one would think no temptations should have prevailed, fall; and that so foully? Then "let him that thinks he standeth, take heed lest he fall." O be not high minded, but fear.

Inf. 2. Did Christ stand his ground, and go through with his suffering-work, when all that had followed him, forsook him? Then a resolved adherence to God, and duty, though left alone, without company or encouragement, is Christ-like, and truly excellent. You shall not want better company than that which has forsaken you in the way of God. Elijah complains, 1 Kings 19: 10 "They have forsaken thy covenant, thrown down thine altars, and slain thy prophets with the sword; and I, even I only, am left, and they seek my life, to take it away" And yet all this did not damp or discourage him in following the Lord; for still he was very jealous for the Lord God of Hosts.

Paul complains, 2 Tim 4: 16 "At my first answer no man stood by me, all men forsook me: nevertheless the Lord stood with me." And as the Lord stood by him, so he stood by his God alone, without any aids or support from men. How great an argument of integrity is this! He that professes

Christ for company, will also leave him for company. But to be faithful to God, when forsaken of men; to be a Lot, in Sodomy a Noah, in a corrupted generation; oh, how excellent is it! It is sweet to travel over this earth to heaven, in the company of the saints, that are bound it thither with us, if we can; but if we can meet no company, we must not be discouraged to go on. It is not unlike, but before you have gone many steps farther, you may have cause to say, as one did once, Never less alone, than when alone.

Inference 3. Did the disciples thus forsake Christ, and yet were all recovered at last? Then, though believers are not privileged from backsliding, yet they are secured from final apostasy and ruin. The new creature may be sick, it cannot die. Saints may fall, but they shall rise again, Micah 7: 8. The highest flood, of natural zeal and resolution, may ebb, and be wholly dried up; but saving grace is "a well of water, still springing up into everlasting life," John 4: 14. God's unchangeable election, the frame and constitution of the New Covenant, the meritorious and prevalent intercession of Jesus Christ, do give the believer abundant security against the danger of a total and final apostasy. "My Father, which gave them me, saith Christ, is greater than all: and none is able to pluck them out of my Father's hand," John 10: 29.

And again, "The foundation of God standeth sure, having this seal; the Lord knoweth who are his," 2 Tim. 2: 19. Every person committed to Christ by the Father, shall be brought by him to the Father, and not one wanting.

God has also so framed and ordered the new covenant, that none of those souls, who are within the blessed clasp and bond of it can possibly be lost. It is settled upon immutable things: and we know all things are as their foundations be, Heb. 6: 18, 19. Among the many glorious promises contained in the bundle of promises, this is one, "I will not turn away from them, to do them good; but I will put my fear in their hearts, that they shall not depart from me."

And as the fear of God in our hearts, pleads in us against sin, so our potent intercessor in the heavens pleads for us with the Father; and by reason thereof, we cannot finally miscarry, Rom. 8: 34, 35. Upon these grounds, we may (as the apostle in the place last cited does) triumph in that full security which God has given us; and say, What "shall separate us from the love of God?" Understand it either of God's to us, as Calvin, Beza, and Martyr do; or of our love to God, as Ambrose and Augustine do: it is true in both senses, and a most comfortable truth.

Inference 4. Did the sheep fly, when the shepherd was smitten; such men, and so many forsake Christ in the trial? Then learn how sad a thing it is for the best of men to be left to their own carnal fears in a day of temptation: This was it that made those good men shrink away so shamefully from Christ in that trial: "The fear of man brings a snare," Prov. 29: 25. In that snare these good souls were taken, and for a time held fast.

Oh what work will this unruly passion make, if the fear of God do not over-rule it! Is it not a shame to a Christian, a man of faith to see himself out done by an Heathen? Shall natural conscience and courage make them stand and keep their places in times of danger; when we shamefully turn our backs upon duty, because we see duty and danger together?

When the emperor Vespasian had commanded Fluidius Priscus not to come to the senate; or, if he did, to speak nothing but what he would have him; the senator returned this brave and noble answer, "That as he was a senator, it was fit he should be at the senate; and if, being there, he were required to give his advice, he would speak freely, that which his conscience commanded him." The emperor threatening that then he should die; he returned thus, "Did I ever tell you that I was immortal? Do you what you will, and I will do what I ought. It is in your power to put me to death unjustly, and in me to die constantly." O think, what mischief you; fears may do yourselves, and the discovery of them to others. O learn to trust God with your lives, liberties, and comforts, in the way of your duty; and at that time you are afraid trust in him: and do not magnify poor dust and ashes, as to be scared, by their threat, from your God and your duty. The politic design of Satan herein, is to affright you out of your coverts, where you are safe, into the net. I will enlarge on this no farther; I have elsewhere laid down fourteen rules for the cure of this, in what of mine is public.

Inf. 5. Learn hence, How much a man may differ from himself, according as the Lord is with him, or withdrawn from him. The Christian does not always differ from other men, but sometimes from himself also: yea, so great is the difference betwixt himself and himself, as if he were not the same man. And where is he that does not so experience it? Sometimes bold and courageous, despising dangers, bearing down all discouragements in the strength of zeal, and love to God: at another time faint, feeble, and discourage at every petty thing. Whence is this but from the different administrations of the Spirit, who sometimes gives forth more, and sometimes less, of his gracious influence. These very men that flinched now, when the Spirit was more abundantly shed forth upon them, could boldly own Christ before the council, and despised all dangers for his sake.

A little dog, if his master be by, and encourage him, will venture upon a greater beast than himself. Peter stood at the door without, when the other disciple, (or one of the other disciples, as the Syrian turns it, and Grotius approves it as the best), i.e. one of the private disciples that lived at

Jerusalem, went in so boldly, John 18: 16, 17. We are strong or weak, according to the degrees of assisting grace. So that as you cannot take the just measure of a Christian by one act, so neither must they judge of themselves, by what they sometimes feel in themselves.

But when their spirits are low, and their hearts discouraged, they should rather say to their souls, "Hope in God, for I shall yet praise him:" It is low with me now, but it will be better.

Inf. 6. Was the sword drawn against the Shepherd, and he left alone to receive the mortal strokes of it? How should all adore both the justice and mercy of God so illustriously displayed herein! Here is the triumph of divine justice, and the highest triumph that ever it had, to single forth the chief Shepherd, the man that is God's fellow, and sheathe its sword in his breast for satisfaction. No wonder it is drawn and brandished with such a triumph; awake rejoicingly, O sword, against my Shepherd, &c. For in this blood shed by it, it has more glory than if the blood of all the men and women in the world had been shed.

And no less is the mercy and goodness of God herein signalised, in giving the sword a commission against the Man, his fellow, rather than against us. Why had he not rather said, awake, O sword, against the men that are mine enemies; shed the blood of them that have sinned against me, than smite the Shepherd, and only scatter the sheep. Blessed be God, the dreadful sword was not drawn and brandished against our souls; that God did not set it to our breasts; that he had not made it fat with our flesh, and bathed it in our blood; that his fellow was smitten, that his enemies might be spared. O what manner of love was this! Blessed be God therefore for Jesus Christ, who received the fatal stroke himself; and has now so sheathed that sword in its scabbard, that it shall never be drawn any more against any that believe in him.

Inf. 7. Were the sheep scattered when the Shepherd was smitten? Learn hence, That the best of men know not their own strength till they come to the trial. Little did these holy men imagine such a cowardly spirit had been in them, till temptation put it to the proof. Let this therefore be a caution for ever to the people of God. You resolve never to forsake Christ, you do well; but so did these, and yet were scattered from him. You can never take a just measure of your own strength, till temptation have tried it. It is said, Deut. 8: 2. that God led the people so many years in the wilderness to prove them; and to know them, (i.e. to make them know) what was in their hearts. Little did they think such unbelief, murmurings, discontents, and a spirit bent to backslidings, had been in them; until their straits in the wilderness gave them the sad experience of these things.

Inf. 8. Did the dreadful sword of divine justice smite the Shepherd, God's own fellow; and at the same time the flock, from whom all its outward comforts arose, were scattered from him? Then learn, That the holiest of men have no reason either to repine or despond, though God should at once strip them of all their outward and inward comforts together. He that did this by the man his fellow, may much rather do it by the man his friend. Smite my Shepherd: there is all comfort gone from the inward man; Scatter the sheep; there is all comfort gone from the outward man. What refreshments had Christ in this world, but such as came immediately from his Father, or those holy ones now scattered from him? In one day he loseth both heavenly and earthly comforts. Now, as God dealt by Christ, he may, at one time or other, deal with his people. You have your comforts from heaven; so had Christ, in a fuller measure than ever you had, or can have. He had comforts from his little flock; you have your comforts from the society of the saints, the ordinances of God, comfortable relations, &c. Yet none of these are so firmly settled upon you, but you may be left destitute of them all in one day. God did take all comfort from Christ, both outward and inward; and are we greater than he? God sometimes takes outward, and leaves inward comfort; sometimes he takes inward, and leaves outward comfort: but the time may come, when God may strip you of both.

This was the case of Job, a favourite of God, who was blessed with outward and inward comforts; yet a time came when God stripped him of all, and made him poor to a proverb, as to all outward comfort; and the venom of his arrows drank up his spirit, and the inward comforts thereof.

Should the Lord deal thus wish any of you, how seasonable and relieving will the following considerations be?

First. Though the Lord deal thus with you, yet this is no new thing; he has so dealt with others, yea with Jesus Christ that was his fellow. If these things were done in the green tree, in him that never deserved it for any sin of his own, how little reason have we to complain? Nay,

Secondly. Therefore did this befell Jesus Christ before you, that the like condition might be sanctified to you, when you shall be brought into it. For therefore did Jesus Christ pass through such varieties of conditions, on purpose that he might take away the curse, and leave a blessing in those conditions, against the time that you should come into them. Moreover,

Thirdly, Though inward comforts and outward comforts were both removed from Christ, in one day, yet he wanted not support in the absence of both. How relieving a consideration is this! John 16: 32. "Behold, (saith he) the hour comes, yea, is now come that ye shall be scattered, every man to his own, and shall leave me alone; and yet I am not alone, because the Father is with me."

With me by way of support, when not by way of comfort. Thy God, Christian, can in like manner support thee, when all sensible comforts shrink away together from thy soul and body in one day.

Lastly, It deserves a remark, that this comfortless forsaken condition of Christ, immediately preceded the day of his greatest glory and comfort. Naturalists observe, the greatest darkness is a little before the dawning of the morning. It was so with Christ, it may be so with thee. It was but a little while and he had better company than theirs that forsook him. Act therefore your faith upon this, that the most glorious light usually follows the thickest darkness. The louder your groans are now, the louder your triumphs hereafter will be. The horror of your present, will but add to the lustre of your future state.

Sermon 29: Of the manner of Christ's Death, in respect of the Patience thereof

Isaiah 53:7
He was oppressed, and he was afflicted, yet he opened not his mouth: he is brought as a lamb to the slaughter, and as a sheep before her shearers is dumb, so he openeth not his mouth.

How our Lord Jesus Christ carried on the work of our redemption in his humble state, both in his incarnation, life, and death, has in part been discovered in the former sermons. I have shewed you the kind or nature of that death he died; and am now engaged, by the method proposed, to open the manner of his death. The solitariness or loneliness of Christ in his sufferings, was the subject of the last sermon. The patience and meekness of Christ in his sufferings, come in order, to be opened in this.

This chapter treats wholly of the sufferings of Christ, and the blessed fruits thereof. Hornbeck tells us of a learned Jew, "that ingenuously confessed this very chapter converted him to the Christian faith. And such delight he had in it, that he read it more than a thousand times over." Such is the clearness of this prophecy, that he who penned it, is deservedly stiled the evangelical prophet. I cannot allow time to annualise the chapter; but my work lying in the seventh verse, I shall speak to these two branches or parts of it, viz. The grievous sufferings of Christ, and the glorious ornament he put upon them.

First, Christ's grievous sufferings; "he was afflicted, and he was oppressed, brought to the slaughter, and shorn as a sheep," i.e. he lost both fleece and blood, life, and comforts of life. "He was oppressed;" the word signifies both "to answer and oppress, humble or depress." The other word, rendered afflicted, signifies "to exact and afflict," and so implies Christ to stand before God, as a surety before the creditor; who exacts the utmost satisfaction from him, by causing him to suffer according to the utmost rigour and severity of the law. It did not suffice that he was shorn as a sheep, i.e. that he was stripped and deprived of his riches, ornaments and comforts; but his blood and life must go for it also. He is brought to the slaughter. These were his grievous sufferings.

Secondly, Here is the glorious ornament he put upon those grievous sufferings, even the ornament of a meek and patient spirit. He opened not his mouth: but went as a sheep to be shorn, or a lamb to the slaughter. The lamb goes as quiet to the slaughter-house, as to the fold. By this lively and lovely similitude, the patience of Christ is here expressed to us. Yet Christ's dumbness and silence is not to be understood simply, but universally; as though he spake nothing at all when he suffered; for he uttered many excellent and weighty words upon the cross, as you shall hear in the following discourses; but it must be understood respectively, i.e. he never opened his mouth repiningly, passionately, or revengefully, under his greatest tortures and highest provocations. Whence the note is,

Doct. That Jesus Christ supported the burden of his sufferings, with admirable patience and meekness of spirit.

It is a true observation, that meekness inviteth injury, but always to its own cost. And it was evidently verified in the sufferings of Christ. Christ's meekness triumphed over the affronts and injuries of his enemies, much more than they triumphed over him. Patience never had a more glorious triumph, than it had upon the cross.

The meekness and patience of his spirit, amidst injuries and provocations, is excellently set forth in 1 Pet. 2: 22, "Who did no sin, neither was guile found in his mouth: who when he was reviled, reviled not again; when he suffered he threatened not, but committed himself to him that judgeth righteously."

In this point we have these three things to open doctrinally.
1. The burden of sufferings, and provocations that Jesus Christ was oppressed with.
2. The meekness and admirable patience with which he supported that burden.
3. The causes and grounds of that perfect patience which he then exercised.

First, The burden of sufferings and provocations which Christ supported, was very great; for on him met all sorts and kinds of trouble at once, and those in their highest degrees and fullest strength. Troubles in his soul, and these were the soul of his troubles. His soul was laden with spiritual horrors and troubles, as deep as it could swim, Mark 14: 33. "He began to be sore amazed and very heavy." The wrath of an infinite dreadful God beat him down to the dust. His body full of pain and exquisite tortures in every part. Not a member or sense but was the seat and subject of torment.

His name and honour suffered the vilest indignities, blasphemies, and horrid reproaches that the malignity of Satan and wicked men could belch out against it. He was called a blasphemer, seditious, one that had a devil, a glutton, a wine-bibber, a friend of publicans and harlots, the carpenter's son, this fellow. He that was God's fellow, as you heard lately, now this fellow. Contempt was poured upon all his offices. Upon his kingly office, when they crowned him with thorns, arrayed him with purple, bowed the knee in mockery to him and cried, "Hail king of the Jews." His prophetical, office, when they blinded him, and then bid him "prophesy who smote him." His priestly office, when they reviled him on the cross, saying, "He saved others, himself he cannot save." They scourged him, spit in his face; and smote him on the head and face. Besides, the very kind of death they put him to, was reproachful and ignominious; as you heard before.

Now all this, and much more than this, meeting at once upon an innocent and dignified person; one that was greater than all; that lay in the bosom of God; and from eternity had his smiles and honours; upon one that could have crushed all his enemies as a moth; I say, for him to bear all this, without the least discomposure of spirit, or breach of patience, is the highest triumph of patience that ever was in the world. It was one of the greatest wonders of that wonderful day:

Secondly, And that is the next thing we have to consider, even this almighty patience and unpatterned meekness of Christ, supporting such a burden with such evenness and steadiness of spirit. Christian patience, or the grace of patience, is an ability or power to suffer hard and heavy things, according to the will of God.

It is a power, and a glorious power, that strengthens the suffering soul to bear. It is our passive fortitude, Col. 1: 11. "Strengthened with all might, according to his glorious power, unto all patience, and long suffering, with joyfulness;" i.e. strengthened with the might or power of God himself: Or such as might appear to be the proper impress and image of that divine power, who is both its principle and pattern. For the patience which God exercises towards sinners, that daily wrong and load him, is called power, and great power, Numb. 14: 17. "Let the power of my Lord be great, as thou hast spoken, saying, The Lord is longsuffering, forgiving," &c. Hence it is observed, Prov. 24: 10. That the loss or breaking of our patience under adversity, argues a decay of strength in the soul. "If thou faint in the day of adversity, thy strength is small."

It is a power or ability in the soul, to bear hard, heavy, and difficult things. Such only are the objects of patience. God has several sorts of burdens to impose upon his people. Some heavier, others lighter; some to be carried but a few hours, others many days; others all our days: some more spiritual, bearing upon the soul, some more external, touching or punishing the flesh immediately; and the spirit by way of sympathy: and sometimes both sorts are laid on together. So they were at this time on Christ. His soul burdened as deep as it could swim; full of the sense, the bitter sense and apprehension of the wrath of God: his body filled with tortures: in every member and sense grief took up its lodging. Here was the highest exercise of patience.

It is a power to bear hard and heavy things, according to the will of God. Considering it in that respect, patience, the Christian grace, differs from patience the moral virtue. So the apostle describes it, 1 Pet. 4: 19. "Let them that suffer according to the will of God," &c. i.e. who exercise patience graciously, as God would have them.

And then our patience is, as Christ's most exactly was, according to the will of God; when it is as extensive, as intensive, and as protensive as God requires it to be.

First, When it is as extensive, as God would have it. So was Christ's patience. It was a patience that stretched and extended itself to all, and every trouble and affliction, that came upon him. Troubles came upon him in troops, in multitudes. It is said, Psal. 40: 12. "Innumerable evils have compassed me about." Yet he found patience enough to receive them all. It is not with us. Our patience is often worn out. And like sick people, we fancy, if we were in another chamber, or bed, it would be better. If it were any other trouble than this, we could bear it. Christ had no exceptions at any burden his Father would lay on. His patience was as large as his trouble, and that was large indeed.

Secondly, It is then according to the will of God, when it is as intensive as God requires it to be, i.e. in the apostle's phrase, Jam. 1: 4. When it has its perfect work, or exercise; when it is not only extended to all kinds of troubles; but when it works in the highest and most perfect degree. And then may patience be said to be perfect (as it was in Christ) when it is *plenum sui, et prohibens alieni*, full of itself, and exclusive of its opposite. Christ's patience was full of itself, (i.e.) it included all that belonged to it. It was full of submission, peace, and serenity; full of obedience and complacency in his Father's will. He was in a perfect calm. As a lamb or sheep, (saith the text) that howls not, opposes not, but is dumb and quiet. And as his external behaviour, so his internal frame and temper of soul was most serene and calm. Not one repining thought against God. Not one revengeful thought against man once ruffled his spirit, "Father forgive them, for they know not what they do," was all the hurt he wished his worst enemies. And as it included all that belonged to it, so his perfect patience excluded all its opposites. No discontents, murmurings, despondencies had place in his heart. So that his patience was a most intensive, perfect patience. And as it was as extensive, and as intensive, so it was,

Thirdly, As protensive as God required it to be, (i.e.) it held out to the end of his trial. He did not faint at last. His troubles did not out-live his patience. He indeed was strengthened with all might unto all patience, and long suffering. This was the patience of Christ our perfect pattern. He had not only patience but longanimity.

Thirdly, In the last place, let us inquire into the grounds and reasons of this his most perfect patience. And if you do so, you shall find perfect holiness, wisdom, fore knowledge, faith, heavenly mindedness, and obedience, at the root of this perfect patience.

First, This admirable patience and meekness of Christ, was the fruit and offspring of his perfect holiness. His nature was free from those corruptions, that ours groan and labour under; otherwise he could never have carried it at this rate. Take the meek Moses who excelled all others in that grace, and let him be tried in that very grace, wherein he excels, and see how "unadvisedly he may speak with his lips," Psal. 106: 33. Take a Job, whose famous patience is trumpeted and resounded over all the world; ye have heard of the patience of Job; and let him be tried by outward and inward troubles, meeting upon him in one day; and even a Job may curse the day wherein he was born. Envy, revenge, discontent, despondencies, are weeds naturally springing up in the corrupt soil of our sinful natures, "I saw a little child grow pale with envy," said Austin. And the spirit that is in us, lusteth unto envy, (saith the apostle) Jam. 4: 5. The principles of all these evils being in our natures, they will show themselves in time of trial. The old man is fretful and passionate. But it was otherwise with Christ. His nature was like a pure crystal glass, full of pure fountain water, which though shaken and agitated never so much, cannot show, because it has no dregs. "The prince of this world comes, and has nothing in me," John 14: 30. No principle of corruption, for a handle to temptation. Our high-priest was holy, harmless, undefiled, separate from sinners, Heb. 7: 26.

Secondly, The meekness and patience of Christ proceeded from the infinite wisdom with which he was filled. The wiser any man is, the more patient he is. Hence meekness, the fruit, is denominated from patience, the root that bears it, Jam. 3: 13. "The meekness of wisdom." And anger is lodged in folly, its proper cause, Eccl. 7: 9. "Anger resteth in the bosom of fools." Seneca would allow no place for passion in a wise man's breast. Wise men use to ponder, consider, and weigh things deliberately in their judgements, before they suffer their affections and passions to be stirred and enraged. Hence come the constancy and serenity of their spirits. As wise Solomon has observed, Prov. 17: 27. "A man of understanding is of an excellent (or as the Hebrew is) a cool, spirit."

Now wisdom filled the soul of Christ. He is wisdom in the abstract, Prov. 8. In him are hid all the treasures of wisdom, Col. 2: 3. Hence it was that he was no otherwise moved with the revilings and abuses of his enemies, than a wise physician is with the impertinencies of his distempered, and crazy patient.

Thirdly, And as his patience flowed from his perfect wisdom and knowledge, so also from his foreknowledge. He had a perfect prospect of all those things from eternity, which befell him afterwards. They came not upon him by way of surprisal. And therefore he wondered not at them when they came, as if some strange thing had happened. He foresaw all these things long before, Mark 8: 31. "And he began to teach them, that the Son of man must suffer many things, and be rejected of the elders, and chief priests, and scribes, and be killed." Yea, he had compacted and agreed with his Father to endure all this for our sakes, before he assumed our flesh. Hence, Isa. 1. 6. "I gave my back to the smiters, and my cheeks to them that plucked off the hair. I hid not my face from shame and spitting."

Now look as Christ in John 16: 4. obviates all future offences his disciples might take at suffering for his sake, by telling them beforehand what they must expect. "These things (saith he) I told you, that when the time shall come, ye may remember that I told you of them:" So he, foreknowing what himself must suffer, and having agreed so to do, bare those sufferings with singular patience. "Jesus therefore knowing all things that should come upon him, went forth, and said unto them, whom seek ye?" John 18: 4.

Fourthly, As his patience sprang from his fore-knowledge of his sufferings; so from his faith which he exercised under all that he suffered in this world. His faith looked through all those black and dismal clouds, to the joy proposed, Heb. 12: 2. He knew that though Pilate condemned, God would justify him, Isa. 50: 4, 5, 6, 7, 8. And he set one over-against the other: he balanced the glory, into which he was to enter, with the sufferings, through which he was to enter into it. He acted faith upon God for divine support and assistance under suffering, as well as for glory, the fruit and reward of them, Psal. 16: 7, 8, 9, 10, 11. I have set (or as the apostle varies it) "I foresaw the Lord always before me; because he is at my right hand I shall not be moved. Therefore my heart is glad, and my glory rejoiceth." There is faith acted by Christ, for strength to carry him through. And then it follows, "My flesh also shall rest in hope; for thou wilt not leave my soul in hell, neither wilt thou suffer thine holy one to see corruption. Thou wilt show me the path of life. In thy presence is fulness of joy; at thy right-hand there are pleasures for evermore." There is his faith acting spoil the glory into which he was to enter, after he had suffered these things: this filled him with peace.

Fifthly, As his faith, eyeing the glory into which he was passing, made him endure all things; so the heavenliness of his Spirit also filled him with a heavenly tranquillity and calmness of spirit under all his abuses and injuries. It is a certain truth, that the more heavenly any man's spirit is, the more sedate, composed and peaceful. "As the higher heavens (saith Seneca) are more ordinate and tranquil; there are neither clouds nor winds, storms nor tempests; they are the inferior heavens that lighten and thunder: the nearer the earth the more tempestuous and unquiet: even so the sublime and heavenly mind is placed in a calm and quiet station."

Certainly that heart which is sweetened frequently with heavenly, delightful communion with God, is not very apt to be embittered with wrath, or soured with revenge against men. The peace of God does "brabeuein", appease and end all strifes and differences, as an umpire: so much that word, Col. 3: 15. imports. The heavenly Spirit marvellously affects a sedate and quiet breast.

Now, never was there such a heavenly soul on earth, since man inhabited it, as Christ was: he had most sweet and wonderful communion with God: he had meat to eat, which others, yea, and those his greatest intimates, knew not of. The Son of man was in heaven upon earth, John 3: 13. Even in respect of that blessed heavenly communion he had with God, as well as in respect of his immense Deity: and that his heart was in heaven when he so patiently endured and digested the pain and shame of the cross is evident from Heb. 12: 2. "For the joy set before him, he endured the cross, despising the shame." See where his eye and heart were, when he went as a lamb to the slaughter.

Sixthly, And lastly, As his meekness and patience sprang from the heavenliness and sublimity of his spirit; so likewise, from the complete and absolute obedience of it to his Father's will and pleasure: he could most quietly submit to all the will of God, and never regret at any part at the work assigned him by his Father. For thou must know, that Christ's death in him was an act of obedience; he all along eyeing his Father's command and counsel in what he suffered, Phil. 2: 7, 8. John 18: 11. Ps. 40: 6, 7, 8. Now look, as the eyeing and considering the hand of God in an affliction, presently becalms and quiets a gracious soul; as you see in David, 2 Sam. 16: 11. "Let him alone, it may be God that has bid him curse David;" So much more it quieted Jesus Christ, who was privy to the design and end of his Father, with whose will he all along complied; looking on Jews and Gentiles but as the instruments ignorantly fulfilling God's pleasure, and serving that great design of his Father; this was big patience, and these the grounds of it.

Use 1. I might variously improve this point; but the direct and main use of it is, to press us to a Christ-like patience in all our sufferings and troubles. And seeing in nothing we are more generally defective, and that defects of Christians herein, are so prejudicial to religion, and uncomfortable to themselves; I resolve to wave all other uses, and spend the remaining time wholly upon this branch; even a persuasive to Christians unto all patience, in tribulations; to imitate their lamb-like Saviour. Unto this (Christians) you are expressly called, 1 Pet. 2: 21, 22. "Because Christ also suffered for us, leaving us an example, that we should follow his steps. Who did no sin, neither was guile found in his mouth; who when he was reviled, reviled not again; when he suffered, he threatened not; but committed himself to him that judgeth righteously." Here is your pattern; a perfect pattern! a lovely and excellent pattern! Will you be persuaded to the imputation of Christ herein? Methinks I should persuade you to it: yea, every thing about you persuades to patience in your sufferings, as well as I: look which way you will, upward or downward, inward or outward, backward or forward, to the right-hand, or to the left, you shall find all things persuading and urging the doctrine of patience upon you.

First, Look upwards, when tribulations come upon you: look to that sovereign Lord, that commissionates and sends them upon you. You know troubles do not rise out of the dust, nor spring out of the ground, but are framed in heaven, Jer. 18: 11. "Behold I frame evil, and devise a device against you." Troubles and afflictions are of the Lord's framing and devising, to reduce his wandering people to himself: much like that device of Absalom, in setting Joab's field of corn on fire, to bring Joab to him, 2 Sam. 14: 30. In the frame of your afflictions, you may observe much of divine wisdom in the choice, measure, and season of your troubles: sovereignty, in electing the instruments of your affliction; in making them as afflictive as he pleaseth; and in making them obedient both to his call, in coming and going, when he pleaseth. Now, could you in times of trouble look up to this sovereign hand, in which your souls, bodies, and all their comforts and mercies are; how quiet would your hearts be! Psal. 39: 9. "I was dumb, and opened not my mouth, because it is thy doing." 1 Sam. 3: 18. "It is the Lord, let him do what seemeth him good." Oh, when we have to do with men, and look no higher, how do our spirits swell and rise with revenge and impatience! But if you once come to see, that man as a rod in your Father's hand, you will be quiet; Psal. 46: 10. "Be still, and know that I am God;" q.d. consider with whom you have to do; not with your fellow, but with your God, who can puff you to destruction with one blast of his mouth; in whose hand you are, as the clay in the potter's hand. It is for want of looking up to God in our troubles, that we fret, murmur, and despond at the rate we do.

Secondly, Look downward, and see what is below you, as well as up to that which is above you. You are afflicted, and you cannot bear it. Oh! no trouble like your trouble! never man in such a case as you are! Well, well, cast the eye of your mind downward, and see those who lie much lower than you. Can you see none on earth in a more miserable state than yourselves? Are you at the very bottom, and not a man below you? sure there are thousands in a sadder case than you on earth. What is your affliction? Have you lost a relation? others have lost all. Have you lost an estate, and are become poor? Well, but there are some you read of, Job 30: 4, 5, 6, 7. "Who cut up mallows by the bushes, and juniper-roots for their meat. They are driven forth from among men, they cried after them as after a thief. They dwell in the cliffs of the valleys, in caves of the earth, and in the rocks. Among the bushes they braved, under the nettles they were gathered together." What difference, as to manner of life, do you find between the persons here described, and the wild beasts, that herd together in a desolate p]ace? Are you persecuted and afflicted for Christ's sake? What think you of their sufferings, Heb. 11: 36, 37. "Who had trial of cruel dockings; yea, moreover of bands and imprisonments: they were stoned, they were sawn asunder, were tempted, were slain with the sword, they wandered about in sheep skins and goat skins, being destitute, afflicted, tormented." And are you better than they? I know not what you are; but I am sure, these were such "of whom the world was not worthy," ver. 38.

Or are your afflictions more spiritual and inward? Say not the Lord never dealt more bitterly with the soul of any, than he has with yours. What think you of the case of David, Heman, Job, Asaph, whose doleful cries, by reason of the terrors of the Almighty, are able to melt the stoniest heart that reads their stories? the Almighty was a terror to them: the arrows at God were within them; they roared by reason of the disquietness of their hearts.

Or are your afflictions outward and inward together; an afflicted soul in an afflicted body? Are you fallen, like the ship in which Paul sailed, into a place where two seas meet! Well, so it was with Paul, Job, and many other of those worthies gone before you. Sure you may see many on earth who have been, and are in far lower and sadder states than yourselves.

Or if not on earth, doubtless, you will yield there are many in hell, who would be glad to change conditions with you, as bad as you think yours to be. And were not all these mounded out of the same lump with you? Surely, if you can see any creature below you, especially any reasonable being, you have no reason to return so ungratefully upon your God, and accuse your Maker of severity; or charge God foolishly. Look down, and you shall see grounds enough to be quiet.

Thirdly, Look inward, you discontented spirits, and see if you can find nothing there to quiet you. Cast year eye into your own hearts; consider either the corruptions or the graces that are there. Cannot you find weeds enough there, that need such winter breather as this to rot them? Has not that proud heart need enough of all this to humble it? That carnal heart need of such things as these to mortify it? That backsliding, wandering heart need of all this to reduce and recover it to its God? "If need be, ye are in heaviness," 1 Pet. 1: 6. O Christian! Didst thou not see need of this before thou camest into trouble? Or has not God shown thee the need of it since thou wast under the rod? It is much thou shouldest not see it; but be assured, if thou dost not, thy God does: he knows thou wouldest be ruined for ever, if he should not take this course with thee.

Thy corruptions require all this to kill them. Thy lusts will take all this, it may be more than this, and all little enough. And as your corruptions call for it, so do year graces too. Wherefore think ye the Lord planted the principles of faith, humility, patience, &c. in your souls? What, were they put there for nothing? Did the Lord intend they should lie sleeping in their drowsy habits? Or were they not planted there in order to exercise? And how shall they be exercised without tribulations? Can you tell? Does not "tribulation work patience, and patience experience, and experience hope?" Rom. 5: 3, 4. Is not "the trial of your faith much more precious, than of gold which perishes," 1 Pet. 1: 7. O look inward, and you will be quiet.

Fourthly, Look outward, and see who stands by and observes your carriage under trouble. Are there not many eyes upon you: yea, many envious observers round about you. It was David's request, Psal. 5: 8. "Lead me, O Lord, in thy righteousness, because of mine enemies;" or, as the Hebrew word there might be rendered, because of mine observers or watchers. There is many an envious eye upon you. To the wicked there can scarcely be an higher gratification and pleasure, than to see your carriage under trouble so like their own; for thereby they are confirmed in their prejudices against religion, and in their good opinion of themselves. These may talk and profess more than we; but when they are tried, and put to it, it appears plainly enough, their religion enables them to do no more than we do; they talk of heaven's glory, and their future expectancies; but it is but talk, for it is apparent enough their hopes cannot balance a small afflictions with all the happiness they talk of. Oh, how do you dishonour Christ before his enemies, when you make them think all your religion lies in talking of it! Consider who looks on.

Fifthly, Look backward, and see if there be nothing behind you that may hush and quiet your impatient spirits; consult the multitude of experiences past and gone; both your own and others. Is this the first strait that ever you were in? If so, you have reason to be quiet, yet to bless God that has spared you so long, when others have had their days filled up with sorrow. But if you have been in troubles formerly, and the Lord has helped you; if you have past through the fire, and not been burnt; through the waters, and not drowned; if God has stood by you, and hitherto helped you. O what cause have you to be quiet now, and patiently wait for the salvation of God! Did he help you then, and cannot he do so now? Did he give waters, and cannot he give bread also? Is he the God of the hills only, and not the God of the valleys also? O call to mind the days of old, the years of the right hand of the Most High. "These things I call to mind, therefore I have hope," Lam. 3: 21. Have you kept no records of past experiences? How ungrateful then have you been to your God, and how injurious to yourselves, if you have not read them over in such a day as this? for to that end were they given you.

O when you shall consider what a God he has been to you, at a pinch; how faithfully Jehovah-jireh has stood by you; that this is not the first time your hearts and hopes have been low; as well as your condition, and yet God has raised you again; surely you will find your present troubles made light, by a glance back upon your past experiences.

Sixthly, Look forward, to the end of your troubles; yea, look to a double end of them, the end of their duration, and the end of their operation. Look ye to the end of their duration, and that is just by you: they shall not be everlasting troubles, if you be such as fear the Lord. "The God of all grace, who hath called us unto his eternal glory by Jesus Christ, after that ye have [suffered a while] make you perfect," 1 Pet. 5: 10. "These light afflictions are but for a moment," 2 Cor. 4: 18. They are no more comparatively, with that vast eternity that is before you. Alas! what are a few days and nights of sorrows, when they are past? Are they not swallowed up as a spoonful of water in the vast ocean? But more especially look to the end of their operation. What do all these afflictions tend to and effect? Do they not work out an exceeding weight of glory? Are you not by them made partakers of his holiness?" Heb. 12: Is not this all the fruit to take away your sins? What, and be impatient at this; fret and repine, because God is, this way, perfecting your happiness? O ungrateful soul! Is this a due requital of that love that disdains not to stoop to so low an employment, as to scour and cleanse your souls, that they might be shining vessels of honour to all eternity?

O look forward to the end of your troubles: the end of their duration and operation.

Seventhly, Look to the right-hand, and see how you are shamed, convinced and silenced by other Christians; and it may be such too, as never made that profession you have done; and yet can not only patiently bear the afflicting hand of God, but are blessing, praising, and admiring God under their troubles; whilst you are sinning against, and dishonouring him under smaller ones. It may be you will find some poor Christians that know not where to have their next bread, and yet are speaking of the bounty of their God; while you are repining in the midst of plenty. Ah! if there be any ingenuity in you, let this shame you. If this will not, then,

Eighthly, Look to your left-hand, and there you will see a sad sight, and what one would think should quiet you. There you may see a company of wicked, graceless wretches, carrying themselves under their troubles, but too much like yourselves. What do they more, than fret and murmur, despond and sink, mix sin with their afflictions, when the rod of God is upon them?

It is time for thee to leave off, when thou sees how near thou art come to them, whom thou hopest thou shalt never be ranked and numbered with. Reader, such considerations as these, I am persuaded, would be of singular use to thy soul at such a time, but above all, thine eyeing the great pattern of patience, Jesus Christ; whose Lamb- like damage, under a trial, with which thine is not to be named the same day, is here recommended to thee. O how should this transform thee into a lamb, for meekness also!

Sermon 30: Of the Instructiveness of the Death of Christ, in his seven last Words; the first of which is here illustrated

Luke 23:34
Then said Jesus, Father, forgive them; for they know not what they do.

    The manner in which Christ died has already been opened in the solitude and patience in which he died. The third, to wit, the instructiveness of his death, now follows, in these seven excellent and weighty sayings, which dropped from his blessed lips upon the tree, whilst his sacred blood dropped on the earth from his wounded hands and feet; so that on the cross he exercised both his priestly and prophetical office together, redeeming us by his blood, and instructing us by his words.

    These seven words of Christ upon the cross are his last words, with which he breathed out his soul. The last words of a dying man are remarkable; the scripture puts a remark upon them, 2 Sam. 23: 1. "Now these be the last words of David." How remarkable are the last words of Christ.

    These words are seven in number; three directed to his Father, and four more to those about him. Of the former sort this is one, Father, forgive them, &c. In which we have, First, The mercy desired by Christ, and that is forgiveness. Secondly, The persons for whom it is desired, [Them,] that is, those cruel and wicked persons that were now imbruing their hands in his blood. And, Thirdly, The motive or argument urged to procure that mercy from his Father, for they know not what they do.

    First, The mercy prayed for, that is, forgiveness; Father, forgive. Forgiveness is not only a mercy, a spiritual mercy, but one of the greatest mercies a soul can obtain from God, without which, whatever else we have from God, is no mercy to us. So great a mercy is forgiveness, that David calls him blessed, or rather admires the blessedness of him, "whose transgression is forgiven, whose sin is covered." This mercy, this best of mercies, he requests for them, Father, forgive them.

    Secondly, The persons for whom he requests forgiveness, are the same that with wicked hands crucified him. Their fact was the most horrid that ever was committed by men: they not only shed innocent blood, but the blood of God; the best of mercies is by him desired for the worst of sinners.

    Thirdly The motive or argument urged to procure this mercy for them, is this for they know not what they do. As if he should say, Lord, what these poor creatures do, is not so much out of malice to me as the Son of God; but it is from their ignorance. Did they know who, and what I am, they would rather be nailed to the cross themselves, than do it. To the same purpose the apostle saith, 1 Cor. 2: 8. "Whom none of the princes of this world knew; for had they known it, they would not have crucified the Lord of glory." Yet this is not to be extended to all that had an hand in the death of Christ, but to the ignorant multitude, among whom, some of God's elect were, who afterwards believed in him, whose blood they spilt, Acts 3: 17. "And now, brethren, I wet that through ignorance ye did it." For them this prayer of Christ was heard. Hence the notes are,

    Doct. 1. That ignorance is the usual cause of enmity to Christ.

    Doct. 2. That there is forgiveness with God for such as oppose Christ through ignorance.

    Doct. 3. That to forgive enemies, and beg forgiveness for them is the true character and property of the Christian spirit.

    These observations contain so much practical truth, that it would be worth our time to open and apply them distinctly,

    Doct. 1. That ignorance is the usual cause of enmity to Christ.

    "These things (saith the Lord) will they do, because they have "not known the Father, nor me," John 16: 3. What thing does he mean? Why, kill and destroy the people of God, and therein suppose they do God good service, (i.e.) think to oblige and gratify the Father, by their butchering his children. So Jer 9: 3. "They proceed from evil to evil; and have not known me, " saith the Lord," q.d. Had they the knowledge of God, this would check and stop them in their ways of wickedness? and so Psal. 74: 20. "The dark places of the earth are full of the habitations of cruelty."

Three things must be inquired into, viz. what their ignorance of Christ was. Whence it was. And how it disposed them to such enmity against him.

First. What was their ignorance who crucified Christ? Ignorance is two-fold, simple, or respective. Simple ignorance is not supposable in these persons, for in many things they were a knowing people. But it was respective, particular ignorance, Rom. 9: 25. "Blindness in part is happened to Israel." They knew many other truths, but did not know Jesus Christ; in that their eyes were held. Natural light they had; yea, and scripture light they had; but in this particular, that this was the Son of God, the Saviour of the world, therein they were blind and ignorant.

But how could that be! Had they not heard at least of his miraculous works? Did they not see how his birth, life and death, squared with the prophecies, both in time, place, and manner? Whence should this their ignorance be when they saw, or at least might have seen, the scriptures fulfilled in him; and that he came among them in a time when they were big with expectations of the Messiah?

It is true, indeed, they knew the scriptures; and it cannot but be supposed the fame of his mighty works had reached their ears: But yet,

First, Though they had the scriptures among them, they misunderstood them; and did not rightly measure Christ by that right rule. You find, John 7: 52. how they reason with Nicodemus against Christ; "Art thou also of Galilee? Search, and see: for out of Galilee ariseth no prophet." Here is a double mistake: First, They supposed Christ to arise out of Galilee, whereas he was of Bethlehem, though much conversant in the parts of Galilee: And, Secondly, They thought, because they could find no prophet had arisen out of Galilee, therefore none should.

Another mistake that blinded them about Christ, was from their conceit that Christ should not die, but live for ever, John 12: 34. "We have heard out of the law, that Christ abideth for ever: and how sayest thou, the Son of man must be lifted up? who is the Son of man?" That scripture which probably they urge against the mortality of Christ, is Isa. 9: 7. "Of the increase of his government and peace, there shall be no end, upon the throne of David," &c. In like manner, John 7: 27. we find them in another mistake; "We know this man whence he is; but when Christ comes, no man knoweth whence he is." This, likely, proceeded from their misunderstanding of Micas 5: 2. "His going forth have been from of old, from everlasting." Thus were they blinded about the person of Christ, by misinterpretations of scripture-prophecies

Secondly, Another thing occasioning their mistake of Christ, was the outward meanness and despicableness of his condition. They expected a pompous Messiah, one that should come with state and glory, becoming the king of Israel. But when they saw him in the form of a servant, coming in poverty, not to be ministered unto, but to minister, they utterly rejected him: "We hid as it were our faces from him; he was despised and we esteemed him not," Isa. 53: 3. Nor is it any great wonder these should be scandalised at his poverty when the disciples themselves had such carnal apprehensions of his kingdom, Mark 10: 37, 38.

Thirdly, Add to this, their implicit faith in the learned rabbis and doctors, who utterly misled them in this matter, and greatly prejudiced them against Christ. "Lo, (said they) he speaketh boldly, and they say nothing to him. Do the rulers know indeed that this is the very Christ?" They pinned their faith upon the rulers sleeves, and suffered them to carry it whether they would. This was their ignorance, and these its causes.

Thirdly, Let us see, in the next place, how this disposed them to such enmity against Christ. And this it does three ways.

First, Ignorance disposes men to enmity and opposition to Christ, by removing those hindrances that would otherwise keep them from it, as checks and rebukes of conscience, by which they are restrained from evil; but conscience binding and reproving in the authority and virtue of the law of God, where that law is not known, there can be no reproofs; and therefore we truly say, That ignorance is virtually every sin.

Secondly, Ignorance enslaves and subjects the soul to the lusts of Satan; he is "the ruler of the darkness of this world," Eph. 6: 12. There is no work so base and vile, but an ignorant man will undertake it.

Thirdly, Nay, which is more, if a man be ignorant of Christ, his truths, or people, he will not only oppose, and persecute, but he will also do it conscientiously, i. e. he will look upon it as his duty so to do, John 16: 3. Before the Lord opened Paul's eyes, "he verily thought that he ought to do many things contrary to the name of Christ." Thus you have a brief account what, and whence their ignorance was, and how it disposed and prepared them for this dreadful work. Hence we learn,

Inference 1. How falsely is the gospel charged as the cause of discord and trouble in the world. It is not light, but darkness, that makes men fierce and cruel: as light increases, so does peace, Isa. 11: 6, 9. "The wolf also shall dwell with the lamb, and the leopard lie down with the kid;

The Fountain of Life Opened Up

and the calf and the young lion, and the fatling together; and a little child shall lead them; they shall not hurt nor destroy in all my holy mountain; for the earth shall be full of the knowledge of the Lord, as the waters cover the sea." What a sad condition would the world be in without gospel light! all places would be dens of rapine, and mountains of prey. Certainly we owe much of our civil liberty, and outward tranquillity to gospel-light. If a sword, or variance, at any time, follow the gospel, it is but an accidental, not a direct and proper effect of it.

Inf. 2. How dreadful is it to oppose Christ and his truth knowingly, and with open eyes? Christ pleads their ignorance as an argument to procure their pardon. Paul himself was once filled with rage and madness against Christ and his truths: it was well for him that he did it ignorantly: had he gone against his light and knowledge, there had been little hope of him, 1 Tim. 1: 13. "I was a blasphemer, a persecutor, and injurious; but I obtained mercy, because I did it ignorantly, and in unbelief." I do not say, it is simply impossible for one that knowingly and maliciously opposes and persecutes Christ and his people, to be forgiven, but it is not usual, Heb. 6: 4, 5. There are few instances of it.

Inf. 3. What an awful majesty sits upon the brow of holiness, that few dare to oppose it that see it! There are few or none so daringly wicked, to fight against it with open eyes; 1 Pet. 3: 13. "Who will harm you whilst ye are followers of that which is good:" q. d. who dare be so hardy to set upon known godliness, or afflict and wrong the known friends of it? The true reason why many Christians speed so bad, is not because they are godly, but be cause they do not manifest the power of godliness more than they do: their lives are so like the lives of others, that they are often mistaken for others. Cyprian brings in the wicked of his time, thus scoffing at professors, "behold, they that boast themselves to be redeemed from the tyranny of Satan, and to be dead to the world, how are they overcome by the lusts of it, as well as other men:" Look as the poverty and meanness of Christ's outward condition was a ground of their mistake of him then, so the poverty and meanness of our love to God, heavenly mindedness, and mortification to this world, is a disguise to professors, and cause why they are not more owned and honoured in the consciences of men at this day. For holiness, manifested in its power, is so awfully glorious, that the consciences of the vilest cannot but honour it, and do obeisance to it, Mark 6: 20. "Herod feared John, for he was a just man."

Inf. 4. The enemies of Christ are objects of pity. Alas, they're blind, and know not what they do. It is pity that any other affection than pity, should stir in our hearts towards them. Were their eyes but open, they would never do as they do: we should look upon them as the physician does upon his sick distempered patient. Did they but see with the same light you do, they would be as far from hating Christ, or his ways, as you are, Simul ac desinunt ignorere, desinunt odisse; as soon as they cease to be ignorant, they cerise to hate, saith Tertullian.

Inf. 5. How needful is it before we engage ourselves against any person or way, to be well satisfied and resolved that it is a wicked person or practice that we oppose? You see the world generally runs upon a mistake in this matter. O beware of doing you know not what! for though you do you know not what, Satan knows what he is doing by you: he blinds your eyes, and then sets you to work, knowing that if you should but see what you are doing, you would rather die than do it: you may now do you know not what but you may afterwards have time enough to reflect on, and lament what you have done: you may now do you know not what, and hereafter you may not know what to do. O beware what you now do!

Doct. 2. That there is forgiveness with God, for such as oppose Christ out of ignorance.

If all manner of sin and blasphemy shall be forgiven to men, then this, as well as others, Mat. 12: 31. We are not, with Theophilact, to understand that place of the certainty of pardon; much less, with Origin, of the desert of it; nor yet, with Jansenius, of the facility at it, but rather of the possibility of forgiveness: it shall be so to some; it may be so to you; even those whose wicked hands had crucified Christ, may receive remission by that blood they shed, Acts 2: 23, 38. compared.

I have two things here to do: First, To open the nature of the forgiveness, and show you what it is. Secondly, To evince the possibility of it, for such as, mistakingly, oppose Christ.

For the First, Forgiveness is God's gracious discharge of a believing penitent sinner, from the guilt of all his sin, for Christ's sake.

It is Gods discharge: there is indeed fraternal forgiveness, by which one man forgives another; so far as he is interested in the wrong, Luke 6: 87. There is also a ministerial forgiveness, whereby the minister of Christ, as his mouth, and in his name, declares the pardon, or ministerially applies the promises of pardon to penitent offenders, John 20: 23. But none can absolutely and properly forgive sin, but God only, Mark 2: 7. The primary, and principal wrong is done to him; Psal. 51: 4. " Against thee, and thee only" (i.e.) thee mainly or especially, " have I sinned." Hence sins are metonimically called debts, debts to God, Mat. 6: 12. Not that we owe them to God, or ought to sin against him; but as pecuniary debts obliges him that owes it to the penalty, if he satisfy not for it; so do our sins. And who can discharge the debtor, but the creditor?

It is gracious act to discharge. "I, even I, am he that blotteth out thy transgression for mine own name sake," Isa. 43: 25. And yet sin is not so forgiven, as that God expects no satisfaction at all; but as expecting none from us, because God has provided a surety for us, from whom he is satisfied, Eph. 1: 7. "In whom we have redemption through his blood, the forgiveness of sins, according to the riches of his grace."

it is a gracious discharge from the guilt of sin. Guilt is that which pardon properly deals with. Guilt is an obligation to punishment. Pardon is the dissolving that obligation. Guilt is a chain with which sinners are bound and fettered by the law. Pardon is that Aquafortis that eats it asunder, and makes the prisoner a free man. The pardoned soul is a discharged soul, Rom. 8: 53. "Who shall lay any thing to the charge of God's elect? It is "God that justifieth, who shall condemn? It is Christ that died."

It is God's discharge of a believing penitent sinner. Infidelity and impenitence, are not only sins in themselves, but such sins as bind fast all other sins upon the soul. "By him, all that believe are justified from all things," Acts 10: 43. So Acts 3: 19. "Repent therefore, that your sins may be blotted out." This is the method in which God dispenseth pardon to sinners.

Lastly, It is for Christ's sake we are discharged; he is the meritorious cause of our remission, "As God, for Christ's sake, has forgiven you," Eph. 4: 32. It is his blood alone that meritoriously procures our discharge.

This is a brief and true account of the nature of forgiveness.

Secondly, Now to evince the possibility of forgiveness, for such as ignorantly oppose Christ, let these things be weighed:

First, Why should any poor soul, that is now humbled for its enmity to Christ in the days of ignorance, question the possibility of forgiveness, when this effect does not exceed the power of the cause; nay, when there is more efficacy in the blood of Christ, the meritorious cause, than is in this effect of it? There is power enough in that blood, not only to pardon thy sins, but the sins of the whole world, were it actually applied, 1 John 2: 2. There is not only a sufficiency, but also a redundancy of merit, in that precious blood. Surely then thy enmity to Christ, especially, before thou knewest him, may not look like an unpardonable iniquity in thine eyes.

Secondly, And as this sin exceeds not the power of the meritorious cause of forgiveness; so neither is it any where excluded from pardon, by any word of God. Nay, such is the extensiveness of the promise to believing penitents, that this case is manifestly included, and forgiveness tendered to thee in the promises, Isa. 55: 7. "Let the wicked forsake his way, and the unrighteous man his thoughts; and let him return unto the Lord, and he will have mercy on him, and to our God, for he will abundantly pardon." Many such extensive promises there are in the scriptures: and there is not one parenthesis in all these blessed pages, in which this case is excepted.

Thirdly, And it is yet more satisfactory; that God has already actually forgiven such sinners; and that which he has done, he may again do: yea, therefore he has done it to some, and those eminent for their enmity to Christ, that others may be encouraged to hope for the same mercy, when they also shall be, in the same manner, humbled for it. Take one famous instance of many; it is that of Paul in 1 Tim. 1: 13, 16. "Who was before a blasphemer, a persecutor, and injurious. But I obtained mercy, because I did it ignorantly in unbelief. - Howbeit for this cause I obtained mercy, that in me first Jesus Christ might show forth all long-suffering, for a pattern to them which should hereafter believe on him to everlasting life." It is no small encouragement to a sick man, to hear of some that have been recovered out of the same disease, and that prevailing in an higher degree than in himself.

Fourthly, Moreover, it is encouraging to consider, That when God had cut off others in the way of their sin, he has hitherto spared thee. What speaks this but a purpose of mercy to thy soul? Thou shouldest account the long-suffering of God thy salvation, 2 Pet. 3: 15. Had he smitten thee in the way of thy sin and enmity to Christ, what hope had remained! But in that he has not only spared thee, but also given thee a heart ingenuously ashamed, and humbled for thy evils: does not this speak mercy for thee; surely it looks like a gracious design of love to thy soul.

Inference 1. And is there forgiveness with God for such as have been enemies to Christ, his truths, and gospel? Then certainly there is pardon and mercy for the friends of God, who involuntarily fall into sin, by the surprisals of temptation, and are broken for it, as ingenuous children for offending a good Father. Can any doubt, if God have pardon for such enemies, he has none for children? If he have forgiveness for such as shed the blood of Christ with wicked hands, has he not much more mercy and forgiveness for such as love Christ, and are more afflicted for their sin against him, than all other troubles they have in the word? Doubt it not, but he who receives enemies into his bosom, will much more receive and embrace children, though offending ones.

How pensive do the dear children of God sometimes sit, after their lapse into sin? Will God ever pardon this? will he be reconciled again? May I hope his face shall be to me, as in former times? Pensive soul! if thou didst but know the largeness, tenderness, freeness of that grace, which yearns over enemies, and has given forth thousands, and ten thousands of pardons to the worst of sinners, thou wouldst not sink at that rate.

Inf. 2. Is there pardon with God for enemies? How inexcusable then are all they that persist and perish in their enmity to Christ! sure their destruction is of themselves. Mercy is offered to them, if they will receive it, Isa. 55: 7. Proclamation is made in the gospel, that if there be any among the enemies of Christ, who repent of that they have been, and done against him, and are now unfeignedly willing to be reconciled, upon the word of a King, they shall find mercy: But "God shall wound the head of the enemies, and the hairy scalp of such a one as goes on still in his trespasses," Psal. 68: 21. "If he turn not, he will whet his sword; he has bent his bow, and made it ready; he has also prepared for him the instruments of death: He ordaineth his arrows against the persecutors," Psal. 7: 12.

This lays the blood of every man that perishes in his enmity to Christ, at his own door; and vindicates the righteousness of God, in the severest strokes of wrath upon them: This also will be a cutting thought to their hearts eternally: I might once have had pardon, and I refused it: the gospel trumpet sounded a parley: fair and gracious terms were offered, but I rejected them.

Is there mercy with God and forgiveness, even for his worst enemies, upon their submission; How unlike to God then are all implacable spirits! Some there are that cannot bring their hearts to forgive an enemy; "to whom revenge is sweeter than life." 1 Sam. 24: 16. "If a man find his enemy, will he let him go?" This is hell fire, a fire that never goes out. How little do such poor creatures consider, if God should deal by them, as they do by others, what words could express the misery of their condition! It is a sad sin, and a sad sign, a character of a wretched state, wherever it appears. Those that have found mercy, should be ready to show mercy: and they that expect mercy themselves, should not deny it to others. This brings us upon the third and last observation, viz.

Doct. 3 That to forgive enemies, and beg forgiveness for them, is the true character and property of the Christian spirit.

Thus did Christ: "Father forgive them." And thus did Stephen, in imitation of Christ, Acts 7: 59, 60. "And they stoned Stephen, calling upon God, and saying, Lord Jesus receive my spirit. And he kneeled down, and cried with a loud voice, Lord, lay not this sin to their charge." This suits with the rule of Christ, Mat. 5: 44, 45. "But I say unto you, love your enemies; bless them that curse you, do good to them that hate you, and pray for them which despitefully use you and persecute you; that ye may be the children of God your Father which is in heaven."

Here I shall first open the nature of this duty, and show you what a forgiving spirit is; and then the excellency of it, how well it becomes all that call themselves Christians.

First, Let us enquire what this Christian forgiveness is. And that the nature of it may the better appear, I shall show you both what it is not, and what it is.

First, It consists not in a Stoical insensibility of wrongs and injuries. God has not made men as insensible, stupid blocks, that have no sense or feeling of what is done to them. Nor has he made a law inconsistent with their very natures that are to be governed by it: but allows us a tender sense of natural evils, though he will not allow us to revenge them by moral evils: nay, the more deep and tender our resentments of wrongs and injuries are, the more excellent is our forgiveness of them; so that a forgiving spirit does not exclude sense of injuries, but the sense of injuries graces the forgiveness of them.

Secondly, Christian forgiveness is not a politic concealment of our wrath and revenge, because it will be a reproach to discover it; or, because we want opportunity to vent it. This is carnal policy, not Christian meekness. So far from being the mark of a gracious spirit, that it is apparently the sign of a vile nature. It is not Christianity to repose, but depose injuries.

Thirdly, Nor is it that moral virtue for which we are beholden to an easier and better nature, and the help of moral rules and documents. There are certain virtues attainable without the change of nature, which they call homilitical virtues, because they greatly adorn and beautify nature; such as temperance, patience, justice, &c. These are of singular use to conserve peace and order in the world: and without them, (as one aptly speaks) the world would soon break up, and its civil societies disband. But yet, though these are the ornaments of nature, they do not argue the change of nature. All graces, in the exercises of them, involve a respect to God: And for the being of them, they are not by natural acquisition, but supernatural infusion.

Fourthly, and lastly, Christian forgiveness is not an injurious giving up of our rights and properties to the lust of everyone that has a mind to invade them. No; these we may lawfully defend and preserve, and are bound so to do; though, if we cannot defend them legally, we must not avenge our wrongs unchristianly: This is not Christian forgiveness. But, then positively,

It is a Christian lenity, or gentleness of mind, not retaining, but freely passing by the injuries done to us, in obedience to the command of God.

It is a levity, or gentleness of mind. The grace of God demulces the angry stomach; calms the tumultuous passions; new-moulds our sour spirits, and makes them benign, gentle and easy to be entreated; Gal. 5: 22. "The fruit of the Spirit is love, joy, peace, long suffering, gentleness," &c.

This gracious levity inclines the Christian to pass by injuries; so to pass them by, as neither to retain then revengefully in the mind, or requite them when we have opportunity with the hand: Yea, and that freely, not by constraint, because we cannot avenge ourselves, but willingly. We abhor to do it when we can. So that as a carnal heart thinks revenge its glory, the gracious heart is content that forgiveness should be his glory. I will be even with him, saith nature: I will be above him, saith grace: it is his glory to pass over transgression, Prov. 19: 11.

And this it does in obedience to the command of God: Their own nature inclines them another way. "The spirit that is in us lusteth to envy; but he giveth more grace," James 4: 5. It lusteth to revenge, but the fear of God represseth those motions. Such considerations as these God has forbidden me; yea, and God has forgiven me, as well as forbidden me: they prevail upon him when nature urges to revenge the wrong. "Be kind one to another, tender-hearted, forgiving one another, even as God for Christ's sake has forgiven you," Eph. 4: 32. This is forgiveness in a Christian sense.

Secondly, And that this is excellent, and singularly becoming the profession of Christ, is evident; inasmuch as,

This speaks your religion excellent, that can mould your hearts into that heavenly frame, to which they are so averse, yea, contrarily disposed by nature. It is the glory of Pagan morality, that it can abscondere vitia, hide and cover men's lusts and passions. But the glory of Christianity lies in this, that it can abscindere vitia, not hide, but destroy, and really mortify the lusts of nature. Would Christians but live up to the excellent principles of their religion, Christianity shall be no more out-vied by heathenish morality. The greatest Christian shall be no more challenged to imitate Socrates, if he can. We shall utterly spoil that proud boast, "that the faith of Christians is out-done by the infidelity of Heathens." Christians yield not to-day to Heathens! Let all the world see the true greatness, heavenliness, and excellency of our represented pattern; and by true mortification of your corrupt natures, enforce an acknowledgement from the world, that a greater than Socrates is here. He that is really a meek, humble, patient, heavenly Christian, wins this glory to his religion, that it can do more than all other principles and rules in the world. In nothing were the most accomplished Heathens more defective than this forgiving of injuries: It was a thing they could not understand, or, if they did, could never bring their hearts to it; witness that rule of their great Tally: "It is the first office of justice, (saith he), to hurt no man, except first provoked by an injury." The addition of that exception spoiled his excellent rule.

But now Christianity teaches, and some Christians have attained it, to receive evil, and return good, 1 Cor. 4: 12,13. "Being reviled, we bless; being persecuted, we suffer it: being defamed, we intreat." This certainly is that meekness wrought in us by the wisdom that is from above, James 3: 17.

This makes a man sit sure in the consciences of others, who, with Saul, must acknowledge, when they see themselves so outdone, "Thou art more righteous than I," 1 Sam. 24: 16, 17. Had we been so much injured, and had such opportunities to revenge them, we should never have passed them by, as these men did.

This impresses and stamps the very image of God upon the creature, and makes us like our heavenly Father, who does good to his enemies, and sends down showers of outward blessings upon them, that pour out floods of wickedness daily to provoke him, Mat. 5: 44, 45. In a word, this Christian temper of spirit gives a man the true possession and enjoyment of himself. So that our breasts shall be as the Pacific sea, smooth and pleasant, when others are as the raging sea, foaming and casting up mire and dirt.

Inference 1. Hence we clearly infer, That the Christian religion, exalted in its power, is the neatest friend to the peace and tranquillity of states and kingdoms. Nothing is more opposite to the true Christian spirit, than implacable fierceness, strife, revenge, tumults and uproars. It teaches men to do good and receive evil: to receive evil, and return good. "The wisdom that is from above, is first pure, then peaceable, gentle, and easy to be intreated; full of mercy and good fruits; without partiality, and without hypocrisy; and the fruit of righteousness is sown in peace of them that make peace," James 3: 17,18.

The church is a dove for meekness, Cant. 6: 9. When the world grows full of strife, Christians then grow weary of the world, and sigh out the Psalmist's request, "O that I had the wings of a dove! that I might fly away and be at rest." Strigellius desired to die, that he might be freed ab implacabilibus odiis theologorum, "from the implacable strife of contending divines."

The rule by which they are to walk, is, "If it be possible, as much as lieth in you, live peaceably with all men. Dearly beloved, avenge not yourselves, but rather give place unto wrath;

for it is written, Vengeance is mine, I will repay it, saith the Lord," Rom. 12: 18, 19. It is not religion, but lusts that make the world so unquiet, James 4: 1, 2. Not godliness, but wickedness, that makes men bite and devour one another. One of the first effects of the gospel, is to civilise those places where it comes, and settle order and peace among men. How great a mistake and evil then is it to cry out, when atheism and irreligion have broken the civil peace; this is the fruit of religion! this is the effect of the gospel! Happy would it be if religion did more obtain in all nations. It is the greatest friend in the world to their tranquillity and prosperity.

Inf. 2. How dangerous a thing is it to abuse and wrong meek and forgiving Christians? Their patience and easiness to forgive often invites injury, and encourages vile spirits to insult and trample upon them: but if men would seriously consider it, there is nothing in the world should more scare and affright them from such practices than this. You may abuse and wrong them, they must not avenge themselves, nor repay evil for evil: true, but because they do not, the Lord will; even the Lord to whom they commit the matter; and he will do it to purpose, except ye repent.

"Be patient therefore, brethren, unto the coming of the Lord," James 5: 7. Will ye stand to that issue? had you rather indeed have to do with God than with men? When the Jews put Christ to death, "he committed himself to him that judgeth righteously, 1 Pet. 2: 22, 23. And did that people get any thing by that: did not the Lord severely avenge the blood of Christ on them and their children? yea, do not they and their children groan under the doleful effects of it to this day? If God undertakes, (as he always does) the cause of his abused, meek, and peaceable people, he will be sure to avenge it seven fold more than they could. His little finger will be heavier then their loins. You will get nothing by that.

Inf. 3. Lastly, Let us all imitate our pattern Christ, and labour for meek forgiving spirits. I shall only propose two inducements to it: the honour of Christ, and your own peace: two dear things indeed to a Christian. His glory is more than your life, and all that you enjoy in this world. O do not expose it to the scorn and derision of his enemies. Let them not say, How is Christ a lamb, when his followers are lions? How is the church a dove, that smites and scratches like a bird of prey? Consult also the quiet of your own spirits. What is life worth, without the comfort of life? what comfort can you have in all that you do possess in the world, as long as you have not the possession of your own souls? If your spirits be full of tumult and revenge, the spirit of Christ will grow a stranger to you: that dove delights in clean and quiet breasts. O then imitate Christ in this excellency also!

Sermon 31: The second excellent Word of Christ upon the Cross, illustrated

John 19:27
Then saith he to the disciple, Behold thy mother!

We now pass to the consideration of the second memorable and instructive word of our Lord Jesus Christ upon the cross, contained in this scripture. Wherein he has left us an excellent pattern for the discharge of our relative duties. It may be well said, the gospel makes the best husbands and wives, the best parents and children, the best masters and servants in the world; seeing it furnishes them with the most excellent precepts, and proposes the best patterns. Here we have the pattern of Jesus Christ presented to all gracious children for their imitation, teaching them how to acquit themselves towards their parents, according to the laws of nature and grace. Christ was not only subject and obedient to his parents whilst he lived, but manifested his tender care even whilst he hanged in the torments of death upon the cross. "Then saith he to the disciple, Behold thy mother."

The words contain an affectionate recommendation of his distressed mother to the care of a dear disciple, a bosom friend; wherein let us consider the design, manner, and season of this recommendation.

First, The design and end of it, which, doubtless, was to manifest his tender respect and care for his mother, who was now in a most distressed comfortless state. For now was Simeon's prophecy Luke 2: 35. fulfilled, in the trouble and anguish that filled her soul, yea, a sword also shall pierce through thine own soul, that the thoughts of many hearts may be revealed. Her soul was pierced for him, both as she was his mother, and as she was a mystical member of him, her head, her Lord: and therefore he commends her to the beloved disciple that lay in his bosom, saying, "Behold thy mother," i. e. let her be to thee as thine own mother. Let thy love to me be now manifested in thy tender care for her.

Secondly, The manner of his recommending her, is both affectionate and mutual. It was very affectionate and moving, Behold, thy mother, q. d. John, I am now dying, leaving all human society and relations, and entering into a new state, where neither the duties of natural relations are exercised, nor the pleasures and comforts of them enjoyed. It is a state of dominion over angels and men, not of subjection and obedience; this I now leave to thee. Upon thee do I devolve both the honour and duty of being in my stead and room to her, as to all dear and tender care over her.

John, "Behold thy mother;" and as it is affectionate, so it is mutual, ver. 26. And to his mother he said, "Woman, behold thy son;" not mother, but woman, intimating not only the change of state and conditions with him, but also the request he was making for her to the disciple with whom she was to live, as a mother with a son.

And all this he designs as a pattern to others.

Thirdly, The season or time when his care for his mother so eminently manifested itself, was when his departure was at hand, and he could no longer be a comfort to her, by his bodily presence; yea, his love and care then manifested themselves, when he was full of anguish to the very brim, both in his soul and body; Yet all this makes him not in the least unmindful of so dear a relation. Hence the doctrinal note is,

Doct. That Christ's tender care of his mother, even in the time of his greatest distress; is an excellent pattern for all gracious children to the end of the world.

"There are three great foundations, or bonds of relations, on which all family government depends." Husbands and wives, parents and children, masters and servants. The Lord has planted in the souls of men, affections suitable to these relations, and to his people he has given grace to regulate those affections, appointed duties to exercise those graces, and seasons to discharge those duties. So that, as in the motion of a wheel every spoke takes its turn, and bears its stress; in like manner, in the whole round of a Christian's conversation, every affection, grace, and duty, at one season or other, comes to be exercised.

But yet grace has not so far prevailed in the sanctification of any man's affections, but that there will be excesses or defects in the exercise of them towards our relations; yea, and in this the most eminent saints have been eminently defective. But the pattern I set before you this day, is a perfect pattern. As the church finds him the best of husbands, so to his parents he was the best of sons; "and being the best, and most perfect, is therefore the rule and measure of all others." Christ knew how those corruptions we draw from our parents are returned in their bitter fruits upon them again, to the wounding of their very hearts; and therefore it pleased him to commend obedience and love to parents, in his own example to us.

It was anciently a proverb among the heathen, in sole Sparta, expedite senescere. It is good to be an old man, or women, only in Sparta. The ground of it was the strict laws that were among the Spartans, to punish the rebellions and disobedience of children to their aged parents. And shall it not be good to be an old father and mother in England, where the gospel of Christ is preached, and such an argument as this now set before you urge; an argument which the Heathen world was never acquainted with? Shall parents here be forced to complain with the eagle in the fable, that they are smitten to the heart, by an arrow winged with their own feathers? Or, as a tree cleft in pieces by the wedges that were made of its own body? God forbid.

To prevent such sad occasions of complaints as these, I desire all that sustain the relation of children, into whose hands providence shall cast this discourse, seriously to ponder this example of Christ, proposed for their imitation in this point. Wherein we shall first consider what duties belong to the relation of children: secondly, how Christ's example enforces those duties, and then suitably apply it.

First, Let us examine what duties pertain to the relation of children, and they are as truly, as commonly branched out into the following particulars.

First, Fear and reverence are due from children to their parents, by the express command of God, Lev. 19: 3. Ye shall fear every man his mother and his father. The Holy Ghost purposely inverts the order, and puts the mother first, because she, by reason of her blandishments, and fond indulgence, is most subject to the irreverence and contempt of children. God has clothed parents with his authority. They are intrusted by God with them, and are accountable to him for the souls and bodies of their children; and he expects that you reverence them, although, in respect of outward estate, or honour, you be never so much above them. Joseph, though Lord of Egypt, bowed down before his aged father, with his face to the earth, Gen. 48: 12. Solomon, the most magnificent and glorious king that ever swayed a sceptre, when his mother came to speak with him for Adonijah, he rose up to meet her, and bowed himself to her, and caused a seat to be set up for the king's mother, and set her upon his right hand, 2 Kings 2: 19.

Secondly, Dear and tender love is due from children to their parents: and to show how strong and dear that love ought to be, it is joined with the love you have for your own lives; as it appears in that injunction, to deny both for Christ's sake, Mat. 10: 37. The bonds of nature are strong and direct betwixt parents and children. What is the child but a piece of the parent wrapped up in another skin? O the care, the cost, the pity, the tenderness, the pains, the fears they have expressed for you. It is worse than Heathenish ingratitude, not to return love for love. This filial love is not only in itself a duty, but should be the root or spring of all your duties to them.

Thirdly, Obedience to their commands is due to them, by the Lord's strict and special command, Eph. 6: 1. "Children obey your parents in the Lord, for this is right; honour thy father and thy mother, which is the first commandment with promise." Filial obedience is not only founded upon the positive law of God, but also upon the law of nature; for though the subjection of children to parents is due to them by natural right; therefore, saith the apostle, this is right, (i.e.) right both according to natural and positive law. However, this subjection and obedience is not absolute and universal. God has not divested himself of his own authority, to clothe a parent with it. Your obedience to them must be in the Lord," i.e. in such things as they require you to do in the Lord's authority. In things consonant to that divine and holy will, to which they, as well as you must be subject; and therein you must obey them. Yea, even the wickedness of a parent exempts not from obedience, where his command is not so. Nor, on the other side, must the holiness of a parent sway you, where his commands and God's are opposite. In the former case, the Canonists have determined, "that the command must be distinguished from the person." In the latter, it is a good rule, "My parents must be loved, but my God must be preferred."

Yield yourselves, therefore, cheerfully to obey all that which they lawfully enjoin, and take heed of that black character fixed on the Heathens who know not God, be not found upon you, "disobedience to parents," Rom. 1: 30. Remember, your disobedience to their just commands rises higher, much higher, than an affront to their personal authority; it is disobedience to God himself, whose commands second, and strengthen theirs upon you.

Fourthly, Submission to their discipline and rebukes, is also your duty, Heb. 12: 9. "We had fathers of our own flesh that corrected us, and we gave them reverence." Parents ought not to abuse their authority. "Cruelty in them is a great sin, wrath and rebellion in a child against his parents, is monstrous." It is storied of Elian, that having been abroad, at his return, his father asked him what he had learned since he went from him; he answered, you will know shortly; I have learned to bear your anger quietly, and submit to what you please to inflict. Two considerations should especially mould others into the like frame, especially to their godly parents. The end for which, and the manner in which they manifest their anger to their children. Their end is to save your souls from hell. They judge it better for you to hear the voice of their anger, than the terrible voice of the wrath of God: to feel their hand than his. They know, if you fall into the hands of the living God, you will be handled in another manner.

And for the manner in which they rebuke and chasten, it is with grief in their hearts, and tears in their eyes. Alas! it is no delight to them to cross, vex, or afflict you. Were it not mere conscience of their duty to God, and tender love to your souls, they would neither chide nor smite: and when they do, how do they afflict themselves in afflicting you! When their faces are full of anger, their bowels are full of compassion for you; and you have no more reason to blame them for what they do, than if they cry out and violently snatch at you, when they see you ready to fall from the top of a rock.

Fifthly, faithfulness to all their interests is due so them, by the natural and positive law of God. What in you lies, you are bound to promote, not to waste and scatter their substance: to assist, not to defraud them. Whoso robbeth his father or mother, and saith, it is no transgression, the same is a companion of a destroyer, Prov. 28: 24. This, saith one, as far excels your wronging another, as parricide is a greater crime than man-slaughter, or as Reuben's incest was beyond common fornication. God never meant you should grow up about your parents, as suckers about a tree, to impoverish the root. But for a child, out of covetousness after what his parents have, secretly to wish their death, is a sin so monstrous, as should not be once named, much less found among persons professing Christianity. To desire their death, from whom you had your life, is unnatural wickedness: to dispose of their goods, much more of yourselves, without their consent, is (ordinarily) the greatest injustice to them. Children are obliged to defend the estate and persons of their parents, with the hazard of their own. As arrows are in the hand of a mighty man, so are children of the youth. Happy is the man that has his quiver full of them. They shall not be ashamed, but they shall speak with the enemy in the gates. Psal. 127: 5.

Sixthly, And more especially, requital of all that love, care, and pains they have been at for you, is your duty so far as God enables you, and those things are requitable, 1 Tim. 5: 4. "Let them learn to show piety at home, and requite their parents." The word is "antipelargein", and signifies to play the stork, to imitate that creature of whom it is said, that the young do tenderly feed the old ones, when they are no longer able to fly abroad and provide for themselves. Hence those that want bowels of natural affection to their relations, are said to be "asogmoi", Rom. 1: 30. worse than storks. Oh, it is a shame that birds and beasts should show more tenderness to their dams than children to their parents.

It is a saying frequent among the Jews, "A child should rather labour at the mill than suffer his parents to want." And to the same sense is that other saying, "Your parents must be supplied by you if you have it; if not, you ought to beg for them, rather than see them perish." It was both the comfort and honour of Joseph, that God made him an instrument of so much succour and comfort to his aged father and distressed family, Gen. 47: 13. And you are also to know, that what you do for them, is not in the way of an alms, or common charity. For the apostle saith, it is but your requiting them, and that is justice, not charity. And it can never be a full requital. Indeed the apostle tells us, 2 Cor. 12: 14. That parents lay up for their children, and not children for their parents, and so they ought; but, sure, if providence blast them, and bless you, an honourable maintenance is their due. Even Christ himself took care for his mother.

Secondly, You have had a brief account of the duties of this relation; next, let us consider how Christ's example, who was so subject to them in his life, Luke 2: 51. and so careful to provide at his death, enforces all those duties upon children, especially upon gracious children. And this it does two ways, both as it has the obliging power of a law; and as he himself will one day sit in judgement to take an account how we have imitated him in these things.

First, Christ's example in this has the force and power of a law, yea, a law of love, or a law lovingly constraining you to an imitation of him. If Christ himself will be your pattern, if God will be pleased to take relations like yours, and go before you in the discharge of relative duties; Oh, how much are you obliged to imitate him, and tread in all his footsteps! This was by him intended as a precedent, or pattern, to facilitate and direct your duties.

Secondly, He will come to take an account how you have answered the pattern of obedience, and tender care he set before you in the days of his flesh. What wilt the disobedient plead in that day? He that heard the groans of an afflicted father or mother, will now come to reckon with the disobedient child for them; and, the glorious example of Christ's own obedience to, anti tenderness of his relations, will, in that day, condemn and aggravate, silence and shame such wretched children as shall stands guilty before his bar.

Inference 1. Has Jesus Christ given such a famous pattern of obedience and tenderness to parents? Then there can be nothing of Christ in stubborn, rebellious, and careless children, that regard not the good or comfort of their parents. The children of disobedience cannot be the children of God. If providence directs this to the hands of any that are so, my heart's desire and prayer for them is, that the Lord would search their souls by it, and discover their evils to them, whilst they shall read the following queries.

First Query, Have you not been guilty of slighting your parents by irreverent words or carriages; the old man or woman? To such I commend the consideration of that scripture, Prov. 30:17, which, methinks, should be to them as the hand-writing that appeared upon the plaister of the wall to Belshazzar. "The eye that mocketh at his father, and despiseth to obey his mother, the ravens of the valley shall pick it out, and the young eagles shall eat it." That is, they shall be brought to an untimely end, and the birds of the air shall eat that eye, that had never seen but for that parent that was despised by it.

It may be you are vigorous and young, they decayed and wrinkled with ages: but, saith the Holy Ghost, "Despise not thy mother when she is old," Prov. 23: 22. Or when she is wrinkled, as the Hebrew signifies. It may be you are rich, they poor; own, and honour them in their poverty, and despise them not. God will requite it with his hand if you do.

Second Query, Have you not been disobedient to the commands of parents? a son of Belial is a son of wrath, if God give not repentance to life. Is not this the black brand set upon the Heathens, Rom. 1: 30. Have not many repented this upon a ladder, with a halter about their necks? Wo to him that makes a father or mother complain, as the tree in the fable, that they are cleft asunder with the wedges that are cut out of their own bodies.

Third Query, Have you not risen up rebelliously against, and hated your parents for chastening your bodies, to save your souls from hell? Some children (saith one) will not take that from a parent, which beasts, yea, and savage beasts too, bears and lions, will take from their keepers. What is this but to resist an ordinance of God for your good? and, in rebelling against them, to rebel against the Lord? Well, if they do not, God will take the rod into his own hand, and him you shall not resist.

Fourth Query, Have you not been unjust to your parents, ant defrauded them? first, help to make them poor, and then despise them because they are poor. O horrid wickedness! What a complicated evil is this! Thou art, in the language of the scripture, a companion with destroyers, Prov. 28: 24. This is the worst of theft, in God's account. You may think you make bold with them, but how bold do you make with conscience, and the command of God?

Fifth Query, Are you not, or have you not been ungrateful to parents? Leaving then to shift for themselves, in those straits you have helped to bring them into. O consider it, children, this is an evil which God will surely avenge, except ye repent. that! to be hardened against thine own flesh; to be cruel to thine own parents, that with so much tenderness fed thee, when else thou had perished! I remember Luther gives us a story of one, (and oh that it might be a warning to all that hear it), who had made over all that he had to his son, reserving only a maintenance for himself; at last his son despised him, and grudged him the very meat he eat; and one day the father coming in, when the son and his wife were at dinner upon a goose, they shuffled the meat under the table; but see the remarkable vengeance of God upon this ungracious, unnatural son: the goose was turned into a monstrous toad, which seized upon this vile wretch, and killed him. If any one of you be guilty of these evils, to humble you for them, and reclaim you from them, I desire these six considerations may be laid to heart.

First, That the effects of your obedience, or disobedience will stick upon you and yours to many generations. If you be obedient children in the Lord, both you and yours may reap the fruits of that your obedience, in multitudes of sweet mercies, for many generations. So runs the promise, Eph. 6: 22. "Honour thy father and mother, which is the first commandment with promise, that it may be well with thee, and thou mayest live long on the earth." You know what an eye of favour God cast upon the Recabites for this, Jer. 35: 8. from the 14th to the 20th verse: and as his blessings are, by promise, entailed on the obedient, so his curse upon the disobedient, Prov. 20: 20. "Whoso curseth his father or his mother, his lamp shall be put out in obscure darkness;" i.e. the lamp of his life quenched by death, yea, say others, and his soul also by the blackness of darkness in hell.

Secondly, Though other sins do, this sin seldom escapes exemplary punishment, even in this world. Our English history tells us of a yeoman in Leicestershire, who had made over all he had to his son, to prefer him in marriage, reserving only a bare maintenance at his son's table: afterward, upon some discontent, the son bid his father get out of his house. The next day Mr. Goodman, the minister of the parish, meeting the young man walking about his ground, asked him, How he did? He answered, very well; but before the minister was gone far from him, his bowels fell out, which he carried in his hands, got to his house, sent for Mr. Goodman, bitterly bewailed his sin against his father, and so died. And Dr. Taylor, in his great exemplar, tells us of another, that, upon discontent with his father, wished the house might be on fire, if ever he came any more into his father's house: afterwards, coming, in, it was fired indeed, and this wicked son only consumed. I could multiply instances of this nature, (for indeed that righteous judgement of God has multiplied them,) but this only for a taste.

Thirdly, Heathens will rise up in judgement against you, and condemn you. They never had such precepts nor precedents as you, and yet some of the better natured Heathens would rather chosen death, than to do as you do. You remember the story of Croesus' dumb son, whose dear affections could make him speak when he saw Croesus in danger; though he never spake before, yet then he could cry out, "O do not kill my father!" But what speak I of Heathens! the stork in the heavens, yea, the beasts of the earth, will condemn the disobedience of children.

Fourthly, These are sins inconsistent with the true fear of God, in whomsoever they are found. That a man is indeed, which he is in his family, and among his relations. He that is a bad child can never be a good Christian. Either bring testimonies of your godliness from your relations, or it may be well suspected to be no better than counterfeit. Never talk of your obedience to God, whilst your disobedience to the just commands of your parents gives you the lie.

Fifthly, A parting time is coming when death will break up the family, and when that time comes, oh! how bitter will the remembrance of these things be! when you shall see a father or a mother lying by the wall, what a cut will it be to remember your miscarriages and evils! They are gone out of your reach, you cannot now, if you would, give them any satisfaction for what you have done against them; but, oh, how bitter will the remembrance of these things be at such a time! Surely, this will be more unsupportable to you than their death, if the Lord open your eyes, and give you repentance; and if not, then,

Sixthly, What a terrible thing will it be, to have a father or mother come in as witnesses against you at Christ's bar? As well as they loved you, and as dear as you were to them in this world, they must give evidence against you then. Now, what a fearful thing is it for you but to imagine your parents to come before the Lord, and say, Lord, I have given this child many hundred reproofs for sin; I have counselled, persuaded, and used all means to reclaim him, but in vain; he was a child of disobedience, nothing could work upon him: what think you of this?

Inf. 2. Have you such a pattern of obedience, and tender love to parents? Then, children, imitate your pattern, as it becomes Christians, and take Christ for your example. Whatsoever your parents be, see that you carry it towards them becoming such as profess Christ

First, If your parents be godly, O beware of grieving them by any unbecoming carriage. Art thou a Christian indeed? thou wilt then reckon thyself obliged in a double bond, both of grace and nature, to them: O what a mercy would some children esteem it, if they had parents fearing the Lord, as you have!

Secondly, If they be carnal, walk circumspectly, in the most precise and punctual discharge of your duties, for how knowest thou, O child, but hereby thou mayest win thy parents? Wouldst thou but humbly, and seriously entreat, and persuade them to mind the ways of holiness, speaking to them at fit seasons, with all imaginable humility and reverence, insinuating your advice to duties, or trouble for their evils, rather by relating some pertinent history, or proposing some excellent example, leaving, their own conscience to draw the conclusion, and make application, than to do it yourselves; it is possible they may ponder your words in their hearts, as Mary did Christ's, Luke 2: 49, 51. And would you but back all this with your earnest cries to heaven for them, and your own daily example, that they may have nothing from yourselves to retort upon you; and thus wait with patience for the desired effect: O what blessed instruments might you be of their everlasting good!

Inf. 3. To conclude, Let those that have such children as fear the Lord, and endeavour to imitate Christ in those duties, account them a singular treasure and heritage from the Lord, and give them all due encouragement to their duties.

How many have no children at all, but are as a dry tree! and how many have such as are worse than none? The very reproach and heart breaking of their parents, that bring down their hoary heads with sorrow to the grave.

If God have given you the blessing of godly children, you can never be sufficiently sensible of, or thankful for such a favour. O that ever God should honour you to bring forth children for heaven! what a comfort must this be to you, whatever other troubles you meet with abroad, when you come home among godly relations, that are careful to sweeten your own family to you by their obedience! especially, what a comfort is it, when you come to die, that you leave them within the covenant, entitled to Christ, and so need not be anxious how it shall be with them when you are gone? Take heed of discouraging or damping such children from whom so much glory is like to rise to God, and so much comfort to yourselves. Thus let Christ's pattern be improved, who went before you in such eminent holiness, in all his relations, and left you an example that you should follow his steps.

Sermon 32: The third of Christ's last Words upon the Cross, illustrated

Luke 23:43
And Jesus said unto him, Verily I say unto thee, Today shalt thou be with me in paradise.

In this scripture you have the third excellent saying of Christ upon the cross, expressing the riches of free grace to the penitent thief; a man that had spent his life in wickedness, and for his wickedness was now to lose his life. His practice had been vile and profane, but now his heart was broken for it; he proves a convert, yea, the first fruits of the blood of the cross. In the former verse he manifests his faith, "Lord, remember me, when thou comest into thy kingdom. In this Christ manifests his pardon and gracious acceptance of him; "Verily I say unto thee, to-day shalt thou be with me in paradise." In which promise are considerable, the matter of it, the person to whom it is made, the time set for its performance, and the confirmation of it for his full satisfaction.

First, The matter or substance of the promise made by Christ, viz. That he shall be with him in paradise. By paradise he means heaven itself, which is here shadowed to us by a place of delight and pleasure. This is the receptacle of gracious souls, when separated from their bodies. And that paradise signifies heaven itself, and not a third place, as some of the fathers fondly imagine, is evident from 2 Cor. 12: 2, 4. where the apostle calls the same place by the names of the third heaven, and the paradise. This is the place of blessedness designed for the people of God. So you find, Rev. 2: 7. "To him that overcometh will I give to eat of the tree of life, which is in the midst of the paradise of God;" i.e. to have the fullest and most intimate communion with Jesus Christ in heaven. And this is the substance of Christ's promise to the thief: Thou, i.e. thou in spirit, or thou in the noblest part, thy soul which here bears the image of the whole person; "Thou shalt be with me in paradise."

Secondly, The person to whom Christ makes this excellent and glorious promise: it was to one that had lived lewdly and profanely; a very vile and wretched man, in all the former part of his time, and, for his wickedness, now justly under condemnation; yea, to one that had reviled Christ, after that sentence was executed on him. However, now at last the Lord gave him a penitent believing heart. Now, almost at the last gasp, he is soundly, in an extraordinary way converted; and, being converted, he owns and professes Christ amidst all the shame and reproach of his death; vindicates his innocence, and humbly supplicates for mercy; "Lord, remember me when thou comest into thy kingdom."

Thirdly, The set time for the performance of this gracious promise: Today, this very day, shalt thou be with me in glory: Not after the resurrection, but immediately from the time of thy dissolution, thou shalt enjoy blessedness. And here I cannot but detect the cheat of those that deny an immediate state of glory to believers after death; who, (to the end this scripture might not stand in full opposition to their, as uncomfortable, as unsound opinion), loose the whole frame of it, by drawing one pin, yea, by transposing but a comma, putting it at the word day, which should be at the word thee; and so reading it thus, "Verily I say unto thee to-day," referring the word "day" to the time that Christ made the promise, and not to the time of its performance. But if such a liberty as this be yielded, what may not men make the scriptures speak? There can be no doubt, but Christ, in this expression, fixes the time for his happiness; "To-day thou shalt be with me.

Fourthly, and lastly, You have here the confirmation and seal of this most comfortable promise to him, with Christ's solemn asseveration; "Verily I say unto thee." Higher security cannot be given. I that am able to perform what I promise, and have not out promised myself; for heaven and the glory thereof, are mine: I that am faithful and true to my promises, and have never forfeited my credit with any; I say it, I solemnly confirm it; "Verily I say unto thee, to-day thou shalt be with me in paradise." Hence we have three plain obvious truths, for our instruction and consolation.

Doct. 1. That there is a future eternal state, into which souls pass at death.

Doct. 2. That all believers are, at their death, immediately received into a state of glory and eternal happiness.

Doct. 3. That God may, though he seldom does, prepare men for this glory, immediately before their dissolution by death.

These are the useful truths resulting from this remarkable word of Christ to the penitent thief. We will consider and improve them in the order proposed.

Doct. 1. That there is a future eternal state, into which souls pass at death.

This is a principal foundation-stone to the hopes and happiness of souls. And seeing our hopes must needs be as their foundation and ground work is, I shall briefly establish this truth by these five arguments. The being of a God evinces it. The scriptures of truth plainly reveal it. The consciences of all men have presentiments of it. The incarnation and death of Christ is but a vanity without it; and the immortality of human souls plainly discovers it.

Arg. 1. The being of a God undeniably evinces a future state for human souls after this life. For, if there be a God who rules the world which he has made, he must rule it by rewards and punishments, equally and righteously distributed to good and bad; putting a difference betwixt the obedient and disobedient. the righteous and the wicked. To make a species of creatures capable of a moral government, and not to rule them at all, is to make them in vain, and is inconsistent with his glory, which is the last end of all things. To rule them, but not suitably to their natures, consists not with that infinite wisdom from which their beings proceeded, and by which their workings are ruled and ordered. To rule them, in a way suitably to their natures, viz. by rewards and punishments, mid not to perform, or execute them at all, is utterly incongruous with the veracity and truth of him that cannot lie: this were to impose the greatest cheat in the world upon men, and can never proceed from the holy and true God. So then, as he has made a rational sort of creatures, capable of moral government by rewards and punishments; so he rules them in that way which is suitable to their natures, promising "it shall be well with the righteous, and ill with the wicked." These promises and threatening can be no cheat, merely intended to scare and fright, where there is no danger, or encourage where there is no real benefit; but what he promises, or threatens, must be accomplished, and every word of God take place and be fulfilled. But it is evident that no such distinction is made by the providence of God (at least ordinarily and generally) in this life; but all things coins alike to all; and as with the righteous, so with the wicked. Yea, here it goes ill with them that fear God; they are oppressed; they receive their evil things, and wicked men their good; therefore we conclude, the righteous Judge of the whole earth, will, in another world, recompense to every one according as his work shall be.

Arg. 2. Secondly, And as the very being of God evinces it, so the scriptures of truth plainly reveal it. These scriptures are the pandect, or system of the laws, for the government of man; which the wise and holy Ruler of the world has enacted and ordained for that purpose. And in them we find promises made to the righteous, of a full reward for all their obedience, patience, and sufferings in the next life or world to come; and threatening, made against the wicked, of eternal wrath and anguish, as the just recommence of their sin in hell for ever, Rom. 2: 5, 6, 7, 8, 9, 10. "Thou treasures up to thyself wrath against the day of wrath, and revelation of the righteous judgement of God; who will render to every man according to his deeds: to them who, by patient continuance in well doing, seek for glory, and honour, and immortality, eternal life: but unto them that are contentious, and obey not the truth, but obey unrighteousness, indignation and wrath, tribulation and anguish, upon every soul of man that does evil, &c." So 2 Thess. 1: 4, 5, 6, 7. "So that we ourselves glory in you, in the churches of God, for your patience and faith in all your persecutions and tribulations that ye endure: which is (a manifest token) of the righteous judgement of God, that ye may be counted worthy of the kingdom of God for which ye also suffer; seeing it is a righteous thing with God to recompense tribulation to them that trouble you: and to you who are troubled rest with us, when the Lord Jesus shall be revealed from heaven in flaming fire, &c." To these plain testimonies, multitudes might be added, if it were needful. Heaven and earth shall pass away, but these words shall never pass away.

Arg. 3. Thirdly, As the scriptures reveal it, so the consciences of all men have borne presentiments of it. Where is the man whose conscience never felt any impressions of hope, or fear, from a future world? If it is said, these may be but the effects and force of discourse, or education; we have read such things in the scriptures, or have heard it by preachers; and so raise up to ourselves hopes and fears about it. I demand, how the consciences of the Heathens, who have neither scriptures nor preachers, came to be impressed with these things? Does not the apostle tell us, Rom. 2: 15. "That their consciences in the mean while work upon these things?" their thoughts, with reference to a future state, accuse, or else excuse, i.e. their hearts are cheered and encouraged by the good they do, and terrified with fears about the evils they commit. Whereas, if there were no such things, conscience would neither accuse nor excuse for good or evil done in this world.

Arg. 4. Fourthly, The incarnation and death of Christ, are but vanity without it. What did he propose to himself, or what benefit have we by his coming, if there be no such future state? Did he take our nature, and suffer such terrible things in it for nothing! If you say, Christians have much comfort from it in this life: I answer, the comforts they have are raised by faith and expectation of the happiness to be enjoyed, as the purchase of his blood, in heaven. And if there be no such heaven to which they are appointed, no hell from which they are redeemed, they do but comfort themselves with a fable, and bless themselves with a thing of nought: their comfort is no greater than the comfort of a beggar, that dreams he is a king, and when he awakes, finds himself a beggar still. Surely the ends of Christ's death were to deliver us from the wrath to come, 1 Thess. 1: 10. not from an imaginary, but a real hell, to bring us to God, 1 Pet. 3: 18. to be the author of eternal salvation to them that obey him, Heb. 5: 9.

Arg. 5. Fifthly and lastly, The immortality of human souls, puts it beyond all doubt. The soul of man, vastly differs from that of a beast, which is but a material form, and so wholly depending on, that it must need perish with matter. But it is not so with ours: Ours are reasonable spirits, that can live and act in a separated state from the body, Eccles. 3: 21. "Who knoweth the spirit of man, that goes upward; and the spirit of a beast, that goes downward to the earth?" For if a man dispute whether man be rational, this his very disputing it proves him to be so: so our disputes, hopes, fears, and apprehensions of eternity, prove our souls immortal, and capable of that state.

Inference 1. Is there an eternal state, into which souls pass after this life? How precious then is present time, upon the improvement whereof that state depends. O what a huge weight has God hanged upon a small wire! God has set us here in a state of trial: "According as we improve these few hours, so will it fare with us to all eternity." Every day, every hour, nay, every moment of your present time has an influence into your eternity. Do you believe this? What! and yet squander away precious time so carelessly, so vainly! How do these things consist? When Seneca heard one promise to spend a week with a friend that invited him, to recreate himself with him; he told him, he admired he should make such a rash promise! What (said he) cast away so considerable a part of your life? How can you do it? Surely, our prodigality in the expense of time, argues we have but little sense of great eternity.

Inference 2. How rational are all the difficulties, and severities of religion, which serve to promote and secure a future eternal happiness? So vast is the disproportion betwixt time and eternity, things seen, and not seen as yet, the present vanishing, and future permanent state, that he can never be justly reputed a wise man, that will not let go the best enjoyment he has on earth, if it stand in the way of his eternal happiness. Nor can that man ever escape the just censure of notorious folly, who, for the gratifying of his appetite and present accommodation of his flesh, lets go an eternal glory in heaven. Darius repented heartily that he lost a kingdom for a draught of water; O, said he, "for how short a pleasure have I sold a kingdom!" It was Moses' choice, and his choice argued his wisdom, he chose rather "to suffer afflictions with the people of God, than to enjoy the pleasures of sin, which are but for a season," Heb. 11: 25. Men do not account him a fool, that will adventure a penny, upon a probability to gain ten thousand pounds. But sure the disproportion betwixt time and eternity is much greater.

Inf. 3. If there certainly be such an eternal state into which souls pass immediately after death; How great a change then does death make upon every man and upon every man and woman? O what a serious thing is it to die! It is your passage out of the swift river of time, into the boundless and bottomless ocean of eternity. You that now converse with sensible objects, with men and women like yourselves, enter then into the world of spirits. You that now see the continual revolutions of days and nights, passing away one after another, will then be fixed in a perpetual NOW. O what a serious thing is death! You throw a cast for eternity when you die. If you were to cast a die for your natural life, O! how would your hand shake with fear, how it would fall! But what is that to this?

The souls of men are, as it were, asleep now in their bodies; at death they awake, and find themselves in the world of realities. Let this teach you, both how to carry yourselves towards dying persons when you visit them; and to make every day some provision for that hour yourselves. Be serious, be plain, be faithful with others that are stepping into eternity; be so with your own souls every day. O remember what a long word, what an amazing thing eternity is! especially considering,

Doct. 2. That all believers are, at their death, immediately received into a state of glory and eternal happiness.

This day shalt thou be with me.

This the Atheist denies: He thinks he shall die, and therefore resolves to live as the beasts that perish. Beryllus, and some others after him, taught, that there was indeed a future state of happiness and misery for souls, but that they pass not into it immediately upon death and separation from the body, but shall sleep till the resurrection, and then awake and enter into it. But is not that soul asleep, or worse, that dreams of a sleeping soul till the resurrection? Are souls so wounded and prejudiced by their separation from the body, that they cannot subsist or act separate from it? Or have they found any such conceit in the scriptures? Not at all. The scriptures take notice of no such interval; but plainly enough denies it, 2 Cor. 5: 8. "We are confident, I say, and willing rather to be absent from the body, and present with the Lord." Mark it, no sooner parted from the body, but present with the Lord. So Phil. 1: 23. "I desire to be dissolved, and to be with Christ, which is far better." If his soul was to sleep till the resurrection, how was it far better to be dissolved, than to live? Sure Paul's state in the body had been far better than his state after deaths if this were so; for here he enjoyed much sweet communion with God by faith, but then he should enjoy nothing.

To confirm this dream, they urge, John 14: 3. "If I go away, I will come attain, and receive you to myself". As if the time of Christ's receiving his people to himself, should not come, until his second coming at the end of the world. But though he will then collect all believers into one body, and present them solemnly to his Father; yet that hinders not, but he may, as indeed he does, receive every particular believing soul to himself at death, by the ministry of angels. And if not, how is it that when Christ comes to judgement, he is attended with ten thousand of his saints, that shall follow him when he comes from heaven? Jude 14. You see then the scripture puts no interval betwixt the dissolution of a saint, and his glorification: It speaks of the saints that are dead, as already with the Lord: And the wicked that are dead, as already in hell, calling them spirits in prison, 1 Pet. 3: 19, 20. assuring us, that Judas went presently to his own place, Acts 1: 25. And to that sense, is the parable of Dives and Lazarus, Luke 16: 22.

But let us weigh these four things more particularly, for our full satisfaction in this point.

Arg. 1. First, Why should the happiness of believers be deferred, since they are immediately capable of enjoying it, as soon as separated from the body? Alas, the soul is so far from being assisted by the body (as it is now) for the enjoyment of God; that it is either clogged or hindered by it: So speaks the apostle, 2 Cor. 5: 6, 8. "Whilst we are at home in the body, we are absent from the Lord;" i.e. our bodies prejudice our souls, obstruct and hinder the fulness and freedom of their communion: When we part from the body, we go home to the Lord! then the soul is escaped as a bird out of a cage or snare. Here I am prevented by an excellent pen, which has judiciously opened this point: To whose excellent observations I only add this; That if the entanglements, snares, and prejudices of the soul are so great and many in its embodied estate, that it cannot so freely dilate itself and take in the comforts of God by communion with him, then surely the laying aside of that clog, or the freeing of the soul from that burden, can be no bar to its greater happiness, which it enjoys in its separated state.

Arg. 2. Secondly, Why should the happiness and glory of the soul be deferred, unless God had some farther preparative work to do upon it, before it be fit to be admitted into glory? But surely, here is no such work wrought upon it after its separation by death: all that is done of that kind, is done here. When the compositum is dissolved, all means, duties, and ordinances are ceased. The working day is then ended, and night comes, when no man can work, John 9: 3. To that purpose are those words of Solomon, Eccles. 9: 10. "Whatsoever thy hand findeth to do, do it with all thy might; for there is no wisdom, nor knowledge, nor device in the grave whither thou goest." So that our glorification is not deferred, in order to our fuller preparation for glory. If we are not fit when we die, we can never be fit: all is done upon us that ever was intended to be done; for they are called, Heb. 12: 23. the spirits of the just made perfect.

Arg. 3. Thirdly, Again, Why should our salvation slumber, when the damnation of the wicked does not slumber? God defers not their misery; and surely he will not defer our glory. If he be quick with his enemies, he will not be slow and dilatory with his friends. It cannot be imagined, but he is as much inclined to acts of favour to his children, as to acts of justice to his enemies; these are presently damned, Jude, ver. 7. Acts 1: 25. 1 Pet. 3: 19, 20. And what reason why believers, yea, every believer, as well as this in the text, should not be, that very day in which they die, with Christ in glory?

Arg. 4. Fourthly, and lastly, How do such delays consist with Christ's ardent desires to have his people with him where he is, and with the vehement longings of their souls to be with Christ? You may see those reflected flames of love and desire of mutual enjoyment betwixt the bridegroom and his spouse in Rev. 22: 17, 20. Delays make their hearts sick: the expectation and faith in which the saints die, is to be satisfied then; and surely God will not deceive them. I deny not but their glory will be more complete when the body, their absent friend, is reunited, and made to share with them in their happiness; yet that hinders not, but meanwhile the soul may enjoy its glory, whilst the body takes its rest, and sleeps in the dust.

Inference 1. Are believers immediately with God after their dissolution? Then how surprisingly glorious will heaven be to believers! Not that they are in it before they think of it, or are fitted for it; no, they have spent many thoughts upon it before, and been long preparing for it; but the suddenness and greatness of the change is amazing to our thoughts. For a soul to be now here in the body, conversing with men, living among sensible objects, and within a few moments to be with the Lord; this hour on earth, the next in the third heaven; now viewing this world, and anon standing among an innumerable company of angels, and the spirits of the just made perfect: O what

The Fountain of Life Opened Up

a change is this! What! but wink, and see God! Commend thy soul to Christ, and be transferred in the arms of angels into the invisible world, the world of spirits! To live as angels of God? To live without eating, drinking. sleeping! To be lifted up from a bed of sickness to a throne of glory! To leave a sinful, troublesome world, a sick and pained body, and be in a moment perfectly cured, and feel thyself perfectly well, and free from all troubles and distempers! You cannot think what this will be! Who can tell what sights, what apprehensions, what thoughts, what frames believing souls have, before the bodies they left are removed from the eyes of their dear surviving friends!

Inf. 2. Are believers immediately with God after their dissolution? Where then shall the unbelievers be, and in what state will they find themselves immediately after death has closed their eyes? Ah! what will the case of them be that go the other way?

To be plucked out of house and body, from among friends and comforts, and thrust into endless miseries, into the dark vault of hell, never to see the light of this world any more; never to see a comfortable sight; never to hear a joyful sound; never to know the meaning of rest, peace, or delight any more. O what a change is here! To exchange the smiles and honours of men, for the frowns and fury of God; to be clothed with flames, and drink the pure unmixed wrath of God, who were but a few days since clothed in silks, and filled with the sweet of the creature! How is the state of things altered with them! It was the lamentable cry of poor Adrian, when he felt death approaching: "O my poor wandering soul! alas! whither art thou going! Where must thou lodge this night! Thou shalt never jest more, never be merry more!"

Your term in your houses and bodies is out, and there is another habitation provided for you; but it is a dismal one! When a saint dies, heaven above is as it were moved to receive and entertain him; at his coming, he is received into everlasting habitations, into the inheritance of the saints in light. When an unbeliever dies, we may say of him alluding to Isa. 14: 9. "Hell from beneath is moved for him, to meet him at his coming; it stirreth up the dead for him." No more sports, nor plays, nor cups of wine, nor beds of pleasure: the more of these you enjoyed here, the more intolerable will this change be to you. If saints are immediately with God, others must be immediately with Satan.

Inf. 3. How little cause have they to fear death, who shall be with God so soon after their death? Some there are that tremble at the thoughts of death; that cannot endure to hear its name mentioned; they would rather stoop to any misery here, yea, to any sin, than die, because they are afraid of the exchange. But you that are interested in Christ, need not do so; you can lose nothing by the exchange: the words Death, Grave, and Eternity, should have another kind of sound in your ears, and make contrary impressions upon your hearts. If your earthly tabernacles cast you out, you shall not be found naked; you have "a building of God, a house not made with hands, eternal in the heavens;" and it is but a step out of this into that. O what fair, sweet, and lovely thoughts should you have of that great and last change! But what speak I of your fearlessness of death? Your duty lies much higher than that far.

Inf. 3. If believers are immediately with God, after their dissolution, then it is their duty to long for that dissolution, and cast many a longing look towards their graves. So did Paul, I desire to be dissolved, and to be with Christ, which is far better. The advantages of this exchange are unspeakable: You have gold for brass; wine for water; substance for shadow: solid glory for very vanity. Oh! if the dust of this earth were but once blown out of your eyes, that you might see the divine glory, how weary would you be to live? How willing to die; But then be sure your title be sound and good: leave not so great a concernment to the last; for, though it is confessed, God may do that in an hour, that never was done all your days, yet it is not common; which brings to our third and last observation.

Doct. 3. That God may, though he seldom does, prepare men for glory immediately before their dissolution by death.

There is one parable, and no more, that speaks of some that were called at the last hour, Matt. 20: 9, 10. And there is this one instance in the text, and no more, that gives us an account of a person so called. We acknowledge God may do it, his grace is his own, he may dispense it how and where he pleaseth: we must always salve divine prerogative. Who shall fix bounds, or put limits to free grace, but God himself, whose it is? If he do not ordinarily show such mercies to dying sinners (as indeed he does not); yet it is not because he cannot, but because he will not; not because their hearts are so hardened by long custom in sin, that his grace cannot break them, but because he most justly withholds that grace from them. When blessed Mr. Bilney, the martyr, heard a minister preaching thus: O thou old sinner, thou hast lain these fifty years rotting in thy sin, dost thou think now to be saved? That the blood of Christ shall save thee? O, said Mr. Bilney, what preaching of Christ is this? If I had heard no other preaching than this, what had become of me? No, no, old sinners, or young sinners, great or small sinners, are not to be beaten off from Christ, but encouraged to repentance and faith; for who knows but the bowels of mercy may yearn at last upon one that has all along rejected it? This thief was as unlikely ever to receive mercy, but a few hours before he died, as any person in the world could be.

But surely this is no encouragement to neglect the present seasons of mercy, because God may show mercy hereafter; or to neglect the ordinary, because God sometimes manifests his grace in ways extraordinary. Many, I know, have hardened themselves in ways of sin, by this example of mercy. But what God did at this time, for this man, cannot be expected to be done ordinarily for us, and the reasons thereof are:

Reason 1. First, Because God has vouchsafed us the ordinary and standing means of grace, which this sinner had not; and therefore we cannot expect such extraordinary and unusual conversion as he had. This poor creature never heard in all likelihood, one sermon preached by Christ, or any of his apostles: He lived the life of a highwayman, and concerned not himself about religion. But we have Christ preached freely, and constantly in our assemblies: We have line upon line, precept upon precept: and when God affords the ordinary preaching of the gospel, he does not use to work wonders. When Israel was in the wilderness, then God gave them bread from heaven, and clave the rocks to give them drink; but when they came to Canaan, where they had the ordinary means of subsistence, the manna ceased.

Reason 2. Secondly, Such a conversion as this, may not be ordinarily expected by any man, because such a time as that will never come again: it is possible, if Christ where to die again, and thou to be crucified with him, thou mightest receive thy conversion in such a miraculous and extraordinary way; but Christ dies no more; such a day as that will never come again.

Mr. Fenner, in his excellent discourse upon this point, tells us, That as this was an extraordinary time, Christ being now to be installed in his kingdom, and crowned with glory and honour; so extraordinary things were now done; as when kings are crowned, the streets are richly hanged, the conduits run with wine, great malefactors are then pardoned, for then they show their munificence and bounty; it is the day of the gladness of their hearts. But let a man come at another time to the conduits, he shall find no wine, but ordinary water there. Let a man be in the jail at another time, and he may be hanged; veer, and have no reason but to expect and prepare for it. What Christ did now for this man, was at an extraordinary time.

Reason 3. Thirdly, Such a conversion as this may not ordinarily be expected; for as such a time will never come again, so there will never be the like reason for such a conversion any more: Christ converted him upon the cross, to give an instance of his divine power at that time, when it was almost wholly clouded: Look, as in that day the divinity of Christ brake forth in several miracles, as the preternatural eclipse of the sun, the great earthquake, the rending of the rocks and vail of the temple; so in the conversion of this man in such an extraordinary way, and all, to give evidence of the divinity of Christ, and prove him to be the Son of God whom they crucified; but that is now sufficiently confirmed, and there will be no more occasion for miracles to evidence it.

Reason 4. Fourthly. None has reason to expect the like conversion, that enjoys the ordinary means; because, though in this convert we have a pattern of what free grace can do, yet, as divines pertinently observe, it is a pattern without a promise; God has not added any promise to it, that ever he will do it for any other; and where we have not a promise to encourage our hope, our hope can signify but little to us.

Inference 1. Let those that have found mercy in the evening of their life, admire the extraordinary race that therein has appeared to them. O that ever God should accept the bran, when Satan has had the flour of thy days! The fore-mentioned reverend author tells us of one Marcus Caius Victorius, a very aged man in the primitive times, who was converted from Heathenism to Christianity in his old age. This man came to Simplicianus, a minister, and told him, he heartily owned and embraced the Christian faith. But neither he nor the church would trust him for a long time; and the reason was, the unusualness of a conversion at such an age. But after he had given them good evidence of the reality thereof, there were acclamations and singing of Psalms, the people every where crying, Marcus Caius Victorius is become a Christian. This was written for a wonder! Oh! if God have wrought such wondrous salvation for any of you, what cause have you to do more for him than others! What! to pluck you out of hell when one foot was in! To appear to you at last, when so hardened by long custom in sin, that one might say, "Can the Ethiopian change his skin, or the leopard his spots? Oh! what riches of mercy halve appeared to you!

Inf. 2. Let this convince and startle such, as even to their gray hairs, remain in an unconverted state, who are where they were when they first came into the world, yea, rather further off by much.

Bethink yourselves, ye that are full of days, and full of sin, whose time is almost done, and your great work not begun: who have but a few sands more in the upper part of the glass to run down, and then your conversion will be impossible; your sun is setting; your night is coming; the shadows of the evening, are stretched out upon you; you have one foot in the grave, and the other in hell. O think, if all sense and tenderness be not withered up as well as natural verdure; think with yourselves how sad a case you are in: God may do wonders, but they are not seen every day, then they would cease to be wondered at. O strive, strive, while you have a little time, and a few helps and means more; strive to get that work accomplished now that was never done yet; defer it no longer, you have done so too much already.

It may be (to use Seneca's expression) you have been these sixty, seventy, or eighty years, beginning to live, about to change your tactics; but hitherto you still continue the same. Do not you see how Satan has gulled, and cheated you with vain purposes, till he has brought you to the very brink of the grave and hell? O it is time now to make a stand, and pause a little where you are, and to what he has brought you. The Lord at last give you an eye to see, and an heart to consider.

Inf. 3. Lastly, Let this be a call and caution to al young ones to begin with God betime, and take heed of delays till the last, so as many thousands have done before them to their eternal ruin. Now is your time, if you desire to be in Christ; if you have any sense of the weight and worth of eternal things upon your hearts: I know your age is voluptuous, and delights not the serious thoughts of death and eternity: you are more inclined to mind your pleasures, and leave these grave and serious matters to old age: but let me persuade you against that, by these considerations.

First, O set to the business of religion now, because this is the moulding age. Now your hearts are tender, and your affections flowing: now is the time when you are most likely to be wrought upon.

Secondly, Now, because this is the freest part of your time. It is in the morning of your life, as in the morning of the day: if a man have any business to be done, let him take the morning for it; for in the after part of the day a hurry of business comes on, so that you either forget it, or want opportunity for it.

Thirdly, Now, because your life is immediately uncertain; you are not certain that ever you shall attain the years of your fathers: there are graves in the church-yard just of your length; and souls of all sorts and sizes in Golgotha, as the Jews proverb is.

Fourthly, Now, because God will not spare you because you are but young sinners, little sinners, if you die Christless. If you are not; as you think, old enough to mind Christ, surely, if you die Christless, you are old enough to be damned: there is the small spray, as well as great logs in the fire of hell.

Fifthly, Now, because your life will be the more eminently useful, and serviceable to God, when you know him betimes, and begin with him early. Austin repented, and so have many thousands since, that he began so late, and knew God no sooner.

Sixthly, Now, because your life will be the sweeter to you, when the morning of it is dedicated to the Lord. The first fruits sanctify the whole harvest: this will have a sweet influence into all your days, whatever changes, straits, or troubles you may afterwards meet with.

John Flavel

Sermon 33: The fourth excellent Saying of Christ upon the Cross, illustrated

Matthew 27:46

And about the ninth hour Jesus cried with a loud voice, saying, Eli, Eli, lama sabachthani? that is to say, My God, my God, why hast thou forsaken me?

This verse contains the fourth memorable saying of Christ upon the cross; words able to rend the hardest heart in the world: it is the voice of the Son of God in an agony: his sufferings were great, very great before, but never in that extremity as now; when this heaven rending and heart melting out-cry brake from him upon the cross, Eli, Eli, lama sabachthani? In which are considerable, the time, matter, and manner of this his sad complaint.

First, The time when it was uttered, "about the ninth hour," i.e. about three of the clock afternoon. For as the Jews divided the night into four quarters, or watches; so they divided the day, in like manner, into four quarters, or greater flours; which had their names from that hour of the day that closed the quarter. so that beginning their account of their lesser hours from six in the morning, which with them was the first, their ninth hour answered to our third afternoon. And this is heedfully marked by the evangelists, on purpose to show us how long Christ hanged in distress upon the cross both in soul and body, which at least was full three hours: towards the end whereof his soul was so filled, distressed, and overwhelmed, that this doleful cry brake from his soul, in bitter anguish, "My God, my God," &c.

Secondly. The matter of the complaint. It is not of the cruel tortures he felt in his body, nor of the scoffs and reproaches of his name; he mentions not a word of these, they were all swallowed up in the sufferings within, as the river is swallowed up in the sea, or the lesser flame in the greater. He seems to neglect all these, and only complains of what was more burdensome than ten thousand crosses; even his Father's deserting him, "My God, my God, why hast thou forsaken me?" It is a more inward trouble that burdens him, darkness upon his spirit, the hidings of God's face from him, an affliction he was totally a stranger to till now; here he lays his hand in this complaint. This was the pained place, to which he points in this dolorous outcry.

Thirdly. The manner in which he utters his sad complaint, and that was with a remarkable vehemency, "he cried with a loud voice," not like a dying man, in whom nature was spent, but as one full of vigour, life, and sense. He gathered all his spirits together, stirred up the whole power of nature, when he made this grievous outcry. There is in it also an emphatical reduplication which shows with what vehemency it was uttered; not singly, my God, but he doubles it, "My God, my God," as distressed persons use to do. So Elisha, when Elijah was separated from him by the chariots and horses of fire, cries out, "My father, my father."

Nay, moreover, to increase the force and vehemency of this complaint, here is an affectionate interrogation, "Why hast thou forsaken me?" Questions, especially such as this, are full of spirits. It is as if he were surprised by the strangeness of this affliction: and rousing up himself with an unusual vehemency, turns himself to the Father, and cries, Why so, my Father? O what dost thou mean by this! What! hide that face from me that was never hid before! What! and hide it from me now, in the depth of my other torments and troubles! O what new, what strange things are these!

Lastly, here is an observable variation of the language in which this astonishing complaint was uttered; for he speaks both Hebrew and Syrian in one breath, Eli, Eli lama, are all Hebrew, sabachthani is a Syrian word, used here for emphasis sake. Hence we observe,

Doct. That God in design to heighten the sufferings of Christ to the uttermost, forsook him in the time of his greatest distress; to the unspeakable affliction and anguish of his soul.

This proposition shall be considered in three parts: The desertion itself; the design or end of it; the effect and influence it had on Christ.

First, The desertion itself. Divine desertion generally considered, is God's withdrawing himself from any, not as to his essence, that fills heaven and earth, and constantly remains the same; but it is the withdrawment of his favour, grace, and love: when these are gone, God is said to be gone. And this is done two ways, either absolutely, and wholly, or respectively, and only as to manifestation. In the first sense, devils are forsaken of God. They once were in his favour and love, but they have utterly and finally lost it. God is so withdrawn from them, as that he will never take them into favour any more. In the other sense he sometimes forsakes his dearest children, i.e. he removes all sweet manifestations of his favour and love for a time, and carries it to them as a stranger, though his love be still the same.

And this kind of desertion, which is respective, temporary, and only in regard of manifestation, is justly distinguished from the various ends and designs of it, into probational, cautional, castigatory, and penal. Probational desertions are only for the proof and trial of grace. Cautional desertions are designed to prevent sin. Castigatory desertions are God's rods to chastise his people for sin. Penal desertions are such as are inflicted as the just reward of sin, for the reparation of that wrong sinners have done by their sins. Of this sort was Christ's desertion. A part of the curse, and a special part. And his bearing it was no small part of the reparation, or satisfaction he made for our sins.

More particularly, to open the nature of this desertion of Christ by his Father, there being much of intricacy and difficulty in it; I shall proceed in the explication of it negatively, and positively.

First, Negatively. When Christ cries out of God's forsaking him, he does not mean, that he had dissolved the personal union of the two natures. Not as if the marriage-knot which united our nature to the person of Christ was loosed, or a divorce made betwixt them: No, for when he was forsaken of God, he was still true and real God-man, in one person.

Secondly, When Christ bewails the father's forsaking him, he does not mean, that he pulled away the prop of divine support from him, by which he had till then endured the tortures and sufferings that oppressed him: no, though the Father deserted, yet he still supported him. And so much is intimated in these words of Christ, Eli, Eli, which signifies, my strong One, my strong One. God was with him by way of support, when withdrawn as to manifestations of love and favour. In respect of God's supporting essence which was with Christ at this time, it is said, Isa. 42: 1. "Behold my servant, whom I uphold:" and John 16: 32. "I am not alone, but my father is with me." So that this cannot be the meaning of it.

Thirdly, Much less is it his meaning? that God had left him, as to inherent grace and sanctification; recalling that spirit of holiness which had anointed him above his fellows: no, when he was forsaken, he remained as holy as ever: he had indeed less comfort, but not less holiness than before. Such a desertion had irritated and made void the very end of his death. And his sacrifice could never have yielded such a fragrant odour to God as it did, Eph. 5: 2.

Fourthly, The love of God was not so withdrawn from Christ, as that the Father had now no love for him, nor delight in him. That is impossible, he can no more cease to love Christ, than to love himself. his love was not turned into wrath; though his wrath only was now manifested to him as our surety; and hid his love from him as his beloved Son.

Fifthly, Nor was Christ forsaken by his Father finally, upon what account soever it was that he was forsaken: no, it was but for a few hours that the dark cloud dwelt upon his soul; it soon passed away, and the bright and glorious face of God shone forth again as bright as ever, Psal. 22: 1, 24. compared.

Sixthly, and lastly, It was not a mutual desertion, or a desertion on both parts; the Father forsook him, but he forsook not his Father. When God withdrew, he followed him, crying, "My God, my God."

Yet to speak positively of it; though he did not dissolve the personal union, nor cut off divine supports, nor remove his inherent grace, nor turn his Father's love into hatred, nor continue for ever, nor yet was it on both parts, Christ's forsaking God, as well as God's forsaking Christ: yet I say it was,

First, A very sad desertion, the like unto which in all respects never was experienced by any, nor can be to the end of the world. All his other sufferings were but small to this; they bore upon his body, this upon his soul; they came from the hands of vile men, this from the hands of a dear Father. He suffered both in body and soul; but the sufferings of his soul were the very soul of his sufferings. Under all his other sufferings he opened not his mouth; but this touched the quick, that he could not but cry out, "My God, my God, why best thou forsaken me?"

Secondly, As it was sad, so it was a penal desertion, inflicted on him for satisfaction for those sins of ours, which deserved that God should forsake us for ever, as the damned are forsaken by him. So that this cry (as one observes) was like the perpetual shriek of them that are cast away for ever: this was that hell, and the torments of it which Christ, our surety, suffered for us. For look, as there lies a twofold misery upon the damned in hell, viz. pain of sense, and pain of sense; so upon Christ answerable, there was not only an impression of wrath, but also a subtraction or withdrawment of all sensible favour and love. Hence it is said by himself, John 12: 27. And now my soul, "tetaraktai" is troubled. The word signifies, troubled as they that are in hell are troubled.

Though God did not leave his soul in hell, as others are, he having enough to pay the debt which they have not, yet in the torments thereof, at this time, he was; yea, his sufferings at this time in his soul were equivalent to all that which our souls should have suffered there to all eternity.

Thirdly, It was a desertion that was real, and not fictitious. He does not personate a deserted soul, and speak as if God had withdrawn the comfortable sense and influence of his love from him; but the thing was so indeed. The Godhead restrained and kept back, for this time, all its joys, comforts and sense of love from the manhood, yielding it nothing but support. This bitter doleful outcry of Christ gives evidence enough of the reality of it: he did not feign, but feel the burdensomeness of it.

Fourthly, This desertion fell out in the time of Christ's greatest need of comfort that ever he had in all the time of his life on earth. His Father forsook him at that time, when all earthly comforts had forsaken him, and all outward evils had broken in together upon him; when men, yea, the best of men stood afar off, and none but barbarous enemies were about him. When pains and shame, and all miseries even weighed him down; then, even then, to complete and fill up his suffering, God stands afar off too.

Fifthly, and lastly, It was such a desertion as left him only to the supports of his faith. He had nothing else now but his Father's covenant and promise to hang upon. And indeed, as a judicious author pertinently observes, the faith of Christ did several ways act and manifest itself, in these very words of complaint in the text.

For though all comfortable sights of God and sense of love were obstructed, yet you see his soul cleaves fiducially to God for all that: My God, &c. Though sense and feeling speak as well as faith, yet faith speaks first, My God, before sense speaks a word of his forsaking. His faith presented the complaint of sense; and though sense comes in afterwards with a word of complaint, yet here are two words of faith to one of sense: it is, "My God, my God," and but one word of forsaking. As his faith spake first, so it spake twice, when sense and feeling spake but once: yea, and as faith spake first, and twice as much as sense, so it spake more confidently than sense did. He lays a confident claim to God as his God; "My God, my God," and only queries about his forsaking of him, "Why hast thou forsaken me?" This is spoken more dubiously, the former more confidently.

To be short, his faith laid hold on God, under a most suitable title, or attribute, Eli, Eli, "my strong One, my strong One," q. d. O thou, with whom is infinite and everlasting strength; thou that hast hitherto supported my manhood, and according to thy promise upheld thy servant; what! wilt thou now forsake me? My strong One, I lean upon thee. To these supports and refuges of faith this desertion shut up Christ: by these things he stood, when all other visible and sensible comforts shrunk away, both from his soul and body. This is the true, though brief account of the nature and quality of Christ's desertion.

Secondly, In the next place, let us consider the designs and ends of it; which were principally satisfaction and sanctification: Satisfaction for those sins of ours which deserved that we should be totally and everlastingly forsaken of God. This is the desert of every sin, and the damned do feel it, and shall to all eternity: God is gone from them for ever, not essentially; the just God is with them still, the God of power is still with them, the avenging God is ever with them; but the merciful God is gone, and gone for ever. And thus would he have withdrawn himself from every soul that sinned, had not Christ borne that punishment for us in his own soul: If he had not cried, "My God, my God, why hast thou forsaken me?" we must have howled out this hideous complaint in the lowest hell for ever, O righteous God! O dreadful! O terrible God! thou hast for ever forsaken me!

And as satisfaction was designed in this desertion of Christ, so also was the sanctification of all the desertion of the saints designed in it. For he having been forsaken before us, and for us, whenever God forsakes us, that very forsaking of his is sanctified, and thereby turned into a mercy to believers. Hence are all the precious fruits and effects of our desertions: such are the earnest excitations of the soul to prayer, Psal. 78: 2. Psal. 88: 1, 9. The antidoting the tempted soul against sin. The reviving of ancient experiences, Psal. 77: 5. Enchanting the value of the divine presence with the soul, and teaching it to hold Christ faster than ever before, Cant. 3: 1, 2, 3, 4, 5. These, and many more, are the precious effects of sanctified desertion; but how many, or how good soever these effects are, they all owe themselves to Jesus Christ, as the author of them; who, for our sakes would pass through this sad and dark state, that we might find those blessings in it. So then, the Godhead's suspending of all the effects of joy and comfort from the humanity of Christ at this time, which had not ceased to flow into it, in an ineffable measure and manner, till now, must needs be both a special part of Christ's satisfaction for us, and consequently, that which makes all our temporary desertions rather mercies and blessings, than curses to us.

Thirdly, Let us, in the next place, consider the effects and influence this desertion had upon the spirit of Christ.

And though it did not drive him to despair, as the Papists falsely charge Mr. Calvin to have affirmed; yet it even amazed him, and almost swallowed up his soul in the deeps of trouble and consternation. This cry is a cry from the deeps, from a soul oppressed even to death. Never was the Lord Jesus so put to it before; it is a most astonishing outcry.

Let but five particulars be weighed, and you will say, never was there any darkness like this: no sorrow like Christ's sorrow in his deserted state: For,

First, Apprehend, reader, this was a new thing to Christ, and that which he never was acquainted with before. From all eternity until now there had been constant and wonderful outlets of love, delight, and joy, from the bosom of the Father, into his bosom. He never missed his Father before: never saw a frown, or a veil, upon that blessed face before. This made it an heavy burden indeed, the words are words of admiration and astonishment; "My God, my God, why hast thou forsaken me?" thou that never midst so before, hast forsaken me now.

Secondly, As it was a new thing to Christ, and therefore the more amazing, so it was a great thing to Christ; so great, that he scarce knew how to support it. Had it not been a great trial indeed, so great a spirit as Christ's was would never have so drooped under it, and made so sad a complaint of it. It was so sharp, so heavy an affliction to his soul, that it caused him, who was meek under all other sufferings as a lamb, to roar under this like a lion; for so much those words of Christ signify, Psal. 22: 1. "My God, my God, why hast thou forsaken me? Why art thou so far from the voice of my roaring?" It comes from a root, that signifies "to howl, or roar as a lion; and rather signifies the noise made by a wild beast, than the voice of a man."

And it is as much as if Christ had said, O my God, no words can express my anguish: I will not speak, but roar, howl out my complaint; pour it out in vollies of groans: I roar as a lion. It is no small matter will make that majestic creature to roar: and sure, so great a spirit as Christ's would not have roared under a slight burden.

Thirdly, As it was a great burden to Christ, so it was a burden laid on in the time of his greatest distress. When his body was in tortures, and all about him was black, dismal, and full of horror and darkness. He fell into this desertion at a time when he never had the like need of divine supports and comforts, and that aggravated it.

Fourthly, It was a burden that lay upon him long, even from the time his soul began to be sorrowful and sore amazed in the garden, till his very death. If you were but to hold your finger in the fire for two minutes, you would not be able to bear it. But what is the finger of a man to the soul of Christ? Or what is a material fire to the wrath of the great God!

Fifthly, So heavy was this pressure upon Christ's soul, that in probability it hastened his death; for it was not usual for crucified persons to expire so soon; and those that were crucified with him were both alive after Christ was gone. Some have hanged more than a day and a night, some two full days and nights, in those torments alive; but never did any feel inwardly what Christ felt. He bare it till the ninth hour, and then makes a fearful outcry and dies. The uses follow.

Inference 1. Did God forsake Christ upon the cross as a punishment to him for our sins? Then it follows, That as often as we have sinned, so oft have we deserved to be forsaken of God. This is the just recompence and demerit of sin. And, indeed, here lies the principal evil of sin, that it separates betwixt God and the soul. This separation is both the moral evil that is in it, and the penal evil inflicted by the righteous God for it. By sin we depart from God, and, as a due punishment of it, God departs from us. This will be the dismal sentence in the last day, Matt. 25: "Depart from me, ye cursed." Thenceforth there will be a gulph fixed betwixt God and them, Luke 19: 20. No more friendly intercourses with the blessed God for ever. The eternal shriek of the damned is, Wo and alas, God has forsaken us for evermore. Ten thousand worlds can nowise recompense the loss of one God. Beware, sinners, how you say to God now, Depart from us, we desire not the knowledge of thy ways, lest he say, Depart from me, you shall never see my face.

Inf. 2. Did Christ never make such a sad complaint and outcry, till God hid his face from him? Then the hiding of God's face is certainly the greatest misery that can possibly befal a gracious soul in this world. When they scourged, buffeted, and smote Christ, yea, when they nailed him to the tree, he opened not his mouth; but when his father hid his face from him, then he cried out; yea, his voice was the voice of roaring: this was more to him than a thousand crucifyings. And, surely, as it was to Christ, so is it to all gracious souls, the saddest stroke, the heaviest burden that ever they felt. When David forbade Absalom to come to Jerusalem, to see his father, he complains in 2 Sam. 14: 32. "Wherefore, (saith he) am I come from Geshur, if I may not see the king's face?" So does the gracious soul bemoan itself; Wherefore am I redeemed, called, and reconciled, if I may not see the face of my God?

It is said of Tully, when he was banished from Italy, and of Demosthenes, when he was banished from Athens, that they wept every time they looked towards their own country: and, is it strange that a poor deserted believer should mourn every time he looks heaven ward? Say, Christian, did the tears never trickle down thy cheeks when thou lookedst towards heaven, and couldst not see the face of thy God, as at other times? If two dear friends cannot part, though it be but for a season, but that parting must be in a shower; blame not the saints if they sigh and mourn bitterly when the Lord, who is the life of their life, depart, though but for a season, from them; for if God depart, their sweetest enjoyment on earth, the very crown of all their comforts is gone; and what will a king take in exchange for his crown? What can recompense a saint for the loss of his God! Indeed, if they had never seen the Lord, or tasted the incomparable sweetness of his presence, it were another matter; but the darkness which follows the sweetest light of his countenance, is double darkness.

And that which does not a little increase the horror of this darkness is, that when their souls were thus benighted, and the sun of their comfort is set; then does Satan, like the wild beasts of the desert, creep out of his den, and roar upon them with hideous temptations. Surely this is a sad state, and deserves tender pity! Pity is a debt due to the distressed, and the world shows not a greater distress than this. If ever you have been in troubles of this kind yourselves, you will never slight others in the same case: nay, one end of God's exercising you with troubles of this nature, is to teach you compassion towards others in the same case. Do they not cry to you, as Job 19: 21. "Have pity have pity upon me, O ye my friends, for the hand of God has touched me." Draw forth bowels of mercy and tender compassion to them; for, either you have been, or are, or may be in the same case yourselves: however, if men do not, to be sure, Christ, that has felt it before them, and for them, will pity them.

Inf. 3. Did God really forsake Jesus Christ upon the cross? Then from the desertion of Christ, singular consolation springs up to the people of God; yea, manifold consolation. Principally it is a support in these two respects, as it is preventive of your final desertion and a comfortable pattern to you in your present sad desertions.

First, Christ's desertion is preventive of your final desertion: because he was forsaken for a time, you shall not be forsaken for ever: for he was forsaken for you: and God's forsaking him, though but for a few hours, is equivalent to his forsaking you for ever. It is every way as much for the dear Son of God, the darling delight of his soul, to be forsaken of God for a time; as if such a poor inconsiderable thing as thou art, should be cast off to eternity. Now this being equivalent, and borne in thy room, must needs give thee the highest security in the world, that God will never finally withdraw from thee: had he intended to have done so, Christ had never made such a sad outcry as you hear this day, "My God, my God, why hast thou forsaken me?"

Secondly, Moreover, this sad desertion of Christ becomes a comfortable patterns to poor deserted souls in divers respects: and the proper business of such souls, at such times, is to eye it believingly, in these six respects.

First, Though God deserted Christ, yet at the same time he powerfully supported him: his omnipotent arms were under him, though his pleased face was hid from him: he had not indeed his smiles, but he had his supports. So, Christian, just so shall it be with thee: thy God may turn away his face, but he will not pluck away his arm. When one asked holy Mr. Baines, how the case stood with his soul, he answered, supports I have, though suavities I want. Our father, in this, deals with us, as we ourselves sometimes do with a child that is stubborn and rebellious. We turn him out of doors, and bid him begone out of our sight: and there he sighs and weeps; but however, for the humbling of him, we will not presently take him into house and favour: yet we order, or at least, permit the servants to carry him meat and drink. Here is fatherly care and support: though no former smiles, or manifested delights.

Secondly, Though God deserted Christ, yet he deserted not God: his Father forsook him, but he could not forsake his Father, but followed him with this cry, "My God my God, why hast thou forsaken me?"

And is it not even so with you? God goes off from your souls, but you cannot go off from him. No, your hearts are mourning after the Lord, seeking him carefully with tears: complaining of his absence, as the greatest evil in this world. This is Christ-like: so it was with the spouse, Cant. 3: 1, 2. Her beloved had withdrawn himself, and was gone; but was she content to part with him so? No such thing. "By night, on my bed, I sought him whom my soul loveth; I sought him, but I found him not; I will arise now, and go about the city," &c.

Thirdly, Though God forsook Christ, yet he returned to him again. It was but for a time, not for ever. In this also does his desertion parallel yours. God may, for several wise and holy reasons, hide his face from you, but not so as it is hid from the damned, who shall never see it again. This cloud shall pass away; this night shall have a bright morning: "For (saith thy God) I will not contend for ever, neither will I be always wrath; for the spirit shall fail before me, and the souls which I have made." As if he should say, I may contend with him for a time, to humble him, but not for ever, lest, instead of a sad child, I should have a dead child. Oh the tenderness even of a displeased father!

Fourthly, Though God forsook Christ, yet at that time he could justify God. So you read, Psal. 22: 2, 3. "O my God (saith he) I cry in the day time, but thou hearest not; and in the night season, and am not silent: but thou art holy." Is not thy spirit, according to the measure, framed like Christ's

The Fountain of Life Opened Up

in this; canst thou not say, even when he writes bitter things against thee, he is a holy, faithful, and good God for all this? I am deserted but not wronged. There is not one drop of injustice in all the sea of my sorrows. Though he condemn me, I must, and will justify him; this also is Christ-like.

Fifthly, Though God took from Christ all visible and sensible comforts, inward as well as outward; yet Christ subsisted, by faith, in the absence of them all: his desertion put him upon the acting of his faith. "My God, my God", are words of faith, the words of one that wholly depends upon his God: and is it not so with you too? Sense of love is gone, sweet sights of God shut up in a dark cloud? well, what then? Must thy hands presently hang down, and thy soul give up all its hopes? What! Is there no faith to relieve in this case? Yes, yes, and blessed be God for faith. "Who is among you that feareth the Lord, and obeyeth the voice of his servants, that walketh in darkness, and has no light; let him trust in the name of the Lord, and stay himself upon his God," Isa. 50: 10. To conclude,

Sixthly, Christ was deserted, a little before the glorious morning of light and joy dawned upon him. It was a little, a very little while, after this sad cry, before he triumphed gloriously; and so it may be with you: heaviness may endure for a night, but joy and gladness will come in the morning. You know how Mr. Glover was transported with joy, and cried out, as a man in a rapture, O Austin! he is come, he is come, he is come, meaning the Comforter, who for some time had been absent from his soul.

But, I fear I am absolutely and finally forsaken.

Why so? Do you find the characters of such a desertion upon your soul? Be righteous judges, and tell me, whether you find an heart willing to forsake God? Is it indifferent to you whether God ever return again or no? Are there no mournings, meltings, or thirsting after the Lord? Indeed, if you forsake him, he will cast you off for ever; but can you do so? Oh, no, let him do what he will, I am resolved to wait for him, cleave to him, mourn after him, though I have no present comfort from him, no assurance of my interest in him; yet will I not exchange my poor weak hopes for all the good in this world.

Again, you say God has forsaken you, but has he let loose the bridle before you? To allude to Job 30: 11. Has he taken away from your souls all conscientious tenderness of sin, so that now you can sin freely, and without any regret? If so, it is a sad token indeed: tell me, soul, if thou, indeed, judgest God will never return in loving kindness to thee any more; why hast thou not then give thyself over to the pleasures of sin, and fetch thy comforts that way, from the creature, since thou can't have no comfort from thy God? Oh, no, I cannot do so; if I die in darkness and sorrow, I will never do so: my soul is as full of fear and hatred of sin as ever, though empty of joy and comfort. Surely, these are no tokens of a soul finally abandoned by its God.

Inf. 4. Did God forsake his own Son upon the cross; Then the dearest of God's people may, for a time, be forsaken of their God. Think it not strange, when you, that are the children of light, meet with darkness, yea, and walk in it; neither charge God foolishly; nor say he deals hardly with you. You see what befall Jesus Christ, whom his soul delighted in: It is doubtless your concernment to expect and prepare for days of darkness. You have heard the doleful cry of Christ, "My God, my God, why hast thou forsaken me?" You know how it was with Job, David, Heman, Asaph, and many others, the dear servants of God, what heart melting lamentations they had made upon this account; and are you better than they? Oh, prepare for spiritual troubles; I am sure you do enough every day to involve you in darkness. Now, if at any time this trial befall you, mind these two seasonable admonitions, and lay them up for such a time.

Admonition 1. First, Exercise the faith of adherence, when you have lost the faith of evidence. When God takes away that, he leaves this: that is necessary to the comfort, this to the life of his people. It is sweet to live in views of your interest, but if they be gone, believe and rely on God, for an interest. Stay yourselves on your God when you have no light, Isa 50: 10. Drop this anchor in the dark, and do not reckon all gone when evidence is gone: never reckon yourselves undone whilst you can adhere to your God. Direct acts are noble acts of faith, as well as reflexive ones; yea, and in some respects to be preferred to them. For,

First, As your comfort depends on the evidencing acts of faith, so your salvation upon the adhering act of faith. Evidence comforts, affiance saves you; and, sure, salvation is more than comfort.

Secondly, Your faith of evidence has more sensible sweetness, but your faith of adherence is of more constancy and continuance: the former is as a flower in its month, the latter sticks by you all the year.

Thirdly, Faith of evidence brings more joy to you, but faith of adherence brings more glory to God: for thereby you trust him when you cannot see him; yea, you believe not only without, but against sense and feeling; and, doubtless, that which brings glory to God, is better than that which brings comfort to you. O then exercise this, when you have lost that.

Admonition 2. Secondly, Take the right method to recover the sweet light which you have sinned away from your souls. Do not go about from one to another complaining; nor yet sit down desponding under your burden. But,

First, Search diligently after the cause of God's withdrawment: urge him hard, by prayer, to tell thee wherefore he contends with thee, Job 10: 2. Say, Lord, what have I done that so offends thy Spirit? What evil is it which thou so rebukest? I beseech thee shew me the cause of thine anger: have I grieved thy Spirit in this thing, or in that? Was it my neglect of duty, or my formality in duties? Was I not thankful for the sense of thy love, when it was shed abroad in my heart? O Lord, why is it thus with me?

Secondly, Humble your souls before the Lord for every evil you shall be convinced of: tell him, it pierces your heart, that you have so displeased him, and that it shall be a caution to you, whilst you live, never to return again to folly: invite him again to your souls, and mourn after the Lord till you have found him: If you seek him, he will be found of you, 2 Chron. 15: 2. It may be you shall have a thousand comforters come about your sad souls, in such a time to comfort them: this will be to you instead of God, and that will repair your loss of Christ: despise them all, and say, I am resolved to sit as a widow till Christ return; he, or none, shall have my love.

Thirdly, Wait on in the use of means till Christ return. O be not discouraged; though he tarry, wait you for him; for, blessed are all they that wait for him.

Sermon 34: The fifth excellent Saying of Christ upon the Cross, illustrated

John 19: 28.
After this, Jesus knowing that all things were now accomplished, that the scripture might be fulfilled, saith, I thirst.

It is as truly, as commonly said, death is dry: Christ found it so, when he died. When his spirit laboured in the agonies of death, then he said, I thirst.

This is the fifth word of Christ upon the cross, spoken a little before he bowed the head and yielded up the ghost. It is only recorded by this evangelist; and, there are four things remarkable in this complaint of Christ, viz. The person complaining: the complaint he made: the time when, and the reason why he so complained.

First, The person complaining. Jesus said, I thirst. This is a clear evidence, that it was no common suffering: great and resolute spirits will not complain for small matters. The spirit of a common man will endure much, before it utters any complaint. Let us therefore see,

Secondly, The affliction, or suffering, he complains of; and that is thirst. There are two sorts of thirst, one natural and proper, another spiritual and figurative: Christ felt both at this time. His soul thirsted, in vehement desires and longings, to accomplish and finish that great and difficult work he was now about; and his body thirsted, by reason of those unparalleled agonies it laboured under, for the accomplishing thereof: but it was the proper natural thirst he here intends, when he said, I thirst. Now, "this natural thirst," of which he complains, "is the raging of the appetite for moist nourishment, arising from scorching up of the parts of the body for want of moisture." And, amongst all the pains and afflictions of the body, there can scarcely be named a greater, and more intolerable one, than extreme thirst. The most mighty and valiant have stooped under it. Mighty Samson, after all his conquests and victories, complains thus, Judges 15: 18. "And he was sore athirst, and called on the Lord, and said, Thou hast given this great deliverance into the hand of thy servant, and now shall I die for thirst, and fall into the hands of the uncircumcised?" Great Darius drank filthy water, defiled with the bodies of the slain, to relieve his thirst, "and protested, never any drink was more pleasant to him." Hence, Isa. 41: 17, thirst is put to express the most afflicted state, "When the poor and needy seek water, and there is none, and their tongue faileth for thirst, I the Lord will hear them;" i.e. when my people are in extreme necessities, under any extraordinary pressures and distresses, I will be with them, to supply and relieve them. Thirst causes a most painful compression of the heart, when the body, like a sponge, sucks and draws for moisture, and there is none. And this may be occasioned, either by long abstinence from drink, or by the labouring and expense of the spirits under grievous agonies and extreme tortures; which, like a fire within, soon scorch up the very radical moisture.

Now, though we find not that Christ tasted a drop since he sat with his disciples at the table; after that no more refreshments for him in this world: yet that was not the cause of this raging thirst; but it is to be ascribed to the extreme sufferings which he so long had conflicted with, both in his soul and body. These preyed upon him, and drank up his very Spirits. Hence came this sad complaint, I thirst.

Thirdly, Let us consider the time when he thus complained. "When all things were now accomplished," saith the text, i.e. when all things were even ready to be accomplished in his death. A little, a very little while before his expiration, when the pangs of death began to be strong upon him: and so it was both a sign of death at hand, and of his love to us, which was stronger than death, that would not complain sooner, because he would admit of no relief, nor take the least refreshment, until he had done his work.

Fourthly, and lastly, Take notice of the design and end of his complaint: "that the scripture might be fulfilled, he saith, I thirst;" i.e. that it might appear, for the satisfaction of our faith, that whatsoever had been predicted by the prophets, was exactly accomplished, even to a circumstance in him. Now it was foretold of him, Psal 69: 21. "They gave me gall for my meat, and, in my thirst, they gave me vinegar to drink;" and herein it was verified. Hence the note is,

Doct. That such were the agonies and extreme sufferings of our Lord Jesus Christ upon the cross, as drank up his very spirits, and made him cry, I thirst.

"If I, (said one) should live a thousand years, and every day die a thousand times the same death for Christ that he once died for me, yet all this would be nothing to the sorrows Christ endured in his death." At this time the bridegroom Christ might have borrowed the words of his spouse, the church, Lam. 1: 12. "It is nothing to you, all ye that pass by? See and behold, if there be any sorrow like unto my sorrow which is done unto me, wherewith the Lord has afflicted me in the day of his fierce anger."

Here we are to enquire into, and consider the extremities and agonies Christ laboured under upon the cross, which occasioned this sad complaint of thirst; and then make application, in the several inferences of truth deducible from it.

Now the sufferings of our Lord Jesus Christ upon the cross were two fold, viz. His corporeal, and spiritual sufferings: we shall open them distinctly, and then show how both these meeting together upon him in their fulness and extremity, must needs consume his very radical moisture, and make him cry, I thirst. To begin with the first.

First, His corporeal and more external sufferings were exceeding great, acute, and extreme sufferings; for they were sharp, universal, continual, and unrelieved by any inward comfort.

First, They were sharp sufferings; for his body was racked or digged in those parts where sense more eminently dwells: in the hands and feet the veins and sinews meet, and their pain and anguish meet with them; Psal. 22: 16. "They digged my hands and my feet." Now Christ by reason of his exact and excellent temper of body, had doubtless more quick, tender and delicate senses than other men: his body was so formed, that it might be a capacious vessel, to take in more sufferings than any other body could. Sense is, in some, more delicate and tender, and in others dull and blunt, according to the temperament and vivacity of the body and spirits; but in none as it was in Christ, whose body was miraculously formed on purpose to suffer unparalleled miseries. and sorrows in: "A body hast thou fitted me," Heb. 10: 5. Neither sin nor sickness had any way enfeebled or dulled it.

Secondly, As his pains were sharp, so they were universal, not affecting one, but every part; they seized every member; from head to foot, no member was free from torture: for, as his head was wounded with thorns, his back with bloody lashes, his hands and feet with nails, so every other part was stretched and distended beyond its natural length, by hanging upon that cruel engine of torment, the cross. And as every member, so every particular sense, was afflicted; his sight with vile wretches, cruel murderers that stood about him; his hearing with horrid blasphemies, belched out against him; his taste with vinegar and gall, which they gave to aggravate his misery; his smell with that filthy Golgotha where he was crucified, and his feeling with exquisite pains in every part; so that he was not only sharply, but universally tormented.

Thirdly, These universal pains were continual, not by fits, but without any intermission. He had not a moment's ease by the cessation of pains; wave came upon wave, one grief driving on another, till all God's waves and billows had gone over him. To be in extremity of pain, and that without a moment's intermission, will quickly pull down the stoutest nature in the world.

Fourthly, and lastly, As his pains were sharp, universal and continual, so they were altogether unrelieved by his understanding part. If a man have sweet comforts flowing into his soul from God, they will sweetly demulce and allay the pains of the body: this made the martyrs shout amidst the flames. Yes, even inferior comforts and delights of the mind, will greatly relieve the oppressed body.

It is said of Possidonius, that, in a great fit of the stone, he solaced himself with discourses of moral virtue, and when the pain twinged him, he would say, "O pain thou does nothing, though thou art a little troublesome, I will never confess thee to be evil." And Epicures, in the fits of the colic, refreshed himself, ob memoriam inventorum, i.e. by his inventions in philosophy.

But now Christ had no relief this way in the least; not a drop of comfort came from heaven into his soul to relieve it, and the body by it: but, on the contrary, his soul was filled up with grief, and had an heavier burden of its own to bear than that of the body; so that instead of relieving, it increased unspeakably the burden of its outward man. For,

Secondly, Let us consider these inward sufferings of his soul how great they were, and how quickly they spent his natural strength, and turned his moisture into the drought of summer. And,

First, His soul felt the wrath of an angry God, which was terribly impressed upon it. The wrath of a king is as the roaring of a lion; but what is that to the wrath of a Deity? See what a description is given of it in Nahum 1: 6. "Who can stand before his indignation: and who can abide in the fierceness of his anger? His fury is poured out like fire, and the rocks are thrown down by him." Had not the strength that supported Christ been greater than that of rocks, this wrath had certainly overwhelmed and ground him to powder.

The Fountain of Life Opened Up

Secondly, As it was the wrath of God that lay upon his soul, so it was the pure wrath of God, without any allay or mixture: not one drop of comfort came from heaven or earth; all the ingredients in his cup were bitter ones: There was wrath without mercy; yea, wrath without the least degree of sparing mercy; "for God spared not his own Son," Rom. 8: 32. Had Christ been abated or spared, we had not. If our mercies must be pure mercies, and our glory in heaven pure and unmixed glory, then the wrath which lie suffered must be pure and unmixed wrath. Yea,

Thirdly, As the wrath, the pure unmixed wrath of God, lay upon his soul, so all the wrath of God was poured out upon him, even to the last drop; so that there is not one drop reserved for the elect to feel. Christ's cup was deep and large, it contained all the fury and wrath of an infinite God in it! and yet he drank it up: he bare it all, so that to believing souls, who come to make peace with God through Christ, he saith, Isa. 27: 4. "Fury is not in me." In all the chastisements God inflicts upon his people, there is no vindictive wrath; Christ bore it all in his own soul and body on the tree.

Fourthly, As it was all the wrath of God that lay upon Christ, so it was wrath aggravated, in divers respects beyond that which the damned themselves do suffer. That is strange you will say; can there be any sufferings worse than those the damned suffer, upon whom the wrath of an infinite God is immediately transacted, who holds them up with the arm of his power, while the arm of his justice lies on eternally? Can any sorrows be greater than these? Yes; Christ's sufferings were beyond theirs in divers particulars.

First, None of the damned were ever so near and dear to God as Christ was: they were estranged from the womb, but Christ lay in his bosom. When he smote Christ, he smote "the man that was his fellow," Zech. 13: 7. But in smiting them, he smites his enemies. When he had to do, in a way of satisfaction, with Christ, he is said not to spare his own son, Rom. 8: 32. Never was the fury of God poured out upon such a person before.

Secondly, None of the damned had ever so large a capacity to take in a full sense of the wrath of God as Christ had. The larger any one's capacity is to understand and weigh his troubles fully, the more grievous and heavy is his burden. If a man cast vessels of greater and lesser quantity into the sea, though all will be full, yet the greater the vessel is, the more water it contains. Now Christ had a capacity beyond all mere creatures to take in the wrath of his Father; and what deep and large apprehensions he had of it may be judged by his bloody sweat in the garden, which was the effect of his mere apprehensions of the wrath of God. Christ was a large vessel indeed; as he is capable of more glory, so of more sense and misery than any other person in the world.

Thirdly, The damned suffer not so innocently as Christ suffered; they suffer the just demerit and recompence of their sin: They have deserved all that wrath of God which they feel, and must feel for ever: It is but that recompence which was meet; but Christ was altogether innocent: He had done no iniquity, neither was guile found in his mouth; yet it pleased the Lord to bruise him. When Christ suffered, he suffered not for what he had done; but his sufferings were the sufferings of a surety, paying the debts of others. "The Messiah was cut off, but not for himself," Dan. 9: 26. Thus you see what his external sufferings in his body, and his internal sufferings in his soul were.

Thirdly, In the last place, it is evident that such extreme sufferings as these, meeting together upon him, must needs exhaust his very spirits, and make him cry, I thirst. For let us consider,

First, What mere external pains, and outward afflictions can do. These prey upon, and consume our spirits. So David complains, Psal. 39: 11. "When thou with rebukes correctest man for iniquity; thou makes his beauty to consume away as a moth," i.e. look, as a moth frets and consumes the most strong and well wrought garment, and makes it scary and rotten without any noise; so afflictions waste and wear out the strongest bodies. They make bodies of the firmest constitution like an old rotten garment: They shrivel and dry up the most vigorous and flourishing body, and make it like a bottle in the smoke, Psal. 119: 83.

Secondly, Consider what mere internal troubles of the soul can do upon the strongest body: They spend its strength, and devour the spirits. So Solomon speaks, Prov. 17: 22. "A broken spirit drieth the bones," i.e. it consumes the very marrow with which they are moistened. So Psal. 32: 3, 4. "My bones waxed old, and through my roaring all the day long: for day and night thy hand was heavy on me: my moisture (or chief sap) is turned into the drought of summer." What a spectacle of pity was Francis Spira become, merely through the anguish of his spirit? a spirit sharpened with such troubles, like a keen knife, cuts through the sheath. Certainly, whoever has had any acquaintance with troubles of soul, knows, by sad experience, how, like an internal flame, it feeds and preys upon the very spirits, so that the strongest stoop and sink under it. But,

Thirdly, When outward bodily pains shall meet with inward spiritual troubles, and both in extremity shall come in one day; how soon must the firmest body fail and waste away like a candle lighted at both ends? Now strength fails a-pace, and nature must fall flat under this load. When the ship in which Paul sailed, fell into a place where two seas met, it was quickly wrecked; and so will the best constituted body in the world, if it fall under both these troubles together the soul and body sympathise with each other under trouble, and mutually relieve each other.

If the body be sick and full of pain, the spirit supports, cheers, and relieves it by reason and resolution all that it can; and if the spirit be afflicted the body sympathises and helps to bear up the spirit; but now, if the one be over laden with strong pains, more than it can bear, and calls for aid from the other, and the other be oppressed with intolerable anguish, and cries out under a burden greater than it can bear, so that it can contribute no help, but instead thereof adds to its burden, which before was above its strength to bear, then nature must needs fail, and the friendly union betwixt soul and body suffer a dissolution by such an extraordinary pressure as this. So it was with Christ, when outward and inward sorrows met in one day in their extremity upon him. Hence the bitter cry, I thirst.

Inference 1. How horrid a thing is sin! How great is to that evil of evils, which deserves that all this should be inflicted and suffered for the expiation of it!

The sufferings of Christ for sin give us the true account, and fullest representation of its evil. "The law (saith one) is a bright glass, wherein we may see the evil of sin; but there is the red glass of the sufferings of Christ, and in that we may see more of the evil of sin, than if God should let us down to hell, and there we should see all the tortures and torments of the damned. If we should see them how they lie sweltering under God's wrath there, it were not so much as the beholding of sin through the red glass of the sufferings of Christ."

Suppose the bars of the bottomless pit were broken up; and damned spirits should ascend from thence, and come up among us, with the chains of darkness rattling at their heels, and we should hear the groans, and see the ghastly paleness and trembling of those poor creatures upon whom the righteous God has impressed his fury and indignation, if we could hear how their consciences are lashed by the fearful scourge of guilt, and how they shriek at every lash the arm of justice gives them.

If we should see and hear all this, it is not so much as what we may see in this text, where the Son of God, under his sufferings for it, cries out, I thirst. For, as I shewed you before, Christ's sufferings, in divers respects, were beyond theirs. O then, let not thy vain heart slight sin, as if it were but a small thing! If ever God shew thee the face of sin in this glass, thou wilt say, there is not such another horrid representation to be made to a man in all the world. Fools make a mock at sin, but wise men tremble at it.

Inf. 2. How afflictive and intolerable are inward troubles. Did Christ complain so sadly under them, and cry, I thirst? Surely then they are not such light matters as many are apt to make of them. If they so scorched the very heart of Christ, dried up the green tree, preyed upon his very spirits, and turned his moisture into the drought of summer, they deserve not to be slighted, as they are by some. The Lord Jesus was fitted to bear and suffer as strong troubles as ever befell the nature of man, and he did bear all other troubles with admirable patience; but when it came to this, when the flames of God's wrath scorched his soul, then he cries, I thirst.

David's heart was, for courage, as the heart of a lion; but when God exercised him with inward troubles for sin, then he roars out under the anguish of it, "I am feeble, and sore broken; I have roared, by reason of the disquietness of my heart. My heart panteth, my strength faileth me: As for the light of mine eyes, it is also gone from me," Psal. 38: 8, 10. "A wounded spirit who can bear!" Many have professed that all the torments in the world are but toys to it; the racking fits of the gout, the grinding tortures of the stone, are nothing to the wrath of God upon the conscience. What is the worm that never dies but the efficacy of a guilty conscience? This worm feeds upon, and gnaws the very inwards, the tender and most sensible part of man and is the principal part of hell's horror. In bodily pains, a man may be relieved by proper medicines; here nothing but the blood of sprinkling relieves. In outward pains, the body may be supported by the resolution and courage of the mind; here the mind itself is wounded. O let none despise these troubles, they are dreadful things!

Inf. 3. How dreadful a place is hell, where this cry is heard for ever, I thirst! There the wrath of the great and terrible God flames upon the damned for ever, in which they thirst, and none relieves then. If Christ complained, I thirst, when he had conflicted but a few hours with the wrath of God; what is their state then, that are to grapple with it for ever? When millions of years are past and gone, ten thousand millions more are coming on. There is an everlasting thirst in hell, and it admits of no relief. There are no full cups in hell, but all eternal, unrelieved thirst. Think on this ye that now add drunkenness to thirst, who wallow in all sensual pleasures, and drown nature in an excess of luxury. Remember what Dives said in Luke 16: 24. "And he cried and said, Father Abraham, have mercy on me, and send Lazarus that he may dip the tip of his finger in water, and cool my tongue, for I am tormented in this flame." No cups of water, no bowls of wine in hell. There, that throat will be parched with thirst, which is now drowned with excess. The songs of the drunkard turned into cowlings. If thirst in the extremity of it be now so insufferable, what is that thirst which is infinitely beyond this in measure, and never shall be relieved? Say not it is hard that God should deal thus with his poor creatures. You will not think it so, if you consider what he

The Fountain of Life Opened Up

exposed his own dear Son to, when sin was but imputed to him. And what that man deserves to feel, that has not only merited hell, but, by refusing Christ the remedy, the hottest place in hell.

In this thirst of Christ we have the liveliest emblem of the state of the damned, that ever was presented to men in this world. Here you see a person labouring in extremity, under the infinite wraths of the great and terrible God lying upon his soul and body at once, and causing him to utter this doleful cry, I thirst. Only Christ endured this but a little while, the damned must endure it for ever: in that they differ, as also in the innocence and ability of the persons suffering, and in the end for which they suffer. But, surely, such as this will the cry of those souls be that are cast away for ever. O terrible thirst!

Inf. 4. How much do nice and wanton appetites deserve to be reproved? The Son of God wanted a draught of cold water to relieve him, and could not have it. God has given us variety of refreshing creatures to relieve us, and we despise them. We have better things than a cup of water to refresh and delight us when we are thirsty, and yet are not pleased. O that this complaint of Christ on the cross, I thirst, were but believingly considered, it would make you bless God for what ye now despise, and beget contentment in you for the meanest mercies, and most common favours in this world. Did the Lord of all things cry, I thirst, and had nothing in his extremity to comfort him; and dost thou, who hast a thousand times over forfeited all temporal as well as spiritual mercies, condemn and slight the good creatures of God! What, despise a cup of water, who deserves nothing but a cup of wrath from the hand of the Lord! O lay it to heart, and hence learn contentment with any thing.

Inf. 5. Did Jesus Christ upon the cross cry, I thirst? Then believers shall never thirst eternally. Their thirst shall be certain satisfied.

There is a threefold thirst, gracious, natural, and penal. The gracious thirst is the vehement desire of a spiritual heart after God. Of this David speaks, Psal. 42: 1, 2. "As the hart panteth after the water-brooks, so panteth my soul after thee, O God. My soul thirsteth for God, for the living God, when shall I come and appear before God?" And this is indeed a vehement thirst; it makes the soul break with the longings it has after God, Psal. 119. It is a thirst proper to believers, who have tasted that the Lord is gracious.

Natural thirst is (as before was noted) a desire of refreshment by humid nourishment, and it is common both to believers and unbelievers in this world. God's dear saints have been driven to such extremities in this life, that their tongues have even failed for thirst. "When the poor and needy seek water, and there is none, and their tongue faileth for thirst," Isa. 41: 17. And of the people of God in their captivity, it is said, Lam. 4: 4. "The tongue of the sucking child cleaveth to the roof of his mouth for thirst. The young children ask bread, and no man breaketh it unto them. They that feed delicately are desolate in the streets; they that were brought up in scarlet embrace dung hills." To this many that fear the Lord have been reduced.

A penal thirst, is God's just denying of all refreshments or relief to sinners in their extremities, and that as a due punishment for their sin. This believers shall never feel, because when Christ thirsted upon the cross, he made full satisfaction to God in their room. These sufferings of Christ, as they were ordained for them, so the benefits of them are truly imputed to them. And for the natural thirst, that shall be satisfied: for in heaven we shall live without these necessities and dependencies upon the creature; we shall be equal with the angels in the way and manner of living and subsisting, "isangeloi eisin", Luke 20: 6. And for the gracious thirsting of their souls for God, it shall be fully satisfied. So it is promised, Mat. 5: 6. "Blessed are they which hunger and thirst after righteousness, for they shall be filled:" They shall then depend no more upon the stream, but drink from the overflowing fountain itself, Psal. 36: 8 "They shall be abundantly satisfied with the fatness of thy house, and thou shalt make them drink of the river of thy pleasures: for with thee is the fountain of life, and in Thy light shall we see light:" There they shall drink and praise, and praise and drink for evermore; all their thirsty desires shall be filled with complete satisfaction. O how desirable a state is heaven upon this account! and how should we be restless till we come thither; as the thirsty traveller is until he meet that cool, refreshing spring he wants and seeks for. This present state is a state of thirsting, that to come of refreshment and satisfaction. Some drops indeed come from the fountain by faith, hut they quench not the believer's thirst; rather like water sprinkled on the fire, they make it burn the more: but there the thirsty soul has enough.

O bless God, that Jesus Christ thirsted under the heat of his wrath once, that you might not be scorched with it for ever. If he had not cried, I thirst, you must have cried out of thirst eternally, and never be satisfied.

Inf. 6. Lastly; Did Christ in the extremity of his sufferings cry, I thirst? Then how great, beyond all compare, is the love of God to sinners, who for their sakes exposed the Son of his love to such extreme sufferings?

Three considerations marvellously heighten that love of the Father.

First, His putting the Lord Jesus into such a condition. There is none of us would endure to see a child of our own lie panting, and thirsting in the extremity of torments, for the fairest inheritance on earth; much less to have the soul of a child conflicting with the wrath of God, and making such heart-rending complaints as Christ made upon the cross, if we might have the largest empire in the world for it: yet, such was the strength of the love of God to us, that he willingly gave Jesus Christ to all this misery and torture for us. What shall we call this love? O the height, length, depth, and breadth of that love which passeth knowledge! The love of God to Jesus Christ was infinitely beyond all the love we have for our children, as the sea is more then a spoonful of water: and yet, as dearly as he loved him, he was content to expose him to all this, rather than we should perish eternally.

Secondly, As God the Father was content to expose Christ to this extremity, so in that extremity to hear his bitter cries, and dolorous complaints, and yet not relieve him with the least refreshment till he fainted and died under it. He heard the cries of his Son; that voice, I thirst, pierced heaven, and reached the Father's ear; but yet he will not refresh him in his agonies, nor abate him any thing of the debt he was now paying, and all this for the love he had to poor sinners. Had Christ been relieved in his sufferings, and spared, then God could not have pitied or spared us. The extremity of Christ's suffering was an act of justice to him; and the greatest mercy to us that ever could be manifested. Nor indeed (though Christ so bitterly complains of his thirst) was he willing to be relieved, till he had finished his work. O love unspeakable! He does not complain, that he might be relieved, but to manifest how great that sorrow was which his soul now felt upon our account.

Thirdly, And it should never be forgotten, that Jesus Christ was exposed to these extremities of sorrow for sinners, the greatest of sinners, who deserved not one drop of mercy from God. This commends the love of God singularly to us, in that "whilst we were yet sinners, Christ died for us," Rom. 5: 1. Thus the love of God in Jesus Christ still rises higher and higher in every discovery of it. Admire, adore, and be ravished with the thoughts of this love!

Thanks be to God for this unspeakable gift.

Sermon 35: The sixth excellent Saying of Christ upon the Cross, illustrated

John 19: 30.
When Jesus therefore had received the vinegar, he said, It is finished: and he bowed his head, and gave up the ghost.

It is finished. This is the sixth remarkable world of our Lord Jesus Christ upon the cross, uttered as a triumphant shout when he saw the glorious issue of all his sufferings now at hand.

It is but one word in the original; but in that one word is contained the sum of all joy; the very spirit of all divine consolation. The ancient Greeks reckoned it their excellency to speak much in a little: "to give a sea of matter in a drop of language." What they only sought, is here found. I find some variety, (and indeed variety rather than contrariety), among expositors about the relation of these words. Some are of opinion, that the antecedent is the legal types and ceremonies; and so make this to be the meaning; It is finished: that is, all the types and prefigurations that shadowed forth the redemption of souls, by the blood of Christ, are now fulfilled and accomplished. And, doubtless, as this is itself a truth, so it is such a truth as may not be excluded, as foreign to the true scope and sense of this place. And though it be objected, that many types and prefigurations remained at this time unsatisfied, even all that looked to the actual death at Christ, his continuance in the state of the dead, and his resurrection; yet it is easily removed, "by considering that they are said to be finished, because they were just finishing, or ready to be finished: and it is as if Christ had said, I am now putting the last hand to it", a few moments of time more will complete and finish it. I have the sum now in my hand, which will fully satisfy and pay God the whole debt.

It is now but bow the head, and the work is done, and all the types therein fulfilled. So that this cannot exclude the fulfilling of the types in the death of Christ, from their just claim to the sense of this place. But yet, thought we cannot here exclude this sense, we cannot allow it to be the whole or principal sense: for lo! a far greater truth is contained herein, even the finishing or completing of the whole design and project of our redemption, and therein of all the types that prefigured it. Both these judicious Calvin conjoins, making the completing of redemption the principal; and the fulfilling of all the types the collateral and less principal sense of it.

Yet it must be observed, when we say, Christ finished redemption-work by his death, the meaning is not that his death alone did finish it; for his abode in the grave, resurrection, and ascension, had all of them their joint influence therein; but these being shortly to follow, all are included in the scope of this place. According then to the principal scope of the place, we observe,

Doct. That Jesus Christ has perfected and completely finished the great work of redemption, committed to him by God the Father.

To this great truth the apostle gives a full testimony, Heb. 10: 14 "By one offering he has perfected for ever them that are sanctified." And to the same purpose speaks Christ, John 17: 4. "I have glorified thee on earth! I have finished the work thou gavest me to do." Concerning this work, and the finishing thereof by Jesus Christ upon the cross, we shall enquire what this work was; how Christ finished it; and what evidence can be produced for the finishing of it.

First, What was the work which Christ finished by his death?

It was the fulfilling the whole law of God in our room, and for our redemption, as a sponsor or surety for us. The law is a glorious thing; the holiness of God, that fiery attribute, is engraven or stamped upon every part of it; Deut. 33: 2. "From his right hand went a fiery law." The jealousy of the Lord watched over every point and tittle of it, for his dreadful and glorious name was upon it; it cursed every one that continued noe in all things contained therein, Gal. 3: 10. Two things, therefore, were necessarily required in him that should perfectly fulfil it, and both found in our Surety, and in him only, viz. a subjective and effective perfection.

First, A subjective perfection. He that wanted this, could never say, It is finished. Perfect working always follows a perfect Being. That he might therefore finish this great work of obedience, and therein the glorious design of our redemption; lo! in what shining and perfect holiness was he produced! Luke 1: 35. "That holy thing that shall be born of thee, shall be called the Son of God." And indeed, "such an High-priest became us, who is holy, harmless, undefiled, separate from sinners," Heb. 7:26. So that the law could have no exception against his person; nay, it was never so honoured since its first promulgation, as it was by having such a perfect and excellent person as Christ to stand at its bar, and give it due reparation.

Secondly, There must be also an effective perfection, or a perfection of working and obeying, before it could be said, It is finished. This Christ had; for he continued in all things written in the law, to do them: He fulfilled all righteousness, as it behaved him to do, Mat. 3: 15. He did all that was required to be done, and suffered all that was requisite to be suffered; he did and suffered all that was commanded or threatened, in such perfection of obedience, both active and passive, that the pure eye of divine justice could not find a flaw in it; and so finished the work his Father gave him to do; and this work finished by our Lord Jesus Christ was both a necessary, difficult, and precious work.

First, It was a necessary work which Christ finished upon the cross; necessary, upon a threefold account.

Opus necessarium ex parts Patris; It was necessary on the Father' account: I do not mean that God was under any necessity, from his nature, of redeeming us this or any other way; for our redemption is opus liberi concilii, an act of the free counsel of God; but when God had once decreed and determined to redeem and save poor sinners by Jesus Christ, then it became necessary that the counsel of God should be fulfilled; Acts 4: 28. "To do whatsoever thy hand and counsel had before determined to be done."

Secondly, Ex parte Filii. It was necessary with respect to Christ, upon the account of that precious compact that was betwixt the Father and him about it. Therefore it is said by Christ himself, Luke 22: 22. "Truly the Son of man goes as it was determined," i.e. as it was fore agreed and covenanted; under the necessity of fulfilling his engagement to the Father, he came into the world; and being come, he still minds his engagement, John 9: 3. "I must work the works of him that sent me."

Thirdly, Ex parte nostri. Yea, and it was no less necessary upon our account that this work should be finished; for, had not Christ finished this work, sin had quickly finished all our lives, comforts, and hopes. Without the finishing this work, not a son or daughter of Adam could ever have seen the face of God. Therefore it is said, John 3: 14, 15. "As Moses lifted up the serpent in the wilderness, so [must] the Son of man be lifted up; that whosoever believeth in him should not perish, but have everlasting life." On all these accounts the finishing of this work was necessary.

Secondly, As it was necessary this work should be finished, so the finishing of it was exceeding difficult: It cost many a cry, many groan, and many a tear, before Christ could say, It is finished. All the angels in heaven were not able, by their united strength, to lift that burden one inch from the ground, which Christ bare upon his shoulders, yea, and bare it away. But how heavy a burden this was, may in part appear by his agony in the garden, and the bitter outcries he made upon the cross, which in their proper places have been opened.

Thirdly, and lastly, It was a most precious work which Christ finished by his death; that work was dispatched and finished in few hours, which will be the matter of everlasting songs and triumphs to the angels and saints to all eternity. O it was a precious work! The mercies that now flow out of this fountain, viz. justification, sanctification, adoption, &c. are not to be valued; besides the endless happiness and glory of the world to come, which cannot enter into the heart of man to conceive. If the angels sang when the foundation-stone was laid, what shouts, what triumphs shall there be among the saints, when this voice is heard, It is finished!

Secondly, Let us next inform ourselves how, and in what manner Jesus Christ finished this glorious work; and if you search the scriptures upon that account, you will find that he finished it obediently, freely, diligently, and fully.

First, This blessed work was finished by Jesus Christ most obediently, Phil. 2: 8. "He became obedient to death, even the death of the cross." "His obedience was the obedience of a servant, though not servile obedience." So it was foretold of him, before he touched this work, Isa. 1. 5. "The Lord God has opened mine ear, and I was not rebellious, neither turned away back;" i.e. My Father told me the very worst of it; he told me what hard and heavy things I must undergo, if ever I finished this design of redemption; and I was not rebellious, i.e. I heartily submitted to, and accepted all those difficulties; for there is a Meiosis in the words; I was content to stoop to the hardest and most ignominious part of it, rather than not finish it.

Secondly, As Christ finished it obediently, so he finished it freely. Freedom and obedience in acting are not at all opposite to, or exclusive of each other. Moses' mother nursed him in obedience to the command of Pharaoh's daughter, yet most freely with respect to her own delight and contentment in that work. So it is said of Christ, and that by his own mouth, John 10: 17, 18. "Therefore does my Father love me, because I lay down my life, that I might take it again. No man taketh it from me, but I lay it down of myself: I have power to lay it down, and I have power to take

The Fountain of Life Opened Up

it up again. This commandment have I received of my Father." He liked the work for the end's sake. When he had a prospect of it from eternity, then were his delights with the sons of men: then he rejoiced in the habitable parts of the earth, Prov. 8: 30, 31. And when he came into the world about it, with what a full and free consent did his heart echo to the voice of his Father calling him to it; just as you shall sometimes hear an echo answering your voice two or three times over, Psal. 40. "Lo, I come: I delight to do thy will: thy law is within my heart." He finished the work freely.

Thirdly, As he finished it freely, so he finished it diligently; he wrought hard from the morning of his life to the end of it: he was never idle wherever he was, but "went about doing good," Acts 10: 38. Sometimes he was so intent upon his work, that "he forget to eat bread," John 4: 30, 31. As the life of some men is but a diversion from one trifle to another, from one pleasure to another; so the whole life of Christ was spent and taken up betwixt one work and another: never was a life so filled up with labour: the very moments of his time were all employed for God to finish this work.

Fourthly, and lastly, He finished it completely and fully. All that was to be done by way of impetration and meritorious redemption is fully done; no hand can come after his; angels can add nothing to it. "That is perfected to which nothing is wanting, and to which nothing can be added." Such is the work Christ finished. Whatever the law demanded is perfectly paid; whatever a sinner needs, is perfectly obtained and purchased; nothing can be added to what Christ has done; he put the last hand to it, when he said, It is finished. Thus you see what the work was, and how Christ finished it.

Thirdly, In the last place, let us consider what assurance or evidence we have that Christ has so finished redemption-work: and if you pursue that enquiry, you will find these, among other plain evidences of it.

First, When Christ died, redemption-work must needs be finished, inasmuch as the blood, as well as the obedience of Christ, was of infinite value and efficacy, sufficiently able to accomplish all the ends for which it was shed; "and that not by divine acceptation, but upon the account of its proper value." This effect, viz. the finishing redemption-work meritoriously by Christ, does not exceed the power of the cause to which we assign it, viz. the death of Christ. And if there be a sole sufficient cause in act, what hinders but the effect should follow? There was certainly enough in Christ's blood to satisfy the utmost demand of justice: when that therefore is actually shed, justice is fully paid, and, consequently, the souls for whom, and in whose names it is paid, are fully redeemed from the curse by the merit thereof.

Secondly, It is apparent that Christ finished the work, by the discharge or acquittance God the Father gave him, when he raised him from the dead, and set him at his own right hand. If Christ, the sinner's surety, be, as such, discharged by God the creditor, then the debt is fully paid. Now Christ was justified, and cleared at his resurrection, from all charges and demands of justice; therefore it ix said, 1 Tim. 3:16 that he was justified in the spirit, i.e. openly discharged by that very act of the Godhead, his raising him from the dead. For when the grave was opened, and Christ arose, it was to him as the opening of the prison-doors, and setting a surety at liberty, who was confirmed for another man's debt. To the same sense Christ speaks of his ascension, John 16: 10. "The Spirit (saith he) shall convince the world of righteousness," i.e. of a complete and perfect righteousness in me, imputable to sinners for their perfect justification. And whereby shall he convince and satisfy them that is so? Why, by this, "Because I go to the Father, and ye see me no more." There is a great deal of force and weight in those words, "because ye see me no more:" for it amounts to this much; by this you shall be satisfied I have fully and completely performed all righteousness, and that, by my active and passive obedience; I have so fully satisfied God for you, as that you shall never be charged or condemned; because, when I go to heaven, I shall abide there in glory with nay Father, and not be sent back again, as I should, if any thing had been omitted by me. And this the apostle gives you also in so many plain words, Heb. 10: 12, 13, 14. "After he had offered one sacrifice for sins, for ever sat down on the right hand of God." And what does he infer from that, but the very truth before us, verse 14 that "by one offering he hath perfected for ever them that are sanctified?"

Thirdly, It is evident Christ has finished the work, by the blessed effects of it upon all that believe in him: for by virtue of the completeness of Christ's work, finished by his death, their consciences are now rationally pacified, and their souls at death, actually received into glory; neither of which could be, if Christ had not in this world finished the work. If Christ had done his work imperfectly, he could not have given rest and tranquillity to the labouring and burdened souls that come to him, as now he does, Mat. 11: 28. Conscience would still be hesitating, trembling, and unsatisfied, and had he not finished his work, he could not have had entrance through the vail of his flesh into heaven, as all that believe in him have, Heb. 10: 19, 20. If he had but almost done that work, we had been but almost saved, that is, certainly damned. And thus you see briefly the evidences, that the work is finished.

Inf. 1. Has Christ perfected and completely finished all his work for us? How sweet a relief is this to us that believe in him against all the defects and imperfections of all the works of God, that are wrought by us. There is nothing, finished that we do: all our duties are imperfect duties; they come off lamely, and defectively from our hands. It is Christ's charge against the church of Sardis, Rev. 3: 2. I have not found thy works "pepleromena" perfect, or filled up before God. O there is much impudence and vanity in the best of our duties: but here is the grand relief, and that which answers to all the grounds of our doubts and fears upon that account; Jesus Christ has finished all his work, though we can finish none of ours: and so, though we be defective, poor, imperfect creatures, in ourselves, yet, notwithstanding, we are complete in him, Col. 2: 9, 10. Though we cannot perfectly obey, or fulfil one command of the law, yet is "the righteousness of the law fulfilled in us that believe," Rom. 8: 4. Christ's complete obedience being imputed to us, makes us complete, and without fault before God.

It is true, we ought to be humbled for our defects, and troubled for every failing in obedience; but we should not be discouraged, though multitudes of weaknesses be upon us, and many infirmities compass us about, in every duty we put our hand to: though we have no righteousness of our own; yet of God, Christ is made unto us righteousness; and that righteousness of his is infinitely better than our own: instead of our own, we have his. O blessed be God for Christ's perfect righteousness!

Inf. 2. Did Christ finish his work with his own hand? How dangerous and dishonourable a thing is it to join any thing of our own to the righteousness of Christ, in point of justification before God. Jesus Christ will never endure this; it reflects upon his work dishonourably; he does not (in this case) affect social glory: not I, and my God; I, and my Christ, did this; he will be all, or none, in your justification. If he have finished the work, what need of our additions? And if not, to what purpose are they? Can we finish that which Christ himself could not? But we would fain be sharing with him in this honour, which he will never endure. Did he finish the work by himself, and will he ever divide the glory and praise of it with us? No, no, Christ is no half Saviour. O it is an hard thing, to bring these shroud hearts to live upon Christ for righteousness: we would fain add our penny to make up Christ's sum. But if you would have it so, or have nothing to do with Christ, you and your penny must perish together, Isa. 50 ult. God gives us the righteousness of Christ, as he gave manna to the Israelites in the wilderness. It is said, Deut. 8: 16. "That he fed them with manna in the wilderness, that he might humble them." The quality of the food was not humbling, for it was angels fools, but the manner of giving it was so: they must live by faith upon God for it, from day to day. This was not like other food, produced by their own labour. Certainly God takes the right way to humble proud nature, in calling sinners wholly from their own righteousness to Christ's for their justification.

Inf. 3 .Did Christ finish his work for us: Then there can be no doubt, but he will also finish his work "in" us. As he began the work of our redemptions, and finished it: so he that has begun the good work in you, will also finish it upon your souls. And at this the apostle saith, "He is confident," Phil. 1: 6. Jesus Christ is not only called the author, but also the finisher of our faith, Heb. 12: 2. If he begin it, no doubt but he will finish it. And indeed the finishing of his own work of redemption without us, gives full evidence that he will finish his work of sanctification within us; and that because these two works of Christ have a respect and relation to each other; and such a relation, that the work he finished by his own death, resurrection, and ascension, would be in vain to us, if the work of sanctification in us should not in like manner be finished. Therefore, as he presented a perfect sacrifice to God, and finished redemption-work; so will he present every man perfect and complete, for whom he offered up himself, for he will not lose the end of all his sufferings at last. To what purpose would his meritorious impetration be, without complete and full application? Be not therefore discouraged at the defects and imperfections of your inherent grace: be humbled for them, but be not dejected by them: this is Christ's work, as well as that: that work is finished, and so will this.

Inf. 4. Is Christ's work of redemption a complete and finished work? How excellent and comfortable beyond all compare, is the method and way of faith! Surely the way of believing is the most excellent way in which a poor sinner can approach God, for it brings before him a complete, entire, perfect righteousness; and this must needs be most honourable to God, most comfortable to the soul that draws nigh to God. O what a complete, finished perfect thing is the righteousness of Christ! the searching eye of the holy and jealous God cannot find the least flaw or defect in it. Let God or conscience look upon it; turn it every way; view it on every side; thoroughly weigh and examine it, it will appear a pure, a perfect piece, containing in it whatsoever is necessary for the reconciling of an angry God, or pacifying of a distressed and perplexed soul. How pleasing, therefore, and acceptable to God must be that faith, which presents so complete and excellent an atonement to him! Hence the acting of our faith upon Christ for righteousness, the approaches of faith to God with such an acceptable present, is called the work of God; that is, the most grateful, acceptable, and well pleasing work to God that a creature can perform; John 6: 29. "This is the work of God, that ye believe." One act of faith pleases him more, than if you should toil all your lives at a task of obedience to the law. As it is more for God's honour and thy comfort, to pay all thou owest him at one payment, in one full sum, than to be paying by very small degrees, and never be able to make full payment, or see the bond cancelled; so this perfect work only produces perfect peace.

Inf. 5. Did Christ work, and work out all that God gave him to do, till he had finished his work? How necessary then is a laborious working life to all that call themselves Christians? The life of Christ, you sees, was a laborious life. Shall he work and we play? Shall a zealous, active, working Christ be reproached with idle, negligent and lazy followers? O work, and work out your own salvation with fear and trembling, Phil. 2: 12.

Object. But if Christ wrought so hard, we may sit still. If he finished the work, nothing remains for us to do.

Solut. Nothing of that work which Christ did, remains for you to do. It is your commendation and duty to leave all that to Christ: but there is other work for you to do; yea, store of work lying upon your hands. You must work as well as Christ, though not for the same ends Christ did. He wrought hard to satisfy the law, by fulfilling all righteousness. He wrought all his life long, to work out a righteousness to justify you before God. This work falls to no hand but Christ's: but you must work, to obey the commands of Christ into whose right ye are come by redemption: you must work to testify your thankfulness to Christ, for the work finished for you: you must work, to glorify God by your obedience: let your light so shine before men. For these, and divers other such ends and reasons, your life must be a working life. God preserve all his people from the gross and vile opinions of Antinomian libertines, who cry up grace and decry obedience: who under specious pretences of exalting a naked Christ upon the throne, do indeed strip him naked of a great part of his glory, and vilely dethrone him. My pen shall not English what mine eyes have read. Tell it not in Gath.

But for thee, reader, be thou a follower of Christ, imitate thy pattern; yea, let me persuade thee, as ever thou hopest to clear up thine interest in him, imitate him in such particulars as these that follow.

First, Christ began early to work for God; he took the morning of his life, even the very beginning of it, to work for God: "How is it (said he to his parents, when he was but a child of about twelve years old) that ye sought me? Wist ye not that I must be about my Father's business?" Reader, if the morning of thy life be not gone, O devote it to the work of God as Christ did: if it be, ply thy work the closer in the afternoon of thy life. If a man have any great and necessary business to do, it is good doing it in the morning; afterwards a hurry of business and diversion comes on.

Secondly, As Christ began betime, so he followed his work close: he was early up, and he wrought hard, so hard, that "he forget to eat bread." John 4: 31, 32. So zealous was he in his Father's work, that his friends thought "that he had been beside himself," Mark 3: 21. So zealous that "the zeal of God's house eat him up." He flew like a seraphim, in a flame of zeal, about the work of God. O be not ye like snails. What Augustus said of the young Roman, well becomes the true Christian, "whatsoever he does, he does it to purpose."

Thirdly, Christ often thought upon the shortness of his time, and wrought hard because he knew his working-time would be but little. So you find it, John 9: 4. "I must work the works of him that sent me, whilst it is day; the night comes, when no man can work." O in this be like Christ: rouse your hearts to diligence with this consideration. If a man have much to write, and be almost come to the end of his paper, he will write close, and thereby put much matter in a little room.

Fourthly, He did much work for God in a very silent manner: he wrought hard, but did not spoil his work, when he had wrought it, by vain ostentation. When he had expressed his charity in his acts of mercy and bounty to men, he would humbly seal up the glory of it, with this charge; "see ye tell no man of it", Matt. 8: 4. He affected no popular air. All the angels in heaven could not do what Christ did, and yet he called himself a worm, for all that, Psal. 22: 6. O imitate your pattern; Work hard for God, and let not pride blow upon it, when you have done. It is hard for a man to do much, and not value him self for it too much.

Fifthly, Christ carried on his work for God resolvedly: no discouragements would beat him off, though never any work met with more from first to last. How did Scribes and Pharisees, Jews, Gentiles, yea, devils set upon him, by persecutions, and reproaches, violent oppositions, and subtle temptations; but yet, he goes on with his Father's work for all that: he is deaf to all discouragements. So it was foretold of him, Isa. 42: 4. "He shall not fail, nor be discouraged." O that more of this spirit of Christ were in his people: O that, in the strength of love to Christ, and zeal for the glory of God, you will pour out your hearts in service, and, like a river, sweep down all discouragements before you.

Sixthly, He continued working, whilst he continued living: His life and labour ended together: He fainted not in his work: Nay, the greatest work he did in this world, was his last work. O be like Christ in this, be not weary of well doing: Give not over the work of God, while you can move hand and tongue to promote it, and see that your last works be more than your first. O let the motions of your soul after God be, as all natural motions are, swiftest when nearest the centre. Say not it is enough, whilst there is any capacity of doing more for God. In these things, Christians, be like your Saviour.

Inf. 6. Did Christ finish his work? Look to it Christian, that ye also finish your work which God has given your to do: That you may with comfort say, when death approaches, as Christ said, John 17: 4. "I have glorified thee on earth, I have finished the work thou gavest me to do; and now, O Father, glorify thou me with thine own self." Christ had a work committed to Him, and he finished it; you have a work also committed to you: O see that you may be able to say, it is finished when your time is so: O work out your own salvation with fear and trembling; and, that I may persuade you to it, I beseech you lay these considerations close to heart.

First, If your work be not done before you die, it can never be done when you are dead. "There is no work nor knowledge, nor device in the grave, whither thou goest," Eccl. 9: 5, 10. They that go down to the pit cannot celebrate the name of God, Isa 38: 18. Death binds up the hand from working, any more; strikes dumb the tongue that it can speak no more; for then the composition is dissolved. The body, which is the soul's instrument to work by, is broken and thrown aside: the soul itself presented immediately before the Lord, to give an account of all its works. O therefore, seeing the night comes, when no man can work, as Christ speaks, John 9: 4. make haste and finish your work.

Secondly, If you finish not your work, as the season of working, so the season of mercy will be over at death. Do not think, you that have neglected Christ all your lives, you that could never be persuaded to a laborious holy life, that ever your cries and entreaties shall prevail with God for mercy, when your season is past: No, it is too late, "Will God hear his cry, when troubles come upon him?" Job 27: 9. The season of mercy is then over; as the tree falls, so it lies: Then he that is holy shall be holy still, and he that is filthy shall be filthy still. Alas, poor souls, you come too late: "The master of the house is risen up, and the doors are shut," Luke 19: 42. The season is over: happy had it been if ye had known the day of your visitation.

Lastly, If your work be not finished when you come to die, you can never finish your lives with comfort. He that has not fished his stork with care, can never finish his course with joy. O what a dismal case is that soul in, that finds itself surprised by death in an unready posture! To lie shivering upon the brink of the grave, saying, Lord, what will become of me! O I cannot, I dare not die! For the poor soul to shrink back into the body, and cry, Oh, it were better for me to do any thing than die. Why, what is the matter? Oh, I am in a Christless state and dare not go before that awful judgement-seat. If I had in season made Christ sure, I could then die with peace. Lord, what shall I do? How dost thou like this, reader? Will this be a comfortable close! When one asked a Christian that constantly spent six hours every day in prayer, why he did so? He answered, Oh, I must die, I must die. Well then, look to it that you finish your work as Christ also did his.

Sermon 36: The seventh and last Word with which Christ breathed out his Soul, illustrated

Luke 23: 46.
And when Jesus had cried with a loud voice, he said, Father, into thy hands I commend any spirit; and having said thus, he gave up the ghost.

These are the last of the last words of our Lord Jesus Christ upon the cross, with which he breathed out his soul. They were David's words before him, Psal. 31: 5. and for substance, Stephen's after him, Acts 7: 27. They are words full, both of faith and comfort; fit to be the last breathing of every gracious soul in this world. They are resolved into these five particulars:

First, The person depositing, or committing: The Lord Jesus Christ, who in this, as well as in other things, acted as a common person, as the head of the church. This must be remarked carefully, for therein lies no small part of a believer's consolation: When Christ commends his soul to God, he does as it were bind up all the souls of the elect in one bundle with it, and solemnly presents them all with his, to his Father's acceptance: To this purpose one aptly renders it.

"This commendation made by Christ, turns to the singular profit and advantage of our souls; inasmuch as Christ, by this very prayer, has delivered them into his Father's hand, as a precious treasure, whenever the time comes that they are to be loosed from the bodies which they now inhabit." Jesus Christ neither lived nor died for himself, but for believers; what he did in this very act, refers to them as well as to his own soul: You must look therefore upon Christ, in it is last and solemn act of his life, as gathering all the souls of the elect together, and making a solemn tender of them all, with his own soul to God.

Secondly, The depository, or person to whom he commits this precious treasure, and that was to his own Father: "Father, into thy hands I commend my spirit." Father is a sweet encouraging, assuring title: Well may a son commit any concernment, how dear soever, into the hands of a father, especially such a son into the hands of such a father. "By the hands of the Father into which he commits his soul, we are not to understand the naked or mere power, but the fatherly acceptation and protection of God."

Thirdly, The depositum, or thing committed into this hand, [my spirit] i.e. my soul, now instantly departing, upon the very point of separation from my body. The soul is the most precious of all treasures, it is called the darling, Psal. 35: 17. or, "the only ones," i.e. that which is most excellent, and therefore most dear and precious: A whole world is but a trifle, if weighed, for the price of one soul, Mat. 16: 26. This inestimable treasure he now commits into his Father's hands.

Fourthly, The Act by which he puts it into that faithful hand of the Father, "parathesomai", I commend. We rightly render it in the present tense, though the word be future: For, with these words he breathed out his soul. This word is of the same import with "sunhiemi" I present, or tender it into thy hands; It was in Christ an act of Faith, a most special and excellent act intended as a precedent for all his people.

Fifthly, and Lastly, The last thing observable is, the manner in which he uttered these words, and that was with a loud voice; he spake it that all might hear it, and that his enemies, who judged him now destitute and forsaken of God, might be convinced that he was not so, but that he was dear to his Father still, and could put his soul confidently into his hands: "Father, into thy hands I commend my spirit." Talking then these words, not only as spoken by Christ, the head of all believers, and so commending their souls to God with his own, but also as a pattern, teaching them what they ought to do themselves, when they come to die. We observe,

Doct. That dying believers are both warranted, and encouraged, by Christ's example, believingly to commend their precious souls into the hands of God.

Thus the apostle directs the faith of Christians, to commit their souls to God's tuition and fatherly protection, when they are either going into prisons, or to the stake for Christ, 1 Pet. 4: 9. "Let them (saith he) that suffer according to the will of God, commit the keeping of their souls to him in well doing, as unto a faithful Creator."

This proposition we will consider in these two main branches of it, viz. what is implied and carried in the soul's commending itself to God by faith, when the time of separation is come. And what warrant or encouragement gracious souls have for so doing.

First, What is implied in this act of a believer, his commending or committing, his soul into the hands of God at death?

And if it be thoroughly weighed, you will find these six things, at least, carried in it.

First, It implies this evidently in it, That the soul outlives the body, and fails not, as to its being, when its body fails; it feels the house in which it dwelt, dropping into ruins, and looks out for a new habitation with God. "Father, into thy hands I commend my spirit." The soul understands itself a more noble being than that corruptible body, to which it was united, and is now to leave in the dust: it understands its relation to the Father of spirits, and from him it expects protection and provision in its unbodied state; and therefore into his hands it puts itself. If it vanished, or breathed into air, and did not survive the body, if it were annihilated at death, it were but a mocking of God to say, when we die, "Father, into thy hands I commend my spirit."

Secondly, It implies the soul's true rest to be in God. See which way its motions and tendencies are, not only in life, but in death also. It bends to its God: It reposes, it even puts itself upon its God and Father; "Father, into thy hands." God is the centre of all gracious spirits. While they tabernacle here, they have no rest but in the bosom of their God: when they go hence, their expectation and earnest desires are to be with him. It had been working after God by gracious desires before, it had cast many a longing look heaven-ward before; but when the gracious soul comes near its God (as it does in a dying hour) "then it even throws itself into his arms;" as a river, that after many turnings and windings, at last is arrived to the ocean; it pours itself with a central force into the bosom of the ocean, and there finishes its weary course. "Nothing but God can please it in this world, and nothing but God can give it content when it goes hence." It is not the amenity of the place, whither the gracious soul is going, but the bosom of the blessed God, who dwells there, that it so vehemently pants after; not the Father's house, but the Father's arms and bosom: "Father, into thy hands I commend my spirit: Whom have I in heaven but thee? And on earth there is none that I desire in comparison of thee, Psal. 73: 24,25.

Thirdly, It also implies the great value believers have for their souls. That is the precious treasure; and their main solicitude and chief care, is to see it secured in a safe hand: "Father, into thy hands I commit my spirit:" They are words speaking the believer's care for his soul, that it may be safe, whatever becomes of the vile body. A believer when he comes nigh to death, spends but few thoughts about his body, where it shall be laid, or how it shall be disposed of: He trusts that in the hands of friends; but as his great care all along was for his soul, so he expresses it in these his very last breathing, in which he commends it into the hands of God: It is not, Lord Jesus receive my body, take care of my dust, but receive my Spirit: Lord, secure the jewel, when the casket is broken.

Fourthly, These words imply the deep sense that dying believers have of the great change that is coming upon them by death; when all visible and sensible things are shrinking away from them, and failing. They feel the world and the best comforts of it failing: Every creature and creature comfort failing: For, at death we are said to fail, Luke 16: 9. Hereupon the soul clasps the closer about its God, cleaves more close than ever to him: "Father, into thy hands I commend my spirit." Not that a mere necessity puts the soul upon God; or that it cleaves to God, because it has then nothing else to take hold on: No, it chose God for its portion, when it was in the midst of all its outward enjoyments, and had as good security as other men have for the long enjoyment of them: but my meaning is, that although gracious souls have chosen God for their portion, and do truly prefer him to the best of their comforts; yet in this compounded state, it lives not wholly upon its God, but partly by faith, and partly by sense; partly upon things seen, and partly upon things not seen. The creatures had some interest in their hearts; alas, too much: but now all these are vanishing, and it sees they are so. I shall see man no more, with the inhabitants of the world, (said sick Hezekiah;) hereupon it turns itself from them all, and casts itself upon God for all its subsistence, expecting now to live upon its God entirely, as the blessed angels do; and so, in faith, they throw themselves into his arms: "Father, into thy hands I commend my spirit."

Fifthly, It implies the atonement of God, and his full reconciliation to believers, by the blood of the great Sacrifice; else they durst never commit their souls into his hands: "For it is a fearful thing to fall into the hands of the living God," Heb. 12: 29. i.e. of an absolute God, a God unatoned by the offering up of Christ. The soul dare no more cast itself into the hand of God, without such an atoning sacrifice, than it dares approach to a consuming fire; And, indeed, the reconciliation of God by Jesus Christ, as it is the ground of all our acceptance with God; for we are made accepted in the beloved: So it is plainly carried in the order or manner of the reconciled soul, committing itself to him: For, it first casts itself into the hands of Christ, then into the hands of God by him. So Stephen, when dying, "Lord Jesus receive my spirit:" And by that hand it would be put into his Father's hands.

Sixthly, and lastly, It implies both the efficacy and excellency of faith, in supporting and relieving the soul at a time when nothing else is able to do it; Faith is its conductor, when it is at the greatest loss and distress that ever it met with: it secures the soul when it is turned out of the body; when heart and flesh fail, this leads it to the rock that fails not: it sticks by that soul till it sees it safe through all the territories of Satan, and safe landed upon the shore of glory; and then is swallowed up in vision: many a favour it has shown the soul while it dwelt in its body. The great service it did for the soul was in the time of its espousals to Christ. This is the marriage knot, the blessed bond of union between the soul and Christ. Many a relieving sight, secret and sweet support it has received from its faith since that; but, surely, its first and last works are its most glorious works. By faith it first ventured itself upon Christ; threw itself upon him in the deepest sense of its vileness and utter unworthiness, when sense, reason, and multitudes of temptations stood by, contradicting and discouraging the soul: by faith it now casts itself into his arms, when it is launching out into vast eternity.

They are both noble acts of faith; but the first no doubt, is the greatest and most difficult: for, when once the soul is interested in Christ, it is no such difficulty to commit itself into his hands, as when it has no interest at all in him. It is easier for a child to cast himself in the arms of his own father, in distress, than for one that has been both a stranger and an enemy to Christ, to cast itself upon him, that he may be a father and a friend to it.

And this brings us upon the second enquiry I promised to satisfy, viz.

Secondly, What warrant or encouragement have gracious souls to commit themselves at death into the hands of God? I answer, Much every way; all things encourage and warrant its so doing: For,

First, This God, to whom the believer commits himself at death, is its Creator: the Father of its being; he created and inspired it, and so it has the relation of a creature to a Creator: yea, of a creature now in distress, to a faithful Creator, 1 Pet. 4: 19. "Let them that suffer according to the will of God, commit the keeping of their souls to him in well doing; as to a [faithful Creator]." It is very true, this single relation, in itself, gives little ground of encouragement, unless the creature had conserved that integrity in which it was originally created. And they that have no more to plead with God for acceptance, by their relation to him as creatures to a Creator, will doubtless find that word made good to their little comfort, Isa. 27: 11. "It is a people of no understanding, therefore he that made them, will not have mercy on them; and he that formed them, will show them no favour." But now, grace brings that relation into repute: holiness ingratiates us again, and revives the remembrance of this relation; so that believers only can plead this.

Secondly, As the gracious soul is his creature, so it is his redeemed creature; one that he has bought, and that with a great price, even with the precious blood of Jesus Christ, 1 Pet. 1: 18. This greatly encourages the departing soul, to commit itself into the hands of God; so you find, Psal. 31: 5. "Into thy hands do I commend my spirit, thou hast redeemed it, O Lord God of truth." Surely this is mighty encouragement, to put itself upon God in a dying hour. Lord, I am not only thy creature, but thy redeemed creature; one that thou hast bought with a great price: O, I have cost thee dear! for my sake Christ came from thy bosom, and is it imaginable, that after that thou hast in such a costly way, even by the expense of the precious blood of Christ, redeemed me, thou shouldst at last exclude me? Shall the ends both of creation and redemption of this soul be lost together? will God form such an excellent creature as my soul is, in which are so many wonders of the wisdom and power of its Creator? will he be content, when sin has marred the frame, and defaced the glory of it, to recover it to him self again, by the death of his own dear Son, and after all this, cast it away, as if there were nothing in all this? "Father, into thy hands I commend my spirit:" I know thou wilt have a respect to the work of thy hands; especially to a redeemed creature, upon which thou best expended so great sums of love, which thou hast bought at so dear a rate.

Thirdly, Nay, that is not all; the gracious soul may confidently and securely commit itself into the hands of God, when it parts with its body at death; not only because it is his creature, his redeemed creature, but because it is his renewed creature also: and this lays a firm ground for the believer's confidence and acceptance; not that it is the proper cause, or reason of its acceptance, but as it is the soul's best evidence, that it is accepted with God, and shall not be refused by him, when it comes to him at death: for, in such a soul, there is a double workmanship of God, both glorious pieces, though the last exceeds in glory. A natural workmanship, in the excellent frame of that noble creature, the soul; and a gracious workmanship upon that again; a new creation upon the old; glory upon glory. "We are his workmanship, created in Christ Jesus," Eph. 2: 10. The Holy Ghost came down from heaven on purpose to create this new workmanship; to frame this new creature; and indeed, it is the top and glory of all God's works of wonders in this world; and must needs give the believer encouragement to commit itself to God, whether at such a time, it shall reflect either upon the end of the work, or upon the end of the workman; both which meet in the salvation of the soul so wrought upon, the end of the neck is our glory. By this "we are made meet to be partakers of the inheritance of the saints in light," Col. 1: 12. It is also the design and end of him that wrought it, 2 Cor. 5: 5. "Now he that has wrought us for the self same thing, is God." Had he not designed thy soul for glory, the Spirit should never have come upon such a sanctifying design as this: surely it shall not fail of a reception into glory, when it is cast out of this tabernacle: such a work was not wrought in vain, neither can it ever perish: when once sanctification comes upon a soul, it so roots itself in the soul, that where the soul goes, it goes; gifts indeed, they die: all natural excellency and beauty, that goes away at death, Job 4 ult. but grace ascends with the soul; it is a sanctified, when a separate sent. And can God shut the door of glory upon such a soul, that by trace is made meet for the inheritance? O, it cannot be!

Fourthly, As the gracious soul is a renewed soul, so it is also a sealed soul; God has sealed it in this world for that glory, into which it is now to enter at death. All gracious souls are sealed objectively, i.e. they have those works of grace wrought on their souls which do, (as but now was said,) ascertain and evidence their title to glory; and in many are sealed formally; that is, the Spirit helps them clearly to discern their interest in Christ, and all the promises. This both secures heaven to the soul in itself, and becomes also an earnest or pledge of that glory in the unspeakable joys and comforts that it produces in the soul: So you find, 2 Cor. 1: 22. "Who has sealed us, and given us the earnest of the Spirit in our hearts." God's sealing, us gives his security; his objective seal makes it sure in itself, its formal seal makes it so to us. but, if over and above all this, he will please, as a fruit of that his sealing, to give us those heavenly inexpressible joys and comforts which are the fruit of his formal sealing-work, to be an earnest, a foretaste and hansel of that glory, how can the soul that has found all this, fear in the least at a rejection by its God, when at death it comes to him? Surely, if God have sealed, he will not refuse you; if he have given his earnest, he will not shut you out; God's earnest is not given in jest.

Fifthly, Moreover, every gracious soul may confidently cast itself into the arms of its God, when it goes hence, with "Father, into thy hands I commit my spirit." Forasmuch as every gracious soul; is a soul in covenant with God; and God stands obliged by his covenant and promise to such, not to cast them out, when they come unto him. As soon as ever thou became his, by regeneration, that promise became thine, Heb. 13: 5. "I will never leave you, nor forsake you." And will he leave the soul at a time when it never had more need of a God to stand by it, than it has then? Every gracious soul is entitled to that promise, John 14: 3. "I will come again, and receive you to myself." And will he fail to make it good when the time of the promise is come, as at death it is? It cannot be. multitudes of promises; the whole covenant of promises, give security to the soul against the fears of rejections, or neglect by God. And the soul's dependence upon God and his promise; its very casting itself upon him, from the encouragement the word gives it, add to the engagement upon God. When he sees a poor soul that he has made, redeemed, sanctified sealed, and by solemn promise engaged himself to receive, coming to him at death, firmly depending upon his faithfulness that has promised, saying, as David, 2 Sam. 23: 5, Though Lord, there be many defects in me, yet thou hast made a covenant with me, well ordered in all things, and sure; and this is all my salvation, and all my hope." Lord, I am resolved to send out my soul in an act of faith; I will venture it upon the credit of thy promise. How can God refuse such a soul? How can he put it off, when it so puts itself upon him?

Sixthly, But this is not all; the gracious soul sustains many intimate and dear relations to that God into whose hands it commends itself at death. It is his spouse, and the consideration of such a day of espousals, may well encourage it to cast itself into the bosom of Christ, its head and husband: it is a member of his body, flesh and bones, Eph. 5: 30. It is his child, and he its everlasting Father, Isa. 9: 6. It is his friend. "Henceforth (saith Christ,) I call you not servants, but friends," John 15: 15. What confidence may these, and all other the dear relations Christ owns to the renewed soul, beget, in such an hour as this is! that husband can throw off the dear wife of his bosom; Who in distresses casts herself into his arms! What father can shut the door upon a dear child that comes to him for refuge, saying, Father, into thy hands I commit myself!

Seventhly, and lastly, The unchangeableness of God's love to his people, gives confidence they shall in no wise be cast out. They know Christ was the same to them at last as he was at first: the same in the pangs of death, as he was in the comforts of life: having loved his own which were in the world, he loved them to the end, John 13: 1. He does not love as the world loves, only in prosperity; but they are as dear to him when their beauty and strength are gone, as when they were in the greatest flourishing. If we live, we live to the Lord; and if we die, we die to the Lord; so then, whether we live or die, we are the Lord's, Rom. 14: 8. Take in all these things, and weigh them both apart, and together, and see whether they amount not to a full evidence of the truth of this point, that dying believers are both warranted and encouraged to commend their souls into the lands of God; whether they have not every one of them cause to say as the apostle did, 2 Tim. 1: 12 "I know whom I have believed, and am persuaded that he is able to keep that which I have committed to him against that day." The improvements of all this you have in the following practical deductions.

Deduction I. Are dying believers only warranted and encouraged thus to commend their souls into the hands of God? What a sad strait then must all dying unbelievers be in about their souls? Such souls will fall into the hands of God, but that is their misery, not their privilege: they are not put by faith into the hands of mercy, but fall by sin into the hands of justice: not God, but the devil is their father, John 8: 4. Whither should the child go but to its own father? They have not one of those aforementioned encouragements to cast themselves into the hands of God, except the naked relation they have to God as their Creator, and that is as good as none, without the new creation. If they have nothing but this to plead for their salvation, the devil has as much to plead as they. It is the new creature that brings the first creation into repute again with God.

O dismal! O deplorable case! A poor soul is turning out of house and home, and knows not where to go; it departs, and immediately falls into the hands of justice. The devil stands by, waiting for such a soul (as a dog for a crust) whom God will throw to him. Little! ah little, do the friends of such a one think, whilst they are honouring his dust by a splendid and honourable funeral, what a case that poor soul is in that lately dwelt there; and what fearful straits and extremities it is now exposed to! He may cry, indeed, Lord! Lord! open to me, as in Mat. 7: 22. But to how little purpose are these vain cries! Will God hear him when he cries? Job 27: 9. It is a lamentable case!

Deduction 2. Will God graciously accept, and faithfully keep what the saints commit to him at death? How careful then should they be to keep what God commits to them, to be kept for him while they live? You have a great trust to commit to God when you die, and God has a great trust to commit to you whilst you live: you expect that he should faithfully keep what then you shall commit to his keeping, and he expects you should faithfully keep what he now commits to your keeping. O keep what God commits to you, as you expect he should keep your souls when you commit them unto him. If you keep his truths, he will keep your souls. "Because thou hast kept the word of my patience, I also will keep thee, &c." Rev. 3: 10. Be faithful to your God, and you shall find him faithful to you. None can pluck you out of his hand; see that nothing wrest his truths out of your hands. "If we deny him, he also will deny us," 2 Tim. 2: 12. Take heed lest those estates you have gotten as a blessing, attending the gospel, prove a temptation to you to betray the gospel. "Religion (saith one) brings forth riches, but the daughter devours the mother." How can you expect acceptance with God, who have betrayed his truth, and dealt perfidiously with him.

Deduction 3. If believers may safely commit their souls into the hands of God, how confidently may they commit all lesser interests and lower concernments into the same hand? Shall we trust him with our souls, and not with our lives, liberties or comforts. Can we commit the treasure to him and not a trifle? Whatever you enjoy in this world, is but a trifle to your souls. Sure, if you can trust him for eternal life for your souls, you may much more trust him for the daily bread for your bodies. I know it is objected, that God has made over temporal things to his people upon conditional promises, and an absolute faith can never be grounded upon conditional promises.

But what means this objection? Let your faith be but suitable to these conditional promises, i.e. believe they shall be made good to you so far as God sees them good for you: do you but labour to come up to those conditions required in you, and thereby God will have more glory, and you more comfort: If your prayers for these things proceed from pure ends, the glory of God, not the satisfaction and gratification of your lusts: If your desires after them be moderate as to the measure, content with that proportion the Infinite Wisdom sees fittest for you: If you take God's way to obtain them, and dare not strain conscience, or commit a sin, though you should perish for want: If you can patiently wait God's time for enlargements from your straits, and not make any sinful haste, you shall be surely supplied; and he that remembers your souls will not forget your bodies. But we live by sense, and not by faith; present things strike our affections more powerfully than the invisible things that are to come. The Lord humble his people for this.

Deduction. 4. Is this the privilege of believers, that they can commit their souls to God in a dying hour? Then how precious, how useful a grace is faith to the people of God, both living and dying?

All the graces have done excellently, but faith excels then all: faith is the Phoenix grace, the queen of graces: deservedly it is stiled precious faith, 2 Pet. 1: 1. The benefits and privileges of it in this life are unspeakable: and as there is no comfortable living, so no comfortable dying without it.

First, While we live and converse here in the world, all our comfort and safety is from it; for all our union with Christ, the fountain of mercies and blessings, is by faith, Eph. 3: 17. "that Christ may dwell in your hearts by faith." No faith, no Christ: all our communion with Christ is by it: he that cometh to God must believe, Heb. 11: 6. The soul's life is wrapt up in this communion with God, and that communion in faith. All communications from Christ depend upon faith; for look, as all communion is founded in union, so from our union and communion are all our communications. All communications of quickening, comforts, joy, strength, and whatsoever serves to the well-being of the life of grace, are all through that faith which first knits us to Christ, and still maintains our communion with Christ; believing we rejoice, 1 Pet. 1: 8. The inner man is renewed, whilst we look to the things that are not seen, 2 Cor. 4: 18.

Secondly, And as our life, and all the supports and comforts of it here, are dependent on faith, so you see our death, as to the safety and comfort of our souls then, depends upon our faith: he that has no faiths cannot commit his soul to God, but rather shrinks from God. Faith can do many sweet offices for your souls upon a death-bed, when the light of this world is gone, and all joy ceases on earth: it can give us sights of things invisible in the other world, and those sights will breathe life into your souls, amidst the very pangs of death.

Reader, do but think what a comfortable foresight of God, and the joys of salvation, will be to thee, when thine eye-strings are breaking; faith can not only see that beyond the grave, which will comfort, but it can cleave to its God, and clasp Christ in a promise, when it feels the ground of all sensible comforts trembling, and sinking under thy feet: "My heart and my flesh faileth, but God is the strength (or rock) of my heart, and my portion forever." Reeds fail, but the rock is firm footing; yea, and when the soul can no longer tabernacle here, it can carry the soul to God, cast it upon him, with "Father, into thy hands I commend my spirit." O precious faith!

Deduction 5. Do the souls of dying believers commend themselves into the hands of God? Then let not the surviving relations of such sorrow as men that have no hope. A husband, a wife, a child, is rent by death out of your arms: well, but consider into what arms, into what bosom they are commended. Is it not better for them to be in the bosom of God, than in yours? Could they be spared so long from heaven, as to come back again to you but an hour, how would they he displeased to see your tears, and hear your cries and sighs for them: They would say to you as Christ said to the daughters of Jerusalem, "Weep not for me, but weep for yourselves, and for your children." I am in a safe land, I am out of the reach of all storms and troubles. O did you but know what their state is, who are with God, you would be more than satisfied about them.

Deduction 6. Lastly, I will close all with a word of counsel. Is this the privilege of dying believers, to commend their souls into the hands of God.? Then as ever you hope for comfort, or peace in your last hour, see that your souls be such, as may be then fit to be commended into the hands of an holy and just God: See that they be holy souls; God will never accept them if they be not holy, "Without holiness no man shall see God," Heb. 12: 24. "He that has this hope, (viz. to see God) purifieth himself even as he is pure," 1 John 3: 3. Endeavours after holiness are inseparably connected with all rational expectations of blessedness. Will you put an unclean, filthy, defiled thing into the pure hand of the most holy God? O see they be holy, and already accepted in the beloved, or use to them when they take their leave of those tabernacles they now dwell in. The gracious soul may confidently say then, Lord Jesus! into thy hand I commend my spirit. O let all that can say so then, now say,

Thanks be to God for Jesus Christ.

Sermon 37: Christ's Funeral illustrated, in its Manner, Reasons, and excellent Ends

John 9: 40, 41, 42.

Then took they the body of Jesus, and wound it in linen clothes with the spices, as the manner of the Jews is to bury. Now in the place where he was crucified there was a garden; and in the garden a new sepulchre, wherein was never man yet laid. There laid they Jesus therefore because of the Jews' preparation day; for the sepulchre was nigh at hand.

You have heard the last words of dying Jesus commending his spirit into his Father's hands. And now the life of the world hangs dead upon a tree. The light of the world, for a time, muffled up in a dismal cloud. The Sun of Righteousness set in the region and shadow of death. The Lord is dead, and he that wears the keys of the grave at his girdle, is now himself to be locked up in the grave.

All you that are the friends and lovers of Jesus, are this day invited to his funeral: such a funeral as never was since graves were first digged. "Come see the place where the Lord lay." There are six remarkable particulars, about this funeral, in these three verses.

1. The preparations that were made for it, and that was mainly in two particulars, viz. the begging and perfuming of the body. His body could not be buried, till, by begging, his friends had obtained it as a favour from his judge. The dead body was by law in the power of Pilate, who adjudged it to death, as the bodies of those that are hanged, are in the power of the judge to dispose of them as he pleases. And when they had gotten it from Pilate, they wind it in fine linen clothes with spices. But what need of spices to perfume that blessed body? His own love was perfume enough to keep it sweet in the remembrance of his people to all generations: however, by this they will manifest, as far as they are able, the dear affection they have for him

2. The Bearers that carried his body to its grave, Joseph of Arimathea, and Nicodemus, two secret disciples; they were both men of estate and honour: none could imagine that these would have appeared at a time of so much danger, with such boldness for Christ; that ever they would have gone openly, and boldly to manifest their love to Christ, when dead, who were afraid to come to him (except by night) when he was living. But now a spirit zeal and courage is come upon them, when those that made greater and more open confessions of him are gone.

3. The Attendants who followed the hearse, were the women that followed him out of Galilee: among whom the two Maries, and the mother of Zebedee's children (whom Marls calls Salome) are only named.

4. The grave, or sepulchre, where they laid him. It was in Joseph's new tomb, which he had prepared in a garden near unto Golgotha, where our Lord died. Two things are remarkable about this tomb; it was another's tomb, and it was a new tomb. It was another's; for he had not a house of his own to lay his body in when dead. As he lived in other men's houses, so he lay in another man's tomb; and it was a new tomb, wherein never man was yet laid. Doubtless there was much of providence in this; for had any other been laid there before him, it might have proved an occasion both to shake the credit and slur the glory at his resurrection, by pretending it was some former body, and not the Lord's, that rose out of it. In this also divine Providence had a respect to that prophecy, Isa. 53: 9 which was to be fulfilled at his funeral "He made his grave with the rich, because he had done no violence," &c.

5. The disposition of the body in that tomb. It is true, there is no mention made of the groans and tears with which they laid him in his sepulchre; yet we may well presume, they were not wanting in plentiful expressions of their sorrow that way; for as they wept, and smote their breasts when he died, Luke 23: 48 so no doubt, they laid him with melting hearts, and flowing eyes in his tomb, when dead.

6. And lastly, The last remarkable particular in the text, is the solemnity with which his funeral rites were performed, and they were all suitable to his humbled state: it was, indeed, a funeral as decently ordered, as the straits of time, and state of things would then permit; but there was nothing of pomp or outward state at all observed: few marks of honour set by men upon it; only the heavens adorned it with divers miraculous works, which in their proper place will be spoken to. Thus was he laid in his grave, where he continued for three incomplete days and nights in the territories of death, in the land of darkness and forgetfulness: partly to correspond with Jonah his type, and partly to ascertain the world of the reality of his death. Whence our observation is,

Doct. That the dead body of our Lord Jesus Christ was decently interred by a small number of his own disciples, and continued in the state of the dead for a time.

This observation containing matter of fact, and that so plainly and faithfully delivered to us by the pens of the several evangelists, we need do no more, to prepare it for our use, than to satisfy these two enquiries: why had Christ any funeral at all, since his resurrection was so soon to follow his death? And what manner of funeral Christ had?

First, Why had Christ any funeral at all, since he was to rise again from the dead, within that space of time that other men commonly have to lie by the wall before their interment; and had it continued longer unburied, it could see no corruption, having never been tainted by sin? Why, though there was no need of it at all upon that account that a funeral is needful for other bodies, yet there were these four weighty ends and reasons for it.

Reason 1. First, it was necessary Christ should be buried, to ascertain his death; else it might have been looked upon as a cheat: for, as they were ready enough to impose so gross a cheat upon the world at his resurrection, "That the disciples came by night, and stole him away," much more would they have denied at once the reality, both of his death and resurrection, had he not been so perfumed and interred. But this cut off all pretensions; for in their kind of embalming, his mouth, ears and nostrils were all filled with their spices and odours; bound up in linen, and laid long enough in the tomb to give full assurance to the world of the certainty of his death; so that there could be no latent principle of life in him. Now, since our eternal life is wrapt up in Christ's death, it can never be too firmly established. To this, therefore, we may well suppose Providence had special respect in his burial, and the manner of it.

Reason 2. Secondly, He must be buried, to fit the types and prophecies that went before. His abode in the grave was prefigured by Jonah's abode three days and nights in the belly of the whale, Matt. 12: 40. So must the Son of man be three days and three nights in the heart of the earth. Yea, the prophet had described the very manner of his funeral, and, long before he was born, foretold in what kind of tomb his body should be laid, Isa. 53: 9 "He made his grave with the wicked, and with the rich in his death:" pointing, by that expressions at this tomb of Joseph, who was a rich man; and the scriptures cannot be broken.

Reason 3. Thirdly, He must be buried, to complete his humiliation; this being the lowest step he could possibly descend to in his abased state. They have brought me to the dust of death: lower he could not be laid; and so low he must lay his blessed head, else he had not been humbled to the lowest.

Reason 4. Fourthly, But the great end and reason of his interment was the conquering of death in its own dominion and territories; which victory over the grave furnished the saints with that triumphant "epinikion" song of deliverance, 1 Cor. 15: 55. "O death! where is thy sting? O grave! where is thy destruction?" Our graves would not be so sweet and comfortable to us, when we come to lie down in them, if Jesus had not lain there before us and for us. Death is a dragon, the grave its den; a place of dread and terror; but Christ goes into its den, there grapples with it, and for ever overcomes it; disarms it of all its terror; and not only makes it to cease to be inimical, but to become exceeding beneficial to the saints; a bed of rest, and a perfumed bed; they do but go into Christ's bed, where he lay before them. For these ends he must be buried.

Secondly, Next let us enquire what manner of funeral Christ had?

And if we intently observe it, we shall find many remarkable properties in it.

First, We shall find it to be a very obscure and private funeral. Here was no external pomp or gallantry: Christ affected it not in his life, and it was no way suitable to the ends and manner of his death. Humiliation was designed in his death; and state is inconsistent with such an end; besides, he died upon the tree; and persons so dying, do not use to have much ceremony and state at their funerals. Three things show it to be a very humble and obscure funeral, as to what concerned outward glory, with which the great ones of the earth are usually interred. For,

1. The dead body of the Lord was not brought from his own house, as other men's commonly are, but from the tree. They begged it of his judge. Had they not obtained this favour from Pilate, it must have been buried in Golgotha; it had been tumbled into a pit digged under the cross.

2. As it was first begged, then buried, so it was attended with a very poor train: a few sorrowful women followed the bier. Other men are accompanied to their graves by their relations and friends: the disciples were all scattered from him; afraid to own him dying, and dead.

3. And these few that were resolved to give him a funeral, are forced, by reason of the straits of time, to do it in great haste. Time was short; they take the next sepulchre they can get, and hurry him away that evening into it; for the preparation for the passover was at hand. This was the obscure funeral which the body of the Lord had. Thus was the Prince of the kings of the earth, who has the keys of death and hell, laid into his grave.

Secondly, Yet though men could bestow little honour upon it, the heavens bestowed several marks of honour upon it: adorned it with divers miracles, which wiped off the reproach of his death from him. These miracles were antecedent to his interment, or concomitants of it.

1. There was that extraordinary and preternatural eclipse of the sun; such an eclipse as was never seen since it first shone in heaven; the sun fainted at the sight of such a rueful spectacle, and clothed the whole heaven in black. The sight of this caused a great philosopher, who was then far from the place where this unparalleled tragedy was acting, to cry out upon the sight of it, "Either the God of nature now suffers, or the frame of the world is now dissolved." The same Dionysius, writing to Apollophanes, a philosopher, who would not embrace the Christian faith, thus goes about to convince him. "What thinkest thou, (saith he) of the eclipse when Christ was crucified? were we not both of us at Heliopolis, and standing in the same place? Did we not see the moon in a new manner following the sun: and not in the conjunction, but from the ninth hour until the evening, by a reason unknown in nature, directly opposite to the sun? Didst thou not then, being greatly terrified, say unto me, O my Dionysius, what strange communications of the heavenly bodies are these?"

Such a preternatural eclipse is remembered in no other history; for it was not in time of conjunction, but opposition, the moon being then at full. From the sixth to the ninth hour, the sun and moon were together in the midst of heaven; but in the evening she appeared in the east, her own place, opposite to the sun. And then miraculously returning from east to west, did not pass by the sun, and set in the west before it, but kept it company for the space of three hours, and then returned to the east again. And whereas in all other natural eclipses, the shadow always begins on the western parts of the body of the sun, and that part is also first cleared; it was quite contrary in this; for though the moon was opposite to the sun, and distant from it the whole breadth of heaven, yet with a miraculous swiftness it overtook the sun, darkened first the eastern part of it, and soon prevailed over its whole body; which caused darkness over all the land; i.e. say some, over the whole earth; or, as others, over the whole land of Jewry; or, as others, over the whole horizon, and all places of the same altitude and latitude, which is most probable.

Secondly, And as Christ's funeral was adorned with such a miraculous eclipse, which put the heavens and earth into mourning; so thee rocks did rend: the vail of the temple rent in twain from top to bottom; the graves opened, and the dead bodies of many saints arose and went into the holy city, and were seen of many. The rending of the rocks was a sign of God's fierce indignation, Nahum 1: 6, and a discovery of the greatness of his power; shewing them what they deserved, and what he could do to them that had committed this horrid fact; though he rather chose at this time to show the dreadful effects of it upon inanimate rocks, than rocky hearted sinners; but especially it served to convince the world, that it was none other but the Son of God that died; which was farther manifested by these concomitant miracles.

As for the rending in twain of the vail, it was a notable miracle, plainly shewing that all ceremonies were now accomplished and abolished; no more veils now: as also that believers have now most free access into heaven. At that very instant when the vail rent, the high priest was officiating in the most holy place, and the vail which hid him from the rest of the people, being rent, they might freely see him about his work in the holy of holies; a lively emblem of our High-priest, whom now we see by faith in the heavens there performing his intercession work for us.

The opening of the graves, plainly shewed the design and end of Christ's going into it; that it might not have dominion over the bodies of the saints, but being vanquished and destroyed by Christ, lets go all that are his whom he ransomed from the grave as a prey out of its paws: a specimen whereof was given in those holy ones that rose at that time and appeared to many in the holy city. Thus was the funeral of our Lord performed by men: Thus was it adorned by miracles from heaven.

Use. And now we have seen Jesus interred; he that wears at his girdle the keys of hell and death, himself locked up in the grave. What shall I say of him whom they now laid in the grave? shall I undertake to tell you what he was, what he did, suffered, and deserved? Alas! the tongues of angels must pause and stammer in such a work. I may truly say, as Nazianzen said of Basil, "No tongue but his own can sufficiently commend and praise him." He is a sun of righteousness; a fountain of life; a bundle of love. Of him it might be said in that day, Here lies lovely Jesus, in whom is treasured up whatsoever an angry God can require for his satisfaction, or an empty creature for his perfection; before him was none like him, and after shall none arise comparable to him. "If every leaf and spire of grass," (saith one,) "nay, all the stars, sands and atoms, were so many souls and seraphims, whose love should double in them every moment to all eternity, yet would it fall infinitely short of what is due to his worth and excellency. Suppose a creature composed of all the choice endowments that ever dwelt in the best of men since the creation of the world, in whom you find a meek Moses, a strong Samson, a faithful Jonathan, a beautiful Absalom, a rich and wise Solomon; nay, and add to this, the understanding, strength, agility, splendour, and holiness of all the angels, it would all amount but to a dark shadow of this incomparable Jesus."

"Who ever weighed Christ in a pair of balances?" saith another. "Who has seen the foldings and plaits, the heights and depths of that glory that is in him! O for such a heaven, as but to stand afar off and see, and love, and long for him, while time's thread be cut, and this great work of creation dissolved!--O, if I could yoke in among the throng of angels and seraphim, and now glorified saints, and could raise a new love song of Christ before all the world! I am pained with wondering at new opened treasures in Christ. If every finger, member, bone and joint, were a torch burning in the hottest fire in hell, I would they could all send out love praises, high songs of praise for evermore, to that plant of renown, to that royal and high Prince, Jesus my Lord. But, alas! his love swelleth in me, and finds no vent.--I mar his praises, nay, I know no comparison of what Christ is, and what he is worth. All the angels, and all the glorified, praise him not so much as in halves. Who can advance him, or utter all his praise?--O, if I could praise him, I would rest content to die of love for him. O, would to God I could send in my praises to my incomparable Well-beloved, or cast my love-songs of that matchless Lord Jesus over the walls, that they might light in his lap before men and angels!--But when I have spoken of him till my head rive, I have said just nothing; I may begin again. A Godhead, a Godhead, is a world's wonder! Set ten thousand thousand new made worlds of angels and elect men, and double them in number ten thousand thousand thousand times: let their hearts and tongues be ten thousand times more agile and large than the hearts and tongues of the seraphim, that stand with six wings before him; when they have said all for the glorifying and praising of the Lord Jesus, they have spoken little or nothing. O that I could even wear out this tongue in extolling his highness! But it is my daily admiration, and I am confounded with his incomparable love,"

Thus have his enamoured friends faintly expressed his excellencies; and if they have therein done any thing, they have shown the impossibility of his due praises.

Come and see, believing souls, look upon dead Jesus in his winding-sheet by faith, and say, Lo, this is he, of whom the church said, "My beloved is white and ruddy:" his ruddiness is now gone, and a death paleness has prevailed over all his body, but still as lovely as ever, yea, altogether lovely.

If David, lamenting the death of Saul and Jonathan, said, "Daughters of Jerusalem, weep over Saul, who clothed you in scarlet, with other delights; who put ornaments of gold upon your apparel;" Much rather may I say, Children of Zion, weep over Jesus, who clothed you with righteousness, and the garments of salvation.

This is he who quitted the throne of glory; left the bosom of unspeakable delights; came in a body of flesh, produced in perfect holiness; brake through many and great impediments, (thy great unworthiness, the wrath of God and man,) by the strength of love to bring salvation home to thy soul. Can he that believingly considers this, do less than faint at the sense of that love that brought him to the dust of death, and cry out with that father, "My Lord was crucified!" But I will insist no longer upon generals; but draw down the particulars of Christ's funeral to your use, in the following corollaries,

Corollary 1. Was Christ buried in this manner? Then a decent and mournful funeral, where it can be had, is very laudable among Christians.

I know the souls of the saints have no concernment for their bodies, nor are they solicitous how the body is treated here; yet there is a respect due to them, as they are the temples wherein God has been served, and honoured by those holy souls that once dwelt in them, as also upon the account of their relation to Christ, even when they lie by the walls; and the glory that will be one day put upon them, when they shall be changed, and made like unto Christ's glorious body. Upon such special accounts as these, their bodies deserve an honourable treatment, as well as upon the account of humanity, which owes this honour to the bodies of all men.

To have no funeral, is accounted a judgement, Eccles. 7: 4. or to be tumbled into a pit without any to lament us, is as lamentable. We read of many solemn and mournful funerals in scriptures, wherein the people of God have affectionately paid their respects and honours to the dust of the saints, as men that were deeply sensible of their worth, and how great a loss the world sustains by their remove. Christ's funeral had as much of decency and solemnity in it, as the time would permit; though he was a stranger to all pomp, both in life and death.

Corol. 2. Did Joseph and Nicodemus so boldly appear at a time of so much danger, to beg the body, and give it a funeral? Let it be for ever a caution to strong Christians, not to despise or glory over the weak. You see here a couple of poor, low spirited, and timorous persons, that were afraid to be seen in Christ's company, when the other disciples professed their readiness to die with him: yet those flee, and these appear for him, when the trial comes indeed. If God desert the strong, and assist the weak, the feeble shall be as David, and the strong as tow. I speak not this to discourage any man from striving to improve inherent graces to the utmost; for it is ordinarily found in experience, that the degrees of assisting grace, are given out according to the measures of inherent grace: but I speak it to prevent a sin incident to strong Christians, which is to despise the weak, which God corrects by such instances and examples as this before us.

Corol. 3. Hence we may be assisted in discerning the depths of Christ's humiliation for us: And see from what, to what his love brought him. It was not enough, that he who was in the form of God, became a creature, which was an infinite stoop, nay, to be made a Man, an inferior order of creatures; nay, to be a poor man, to spend his days in poverty and contempt, but also to be a dead corpse for our sakes. O what manner of love is this!

Now, the deeper the humiliation of the Son of God was, the more satisfactory to us it must needs be, for as it shows us the heinousness of sin, that deserves all this, so the fulness of Christ's satisfaction, whereby he makes up that breach. O, it was deep humiliation indeed! how unlike himself is he now become! does he look like the Son of God? What! the Son of God, whom all the angels adore, to be hurried by three or four persons into his grave in an evening! to be carried from Golgotha to the grave in this manner, and there lie as a captive to death for a time! Never was the like change of conditions; never such an abasement heard of in the world.

Corol. 4. From this funeral of Christ results the purest, and strongest consolation and encouragement to believers, against the fears of death and the grave. If this be so, that Jesus has lain in the grave before you; let me say then to you, as the Lord spake to Jacob, Gen. 46: 2, 3. "Fear not to go down into Egypt, for I will go down with thee, and I will also surely bring thee up again." So here, fear not believer, to go down to the grave, for God will be with thee there, and will surely bring thee up thence. This consideration that Jesus Christ has lain in the grave himself, gives manifold encouragements to the people of God, against the terrors of the grave.

First, The grave received, but could not destroy Jesus Christ: death swallowed him, as the whale did Jonah his type, but could not digest him when it had swallowed him, but quickly delivered him up again. Now Christ's lying in the grave, as the common head and representative of believers, what comfort should this inspire into their hearts: for, as it fared with Christ's body personal, so it shall with Christ's body mystical: it could not retain him; it shall not for ever retain them. This resurrection of Christ out of his grave, is the very ground of our hope for a resurrection out of our graves. "Christ is risen from the dead, and become the first fruits of them that slept," 1 Cor. 15: 20.

Secondly, As the union betwixt the body of Christ, and the Divine nature was not dissolved, when that body was laid in the grave, so the union betwixt Christ and believers is not, cannot be dissolved, when their bodies shall be laid in their graves. It is true, the natural union betwixt his soul and body was dissolved for a time; but the hypostatical union was not dissolved, no, not for a moment: that body was the body of the Son of God, when it was in the sepulchre. In like manner, the natural union betwixt our souls and bodies is dissolved by death; but the mystical union betwixt us and Christ, yea, betwixt our very dust and Christ, can never be dissolved.

Thirdly, As Christ's body, when it was in the grave, did there rest in hope, and was assuredly a partaker of that hope; so it shall fare with the dead bodies of the saints, when they lay them down also in the dust: "My flesh also shall rest in hope," saith Christ, Psal. 16: 9, 10, 11. In like manner the saints commit their bodies to the dust in hope: "The righteous has hope in his death," Prov. 14: 32. And as Christ's hope was not a vain hope, so neither shall their hope be vain.

Fourthly, and lastly, Christ's lying in the grave before us, has quite changed, and altered the nature of the grave; so that it is not what it was: it was once a part of the curse. "Dust thou art, and unto dust thou shalt return," was a part of the threatening, and curse for sin. The grave had the nature and use of a prison, to keep the bodies of sinners against the great assizes, and then deliver them up into the hands of a great and terrible God; but now it is no prison, but a bed of rest: yea, and a perfumed bed, where Christ lay before us. Which is a sweet consideration of the grave indeed; "They shall enter into peace, they shall rest in their beds," Isa. 57:2. O then let not believers stand in fear of the grave. He that has one foot in heaven need not fear to put the other into the grave. "Though I walk through the valley of the shadow of death, I will fear no evil, for thou ant with me," Psal. 23: 4.

Indeed, the grave is a terrible place to them that are out of Christ; death is the Lord's sergeant to arrest them; the grave is the Lord's prison to secure them. When death draws them into the grave, it draws them thither as a lion does his prey into the den to devour it. So you read, Psal. 49: 14.

"Death shall feed (or prey) upon them." Death there reigns over them in its full power, Rom. 5: 14. And though at last it shall render them again to God, yet it were better for them to lie everlastingly where they were, than to rise to such an end; for they are brought out of their graves, as a condemned prisoner out of the prison, to go to execution. But the case of the saints is not so; the grave (thanks be to our Lord Jesus Christ!) is a privileged place to them, whilst they sleep there; and when they awake, it will be with singing. When they awake, they shall be satisfied with his likeness.

Corollary 5. Lastly, Since Christ was laid in his grave, and his people reap such privileges by it; as ever you expect rest or comfort in your graves, see that you get union with Christ now.

It was an ancient custom of the Jews, to put rich treasures into the graves with their friends, as well as to bestow much upon their sepulchres. It is said, Hircanus opened David's sepulchre, and took out of it three thousand talents of gold and silver. And to this sense many interpret that act of the Chaldeans, Jer. 8: 1. "At that time, saith the Lord, they shall bring out the bones of the kings of Judas, and the bones of his princes, &c. And they shall spread them before the sun and moon," &c. This is rather conceived to be an act of covetousness than cruelty: they shall ransack their graves for the treasure that is hid there among their bones. It is possible the case so stands with many of you, that you have no great matter to bestow upon your funerals, nor are they like to be splendid; no stately monuments; no hidden treasure; but if Christ be yours, you carry that with you to your graves, which is better than all the gold and silver in the world. What would you be the better if your coffin were made of beaten gold, or your grave-stone set thick with glittering diamonds? But if you lie in the Lord, i.e. interested in and united to the Lord, you shall carry six grounds of comfort with you to your graves, the least of which is not to be purchased with the wealth of both the Indies.

First, The first ground of comfort which a believer carries with him to the grave, is, that the covenant of God holds firmly with his very dust, all the days of its appointed time in the grave. So much Christ tells us, Matt. 22: 31, 32. "I am the God of Abraham, and the God of Isaac, and the God of Jacob: God is not the God of the dead, but of the living;" q. d. Abraham, Isaac, and Jacob, are naturally dead; but inasmuch as God, long after their deaths, proclaimed himself their God still, therefore they are all alive, foederally alive to God: they live, i.e. their covenant-relation lives still. "Whether we live, or whether we die, (saith the apostle) we are the Lord's," Rom. 14: 7, 8, 9. Now, what an encouragement is here! I am as much the Lord's in the state of the dead, as I was in the state of the living: death puts an end to all other relations and bonds, but the bond of the covenant rots not in the grave: that dust is still the Lord's.

Secondly, As God's covenant with our very bodies is indissolvable, so God's love to our very dust is inseparable. "I am the God of Abraham." God looks down from heaven into the graves of his saints with delight, and looks on that pile of dust with complacency, which those that once loved it cannot behold without loathing. The apostle is express, Rom. 8: 33, that death separates not the believer from the love of God. As at first it was not our natural comeliness or beauty that drew, or engaged his love to us; so neither will he cease to love us when that beauty is gone, and we become objects of loathing to all flesh. When a husband cannot endure to see a wife, or a wife her husband; but saith of them that were once dear and pleasant, as Abraham of his beloved Sarah, "Bury my dead out of my sight;" yet then the Lord delights in it as much as ever. The goldsmith does not value the dust of his gold, as God values the dust of his saints, for all these precious particles are united to Christ.

Thirdly, As God's love will be with you in the grave, so God's providence shall take order about your graves, when they shall be digged for you. And be sure he will not dig your graves till you are fit to be put into them: he will bring you thither in the best time; Job 5: 26. "Thou shalt come to thy grave as a shock of corn in its season:" you shall be ripe and ready before God house you there. It is said of David, that "after he had served his generation by the will of God, he fell asleep," Acts 13: 36. O what a holy and wise will is that will of God, that so orders our death! And how equal is it, that our will should be concluded by it?

Fourthly, If you be in Christ, as God's covenant holds with you in the grave, his love is inseparable from your dust, his providence shall give order when it shall be digged for you, so, in the next place, his pardons have loosed all the bonds of guilt from you, before you lie down in the grave: so that you shall not die in your sins. Ah, friends, what a comfort is this! that you are the Lord's free men in the grave! sin is a bad bed-fellow, and a worse grave fellow. It is a grievous threatening, John 8: 24. "Ye shall die in your sins." Better be cast alive into a pit among dragons and serpents, than dead in your graves among your sins. O what a terrible word is that, Job 20: 11. "His bones are full of the sins of his youth, which shall lie down with him in the dust!" But from the company of sin, in the grave, all the saints are delivered. God's full, free, and final pardons have shut guilt out of your graves.

Fifthly, Whenever you come to your graves, you shall find the enmity of the grave slain by Christ: it is no enemy; nay, you will find it friendly, a privileged place to you: it will be as sweet to you that are in Christ, as a soft bed in a still quiet chamber to one that is weary and sleepy. Therefore, it is said, 1 Cor. 3: 21, 22. "Death is yours;" yours is a privilege; your friend: there you shall find sweet rest in Jesus; be hurried, pained, troubled no more.

Sixthly, To conclude: if in Christ, know this for your comfort, that your own Lord Jesus Christ keeps the keys of all the chambers of death: and as he unlocks the door of death, when he lets you in, so he will open it again for you when you awake, to let you out; and from the time he opens to let you in, till the time he opens to let you out, he himself wakes and watches by you while you sleep there. "I (saith he) have the keys of death," Rev. 1: 18. O then, as you expect peace or rest in the chambers of death, get union with Christ. A grave with Christ is a comfortable place.

John Flavel

Sermon 38: Wherein four weighty Ends of Christ's Humiliation are opened, and particularly applied

Isa. 53:11
He shall see the travail of his soul, and be satisfied.

We are now arrived at the last particular place which we designed to speak to in Christ's state of humiliation, namely, the designs and blessed ends for which he was so deeply abased. It is inconsistent with the prudence of a common agent, to be at vast expenses of time, pains, and cost, and not to propound to himself a design worthy of all those expenses. And it is much less imaginable, that Christ should so stupendously abase himself, by stooping from the bosom of his Father to the state of the dead, where our last discourse left him, it there had not been some excellent and glorious thing in his eye, the attainment whereof might give him a content and satisfaction, equivalent to all the sorrows and abasements he endured for it.

And so much is plainly held forth in this scripture, "He shall see the travail of his soul, and be satisfied." In which words three things fall under our consideration.

First, The travailing pangs of Christ. So the agonies of his soul and torments of his body are fitly called, not only because of the sharpness and acuteness of them, being in that respect like the sharpness and acuteness of them, being in that respect like birth-pangs of a travailing women, for so this word signifies, but also because they fore-run, and make way for the birth, which abundantly recompenses all those labours. I shall not here insist upon the pangs and agonies endured by Christ in the garden, or upon the cross, which the prophet stiles "the travail of his soul," having, in the former sermons, opened it largely in its particulars, but pass to the

Second Thing considerable in these words, and that is the assured fruits and effects of this his travail; he shall see the travail of his soul. By seeing, understand the fruition, obtainment, or enjoyment of the end of his sufferings. He shall not shed his blood upon an hazard; his design shall not miscarry; but he shall certainly see the ends he aimed at, accomplished.

And Thirdly, This shall yield him great satisfaction: as a "woman forgets her sorrow, for joy that a man is born into the world," John 16: 21. he shall see it and be satisfied. As God, when he had finished the work of creation, viewed that his work with pleasure and satisfaction; so does our exalted Redeemer, with great contentment, behold the happy issues of his hard sufferings. It affords pleasure to a man to see great affairs, by orderly conduct, brought to happy issues. Much more does it yield delight to Jesus Christ to see the results of the most profound wisdom and love wherein he carried on redemption work. All runs into this doctrine,

Doct. That all the blessed designs and ends for which the Lord Jesus Christ humbles himself to the death of the cross, shall certainly be attained, to his full content and satisfaction.

My present business is not to prove, that Christ shall certainly obtain what he died for; nor to open the great satisfaction and pleasure which will arise to him out of those issues of his death, but to point at the principal ends of his death: making some brief improvement as we pass along.

First, Then let us enquire into the designs and ends of Christ's humiliation, at least the main and principal ones; and we shall find, that as the sprinkling of the typical blood in the Old Testament was done for four weighty ends or uses, answerable, the precious and invaluable blood of the Testator and surety of the New Testament is shed for four weighty ends also.

First, That blood was shed and applied to deliver from danger; Exod. 12: 13. "And the blood shall be to you for a token upon the houses where you are; and when I see the blood, I will pass over you: and the plague shall not be upon you, to destroy you, when I smite the land of Egypt."

Secondly, The blood that was shed to make an atonement betwixt God and the people; Lev. 4: 20. "And he shall do with the bullock as he did with the bullock for a sin-offering; so shall he do with this, and the priest shall make an atonement for them, and it shall be forgiven them."

Thirdly, That blood was shed to purify persons from their ceremonial pollutions, Lev. 14: 6, 7. "He shall dip the cedar wood, and scarlet, and hyssop, with the living bird, in the blood of the bird that was killed over the running water, and he shall sprinkle upon him that is to be cleansed from the leprosy seven times; and shall pronounce him clean, and shall let the living bird loose in the open field."

Fourthly, That blood was shed to ratify and confirm the testament or covenant of God with the people, Exod. 24: 8. "And Moses took the blood, and sprinkled it on the people, and said, "Behold the blood of the covenant, which the God has made with you concerning all these words." These were the four main ends for shedding and sprinkling, that typical blood. Suitably, there are four principal ends for shedding and applying Christ's blood. As that typical blood was shed to deliver from danger, so this was shed to deliver from wrath, even the wrath to come. That was shed to make an atonement, so was this. That was shed to purify persons from uncleanness, so was this. That was shed to confirm the Testament, so was this. As will appear in the following particulars more at large.

First, One principal design and end of shedding the blood of Christ was to deliver his people from danger, the danger of that wrath which burns down to the lowest hell. So you find, 1 Thess. 1:10, "Even Jesus who delivered us from wrath to come." Here our misery is both specified and aggravated. Specified, in calling it wrath, a word of deep and dreadful signification. The damned best understand the importance of that word. And aggravated, in calling it wrath to come, or coming wrath. Wrath to come implies both the futurity and perpetuity of this wrath. It is wrath that shall certainly and inevitably come upon sinners. As sure as the night follows the day, as sure as the winter follows the summer, so shall wrath follow sin, and the pleasures thereof. Yea, it is not only certainly future, but when it comes it will be abiding wrath, or wrath still coming. When millions of years and ages are past and gone, this will still be wrath to come. Ever coming as a river ever flowing.

Now from this wrath to come, has Jesus delivered his people by his death. For that was the price laid down for their redemption from the wrath of the great and terrible God, Rom. 5: 9. "Much more then, being justified by his blood, we shall be saved from wrath through him." The blood of Jesus was the price that ransomed man from this wrath. And it was shed not only to deliver them from wrath to come, but to deliver them freely, fully, distinguishingly, and wonderfully from it.

First, Freely, by his own voluntary interposition and susception oft the mediatorial office, moved thereunto by his own bowels of compassion, which yearned over his elect in their misery. The saints were once a lost generation, that had sold themselves, and their inheritance also; and had not wherewithal to redeem either: but they had a near kinsman (even their elder brother by the mother's side) to whom the right of redemption did belong who being a mighty man of wealth, the heir of all things, undertook to be their God; and out of his own proper substance to redeem both them and their inheritance. Them, to be his own inheritance, Eph. 1: 10. and heaven, to be theirs, 1 Pet. 1: 4. All this he did most freely, when none made supplication to him. No sighing of the prisoners came before him. He designed it for us before we had a being. And when the purposes of his grace were come to their parturient fulness, then did he freely lay out the infinite treasures of his blood to purchase our deliverance from wrath.

Secondly, Christ by death has delivered his people fully. A full deliverance it is, both in respect of time and degrees. A full deliverance in respect of time. It was not a reprieve, but a deliverance. He thought it not worth the shedding of his blood to respite the execution for a while. Nay, in the procurement of their eternal deliverance from wrath, and in the purchase of their eternal inheritance, he has but an even bargain, not a jot more than his blood was worth. Therefore is he become "the author of eternal salvation to them that obey him," Heb. 5: 9. And as it is full in respect of time, so likewise in respect of degrees. He died not to procure a mitigation or abatement of the rigour or severity of the sentence, but to rescue his people fully from all degrees of wrath. So that there is no condemnation to them that are in Christ, Rom. 8: 1. All the wrath of God to the last drop, was squeezed out into that bitter cup which Christ drank off, and wrung out the very dregs thereof.

Thirdly, This deliverance obtained for us by the death of Christ is a special and distinguishing deliverance. Not common to all, but peculiar to some; and they by nature no better than those that are left under wrath. Yea, as to natural disposition, moral qualifications, and external endowments, oftentimes far inferior to them that perish. How often do we find a moral righteousness, an harmless innocence, a pretty ingenuity, a readiness to all offices of love, in them that sue notwithstanding left under the dominion of other lusts, and under the damning sentence of the law; whilst on the other side, proud, peevish, sensual, morose, and unpolished natures, are chosen to be the subjects of this salvation? "You see your calling, brethren," 1 Cor. 1: 26.

Fourthly and lastly, It is a wonderful salvation. It would weary the arm of an angel to write down all the wonders that are in this salvation. That ever such a design should be laid, such a project of grace contrived in the heart of God, who might have suffered the whole species to perish. That it should only concern man, and not the angels, by nature more excellent than us; that Christ should be pitched upon to go forth upon this glorious design. That he should effect it in such a way, by taking our nature and suffering the penalty of the law therein. That our deliverance should be wrought out and finished when the Redeemer and his design seemed both to be lost and perished. These with many more are such wonders as will take up eternity itself to search, admire, and adore them.

Before I part from this first end of the death of Christ, give me leave to deduce two useful corollaries from it, and then proceed to a second.

Coroll. 1. Hath Christ by death delivered his people from the wrath to come? How ungrateful and disingenuous a thing must it be then for those that have obtained such a deliverance as this, to repine and grudge at those light afflictions they suffer for a moment upon Christ's account in this world!

Alas! what are these sufferings, that we should grudge at them? Are they like those which the Redeemer suffered for our deliverance? Did ever any of us endure for him what he endured for us? Or is there any thing you can suffer for Christ in this world, comparable to this wrath to come, which you must have endured, had he not, by the price of his own blood, rescued you from it.

Readers wilt thou but make the comparison in thine own thoughts, in the following particulars, and then pronounce when thou best duly compared.

First, What is the wrath of man to the wrath of God? What is the arm of a creature to the anger of a Deity? Can man thunder with an arm like God?

Secondly, What are the sufferings of the vile body here, to the tortures of a soul and body in hell? The torments of the soul, are the very soul of torments

Thirdly, What are the troubles of a moment to that wrath, which, after millions of years are gone, will still be called wrath to come? O what comparison betwixt a point of hasty time, and the interminable duration of vast eternity!

Fourthly, What comparison is there betwixt the intermitting sorrows and sufferings of this life, and the continued uninterrupted wrath to come? Our troubles here are not constant, there are gracious relaxations, lucid intervals here; but the wrath to come allows not a moment's case or mitigation.

Fifthly, What light and easy troubles are those, which, being put into the rank and order of adjuvant causes, work under the influence and blessing of the first cause, to the everlasting good of them that love God, compared with that wrath to come, out of which no good effects or issues are possible to proceed to the souls on which it lies?

Sixthly, and lastly, How much more comfortable is it, to suffer in fellowship with Christ and his saints for righteousness sake, than to suffer with devils and reprobates for wickedness sake? Grudge not then, O ye that are delivered by Jesus from wrath to come, at any thing ye do suffer, or shall suffer from Christ, or for Christ in this world.

Corol. 2. If Jesus Christ has delivered his people from the wrath to come, how little comfort can any man take in this present enjoyments and accommodations in the world, whilst it remains a question with him, whether he be delivered from the wrath to come? It is well for the present, but will it be so still? Man is a prospecting creature, and it will not satisfy him that his present condition is comfortable, except he have some hopes it shall be so hereafter. It can afford a man little content that all is easy and pleasant about him now, whilst such passages and terrible hints of wrath to cone are given him by his own conscience daily. O, methinks such a thought as this, what if I am reserved for the wrath to come? should be to him, as the fingers appearing upon the plaster of the wall were to Belteshazzar in the height of a frolic. It is a custom with some of the Indians, when they have taken a prisoner (whom they intend not presently to eat) to bring him with great triumph into the village, where he dwelleth that has taken him; and placing him in the house of one that was slain in the wars, as it were to re- celebrate his funeral, they give him his wives or sisters to attend on him, and use at his pleasure: they apparel him gorgeously, and feed him with all the dainty meats that may be had; affording him all the pleasure that can be devised; when he has passed certain months in all these pleasures, and (like a capon) is made fat with delicate fare, they assemble themselves upon some festival day, and in great pomp bring him to the place of execution, where they kill and eat him.

Such are all the pleasures and enjoyments of the wicked, which feed them for the day of slaughter. How little stomach can a man have to those dainties that understands the end and meaning of them! Give not sleep therefore to thine eyes, reader, till thou hast got good evidence, that thou art of that number whom Jesus has delivered from the wrath to come. Till thou canst say, he is a Jesus to thee. This may be made out to thy satisfaction three ways.

The Fountain of Life Opened Up

First, If Jesus have delivered thee from sin, the cause of wrath, thou mayest conclude he has delivered thee from wrath, the effect and fruit of sin. Upon this account the sweet name of Jesus, was imposed upon him, Mat. 1: 21. "Thou shalt call his name Jesus, for he shall save his people from their sins." Whilst a man lies under the dominion and guilt of sin, he lies exposed to wrath to come; and when he is delivered from the guilt and power of sin, he is certainly delivered from the danger of this coming wrath. Where sin is not imputed, wrath is not threatened.

Secondly, If thy soul do set an inestimable value on Jesus Christ, and be endeared to him upon the account of that inexpressible grace manifested in this deliverance, it is a good sign thy soul has a share in it. Mark what an epithet the saints give Christ upon this account, Col. 1: 12, 13. "Giving thanks to the Father, who has delivered us from the power of darkness, and translated us into the kingdom of his dear Son." Christ is therefore dear and dear beyond all compare to his saved ones. I remember it is storied of the poor enthralled Grecians, that when Titus Flaminius had restored their ancient liberties, and proclamation was to be made in the marketplace by an herald; they so pressed to hear it, that the herald was in great danger of being stifled and pressed to death among the people; but when the proclamation was ended, there were heard such shouts and joyful acclamations, that the very birds of the air fell down astonished with the noise, while they continued to cry, "Soter, Sorter", a Saviour, a Saviour; and all the following night they continued dancing and singing about his pavilion.

If such a deliverance so endeared them to Titus, how should the great deliverance from wrath to come, endear all the redeemed to love their dear Jesus? This is the native effect of mercy upon the soul that has felt it.

Thirdly. To conclude, A disposition and readiness of mind to do, or endure any thing for Christ's sake, upon the account of his deliverance from the wrath to come; is a good evidence you are so delivered, Col. 1: 10, 11. "That we may walk worthy of the Lord to all pleasing, being fruitful in every good work." There is readiness to do for Christ. "Strengthened with all might, according to his glorious power, unto all patience and long-suffering with joyfulness." There is a cheerful readiness to endure any thing for Christ. And how both these flow from the sense of this great deliverance from wrath, the 12th verse will inform you, which was but now cited. O then, be serious and assiduous in the resolution of this grand case. Till this be resolved, nothing can be pleasant to thy soul.

End 2. As the typical blood was shed and sprinkled to deliver from danger, so it was shed to make atonement, Lev. 4: 20. "He shall expiate (we translate atone) the sin." The word imports both. And the true meaning is, that by the blood of the bullock, all whose efficacy stood in its relation to the blood of Christ, signified and shadowed by it, the people, for whom it was shed, should be reconciled to God, by the expiation and remission of their sins. And what was shadowed in this typical blood, was really designed and accomplished by Jesus Christ, in the shedding of his blood.

Reconciliation of the elect to God, is therefore another of those beautiful births which Christ travailed for. So you find it expressly, Rom. 5: 10. "If when we were enemies, we were reconciled to God by the death of his Son." This [if] is not a word of doubting, but argumentation. The apostle supposes it is a known truth, or principle yielded by all Christians, that the death of Christ was to reconcile the elect to God. And again he affirms it with like clearness, Col. 1: 20. "And having made peace by the blood of his cross, by him to reconcile all things." And that this was a main and principal end designed both by the Father and Son in the humiliation of Christ, is plain from 2 Cor. 5: 18, 19. "God was in Christ reconciling the world to himself." God filled the humanity with grace and authority. The Spirit of God was in him to qualify him. The authority of God was in him by commission, to make all he did valid. The grace and love of God to mankind was in him, and one of the principal effects in which it was manifested, was this design upon which he came, viz. to reconcile the world to God. Upon which ground Christ is called the "propitiation for our sins," 1 John 2: 2. "Now reconciliation or atonement is nothing else but the making up of the ancient friendship betwixt God and men which sin had dissolved, and so to reduce these enemies into a state of concord, and sweet agreement." And the means by which this blessed design was effectually compassed, was by the death of Christ, which made complete satisfaction to God, for the wrong he had done him. There was a breach made by sin betwixt God and angels, but that breach is never to be repaired or made up; since, as Christ took not on him their nature, so he never intended to he a mediator of reconciliation betwixt God and them. That will be an eternal breach. But that which Christ designed, as the end of his death, was to reconcile God and man. Not the whole species, but a certain number, whose names were given to Christ. Here I must briefly open, 1. How Christ's death reconciles. 2. Why this reconciliation is brought about by his death, rather than any other way. 3. What are the articles according to which it is made. And 4. What manner of reconciliation this is.

First, How Christ reconciles God and man by his death. And it must needs be by the satisfaction his death made to the justice of God for our sins. And so, reparation being made, the enmity ceases. Hence it is said, Isa. 53: 5. "the chastisement of our peace was upon him, and by his stripes we are healed." That is (as our English Annotators well explain it) he was chastised to procure our peace, by removal of our sins, that set God and us asunder, the guilt thereof being discharged with the price of his blood.

Now this reconciliation is made and continued betwixt God and us, three ways; namely, by the oblation of Christ, which was the price that procured it, and so we were virtually meritoriously reconciled. By the application of Christ and his benefits to us through faith, and so we are actually reconciled. And by the virtual continuation of the sacrifice of Christ in heaven, by his potent and eternal intercession, and so our state of reconciliation is confirmed, and all future breaches prevented. But all depends, as you see, upon the death of Christ. For had not Christ died, his death could never be applied to us, nor pleaded in heaven for us. How the death of Christ meritoriously procures our reconciliation, is evident from that fore-cited scripture, Rom. 5: 10. "When we were enemies we were reconciled to God by the death of his Son," i.e. Christ's death did meritoriously or virtually reconcile us to God, who, as to our state, were enemies long after that reconciliation was made. That the application of Christ to us by faith, makes that virtual reconciliation to become actual, is plain enough from Eph. 2: 16, 17. "And that he might reconcile both unto God in one body by the cross, having slain the enmity thereby. And came and preached peace to you that were afar off, and to them that were nigh." Now therefore (as it is added, verse 19.) "Ye are no more strangers and foreigners, but fellow-citizens with the saints," &c. And that this state of friendship is still continued by Christ's intercession within the vail, so that there can be no breaches made upon the state of our peace, notwithstanding all the daily provocations we give God by our sins, is the comfortable truth which the apostle plainly asserts, after he had given a necessary caution to prevent the abuse of it, in 1 John 2: 1, 2. "My little children, these things I write unto you that ye sin not; and if any man sin, we have an Advocate with the Father, Jesus Christ the righteous; and he is the propitiation," &c. Thus Christ reconciles us to God by his death.

Secondly, And if you enquire why this reconciliation was made by the death of Christ, rather than any other way, satisfaction is at hand, in these two answers.

First, That we can imagine no other way by which it could be compassed. And,

Secondly, If God could have reconciled us as much by another way, yet he could not have obliged us so much by doing it in another way, as he has by doing it this way. Surely, none but he that was God manifested in our flesh could offer a sacrifice of sufficient value to make God amends for the wrong done him by one sin, much less for all the sins of the elect. And how God should (especially after a peremptory threatening of death for sin) readmit us into favour without full satisfaction, cannot be imagined. He is indeed inclined to acts of mercy, but none must suppose him to exercise one attribute in prejudice to another. That his justice must be eclipsed, whilst his mercy shines. But allow that Infinite Wisdom could have found out another means of reconciling us as much, can you imagine, that in any other way he could have obliged us as much, as he has done by reconciling us to himself by the death of his own Son? It cannot be thought possible. This therefore was the most effectual, just, honourable, and obliging way to make up the peace betwixt him and us.

Thirdly, This reconciliation, purchased by the blood of Christ, is offered unto men by the gospel, upon certain articles and conditions; upon the performance whereof it actually becomes theirs; and without which, notwithstanding all that Christ has done and suffered, the breach still continues betwixt them and God. And let no man think this a derogation from the freeness and riches of grace, for these things serve singularly to illustrate and commend the grace of God to sinners.

As he consulted his own glory, in the terms on which he offers us our peace with him: so it is his grace which brings up souls to those terms of reconciliation. And surely he has not suspended the mercy of our reconciliation upon unreasonable or impossible conditions. He has not said, if you will do as much for me, as you have done against me, I will be at peace with you; but the two grand articles of peace with God, are repentance and faith. In the first, we lay down arms against God, and it is meet it should be so, before he readmits us into a state of peace and favour; in the other, we accept Christ and pardon through him with a thankful heart, Yielding up ourselves to his government, which is equally reasonable.

These are the terms on which we are actually reconciled to God. "Let the wicked forsake his way, and the unrighteous man his thoughts; and let him turn to the Lord, and he will have mercy on him; and to our God, for he will abundantly pardon." So Rom. 5: 1. "Being justified by faith, we have peace with God." And surely it would not become the holy God to own, as his friend and favourite, a man that goes on perversely and impenitently in the way of sin; not so much as acknowledging, or once bewailing the wrong he has done him, purposing to do so no more; or to receive into amity one that slights and rejects the Lord Jesus, whose precious blood was shed to procure and purchase peace and pardon for sinners.

But if there be any poor soul, that saith in his heart, it repents me for sinning against God, and is sincerely willing to come to Christ, upon gospel-terms, he shall have peace. And that peace,

Fourthly, Is no common peace. The reconciliation which the Lord Jesus died to procure for broken-hearted believers, it is,

First, A firm well-bottomed reconciliation, putting the reconciled soul beyond all possibility of coming under God's wrath any more, Isa. 54: 10. "Mountains may depart, and hills be removed, but the covenant of this peace cannot be removed." Christ is a surety, by way of caution, to prevent the new breaches, 2 John 1: 2.

Secondly, This reconciliation with God is the fountain out of which all our other comforts flow to us; this is plainly included in those words of Eliphaz to Job, chap. 22: 21. "Acquaint now thyself with him, and be at peace, thereby good shall come upon thee." As trade flourishes, and riches come in when peace is made betwixt states and kingdoms; so all spiritual and temporal mercies flow into our bosoms, when once we are reconciled to God. What the comfort of such a peace will be in a day of straits and dangers, and what it will be valued at in a dying day, who but he that feels it can declare? And yet such an one cannot fully declare it, for it passes all understanding, Phil. 4: 7. We shall now make some improvements of this, and pass on to the third end of the death of Christ.

Inference 1. If Christ died to reconcile God and man, how horrid an evil then is sin! And how terrible was that breach made betwixt God and the creature by it, which could no other way be made up by the death of the Son of God! I remember I have read, that when a great chasm or breach was made in the earth by an earthquake, and the oracle was consulted how it might be closed; this answer was returned, That breach can never be closed, except something of great worth be thrown into it. Such a breach was that which sin made, it could never be reconciled but by the death of Jesus Christ, the most excellent thing in all the creation.

Inf. 2. How sad is the state of all such as are not comprised in the articles of peace with God! The impenitent unbeliever is excepted. God is not reconciled to him; and if God be his enemy, how little avails it, who is his friend? For, if God be a man's enemy, he has an Almighty enemy in him, whose very frown is destruction, Deut. 32: 40, 41, 42, "I lift up my hand to heaven and say, I live for ever. If I whet my glittering sword, and my hand take hold on judgement, I will render vengeance to my enemies, and I will reward them that hate me. I will make mine arrows drunk with blood, (and my sword shall devour flesh) and that with the blood of the slain and the captives, from the beginning of revenges upon the enemy."

Yea, he is an unavoidable enemy. Fly to the utmost parts of the earth, there shall his hand reach thee, as it is Psal. 139: 10. The wings of the morning cannot carry thee out of his reach. If God be your enemy, you have an immortal enemy, who lives for ever to avenge himself upon his adversaries. And what wilt thou do when thou art in Saul's case? 1 Sam. 28: 15, 16. Alas, whither wilt thou turn? To whom wilt thou complain? But what wilt thou do, when thou shalt stand at the bar, and see that God, who is thine enemy, upon the throne? Sad is their case indeed, who are not comprehended in the articles of peace with God.

Inf. 3. If Christ died to reconcile us to God, give diligence to clear up to your own souls, your interest in this reconciliation. It Christ thought it worth his blood to purchase it, it is worth your care and pains to clear it. And what can better evidence it, than your conscientious tenderness of sin, lest you make new breaches. Ah, if reconciled, you will say, as Ezra 9: 14. "And now our God, seeing thou hast given us such a deliverance as this; should we again break thy commandments?" If reconciled to God, his friends will be your friends, and his enemies your enemies. If God be your friend, you will be diligent to please him, John 15: 10, 14. He that makes not peace with God is an enemy to his own soul. And he that is at peace, but takes no pains to clear it, is an enemy to his own comfort. But I must pass from this to the third end of Christ's death.

End 3. You have seen two of those beautiful births of Christ's travail, and lo, a third comes, namely, The sanctification of his people. Typical blood was shed, as you heard, to purify them that were unclean; and so was the blood of Christ shed to purge away the sins of his people: so speaks the apostle expressly, Eph. 5: 25, 26. "Christ gave himself for the church, that he might sanctify and cleanse it." And so he tells us himself, John 17: 29. "And for their sakes I sanctify myself," i.e. consecrate or devote myself to death, "That they also might be sanctified through the truth." Upon the account of this benefit received by the blood of Christ, is that Doxology, which, in a lower strain, is now sounded in the churches, but will be matter of the Lamb's song in heaven, Rev. 1: 5, 6. "To him that loved us, and washed us from our sins, in his own blood, - be glory and honour for ever." Now, there is a twofold evil in sin, the guilt of it, and the pollution of it. Justification properly cures the former, sanctification the latter; but both justification and sanctification flow unto sinners out of the death of Christ. And though it is proper to say the Spirit sanctifies, yet, it is certain, it was the blood of Christ that procured for us the Spirit of sanctification. Had not Christ died, the Spirit had never come down from heaven upon any such design.

The pouring forth of Christ's blood for us, obtained the pouring forth of the spirit of holiness upon us. Therefore the Spirit is said to come in his name, and to take of his, and shew it unto us. Hence it is said, 1 John 5: 6. "He came both by blood and by water;" by blood, washing away the guilt; by water, purifying from the filth of sin. Now this fruit of Christ's death, even our sanctification, is a most incomparable mercy. For, do but consider a few particular excellencies of holiness.

First, Holiness is the image and glory of God. His image, Col. 3: 10. and his glory, Exod. 15: 11. "Who is like unto thee, O Lord, glorious in holiness." Now, when the guilt and filth of sin are washed off, and the beauty of God put upon the soul in sanctification, O what a beautiful creature is the soul now! So lovely in the eyes of Christ, even in its imperfect holiness, that he saith, Cant. 6: 5. "Turn away thine eyes from me, for they have overcome me." So we render it, but the Hebrew word signifies, "they have made me proud, or puffed me up. It is beam of divine glory upon the creature, enamouring the very heart of Christ.

Secondly, As it is the soul's highest beauty, so it is the soul's best evidence for heaven. "Blessed are the pure in heart, for they shall see God," Matt. 5: 8. "And without holiness no man shall see God," Heb. 12: 14. No gifts, no duties, no natural endowments will evidence a right in heaven, but the least measure of true holiness will secure heaven to the soul.

Thirdly, As holiness is the soul's best evidence for heaven, so it is a continual spring of comfort to it in the way thither. The poorest and sweetest pleasures in this world are the results of holiness, "till we come to live holy, we never live comfortably. Heaven is epitomised in holiness.

Fourthly, And to say no more; it is the peculiar mark by which God has visibly distinguished his own from other men, Psal. 4: 3 "The Lord has set apart him that is godly for himself," q. d. this is the man, and that the woman, to sham I intend to do good for ever. This is a man for me. O holiness, how surpassingly glorious art thou!

Inference 1. Did Christ die to sanctify his people, how deep then is the pollution of sin, that nothing but the blood of Christ can cleanse it! All the tears of a penitent simmer, should he shed as many as there have fallen drops of rain since the creation to this day, cannot wash away one sin. The everlasting burnings in hell cannot purify the flaming conscience from the least sin. O guess at the wound by the largeness and length of this tent that follows the mortal weapons, Sin.

Inf. 2. Did Christ die to sanctity his people? Behold then the love of a Saviour. "He loved us, and washed us from our sins in his own blood." He did not shed the blood of beasts, as the priests of old did, but his own blood, Heb. 9: 12. And that not common, but precious blood, 1 Pet. 1: 1, 19. The blood at God; one drop of which out-values the blood that runs in the veins of all Adam's posterity. And not some of that blood, but all, to the last drop. He bled every vein dry for us: and what remained lodged about the heart of a dead Jesus, was let out by that bloody spear which pierced the Pericardium: so that he bestowed the whole treasure of his blood upon us. And thus liberal was he of his blood to us when we were enemies. This then is that heavenly Pelican that feeds his young with his own blood. O what manner of love is this! But I must hasten.

End 4. As Christ died to sanctify his people; so he died also to confirm the New Testament to all those sanctified ones. So it was in the type, Exod. 24: 8. and so it is in the text. "This is the New Testament in my blood," Mat. 26: 28. i.e. ratified and confirmed by my blood. For, where a testament is, there must also of necessity be the death of the testator, Heb. 9: 16. So that now all the blessings and benefits bequeathed to believers in the last will and testament of Christ, are abundantly confirmed and secured to them by his death. Yea, he died on purpose to make that testament of force to them. Men make their wills and testaments, and Christ makes his. What they bequeath, and give in their wills, is a free and voluntary act, they cannot be compelled to do it. And what is bequeathed to us in this testament of Christ, is altogether a free and voluntary donation. Other testators use to bequeath their estates to their wives and children, and near relations; so does this testator; all is settled upon his spouse, the church, upon believers, his children. A stranger intermeddles not with these mercies. They give all their goods and estates, that can that way be conveyed, to their friends that survive them. Christ giveth to his church, in the New Testament, three sorts of goods.

First, All temporal good things, 1 Tim. 6: 1. Matt. 6: 33. i.e. the comfort and blessing of all, though not the possession of much. "As having nothing, and yet possessing all things," 2 Cor. 6: 10.

Secondly, All spiritual good things are bequeathed to them in this testament, as remission of sin, and acceptation with God, which are contained in their justification, Rom. 3: 24, 25, 26. Sanctification of their natures, both initial and progressive, 1 Cor. 1: 30. Adoption into the family of God, Gal. 3: 26. The ministry of angels, Heb. 1: 14. Interest in all the promises, 2 Pet. 1: 4. Thus all spiritual good things are in Christ's testament conveyed to them. And as all temporal and spiritual, so,

Thirdly, All eternal good things. Heaven, glory, and eternal life, Rom. 8: 10, 11. No such bequests as these were ever found in the testaments of princes. That which kings and nobles settle by will upon their heirs, are but trifles to what Christ has conferred in the New Testament upon his people. And all this is confirmed and ratified by the death of Christ, so that the promise is sure, and the estate indefeasible to all the heirs of promise.

How the death of Christ confirmed the New Testament is worth our enquiry. The Socinians, as they allow no other end of Christ's death, but the confirmation of the New Testament, so they affirm he did it only by way of testimony, or witness-bearing in his death. But this is a vile derogation from the efficacy of Christ's blood, to bring it down into an equality with the blood of martyrs. As if there were no more in it than was in their blood.

But know, reader, Christ died not only, or principally, to confirm the Testament by his blood, as witness to the truth of those things, but his death rectified it as the death of a testator, which makes the New Testament irrevocable. And so Christ is called in this text. Look as when a man has made his will, and is dead, that will is presently in force, and can never be recalled. Besides, the will of the dead, is sacred with men. They dare not cross it. It is certain the last will and testament of Christ is most sacred, and God will never annul or make it void. Moreover, it is not with Christ as with other testators, who die, and must trust the performance of their wills with their executors, but as he died to put it in force, so he lives again to be the executor of his own testament. And all power to fulfil his will is now in his own hands, Rev. 1: 18.

Inference 1. Did Christ die to confirm the New Testament, in which such legacies are bequeathed to believers. How are all believers concerned then to prove the will of a dead Jesus! My meaning is, to clear their title to the mercies contained in this blessed testament. And this may be done two ways. By clearing to ourselves our covenant-relations to Christ. And by discovering those special covenant-impressions upon our hearts, to which the promises therein contained, do belong.

First, Examine your relations to Christ. Are you his spouse? Have you forsaken all for him? Psal. 45: 10. Are you ready to take your lot with him, as it falls in prosperity or adversity? Jer. 2: 2. And are you loyal to Christ! "Thou shalt be for me, and not for another," Hos. 3: 3. Do you yield obedience to him as your Head and Husband? Eph. 6: 24. then you may be confident you are interested in the benefits and blessings of Christ's last will and testament; for can you imagine Christ will make a testament and forget his spouse? It cannot be. If he so loved the church as to give himself for her, much more what he has is settled on her. Again, are you his spiritual seed, his children by regeneration? Are you born of the Spirit? John 3. Do you resemble Christ in holiness? 1 Pet. 1: 14, 15. Do you find a reverential fear of Christ carrying you to obey him in all things? Mal. 1: 6. Are you led by the Spirit of Christ? "As many as are so led, they are the sons of God," Rom. 8: 14. To conclude, Have you the spirit of adoption, enabling you to cry, Abba, Father? Gal. 4: 6. that is, helping you in a gracious manner, with reverence mixed with filial confidence, to open your hearts spiritually to your Father on all occasions? If so, you are children; and if children, doubt not but you have a rich legacy in Christ's last will and testament. He would not seal up his testament, and forget his dear children.

Secondly, You may discern your interest in the new testament or covenant (for they are substantially the same thing) by the new covenant impressions that are made on your hearts, which are so many clear evidences of your right to the benefits it contains. Such are spiritual illuminations, Jer. 31: 34. gracious softness and tenderness of heart, Ezek. 11: 19. the awful dread and fear of God, Jer. 32: 43. the copy or transcript of his laws on your hearts in gracious correspondent principles, Jer. 31: 33. These things speak you the children of the covenant, the persons on whom all these great things are settled.

Inf. 2. To conclude, it is the indispensable duty of all on whom Christ has settled such mercies, to admire his love, and walk answerably to it.

First, Admire the love of Christ. O how intense and ardent was the love of Jesus! who designed for you such an inheritance, with such a settlement of it upon you! These are the mercies with which his love had travailed big from eternity, and now he sees the travail of his soul, and you also have seen somewhat of it this day. Before this love let all the saints fall down astonished, humbly professing that they owe themselves, and all they are, or shall be worth, to eternity, to this love.

Secondly, And be sure you walk becoming persons for whom Christ has done such great things. Comfort yourselves under present abasures with your spiritual privileges, James 2: 5. and let all your rejoicing be in Christ, and what you have in him, whilst others are blessing themselves in vanity. Thus we have finished the state of Christ's humiliation, and thence proceed to the second state of his exaltation.

An Introduction to the State of Exaltation.

Having finished what I designed to speak to, about the work of redemption, so far as it was carried on by Christ in his humble state, we shall now view that blessed work as it is further advanced and perfected in his state of exaltation.

The whole of that world was not to be finished on earth in a state of suffering, and abasure, therefore the apostle makes his exaltation, in order to the finishing of the remainder of his work so necessary a part of his priesthood, that without it he could not have been a priest, Heb. 8: 4. "If he were on earth he should not be a priest," i.e. if he should have continued always here, and had not been raised again from the dead, and taken up into glory, he could not have been a complete and perfect priest.

For look, as it was not enough for the sacrifice to be slain without, and his blood left there; but after it was shed without, it must be carried within the vail, into the most holy place before the Lord, Heb. 9: 7, so it was not sufficient that Christ shed his own blood on earth, except he carry it before the Lord into heaven, and there perform his intercession-work for us.

Moreover, God the Father stood engaged in a solemn covenant to reward him for his deep humiliation, with a most glorious and illustrious advancement, Isa. 49: 5, 6, 7. And how God (as it became him) made this good to Christ, the apostle very clearly expresses, Phil. 2: 9.

Yea, justice required it should be so. For how could our surety be detained in the prison of the grave, when the debt for which he was imprisoned was by him fully discharged, so that the law of God must acknowledge itself to be fully satisfied in all its claims and demands? His resurrection from the dead was, therefore, but his discharge or acquittance upon full payment. Which could not in justice be denied him.

And, indeed, God the Father lost nothing by it, for there never was a more glorious manifestation made of the name of God to the world, than was made in that work. Therefore it is said, Phil. 2: 11. speaking of one of the designs of Christ's exaltation, it was, (saith the apostle), "That every tongue should confess that Jesus Christ is Lord, to the glory of God the Father." O how is the love of God to poor sinners illustriously, yea, astonishingly, displayed in Christ's exaltation. When, to show the complacency and delight, which he took in our recovery, he has openly declared to the world, that his exalting Christ to all that glory, such as no mere creature ever was, or can be exalted to, was bestowed upon him as a reward for that work, that most grateful work at our redemption, Phil. 2: 9. Wherefore God also has highly exalted him; there is an "emphatical pleonasm in that word," our English is too flat to deliver out the elegance of the original, it is super-exaltation. The Syriac renders it, "he has multiplied his sublimity." The Arabic, "he has heightened him with an height." Justin, "he has famously exalted him." Higher he cannot raise him, a greater argument of his high satisfaction and content in the recovery of poor sinners cannot be given. For this, therefore, God the Father shall have glory and honour ascribed to him in heaven to all eternity.

Now this singular exaltation of Jesus Christ, as it properly respects his human nature, which alone is capable of advancement; for, in respect of his divine nature, he never ceased to be the Most High. So it was done to him as a common person, and as the Head of all believers, their Representative in this as well as in his other works. God therein shewing what, in due time, he intends to do the persons of his elect, after they, in conformity to Christ, have suffered a while. Whatever God the Father intendeth to do in us, or for us, he has first done it to the person of our Representative, Jesus Christ. And this, if you observe, the scriptures carry in very clear and plain expressions, through all the degrees and steps of Christ's exaltation, viz. his resurrection, ascension, session at the right-hand of God, and returning to judge the world; of which I purpose to speak distinctly in the following sermons.

He arose from the dead as a public person, Col. 3: 1. "If ye then be risen with Christ," saith the apostle, so that the saints have communion and fellowship with him in his resurrection.

He ascended into heaven, as a public person, for so it is said in Eph. 2: 6. "He has raised us up," or exalted us together with Christ. He sits at God's right-hand, as a common person, for so it follows in the next clause, "and has made us sit together in heavenly places in Christ Jesus." We sit there in our Representative. And when he shall come again to judge the world, the saints shall come with him. So it is prophesied, Zech. 14: 5. "The Lord my God shall come, and all the saints with thee." And as they come with Christ from heaven, so they shall sit on thrones with him, judging by way of suffrage. They shall be assessors with the Judge, 1 Cor. 6: 2. This deserves a special remark, that all this honour is given to Christ, as our Head and representative, for thence results abundance of comfort to the people of God. Carry it therefore along with you in your thoughts, throughout the whole of Christ's advancement. Think when you shall hear that Christ is risen from the dead, and is in all that glory and authority in heaven, how sure the salvation of his redeemed is. "For if when we were enemies, we were reconciled to God, by the death of his Son; much more, being reconciled, we shall be saved by his life." Surely, it cannot be supposed, but "he is able to save to the uttermost, all them that come to God by him; seeing he ever lives to make intercession," Heb. 7: 25. Think how safe the people of God in this world are, whose Head is in heaven. It was a comfortable expression of one of the fathers, encouraging himself and others with this truth in a dark day, "Come, (said he) why do we tremble thus, Do we not see our head above water?" If he live,

The Fountain of Life Opened Up

believers cannot die, John 14: 19. "Because I live, ye shall live also."

And let no man's heart suggest a suspicious thought to him, that this wonderful advancement of Christ may cause him to forget his poor people, groaning here below under sin and misery. For the temper and disposition of his faithful and tender heart, is not changed with his condition. He bears the same respect to us as when he dwelt among us. For indeed he there lives and acts upon our account, Heb. 7: 25. 1 John 2: 1, 2.

And how seasonable and comfortable will the meditations of Christ's exaltation be to thee, O believer, when sickness has wasted thy body, withered its beauty, and God is bringing thee to the dust of death! Ah! think then, that that "vile body shall be conformed to the glorious body of Christ," Phil. 3: 21. As God has glorified, and highly exalted his Son, "whose form was marred more than any man's;" so will he exalt thee also. I do not say, to a parity, or equality, in glory with Christ, for, in heaven he will be discerned and distinguished, by his peculiar glory, from all the angels and saints; as the sun is known by its excellent glory from the lesser stars. But we shall be conformed to this glorious Head, according to the proportion of members. O whither will love mount the believer in that day!

Having spoken thus much of Christ's exalted state, to cast some general light upon it, and engage your attentions to it, I shall now according to the degrees of this his wonderful exaltation, briefly open it, under the fore-mentioned heads, viz. his resurrection, ascension, session at the Father's right hand, and his return to judge the world.

Sermon 39: Wherein the Resurrection of CHRIST, with its influences upon the Saints Resurrection, is clearly opened, and comfortably applied, being the first Step of his Exaltation

Matth. 28: 6.
He is not here; for he is risen, as he said: come, see the place where the Lord lay.

We have finished the doctrine of Christ's humiliation, wherein the Sun of righteousness appeared to you, as a setting sun, gone out of sight; but as the sun when it is gone down to us, begins a new day in another part of the world, so Christ, having finished his course, and sock in this world, rises again, and that, in order to the acting, another glorious part of his work in the world above. In his death, he was upon the matter totally eclipsed, but in his resurrection, he began to recover his light and glory again. God never intended that the darling of his soul should be lost in obscure sepulchre. An angel descends from heaven, to roll away the stone, and, with it, the reproach of his death; and to be the heavenly herald, to proclaim his resurrection to the two Mary's, whose love to Christ had, at this time, drawn them to visit the sepulchre, where they lately left him.

At this time (the Lord being newly risen) the keepers were trembling, and become as dead men. So great was the terrible majesty and awful solemnity attending Christ's resurrection; but, to encourage these good souls, the angel prevents them with these good tidings; "He is not here; for he is risen, as he said: come, see the place where the Lord lay:" q. d. Be not troubled, though you have not the end you came for, one sight more of your dear, though dead Jesus; yet you have not lost your labour; for, to your eternal comfort, I tell you, "he is risen, as he said." And to put it out of doubt, come hither and satisfy yourselves, "See the place where the Lord lay."

In which words arts we have both a declaration and confirmation of the resurrection of Christ from the dead.

First. A declaration of it by the angels, both negatively and affirmatively. Negatively, He is not here. Here. indeed you laid him, here you left him, and here you thought to find him as you left him; but you are happily mistaken, He is not here. However, this giving them no satisfaction, so he might continue dead still, thought removed to another place, as indeed they suspected he was, John 20: 13. therefore his resurrection is declared positively and affirmatively; He is risen; "egerte", the word imports, the active power or self-quickening principle, by which Christ raised himself from the state of the dead. Which Luke takes notice of also, Acts 1: 3 where he saith, He shewed, or presented, himself alive after his passion. It was the divine nature, or Godhead of Christ, which revived and raised the manhood.

Secondly, Here is also a plain confirmation of Christ's resurrection, and that, first, From Christ's own prediction, He is risen, as he said. He foretold that which I declare to be now fulfilled. Let it not therefore seem incredible to you. Secondly, by their own sight, "Come, see the place where the Lord lay." The grave has lost its guest; it is now empty; death has lost its prey. It received, but could not retain him, "Come, see the place where the Lord lay." Thus the resurrection of Christ is declared, and confirmed. Hence our observation is,

Doct. That our Lord Jesus Christ, by the almighty power of his own Godhead, revived, and rose from the dead; to the terror and consternation of his enemies, and the unspeakable consolation of believers.

That our Lord Jesus Christ, though laid, was not lost in the grave; but the third day revived and rose again, is a truth confirmed to us by many infallible proofs, as Luke witnesseth, Acts 1: 3. We have testimonies of it, both from heaven and earth, and both infallible. From heaven, we have the testimony of angels, and to the testimony of an angel all credit is due; for angels are holy creatures, and cannot deceive us. The angel tells the two Mary's, in the text, "He is risen." We have testimonies of it from men, holy men, who were eye-witnesses of this truth, to whom he showed himself alive by the space of forty days after his resurrection, by no less than nine solemn apparitions to them. Sometimes five hundred brethren saw him at once, 1 Cor. 15: 6. These were holy persons, who durst not deceive, and who confirmed their testimony with their blood. So that no point of religion is of more confessed truth, and infallible certainty than this before us.

And blessed be God it is so. For if it were not, then were the "gospel in vain," 1 Cor. 15: 14. seeing it hangs the whole weight of our faith, hope, and salvation, upon Christ as risen from the dead. If this were not so, then could the holy, and divinely inspired apostles be found false witnesses, 1 Cor. 15; 15. For they all, with one mouth, constantly, and to the death affirmed it. If Christ be not risen, then are believers yet in their sins," 1 Cor. 15: 17. For our justification is truly ascribed to the resurrection of Christ, Rom. 4: 25. Whilst Christ was dying, and continued in the state of the dead, the price of our redemption was all that while but in paying, the payment was completed, when he revived and rose again. Therefore for Christ to have continued always in the state of the dead, had been never to have completely satisfied; hence the whole force and weight of our justifications depends upon his resurrection. Nay, had not Christ risen, "the dead had perished," 1 Cor. 15: 17. Even the dead who died in the faith of Christ, and of whose salvation there now remains no ground to doubt. Moreover,

Had he not revived and risen from the dead, how could all the types that prefigured it have been satisfied? Surely they must have stood as insignificant things in the scriptures; and so must all the predictions of his resurrection, by which it was so plainly foretold. See Matth. 12: 40. Luke 24: 46. Psal. 16: 10. 1 Cor. 15: 4.

To conclude. Had he not risen from the dead, how could he have been installed in that glory whereof he is now possessed in heaven, and which was promised him before the world was, upon the account of his death and sufferings? "For to this end Christ both died, and rose and revived, that he might be Lord both of the dead and living," Rom. 14: 9. And that, in this state of dominion and glorious advancement, he might powerfully apply the virtues and benefits of his blood to us, which else had been as a precious cordial spilt upon the ground.

So then, there remains no doubt at all of the certainty of Christ's resurrection; it was so, and upon all accounts it must needs be so; for you see how great a weight the scriptures hang upon this nail. And blessed be God it is a nail fastened in a sure place. I need spend no more words to confirm it; but rather choose to explain and open the nature and manner of his resurrection, which I shall do by shewing you four or five properties of it. And the first is this,

First, Christ rose from the dead with awful majesty. So you find it in Mat. 28: 2, 3, 4. "And behold there was a great earthquake; for the angel of the Lord descended from heaven, and came and rolled back the stone from the door, and sat upon it. His countenance was like lightning, and his raiment white as snow. And for fear of him the keepers did shake, and became as dead men." Human infirmity was not able to bear such heavenly majesty as attended the business of that morning. Nature sank under it. This earthquake was, as one calls it, triumpale signum: a sign of triumph, or token of victory, given by Christ, not only to the keepers, and the neighbouring city, but to the whole world, that he had overcome death in its own dominions, and, like a conqueror, lifted up his head above all his enemies. So when the Lord fought from heaven for his people, and gave them a glorious, though but temporal deliverance, see how the prophetess drives on the triumph in that rhetorical song, Judg. 5: 4, 5. Alluding to the most awful appearance of God, at the giving of the law. "Lord, when thou went out of Seir, when thou marchedst out of the field of Edom, the earth trembled, and the heavens dropped, the clouds also dropped water. The mountains melted from before the Lord, even that Sinai from before the Lord God of Israel." Our Lord Jesus went out of the grave, in like manner, and marched out of that bloody field with a pomp and majesty becoming so great a conqueror.

Secondly, And to increase the splendour of that day, and drive on the triumph, his resurrection was attended with the resurrection of many of the saints; who had slept in their graves till then, anrd then were awakened and raised to attend the Lord at his rising. So you read, Mat. 27: 52, 53. "And the graves were opened, and many bodies of the saints, which slept, arose, and came out of the graves, after his resurrection; and went into the holy city and appeared unto many." This wonder was designed, both to adorn the resurrection of Christ, and to give a specimen or pledge of our resurrection; which also is to be in the virtue of his. This indeed was the resurrection of saints and none but saints, the resurrection of many saints, yet it was but a special resurrection, intended only to show what God will one day do for all his saints. And for the present, to give testimony of Christ's resurrection from the dead. They were seen, and known of many in the city, who doubtless never thought to have seen them any more in this world. To enquire curiously, as some do, who they were, what discourse they had with those to whom they appeared, and what became of them afterwards, is a vain thing. God has cast a vail of silence and secrecy upon these things, that we might content ourselves with the written word, and he that "will not believe Moses and the prophets, neither will he believe though one rise from the dead", as these saints did.

Thirdly, As Christ rose from the dead with those satellites or at pendants, who accompanied him at his resurrection; so it was by the power of his own Godhead that he quickened and raised him self; and by the virtue of his resurrection were they raised also, who accompanied him. It was not the angel who rolled back the stone that revived him in the sepulchre, but he resumed his own life; so he tells us, John 10: 18. "I lay down my life that I may take it again." Hence 1 Pet. 3: 18. He is said to be put to death in the flesh, but quickened by the Spirit, i.e. by the power of his Godhead, or divine nature, which is opposed there to flesh, or his human nature. By the eternal Spirit he offered himself up to God, when he died, Heb. 9: 14. i.e. by his own Godhead, not the third person in the Trinity, for then it could not have been ascribed to him as his own act, that he offered up himself. And by the same Spirit he was quickened again.

And, therefore, the apostle well observes, Rom. 1: 4. "That he was declared to be the Son of God with power, by his resurrection from the dead." Now if he had been raised by the power of the Father, or Spirit only, and not by his own, how could he be declared by his resurrection to be the Son of God? What more had appeared in him than in others? For others are raised by the power of God, if that were all. So that in this respect also it was a marvellous resurrection. Never any did, or shall rise as Christ rose by a self-quickening principle. For though many dead saints rose at that time also, yet it was by the virtue of Christ's resurrection that their graves were opened, and their bodies quickened. In which respect he saith, John 11: 25. when he raised dead Lazarus, "I am the resurrection and the life," i.e. the principle of life and quickening, by which the dead saints are raised.

Fourthly, And therefore it may be truly affirmed, that though some dead saints are raised to life before the resurrection of Christ, yet that Christ is "the first-born from the dead," as he is called, Col. 1: 18. For though Lazarus and others were raised, yet not by themselves, but by Christ. It was by his virtue and power, not their own. And though they were raised to life, yet they died again. Death recovered them again, but Christ dies no more. "Death has no dominion over him." He was the first that opened the womb of the earth, the first-born from the dead, that in all things he might have the pre-eminence.

Fifthly, But lastly, Christ rose as a public or common person. "As the first fruits of them that slept," 1 Cor. 15: 20. I desire this may be well understood; for upon this account it is that our resurrection is secured to us by the resurrection of Christ; and not a resurrection only, but a blessed and happy one, for the first-fruits both assured and sanctified the whole crop or harvest.

Now that Christ did rise, as a public person, representing and comprehending all the elect, who were called the children of the resurrection, is plain from Eph. 2: 6. where we are said to be risen with, or in him. So that, as we are said to die in Adam, (who also was a common person) as the branches die in the death of the root; so we are said to be raised from death in Christ, who is the head, root, and representative, of all his elect seed. And why is he called the firstborn, and first begotten frown the dead, but with respect to the whole number of the elect, that are to be born from the dead in their time and order also and as sure as the whole harvest follows the first fruits, so shall the general resurrection of the saints to life eternal follow this birth of the first-born from the dead.

It shall surely follow it I say, and that not only as a consequent follows an antecedent, but as an effect follows its proper cause. Now there is a three-fold casualty, or influence that Christ's resurrection has upon the saints resurrection, of which it is at once the meritorious, efficient, and exemplary cause.

First, The resurrection of Christ is a meritorious cause of the saints resurrection, as it completed his satisfaction, and finished his payment, and so our justification is properly assigned to it, as before was noted from Rom. 4: 25. This his resurrection was the receiving of the acquittance, the cancelling of the bond. And had not this been done, we had still been in our sins, as he speaks, 1 Cor. 15: 7. and so our guilt had been still a bar to our happy resurrection. But now, the price being paid in his death, which payment was finished when he revived; and the discharge then received for us, now there is nothing lies in bar against our resurrect lion to eternal life.

Secondly, As it is the meritorious cause of our resurrection, so it s the efficient cause of it also. For when the time shall come that the saints shall rise out of the dust, they shall be raised by Christ, as their head, in whom the effective principle of their life is. "Your life is hid with Christ in God," as it is Col. 3:3. As when a man awakes out of his sleep, "the animal spirits seated in the brain, being set at liberty by the digestion of those vapours that bound them up, do play freely through every part and member of the body;" so Christ, the believers mystical head, being quickened, the spirit of life, which is in him, shall be diffused through all his members to quicken them also in the morning of the resurrection. Hence the warm animating dew of Christ's resurrection is said to be to our bodies, as the dew of the morning is to the withered, languishing plants, which revive by it, Isa. 26: 19. "Thy dew is as the dew of herbs;" and then it follows, "the

The Fountain of Life Opened Up

earth shall cast forth her dead." So that by the same faith we put Christ's resurrection into the promises, we may put the believer's resurrection into the conclusion. And therefore, the apostle makes them convertibles, reasoning forward, from Christ's to ours; and back again from ours to his, 1 Cor. 15: 12, 13. Which is also the sense of that scripture, Rom. 8: 10, 11. "And if Christ be in you, the body indeed is dead because of sin; but the spirit is life because of righteousness." i.e. Though you are really united to Christ by the Spirit, yet your bodies must die as well as other men's; but your souls shall be presently, upon your dissolution, swallowed up in life. And then it follows, verse 11. "But if the Spirit of him that raised up Jesus from the dead, dwell in you; he that raised up Christ from the dead, shall also quicken your mortal bodies, by his Spirit that dwelleth in you," i.e. though your bodies must die, yet they shall live again in the resurrection; and that by virtue of the Spirit of Christ which dwelleth in you, and is the bond of your mystical union with him your head. You shall not be raised as others are, by a mere word of power, but by the Spirit of life dwelling in Christ your head, which is a choice prerogative indeed.

Thirdly, Christ's resurrection is not only the meritorious and efficient cause, but it is also the exemplary cause or pattern of our resurrection. "He being the first and best, is therefore the pattern and measure of all the rest." So you read, Phil. 3: 21. "Who shall change our vile body that it may be fashioned like unto his glorious body." Now the conformity of our resurrection to Christ's stands in the following particulars. Christ's body was raised substantially the same; so will ours. His body was raised first; so will ours be raised before the rest of the dead. His body was wonderfully improved by the resurrection; so will ours. His body was raised to be glorified; and so will ours.

First, Christ's body was raised substantially the same that it was before; and so will ours. Not another, but the same body. Upon this very reason the apostle uses that identical expression, 1 Cor. 15: 53. "This corruptible must put on incorruption, and this mortal, immortality." Pointing, as it were, to his own body when he spake it; the same body, I say, and that not only specifically the same, (for indeed no other species of flesh is so privileged) but the same numerically, that very body, not a new or another body in its stead. So that it shall be both the what it was, and the who it was. And indeed to deny this is to deny the resurrection itself. For should God prepare another body to be raised in stead of this, it would not be a resurrection, but a creation; for non resurrectio dici poterit, ubi non resurgit quod cecidit. That cannot be called a resurrection, where one thing falls and another risers, as Gregory long since pertinently observed.

Secondly, His body was raised, not by a word of power from the Father, but by his own Spirit. So will ours. Indeed the power of God shall go forth to unburrough sinners, and fetch them forcibly out of their graves; but the resurrection of the saints is to be effected another way; as I opened but now to you. Even by his Spirit which now dwelleth in them. That very Spirit of Christ which effected their spiritual resurrection from sin, shall effect their corporal resurrection also from the grave.

Thirdly, His body was raised first, he had in this, as well as in other things, the pre-eminence; so shall the saints, in respect of the wicked, have the pre-eminence in the resurrection, 1 Thess. 4: 16 "The dead in Christ shall rise first." They are to attend the Lord at his coming, and will be brought forth sooner than the rest of the world, to attend on that service. As the sheriff, with his men, goes forth to meet the judge, before the gaoler brings forth his prisoners.

Fourthly, Christ's body was marvellously improved by the resurrection, and so will ours. It fell in weakness, but was raised in power; no more capable of sorrows, pains and dishonours. In like manner our bodies are "sown in weakness, but raised in strength, sown in dishonour, raised in glory. Sown natural bodies, raised spiritual bodies," as the apostle speaks, 1 Cor. 15: 43, 44. Spiritual bodies, not properly, but analogically. No distemper hang about glorified bodies, nor are they henceforth subject to any of those natural necessities, to which they are now tied. There are no flaw, defects, or deformities, in the children of the resurrection. What members are now defective or deformed, will then be restored to their perfect being and beauty; "for, if the universal death of all parts be rescinded by the resurrection, how much more the partial death of any single member?" or as Tertullian speaks, and from thenceforth they are free from the law of mortality, "They can die no more," Luke 20: 35, 36. Thus shall they be improved by their resurrection.

Fifthly, To conclude, Christ's body was raised from the dead to be glorified and crowned with honour. Oh it was a joyful day to him; and so will the resurrection of the saints be to them, the day of the gladness of their hearts. It will be said to them in that morning, "Awake, and sing, ye that dwell in the dust," as Isa. 26: 19. O how comfortable will be the meeting betwixt the glorified soul, and its new raised body. Much more comfortable than that of Jacob's and Joseph's, after twenty years absence, Gen. 46: 29. Or that of David's with Jonathan, when he came out of the cave to him, 1 Sam. 20: 41. Or that of the father of the prodigal with his son, who "was dead, and is alive, was lost, and is found." As he speaks, Luke 15: And there are three things will make it so.

First, The gratifications of the soul, by the satisfaction of its natural appetite of union with its own body. For even glorified souls in heaven have such an appetition and desire of reunion. In deed, the angels, who are pure spirits, as they never had union with, so they have no inclination to matter; but souls are otherwise tempered and disposed. We are all sensible of its affection to the body now, in its compounded state, we feel the tender care it has for the body, the sympathy with it, and lothness to be separated from it. It is said, 2 Cor. 5: 6. "to be at home in the body." And had not God implanted such an inclination to this its tabernacle in it, it would not have paid that due respect it owes the body while it inhabited in it, nor have regarded what became of it when it left it. This inclination remains still with it in heaven, it reckons not itself completely happy till its old dear companion and partner be with it, and in that sense some understand those words, Job 14: 14. "All the days of my appointed time," i.e. of the time appointed for my body to remain in the grave, will I wait till my change (viz. that which will be made by the resurrection) come; for it is manifest enough he speaks there of the resurrection. Now, when this its inclination to its own body, its longings and hankerings after it, are gratified with a sight and enjoyment of it again, oh what a comfortable meeting will this make it! especially if we consider,

Secondly, The excellent temper and state in which they shall meet each other. For, as the body shall be raised with all the improvements and endowments imaginable, which may render it amiable, and every way desirable, so the soul comes down immediately from God out of heaven, shining in its holiness and glory. It comes perfumed out of those ivory palaces, with a strong scent of heaven upon it. And thus it re-enters its body, and animates it again. But,

Thirdly, And principally, that wherein the chief joy of this meeting consists, is the end for which the glorified soul comes down to quicken and repossess it, namely, to meet the Lord, and ever to be with the Lord. To receive a full reward for all the labours and services it performed to God in this world. This must needs make that day, a day of triumph and exaltation. It comes out of the grave, as Joseph out of his prison, to be advanced to the highest honour. O do but imagine what an ecstasy of joy, and ravishing pleasure it will be, for a soul thus to resume its own body, and say as it were, unto it, come away, my dear, my ancient friend, who servedst and sufferedst with me in the world; come along with me to meet the Lord, in whose presence I have been ever since I parted with thee. Now thy bountiful Lord has remembered thee also, and the day of thy glorification is come. Surely it will be a joyful awaking. For, do but imagine, what a joy it is for dear friends to meet after long separation, how do they use to give demonstrations of their love and delight in each other, by embraces, kisses, tears, &c. Or frame but to yourselves a notion of perfect health, when a sprightly vivacity runs through every part, and the spirits do, as it were, dance before us, when we go about any business as especially to such a business as the business of that day will be, to receive a crown, and a kingdom. Do but imagine then what a sun shine morning this will be, and how the gains and agonies, cold sweats, and bitter groans at parting will be recompensed by the joy of such a meeting?

And thus I have shewed you the certainty of Christ's resurrection, the nature and properties of it, the threefold influence it has on the saints resurrection, and the conformity of ours unto his in these five respects. His body rose substantially the same, so shall ours; his body was raised by the Spirit, so shall ours. Not by the Godhead of Christ as his was, but by the Spirit, who is the bond of our union with Christ. He was raised as the first begotten from the dead, so the dead in Christ shall rise first. His body was improved by the resurrection, so shall ours. From the consideration of all which,

Inference 1. We infer, that if Christ was thus raised from the dead, then death is fairly overcome, and swallowed up in victory: were it not so, it had never let Christ escape out of the grave. The prey of the terrible had never been thus rescued out of its paws. Death is a dreadful enemy, it defies all the sons and daughters of Adam. None durst cope with this king of terrors but Christ, and he, by dying, went into the very den of this dragon, fought with it, and foiled it in the grave, its own territories and dominions, and came off a conqueror. For, as the apostle speaks, Acts 2: 24. "It was impossible it should hold or detain him." Never did death meet with its over match before it met with Christ, and he conquering it for us, and in our names, rising as our representative, now every single saint triumphs over it as a vanquished enemy, 1 Cor. 15: 55. "O death, where is thy sting? O grave, where is thy victory? Thanks be to God, who has given us the victory through our Lord Jesus Christ." Thus, like Joshua, they set the foot of faith upon the neck of that king, and, with an holy scorn, deride its power. "O death, where is thy sting?" If it be objected that it is said, 1 Cor. 15: 26. "The last enemy that is to be destroyed is death." And if so, then it should seem the victory is not yet achieved, and so we do but boast before the victory; it is at hand to reply that the victory over death, obtained by Christ's resurrection, is twofold, either personal and incomplete, or general and complete. He actually overcame it at his resurrection, in his own person, perfectly and virtually for us, as our head; but at the general resurrection of the saints (which his resurrection, as the first-fruits, assures them of) then it will be utterly vanquished and destroyed. Till then, it will exercise some little power over the bodies of the saints, in which respect it is called the last enemy. For sin, the chief enemy that let it in, that was conquered utterly and eradicated when they died; but death holds their bodies in the grave till the coming of Christ, and then it is utterly to be vanquished. For after that they can die no more, 1 Cor. 15: 54. "And then shall be brought to pass that saying that is written, Death is swallowed up in victory." Then, and not till shell, will that conquest be fully completed in our persons, though it be already so in Christ's; now incompletely in ours, and then completely and fully for ever. For the same word which signifies victory does also signify perpetuity, and in this place a final or perpetual conquest. And, indeed, now it smites only with its dart, not with its sting, and that but the believer's body only, and the body but for a time remains under it neither. So that there is no reason why a believer should stand in a slavish fear of it.

Inf. 2. Has Christ, and has his resurrection such a potent and comfortable influence into the resurrection of the saints? Then it is the duty, and will be the wisdom of the people of God, so to govern, dispose, and employ their bodies, as become men and women, that understand what glory is prepared form them at the resurrection of the just. Particularly,

First, Be not fondly tender of them, but employ and use them for God here. How many good duties are lost and spoiled by sinful indulgence to our bodies? Alas! we are generally more solicitous to live long, than to live usefully. How many saints have active, vigorous bodies, yet God has little service from them. If your bodies were animated by some other souls that love God more than van do, and burn with holy zeal to his service, more work would be done for God by your bodies in a day, than is now done in a month. To have an able, healthy body, and not use it for God, for fear of hurting it, is as if one should give you a strong and stately horse, upon condition you must not work or ride him. Wherein is the mercy of having a body, except it be employed for God? Will not its reward at the resurrection be sufficient for all the pains you nor put it to in his service?

Secondly, See that you preserve the due honour of your bodies. "Possess them in sanctification and honour," 1 Thess. 4: 4. O, let not these eyes be now defiled with sin, by which you shall see God. Those ears be inlets to vanity, which shall hear the Hallelujahs of the blessed. God hath designed honour for your bodies, O, make them not either the instruments or objects of sin. There are sins against the body, 1 Cor. 6: 18. Preserve your bodies from those defilements, for they are the temple of God; "If any man defile the temple of God, him shall God destroy," 1 Cor. 3: 17.

Thirdly, Let not the contentment and accommodation of your bodies draw your soul into snares, and bring them under the power of temptations to sin. This is a very common case. O how many thousands of precious souls perish eternally for the satisfaction of a vile body for a moment? Their souls must, because their bodies cannot suffer. It is recorded to the immortal honour of these worthies, in Heb. 11: 35. "That they accepted not deliverance, that they might obtain a better resurrection." They might have had a temporal resurrection from death to life, from reproach to honour, from poverty to riches, from pains to pleasure; but upon such terms they judged it not worth acceptance. They would not expose their souls to secure their bodies. They had the same natural affections that other men have. They were made of as tender flesh as we are, but such was the care they had of their souls, and the hope of a better resurrection, that they listened not to the complaints and whinings of their bodies. O, that we were all in the same resolutions with them.

Fourthly, With-hold not, upon the pretence of the wants your own bodies may be in, that which God and conscience bid you to communicate for the refreshment of the saints, whose present necessities require your assistance. O, be not too indulgent to your own flesh, and cruel to others. Certainly, the consideration of that reward which shall be given you at the resurrection, for every act of Christian charity, is the greatest spur and incentive in the world to it. And to that end it is urged as a motive to charity, Luke 14: 13, 14. "When thou makes a feast, call the poor, the maimed, the lame, the blind, and thou shalt be blessed; for they cannot recompense thee: for thou shalt be recompensed at the resurrection of the justly". It was the opinion of an eminent moderns divines, that no man living, fully understands and believes that scripture, Mat. 25: 40. "In as much as you have done it to one of the least of these my brethren, you have done it unto me." How few saints would be exposed to daily wants and necessities, if that scripture were but fully understood and believed!

Inf. 3. Is Christ risen from the dead, and that as a public person and representative of believers? How are we all concerned then to secure to ourselves an interest in Christ, and consequently in this blessed resurrection? What consolation would be left in this world, if the hope of the resurrection were taken away? It is this blessed hope that must support you under all the troubles of life, and in the agonies of death. The securing of a blessed resurrection to yourselves, is therefore the most deep concernment you have in this world. And it may be secured to yourselves, if, upon serious heart-examination, you can discover the following evidences.

Evidence 1. First, If you are regenerated creatures, brought forth in a new nature to God, for we are "begotten again to a lively hope, by the resurrection of Jesus Christ from the dead." Christ's resurrection is the ground work of our hope. And the new birth is our title or evidence of our interest in it. So that until our souls are partakers of the spiritual resurrection from the death of sin, we can have no assurance our bodies shall be partakers of that blessed resurrection to life.

"Blessed and holy (saith the Spirit), is he that has part in the first resurrection, on such the second death has no power," Rev. 20: 6. Never let unregenerate souls expect a comfortable meeting with their bodies again. Rise they shall by God's terrible citation, at the sound of the last trump, but not to the same end that the saints arise, nor by the same principle. They to whom the spirit is now a principle of sanctification, to them he will be the principle of a joyful resurrection. See then that you get gracious souls now, or never expect glorious bodies then.

Evidence. "If you be dead with Christ, you shall live again by the life of Christ. If we have been planted together in the likeness of his death, we shall be also in the likeness of his resurrection," Rom. 6: 5. "sumfutoi", planted together. Some refer it to believers themselves; Jews and Gentiles are planted together in Christ. So Erasmus, "Believers grow together like branches upon the same root," which should powerfully enforce the great gospel duty of unity among themselves. But I would rather understand it, with reference to Christ and believers, with whom believers are in other scriptures said to suffer together, and be glorified together; to die together, and live together; to be crucified together, and buried together; all noting the communion they have with Christ, both in his death, and in his life. Now, if the power of Christ's death, i.e. the mortifying influence of it, have been upon our hearts, killing their lusts, deadening their affections, and flattening their appetites to the creature, then the power of his life, or resurrection, shall come (like the animating dew) upon our dead withered bodies, to revive and raise them up to live with him in glory.

Evidence 3. If your hearts and affections be now with Christ in heaven, your bodies in due time shall be there also, and conformed to his glorious body. So you find it, Phil. 3: 20, 21. "For our conversation is in heaven, from whence we look for the Saviour, the Lord Jesus Christ, who shall change our vile body, that it may be fashioned like unto his own glorious body." "The body is here called vile, or the body of our vileness." Not as God made it, but as sin has marred it. Not absolutely, and in itself, but relatively, and in comparison of what it will be in its second edition, at the resurrection. Then those scattered bones and dispersed dust, like pieces of old broken battered silver, will be new cast, and wrought in the best and newest fashion, even like to Christ's glorious body. Whereof we have this evidence, that our conversation is already heavenly. The temper, frame, and disposition of our souls is already so; therefore the frame and temper of our bodies in due time shall be so.

Evidence 4. If you strive now by any means to attain the resurrection of the dead, no doubt but you shall then attain what you now strive for. This was Paul's great ambition, "that by any means he might attain the resurrection of the dead," Phil. 3: 11. He means not simply a resurrection from the dead, for that all men shall attain, whether they strive for it or no. But by a metonymy of the subject for the adjunct, he intends that complete holiness and perfection, which shall attend the state of the resurrection, so it is expounded, ver. 12. So then, if God have raised in your hearts a vehement desire, and assiduous endeavour after a perfect freedom from sin, and full conformity to God, in the beauties of holiness; that very love of holiness, your present partings, and tendencies after perfection, speak you to be the persons designed for it.

Evidence 5. If you are such as do good in your generation. If you be fruitful and useful men and women in the world, you shall have part in this blessed resurrection, John 5: 28, 29. "All that are in the graves shall hear his voice and shall come forth; they that have done good unto the resurrection of life." Now it is not every act materially good, that entitles a man to this privilege; but the same requisites that the schoolmen assign to make a good prayer, are also necessary to every good work. The person, matter, manner, and end, must be good. Nor is it any single good act, but a series and course of holy actions, that is here meant. What a spur should this be to us all, as (indeed the apostle makes it, closing up the doctrine of the resurrection, with this solemn exhortation, 1 Cor. 15: 58. with which I also close mine) "Therefore, my beloved brethren, be ye steadfast, unmoveable, always abounding in the work of the Lord, for as much as ye know that your labour is not in vain in the Lord."

Thanks be to God for his unspeakable gift.

Sermon 40: The Ascension of Christ illustrated, and variously improved, being the Second Step of his Exaltation

John 20:17.

Jesus saith unto her, Touch me not; for I am not yet ascended to my Father: but go to my brethren, and say unto them, I ascend unto my Father, and your Father; and to my God, and your God.

In all the former sermons, we have been following Christ through his humiliation, from the time that he left the blessed bosom of the Father: and now having finished the whole course of his obedience on earth, and risen again from the dead; we must, in this discourse, follow him back again into heaven, and lodge him in that bosom of ineffable delight and love, which for our sakes, he so freely left. For it was not his end in rising from the dead, to live such a low animal life as this is, but to live a most glorious life, as an enthroned King in heaven: upon which state he was now ready to enter, as he tells Mary in the text, and bids her tell it to the disciples, "Go, tell my brethren, that I ascend to my Father," &c.

In the former verses you find Mary waiting at Christ's sepulchre, in a very pensive frame: exceedingly troubled, because she knew not what was become of Christ, ver. 15. In the next verse, Christ calls her by her name, Mary; she knowing the voice, turned herself, and answered, Rabboni. And as a soul transported with joy, rushes into his arms, as desirous to clasp and embrace him. But Jesus said, "Touch me not," &c.

In which words we have Christ's inhibition, "Touch me not:" Strange that Christ, who rendered himself so kind and tender to all, that not only admitted, but commanded Thomas to put his finger into his wounds, should forbid Mary to touch him, but this was not for want of love to Mary; for he gives another reason for it presently, "I am not yet ascended;" i.e. say some, the time for embracing will be when we are in heaven. Then and there shall be the place and time, we shall embrace one another for evermore. So Augustin. Or, thou dotest too much upon my present state, as if I had now attained the very "akme", culminating point of my exaltation. When as yet I am not ascended, so Cameron and Calvin expound it. Or lastly, Christ would signify hereby that it was not his will and pleasure in so great a juncture of things as this, to spend time now in expressing (this way) her affections to him; but rather to show it by hastening about his service. Which is

The second thing observable, viz. his injunction upon Mary, to carry the tidings of his resurrection to the disciples. In which injunction we have,

First, The persons to whom this message was sent, my brethren, so he calls the disciples. A sweet compellation, and full of love. Much like that of Joseph to his brethren, Gen. 45: 4. save only that there is much more tenderness in this than that; for he twits them in the same breath with what they had done against him: "I am Joseph your brother, whom ye sold;" but in this it is, "Go, tell my brethren," without the least mention of their cowardice or unkindness. And,

Secondly, The message itself; "Tell my brethren, I ascend to my Father, and your Father; to my God, and your God," "anabaino", I ascend. It is put in the present tense, as if he had been ascending; though he did not ascend in some weeks after this; but he so expresses it, to show what was the next part of his work, which he was to act in heaven for them; and how much his heart was set upon it, and longed to be about it, "I ascend to my Father, and your Father; to my God, and your God." Not our Father, or God in common; but mine and yours in a different manner. Yours by right of donation, mine in a different manner. Yours by right of dominion, mine (in reference to my human nature) not only by right of creation, though so too; but also by special covenant and confederation. By predestination of my manhood, to the grace of personal union, by designation of me, to the glorious office of Mediator. My Father, as I am God, by eternal generation. As man, by collation of the grace of union. And your Father by spiritual adoption and regeneration. Thus he is my God, and your God; my Father, and your Father. This is the substance of that comfortable message, sent by Mary to the pensive disciples. Hence the observation is,

Doct. That our Lord Jesus Christ, did not only rise from the dead, but also ascended into heaven; there to dispatch all that remained to be done for the completing the salvation of his people.

So much the apostle plainly witnesseth, Eph. 4: 10. "He that descended, is the same also that ascended up far above all heavens," i.e. all the aspectable heavens. A full and faithful account whereof the several evangelists have given us, Mark 16: 19. Luke 24: 51. This is sometimes called his going away, as John 16: 7. Sometimes his being exalted, Acts 2: 33. Sometimes his being made higher than the heavens, Heb. 7: 26. And sometimes his entering within the vail, Heb. 6: 19, 20. All which are but so many synonymous phrases, expressing his ascension, in a very pleasant variety.

Now for the opening this act of Christ, we will bind up the whole in the satisfaction of these six questions. 1. Who ascended? 2. Whence did he ascend? 3. Whither? 4. When? 5. How? 6. and lastly, Why did he ascend? And these will take in what is needful for you to be acquainted with in this point.

First, Who ascended? This the apostle answers, Eph. 4: 10. "the same that descended," viz. Christ. And himself tells us in the text, "I ascend." "And though the ascension were of Christ's whole person, yet it was but a figurative and improper expression, with respect to his divine nature, but it agrees most properly to the humanity of Christ, which really changed places and conditions by it." And hence it is that it is said, John 16: 28. "I came forth from the Father, and am come into the world;" again, I leave the world, and go to my Father." He goes away, and we see him no more. As God, he is spiritually with us still, even to the end of the world. But as man, "the heavens must contain him till the restitution of all things," Acts 3: 21.

Secondly, Whence Christ ascended?
I answer, more generally, he is said to ascend from this world, to leave the world. That is the terminus a quo, John 16: 28. but more particularly, it was from Mount Olivet, near unto Jerusalem. The very place where he began his last sorrowful tragedy. There, where his heart began to be sadded, there is it now made glad. O, what a difference was there betwixt the frame Christ was in, in that mount before his passion, and this he is now in, at his ascension! But,

Thirdly, Whither did he ascend?
It is manifest it was into the third heavens: the throne of God, and place of the blessed; where all the saints shall be with him for ever. It is said to be far above all heavens; i.e. the heavens which we see, for they are but the pavement of that stately palace of the great King. He is gone (saith the apostle) within the vail, i.e. into the most holy place. And into his Father's house, John 14: 2. And he is also said to go to the "place where he was before," John 6: 62. back again to that sweet and glorious bosom of delight and love, from whence at his incarnation he came.

Fourthly, When did Christ ascend? Was it presently as soon as he arose from the dead?
No, not so, for "after his resurrection (saith Luke) he was seen of them forty days, speaking of the things pertaining to the kingdom of God." And truly the care and love of Christ to his people was very manifest in this his stay with them. He had ineffable glory prepared for him in heaven, and awaiting his coming, but he will not go to possess it, till he had settled all things for the good of his church here. For in this time he confirmed the truth of his resurrection, gave charge to the apostles concerning the discipline and order of his house or kingdom: which was but needful, since he intended that their Acts should be rules to future churches. So long it was necessary he should stay. And when he had set all things in order, he would stay no longer, "lest he should seem to affect a terrene life." And besides, he had work of great concernment to do for us in the other world. He desired to be no longer here, than he had work to do for God and souls. A good pattern for the saints.

Fifthly, How did Christ ascend into heaven?
Here it is worthy our observation, that Christ ascended as a public person or forerunner, in our names, and upon our accounts. So it is said expressly, Heb 6: 20 speaking of the most holy place within the vail; whither (saith he) the forerunner is for us entered. His entering into heaven as our forerunner implies both his public capacity and precedence.

First, His public capacity, as one that went upon our business to God. So he himself speaks, John 14: 2. "I go before to prepare a place for you". To take possession of heaven in your names. The forerunner has respect to others that were to come to heaven after him, in their several generations; for whom he has taken up mansions, which are kept for them against their coming.

Secondly, It notes precedence, he is our forerunner, but he himself had no forerunner. Never any entered into heaven before him, but such as entered in his name, and through the virtue of his name. He was the first that ever entered into heaven directly, immediately, in his own name, and upon his own account. But all the fathers who died before him entered in his name. To the holiest of them all, God would have said as Elisha to Jehoram, 2 Kings 3: 14 Were it not that I had respect to the person of my Son, in whose name and right you come, I would not look upon you . You must go back again, heaven were no place for you. No, not for you, Abraham, nor for you, Moses

Secondly, He ascended triumphantly into heaven. To this good expositors refer that which in the type is spoken of David, when he lodged the ark in its own place, with musical instruments and shootings; but to Christ, in the antitype, when he was received up triumphantly into glory, Psal. 47: 5 "God is gone up with a shout, the Lord with the sound of a trumpet; sing praises to God, sing praises; sing praises unto our King, sing praises."

A cloud is prepared, as a royal chariot, to carry up the King of glory to his princely pavilion. "A cloud received him out of their sight," Luke 24: 51. And then a royal guard of mighty angels surrounded the chariot, if not for support, yet for greater state and solemnity of their Lord's ascension. And oh what jubilations of the blessed angels were heard in heaven! How was the whole city of God moved at his coming! For look as when "he brought his first begotten into the world, he said, let all the angels of God worship him," Heb. 1: 6. So at his return thither again, when he had finished redemption-work, there were no less demonstrations given by those blessed creatures of their delight and joy in it. The very heavens echoed and resounded on that account. Yea, the triumph is not ended at this day, nor ever shall.

It is said, Dan. 7: 13, 14. "I saw, (saith the prophet) in the night visions, and behold one like the Son of man came with the clouds of heaven, and came to the Ancient of days, and they brought him near to him. And there was given him dominion, and glory, and a kingdom; that all people, nations and languages should serve him." This vision of Daniel's was accomplished in Christ's ascension, when they, i.e. the angels, brought him to the Ancient of days, i.e. to God the Father, who, to express his welcome to Christ, gave him glory and a kingdom. And so it is, and ought to be expounded. The Father received him with open arms, rejoicing exceedingly to see him again in heaven; therefore God is said to "receive him up into glory," 1 Tim. 3: 16. For that which, with respect to Christ, is called ascension, is, with respect to the Father, called assumption. He went up, and the Father received him. Yea, received so as none ever was received before him, or shall be received after him.

Thirdly, Christ ascended munificently, shedding forth, abundantly, inestimable gifts upon his church at his ascension. As in the Roman triumphs they did spargere missilia, bestow their largesses upon the people: so did our Lord when he ascended; "wherefore he saith, when he ascended up on high, he led captivity captive; and gave gifts unto men." The place to which the apostle refers, is Psal. 68: 17, 18. where you have both the triumph and munificence with which Christ went up excellently set forth together.

"The chariots of God, (saith the Psalmist) are twenty thousand, even thousands of angels; the Lord is among them, as in Sinai, in the holy place. Thou hast ascended on high, thou hast led captivity captive, thou hast received gifts for men; yea, for the rebellious also, that God might dwell among them." Which words, in their literal sense, are a celebration of that famous victory and triumph of David over the enemies of God, recorded 2 Sam. 8. These conquered enemies bring him several sorts of presents, all which he dedicated to the Lord. The spiritual sense is, that just so our Lord Jesus Christ, when he had overcome by his death on the cross, and now triumphed in his ascension, he takes the parts and gifts of his enemies, and gives them, by their conversion to the church, for its use and service: thus he received gifts, even for the rebellious, i.e. sanctifies the natural gifts and faculties of such as hated his people before, dedicating them to the Lord, in his people's service. Thus, (as one observes) Tertullian, Origin, Austin, and Jerome, came into Canaan, laden with Egyptian gold. Meaning they came into the church richly laden with natural learning and abilities. Austin was a Manichee, Cyprian a magician, learned Bradwardine a scornful, proud naturalist, who once said, when he read Paul's epistles, Dedignar esse parvulus; he scorned such childish things, but afterwards became a very useful man in the church of God. And even Paul himself was as fierce an enemy to the church as breathed on earth, till Christ gave him into his bosom by conversion, and then no mere man ever did the Lord and his people greater service than he. Men of all sorts, greater and smaller lights, have been given to the church. Officers of all sorts were given it by Christ. Extraordinary and temporary, as prophets, apostles, evangelists; ordinary and standing, as pastors, and teachers, which remain to this day, Eph. 4: 8, 9. And those stars are fixed in the church heaven by a most firm establishment, 1 Cor. 12: 28. Thousands now in heaven, and thousands on earth also, are blessing Christ at this day for these his ascension-gifts.

Fourthly, Our Lord Jesus Christ ascended most comfortably, for whilst he was blessing his people, he was parted from them, Luke 24: 50, 51. Therein making good to them what is said by him, John 13: 1. "Having loved his own, he loved them to the end." There was a great deal of love manifested by Christ in this very last act of his in this world. The last sight they had of him in this world was a most sweet and encouraging one. They heard nothing from his lips but love, they saw nothing in his face but love, till he mounted his triumphant chariot, and was taken out of their sight

Surely these blessings at parting were sweet and rich ones. For the matter of them, they were the mercies which his blood had so lately purchased for them. And for their extent, they were not only intended for them who had the happiness to be upon the place with him from whence he ascended; but they reach us as well as them; and will reach the last saint that shall be upon the earth till he come again. For they were but representatives of the future churches, Matt. 28: 20. And in blessing them, he blessed us also. And by this we may be satisfied that Christ carried an heart full of love to his people away with him to heaven; since his love so abounded in the last act that ever he did in this world: and left such a demonstration of his tenderness with them at parting.

Fifthly, He ascended, as well as rose again by his own power. He was not merely passive in his ascension, but it was his own act. He went to heaven. Therefore it is said, Acts 1: 10. He went up, viz. by his own divine power. And this plainly evinceth him to be God, for no mere creature ever mounted itself from earth, far above all heavens, as Christ did.

Sixthly, and lastly, why did Christ ascend?

I answer: His ascension was necessary upon many and great accounts. For,

First, If Christ had not ascended, he could not have interceded, as now he does in heaven for us. And do but take away Christ's intercession, and you starve the hope of the saints. For what have we to succour ourselves with, under the daily surprises of sin, but this, "That if any man sin, we have an advocate [with the Father]" mark that, with the Father; a friend upon the place: one that abides there, on purpose to transact all our affairs, and as a surety for the peace betwixt God and us.

Secondly, If Christ had not ascended, you could not have entered into heaven when you die. For he went to "prepare a place for you," John 14: 2. He was, as I said before, the first that entered into heaven directly, and in his own name; and had he not done so, we would not have entered when we die, in his name. The Fore-runner made way for all that are coming on, in their several generations, after him. Nor could your bodies have ascended after their resurrection, but in the virtue of Christ's ascension. For he ascended, as was said before, in the capacity of our head and representative; to his Father and our Father: For us, and himself too.

Thirdly, If Christ had not ascended, he could not have been inaugurated, and installed in the glory he now enjoys in heaven. This world is not the place where perfect felicity and glory dwell. And then, how had the promise of the Father been made good to him? Or our glory, (which consists in being with, and conformed to him), where had it been? "Ought not Christ to suffer, and to enter into his glory?" Luke 24: 25.

Fourthly, If Christ had not ascended, how could we have been satisfied, that his payment on the cross made full satisfaction to God, and that now God has no more bills to bring in against us? How is it that the Spirit convinceth the world of righteousness, John 16: 9, 10. but from Christ's going to the Father, and returning hither no more? which gives evidence of God's full content and satisfaction, both with his person and work.

Fifthly, How should we have enjoyed the great blessings of the Spirit and ordinances, if Christ had not ascended? And surely, we could not have been without either. If Christ had not gone away, "the Comforter had not come," John 16: 7. he begins where Christ had finished. For he takes of his, and shows it to us, John 16: 14. And therefore it is said, John 17: 39. "The Holy Ghost was not given, because Jesus was not yet glorified." He was then given as a sanctifying spirit, but not given in that measure, as afterwards he was, to furnish and qualify men with gifts for service. And indeed, by Christ's ascension, both his sanctifying, and his ministering gifts were shed forth, more commonly and more abundantly upon men. These fell from him when he ascended, as Elijah's mantle did from him, so that whatsoever good of conversion, edification, support, or comfort you receive from spiritual ordinances, he has shed forth that, which you now see and feel. It is the fruit of Christ's ascension.

Sixthly, and lastly, If Christ had not ascended, how had all the types and prophecies, that prefigured and foretold it, been fulfilled? "And the scriptures cannot be broken," John 10: 35. So that, upon all these accounts, it was expedient that he should go away. It was for his glory, and for our advantage. Though we lost the comfort of his bodily presence by it, yet if "we loved him, we would rejoice he went to the Father," John 14: 28. We ought to have rejoiced in his advancement, though it had been to our loss; but when it is so much for our benefit, as well as his glory, it is a matter of joy on both sides, that he is ascended to his Father, and our Father: to his God, and to our God. From the several blessings flowing to us out of Christ's ascension, it was that he charged his people not to be troubled at his leaving of them, John 14. And hence learn,

Inference 1. Did Christ ascend into heaven? Is our Jesus, our treasure indeed there? Where then should the hearts of believers be, but in heaven, where their ord, their life is? Surely saints, it is not good that your love, and your Lord should be in two several countries, said one that is now with him. Up, and hasten after your lover, that he and you may be together. Christians, you ascended with him, virtually, when he ascended; you shall ascend to him, personally, hereafter; Oh that you would ascend to him, spiritually, in acts of faith, love, and desires daily. Sursum corda, up with your hearts, was the form used by the ancient church at the sacrament. How good were it, if we could say with the apostle, Phil. 3: 20. "Our conversation is in heaven, from whence we look for the Saviour." An heart ascendant, is the beet evidence of your interest in Christ's ascension.

Inf. 2. Did Christ go to heaven as a forerunner? What haste should we make to follow him? He ran to heaven: he ran thither before us. Did he run to glory, and shall we linger? did he flee as an eagle towards heaven, and we creep like snails? Come Christians, "Lay aside every weight, and the sin that so easily besets you, and run with patience the race set before you, looking unto Jesus, Heb. 12: 1, 2. The Captain of our salvation is entered within the gates of the new Jerusalem, and calls to us out of heaven to hasten to him; proposing the greatest encouragements to them that are following after him, saying, "He that overcomes shall sit with me in my throne, as I also overcame, and am set down with my Father in his throne," Rev. 3: 22. How tedious should it seem to us, to live so long at a distance from our Lord Jesus!

Inf. 3. Did Christ ascend so triumphantly, leading captivity captive? How little reason then have believers to fear their conquered enemies? Sin, Satan, and every enemy, were in that day led away in triumph, dragged at Christ's chariot wheels, brought after him as it were in chains. It is a lovely sight to see the necks of those tyrants under the foot of our Joshua. He made at that day, "an open show of them," Col. 2: 15. Their strength is broken for ever. In this he shewed himself more than a conqueror; for he conquered and triumphed too. Satan was then trod under his feet, and he has promised to tread him under our feet also, and that shortly, Rom. 16: 20. some power our enemies yet retain, the serpent may bruise our heel, but Christ has crushed his head.

Inf. 4. Did Christ ascend so munificently, shedding forth so many mercies upon his people? mercies of inestimable value reserved on purpose to adorn that day? O then see that you abuse not those precious ascension-gifts of Christ, but value and improve them as the choicest mercies. Now, the ascension gifts, as I told you, are either the ordinances and officers of the church, (for he then gave them pastors and teachers,) or the Spirit that furnished the church with all its gifts. Beware you abuse not either of these.

First, Abuse not the ordinances and officers of Christ. This is a sin that no nation is plunged deeper into the guilt of, than this nation, and no age more than this. Surely God has written to us the great things of his law, and we have accounted them small things. We have been loose, wanton, sceptical professors for the most part, that have had nice and coy stomachs, that could not relish plain, wholesome truths, except so and so modified to our humours. For this the Lord has a controversy with the nation, and by a sore judgement, he has begun to rebuke this sin already. And I doubt not, before he make an end, plain truths will down with us, and we shall bless God for them.

Secondly, But in the next place, see that you abuse not the Spirit, whom God sent from heaven at his ascension, to supply his bodily absence among us, and is the great pledge of his care for, and tender love to his people. Now take heed that you do not vex him by your disobedience; nor grieve him by your unkindnesses; nor quench him by your sinful neglects of duty, or abuse of light. O deal kindly with the Spirit, and obey his voice: comply with his designs, and yield up yourselves to his guidance and conduct. Methinks, to be intreated by the love of the Spirit, Rom. 15: 30. should be as great an argument as to be intreated for Christ's sake. Now, to persuade all the saints to be tender of grieving the Spirit by sin, let me urge a few considerations proper to the point under hand.

Consid. 1. First, He was the first and principal mercy that Christ received for you at his first entrance into heaven. It was the first thing he asked of God when he came to heaven. So he speaks, John 14: 16, 17. "I will pray the Father, and he shall give you another Comforter, that he may abide with you." No sooner had he set foot upon the place, but the first thing, the great thing that was upon his heart to ask the Father for us was, that the Spirit might forthwith be dispatched, and rent down to his people. So that the Spirit is the first-born of mercies; and deserves the first place in our hearts and esteem.

Consid. Secondly, The spirit comes not in his own name to us, (though, if so, he deserves a dear welcome for his own sake, and for the benefits we receive by him, which are inestimable,) but he comes to us in the name, and in the love, both of the Father, and the Son. As one authorised and delegated by them; bringing his credentials under both their hands and seals, John 15: 26. "But when the Comforter is come, whom I will send to you from the Father:" Mark, I will send him from the Father; and in John 14: 26. the Father is said to "send him in Christ's name." So that he is the messenger that comes from both these great and holy persons. And if you have any love for the God that made you, any kindness for the Christ that died for you, show it by your obedience to the Spirit that comes from them both and in both their names to us, and who will be both offended and grieved, if you grieve him. O therefore give him an entertainment worthy of one that comes to you in the name of the Lord. In the Father's name, and in the Son's name.

Consider. 3 Thirdly, But that is not the only consideration that should cause you to beware of grieving the Spirit, because he is sent in the name of such great and dear persons to you, but he deserves better entertainment than any of the saints give him, for his own sake, and upon his own account, and that upon a double score, viz. of his nature and office.

First, On the account of his nature; for he is God co-equal with the Father and Son in nature and dignity, 2 Sam. 23: 23. "The Spirit of the Lord spake by me, and his word was in my tongue; the God of Israel said; the Rock of Israel spake to me." So that you see he is God. The Rock of Israel. God omnipotent, for he created all things, (Gen. 1: 2; God omnipresent, filling all things, Psal. 139: 7. God omniscient, who knows your hearts, Rom. 9: 1. Beware of him therefore, and grieve him not, for in so doing you grieve God.

Secondly, Upon the account of his office, and the benefits we receive by him. We are obliged, even on the score of gratitude and ingenuity, to obey him; for he is sent in the quality of an advocate to help us to pray; to indite our requests for us; to teach us what and how to ask of God, Rom. 8: 26. He comes to us as a Comforter, John 14: 16. And none like him. His work is to take of Christ's and shew it to us, i.e. to take of his death, resurrection, ascension, yea, of his very present intercession in heaven, and show it to us. He can be with us in a moment, he can, (as one well observes,) tell you what were the very last thoughts Christ was thinking in heaven about you. It was he that formed the body of Christ in the womb, and so prepared him to be a sacrifice for us. He filled that humanity with his unexampled fulness. So fitting and anointing him for the discharge of his office.

It is he that puts efficacy into the ordinances, and without him they would be a dead letter. It was he that blessed them to your conviction and conversion. For if angels had been the preachers, no conversion had followed without the Spirit. It is he that is the vinculum unionis, bond of union betwixt Christ and your souls, without which you could never have had interest in Christ, or communion with Christ. It was he that so often has helped your infirmities, when you knew not what to say; comforted your hearts when they were overwhelmed within you, and you know not what to do; preserved you many thousand times from sin and ruin, when you have been upon the slippery brink of it in temptations. It is he (in his sanctifying-word) that is the best evidence your souls have for heaven. It where endless to enumerate the mercies you have by him. And now, reader, dost thou not blush to think how unworthy thou hast treated such a friend? For which of all these his offices or benefits dost thou grieve and quench him? O grieve not the Holy Spirit whom Christ sent as soon as ever he went to heaven, in his Father's name, and in his own name, to perform all these offices for you.

Inf. 5. Is Christ ascended to the Father as our fore-runner? Then the door of salvation stands open to all believers, and by virtue of Christ's ascension, they also will ascend after him, far above all visible heavens. O my friends, what place has Christ prepared and taken up for you! what a splendid habitation has he provided for you! "God is not ashamed to be called your God; for he has prepared for you a city," Heb. 11: 16. In that city Christ has provided mansions, and resting-places for your everlasting abode, John 14: 2. and keeps them for you till your coming. O how august and glorious a dwelling is that, where sun, and moon, and stars, shall shine as much below your feet, as they are now above your heads? Yea, such is the love Christ has to the believer, that, as one saith, if thou only hadst been the chosen of God, Christ would have built that house for himself and thee. Now it is for himself, for thee, and for many more, who shall inherit with thee. God send us a joyful meeting within the vail with our Fore-runner, and sweeten our passage into it, with many a foresight and foretaste thereof. And, in the meantime, let the love of a Saviour inflame our hearts, so that whenever we cast a look towards that place, where our Fore-runner is for us entered, our souls may say, with melting affections, Thanks be to God for Jesus Christ; and again, Blessed be God for his unspeakable gift.

Sermon 41: The Session of Christ at God's right-hand explained and applied, being the third Step of his glorious Exaltation

Heb 1:3.
When he had by himself purged our sins, sat down on the right hand of the Majesty on high;

Christ being returned again to his Father, having finished his whole work on earth, is there bid by the Father to sit down in the seat of honour and rest. A seat prepared for him at Gods right hand, that makes it honourable; and all his enemies as a footstool under his feet that makes it easy. How much is the state and condition of Jesus Christ changed in a few days! Here he groaned, wept, laboured, suffered, sweat, yea, sweat blood, and found no rest in this world, but when he comes to heaven, there he enters into rest. Sits down for ever in the highest and easiest throne, prepared by the Father for him when he had done his work. "When he had by himself purged our sins, he sat down," &c.

The scope of this epistle is to demonstrate Christ to be the fulness of all legal types and ceremonies, and that whatever light glimmered to the world through them, yet it was but as the light of the day-star, to the light of the sun.

In this chapter, Christ the subject of the epistle, is described; and particularly in this third verse, he is described three ways.

First, By his essential and primeval glory and dignity, he is "ap-augasma", the brightness at his Father's glory, the very splendor of glory, the very refulgency of that son of glory. "The primary reason of that appellation is with respect to his eternal and ineffable generation, light of light, as the Nicene creed expresses it. As a beam of light proceeding from the sun. And the secondary reason of it, is with respect to men," for look as the sun communicates its light and influence to us by its beams, which it projects; so does God communicate his goodness, and manifest himself to us, by Christ. "Yea, he is the express image, or character of his person. Not as the impressed image of the seal upon the wax, but as the engraving in the seal itself." Thus he is described by his essential glory.

Seconds, He is described by the work he wrought here on earth, in his humbled state, and it was a glorious work, and that wrought out by his own single hand, "When he had by himself purged our sins." A work that all the angels in heaven could not do, but Christ did it.

Thirdly, and lastly, He is described by his glory, the which (as a reward of that work) he now enjoys in heaven. "When he had by himself purged our sins, he sat down on the right hand of the Majesty on high," i.e. the Lord clothed him with the greatest power, and highest honour, that heaven itself could afford; for so much this phrase of "sitting down on the right hand of the Majesty" imports, as will appear in the explication of this point, which is the result of this clause, viz.

Doct. That when our Lord Jesus Christ has finished his work on earth, he was placed in the seat of the highest honour, and authority; at the right-hand of God in heaven.

This truth is transformingly glorious. Stephen had but a glimpse of Christ at his Father's right hand, and it caused "his face to shine, as it had been the face of an angel", Acts 7: 56. This, his high advancement, was foretold and promised before the work of redemption was taken in hand, Psal. 110: 1. "The Lord said unto my Lord, sit thou at my right-hand, until I make thine enemies thy footstool." And this promise was punctually performed to Christ, after his resurrection and ascension, in his supreme exaltation, far above all created beings, in heaven and earth, Eph. 1: 20, 21, 22. We shall here open two things in the doctrinal part, viz. What is meant by God's right hand; and what is implied in Christ's sitting there, with his enemies for a footstool.

First, What are we to understand here by God's right hand? It is obvious enough, that the expression is not proper, but figurative and borrowed. God has no hand, right or left; but it is a condescending expression, wherein God stoops to the creature's understanding, and by it he would have us understand honour, power, and nearness.

First, The right hand is the hand of honour, the upper hand, where we place those whom we highly esteem and honour. So Solomon placed his mother in a seat at his right hand, 1 Kings 2: 19. So, in token of honour, God sets Christ at his right hand; which, on that account, in the text, is called the right hand of Majesty. God has therein expressed more favour, delight, and honour to Jesus Christ, than ever he did to any creature. "To which of the angels said he at any time, sit thou on my right hand?" Heb. 1: 13.

Secondly, The right-hand is the hand of power: we call it the weapon hand, and the working hand. And the setting of Christ there, imports his exaltation to the highest authority, and most supreme dominion. Not that God the Father has put himself out of his authority, and advanced Christ above himself; no, "for in that he saith he has put all things under him, it is manifest that he is excepted which did put all things under him," 1 Cor. 15: 27. But to sit as an enthroned king at God's right hand, imports power, yea, the most sovereign and supreme power; and so Christ himself calls the right-hand at which he sits, Matt. 26: 64. "Hereafter ye shall see the Son of man sitting on the right-hand of power."

Thirdly, And as it signifies honour and power, so nearness in place, as we use to say, at one's elbow, and so it is applied to Christ, in Psal. 110: 5. "The Lord at thy right hand, shall strike through kings in the day of his wrath," i.e. the Lord, who is very near thee, present with thee, he shall subdue thine enemies. This then is what we are to understand by God's right-hand, honour, power, and nearness.

Secondly, In the next place let us see what is implied in Christ's sitting at God's right-hand, with his enemies for his footstool. And, if we attentively consider, we shall find that it implies and imports divers great and weighty things in it. As,

First, It implies the perfecting and completing of Christ's work, that he came into the world about. After his work was ended, then he sat down and rested from those labours, Heb. 10: 11, 12. "Every priest standeth daily ministering, and offering oftentimes the same sacrifices: which can never take away sins: but this man when he had once offered one sacrifice for sins, for ever sat down on the right hand of God." Here he assigns a double difference betwixt Christ and the Levitical priests; they stand, which is the posture of servants; he sits, which is the posture of a Lord. They stand daily, because their sacrifices cannot take away sin; he did his work fully, by one offering; and after that, sits or rests for ever in heaven. And this (as the accurate and judicious Dr. Reynolds observes) was excellently figured to us in the ark, which was a lively type of Jesus Christ, and particularly in this, it had rings by which it was carried up and down, till at last it rested in Solomon's temple, with glorious and triumphal solemnity, Psal. 132: 8, 9. 2 Chron. 5: 13. So Christ, while he was here on earth, being anointed with the Holy Ghost and wisdom, went about doing good, Acts 10: 38. and having ceased from his works, did at last enter into his rest, Heb. 5: 10. which is the heavenly temple, Rev. 11: 19.

Secondly, His sitting down at God's right hand, notes the high content and satisfaction of God the Father in him, and in his work. "The Lord said to my Lord, sit thou on my right hand;" the words are brought in as the words of the Father, welcoming Christ to heaven; and (as it were) congratulating the happy accomplishment of his most difficult work. And it is as if he had said," O my Son, what shall be done for thee this day? Thou hast finished a great work, and in all the parts of it acquitted thyself as an able and faithful servant to me; what honours shall I now bestow upon thee? The highest glory in heaven is not too high for thee; come sit at my right hand." O how well is he pleased with Christ, and what he has done! He delighted greatly to behold him here in his work on earth, and by a voice from the excellent glory he told him so, when he spake from heaven to him, saying, "Thou art my beloved Son, in whom I am well pleased," 2 Pet. 1: 17. And himself tells us, John 10: 17. "Therefore does my Father love me, because I lay down my life," &c. for it was a work that the heart of God had been set upon from eternity. He took infinite delight in it.

Thirdly, Christ's sitting down at God's right-hand in heaven, notes the advancement of Christ's human nature to the highest honour; even to be the object of adoration to angels and men. For it is properly his human nature that is the subject of all this honour and advancement; and being advanced to the right hand of Majesty, it is become an object of worship and adoration. Not simply, as it is flesh and blood, but as it is personally united to the second person, and enthroned in the supreme glory of heaven.

O here is the mystery, that flesh and blood should ever be advanced to the highest throne of majesty, and being there installed in that glory, we may now direct our worship to him as God Man; and to this end was his humanity so advanced, that it might be adored and worshipped by all. "The Father has committed all judgement to the Son, that all men should honour the Son, even as they honour the Father." And the Father will accept of no honour divided from his honour. Therefore it is added in the clause, "He that honoureth not the Son, honoureth not the Father which has sent him," John 5: 22, 23. Hence the apostles, in the salutations of their epistles, beg for grace, mercy, and peace, from God the Father, and our Lord Jesus Christ; and in their valedictions, they desire the grace of our Lord Jesus Christ to the churches.

Fourthly, It imports the sovereignty and supremacy of Christ over all. The investiture of Christ, with authority over the empire of both worlds: for this belongs to him that sits down upon his throne. When the Father said to him, Sit at my right-hand, he did therein deliver to him the dispensation and economy of the kingdom. Put the awful sceptre of government into his hand, and so the apostle interprets and understands it, 1 Cor. 15: 25. "He must reign till he have put all his enemies under his feet." And to this purpose, the same apostle accommodates, (if not expounds) the words of the Psalmist, "Thou madest him a little lower than the angels," i.e. in respect of his humbled state on earth, "thou crownedst him with glory and honour, and didst set him over the works of thy hands, thou hast put all things in subjection under his feet," Heb. 2: 7, 8. He is over the spiritual kingdom, the Church, absolute Lord there, Mat. 28: 18, 19, 20. He is also Lord over the providential kingdom, the whole world, Psal. 110: 2. And this providential kingdom, being subordinate to his spiritual kingdom; he orders and rules this, for the advantage and benefit thereof, Eph. 1: 22.

Fifthly, To sit at God's right-hand with his enemies for a footstool, implies Christ to be a conqueror over all his enemies. To have his enemies under his feet, notes perfect conquest and complete victory. As when Joshua set his foot upon the necks of the kings: So Tamerlane made proud Bajazet his footstool. They trampled his name, and his saints under their feet, and Christ will tread them under his feet. It is true indeed this victory is incomplete and in consummate; for now "we see not yet all things put under him, (saith the apostle) but we see Jesus crowned with glory and honour," and that is enough. Enough to show the power of his enemies is now broken; and though they make some opposition still, yet it is to no purpose at all; for he is so infinitely above them, that they must fall before him; it is not with Christ as it was with Abijah, against whom Jeroboam prevailed, because he was young and tender hearted, and could not withstand them. His incapacity and weakness gave the watchful enemy an advantage over him. I say, it is not so with Christ, he is at God's right hand. And all the power of God stands ready bent to strike through his enemies, as it is, Psal. 110: 5.

Sixthly, Christ's sitting in heaven notes to us the great and wonderful change that is made upon the state and condition of Christ, since his ascension into heaven. Ah, it is far otherwise with him now, than it was in the days of his humiliation here on earth. Quantum mutates ab illo! Oh, what a wonderful change has heaven made upon him! It were good (as a worthy of ours speaks), to compare in our thoughts the abasement of Christ, and his exaltation together; as it were in columns, one over against the other. He was born in a stable, but now he reigns in his royal palace. Then he had a manger for his cradle, but now he sits on a chair of state. Then oxen and asses were his companions, now thousands of saints, and ten thousands of angels minister round about his throne. Then in contempt, they called him the carpenter's son, now he obtains a more excellent name than angels. Then he was led away into the wilderness to be tempted of the devil, now it is proclaimed before him, "let all the angels of God worship him." Then he had not a place to lay his head on, now he is exalted to be heir of all things. In his state of humiliation, "he endured the contradiction of sinners;" in his state of exaltation, "he is adored and admired by saints and angels." Then "he had no form or comeliness; and when we saw him, there was no beauty, why we should desire him:" Now the beauty of his countenance shall send forth such glorious beams, as shall dazzle the eyes of all the celestial inhabitants round about him, &c.

O what a change is this! Here he sweated, but there he sits. Here he groaned, but there he triumphs. Here he lay upon the ground, there he sits in the throne of glory. When he came to heaven, his Father did as it were thus bespeak him.

My dear Son, what an hard travail hast thou had of it? What a world of woe hast thou passed through, in the strength of they love to me and mine elect? Thou hast been hungry, thirsty, weary, scourged, crucified, and reproached: Ah, what bad usage hast thou had in the ungrateful world! Not a day's rest for comfort since thou wentest out from me; by now thy suffering days are accomplished; now thy rest is come, rest for evermore. Henceforth sit at my right-hand. Henceforth thou shalt groan, weep, or bleed no more. Sit thou at my right hand.

Seventhly, Christ's sitting at God's right hand, implies the advancement of believers to the highest honour: For this session of Christ's respects them, and there he sits as our representative, in which regard we are made to sit with him in heavenly places, as the apostle speaks, Eph. 2: 6. How secure may we be (saith Tertullian) who do now already possess the kingdom? meaning in our Head, Christ. This (saith another) is all my hope, and all my confidence, namely, that we have a proportion in that flesh and blood at Christ, which is so exalted, and therefore where he reigns, we shall reign; where our flesh is glorified, we shall be glorified. Surely, it is matter of exceeding joy to believe that Christ our Head, our flesh, and blood, is in all this glory at his Father's right-hand. Thus we have opened the sense and importance of Christ's sitting at his Fathers right hand. Hence we infer,

Inference 1. Is this so great an honour to Christ, to sit enthroned at God's right hand? What honour then is reserved in heaven for those that are faithful to Christ, now on the earth? Christ prayed, and his prayer was heard, John 17: 24. "That we may be with him to behold the glory that God has given him;" and what heart can conceive the felicity of such a sight? It made Stephen's face shine as the face of an angel, when he had but a glimpse of Christ at his Father's right hand. "Thine eyes shall see the king in his beauty," Isa. 33: 17. which respected Hezekiah in the type, Christ in the truth. But this is not all, though this be much, to be spectators of Christ in his throne of glory; we shall not only see him in his throne, but also sit with him enthroned in glory. To behold him is much, but to sit with him is more. I remember it was the saying of a heavenly Christian, now with Christ, I should far rather look but through the hole of Christ's door, to see but one half of his fairest and most comely face, [for he looks like heaven] suppose I should never win to see his excellency and glory to the full than to enjoy the flower, the bloom, and chiefest excellency of the glory and riches of ten worlds. And you know how the Queen of the South fainted at the sight of Solomon in his glory. But this sight you shall have of Christ, will change you into his likeness. "We shall be like him (saith the apostle) for we shall see him as he is," 1 John 3: 2. He will place us as it were in his own throne with him. So runs the promise, Rev. 3: 21. "To him that overcometh, I will grant to sit with me in my throne; even as I also overcame, and am set down with my Father in his throne:" and so 2 Tim. 2: 12. "If we suffer with him, we shall also reign with him." The Father set Christ on his right hand, and Christ will set the saints on his right hand. So you know the sheep are placed by the angels at the great day, Mat. 25: and so the church, under the figure of the daughter of Egypt, whom Solomon married, is placed "on the king's right hand, in gold of Ophir," Psal. 45: This honour have all the saints. O amazing love! What, we set on thrones, while as good as us by nature howl in flames! O what manner of love is this! These expressions indeed do not intend that the saints shall be set in higher glory than Christ; or that they shall have a parity of glory with Christ, for in all things he must have the pre-eminence: But they note the great honour that Christ will put upon the saints; as also, that his glory shall be their glory in heaven. "As the glory of the husband redounds to the wife;" and again, their glory will be his glory, 2 Thess. 1: 10. and so it will be a social glory. O, it is admirable to think, whither free grace has already mounted up poor dust and ashes!

To think how nearly related now to this royal, princely Jesus! But how much higher are the designs of grace, that are not yet come to their parturient fulness, they look beyond all this that we now know! "Now are we the sons of God, but it does not yet appear what we shall be," 1 John 3: 2. Ah what reason have you to honour Christ on earth, who is preparing such honours for you in heaven.

Inf. 2. Christ Jesus thus enthroned in heaven then how impossible is it, that ever his interest should miscarry or sink on earth? The church has many subtle and potent enemies. True, but as Haman could not prevail against the Jews, whilst Esther their friend spake for them to the king, no more can they whilst our Jesus sits at his, and our Father's right hand. Will he suffer his enemies that are under his feet, to rise up and pull out his eyes, think you? Surely they that touch his people touch the very apple of his eye," Zech. 2: 8. "He must reign till his enemies are put under his feet," 1 Cor. 15: 25. The enemy under his feet, shall not destroy the children in his arms. He sits in heaven on purpose to manage all to the advantage of his church, Eph. 1: 22. Are our enemies powerful; lo our King sits on the right hand of power: Are they subtle and deep in their contrivance; He that sits on the throne, overlooks all they do. Heaven overlooks hell. "He that sits in heaven beholds," and derides their attempts, Psal. 2: 4. He may permit his enemies to straiten then in one place, but it shall be for their enlargement in another: For it is with the church, as it is with the sea: what it loses in one place, it gets it another; and so really loses nothing. He may suffer them also to distress us in outwards, but shall be recompensed with inward and better mercies; and so we shall lose nothing by that. A footstool you know is useful to him that treads on it, and serves to lift him up higher; so shall Christ's enemies be to him and his, albeit they think not so. What singular benefits the oppositions of his enemies, occasion to his people; I have elsewhere discovered, to which I may refer my reader; and pass to

Inf. 3. Is Christ set down on the right hand of the Majesty in heaven? O with what awful reverence should we approach him in the duties of his worship! Away with light and low thoughts of Christ. Away with formal, irreverent, and careless frames in praying, hearing, receiving, yea, in conferring and speaking of Christ. Away with all deadness, and drowsiness in duties; for he is a great King with whom you have to do. A king, to whom the kings of the earth are but as little bits of clay. Lo, the angels cover their faces in his presence. He is an adorable Majesty.

The Fountain of Life Opened Up

When John had a vision of this enthroned King, about sixty years after his ascension; such was life over-powering glory of Christ, as the sun when it shineth in its strength, that when he saw him, he fell at his fleet as dead, and died it is like he had, if Christ had not laid his hand on him, and said, "Fear not, I am the first and the last; I am he that liveth, and was dead, and behold I am alive for evermore," Rev. 1: 17, 18. When he appeared to Saul in the way to Damascus, it was in glory above the glory of the sun, which overpowered him also, and laid him as one dead upon the ground.

O that you did but know what a glorious Lord you worship and serve. Who makes the very place of his feet glorious, wherever he comes. Surely He is greatly to be feared in the assembly of his saints, and to be had in reverence of all that are round about him. There is indeed a "parresia" boldness or free liberty of speech allowed to the saints, Eph. 3: 12. But no rudeness or irreverence. We may indeed come, as the children of a king come to the father, who is both their awful sovereign, and tender father; which double relation causes a due mixture of love, and reverence in their hearts, when they come before him. You may be free, but not rude, in his presence. Though he be your Father, Brother, Friend; yet the distance betwixt him and you is infinite.

Inference 4. If Christ be so gloriously advanced in the highest throne, then none need to reckon themselves dishonoured, by suffering the vilest things for his sake. The very chains and sufferings of Christ have glory in them. Hence Moses "esteemed the very reproaches of Christ greater riches than the treasures of Egypt," Heb. 11: 26. He saw an excellency in the very worst things of Christ, his reproaches and sufferings, as made him leap out of his honours and riches, into them. He did not, (as one saith) only endure the reproaches of Christ, but counted them treasures. To be reckoned among his honours and things of value. So Thuanus reports of Ludovicus Marsacus, a noble knight of France, when he was led with other martyrs, that were bound with cords, to execution; and he for his dignity was not bound, he cried, give me any chain too, let me be a knight of the same orders. Disgrace itself is honourable, when it is endured for the Lord of Glory. And surely there is (as one phraseth it) a little paradise, a young heaven, in sufferings for Christ. If there were nothing else in it, but that they are endured on his account, it would richly reward all we can endure for him; but if we consider how exceeding kind Christ is to them, that count it their glory to be abased for him; that though he be always kind to his people, (yet if we may so speak) he overcomes himself in kindness, when they suffer for him; it would make men in love with his reproaches.

Inf. 5. If Christ sat not down to rest in heaven, till he had finished his work on earth; then it is in vain for us to think of rest, till we have finished our work, as Christ also did his.

How willing are we to find rest here! To dream of that, which Christ never found in this world, nor any ever found before us. O think not of resting, till you have done working and done sinning. Your life and your labours must end together. "Write (saith the Spirit) blessed are the dead that die in the Lord, for they rest from their labours," Rev. 14: 13. Here you must have the sweat, and there the sweet. It is too much to have two heavens. Here you must be content to dwell in the tents of Cedar, hereafter you shall be within the curtains of Solomon. Heaven is the place of which it may be truly said, that there the weary be at rest. O think not of sitting down on this side heaven. There are four things will keep the saints from sitting down on earth to rest, viz. grace, corruption, devils and wicked men.

First, Grace will not suffer you to rest here. Its tendencies are beyond this world. It will be looking and longing for the blessed hope. A gracious person takes himself for a pilgrim, seeking a better country, and is always suspicious of danger in every place and state. It is still beating up the sluggish heart with such language as that, Mic. 2: 10. "Arise, depart, this is not thy rest, for it is polluted." Its further tendencies and continual jealousies, will keep you from sitting long still in this world.

Secondly, Your corruptions will keep you from rest here. They will continually exercise your spirits, and keep you upon your watch. Saints have their hands filled with work by their own hearts every day. Sometimes to prevent sin; and sometimes to lament it. And always to watch and fear, to mortify and kill it. Sin will not long suffer you to be quiet, Rom. 7: 21, 22, 23, 24. And if a bad heart will not break your rest here, then,

Thirdly, There is a busy devil will do it. He will find you work enough with his temptations and suggestions, and except you can sleep quietly in his arms as the wicked do, there is no rest to be expected. "Your adversary, the devil, goes about as a roaring lion, seeking whom he may devour; whom resist," 1 Pet. 5: 8.

Fourthly, Nor will his servants and instruments let you be quiet on this side heaven. *Their very name speaks their turbulent disposition. "My soul, (saith the holy man) is among lions, and I lie even among them that are set on fire, even the sons of men, whose teeth are spears and arrows," Psal. 57: 4. Well then, be content to enter into your rest, as Christ did into his. He sweat, then sat, and so must you.

Sermon 42: Christ's Advent to Judgement, being the fourth and last Degree of his Exaltation, illustrated and improved

Acts 10: 42.
And he commanded us to preach unto the people, and to testify that it is he which was ordained of God to be the Judge of quick and dead.

Christ enthroned in the highest glory in heaven is there to abide for the effectual and successful government, both of the world, and of the church, until the number given him by the Father, before the world was, and purchased by the blood of the cross, be gathered in; and then comes the judgement of the great day, which will perfectly separate the precious from the vile; put the redeemed in full possession of the purchase of his blood in heaven, and "then shall he deliver up the kingdom to his Father, that God may be all in all."

This last act of Christ, namely, his judging the world, is a special part of his exaltation and honour bestowed upon him, "because he is the Son of man,", John 5:27. In that day shall his glory, as King, and absolute Lord, shine forth as the sun when it shines in its strength. O what an honour will it be to the man Christ Jesus, who stood arraigned and condemned at Pilate's bar, to sit upon the great white throne, surrounded with thousands, and ten thousands of angels! Men and devils waiting upon him to receive the final sentence from his mouth. In this will the glory of Christ's sovereignty and power be eminently and illustriously displayed before angels and men. And this is that great truth which he commanded to be preached and testified to the people, namely, that is it "he which is ordained of God to be the Judge of quick and dead".

Wherein we have four things to be distinctly considered, viz. The subject, object, fountain and truth of the supreme judiciary authority.

First, The subject of it, Christ, it is he that is ordained to be Judge. Judgement is the act of the whole undivided Trinity. The Father and Spirit judge, as well as Christ, in respect of authority and consent, but is its the act of Christ, in respect of visible management and execution, and so it is his per proprietatem by propriety, the Father having conferred it upon him, as the Son of man; but not his per appropriationem, so as to exclude either the Father or Spirit from their authority, for they judge by him.

Secondly, The object of Christ's judiciary authority. The quick and dead, i.e. all that at his coming do live, or ever had lived. This is the Object personal. All men and women that ever sprang from Adam: all the apostate spirits that fell from heaven, and are reserved in chains to the judgement of this great day. And in this personal object, is included the real object, viz. All the actions, both secret and open, that ever they did, 2 Cor. 5:5, Rom. 2:16.

Thirdly, The Fountain of this delegated authority, which is God the Father; for he has ordained Christ to be the Judge. "He is appointed", as the Son of man, to this honourable office and work. The word notes, a firm establishment of Christ in that office by his Father. He is now, by right of redemption, Lord and King. He enacts laws for government, then he comes to judge of men's obedience and disobedience to his laws.

Fourthly, and lastly, Here is the infallible truth, or unquestionable certainty of all this: "He gave us commandment to preach and testify it to the people." We had it in charge from his own mouth; and dare not hide it. Hence the point of doctrine is plainly this,

Doct. That our Lord Jesus Christ is ordained by God the Father to be the Judge of quick and dead.

This truth stands upon the firm basis of scripture authority. You have it from his own hand, John 5: 22. "The Father judges no man, but has committed all judgement to the Son," viz. in the sense before given. And so the apostle, Acts 17: 31. "He has appointed a day, in the which he will judge the world in righteousness, by the man whom he has ordained; whereof he has given assurance," &c. And again, Rom. 2: 16. "In the day when God shall judge the secrets of men by Jesus Christ." Three things will be opened here. First, The certainty of a judgement to come. Secondly, The quality and nature of it. Thirdly, That it is a special part of Christ's exaltation to be appointed Judge in this day.

First, The certainty of a judgement. This is a truth of firmer establishment than heaven and earth. It is no devised fable, no cunning artifice to keep the world in awe! but a thing as confessedly true as it is awfully solemn. For,

First, As the scriptures aforementioned (with these, 2 Cor. 5: 10. Eccles. 12: 14. Matt. 12: 36. and many other, the true and faithful sayings of God) do very plainly reveal it; so the justice and righteousness of God require it should be so. For the Judge of all the earth will do right, Gen. 18: 25. Now righteousness itself requires that a difference be made betwixt the righteous and the wicked: "Say ye to the righteous it shall be well with him; woe to the wicked, it shall be ill with him," Isa. 3: 10. But no such distinction is generally and fully made betwixt one another in this world. Yea, rather the wicked prosper, and the righteous perish, there is a just man that perisheth in his righteousness, and there is a wicked man that prolongeth his life in his wickedness, Eccles. 7: 15. Yea, not only in, but for his righteousness, as it may be fairly rendered.

Here the "wicked devoureth the man that is more righteous than himself," Hab. 1: 13. As the fishes of the sea, where the great and strong swallow up the small and weak. And even in courts of judicature, where the innocent might expect relief; there they often meet with the worst oppressions. How fairly and justly therefore does the wise man infer a judgement to come from this considerations, Eccles. 3: 16, 17, "I saw under the sun the place of judgement that wickedness was there, and the place of righteousness, that iniquity was there; I said in my heart, God shall judge the righteous and the wicked; for there is a time there for every purpose, and for every work," q. d. the judgement to come, is the only relief and support left to poor innocents, to quiet and comfort themselves withal. To the same purpose also is that, Jam. 5: 6, 7. "Ye have condemned and killed the just; and he does not resist you; be patient, therefore, brethren unto the coming of the Lord." It is confessed, that sometimes, God vindicates his providence against the Atheism of the world, by particular strokes upon the wicked; but this is but rare. And as the Father well observes, "if no sin were punished here, no providence would be believed; again, if every sin were openly punished here, no judgement hereafter could be expected." Besides,

Secondly, Man is a reasonable being, and every reasonable being, is an accountable being. He is a subject capable of moral government. His actions have a relation to a law. He is swayed by rewards and punishments. He acts by counsel, and therefore of his actions, he must expect to give an account, as it is Rom. 14: 12. "So then every one of us, shall give an account of himself to God." Especially if we add, that all the gifts of body, mind, estate, time, &c. are so many talents, concredited and betrusted to him by God, and every one of us has one talent at least; therefore a time to render an account for all these talents will come, Matth. 25: 14, 15. We are but stewards, and stewards must give an account, in order whereto, there must be a great audit day.

Thirdly, And what need we seek evidence of this truth, further than our own conscience? Lo, it is a truth engraven legibly upon every man's own breast. Every one has a kind of little tribunal, or privy sessions in his own conscience, which both accuses and excuses for good and evil, which it could never do, were there not a future judgement, of which it is now conscious to itself. In this court, records are now kept of all we do, even of our secret actions and thoughts, which never yet took air; but of no judgement, what need of records? Nor let any imagine, that this may be but the fruit of education and discourse. We have heard of such things, and so are scared by them. For if so, how comes it to obtain so universally? Who could be the author of such a common deception?

Reader, bethink thyself a little; if thou hast a mind (as one saith) to impose a lie upon all the world, what course wouldst thou take? How wouldst thou lay the design? Or why dost thou in this case imagine what thou knowest not how to imagine? It is evident that the very consciences of the Heathens, have these offices of accusing and excusing, Rom. 2: 15. And it is hard to imagine, (as an ingenious author speaks) that a general cheat should bow down the backs of all mankind, and induce so many doubts and fears, and troubles, amongst them; and give an interruption to the whole course of their corrupt living, and that there should be no account of it? And therefore it is undoubted that such a day will come. But I shall rather chose, in the

Second Place, to open the nature and manner of this judgement, than to spend more time in proving a truth, that cannot be denied without violence offered to a man's own light. If then the question be, What manner of judgement will this be? I answer,

First, It will be a great and awful day. It is called the "judgement of the great day," Jude 6. Three things will make it so, the manner of Christ's coming; the work he comes about; and the issues, or events of that work. The manner of Christ's coming, will be awfully solemn, "For the Lord himself shall descend from heaven with a shout, with the voice of the archangel, with the trump of God, and the dead in Christ shall rise first. Then we which are alive and remain, shall be caught up together with them in the clouds, to meet the Lord in the air," &c. 1 Thess. 4: 16, 17. Here Christ breaks out of heaven, with the shouts of angels, "en keleusmai", it signifies such a shout, saith one, as is to be heard among seamen, when after a long and dangerous voyage, they first descry land, crying aloud, with united voices, a shore, a shore. As the poet describes the Italians, when they saw their native country, "lifting up their voices, and making the heavens ring again with Italy, Italy: or as armies shout when the signal of battle is given." Above all which (as some expound it) shall the voice of the Archangel be distinctly heard. And after this shout, the trump of God shall sound. By this tremendous blast, sinners will be affrighted out of their graves; but to the saints, it will carry no more terror, then the roaring of cannons, when armies of friends approach a besieged city, for the relief of them that are within it. The dead being raised, they shall be gathered before the great throne on which Christ shall sit in his glory; and there be divided exactly to the right and left hand of Christ, by the angels. Here will be the greatest assembly that ever met. Where Adam may see his numerous offspring, even as the sand upon the sea shore, which no man can number. And never was there such a perfect division made, (how many divisions soever have been in the world) none was ever like it. The saints in this great Oecumenical assize (as the author stiles it) shall meet the Lord in the air, and there the Judge shall sit upon the throne, and all the saints shall be placed upon bright clouds, as on seats or scaffolds round about him; the wicked remaining below upon the earth, there to receive their final doom and sentence.

These preparatives will make it awful; and much more will the work itself, that Christ comes about, make it so. For it is "to judge the secrets of men," Rom. 2: 16. To sever the tares from the wheat; to make every man's whites and blacks appear; and according as they are found in that trial, to be sentenced to their everlasting and immutable states. O what a solemn thing is this!

And no less will the execution of the sentence on both parts make it a great and solemn day. The heart of man cannot conceive what impressions the voice of Christ, from the throne, will make, both upon believers, and unbelievers.

Imagine Christ upon his glorious throne, surrounded with myriads and legions of angels, his royal guard; a poor unbeliever trembling at the bar; an exact scrutiny made into his heart and life; the dreadful sentence given; and then a cry; and then his delivering him over to the executioners of eternal vengeance, never, never, to see a glimpse of hope or mercy any more.

Imagine Christ, like the general of an army, mentioning with honour, on the head of all the hosts of heaven and earth, all the services that the saints have done for him in this world: then sententially justifying them by open proclamation; then mounting with him to the third heavens, and entering the gates of that city of God, in that noble train of saints and angels intermixed; and so for ever to be with the Lord. O what a great day must this be!

Secondly, As it will be awful and solemn judgement, so it will be a critical and exact judgement, every man will be weighed to his ounces and drachms. The name of the judge is "Kardiognoses", the Searcher of hearts. The judge has eyes as flames of fire, which pierce to the dividing of the heart and reins. It is said, Matth. 12:36. That men shall then "give an account of every idle word that they shall speak." It is a day that will perfectly fan the world. No hypocrite can escape; Justice holds the balances in an even hand: Christ will go to work so exactly, that some divines of good note think, the day of judgement will last as long as this day of the gospel's administration has lasted, or shall last.

Thirdly, it will be an universal judgement, 2 Cor. 5: 10. "We must all appear before the judgement seat of Christ." And Rom. 14: 12. "Every one of us shall give an account of himself to God." Those that were under the law, "and those that having no law, were a law to themselves," Rom. 2: 12. Those that had many talents, and he that had but one talent, must appear at this bar; those that were carried from the cradle to the grave, with him that stooped forage: the rich, and poor; the father, and the child; the master, and servant; the believer, and the unbeliever, must stand forth in that day. "I saw the dead, both small and great, stand before God, and the books were opened," Rev. 20: 12.

Fourthly, It will be a judgement full of convictive clearness. All things will be so sifted to bran, (as we say), that the sentence of Christ, both on saints and sinners, shall be applauded. "Righteous art thou, O Lord, because thou hast judged thus." His judgements will be as the light that goes forth. So that those poor sinners whom he will condemn, shall be first "autokatakritoi", self condemned. Their own consciences shall be forced to confess, that there is not one drop of injustice in all that sea of wrath, into which they are to be cast.

Fifthly, and lastly, It will be a supreme and final judgement, from which lies no appeal. For it is the sentence of the highest, and only Lord. "For as the ultimate resolution of faith is into the word and truth of God, so the ultimate resolution of justice is into the judgement of God." This judgement is supreme and imperial. For Christ is the only Potentate, 1 Tim. 6: 5. and therefore the sentence once passed, its execution is infallible. And so you find it in that judicial process, Matth. 25: ult. just after the sentence is pronounced by Christ, it is immediately added, "these shall go away into everlasting punishment, but the righteous into life eternal." This is the judgement of the great day.

Thirdly, In the last place, I must inform you, that God, in ordaining Christ to be the Judge, has very highly exalted him. This will be very much for his honour: for in this, Christ's royal dignity will be illustrated, beyond whatever it was since he took our nature, till that day; now he will appear in his glory. For,

First, This act of judging pertaining properly to the kingly office, Christ will be glorified as much in his kingly office, as he has been in either of the other. We find but some few glimpses of the kingly office, breaking forth in this world: as, his riding with Hosannas into Jerusalem; his whipping the buyers and sellers out of the temple, his title upon the cross, &c. But these were but faint beams: Now that office will shine in its glory, as the sun in the midst of the heavens. For what were the Hosannas of little children, in the streets of Jerusalem, to the shouts and acclamations of thousands of angels, and ten thousands of saints? what was his whipping the profane out of the temple, to his turning the wicked into hell, and sending his angels to gather out of his kingdom every thing that offendeth? what was a title written be his judge, and fixed on the ignominious tree, to the name that shall now be seen on his vesture, and on his thigh, King of kings, and Lord of lords.

Secondly, This will be a display of his glory in the highest, before the whole world. For they will be present at once, and together, all the inhabitants of heaven, and earth, and hell; angels must be there to attend and minister; those glittering courtiers of heaven must attend his person; so that heaven will, for a time, be left empty of all its inhabitants: men and devils must be there to be judged: and before this great assembly, will Christ appear in royal Majesty. He will, (to allude to that text, Isa. 24:23.) reign before his ancients gloriously. "For he will come to be glorified in his saints, and to be admired in all them that believe," 2 Thess. 1: 10. The inhabitants of the three regions, heaven, earth and hell, shall then rejoice, or tremble before him, and acknowledge him to be supreme Lord and King.

Thirdly, This will roll away for ever the reproach of his death: for Pilate and the High-priest, that judged him at their bars, shall now stand quivering at his bar; with Herod that set him at nought, the soldiers and officers that traduced and abused him: there they that reviled him on the cross, wagging their heads, will stand, with trembling knees, before his throne. For "every eye shall see him, and they also that pierced him," Rev. 1: 7. O what a contemptible person was Christ in their eyes once? As a worm, and no man. Every vile wretch could freely tread and trample on him; but now such will be the brightness of his glory, such the awful beams of majesty, that the wicked shall not stand in his presence, or "be able to rise up," (as that word imports, Psal. 1: 5.) "before him." So that this will be a full and universal vindication of the death of Christ, from all that contempt and ignominy that had attended it. We next improve it.

Inference 1. Is Jesus Christ ordained of God to be the Judge of quick and dead? Great then is the security believers have, that they shall not be condemned in that day. Who shall condemn, when Christ is Judge? If believers be condemned in judgement, Christ must give sentence against them; yea, and they must condemn themselves too. I say, Christ must give sentence, for that is the proper and peculiar office of Christ. And, to be sure, no sentence of condemnation shall in that day be given by Christ against them. For,

First, He died to save them, and he will never cross and overthrow the designs and ends of his own death. That cannot be imagined. Nay,

Secondly, They have been cleared and absolved already. And being once absolved by divine sentence, they can never be condemned afterward. For one divine sentence cannot cross and rescind another. He justified them here in this world by faith: Declared in his word, (which shall then be the rule of judgement, Rom. 2: 16.) that "there is no condemnation to them that are in Christ," Rom. 8: 1. And surely he will not retract his own word, and give a sentence quite cross to his own statute book, out of which he has told us that they shall be judged. Moreover,

Thirdly, The far greatest part of them will have passed their particular judgement, long, before that day, and being therein acquitted by God the Judge of all; and admitted into heaven upon the score and account of their justification; it cannot be imagined that Christ should now condemn them with the world. Nay,

Fourthly, He that judged them is their head, husband, friend, and brother: who loved them, and gave himself for them. O then, with what confidence may they go, even unto his throne? and say, with Job, "Though he try us as fire, we know we shall come forth as gold." We know that we shall be justified. Especially, if we add, that they themselves shall be the assessors with Christ in that day. And, (as a judicious author pertinently observes,) not a sentence shall pass without their votes. "So as that they may by faith not only look upon themselves as already in heaven, sitting with Christ, as a common person, in their right; but they may look upon themselves as judges already. So that if any sin should arise to accuse or condemn, yet it must be with their votes. And what greater security can they have than this, that they must condemn themselves, if they be condemned." No, it is not the business of that day to condemn, but to absolve and pronounce them pardoned and justified, according to the sentence of Acts 3: 19. and Mat. 12: 32. So that its must needs be a time of refreshing, (as all scriptures call it,) to the people of God. You that now believe, shall not come into condemnation, John 5: 24. You that now judge yourselves, shall not be condemned with the world, 1 Cor. 11: 31, 32.

Inf. 2. If Christ be ordained of God to be the Judge of quick and dead, how miserable a case will Christless souls be in at that day! They that are Christless now, will be speechless, helpless, and hopeless then. How will their hands hang down, and their knees knock together! O what pale faces, quivering lips, fainting hearts, and roaring consciences will be among them in that day! O dreadful day! O astonishing sight! to see the world in a dreadful conflagration, the elements netting, the stars falling, the earth trembling, the judgement set, the prisoners brought forth; O who shall endure this day, but those that by union with Christ are secured against the danger and dread of it! Let me demand of poor Christ less souls, whom this day is like to take unawares,

First, Do you think it possible to avoid appearing, after that terrible citation is given to the world by the trump of God? Alas, how can you imagine it? is not the same power that revived your dust, able to bring you before the bar? There is a necessity that you must come forth, 2 Cor. 5: 10. "We [must] all appear." It is not in the sinner's choice, to obey the summons or not.

Secondly, If you must appear, are there no accusers, nor witnesses, that will appear against you, and confront you in the court? What think you, was Satan so often a tempter to you here, and will he not be an accuser there? Yes, nothing surer; for that was the main design of all his temptations. What think you of your own consciences? are they not privy to your secret wickedness; do not they now sometimes whisper in your ears, what you care not to hear of? If they whisper now, they will thunder then, Rom. 2: 15, 16. Will not the Spirit accuse you, for resisting his motions, and stifling thousands of his convictions? Will not your companions in sin accuse you, who drew or were drawn by you to sin? Will not your teachers be your accusers? How many times have you made them complain, Lord, they are iron and brass, they have made their faces harder than a rock; they refuse to return. Will not your very relations be your accusers, to whom you have failed in all your relational duties? Yea, and every one whom you have tempted to sin, abused, defrauded, overreached; all these will be your accusers. So that it is without dispute, you will have accusers enough to appear against you.

Thirdly, Being accused before Jesus Christ what will you plead for yourselves: will you confess, or will you deny the charge. If you confess, what need more? "Out of thine own mouth will I judge thee," saith Christ, Luke 19: 22. If you deny, and plead not guilty, thy Judge is the searcher of hearts, and knows all things. So that it will not at all help thee to make a lie thy last refuge. This will add to the guilt, but not cover it.

Fourthly, If no defence or plea be left thee, then what canst thou imagine should retard the sentence? Why should not Christ go on to that dreadful work? "Must not the Judge of all the earth do right?" Gen. 18: 25. Must not you render to every man according to his deeds? 2 Cor. 5: 10. Yes, no question but he will proceed to that sentence, how terrible soever it be to you to think on it now, or hear it then.

Fifthly, To conclude, if sentence be once given by Christ against thy soul, what in all the world canst thou imagine should hinder the execution? will he alter the thing that is gone out of his mouth? No, Psal. 89: 34. Dost thou hope he is more merciful and pitiful than so? Thou mistakes, if you expect mercy out of that way in which he dispenses it. There will be thousands, and ten thousands that will rejoice in, and magnify his mercy then; but they are such as obey his call, repented, believed, and obtained union with his person here; but for unbelievers, it is against the settled law of Christ, and constitution of the gospel, to show mercy to the despisers of it. But it may be, you think your tears, your cries, your pleadings with him, may move him; these indeed might have done somewhat in time, but they come out of season now. Alas, too late. What the success of such pleas and cries will be, you may see if you will but consult two scriptures, Job 27: 8, 9. "What is the hope of the hypocrite, though he has gained, when God taketh away his soul? Will God hear his cry when trouble comes upon him?" No: And Matt. 7: 22. "Many will say unto me in that day, Lord, Lord, have we not prophesied in thy name, and in thy name have cast out devils, and in thy name have done many wonderful works? And then will I profess unto them, I never knew you; depart from me ye that work iniquity."

And must it come to this dismal issue with you indeed? God forbid it should. Oh then,

Inf. 3. If Christ be appointed of God to be the Judge of all, how are all concerned to secure their interest in him, and therein an eternal happiness to their own souls, by the work of regeneration? Of all the business that men and women have in this world, there is none so solemn, so necessary, and important as this. O my brethren, this is a work, able to drink up your spirits, while you do but think of the consequence of it.

Summon in then thy self-reflecting and considering powers: get alone, reader, and, forgetting all other things, ponder with thyself this deep, dear, eternal concernment of thine. Examine the state of thy own soul. Look into the scriptures, then into thine own heart, and then to heaven, saying, Lord, let me not be deceived in so great a concernment to me as this. O let not the trifles of time wipe off the impressions of death, judgement, and eternity from thy heart. O that long word [Eternity,] that it might be night any day with thee; that the awe of it may be still upon thy Spirit. A gentlewoman of this nation, having spent the whole afternoon, and a great part of the evening at cards, in mirth and jollity, came home late at night, and finding her waiting gentlewoman reading, she looked over her shoulder upon the book, and said, Poor melancholy soul, why dost thou sit here poring so long upon thy book? That night she could not sleep, but lay sighing and weeping; her servant asked her once and again what ailed her; at last she burst out into tears, and said, Oh! it was one word that I cast my eye upon in thy book, that troubles me; there I saw that word Eternity. How happy were I, if I were provided for eternity! Sure it concerns us, seeing we look for such things, to be diligent that we may be found of him in peace. O let not that day come by surprisal upon you. Remember, that as death leaves, so judgement will find you.

Inf. 4. Is Jesus Christ appointed Judge of quick and dead, then look to it, all you that hope to be found of him in peace, that you avoid those sins, and live in the daily practice of those duties, which the consideration of that day powerfully persuades you to avoid or practise. For it not only presses to holiness in actu primu, in the being of it; but in actu secondo, in the daily exercise and practice of it. Do you indeed expect such a day? Oh then,

First, See you be meek and patient under all injuries and abuses for Christ's sake. Avenge not yourselves, but leave it to the Lord, who will do it. Do not anticipate the work of God. "Be patient, my brethren, to the coming of the Lord," James 5: 7,8, 9.

Secondly, Be communicative, public-hearted Christians, studying and devising liberal things, for Christ's distressed members; and you shall have both an honourable remembrance of it, and a full reward of it in that day, Mat. 25: 34, 35.

Thirdly, Be watchful, and sober, keep the golden bridle of moderation upon all your affections; and see that you be not overcharged with the cares and love of this present life, Luke 21: 34, 35. Will you that your Lord come and find you in such a posture? "O let your moderation be known unto all, the Lord is at hand," Phil. 4: 5.

Fourthly, Improve all your Master's talents diligently and carefully. Take heed of the napkin, Matt. 25: 14, 18. Then must you make up your account for them all.

Fifthly, But, above all, be sincere in your profession. Let your hearts be found in God's statutes, that you may never be ashamed; for this day will be the day of manifestation of all hidden things. And nothing is so secret, but that day will reveal it, Luke 12: 1, 2, 3. "Beware of hypocrisy; for there is noting covered, which shall not be revealed; neither hid, that shall not be made known." - Thus I have finished, through divine aids, the whole doctrine of the impetration of redemption by Jesus Christ; we shall wind up the whole in a general exhortation, and I have done.

The General Use

And now, to close up all, let me persuade all those for whom the dear Son of God came from he blessed bosom of the Father; assumed flesh; brake, by the strength of his own love, through all discouragements and impediments; laid down his own life a ransom for their souls; for whom he lived, died, rose, ascended, and lives for ever in heaven to intercede; to live wholly to Christ, as Christ lived and died wholly for them.

O brethren, never was the heathen world acquainted with such arguments to deter them from sin; never acquainted with such motives to urge them to holiness, as I shall this day acquaint you with. My request is, to give up both your hearts and lives to glorify the Father, Son, and Spirit, whose you are, by the holiness and heavenliness of them. Other things are expected tram you than from other men. See that you turn not all this grace that has sounded in your ears into wantonness. Think not because Christ has done so much for you, you may sit still; much less indulge yourselves in sin, because Christ has offered up such an excellent sacrifice for the expiation of it. No, though Christ came to be a curse, he did not come to be a cloak for your sins. "If one died for all then were all dead; that they that live, should not henceforth live to themselves, but to him that died for them," 2 Cor. 5: 15. O keep your lives pure and clean.

Do not make fresh work for the blood of Christ every day. "If you live in the Spirit, see that you walk in the Spirit, Gal. 5: 25, i.e. (saith Cornelius a Lapide very solidly) "Let us shape and order our lives and actions according to the dicates, instinct, and impulses of the Spirit, and of that grace of the Spirit put within us, and planted in our hearts, which tendeth to practical holiness." O let the grace which is in your hearts, issue out into all your religious, civil, and natural actions. Let the faith that is in your hearts appear in your prayers; the obedience of your hearts in hearing; the meekness of your hearts in suffering; the mercifulness of you hearts in distributing; the truth and righteousness of your hearts in trading; the sobriety and temperance of your hearts in eating and drinking. These be the fruits of Christ's sufferings indeed, they are sweet fruits. Let grace refine, ennoble, and elevate all your actions; that you may say, "Truly our conversation is in heaven." Let grace have the ordering of your tongues, and of your hands; the mounding of your whole conversation. Let not humility appear in some actions, and pride in others; holy seriousness in some companies, and vain frothiness in others. Suffer not the fountain of corruption to mingle with, or pollute the streams of grace. Write as exactly as you can, after your copy, Christ. O let there not be (as one well expresses it) here a line, and there a blank; here a word, and there a blot. One word of God, and two of the world. Now a spiritual rapture, and then a fleshly frolic. This day an advance towards heaven, and to-morrow a slide back again towards hell. But be you in the fear of the Lord all the day long. Let there be a due proportion betwixt all the parts of your conversation. Approve yourselves the servants of Christ in all things. "By pureness, by knowledge, by long suffering, by the Holy Ghost, by love unfeigned, by the word of truth, by the power of God, by the armour of righteousness, on the right hand, and on the left," 2 Cor. 6: 6. See then how accurately you walk. - Cut off occasion from them that desire occasion; and in well doing commit yourselves to God, and commend religion to the world. That this is your great concernment and duty, I shall evidence to your consciences, by these following considerations. That of all persons in the world, the redeemed of the Lord are most obliged to be holy; most assisted for a life of holiness; and that God intends to make great use of their lives, both for the conviction and conversion of others.

Consider, First, God has more obliged them to live pure and strict lives. I know the command obliges all men to it, even those that cast away the cords of the commands, and break Christ's bonds asunder, are yet bound by them; and cannot plead a dispensation to live as they do. Yea, and it is not unusual for them to feel the obligations of the command upon their consciences, even when their impetuous lusts hurry them on to the violation of them; but there are special ties upon your souls, that oblige you to holiness more than others. Many special and peculiar engagements you are under. First, from God. Secondly, from yourselves. Thirdly, from your brethren. Fourthly, from your enemies.

First, God has peculiarly obliged you to purity and strictness of life. Yea, every Person in the blessed Trinity has cast his cord over your souls, to bind up your hearts and lives to the most strict and precise obedience of his commands. The Father has obliged you, and that not only by the common tie of creation, which is yet of great efficacy in itself; for, is it reasonable that God should create and form so excellent a piece, and that it should be employed against him? That he should plant the tree, and another eat the fruit of it? But, besides this common engagement, he has obliged you to holiness of life.

First, By his wise and merciful designs and counsels for your recovery and salvation by Jesus Christ. It was he that laid the corner-stone of your salvation with his own hands. The first motion sprang out of his breast. If God had not designed the Redeemer for you, the world had never seen him; he had never left that sweet Bosom for you. It was the act of the Father to give you to the Son to be redeemed, and then to give the Son to be a Redeemer to you. Both of them stupendous and astonishing acts of grace. And in both God acted as a most free Agent. When he gave you to Christ before the beginning of time, there was nothing out of himself that could in the least move him to it. When the Father, Son, and Spirit sat (as I may say) at the council-table, contriving and laying the design for the salvation of a few out of many of Adam's degenerate offspring, there was none came before him to speak one word for thee; but such was the divine Pleasure to insert thy name in that catalogue of the saved. Oh how much owest thou to the Lord for this. And what an engagement does it leave upon thy soul, to obey, please, and glorify him?

Secondly, By his bountiful remunerations of your obedience, which have been wonderful. What service didst thou ever perform for him, for which he has not paid thee a thousand times more than it is worth. Didst thou ever seek him diligently, and not find him a bountiful rewarder? none seek him in vain, unless such only as seek him vainly, Heb. 11: 6. Didst thou ever give a cup of cold water in the name of a disciple, and not receive a disciple's reward? Matt. 10: 42. Hast thou not found inward peace and comfort flowing into thy soul, upon every piece of sincere obedience! Oh what a good Master do saints serve? You that are remiss and inconstant in your obedience, you that are heartless and cold in duties; hear how your God expostulates with you, Jer. 2: 31. "Have I been a wilderness to Israel, or a land of darkness?" q. d. Have I been a hard Master to you? Have you any reason to complain of me? To whomsoever I have been strait handed, surely I have not been so to you. Are fruits of sin like fruits of obedience? Do you know where to find a better Master? Why then are you so shuffling and inconstant, so sluggish and remiss in my work? Surely God is not behind-hand with any of you. May you not say with David, Psal. 119: 56. "This I had, because I kept thy precepts." There are fruits in holiness, even present fruit. It is a high favour to be employed for God. Reward enough that he will accept any thing thou dost. But to return every duty thou representest to him with such comforts, such quickening, such inward and outward blessings into thy bosom, so that thou mayest open the treasury of thine own experiences, view the variety of

The Fountain of Life Opened Up

encouragements and tokens of his love, at several times received in duties; and say, this I had, and that I had, by waiting on God, and serving him. Oh what an engagement is this upon thee to be ever abounding in the work of the Lord! Though thou must not work for wages; yet God will not let thy work go unrewarded. For he is not unrighteous to forget your work and labour of love.

Thirdly, Your Father has further obliged you to holiness and purity of life, by signifying to you (as he has frequently done) thee great delight and pleasure he hath therein. He hath told you, "that such as are upright in the way are his delight," Prov. 11: 20. That he would not have you forget to do good, and to communicate, for with such sacrifices he is well pleased," Heb. 13: 16. You know you cannot "walk worthy of the Lord to all pleasing, [excepts ye be fruitful in every good word and work," Col. 1: 10. And oh what a bond is this upon you to live holy lives! Can you please yourselves in displeasing your Father? If you have the hearts of children in you, sure you cannot. O you cannot grieve his Spirit by loose and careless walking, but you must grieve your own spirits too. How many times has God pleased you, gratified and contented you, and will you not please and content him? This mercy you have asked of him, and he gave it, that mercy and you were not denied; in many things the Lord has wonderfully condescended to please you, and now there is but one thing that he desires of you, and that most reasonable, yea, beneficial for you, as well as pleasing to him, Phil. 1: 27. "Only let your conversation be as becometh the gospel of Jesus Christ." This is the one thing, the great and main thing he expects from you in this world, and will not you do it? Can you expect he should gratify your desires, when you make no more of grieving and displeasing him? Well, if you know what will please God, and yet resolve not to do it, but will rather please your flesh, and gratify the devil than him; pray pull off your wizards, fall into your own rank among hypocrites, and appear as indeed you are.

Fourthly, The Father hath further obliged you to strictness and purity of conversation, by his gracious promises made to such as so walk. He has promised to do great things for you, if you will but do this one thing for him. If you will "order your conversation aright," Psal. 50 ult. He will be your sun and shield, if you walk before him and be upright, Gen. 15: 1. "He will give grace and glory, and no good thing will he withhold from him that walketh uprightly," Psal. 84: 11. And he promises no more to you, than he has made good to others, that have thus walked, and stands ready to perform to you also. If you look to enjoy the good of the promise, you are obliged by all your expectations and hopes to order your lives purely and uprightly. This hope will set you on work to purge your lives, as well as your hearts, from all pollutions, 2 Cor. 7: 1. "Having these promises, let us cleanse ourselves from all filthiness of flesh and spirit, perfecting holiness in the fear of God."

Fifthly, Yea, He hath yet more obliged you to strict and holy lives, by his confidence in you, that you will thus walk and please him. He expresseth himself in scripture, as one that dares trust you with his glory, knowing that you will be tender of it, and dare do no otherwise. But if a man repose confidence in you, and trust you with his concerns, it greatly obliges you to be faithful. What an engagement was that upon Abraham to walk uprightly, when God said of him, Gen. 18: 19. "I know him, that he will commend his children, and his household after him, and they shall keep the way of the Lord," q. d. as for this wicked generation, whom I will speedily consume in my wrath, I know they regard not my laws, they will trample my commands under their feet, they care not how they provoke me, but I expect other things from Abraham, and I am confident he will not fail me. I know him, he is a man of another spirit, and what I promise myself from him, he will make good. And to the like purpose is that in Isa. 63: 7. "I will mention the loving-kindness of the Lord, and the praises of the Lord; according to all that the Lord has bestowed on us, and the great goodness towards the house of Israel, which he has bestowed on them, according to his mercies, and according to the multitude of his loving kindnesses. For he said, Surely they are my people, children that will not lie, (or fail me:) so he was their Saviour." Here you have an ample account of the endearing mercies of God to that people, ver. 7. and the Lord's confident expectations of suitable returns from them, ver. 8. I said, i.e. (speaking after the manner of men in like cases) I made a full account, that after all these endearments and favours bestowed upon them, they would not offer to be disloyal and false to me. I have made them sure enough to myself, by so many bonds of love. Like to which is that expression, Zeph. 3: 7. "I said, surely thou wilt fear me, thou wilt receive instruction." Oh! how great are the expectations of God from such as you! I know Abraham, there is no doubt of him! And again, they are children that will not lie, i.e. they will not fallere fidem datam, break their covenant with me. Or they are my people that will not shrink, as Mr. Coverdale well translates, filii non negantes, such as will be true to me, and answer their covenant-engagements. And again, surely thou wilt fear me, thou wilt receive instruction. And shall not all this engage you to God? What! Neither the ancient and bountiful love of God, in contriving your redemption from eternity, nor the bounty of God, in rewarding all and every piece of service you have done for him? Nor yet the pleasure he takes in your obedience and upright walking? nor the encouraging promises he has made thereto, nor yet his confident expectations of such a life from you, whom he has so many ways obliged and endeared to himself? Will you forget your ancient friend, condemn his rewards, take no delight or care to please him? Slight his promises, and deceive and fail his expectations? "Be astonished, O ye heavens, at this! and be horribly afraid." Consider how God the Father has fastened this fivefold cord upon your souls, and show yourselves Christians; yea, to use the prophet's words, Isa. 46: 8. "Remember this, and show yourselves men."

Secondly, You are further engaged to this precise and holy life, by what the Son has done for you; is not this pure and holy life the very aim, and next end of his death? Did he not shed his blood to "redeem you from your vain conversations?" 1 Pet. 1: 18. Was not this the design of all his sufferings? "That being delivered out of the hands of your enemies, you might serve him in righteousness and holiness all the days of your life," Luke 1: 74, 75. And is not the apostle's inference, 2 Cor. 5: 14, 15. highly reasonable? "If one died for all, then were all dead, and that he died for all, that they which live, should not henceforth live to themselves, but to him that died for them." Did Christ only buy your persons, and not your services also? No, whoever has thy time, thy strength, or any part of either, I can assure thee, Christian, that Christ has paid for it, and thou givest away what is none of thine own to give. Every moment of thy time is his, every talent, whether of grace or nature, is his; and dost thou defraud him of his own? O how liberal are you of your precious words and hours, as if Christ had never made a purchase of them! O think of this, when thy life runs muddy and foul. When the fountain of corruption flows out at thy tongue, in idle frothy discourses; or at thy hand, in sinful unwarrantable actions? Does this become the redeemed of the Lord? Did Christ come from the bosom of his Father for this? Did he groan, sweat, bleed, endure the cross, and lay down his life for this? Was he so well pleased with all his sorrows and sufferings, his pangs and agonies, upon the account of that satisfaction he should have in seeing the travail of his soul? Isa. 53: 11. as if he had said, "Welcome death, welcome agonies, welcome the bitter cup and heavy burden; I cheerfully submit to all this. These are travailing pangs indeed, but I shall see the beautiful birth at last. These throws and agonies shall bring forth many lovely children to God; I shall have joy in them, and glory from them, to all eternity. This blood of mine, these sufferings of mine, shall purchase to me the persons, duties, services, and obedience of many thousands that will love me, and honour me, serve me, and obey me, with their souls and bodies which are mine." And does not this engage you to look to your lives, and keep them pure? Is not every one of Christ's wounds a mouth open to plead for more holiness, more service, and more fruit from you? Oh! what will engage you if this will not? But,

Thirdly, This is not all; as a man when he weigheth a thing, casteth in weight after weight, till the scales are counterpoised; so does God cast in engagement after engagement, and argument upon argument, till thy heart, Christian, be weighed up and won to this heavenly light. And therefore, as Elihu said to Job, chap. 36: 22. "Suffer me a little, and I will show thee what I have yet to speak on God's behalf." Some arguments have already been urged on the behalf of the Father and Son, for purity and cleanness of life; and next I have something to plead on the behalf of the Spirit. I plead now on his behalf, who has so many times helped you to plead for yourselves with God. He that has so often refreshed, quickened, and comforted you, he will be quenched, grieved, and displeased by an impure, loose, and careless conversation; and what will you do then? Who shall comfort you when the Comforter is departed from you? When he that should relieve your souls is far off? O grieve not the holy Spirit of God by which you are sealed, to the day of redemption, Eph. 4: 30. There is nothing grieves him more than impure practices, for he is a holy Spirit. And look, as water damps and quenches the fire, so does sin quench the Spirit, 1 Thess. 5: 19. Will you quench the warm affections and burning desires which he has kindled in your bosoms? If you do, it is a question whether ever you may recover them again to your dying day. The Spirit has a delicate sense. It is the most tender thing in the whole world. He feels the least touch of sin, and is grieved when thy corruptions within are stirred by temptations, and break out to the defiling of thy life; then is the holy Spirit of God, as it were, made sad and heavy within thee. As that word "me lukeite", Eph. 4: 30. may be rendered. For thereby thou resistest his motions, whereby in the way of a loving constraint he would lead and guide thee in the way of thy duty; yea, thou not only resistest his motions, but crossest his grand design, which is to purge and sanctify thee wholly, and build thee up more and more to the perfection of holiness. And when thou thus forsakes his conduct, and crossest his design in thy soul, then does he usually withdraw as a man that is grieved by the unkindness of his friend. He draws in the beams of his evidencing and quickening grace, withholds all his divine cordials, and saith, as it were, to the unkind and disingenuous soul,

"Hast thou thus requited me, for all the favours and kindnesses thou hast received from me? Have I quickened thee, when thou was dead in transgressions? Did I descend upon thee in the preaching of the gospel, and communicate careless life, even the life of God, to thee; leaving others in the state of the dead? Have I shed forth such rich influences of grace and comfort upon thee? Comforting thee in all thy troubles, helping thee in all thy duties; satisfying thee in all thy doubts and perplexities of soul; saving thee, and pulling thee back from so many destructive temptations and dangers? What had been thy condition, if I had not come unto thee? Could the world have

The Fountain of Life Opened Up

converted thee without me? Could ministers, could angels, have done that for thee which I did? And when I had quickened thee, and made thee a living soul, what couldst thou have done, without my exciting and assisting grace? Couldst thou go on in the way of duty, if I had not led thee? How wouldst thou have waded through the deeps of spiritual troubles, if I had not borne thee up? Whither had the temptations of Satan and thine own corruptions carried thee before this day, if I had not stood thy Friend, and come in for thy rescue in the time of need? Did I ever fail thee in thy extremities? Did I ever leave thee in thy dangers? Have I not been tender over thee, and faithful to thee? And now, for which of all these kindnesses, dost thou thus wrong and abuse me? Why hast thou wounded me thus by thy unkindness? Ah! thou hast ill requited my love! And now thou shalt eat the fruit of thy doings. Let thy light now be darkness; thy songs turned into cowlings; the joy of thine heart, the light of thine eyes, the health of thy countenance, even the face of thy God, and the joy of salvation, be hid from thee."

This is the fruit of careless and loose walking. To this sad issue it will bring thee at last, and when it is come to this, thou shalt go to ordinances, and duties, and find no good in them; no life-quickening comfort there. When thy heart which was wont to be enlarged, and flowing, shall be clung up and dry; when thou shalt kneel down before the Lord, and cry, as Elisha, when with the mantle of Elijah, he smote the water, "Where is the Lord God of Elijah?" So thou, where is the God of prayer? Where is the God of duties? But there is no answer: when like Samson, thou shalt go forth and shake thyself, as at other times; but thy strength is gone; then tell me, what thou hast done in resisting, quenching, and grieving the Holy Spirit of God by impure and offensive practices? And thus you see what engagements lie upon you from the Spirit also to walk uprightly, and keep the issues of life pure. I could willingly have enlarged myself upon this last branch, but that a judicious hand has lately improved this argument, to which I shall refer the reader. Thus God has obliged you to circumspect and holy lives.

Secondly, You are under great engagements to keep your lives pure; even from yourselves, as well as from your God. As God has bound you to purity of conversation, so you have bound yourselves. And there are several things in you, and done by you, which wonderfully increase, and strengthen your obligations to practical holiness.

First, Your clearer illumination is a strong bond upon your souls, Eph. 5: 8. "Ye were sometimes darkness, but now ye are light in the Lord; walk as children of the light." You cannot pretend, or plead ignorance of your duty. You stand convinced in your own consciences before God, that this is your unquestionable duty. Christians, will you not all yield to this? I know you readily yield. We live, indeed, in a contentious, disputing age. In other things, our opinions are different. One Christian is of this judgement, another of that: but does he deserve the name of a Christian that dare once question this truth? In this we all meet and close in oneness of mind and judgement, that it is our indisputable duty to live pure, strict, and clean lives. "The grace of God, which has appeared to you, has taught you this truth clearly, and convincingly," Tit. 2: 11, 12. "You have received how you ought to walk, and to please God," 1 Thess. 4: 1. Well then, this being yielded, the inference is plain and undeniable, that you cannot walk as others, in the vanity of their mind; but you must offer violence to your own light. You cannot suffer the corruptions of your hearts to break forth into practice, but you must slight, and put by the notices and rebukes of your own consciences, Jam. 4: 17. "He that knoweth to do good, and does it not, to him it is sin." Yea, sin with a witness. Aggravated sin. Sin of a deeper tincture than that of Heathens. Sin that sadly wastes and violates conscience. Certainly, whoever has, you have no cloak for your sin. Light and lust struggling together; great light and strong lusts: these make the soul a troubled sea that cannot rest. O but when masterless lusts overbear conscience, this impresses horror upon the soul. This brake David's heart, Psal. 51: 6. "Thou hast put knowledge in my inner part", q. d. Ah, Lord! I went against the rebukes of conscience, to the commission of this sin. I had a watchful light set up within me. I knew it was sin. My light endeavoured lovingly to restrain me, and I thrust it aside. Besides, what pleasure in sin can you have? Indeed, such as for want of light know not what they do, or such, whose consciences are seared, and past feeling; they may seek a little pleasure (such as it is) out of sin: but what content or pleasure can you have, so long as your light is ever breaking in upon you, and smiting you for what you do? This greatly increases your obligation to a precise, holy life. Again,

Secondly, You are professors of holiness. You have given in your names to Christ, to be his disciples; and by this your engagements to a life of holiness, are yet further strengthened, 2 Tim. 2: 19. "Let every one that nameth the name of Christ, depart from iniquity." The name of Christ is called upon you, and it is a worthy name, Jam. 2: 7. It is called upon you, as the name of the husband is called upon his wife, Isa. 4: 1. "Let thy name be called upon us." Or, as the name of a Father is called upon his child, Gen. 48: 16. "Let my name be called on them, and the name of my fathers. Well then, you bear the name of Christ as his spouse or children; and will you not live suitably to your name? Every place and relation, every title of honour and dignity has its decorum and becomingness. O how will that worthy name of Christ be blasphemed through you, if you adorn it not with becoming deportment? Better you had never professed any thing, than to set yourselves by your profession in the eye and observation of the world; and then to pour contempt on Jesus Christ, by your scandalous conversations, before the eyes of the world, who will laugh at it. I remember it was a momento given to one of his name by Alexander, recordare nominis Alexandri. Remember (said he) thy name Alexander, and do nothing unworthy of that name. O, that is a heavy charge, Rom. 2: 24. "Through you is the name of God blasphemed among the Heathens." Unhappy man that ever thou shouldst be a reproach to Christ: The herd of wicked men are ignota capita, men of no note or observation. They may sin, and sin again; drink, swear, and tumble in all uncleanness; and it passes away silently; the world takes little notice of it. Their wicked actions make but little noise in the world; but the miscarriages of professors, are like a blazing comet, or an eclipsed sun, which all men gaze at, and make their observations upon; oh then, what manner of persons ought you to be, who bear the worthy name of Christ upon you!

    Thirdly, But more than this, You have obliged yourselves to this life of holiness by your own prayers. How many times have you lifted up your hands to heaven, and cried with David, Psal. 119: 5. "O that my ways were directed to keep thy statutes. Order my steps in thy word, and let no iniquity have dominion over me," ver. 133. Were you in earnest with God, when you thus prayed? did you mean as you said? Or did you only compliment with God? If your hearts and tongues agreed in this request, doubtless it is as much your duty to endeavour, as to desire those mercies and, if not, yet do all these prayers stand on record before the Lord, and will be produced against you as witnesses to condemn you, for your hypocrisy and vanity. How often also have you in your prayers lamented, and bewailed your careless and uneven walkings? You have said with Ezra, chap. 9: 6. "O my God, I am ashamed, and even blush to look up unto thee." And do not your confessions oblige you to greater circumspection and care for time to come? Will you confess, and sin? And sin, and confess? Go to God and bewail your evils, and when you have bewailed them, return again to the commission of them? God forbid you should thus dissemble with God, play with sin, and dye your iniquities with a deeper tincture.

    Fourthly, and lastly, to add no more, You have often reproved or censured others for their miscarriages and falls, which adds to your own obligation, to walk accurately, and evenly. Have you not often reproved your erring brethren? or at least privately censured them, if not duty reproved them, (for to these left-handed blows of secret censurings, we are more apt, than to the fair and open strokes of just and due reproofs (and will you practice the same things you criminals and censure others for? "Thou that teachest another, saith the apostle) teachest thou not thyself?" Rom. 2: 21. So say I, thou that censures or rebukes another, condemnest thou not thyself? Will your rebukes ever do good to others, whilst you allow in yourselves what you condemn in them? And as these reproofs and censures can do them no good, so they do you much evil, by reason of them you are "autokatakritoi", self-condemned persons; and out of your own mouths God will judge you. For you need no other witness than yourselves in this case. Your own tongues will fall upon you. Your censures and reproofs of others will leave you without plea or apology, if you look not to your lives with greater care. And yet will you be careless still? Fear you not the displeasure of God? Nor the wounding and disquieting your own consciences? Surely, these things are of no light value with you, if you be Christians indeed.

    Thirdly, You are yet further engaged to practical holiness upon the account of your brethren, who are not a little concerned and interested therein. For if, through the neglect of your hearts your lives be defiled and polluted, this will be thrown in their faces, and many innocent and upright ones both reproached and grieved upon your account. This mischievous effect holy David earnestly deprecated, Psal. 69: 5, 6. "O God, thou knowest my foolishness, and my sins are not hid from thee; let not them that wait on thee, O Lord God of hosts, be ashamed for my sake. Let not them that seek thee, be confounded for my sake, O God of Israel," q. d. Lord, thou knowest what a weak and foolish creature I am. And how apt to miscarry, if left to myself, and should I, through my foolishness, act unbecoming a saint; how would this shame the faces, and sadden the hearts of thy people! They will be as men confounded at the report of my fall. The fall of one Christian is matter of trouble and shame to all the rest; and, when they shall hear the sad and unwelcome news of your scandalous miscarriages, (which will certainly be the effect of a neglected heart and life) they will say as David concerning Saul and Jonathan, "Tell it not in Gath, publish it not in the streets of Askelon," &c. Or as Tamar concerning Amnon, "And we, whither shall we cause our shame to go?" And for them, they shall be as fools in Israel. Thy loose and careless life will cause them to estrange themselves from thee, and look shy upon thee, as being ashamed to own thee, and canst thou bear that; will it not grieve and pierce your very hearts to see a cloud of strangeness and trouble over the countenances of your brethren? To see yourselves disowned and lightly esteemed by them? This very consideration struck a great favourite in the Persian court to the very heart. It was Ustazanes, who had been governor to Sapores in his minority. And this man for fear denied the

Christian faith, and complied with the idolatrous worship of the king. And one Day (saith the historian) sitting at the court-gate, he saw Simon, the aged archbishop of Seleucia, drawn along to prison, for his constancy in the Christian faith; and, though he durst not openly own the Christian faith he had so basely denied, and confess himself a Christian, yet he could not chuse but rise, and express his reverence to this holy man, in a respective and honourable salutation: but the zealous good man frowned upon him, and turned away his face from him, as thinking such an apostate unworthy of the least respect from him This presently struck Ustazanes to the heart, and drew from him many tears and groans, and thus he reasoned with himself: Simon will not own me, and can I think but that God will disclaim me, when I appear before his tribunal? Simon will not speak unto me, will not so much as look upon me, and can I look for so much as a good word or look from Jesus Christ, whom I leave so shamefully betrayed and denied? Hereupon he threw off his rich courtly robes, and put on mourning, apparel, and professed himself a Christian, and died a martyr O it is a piercing thing to an honest heart, to be cast out of the favour of God's people. If you walk loosely, neither God nor his people look in kindly upon you.

Fourthly, and lastly; Your very enemies engage you to this pure and holy life upon a double ground. You are obliged by them two ways, viz. as they are your bold censurers, and your watchful observers. They censure you as hypocrites, and will you give them ground and matter for such a charge? They say, only your tongues are more holy than other men's, and shall they prove it from your practice? They also observe you diligently; lie at catch, and are highly gratified by your miscarriages. If your lives be loose and defiled, you will not only be a shame to your friends, but the song of your enemies. You will make mirth in hell; and gratify all the enemies of God. This is that they watch for. They are curious observers of your goings And that which makes them triumph at your falls and miscarriages, is not only that deep rooted enmity betwixt the two seeds, but because all your miscarriages and evils are so many absolutions to their consciences, and justifications (as they think) of their ways and practices. For look, as your strictness and holiness does, as it were, cast and condemn them, as Noah, Heb. 11: 7. by his practice, condemned the world, their consciences fly in their faces, when they see your holy and pure conversations. It lays a damp upon them. It works upon their consciences, and causes many smart reflections. So when you fall, you, as it were, absolve their consciences, loose the bonds of conviction you had made fast upon them, and now there is matter of joy put before them.

Oh, say they, whatever these men talk, we see they are no better than we. They can do as we do. They can cozen and cheat for adventure. They can comply with any thing for their own ends; it is not conscience, as we once thought, but mere stomach and humour, that made them so precise. And oh! what a sad thing is this! hereby you shed soul-blood. You fasten the bands of death upon their souls. you kill those convictions, which, for any thing you know, might have made way to their conversion. When you fall, you may rise again; but they may fall at your example, and never rise more. Never have a good opinion of the ways of God, or of his people any more. Upon this consideration, David begs of God, Psal. 5: 8. "Lead me, O Lord, in thy righteousness, because of mine enemies;" (or, as the Hebrew;) my observers, make thy way straight before my face. And thus you see how your very enemies oblige you to this holy and pure conversation also.

Now put all this together, and see to what these particulars will amount. You have heard how God the Father has engaged you to this purity of conversations by his designment of your salvation; rewarded your obedience; his pleasure in it; his promises to it; and his great confidence in you, that you will thus walk before him. The Lord Jesus has also engaged you thereunto by his death and sufferings, whereby you were redeemed from your vain conversations. The Spirit has engaged you, by telling you plainly how much you will grieve and wrong him, resist and quench him, if you do not keep yourselves pure. Yea, you are obliged further, by yourselves; your clear illumination; your high profession; your many prayers and confessions; your many censures and reprehensions of others; do all strengthen your obligation to holiness. Yea, you are obliged further to this holy life by the shame, grief, and trouble your loose walking will bring upon your friends; and the mirth it will make for, and mischief it will do to your enemies; who, thereby, may be made utterly to fall, where, it may be, you only have stumbled: who are justified and absolved, (as before yell heard), by your miscarriages. And now, what think you of all this? Are you obliged or not, to this purity of life? Are all these bonds so tied, that you can set loose, and free yourselves at pleasure from them? If all these things are of no force with you, if none of these bonds can hold you, may it not be questioned, (notwithstanding your profession), whether any spiritual principle, any fear of God, o; love to Christ, be in your souls or no? O, you could not play fast and loose with God? if so, you could not, as Samson, snap these bonds asunder at your pleasure.

Consid. 2. Secondly, As you are more obliged to keep the issues of life pure than others are, so God has given you greater assitances and advantages for it than others have. God has not been wanting to any in helps and means. Even the Heathen, who are without the gospel, will be yet speechless and inexcusable before God; but how much more will you be so? Who, besides the light of nature, and the general light of the gospel, have, First, Such a principle put within you. Secondly, Such patterns set before you. Thirdly, Such an assistant ready to help you. Fourthly, So many rods to quicken you and prevent your wandering: if notwithstanding all these helps, your life be still unholy.

First, Shall men of such principles walk as others do? Shall we lament for you, as David once did for Saul, saying, "There the shield of the mighty was vilely cast away, the shield of Saul; as though he had not been anointed with oil." There the honour of a Christian was vilely cast away, as though he had not been anointed with the Spirit? "You have received an unction from the holy One, which teaches you all things", 1 John 2:20. Another Spirit, far above that which is in other men, 1 Cor. 2:12. And as this spirit which is in you, is fitted for this life of holiness "(for you are his workmanship, created in Christ Jesus to good works", Eph. 2:10.) so this holy spirit of principle, infused into your souls, has such a natural tendency to this holy life, that if you life not purely and strictly, you must offer violence to your own principles and new nature. A twofold help this principle affords you for a life of holiness.

1. First, It pulls you back from sin, as in Joseph; "How can I do this great wickedness, and sin against God?" And it also inclines you powerfully to obedience. It is a curb to sin, and an spur to holiness. It is impossible for all others to live spiritually and heavenly, because they have no new nature to incline them hereunto. And, methinks, it should be hard for you to live carnally, and sensually; and therein cross the very bent and tendency of the new creature, which is formed in you. How can you neglect prayer, as others do, whilst the Spirit, by divine pulsations, is awaking and rousing up your sluggish hearts with such inward motions, and whispers, as that, Psal. 27:8. "Seek my face". Yea, whilst you feel, (during your omissions of duty), something within that bemoans itself, and, as it were, cries for food, pains and gripes you, like an empty stomach, and will not let you be quiet, till it be relieved. How can you let out your hearts to the world, as other men do, when all that while your spirit is restless, and aches like a bone out of joint? And you can never be at ease, till you come back to God, and say, as Psal. 116 "Return to thy rest, O my soul". Is it not hard, yea, naturally impossible, to fix a stone, and make it abide in the fluid air? Does not every creature, in a restless motion, tend to its proper centre, and desire its own perfection? So does this new creature also. You see how the rivers in their course will not be checked, but bear down all the obstacles in their way, et soevior ab obice ibit; a stop does but make them raise the more, and run the swifter afterwards.

There is a central force in these natural motions, which cannot be stopped. And the like may you observe, in the motions of a renewed soul, John 4: 14 "It shall be in him as a well of water springing up." And is it not hard for you to keep it down, or turn its course? How hard did Jeremiah and David find that work? If you do not live holy lives, you must cross your own new nature, and violate the law that is written in your own hearts, and engraven upon your own bowels. To this purpose a late writer speaks; Till you were converted, (saith he) the flesh was predominant, and therefore it was impossible for you to live any other than a fleshly life; for every thing will act according to its predominant principle. Should you not therefore live a spiritual life? Should not the law of God written in your hearts, be legible in your lives? O should not your lives be according to the tendency of your hearts? Thus he: Doubtless this is no small advantage to practical holiness. But,

Secondly, Besides this principle within, you have no small assistance for the purity of life, by these excellent patterns before you. The path of holiness is no untrodden path to you. Christ and his servants have beaten it before you. The life of Christ is your copy, and it is a fair copy indeed, without a blot. Oh! what an advantage is this, to draw all the lines of your actions, according to his example! This glorious, grand example is often pressed upon for your imitation, Heb 12: 2. Looking to Jesus, he has left you an example, that ye should tread in his steps, 1 Pet 2: 21. His life is a living rule to his people; and besides Christ's example, (for you may say, who can live as Christ did? his example is quite above us) you have a cloud of witnesses. A cloud for its directive use, and these men of like passions, temptations, and constitutions with you; who have gone before you in exemplary holiness. The Holy Ghost (intending therein your special help and advantage) has set many industrious pens to sock, to write the lives of the saints, and preserve for your use, their holy sayings, and heavenly actions He bids you "take them for an example," James 5: 10. Oh! what excellent men are passed on before you! what renowned Worthies have led the way! Men, whose conversions were in heaven, whilst they tabernacled on earth. Whilst this lower world had their bodies, the world above had their hearts, and their affections. Their actions, and their designs were all for heaven. Men that improved troubles and comforts; losses and gains, smiles and frowns, and all for heaven. Men that did extract heaven out of spirituals, out of temporals, out of all things; their hearts were full of heavenly meditations, their mouths of heavenly communications, and their practices of heavenly inclination: O what singular help is this! Where they followed Christ, and kept the way, they are propounded for your imitation; and where any of them turned aside, you have a mark set upon that action for your cautions and prevention. Does any strange or unusual trial befall you, in which you are ready to say with the church, Lam. 1:12, "Was there ever any sorrow like unto my sorrow?" Here you may see "the same affliction accomplished in your brethren", 1 Pet. 5:9. Here is a store of good company to encourage you. Do the world and the devil endeavour to turn you from your duty, by loading it with shameful scoffs, or sufferings? In this case you may look to Jesus, who despised the shame; and to your brethren, "who counted it their honour to be dishonoured for the name of Christ", as the original of the text, Acts 5:41, may be translated. Is it a dishonour to thee, to be ranked with Abraham, Moses, David, and such as were the glory of the ages they lived in? Art thou at any time under a faint fit of discouragement, and ready to despond under any burden? Oh, how mayest thou be animated by such examples, when such a qualm comes over thy heart? Some sparks of their holy courage cannot choose but steal into thy breast, whilst thou considerest them. In them, God has set before thee the possibility of overcoming all difficulties, thou seemst men of the same mould, who had the same trials, discouragements and fears, that now thou hast, and yet overcame all. How is thy unbelief checked, when thou sayest, Oh! I shall never reach the end, I shall one day utterly perish! Why dost thou say so? Why may not such a poor creature as thou art, be carried through as well as they? Had not they the same temptations and corruptions with you? Were they not all troubled with an naughty heart, an ensnaring world, and a busy devil, as well as you? Alas! When they put on the divine, they did not put off the human nature; but complained, and feared, as you do; and yet were carried through all.

O what an advantage have you this way! They that first trusted in Christ, had not such helps as you. You stand upon their shoulders. You have the benefit of their experiences. You that are fallen into the last times, have certainly the best helps to holiness, and yet, will not you live strictly and purely? still you put on the name and profession of Christians, and yet be lofty in your spirits; earthly in your designs; neglectful of duty; frothy in your communications? Pray, from which of all the saints did you learn to be proud? Did you learn that from Christ, or any of his? From which of his saints did you learn to be earthly and covetous, passionate or censorious, over-reaching and crafty? If you have read of any such evils committed by them, have you not also read of their shame and sorrow, their repentance and reformations? If you have found any such blots in their lives, it was left there designedly to prevent the like in yours. O, what an help to holiness is this!

Thirdly, And this is not all. You have not only a principle within you, and a pattern before you, but you have also an omnipotent assistant to help, and encourage you throughout your way. Are you feeble and infirm? and is every temptation, even the weakest, strong enough to turn you out of the way of your duty? Lo, God has sent his Spirit to help your infirmities, Rom. 8:26. No matter then how weak you are, how many and mighty your difficulties and temptations are, as long as you have such an assistant to help you. Great is your advantage for a holy life this way also. For,

(1) First, when a temptation to sin presses sore upon you, he pleads with your consciences within, whilst Satan is tempting without. How often has he brought such scriptures to your remembrance, at the very opportunity, as have saved you out of the temptation? If you attend his voice, you may hear such a voice within you as that, Jer. 44:4, "O do not this abominable thing which I have!" What mighty strivings were there in the heart of Spira, as himself relates? He heard, as it were, a voice within him, saying, Do not write, Spira, do not write. To this purpose is that promise, Isa. 30:20, 21 "Thine eyes shall behold thy teachers, and thine ears shall hear a word behind thee, saying, "This is the way, walk ye in it? when you turn to the right hand, and when you turn to the left." Here you have a two-fold help to holiness, the outward teaching of the word, verse 20 and the inward teachings of the Spirit, verse 21. He shall say, this is the way, when ye are turning aside to the right-hand, or to the left Alluding to a shepherd, saith one, who, driving his sheep before him; whistles then in, when he sees them ready to stray.

(2) Secondly, When ye walk homily and closely with God in your duties, and the Spirit encourages you to go on, by those inward comforts, scalings, and joys, you have from him at such times; how often does he entertain your souls in public ordinances, in private duties, with his hidden Manna, with marrow and fatness, with incomparable and unspeakable comforts, and all this to strengthen you in your way, and encourage you to hold on?

(3.) Thirdly, When you are indisposed for duties, and find your hearts empty and dry, he is ready to fill them, quicken and raise them; so that oftentimes the beginning and end of your prayers, hearing or meditations, are as vastly different, as if one man had begun, and another ended the duty. O then, what assistance for a holy life have you! Others indeed are bound to resist temptations, as well as you; but, alas! having no special assistance from the Spirit, what can they do? It may be, they reason with temptation a little while, and in their own strength resolve against it; but how easy a conquest does Satan make, where no greater opposition is made to him than this? Others are bound to hear, meditate, and pray, as well as you; else the neglect of those duties would not be their sin: But, alas, what pitiful work do they make of it! being left to the hardness and vanity of their own hearts, when you spread your sails, you have a gale, but they lie wind bound, heart-bound, and can do nothing spiritually in a way of duty.

Fourthly, and lastly, to mention no more, You have a further advantage to this holy life, by all the rods of God that are at any time upon you. I might show you in many particulars, the advantages this way also, but I shall only present these three to your observation at this time.

First, By these you are clogged, to prevent your straying and wandering. Others may wander even as far as hell, and God will not spend a sanctified rod upon them, to reduce or stop them; but saith, let them alone," Hos. 4: 17. But if you wander out of the way of holiness, he will clog you with one trouble or other to keep van within bounds, 2 Cor. 12: 7. "Lest I should be lifted up, a thorn in the flesh, a messenger of Satan, was sent to buffet me." So David, Psal. 119: 67. "Before I was afflicted, I went astray; but now I have kept thy word." Afflictions are used by God, as thorns by husband men, to stop the gaps and keep you from breaking out of God's way, Hos. 2: 6. "I will hedge up her way with thorns, and build a wall, that she shall not find her paths." A double allusion; 1. To cattle that are apt to stray, I will hedge up thy way with thorns. 2. To the sea, which is apt to overflow the country, I will build a wall to prevent inundations. Holy Basil was a long time sorely afflicted with an inveterate head-ache, he often prayed for the removal of it; at last God removed it, but in the room of it, he was sorely exercised with the motions and temptations of lust; which, when he perceived, he heartily desired his head-ache again, to prevent a worse evil. You little know the ends and uses of many of your afflictions. Are you exercised with bodily weakness? it is a mercy you are so; and if these pains and infirmities were removed, these clogs taken off, you may with Basil, wish for them again, to prevent worse evils. Are you poor? why, with that poverty God has clogged your pride. Are you reproached? with these reproaches God has clogged your ambition. Corruptions are prevented by your afflictions. And, is not this a marvellous help to holiness of life?

Secondly, By your afflictions, your corruptions are not only clogged, but purged. By these God dries up and consumes that spring, of sin that defiles your lives, Isa. 27: 9. "By this therefore shall the iniquity of Jacob be purged; and this is all the fruit to take away sin." God orders your wants to fill your wantonness; and makes your poverty poison to your pride. They are God's physic, to purge ill humours out of your souls. "When they fall by the sword, and by famine, and by captivity, and by spoil, it is to try them, and to purge them, and to make them white?" They are both purges and lavatories to your souls. Others have the same afflictions that you have, but they do not work on them as on you; they are to you as fire for purging, and water for cleansing: and yet, shall not your lives be clean? It is true, (as one well observes upon that place of Daniel,) Christ is the only lavatory, and his blood the only fountain to wash away sin: but, in the virtue and efficacy of that blood, sanctified afflictions are cleansers and purgers too.

A cross without a Christ never made any man better, but with Christ, saints are much the better for the cross. Has God been (as it were) so many days and nights a whitening you, and yet is not the hue of your conversation altered? Has he put you so many times into the furnace, and yet is not the dross separated? The more afflictions you have been under, the more assistance you have had for this life of holiness.

Thirty, By all your troubles, God has been weaning you from the world, the lusts, loves, and pleasures of it; and drawing out your souls to a more excellent life and state than this. He makes your sorrows in this life, give a lustre to the glory of the next. Whoever has, be sure you shall have no rest here; and all, that you may long more ardently for that to come. He often makes you groan, "being burdened, to be clothed with your house from heaven," 2 Cor. 5: 4. And yet will you not be weaned from lusts, customs, and evils of it? O what mariner of persons should you be for heavenly and holy conversations? You stand upon the higher ground. You have, as it were, the wind and tide with you. None are assisted for this life as you are. Put all this together, and see what this second argument contributes toward our further conviction, and persuasion to holy life. Have you received a supernatural principle, fitting you for, and inclining you to holy actions, resisting and holding you buck from sin? Has God also set before you such eminent patterns to encourage and quicken you in your way? Doth the Spirit himself stand ready, so many ways, to assist and help you in all difficulties, and has God hedged up the way of sin with the thorns of affliction, to prevent your wandering, and yet will you turn aside? Will you offer violence to your own principles and new nature? Refuse to follow such leaders as have beaten the way before you? Resist, or neglect his gracious assistance of the blessed Spirit, which he offers you in every need, and venture upon sin, though God has hedged up your way with afflictions? O, how can you do such great wickedness, and sin against such grace as this!

Methinks, I need say no more to convince you how much you are concerned to keep the issues of life pure, none being so much obliged to it, or assisted for it, as you are. But when I remember that Joash lost the complete victory over the Syrians, because he smote not his arrows often enough upon the ground, 2 Kings 13: 8. I shall level one arrow more at this mark: For, indeed, that can never be enough pressed, which can never be enough practised. And therefore,

Consid. 3. Thirdly, It will yet farther appear to be your high concernment, to exact holiness in your conversations, because of the manifold and great uses which God has to make of the visible holiness and purity of your lives, both in this world and that to come. The uses God puts the conversation-holiness of his people in this world unto, are these among others.

First, To win over souls to Christ, and bring them in love with religion. Practical holiness is a very lovely, attractive, and obliging thing. If the heathen could call moral virtue verticordia, turn-heart, from that obliging and winning power it exercises upon the hearts of men; if they could say of it, that were it visible to human eyes, all men would adore it, and fall in love with it; how much rather may we say so of true holiness, made visible in the lives of saints! This is the turn-heart indeed. It makes the souls of men to cling and cleave to the persons in whom it is; as it is prophesied, Zech. 8: 23. of the Jews, when they shall be called, (which shall be a time of great holiness,) "in that day, ten men out of all languages of the nations shall take hold of the skirt of him that is a Jew, saying, we will go with you, for we have heard that God is with you." So much of God as appears in men, so much drawing excellency there is in them. And this is the apostle's argument, 1 John 1:3 "That ye may have fellowship with us." Why, what is there in your fellowship to invite men to you? "Truly our fellowship is with the Father, and with his Son Christ Jesus." Who can choose but to covet their company, that keep company every day with God? Great is the efficacy of visible holiness to work upon the hearts of men; either as a concause, working in fellowship with the word, or as a single instrument, working solitarily without the word.

Where God is pleased to afford the word unto men, there the practical holiness of saints is of singular use, to assist and help it in its operation upon the hearts of men. When the lives of Christians sensibly experience that to the eyes of men, which the gospel does to their ears; when so we preach, and so ye believe and live; when we draw by our doctrines, and you draw with us by your examples; when we hold forth the word of life doctrinally, and you hold it forth practically, as Phil. 2: 16. Where is the heart that can stand before us? O! when the plain and powerful gospel pierces the ears of men, and at the same time, the visible holiness of professors shines so full in their faces, that they must rather put out their own eyes, or else be forced to acknowledge, that God is in you of a truth; then it will work to purpose upon souls. Then will Christ see of the travail of his soul daily.

Yea, if God deny the word to men, yet this practical holiness I am speaking of, may be to them an ordinance for conversion. This way, souls may be won to Christ without the word, as the apostle speaks, 1 Pet. 3: 1. Though pulpits should be silent, and vision fail; yet, if you would this way turn preachers, if your lives may but preach the reality, excellency, and sweetness of Jesus Christ and his ways; and, if you would this way preach down the love of the world, and let men see what poor vanities these are; and preach up the necessity and beauty of holiness; surely you, even you might be honoured to bring many souls to Christ, to turn many to righteousness, and cause many to bless God, on your behalf, in the day of visitation. This is the use God has for the holiness and purity of your lives, and does not this engage you strongly to it? What, not when it may prove the means of eternal the to others? Surely, if you have any bowels of mercy in you, you cannot hide from others that whereby they may be saved. How can you, instead of holding forth the word of life, (which is your manifest duty) visibly hold forth the works of death before men? Have you been beholden to others, and shall none be beholden to you for help towards heaven? Dare you say, let others shift as well as they can, find the way to heaven by themselves if they can, they shall have no benefit by your light? If you be Christians, you are Christians of a different stamp and spirit frown all those we find described in scripture. Should you not rather say as the lepers did, 2 Kings 7: 6. "Do we well to hold our peace," whilst others are perishing? What, shall the lips of ministers, and the lives of Christians, be both silenced together? Shall poor sinners neither hear any thing from us, nor see any thing from you, that may help them to Christ? The Lord have mercy then upon the poor world, and pity it, for its case is desperate. O put on, as the elect of God, bowels of mercy. Destroy not, by the looseness of your conversation, so many souls; for your scandalous miscarriages are like a bag of poison put into the spring which supplies the whole city with water.

Secondly, Another use God has for it, is to recover and salve the credit of religion, which by the apostasies of hypocrites, and scandalous falls of careless Christians, is wounded and exposed to contempt. Much reproach by this means is brought upon religion, and how shall that reproach be rolled away, but by your strictness and purity? By this the world must be convinced that all are not so. Though some be a blot to the name of Christ, yet others are his glory. The more others slur and disgrace religion, the more God expects you to honour and adorn it. I remember Chrysostom brings in the persecutors speaking to two renowned martyrs, after this manner, Nonne videtis alios vestri ordinis hoc fecisse? i.e. Why are you so nice and scrupulous? See you not that others of your rank and profession have done these things? To which they returned this brave answer, Nos hac potissimum ratione viriliter stabimus, i.e. have they done it? For that very reason we will stand out like men, and will never yield to it. There is an holy Antiperistasis in the zeal of a Christian, which makes it, like fire, burn most vehemently in the coldest weather. If men make void God's law, therefore will David love his commandments above gold, Psal. 119: 127. If there be many Pendletons among professors who will betray Christ and his truth to save their flesh; God will have some Sanders to repair that breach, by their constancy and courage in appearing for them.

Thirdly, God makes use of it for the encouragement of his ministers who labour among you. And indeed it is of no small use to refresh their hearts, and strengthen their hands in their painful work: "Now we live (saith the apostle) if ye stand fast in the Lord," 1 Thess. 3: 8. He speaks as if their very life lay at the mercy of the people, because so much of the joy and comfort of it is wrapt up in their regularity and steadfastness. God knows what a hard providence his poor ministers have, and how many discouragements attend them in their work; hear how one of them expresses it, "Ministers would not be gray headed so soon, nor die so fast, notwithstanding their great labours, if they were but successful; but this cuts to the heart, and makes us bleed in secret, that though we do much, yet it comes to nothing. Our work dies therefore we die. Not so much that we labour, as that we labour in vain: When our ministry petrifies, turns hearts into stones, and these taken up and thrown at us, this kills us; the recoiling of our pains kills us. When our peace returns to us; when we spend our strength to make men more nought than they were; this wounds our hearts, which should be considered by sinners. To kill one's self, and one's minister too, who would save them; what a bloody condition is this! Every drop that has fallen from our heart and hand, from our eye-lids and eye-brows, shall be all gathered up, and put as marginal notes by all our labours, and all put in one volume together, and this volume put into your hands at the great day, and opened leaf after leaf, and read distinctly and exactly to you.

Christians, you hear our case, you see our work. Now a little to cheer our spirits in the midst of our hard and killing labours, God sends us to you for a little refreshment, that, by beholding your holy and heavenly conversation, your cheerful obedience, and sweet agreement in the ways of God, we may be comforted over all these troubles, 2 Thess. 1: 3, 4. And will you wound and kill our hearts too? O what a cut will this be!

Fourthly, God has further use for the holiness of your lives; this serves to daunt the hearts, and overawe the consciences of his and your enemies. And sometimes it has had a strange influence and effect upon them. There is a great deal of awful Majesty in holiness, and when it shines upon the conscience of a wicked man, it makes him stoop and do obeisance to it, which turns to a testimony for Christ and his ways before the world. Thus Herod was overawed by the strict and holy life of John; he feared him, knowing that he was a just and holy man, and observed (or preserved and saved) him.

That bloody tyrant was convinced in his conscience of the worth and excellency of that servant of God, and was forced to reverence him for his holiness. So Darius, Dan. 6: 14,18, 19, 20. What conflicts had he with himself about Daniel, whom he had condemned; his conscience condemned him, for condemning so holy and righteous a person. "Then the king went to his palace, and passed the night in fastings; neither were instruments of music brought before him, and his sleep went from him. He goes early in the morning to the den, and cries with a lamentable voice, O Daniel, servant of the living God." How much is this for the honour of holiness, that it conquers the very persecutors of it; and makes them stoop to the meanest servant of God! It is said of Henry II of France, that he was so daunted by the heavenly majesty of a poor taylor that was burnt before him, that he went home sad, and vowed, that he would never be present at the death of such men any more. When Valence the emperor came in person to apprehend Basil, he saw such majesty in his very countenance, that he reeled at the very sight of him; and had fallen backward to the ground, had not his servants stept in to support him. O holiness, holiness, thou art a conqueror. So much, O Christians, as you show of it in your lives, so much you preserve your interest in the consciences of your enemies: cast off this, and they despise you presently.

Fifthly, and lastly, God will use the purity of your conversations to judge and convince the world in the great day. It is true, the world shall be judged by the gospel, but your lives shall also be produced as a commentary upon it; and God will not only show them by the word how they ought to have lived, but bring forth your lives and ways to stop their mouths, by showing how others did live. And this I suppose is intended in that text, 1 Cor. 6:2, "The saints shall judge the world, yea, we shall judge angels;" i.e. our examples are to condemn their lives and practices, as Noah, Heb. 11:7 is said to condemn the world by building the ark, i.e. his faith in the threatening, and obedience to the command, condemned their supineness, infidelity and disobedience. They saw him every day about that work, diligently preparing for a deluge, and yet were not moved with the like fear that he was; this left them inexcusable; so when God shall say in that day to the careless world, did you not see the care, and diligence, the holy zeal, watchfulness, and self-denial of my people, who lived among you? How many times have they been watching and praying, when you have been drinking or sleeping! Was it not easy to reflect when you saw their pains and diligence, Have not I a soul to look after as well as they; a heaven to win or lose, as well as they? O how speechless and inexcusable will this render wicked men, yea, it shall not only be used to judge them, but angels also. How many shocks of temptations have poor saints stood,; whereas they fell without a tempter? They stood not in their integrity, though created in such excellent natures; how much then are you concerned on this very account also to walk exactly! if not instead of judging then, you shall be condemned with them.

And thus you see what use your lives and actions shall be put to; and are these inconsiderable uses? Is the winning over souls to God a small matter? Ii the salving the honour and reputation of godliness a small matter? Is the encouraging the hearts and strengthening of the hands of God's poor ministers, amidst their spending, killing labours, a small matter? Is the awing of the consciences of your enemies, and judging them in the last day, a light thing? Which of these can you call so?

O then, since you are thus obliged to holiness of life, thus singularly assisted for it; and since there are such great dependencies upon it, and uses for it, both now and in the world to come, see that ye be holy in all manner of conversation. See that, "as ye have received Christ Jesus the Lord, so ye walk in him," always remembering, that for this very end, Christ has redeemed, or "delivered you out of the hands of your enemies, that you might serve him without fear, in righteousness and holiness all the days of your lives," Luke 1: 74, 75. And to how little purpose will be all that I have preached, and you have heard, of Christ, if it be not converted into practical godliness? This is the scope and design of it all.

And now, reader, thou art come to the last leaf of this treatise of Christ, it will be but a little while, and thou shalt come to the last page or day of thy life; and thy last moment in that day. Wo to thee, wo and alas for ever; if an interest in this blessed Redeemer be then to get. The world affords not a sadder sight, than a poor Christless soul shivering upon the brink of eternity. To see the poor soul that now begins to awake out of its long dream, at its entrance into the world of realities, to shrink back into the body, and cry, O, I cannot, I dare not die. And then the tears rundown. Lord, what will become of me? O what shall be my eternal lot? This, I say, is as sad a sight as the world affords. That this may not be thy case, reflect upon what thou hast read in these sermons. Judge thyself in the light of them. Obey the calls of the Spirit in them. Let not thy slight and formal spirit float upon the surface of these truths, like a feather upon the water; but get them deeply fixed upon thy spirit, by the Spirit of the Lord; turning them into life and power upon thee; and so animating the whole course and tenor of thy conversation by them, that it may proclaim to all that know thee, that thou art one who esteemest all to be but dross, that thou mayest win Christ.

The End

www.ingramcontent.com/pod-product-compliance
Lightning Source LLC
Chambersburg PA
CBHW020747160426
43192CB00006B/272